# TERRORISM

**Commentary on Security Documents**

**VOLUME 148**

# TERRORISM

## Commentary on Security Documents

## VOLUME 148

## LONE WOLF TERRORISTS

Douglas C. Lovelace, Jr.
Senior National Security Strategist

OXFORD
UNIVERSITY PRESS

OXFORD
UNIVERSITY PRESS

Oxford University Press is a department of the University of Oxford. It furthers the University's objective of excellence in research, scholarship, and education by publishing worldwide. Oxford is a registered trademark of Oxford University Press in the UK and certain other countries.

Published in the United States of America by Oxford University Press
198 Madison Avenue, New York, NY 10016, United States of America



Cataloging-in-Publication information is available from the Library of Congress.

ISSN 1062-4007
Terrorism: Commentary on Security Documents

ISBN 978-0-19-065421-4 (v. 148)

**Note to Readers**

This publication is designed to provide accurate and authoritative information in regard to the subject matter covered. It is based upon sources believed to be accurate and reliable and is intended to be current as of the time it was written. It is sold with the understanding that the publisher is not engaged in rendering legal, accounting, or other professional services. If legal advice or other expert assistance is required, the services of a competent professional person should be sought. Also, to confirm that the information has not been affected or changed by recent developments, traditional legal research techniques should be used, including checking primary sources where appropriate.

*(Based on the Declaration of Principles jointly adopted by a Committee of the American Bar Association and a Committee of Publishers and Associations.)*

## TABLE OF CONTENTS

## VOLUME 148

## LONE WOLF TERRORISTS



## DOCUMENTS

# INTRODUCTION

by
**Douglas C. Lovelace, Jr.**

Following the attacks of September 11, 2001, the United States government has waged war quite successfully against foreign terrorist groups like al Qaeda and the Islamic State. With such terrorist organizations almost decimated, national security experts, law enforcement agencies, and some elements of the U.S. military have turned their attention to the so-called "lone wolf" terrorist, such as the white supremacist James Fields, who killed one woman and injured at least 19 other people at a white nationalist rally in Charlottesville, Virginia, and so-called "lone wolf mass shooters" such as Stephen Paddock, who killed 58 people and injured 546 others during a shooting in Las Vegas. The attention being paid to domestic terrorism as opposed to foreign terrorist organizations increases daily.

It is often unclear whether a lone wolf is a terrorist or a mass murderer who does not espouse an ideological or political motivation. For example, while it appears clear that James Fields acted on his white supremacist views, investigators are still trying to determine what motivated Stephen Paddock. He had no criminal record, did not make a political or ideological statement, had no history of apparent mental illness, and did not exhibit alarming behavior. His mass murder spree was truly horrific, but is far from being the only recent incident of mass killings. In 2012, James Eagan Holmes was convicted of the murder of 12 people and the attempted murder of 70 others in an Aurora, Colorado, movie theater. Although his insanity defense was unsuccessful, he clearly suffered from mental illness at the time of the shooting. He made no political or ideological statements and, therefore, is best classified as a lone wolf mass murderer rather than a terrorist.

Timothy J. McVeigh, on the other hand, is the most infamous lone wolf domestic terrorist in recent decades. His 1995 detonation of an ammonium nitrate bomb in front of the Alfred P. Murrah Federal Building in Oklahoma City killed 168 and injured over 600. Although he had accomplices, he can fairly be considered a lone wolf, since he was self-motivated and did not receive direction from a terrorist cell or other organization. He was a terrorist in that his bombing was intended as revenge for the federal government's 1993 attack on the Branch Davidians' Complex in Waco, Texas, and the Ruby Ridge incident during which federal agents killed members of Randy Weaver's family, including his son and wife. It was domestic terrorism because McVeigh's grievances were domestically generated rather than inspired by a foreign entity. Types of lone wolf murderers include a 15-year-old who shot four of his classmates, angry ex-husbands, and disgruntled workers. As tragic as those murders are, they are not the result of terrorism, which requires an underlying motivation that is political or ideological.

In this volume, we focus on lone wolf terrorists but will discuss lone wolf mass murderers, to the extent necessary to distinguish them from terrorists. To explore the topic of lone wolf terrorists, this volume offers ten documents divided into three sections. Section A includes *Domestic Terrorism: An Overview,* by Jerome P. Bjelopera; *Across the Universe? A Comparative Analysis of Violent Behavior and Radicalization Across Three Offender Types with Implications for Criminal Justice Training and Education,* by John G. Horgan *et al.; Sifting Domestic Terrorism from Hate Crime and Homegrown Violent Extremism,* by Jerome P. Bjelopera; *Report: Lone Wolf Terrorism,* by Lydia Alfaro-Gonzales *et al.*; and *Lone Wolf Terrorism in America: Using Knowledge of Radicalization Pathways to Forge Prevention Strategies,* by Mark S. Hamm and Ramon Spaaij. Section B offers *Stafford Act Assistance and Acts of Terrorism,* by Bruce R. Lindsay; *Preventing Another Boston Marathon Bombing,* a House Homeland Security Report; *Countering Violent Extremism,* a GAO Report to Congressional Requesters; and *The Terrorist Screening Database and Preventing Terrorist Travel,* by Jerome P. Bjelopera, Bart Elias, and Alison Siskin. Section C completes the volume with *The Advocacy of Terrorism on the Internet: Freedom of Speech Issues and the Material Support Statutes,* by Kathleen Ann Ruane.

# A. OVERVIEW OF LONE WOLF TERRORISTS

# COMMENTARY

by
**Douglas C. Lovelace, Jr.**

While lone wolf terrorism is not unprecedented in American history, it has recently taken on increased importance for law enforcement and other investigative agencies. In the United States, the phenomenon can be traced at least as far back as the Anarchist bombings of April and June of 1919. It has continued sporadically since then, motivated by various ideologies and extreme political views, ranging from attempts to incite race wars to attempts to stop abortions. Most lone wolf terrorist attacks in the United States are conducted by domestic terrorists, who feel aggrieved because of domestic policies or conditions, rather than by foreign terrorists or U.S. citizens inspired by foreign terrorist organizations. While the threat is not new, it is more in the public eye as a result of seemingly ubiquitous news coverage and the increased volume and velocity of communications facilitated by the internet.

As discussed previously, lone wolf terrorists are distinguished from lone wolf mass murderers. Also, lone wolf terrorists are divided into two subcategories: lone wolf domestic terrorists and home-grown violent extremists. Domestic terrorists are motivated by organically developed extremist ideologies and grievances. They can include animal rights terrorists, ecological terrorists, anarchists and other anti-government terrorists, militia members, black separatists, white supremacists, and anti-abortionists. Their distinguishing characteristic is that their grievances and ideologies are native to the United States and are not foreign-inspired, as is the case for home-grown violent extremists.

The internet has also made it easier for prospective lone wolf terrorists to learn how to mount successful attacks. International terrorist organizations can now more effectively and efficiently promulgate terroristic tactics, techniques, and procedures. This increased accessibility has led to an increase in the frequency and lethality of lone wolf terrorist attacks. Identifying and intercepting lone wolf terrorists before they strike is difficult. The Federal Bureau of Investigation continually seeks information on individuals who have departed from the political advocacy groups to which they had belonged after becoming too radical for those organizations. While such information may help law enforcement identify potential lone wolf terrorists, the agencies also must respect individual constitutional rights, especially those afforded by the First, Fourth, and Fifth Amendments.

While the United States has not been subject to attacks by lone wolf, foreign-inspired terrorists with the same frequency as have some European countries such as France, Belgium, and Great Britain, the U.S. government has not become complacent. The current administration assesses each overseas terrorist attack for lessons that might be learned by U.S. law enforcement and intelligence agencies. The perpetrators of the November 2015 attacks in Paris, the Brussels bomber in March of 2016, and the Manchester bomber were all European citizens. European officials are deeply concerned about lone wolf radicalization via the internet. They have placed greater emphasis on law enforcement measures, enhanced anti-terrorism laws, enhanced border security, increased surveillance, effective countering of extremist propaganda, improved information sharing, and efforts to reduce radicalization in prisons. All of these are measures which the United States should also be, and in fact is, implementing. However, the challenge of balancing sacrifices of civil liberties with the magnitude and likelihood of the threat is particularly difficult in America's liberal democracy. Such risk management is a very complex and uncertain process.

Today, with most lone wolf terrorists self-radicalizing and isolating themselves from those who might "see something" and "say something," law enforcement has been extraordinarily challenged to preempt the lone wolves' nefarious acts. Making early detection even more difficult, many lone wolves self-radicalize in their own homes, and the process can take only a matter of days, and in some cases hours. The underlying grievance might have been building for some time, but the lone wolf terrorist could well have been cultivating it under the aforementioned constitutional protections. For most lone wolf terrorists' patterns of radicalization, an effective mechanism has not yet developed that would permit timely interdiction by law enforcement.

The FBI believes that an informed and engaged citizenry is essential to managing the lone wolf problem. However, the "see something, say something" instruction can be effective only if the general public understands what signs or behaviors accurately point toward potential lone wolf terrorism. Some indicators would be excessive watching of violent videos, conversations condoning violence as a method of addressing grievances, a significant change in beliefs and behavior, giving away valued belongings, and buying extravagant gifts. Such indicators are usually reported to law enforcement agencies only within communities where law enforcement has cultivated good relations with the general public.

Over the past several years, law enforcement agencies have become increasingly concerned with domestic terrorism, which stems from a variety of often misguided but always extreme beliefs. These can range from distorted views about animal rights, hateful beliefs such as white supremacy, anarchist anti-government sentiments, and opposition to abortion, to name a few. Possession of such views is constitutionally protected, and in most cases, it is not until the beliefs are acted upon in a violent manner that crimes are committed. That is the paradox presented to law enforcement. Police are charged with protecting the public, but in many instances are prevented from taking action until the public has been attacked by a lone wolf.

In the United States, it is not a crime to have a violent thought. It becomes a crime only when the thought is acted upon, i.e., when the crime has been committed and the harm to be prevented has already occurred. Fortunately for law enforcement and the public, there are some important exceptions to this paradoxical situation. Conspiracy statutes, for example, criminalize conspirators who plan to commit a crime and take a substantial step in furtherance of the conspiracy to commit that crime. The substantial step need not be the actual crime; it could be an intermediate step such as surveillance conducted to facilitate the ultimate commission of the crime. Once law enforcement learns of the conspiracy and the substantial step taken in furtherance of it, police may intervene and prevent the ultimate crime from occurring. Learning of the conspiracy and knowing when and where to look for the substantial step require intelligence gathering, an activity that is severely circumscribed when a U.S. citizen is the target.

Having set the context for our examination of lone wolf terrorists, we begin Section A of this volume with *Domestic Terrorism: An Overview*, a Congressional Research Service (CRS) report by Jerome P. Bjelopera. The report provides an excellent introduction to domestic terrorism, and provides a useful discussion of lone wolf domestic terrorists. The context the report provides considerable assistance in understanding the motivations and methods of domestic terrorists. It begins by providing a useful definition of domestic terrorism, explaining why arriving at a consensus definition is more difficult than one might imagine.

After defining domestic terrorism, the report assesses the significance of domestic terrorism and makes a case for why its prevention should be a priority for law enforcement agencies. The report also makes the important point that not all domestic terrorism is physically violent, but all is damaging in one form or another. As for lone wolf domestic terrorists, the report describes leaderless resistance carried out "by persons who (a) operate individually, (b) do not belong to an organized terrorist group or network, and (c) whose modi operandi are conceived and directed by the individual without any direct outside command hierarchy."[1] White supremacists compose a large proportion of domestic lone wolf terrorists. Anti-abortionists and animal rights extremists also have accounted for a number of domestic lone wolves.

In distinguishing lone wolf terrorists from hate crime perpetrators, law enforcement agencies must determine whether the actor was motivated by personal hatred or by a broader ideology. The report correctly observes that since lone wolf terrorists act alone, frequently effective law enforcement approaches such as identifying co-conspirators and proving a conspiracy usually cannot be employed in these types of situations. As a result, preventive and preemptive measures are largely ineffective. The report makes the important point that it is also difficult for law enforcement to identify which individuals have or are acquiring the capability to mount a lone wolf attack, and it also observes that the weapons used are not always guns. While the report correctly notes that lone wolf terrorists do not rehearse with co-conspirators, it should have stated that lone wolves do in fact rehearse. An astute public, informed of the applicable indications and warnings, can assist law enforcement in thwarting attacks, even if the would-be terrorist might not be subject to criminal charges. The report provides a sober assessment of the risk to public security posed by domestic lone wolf terrorists.

The second document in Section A compares lone wolf terrorists with solo mass murderers for the purpose of identifying ways in which their attacks might be thwarted. *Across the Universe? A Comparative Analysis of Violent Behavior and Radicalization Across*

[1] The CRS report quotes this passage from Ramón Spaaij, "The Enigma of Lone Wolf Terrorism: An Assessment," *Studies in Conflict and Terrorism*, vol. 33, no. 9 (2010), 854–70, 856.

*Three Offender Types with Implications for Criminal Justice Training and Education* is an excellent piece of research and analysis that offers valuable observations and conclusions. Moreover, it suggests actions that may reduce the likelihood of successful attacks. The main points it makes include the insight that while lone wolf terrorists and solo mass murderers act for different motivations, their methods, audiences, and weapons are often similar. Their socioeconomic profiles are likewise similar; however, they differ in important respects: motivation, interaction with co-conspirators, behaviors leading up to their attacks, and the degree to which they release indicators of impending attacks. As for motivation, solo mass murderers lack the ideological or political motivation of lone wolf terrorists. The report points out that the majority of solo mass murderers react to perceived grievances against individuals or against categories of persons, while a minority seemingly act spontaneously.

Solo mass murderers do not follow a template for planning and executing their attacks. That fact makes such attacks extremely difficult to preempt. In recent years, both lone wolf terrorists and solo mass murderers have become less prone to making statements of intent, conspiring with sympathetic individuals or groups, experiencing victimization by another individual or group, or acting soon after suffering a traumatic event. Additionally, military experience has become less of a factor over time.

The report lays out a very useful way to conceptualize the complex challenges associated with preventing or preempting lone wolf terrorist and solo mass murderer attacks. The perpetrators sometimes intentionally or inadvertently reveal intent through various indicators. Additionally, law enforcement can learn to identify conditions conducive to attacks and pre-plan appropriate interventions to be made at the right times to reduce the risk of attack while not unnecessarily violating civil liberties. The report concludes that while the methods of lone wolf terrorists and solo mass murderers may differ in some respects, the two types exhibit sufficiently similar pre-attack behaviors to offer opportunities for timely intervention using a common framework. Readers of the report should pay especially close attention to the observations and conclusions presented in chapter 6. They provide law enforcement and the general public with many suggestions on how to join together to manage the risk presented by these two forms of threats.

The third document presented in Section A is a short "CRS Insight" document entitled *Sifting Domestic Terrorism from Hate Crime and Homegrown Violent Extremism*, which helpfully lays out the distinctions between domestic terrorists, perpetrators of hate crimes, and homegrown violent extremists.

The fourth document presented in Section A is the Georgetown University *Report: Lone Wolf Terrorism*. Although this 2015 study is somewhat dated and some of its assumptions have not eventuated, it is still a very important document because of its comprehensive treatment of the lone wolf terrorist phenomenon. It begins by offering a comprehensive definition of lone wolf terrorism: "*The deliberate creation and exploitation of fear through violence or threat of violence committed by a single actor who pursues political change linked to a formulated ideology, whether his own or that of a larger organization, and who does not receive orders, direction, or material support from outside sources." It then presents what the authors believe are* four major trends in domestic lone wolf terrorism: the increased targeting of law enforcement and military personnel, the predominant use of firearms to conduct attacks, the increased use of the internet for radicalization, and individual ideology replacing group ideology as the motivating factor. The claim that domestic lone wolf terrorists overwhelmingly use guns suggests an anti-gun bias. The report fails to acknowledge that the largest loss of life due to lone wolf terrorism in U.S. history was Timothy McVeigh's 1995 truck bombing of the Alfred P. Murrah Federal Building in Oklahoma City. The report also ignores Eric Rudolph's 1996 bombing at Atlanta's Centennial Olympic Park and the 2013 Boston Marathon bombing, among other non–gun-related attacks. Nevertheless, the overall quality of the report is excellent, particularly its fact-based analysis.

Importantly, the report accurately concludes that there is no uniform "profile" of a lone wolf terrorist and that profiling attempts can do more harm than good. However, the report accurately identifies a framework for radicalization that can assist in thwarting terrorist attacks. The authors believe that the interval between the time of adopting an extremist ideology and the time of committing a violent terrorist attack offers meaningful opportunities for intervention. The framework begins with the perception of a personal grievance, followed by receptivity to extremist ideology. The adoption of the ideology leads to moral outrage and anger. The process culminates in the "trigger point," at which the actor becomes convinced that he or she is justified in taking the violent action, and attacks.

The authors correctly observe that this framework is adopted in a lone wolf fashion based on psychological and ideological factors that come to bear on the actor. They might include social isolation, a belief that the world is morally corrupt, rejection or expulsion from a radical group, and a belief than the actor, without substantial assistance, can achieve the ideological or political results desired.

The report offers some recommendations and a caution concerning the identification of lone wolf terrorists. Community reporting, fostered by good public–police relations, can provide critical information to law enforcement. Intelligence gained by undercover police can also be valuable in disrupting attacks. However, surveillance operations must not be such that they destroy trust between the community and the police. Monitoring of communications, especially internet social media platforms, can provide very useful information. Additionally, proactive government efforts to counter internet radicalization can be greatly improved. The report concludes with the finding that a whole-of-government effort at all levels is needed to manage the risk posed by lone wolf terrorists.

The final document presented in Section A of this volume is a Department of Justice report entitled *Lone Wolf Terrorism in America: Using Knowledge of Radicalization Pathways to Forge Prevention Strategies.* As its title implies, the report's major contributions are its explication of radicalization pathways, the understanding of which facilitates the development of prevention strategies. The pathway to radicalization the report describes applies to the majority of lone wolf terrorist attacks carried out in the United States. The first stepping stone along the pathway of radicalization is the place of radicalization. For lone wolf terrorists in the United States, the primary location clearly has become the internet, as the report's authors observe.

The next important feature along the pathway is the formation of a motive for radicalization. The report observes that lone wolf terrorists combine personal with political grievances to form motivation. It would be more accurate to say that lone wolf terrorists come to embrace the belief that political forces give rise to their personal grievances. The report's authors state that affinity with an extremist group is another step in the pathway to radicalization. However, lone wolves today are more likely to form their extreme views from a variety of sources, and not from any one particular extremist group.

The report discusses direct and indirect enablers of lone wolf terrorists. According to the report's authors, those who provide direct support to lone wolves do so unwittingly. However, a lone wolf terrorist may receive intentional direct support from someone who is not willing to assist in the actual conduct of the attack. The terrorist does not necessarily lose his lone wolf status merely because someone along the pathway assisted materially or psychologically.

Perhaps the most important step along the pathway to radicalization is the broadcasting of intent by the lone wolf, because it provides the best opportunity for detection of the plot and preemptive action by law enforcement. The report's authors are correct in noting that broadcasting intent, often in advance of the terrorist act, is common for lone wolf terrorists, though not as much so for lone wolf mass murderers. That is true even in instances when the lone wolf terrorist is not on a suicide mission.Broadcasting venues include emails, videos, social media posts, letters to loved ones, statements to family members and friends, and appearances at protest rallies. While law enforcement agencies do not have the option of legally monitoring all of the listed venues, this option is available with respect to enough of the venues to make this the most important step for interdicting lone wolf terrorists.

The next step the report identifies along the pathway to radicalization is the occurrence of a triggering event that causes the lone wolf to "snap," as it were. The report correctly observes that triggering events are not always sharp, discrete events. They can also be the last in a series of events that accumulate discord in the lone wolf's mind over time. Understanding the well-considered pathway to radicalization presented in this report will assist law enforcement in crafting interdiction strategies and enable members of the general public to assist the police in doing so.

# DOCUMENT NO. 1

# DOMESTIC TERRORISM: AN OVERVIEW

**CRS Report R44921**

**Jerome P. Bjelopera**
Specialist in Organized Crime and Terrorism

August 21, 2017

## Summary

The emphasis of counterterrorism policy in the United States since Al Qaeda's attacks of September 11, 2001 (9/11) has been on jihadist terrorism. However, in the last decade, domestic terrorists—*people who commit crimes within the homeland and draw inspiration from U.S.-based extremist ideologies and movements*—have killed American citizens and damaged property across the country. Not all of these criminals have been prosecuted under federal terrorism statutes, which does not imply that domestic terrorists are taken any less seriously than other terrorists.

The Department of Justice (DOJ) and the Federal Bureau of Investigation (FBI) do not officially designate domestic terrorist organizations, but they have openly delineated domestic terrorist "threats." These include individuals who commit crimes in the name of ideologies supporting animal rights, environmental rights, anarchism, white supremacy, anti-government ideals, black separatism, and beliefs about abortion.

The boundary between constitutionally protected legitimate protest and domestic terrorist activity has received public attention. This boundary is highlighted by a number of criminal cases involving supporters of animal rights—one area in which specific legislation related to domestic terrorism has been crafted. The Animal Enterprise Terrorism Act (P.L. 109-374) expands the federal government's legal authority to combat animal rights extremists who engage in criminal activity. Signed into law in November 2006, it amended the Animal Enterprise Protection Act of 1992 (P.L. 102-346).

This report is intended as a primer on the issue, and four discussion topics in it may help explain domestic terrorism's relevance for policymakers:

- **Level of Activity.** Domestic terrorists have been responsible for orchestrating numerous incidents since 9/11.

- **Use of Nontraditional Tactics.** A large number of domestic terrorists do not necessarily use tactics such as suicide bombings or airplane hijackings. They have been known to engage in activities such as vandalism, trespassing, and tax fraud, for example.
- **Exploitation of the Internet.** Domestic terrorists—much like their jihadist analogues—are often Internet and social-media savvy and use such platforms to share ideas and as resources for their operations.
- **Decentralized Nature of the Threat.** Many domestic terrorists rely on the concept of *leaderless resistance.* This involves two levels of activity. On an operational level, militant, underground, ideologically motivated cells or individuals engage in illegal activity without any participation in or direction from an organization that maintains traditional leadership positions and membership rosters. On another level, the above-ground public face (the "political wing") of a domestic terrorist movement may focus on propaganda and the dissemination of ideology—engaging in protected speech.

## Introduction

Since the terrorist attacks of September 11, 2001 (9/11), domestic terrorists—*people who commit crimes within the homeland and draw inspiration from U.S.-based extremist ideologies and movements*[1]—have not received as much attention from federal law enforcement as their violent jihadist counterparts. This was not necessarily always the case. The Federal Bureau of Investigation (FBI) reported in 1999 that "[d]uring the past 30 years, the vast majority—but not all—of the deadly terrorist attacks occurring in the United States have been perpetrated by domestic extremists."[2]

The U.S. government reacted to 9/11 by greatly enhancing its counterterrorism efforts. This report discusses how *domestic* terrorists broadly fit into the counterterrorism landscape, a terrain that since 9/11 has been largely shaped in response to terrorists inspired by *foreign* ideologies. This report focuses especially on how domestic terrorism is conceptualized by the federal government and issues involved in assessing this threat's significance. Today (perhaps in part because of the government's focus on international terrorist ideologies), it is difficult to evaluate the scope of domestic terrorist activity. For example, federal agencies employ varying terminology and definitions to describe it.

Possibly contributing to domestic terrorism's secondary status as a threat at the federal level, a large number of those labeled as domestic terrorists do not necessarily use traditional terrorist tactics such as bombings or airplane hijackings. Additionally, many

---

1 This conceptualization of the term "domestic terrorism" is derived from a number of U.S. government sources detailed in this report. This report *will not* focus on homegrown violent jihadists. However, when referring to such actors, for this report, "homegrown" describes terrorist activity or plots perpetrated within the United States or abroad by American citizens, permanent legal residents, or visitors radicalized largely within the United States. "Jihadist" describes radicalized Muslims using Islam as an ideological and/or religious justification for belief in the establishment of a global caliphate—a jurisdiction governed by a Muslim civil and religious leader known as a caliph—via violent means. Jihadists largely adhere to a variant of Salafi Islam—the fundamentalist belief that society should be governed by Islamic law based on the Quran and follow the model of the immediate followers and companions of the Prophet Muhammad.

2 Federal Bureau of Investigation, *Terrorism in the United States: 30 Years of Terrorism—A Special Retrospective Edition,* (2000) p. 16.

domestic terrorists do not intend to physically harm people but rather rely on alternative tactics such as theft, trespassing, destruction of property, and burdening U.S. courts with retaliatory legal filings.

While plots and attacks by foreign-inspired homegrown violent jihadists have earned more media attention, domestic terrorists have been busy as well. It is worth noting that in terms of casualties on U.S. soil, an act of domestic terrorism is second only to the events of 9/11. Timothy McVeigh's bombing of the Alfred P. Murrah Federal Building in Oklahoma City on April 19, 1995, claimed 168 lives and injured more than 500 others. Some estimates suggest that domestic terrorists are responsible for carrying out dozens of incidents since 9/11.[3] Much like their jihadist counterparts, domestic terrorists are often Internet savvy and use the medium as a resource for their operations.

Terrorists are typically driven by particular ideologies. In this respect, domestic terrorists are a widely divergent lot, drawing from a broad array of philosophies and worldviews. These individuals can be motivated to commit crimes in the name of ideas such as animal rights, white supremacy, and abortion, for example. However, the expression of these worldviews (minus the commission of crimes) involves constitutionally protected activity.

Aware of the lines between constitutionally protected speech and criminality, domestic terrorists often rope themselves off from ideological (above-ground) elements that openly and often legally espouse similar beliefs. In essence, the practitioners who commit violent acts are distinct from the propagandists who theorize and craft worldviews that could be interpreted to support these acts. Thus, in decentralized fashion, terrorist lone actors (lone wolves) or isolated small groups (cells) generally operate autonomously and in secret, all the while drawing ideological sustenance—*not direction*—from propagandists operating in the free market of ideas.

Domestic terrorists may not be the top federal counterterrorism priority, but they feature prominently among the concerns of some law enforcement officers. For example, in 2011, Los Angeles Deputy Police Chief Michael P. Downing included "black separatists, white supremacist/sovereign citizen extremists, and animal rights terrorists" among his chief counterterrorism concerns.[4] A 2014 national survey of state and local law enforcement officers found that sovereign citizens were "the top concern" among terrorist threats.[5]

The violence related to protests in Charlottesville, VA, on August 12, 2017, also has raised the issue of domestic terrorism, particularly related to public discussions regarding a widely reported incident involving James Alex Fields, who according to witnesses

[3] New America Foundation, *Terrorism in America After 9/11: Part IV, What is the Threat to the United States Today?* https://www.newamerica.org/in-depth/terrorism-in-america/what-threat-united-states-today/.

[4] Bill Gertz, "L.A. Police Use Intel Networks against Terror," *Washington Times*, April 11, 2011. See also Joshua D. Freilich, Steven M. Chermak & Joseph Simone Jr. "Surveying American State Police Agencies About Terrorism Threats, Terrorism Sources, and Terrorism Definitions," *Terrorism and Political Violence*, vol. 21, no. 3 (2009) pp. 450–475. Freilich, Chermak, and Simone found that domestic terrorist groups featured prominently among the concerns of U.S. state police officials.

[5] Jessica Rivinius, "Sovereign Citizen Movement Perceived as Top Terrorist Threat," National Consortium for the Study of Terrorism and Responses to Terrorism, July 30, 2014. For the report, see Carter, David, et al., "Understanding Law Enforcement Intelligence Processes," National Consortium for the Study of Terrorism and Responses to Terrorism, 2014.

drove his car into a group of people protesting a rally featuring white supremacists in Charlottesville on August 12.[6] Fields allegedly killed one person and injured 19 others in the incident. The Department of Justice (DOJ) has opened a civil rights investigation into the incident, presumably pursuing possible hate crime charges.[7] Additionally, Attorney General Jeff Sessions has publicly stated that terrorism investigators are involved in investigating the incident, ostensibly exploring the possibility of characterizing it as an act of domestic terrorism rather than a hate crime.[8]

This report provides background regarding domestic terrorists—detailing what constitutes the domestic terrorism threat as suggested by publicly available U.S. government sources.[9] It illustrates some of the key factors involved in assessing this threat. This report does not discuss in detail either violent jihadist-inspired terrorism or the federal government's role in counterterrorism investigations.

## Domestic Terrorism Defined

Two basic questions are key to understanding domestic terrorism. First, what exactly constitutes "domestic terrorism?" Answering this question is more complicated than it may appear. Some consider all terrorist plots occurring within the homeland as acts of domestic terrorism. According to this perspective, a bombing plot involving U.S. citizens motivated by a foreign terrorist group such as Al Qaeda or the Islamic State constitutes domestic terrorism. While this conceptualization may be true at some level, a practical definition of domestic terrorism distilled from federal sources is much narrower. It suggests that domestic terrorists are Americans who commit ideologically driven crimes in the United States but lack foreign direction or influence—whether tactical or philosophical. This conceptualization excludes homegrown individuals directed or motivated by groups such as Al Qaeda or the Islamic State. Second, what particular *groups* are considered domestic terrorist organizations? The U.S. government does not provide a precise, comprehensive, and public answer to this question. Rather, in broad terms, DOJ has identified a number of general *threats* that embody this issue. The ideological concepts that underpin such threats may inspire criminal activity, such as hate crimes, that do not rise to the level of terrorism. This further complicates defining "domestic terrorism."

### What Is Domestic Terrorism?

In the most general statutory terms, a domestic terrorist engages in terrorist activity that occurs in the homeland. The Federal Bureau of Investigation (FBI, the Bureau) has lead responsibility for terrorism investigations at the federal level.[10]

[6] T. Rees Shapiro et al., "Alleged Driver of Car that Plowed into Charlottesville Crowd Was a Nazi Sympathizer, Former Teacher Says," *Washington Post*, August 13, 2017.

[7] Department of Justice, "Joint Statement from United States Attorney's Office for the Western District of Virginia, Federal Bureau of Investigation and the Civil Rights Division," press release, August, 13, 2017.

[8] Michael Edison Hayden, "Sessions Defends Trump's Comments on Charlottesville, Says Car Ramming Fits Definition of Domestic Terror," *ABC News*, August 14, 2017.

[9] This report does not presume the guilt of indicted individuals in pending criminal cases.

[10] 28 C.F.R. §0.85.

The FBI generally relies on two fundamental sources to define domestic terrorism. First, the Code of Federal Regulations characterizes "terrorism" as including "the unlawful use of force and violence against persons or property to intimidate or coerce a government, the civilian population, or any segment thereof, in furtherance of political or social objectives."[11] Second, 18 U.S.C. Section 2331(5) more narrowly defines "domestic terrorism" and differentiates it from international terrorism and other criminal activity.[12] This definition comes from Section 802 of the USA PATRIOT Act (P.L. 107-56). According to 18 U.S.C. Section 2331(5), domestic terrorism occurs primarily within U.S. territorial jurisdiction, and involves

> (A) . . . acts dangerous to human life that are a violation of the criminal laws of the United States or of any State;
>
> (B) appear to be intended—
>
> > (i) to intimidate or coerce a civilian population;
> >
> > (ii) to influence the policy of a government by intimidation or coercion; or
> >
> > (iii) to affect the conduct of a government by mass destruction, assassination, or kidnapping. . . .[13]

### Enforcement—Joint Terrorism Task Forces

Aside from the FBI, other federal agencies such as the Bureau of Alcohol Tobacco Firearms and Explosives (ATF) and the Internal Revenue Service (IRS) play a role in enforcement efforts to counter domestic terrorism. These agencies—as well as state and local law enforcement representatives—typically cooperate within the framework of Joint Terrorism Task Forces (JTTFs), multi-agency investigative units led by DOJ and the FBI across the country.[14]

JTTFs are teams of police officers, federal agents, analysts, linguists, SWAT experts, and other specialists who investigate terrorism and terrorism-related crimes. Seventy-one of the more than 100 JTTFs operated by DOJ and the FBI were created since 9/11. About 4,000 federal, state, and local law enforcement officers and agents—more than four times the pre-9/11 total—work in them. These officers and agents come from more than 500 state and local agencies and 50 federal agencies.[15]

---

[11] Ibid.

[12] U.S. Congress, Senate Committee on Environment and Public Works, "Responses of John E. Lewis [then Deputy Assistant Director, Federal Bureau of Investigation] to Additional Questions from Senator Obama," *Eco-Terrorism Specifically Examining the Earth Liberation Front and the Animal Liberation Front*, 109th Cong., 1st sess., May 18, 2005, S. Hrg. 109-947 (Washington: GPO, 2007), p. 41. Hereinafter: Responses of John E. Lewis.

[13] 18 U.S.C. §2331(5).

[14] Federal Bureau of Investigation, "Joint Terrorism Task Forces."

[15] Ibid.

The FBI considers JTTFs "the nation's front line on terrorism."[16] They "investigate acts of terrorism that affect the U.S., its interests, property and citizens, including those employed by the U.S. and military personnel overseas."[17] As this suggests, their operations are highly tactical and can involve developing human sources (informants) as well as gathering intelligence to thwart terrorist plots. JTTFs also offer an important conduit for the sharing of intelligence developed from FBI-led counterterrorism investigations with outside agencies and state and local law enforcement.[18]

### Toward a Narrower Definition

The definitions cited above are too broad to capture what the FBI specifically investigates as "domestic terrorism." Besides the statutory definitions regarding the crime of domestic terrorism, the FBI has historically emphasized particular qualities inherent to the *actors* who engage in domestic terrorism. According to the Bureau, domestic *terrorists* do not simply operate in the homeland, but they also *lack foreign direction*.[19] In fact, the Bureau's practical, shorthand definition of domestic terrorism is "Americans attacking Americans based on U.S.-based extremist ideologies."[20] The Department of Homeland Security (DHS) follows this construction.[21]

### Ambiguity Regarding "U.S.-Based Extremist Ideologies"

On the surface, the FBI's shorthand definition for domestic terrorism appears straightforward. However, there is inherent ambiguity to it. Namely, some of the "U.S.-based extremist ideologies" driving what the Bureau views as domestic terrorism have international roots and active followings abroad. The ideologies supporting eco-extremism and animal rights extremism (discussed below) readily come to mind, and people have long committed crimes in their names outside the United States.[22] At least in part, their origins lay in the United Kingdom. Nazism—with its German origins and foreign believers—is an element within domestic white supremacist extremism. Anarchism, the philosophy followed by anarchist extremists, also has long-standing European roots.

---

[16] Federal Bureau of Investigation, "Protecting America against Terrorist Attack: A Closer Look at Our Joint Terrorism Task Forces," May 2009.

[17] Brig Barker and Steve Fowler, "The FBI Joint Terrorism Task Force Officer," *The FBI Law Enforcement Bulletin*, vol. 77, no. 11 (November 2008), p. 13.

[18] Kevin Johnson, "FBI Issues More Top Secret Clearance for Terrorism Cases," USA Today, August 12, 2010; STRATFOR, A Decade of Evolution in U.S. Counterterrorism Operations, Special Report, December 2009.

[19] James F. Jarboe, [then Domestic Terrorism Section Chief, Counterterrorism Division] Federal Bureau of Investigation, Testimony Before the House Resources Committee, Subcommittee on Forests and Forest Health, February 12, 2002. Hereinafter: Jarboe, Testimony.

[20] Federal Bureau of Investigation, "Domestic Terrorism in the Post-9/11 Era," September 7, 2009. Hereinafter: Federal Bureau of Investigation, "Domestic Terrorism."

[21] See Department of Homeland Security, "Domestic Terrorism and Homegrown Violent Extremism Lexicon," November 10, 2011. Hereinafter: Department of Homeland Security, "Domestic Terrorism and Homegrown."

[22] See Gary A. Ackerman, "Beyond Arson? A Threat Assessment of the Earth Liberation Front," *Terrorism and Political Violence, vol. 15, no. 4 (2003), pp. 155–156. Hereinafter: Ackerman, "Beyond Arson?"*

The racist skinhead movement traces its origins abroad—to the United Kingdom—as well. These examples illustrate the FBI's challenge when it emphasizes U.S.-based ideologies in its framing of domestic terrorism.

### Factors Complicating the Descriptions of the Domestic Terrorism Threat

A few more issues make it hard to grasp the breadth of domestic terrorist activity in the United States. First, counting the number of terrorist prosecutions or plots in general has been difficult in the post-9/11 period. Second, there may be some ambiguity in the investigative process regarding exactly when criminal activity becomes domestic terrorism. Third, the federal government appears to use the terms "terrorist" and "extremist" interchangeably when referring to domestic terrorism. It is unclear why this is the case. Finally, and most importantly, which specific *groups* are and should be considered domestic terrorist organizations? The U.S. government does not provide a public answer to this question. Rather, the federal government defines the issue in terms of "threats," not groups.

#### Counting Terrorism Cases

While statutory and practical federal definitions exist for "domestic terrorism," there is little clear sense of the scope of the domestic terrorist threat based on publicly available U.S. government information. Most broadly, it has been said that in much of the post-9/11 period, the federal courts and DOJ may have applied different parameters when sorting, counting, and categorizing *all types* of terrorist prosecutions—let alone domestic terrorism cases.[23] A 2009 study (critiqued by DOJ) found that the U.S. federal district courts, DOJ's National Security Division, and federal prosecutors rely on different criteria to determine whether or not specific cases involve terrorism at all.[24]

A bit more narrowly, in many instances, individuals considered to be domestic terrorists by federal law enforcement may be charged under non-terrorism statutes, making it difficult to grasp from the public record exactly how extensive this threat is. Regarding the prosecution of domestic terrorism cases, no separate federal crime of "domestic terrorism" exists.[25] Also, DOJ has noted that, "[a]lthough we do have at least one specialized [federal] statute aimed at animal enterprise terrorism,[26] domestic terrorism cases often involve firearms, arson or explosive offenses; crimes relating to fraud; and threats and hoaxes."[27] In some instances, the crimes committed by people the FBI describes as domestic terrorism suspects do not violate federal law. When this occurs, the Bureau,

[23] Transactional Records Access Clearinghouse (TRAC), *Who Is a Terrorist? Government Failure to Define Terrorism Undermines Enforcement, Puts Civil Liberties at Risk,* September 8, 2009, http://trac.syr.edu/tracreports/terrorism/215/. DOJ issued a press release that broadly challenged these findings and suggested that TRAC may have omitted certain statistics in its study. TRAC refuted these claims. For the interchange between DOJ and TRAC, see http://trac.syr.edu/tracreports/terrorism/219/.

[24] Ibid.

[25] Greg Myre, "Why the Government Can't Bring Terrorism Charges in Charlottesville," *NPR,* August 14, 2017.

[26] This likely refers to the Animal Enterprise Protection Act from 1992. In late 2006 shortly after the white paper's publication, this act was amended by the Animal Enterprise Terrorism Act.

[27] Department of Justice, *Counterterrorism White Paper,* June 22, 2006, p. 59. Hereinafter: Department of Justice, *White Paper.*

"support[s] [its local] partners any way [it] can—sharing intelligence, offering forensic assistance, conducting behavioral analysis, etc."[28] Thus, individuals considered domestic terrorists by federal law enforcement may not necessarily be federally charged as terrorists.

### Sifting Domestic Terrorism from Other Illegal Activity

It may not be possible for investigators to describe the criminal activity involved early in an investigation as domestic terrorism. In these instances, investigators can work toward clarifying the motives of the suspects involved.[29] Domestic terrorism cases differ from ordinary criminal activity in key ways. Most importantly, unlike ordinary criminals—who are often driven by self-centered motives such as profit and tend to opportunistically seek easy prey—domestic terrorists are driven by a cause or ideology.[30] If the motives involved align with the definition laid out in 18 U.S.C. Section 2331(5), presumably the case becomes a domestic terrorist investigation. In some instances, ideologically motivated actors can also collaborate with profit-driven individuals to commit crimes.

To further cloud matters, another category of criminal activity, hate crime, may appear to involve ideological issues. However, as described by one federal official, a "hate crime" "generally involve[s] acts of personal malice directed at individuals" and is missing the broader motivations driving acts of domestic terrorism.[31] For investigators, distinguishing between "personal malice" and ideologically motivated actions may be difficult in specific cases. This suggests that sorting domestic terrorism from hate crimes depends on the degree of a suspect's intent. Did the suspect articulate an ideology belonging to an extremist movement? The grey area between domestic terrorism and hate crime hints that in some instances, suspects with links to domestic terrorist movements or ideologies supporting domestic terrorism may be charged with hate crimes.[32] It is unclear to what extent this influences how the government understands the threat posed by extremist movements that hold racist beliefs. If some individuals of this ilk commit crimes against police or judges, for example, is the government more apt to label this activity as terrorism while individuals sharing these same racist motivations but targeting ordinary citizens based on race, religion, disability, ethnic origin, or sexual orientation are charged with hate crimes?

---

[28] See CRS Legal Sidebar WSLG1858, *Charlottesville Car Crash Attack: Possibility of Federal Criminal Prosecution,* by Charles Doyle. See also Federal Bureau of Investigation, "Domestic Terrorism."

[29] Responses of John E. Lewis, pp. 41, 42.

[30] In some instances such as those involving white-supremacist prison gangs who espouse extremist beliefs, the profit motive may be paramount in their criminal activity. See Joshua D. Freilich, Steven M. Chermak, and David Caspi, "Critical Events in the Life Trajectories of Domestic Extremist White Supremacist Groups," *Criminology and Public Policy,* vol. 8, no. 3 (August 2009), p. 508. Hereinafter: Freilich, Chermak, and Caspi, "Critical Events."

[31] Responses of John E. Lewis, p. 41.

[32] While this discussion focuses on intent, domestic terrorists can exhibit additional traits that distinguish them from other offenders. For example, as part of their involvement in ideological movements, domestic terrorists often are exposed to more tactical training—in weapons, explosives, arson, reconnaissance, paramilitary discipline—than many more ordinary criminals. See Anti-Defamation League, *Guidebook on Extremism for Law Enforcement,* (2007), p. 9. Hereinafter: Anti-Defamation League, *Guidebook.*

### Two Cases Demonstrating Blurred Lines Between Hate Crime and Domestic Terrorism

When it comes to characterizing ideologically inspired criminal actors for investigative purposes, the FBI occasionally confronts suspects who can be viewed either as terrorists or as perpetrators of hate crimes. Precisely understanding suspect's motives (among other things) can be useful in categorizing his or her case as either a domestic terrorism or hate crime investigation.[33] However, when it comes to prosecution, one can say that such considerations are somewhat more limited, namely because no separate federal crime of "domestic terrorism" exists.[34] Federal prosecutors can pursue hate crimes charges or other criminal offenses that fit the crime.[35] While pursing such non-terrorism charges, prosecutors may avoid publicly describing suspects as domestic terrorists.

#### *Dylann Roof*

On June 17, 2015, Dylann Roof shot and killed nine African Americans in the Emanuel African Methodist Episcopal Church in Charleston, SC. Three churchgoers survived. DOJ pursued a case involving federal hate crimes and firearms charges.[36] Roof was sentenced to death by a federal jury.[37] According to DOJ, before the shooting incident, Roof had posted on a website a manuscript and photos "expressing his racist beliefs." Additionally, DOJ argued that he "wanted to increase racial tensions across the Nation, and sought retribution for perceived wrongs he believed African-Americans had committed against white people."[38] Although it seems that Roof's alleged motives had ideological underpinnings in white supremacy, then-Attorney General Loretta E. Lynch noted in 2015 that DOJ pursued federal hate crimes charges because "[w]e think that this is exactly the type of case that the federal hate crimes statutes were, in fact, conceived to cover."[39]

---

[33] Investigating an individual as a terrorist may confer more resources to an investigation and may offer more investigative options. Regarding the latter, see American Civil Liberties Union, "How the USA PATRIOT Act Redefines 'Domestic Terrorism,'" https://www.aclu.org/other/how-usa-patriot-act-redefines-domestic-terrorism.

[34] Greg Myre, "Why the Government Can't Bring Terrorism Charges in Charlottesville," *NPR*, August 14, 2017.

[35] For a discussion of federal hate crimes, see Department of Justice, "Hate Crime Laws," https://www.justice.gov/crt/hate-crime-laws.

[36] Department of Justice, "Attorney General Lynch Statement Following the Federal Grand Jury Indictment Against Dylann Storm Roof," press release, July 22, 2015. DOJ also sought the death penalty. Department of Justice, "Attorney General Loretta E. Lynch Statement on the Case of Dylann Roof," press release, May 24, 2016.

[37] Department of Justice, "Federal Jury Sentences Dylann Storm Roof to Death," press release, January 10, 2017.

[38] United States v. Dylann Storm Roof, indictment, U.S. District Court, District of South Carolina, June 20, 2015.

[39] Christina Maza, "Why is Dylann Roof Not Facing Charges of Terrorism?" *Christian Science Monitor*, July 24, 2015.

### *Kevin Harpham*

The FBI's public description of the case of confessed would-be bomber Kevin Harpham is an example of how difficult it may be to characterize acts as domestic terrorism. Initially, the FBI viewed the case as domestic terrorism. In 2011, Harpham, motivated by white supremacist ideology, left a bomb—which never detonated—along the route of a parade in Spokane, WA, honoring Dr. Martin Luther King Jr. The FBI's Northwest Joint Terrorism Task Force led the investigation.[40] In prepared public remarks framing the "current state of the terrorism threat" from April 2011, the then-FBI Assistant Director for the Counterterrorism Division noted that Harpham's case was one of "several recent domestic terrorism incidents [that] demonstrate the scope of the threat."[41] Harpham eventually pled guilty to committing a federal hate crime and attempting to use a weapon of mass destruction.[42] Thereafter, the Bureau described the case as the successful prevention of a "horrific hate crime."[43]

## Extremism vs. Terrorism

Another concept that muddies discussion of domestic terrorism is "extremism." The latter term is commonly applied to homegrown actors, whether they be domestic terrorists or adherents of ideologies forwarded by foreign groups such as Al Qaeda. National security expert Jonathan Masters has suggested that many law enforcement officials likely view "extremism" as largely synonymous with "terrorism."[44] Masters has also found that there is a "lack of uniformity in the way *domestic terrorist* activities are prosecuted" in the United States.[45] Presumably, using the term "extremist" allows prosecutors, policymakers, and investigators the flexibility to discuss terrorist-like activity without actually labeling it as "terrorism" and then having to prosecute it as such. This flexibility is certainly an asset to prosecutors. They can charge subjects of FBI domestic terrorism investigations under a wider array of statutes without having to convince a jury that the accused were terrorists. However, for policymakers this flexibility makes it hard to determine the scope of the domestic terrorist threat. One cannot get a clear sense of scope if some individuals are charged and publicly described as terrorists, others are discussed as extremists, and still others enter the public record only as criminals

[40] Department of Justice, "Attempted Bomber Arrested," press release, March 9, 2011.

[41] Mark F. Giuliano, Assistant Director, Counterterrorism Division, Federal Bureau of Investigation, prepared remarks delivered at the Washington Institute for Near East Policy, Stein Program on Counterterrorism and Intelligence, Washington, DC, April 14, 2011, http://www.fbi.gov/news/speeches/the-post-9-11-fbi-the-bureaus-response-to-evolving-threats.

[42] Department of Justice, "Attempted Bomber Pleads Guilty to Federal Hate Crime and Weapons Charge," press release, September 7, 2011.

[43] Federal Bureau of Investigation, "MLK Parade Bomber," January 13, 2012; Department of Justice, press release, "Colville, Wash., Man Indicted for Federal Hate Crime in Attempted Bombing of the MLK Unity March," press release, April 21, 2011.

[44] Jonathan Masters, *Militant Extremists in the United States,* Council on Foreign Relations, Washington, DC, February 7, 2011.

[45] Ibid.

implicated in crimes not necessarily associated with terrorism, such as trespassing, arson, and tax fraud.

### *What Is Extremism?*

The FBI's public formulation of "extremism" suggests two components. First, extremism involves hewing to particular ideologies. Second, it also includes criminal activity to advance these ideologies.[46] Thus, according to this construction, an anarchist believes in a particular ideology—anarchism. An "anarchist extremist" is an anarchist who adopts criminal tactics.[47]

One scholar has indicated a similar bifurcation: First, extremism refers to an ideology outside a society's key values, and for liberal democracies, such ideologies "support racial or religious supremacy and/or oppose the core principles of democracy and human rights." Second, extremism can refer to the use of tactics that ignore the rights of others to achieve an ideological goal.[48]

### *"Homegrown Violent Extremists" Are Not Domestic Terrorists*

The FBI and DHS have popularized the phrase "homegrown violent extremist" (HVE). It separates domestic terrorists from U.S.-based terrorists *motivated by the ideologies of foreign terrorist organizations.* According to DHS and the FBI, a HVE is "a person of any citizenship who has lived and/or operated primarily in the United States or its territories who advocates, is engaged in, or is preparing to engage in ideologically-motivated terrorist activities (including providing support to terrorism) in furtherance of political or social objectives promoted by a foreign terrorist organization, but is acting independently of direction by a foreign terrorist organization."[49] According to the FBI and DHS, an HVE is not a domestic terrorist—they are two distinct categories of terrorist actors.[50]

---

[46] Federal Bureau of Investigation, "Domestic Terrorism: Anarchist Extremism, A Primer," December 16, 2010. The focus of this piece, as the title suggests, is anarchist extremism, not necessarily defining the term "extremism." Hereinafter: Federal Bureau of Investigation, "Anarchist Extremism." This type of formulation—extremism consists of adherence to ideologies *and* criminal activity committed in the name of these ideologies—is replicated in the definitions provided within Department of Homeland Security, "Domestic Terrorism and Homegrown."

[47] Making things more complex, the broader concept of "violent extremism" was used by the Obama Administration. According to the Administration, "violent extremists" are "individuals who support or commit ideologically-motivated violence to further political goals." See *Empowering Local Partners to Prevent Violent Extremism in the United States,* August 2011, p. 1.

[48] Peter R. Neumann, *Prisons and Terrorism: Radicalisation and De-Radicalisation in 15 Countries,* International Centre for the Study of Radicalisation and Political Violence, London, 2010, p. 12. In its *Guidebook on Extremism for Law Enforcement,* Hereinafter: Neumann, *Prisons and Terrorism.* The Anti-Defamation League has defined extremists as: "people who subscribe to extreme ideologies." The group goes on to say, "*extreme* ideologies are those that promote world views so radical that most other people will not agree with them." See Anti-Defamation League, *Guidebook,* p. 3.

[49] This definition appears to differ from the conceptualization of "homegrown jihadists" used in this report by (1) only including individuals *not* directed by a foreign organization and by (2) including all sorts of terrorists motivated by foreign ideologies, not just violent jihadists. See Department of Homeland Security and Federal Bureau of Investigation, Joint Intelligence Bulletin, "Use of Small Arms: Examining Lone Shooters and Small-Unit Tactics," August 16, 2011, p. 3.

[50] Ibid.

### The Lack of an Official Public List

The federal government does not generate an official *and* public list of domestic terrorist organizations or individuals.[51] The development of such a list may be precluded by civil liberties concerns (i.e., inclusion in a publicly available list may impinge on a group's exercise of free speech or its other constitutionally protected activities). However, a lack of official lists or processes to designate groups or individuals as domestic terrorists makes it difficult to assess domestic terrorism trends and evaluate federal efforts to counter such threats. In 2011, an unnamed DHS official cited in a news report stated that "unlike international terrorism, there are no designated domestic terrorist groups. Subsequently, all the legal actions of an identified extremist group leading up to an act of violence are constitutionally protected and not reported on by DHS."[52] Constitutionality aside, the lack of a list may also contribute to a certain vagueness in the public realm about which groups the federal government considers domestic terrorist organizations. While the government does not provide an official and public list of domestic terrorist organizations, it does include domestic terrorists (along with international terrorists) in its Terrorist Screening Database, commonly known as the "Terrorist Watchlist."[53]

The government is much less vague regarding foreign terrorist organizations. They are officially designated as such according to a well-established legally and procedurally proscribed regimen. According to the Department of State's Bureau of Counterterrorism, as of August 16, 2017, the Secretary of State had designated 61 foreign terrorist organizations according to Section 219 of the Immigration and Nationality Act, as amended.[54]

### Toward a Practical Definition: Threats Not Groups

As discussed above, DOJ and the FBI do not list domestic terrorist organizations publicly and officially. This may complicate the understanding that federal policymakers have of what exactly the government considers "domestic terrorism." While not naming specific *groups*, DOJ and the FBI have openly delineated domestic terrorist *threats*. DOJ has identified domestic terrorism threats to include criminal activity by animal rights extremists, ecoterrorists, anarchists, anti-government extremists such as 'sovereign citizens' and unauthorized militias, black separatists, white supremacists, and abortion extremists.[55]

---

[51] See Christopher Bellavita, "Does the U.S. Have Any Domestic Terrorist Groups?" *Homeland Security Watch*, June 29, 2010. Hereinafter: Bellavita, "Domestic Terrorist Groups." See also R. Jeffrey Smith, "Homeland Security Department Curtails Home-Grown Terror Analysis," *Washington Post*, June 7, 2011. Hereinafter: Smith, "Homeland Security." David E. Heller, "Designating Domestic Terrorist Individuals or Groups," (Master's Thesis, Naval Postgraduate School, 2010). Hereinafter: Heller, "Designating Domestic."

[52] Smith, "Homeland Security."

[53] Federal Bureau of Investigation, Terrorist Screening Center, "Frequently Asked Questions." See also Timothy J. Healy, Director, Terrorist Screening Center, Federal Bureau of Investigation, Statement before the House Judiciary Committee, Washington, DC, March 24, 2010; Bellavita, "Domestic Terrorist Groups." For more information on the Terrorist Screening Database, see CRS Report R44678, *The Terrorist Screening Database and Preventing Terrorist Travel*, by Jerome P. Bjelopera, Bart Elias, and Alison Siskin.

[54] For the legal criteria used to designate a foreign terrorist organization, the legal ramifications of designation, and ancillary effects of designation see Department of State, "Foreign Terrorist Organizations," https://www.state.gov/j/ct/rls/other/des/123085.htm.

[55] Department of Justice, *White Paper*, p. 59. See also Federal Bureau of Investigation, "Domestic Terrorism." In recent years, the FBI has switched from "anti-abortion" to abortion extremism, thus including individuals who may commit crimes to protect abortion rights. The FBI's domestic terrorism investigations likely

The actors who constitute each of the domestic terrorist "threats" outlined by DOJ draw upon ideologies whose expression largely involves constitutionally protected activity. The FBI safeguards against cases focused solely on constitutionally protected activities. All FBI investigations have to be conducted for an authorized national security, criminal, or foreign intelligence collection purpose.[56] The purpose of an investigation may not be to solely monitor First Amendment rights.[57]

However, it is unclear how DOJ or the FBI arrive at their list of domestic terrorism threats. This poses at least two fundamental questions:

- How does a particular brand of dissent become ripe for description by DOJ and the FBI as driving a "domestic terrorism" threat?

  What criteria are involved in such a process?

  How many crimes or plots attributed to a specific ideology have to occur to stimulate the identification of a new extremist threat? Is the severity of the crimes linked to an ideology taken into consideration?

- At what point do ideologically driven domestic terrorism threats cease to exist?

  Should there be a means for public petitioning of the government to eliminate various threats as investigative priorities?

*The below discussion of domestic terrorism threats does not necessarily presume the priority of one over the other.*[58] *It is also important to note that instances of animal rights extremism and ecoterrorism within the last fifteen years are more readily available in the public record than cases involving other types of domestic terrorism.*[59] *The extensive use of such examples in this report does not imply the prominence of animal rights extremism or ecoterrorism over other domestic terrorist threats.*

---

cover these categories as well as lone wolves (lone offenders): extremists who commit crimes without the support of a formal organization or network. Some lone wolves are motivated by the ideologies behind the threats outlined by DOJ, but they can fashion their own ideologies as well. In the past, in the area of domestic terrorism, the FBI has distinguished between "special interest terrorism" and "traditional right-wing and left-wing terrorism: "Special interest terrorism differs from traditional right-wing and left-wing terrorism in that extremist special interest groups seek to resolve specific issues, rather than effect widespread political change. Special interest extremists continue to conduct acts of politically motivated violence to force segments of society, including the general public, to change attitudes about issues considered important to their causes. These groups occupy the extreme fringes of animal rights, pro-life, environmental, anti-nuclear, and other movements." It is unclear whether the FBI still uses the categories of "special interest," "left-wing," and "right-wing" terrorism. See Jarboe, Testimony. See also Federal Bureau of Investigation, "What are Known Violent Extremist Groups?" https://www.fbi.gov/cve508/teen-website/what-are-known-violent-extremist-groups. This is from a website designed by the FBI to counter violent extremism. The website, titled "Don't Be a Puppet," addresses teenagers. Regardless, it is one of the few publicly-available sources where the Bureau succinctly describes numerous violent extremist groups or ideologies.

[56] Federal Bureau of Investigation, *Domestic Investigations and Operations Guide*, redacted, October 15, 2011, p. 4-1 through p. 4-2.

[57] Ibid.

[58] The discussion lists the threats in the same order as found in Department of Justice, *White Paper.*

[59] People the FBI or DOJ may characterize as animal rights extremists and ecoterrorists have tended to publicize their activities online.

### Animal Rights Extremists and Environmental Extremists

The term "animal rights extremism" covers criminal acts committed in the name of animal rights.[60] Environmental extremism—most often referred to as "ecoterrorism"—includes criminal acts committed in the name of the environment.[61] These terms are not applied to groups or individuals involved with environmental movements or animal welfare protection/rights activism within the "confines of civil society and the rule of law."[62]

Many of the crimes committed by both animal rights extremists and ecoterrorists are perpetrated by independent small cells or individuals who harass and intimidate their victims.[63] These cells or lone actors engage in crimes such as vandalism, theft, the destruction of property, and arson. Most animal rights extremists and ecoterrorists also eschew physical violence directly targeting people or animals. Regardless, crimes committed by ecoterrorists and animal rights extremists have caused millions of dollars in property damage, and some have involved the intimidation and harassment of victims.[64] These two types of extremism are often discussed together, because the two broader radical *movements* from which they draw their philosophical underpinnings have similar beliefs and overlapping membership.

The two *movements*—the Animal Liberation Front (ALF) and the Earth Liberation Front (ELF)—have the greatest reach among animal rights extremists and ecoterrorists. The ALF and the ELF are too diffuse to be called groups. Neither the ALF nor the ELF maintains formal rosters or leadership structures, for example.[65] However, each communicates a sense of shared identity and attracts people who commit crimes in its name. They achieve this via "above-ground" wings. Largely using websites, ALF and ELF supporters publish literature highlighting movement philosophies, tactics, and accounts (press releases) of recent movement-related criminal activity. Much of this involves protected speech and occurs in the public realm. Press releases allow "underground" extremists to publicly claim responsibility for criminal activity in the name of either movement while maintaining secrecy regarding the details of their operations. The ALF and the ELF do not work alone. Members of other entities such as Stop Huntingdon Animal Cruelty (SHAC) have committed crimes in the name of animal rights, for example.

Additional factors tangle our understanding of the ALF and the ELF. People can simultaneously participate in both. This may partly be true because the movements are so

---

[60] Department of Homeland Security, "Domestic Terrorism and Homegrown."

[61] For the purposes of this report, "ecoterrorists," "eco-extremists," and "environmental extremists" are synonymous. These terms and "animal rights extremism" describe individuals engaged in criminal activity in the name of radical environmental ideologies or animal rights. It is unclear why environmental extremists are frequently dubbed "ecoterrorists" while animal rights extremists do not have a similar commonplace usage applied to them.

[62] See Kevin R. Grubbs, "Saving Lives or Spreading Fear: The Terroristic Nature of Eco-Extremism," *Animal Law*, vol. 16, no. 2 (2010), p. 353–57. Hereinafter: Grubbs, "Saving Lives."

[63] See Federal Bureau of Investigation, "Putting Intel to Work against ELF and ALF Terrorists," June 30, 2008. Hereinafter: FBI, "Putting Intel."

[64] Ibid.

[65] Both the ALF and the ELF focus on criminal activity as central tenets of their philosophies or operational guidelines, and the FBI emphasizes that criminal activity is a key element in the identities of these movements. See FBI, "Putting Intel."

amorphous. The two movements also share similar agendas, and in 1993 they declared solidarity.[66] All of this can play out confusingly in the real world. For example, an individual can commit a crime and claim responsibility for it online in the name of *both* the ALF and the ELF. One case especially highlights intersections between the ALF and the ELF.

In the late 1990s and early 2000s, the FBI uncovered a network that, according to DOJ, committed violent acts in the name of both the ALF and the ELF. The group included about 20 individuals and called itself "the Family." It was reportedly responsible for at least 25 criminal incidents totaling approximately $48 million in damages and disbanded at some point in 2001, due to law enforcement pressure on the group. The Family was responsible for an arson attack in 1998 at the Vail Ski Resort. Eight simultaneous fires damaged radio towers, ski lift towers, restaurants, and the ski patrol office at the Colorado site and totaled over $24 million in losses.[67]

### *Philosophical Underpinnings*

Both the ALF and the ELF rely on and borrow from a number of philosophical underpinnings to rationalize their beliefs and actions. These help forge a common identity among individuals in each movement. These ideas are also key principles professed by more mainstream animal rights or environmental activists engaged in legal protest.

**The ALF: Animal Rights and Speciesism.** The ALF's moral code includes the belief that animals possess basic inalienable rights such as life, liberty, and the pursuit of happiness, and this suggests that animals cannot be owned. According to the ALF, the U.S. legal system—which describes animals as property—is corrupt, and there exists a "higher law than that created by and for the corporate-state complex, a moral law that transcends the corrupt and biased statutes of the US political system."[68] Simply put, the rights of one species do not trump the rights of others. To suggest otherwise is to be prejudiced, according to animal rights adherents.

For the ALF and other animal rights supporters, the favoring of one species, particularly humans, over others has a name: speciesism. For the ALF, speciesism is a "discriminatory belief system as ethically flawed and philosophically unfounded as sexism or racism, but far more murderous and consequential in its implications."[69] Thus, the

[66] U.S. Congress, Senate Committee on Environment and Public Works, "Statement of Carson Carroll, Deputy Assistant Director, Bureau of Alcohol, Tobacco, Firearms, and Explosives," *Eco-Terrorism Specifically Examining the Earth Liberation Front and the Animal Liberation Front,* 109th Cong., 1st sess., May 18, 2005, S. Hrg. 109-947 (Washington: GPO, 2007), p. 43. Hereinafter: Statement of Carson Carroll.

[67] Federal Bureau of Investigation, "Operation Backfire: Help Find Four Eco-Terrorists," November 19, 2008; Department of Justice, "Eleven Defendants Indicted on Domestic Terrorism Charges," press release, January 20, 2006. Hereinafter: Department of Justice, "Eleven Defendants." See also *United States v. Joseph Dibee et al,* Sentencing Memorandum, CR 06-60069-AA, CR 06-60070-AA, CR 06-60071-AA, CR 06-60078-AA, CR 06-60079-AA, CR 06-60080-AA, CR 06-60120-AA, CR-06-60122-AA, CR-06-60123-AA, CR-06-60124-AA, CR-06-60125-AA, CR-60126-AA, U.S. District Court, District of Oregon, May 4, 2007, pp. 6, 8, 19, 20–21. Hereinafter: *U.S. v. Dibee et al.*

[68] North American Animal Liberation Press Office, "History of the Animal Liberation Movement." Hereinafter: NAALPO, "History."

[69] Steven Best and Anthony J. Nocella, II, "Behind the Mask: Uncovering the Animal Liberation Front," in *Terrorists or Freedom Fighters? Reflections on the Liberation of Animals,* ed. Steven Best and Anthony J. Nocella, II (New York: Lantern Books, 2004), p. 24. Hereinafter: Best and Nocella, "Behind the Mask." Best reportedly advises NAALPO, see http://naalpo.posterous.com/our-task-new-essay-by-press-office-advisor-st.

movement couches the theft or illegal release of animals used in research or for economic gain as "liberation." The ALF views the destruction of laboratory infrastructure or tools as the elimination of items used to enslave species who have the same rights as humans. Intimidation of scientists and employees of businesses tied to animal research or testing is rationalized as confrontation with "oppressors" or those who, in the eyes of movement adherents, abuse and murder animals.[70]

**The ELF: An Ideological Mélange.** Ecoterrorists are motivated by a mélange of environmental philosophies. There is no single formula for what constitutes the ideological makeup of an ELF follower, but several concepts likely play key roles in the movement. These are biocentrism, deep ecology, social ecology, and green anarchism. Biocentrism argues for the equality of all organisms.[71] Deep ecology suggests that all species are part of "the larger super-organism that is nature."[72] It criticizes industrialization and views modern human impact on the earth as negative and hearkens back to small communities centered on subsistence agriculture.[73] Social ecology suggests that hierarchical human society leads to social inequalities and environmental harm. Green anarchism ascribes environmental harm to civilization and domestication and embraces the notion of "rewilding," or rejecting civilization and returning to a hunter-gatherer state to preserve one's natural surroundings.[74]

### Anarchist Extremists

According to the FBI, anarchist extremists commit crimes in the name of anarchist ideals.[75] These ideals include belief that

> individual autonomy and collective equality are fundamental and necessary for a functional, civilized society. [Anarchism] resists the existing hierarchical structure of society that gives some people authority and control over others. [According to anarchists] authority imbues power, and power always is used in illegitimate and self-serving ways by those who have it.[76]

Anarchist extremists as well as anarchists engaging in constitutionally protected activity can oppose government, business, or social interests that they view as dangerous. As this suggests, anarchists advocate some form of revolution that realigns authority

P. Michael Conn and James V. Parker, *The Animal Research War* (New York: Palgrave Macmillan, 2008), p. xix. Hereinafter: Conn and Parker, *The Animal.* See also NAALPO, "History" which excerpts Best and Nocella's work.

[70] NAALPO, "History."

[71] Stefan H. Leader and Peter Probst, "The Earth Liberation Front and Environmental Terrorism," *Terrorism and Political Violence*, vol. 15, no. 4 (Spring/Summer 2005), pp. 39–40. Hereinafter: Leader and Probst, "The Earth Liberation Front."

[72] Conn and Parker, *The Animal*, xx.

[73] Leader and Probst, "The Earth Liberation Front," pp. 39–40.

[74] Sean Parson, "Understanding the Ideology of the Earth Liberation Front," *Green Theory and Praxis: The Journal of Ecopedagogy*, vol. 4, no. 2 (2008), pp. 54–58.

[75] Ibid.

[76] Randy Borum and Chuck Tilby, "Anarchist Direct Actions: A Challenge for Law Enforcement," *Studies in Conflict and Terrorism*, vol. 28, no. 3, (2005), p. 202. Hereinafter: Borum and Tilby, "Anarchist Direct Action."

in the societies they desire to transform. However, adherents cannot agree to a single means for attaining revolutionary change.[77]

As one may assume, anarchist activity is decentralized. In fact, a basic, temporary organizational structure—the affinity group—likely plays a larger role in shaping the work of U.S. anarchists than any formal long-lasting entities or networks.[78] Affinity groups are "autonomous militant unit[s] generally made up of between five-to-twenty individuals who share a sense of the causes worth defending and the types of actions they prefer to engage in. The decision-making process is anarchist, that is to say, egalitarian, participatory, deliberative, and consensual."[79] An affinity group often consists of a circle of friends. The friends coalesce around a specific objective and break apart when they achieve their desired ends. Individual groups can band together in "clusters" and clusters can coordinate their efforts, if need be.[80] The efforts can be legal or illegal, violent or nonviolent, covert or open. These structures have a long history among anarchists, but other movements use them as well.[81] Also, anarchists can engage in what they call "black bloc" tactics. These involve secretive planning for public—often criminal—activity in which participants, typically dressed in black, act en-masse.[82] Adding to the sprawling nature of the anarchist movement, some adherents also participate in the ALF and the ELF. These three movements share general philosophical tenets such as opposition to globalization and capitalism.[83]

### "Antifa"

In the aftermath of the violence related to protests in Charlottesville, VA, on August 12, 2017, there has been media attention devoted to the confrontational tactics of antifascist protesters known as "Antifa." Antifa beliefs can dovetail with the broad anti-government and anti-capitalist views that are part of anarchism.[84] One observer has described Antifa as, "a radical pan-leftist politics of social revolution applied to fighting the far right. Its adherents are predominantly communists, socialists and anarchists who reject turning to the police or the state to halt the advance of white supremacy."[85] Antifa beliefs appear to inspire autonomous groups to track the activities of neo-Nazis, and most "anti-fascist organizing is

[77] Ibid., p. 203.

[78] Borum and Tilby, "Anarchist Direct Action," p. 207.

[79] Francis Dupuis-Déri, "Anarchism and the Politics of Affinity Groups," *Anarchist Studies*, vol. 18, no. 1 (2010), p. 41. Hereinafter: Dupuis-Déri, "Anarchism."

[80] CrimethInc. Workers' Collective, *Recipes for Disaster: An Anarchist Cookbook*, (Olympia, WA: CrimethInc. Workers' Collective, 2004), pp. 28–34. Hereinafter: *Anarchist Cookbook.*

[81] Dupuis-Déri, "Anarchism," p. 43.

[82] *Anarchist Cookbook*, pp. 127–130.

[83] Borum and Tilby, "Anarchist Direct Action," p. 208.

[84] "Anarchist Extremists: Antifa," State of New Jersey Office of Homeland Security and Preparedness, June 12, 2017. Hereinafter: "Anarchist Extremists: Antifa." Breanna Cammeron, "Antifa: Left-Wing Militants on the Rise," *BBC News*, August 14, 2017.

[85] Mark Bray, "Who Are the Antifa?" *Washington Post*, August 16, 2017.

nonviolent."[86] However, some Antifa protesters are willing to violently clash with people publicly advocating what Antifa protesters would see as fascist views, particularly white supremacists.[87] Antifa protesters characterize such violence targeting people as defensive.[88]

The FBI has described anarchist extremists as typically being "event driven," meaning

> they show up at political conventions, economic and financial summits, environmental meetings, and the like. They usually target symbols of Western civilization that they perceive to be the root causes of all societal ills—i.e., financial corporations, government institutions, multinational companies, and law enforcement agencies. They damage and vandalize property, riot, set fires, and perpetrate small-scale bombings. Law enforcement is also concerned about anarchist extremists who may be willing to use improvised explosives devices or improvised incendiary devices.[89]

Anarchist extremists in the United States have been involved in illegal activity during mass protests surrounding events such as the 1999 World Trade Organization Ministerial Conference in Seattle, WA.

Anarchist extremists reportedly committed crimes during the 2008 Republican National Convention in St. Paul, MN.[90] To coordinate their protests during the convention, some anarchists formed what they called the "RNC Welcoming Committee" (RNCWC).[91] In September 2007, the RNCWC developed a plan to broadly organize the activities of affinity groups intending to disrupt the convention. Law enforcement infiltrated and undermined these efforts, arresting 800 people, including eight involved with the RNCWC.[92] Initially, in Minnesota state court, the eight "had been charged with felonies: first-degree damage to property and second-degree conspiracy to riot. Prosecutors added a more serious charge of conspiracy to riot in furtherance of terrorism, which

---

86 Ibid.

87 See "Anarchist Extremists: Antifa."

88 Sara Ganim and Chris Welch, "Unmasking the Leftist Antifa Movement," *CNN*, August 20, 2017. They have also engaged in property destruction.

89 Federal Bureau of Investigation, "Anarchist Extremism."

90 Ibid. For information on reported anarchist criminal activity related to the 2008 Republican National Convention, see Department of Justice, "Michigan Man Sentenced for Possessing Molotov Cocktails," press release, March 10, 2009; Department of Justice, "Texas Man Sentenced on Firearms Charges Connected to the Republican National Convention," press release, May 21, 2009; Department of Justice, "Austin, Texas Man Sentenced for Possessing Molotov Cocktails During the Republican National Convention," press release, May 14, 2009. For information on a matter possibly related to the anarchist criminal activity at the 2008 convention, see James C. McKinley Jr., "Anarchist Ties Seen in '08 Bombing of Texas Governor's Mansion," *New York Times*, February 22, 2011.

91 For an archived version of the group's website see http://web.archive.org/web/20080907081250/http://www.nornc.org./.

92 Pat Pheifer, "Guilty Pleas Close Book on '08 Convention Protests," *Minneapolis-St. Paul Star Tribune*, October 19, 2010. Hereinafter: Pheifer, "Guilty Pleas." See also Fred Burton and Scott Stewart, "The Lessons of St. Paul," *STRATFOR*, September 10, 2008.

was later dismissed."[93] Five of the eight pled guilty to gross misdemeanor charges in 2010. The others had all of the charges they faced dismissed.[94]

On April 30, 2012, five men who reputedly had anarchist sympathies were arrested for purportedly scheming to blow up a bridge near Cleveland, OH.[95] One was convicted on charges related to the plot. The four others pled guilty.[96] The plot was apparently timed to coincide with peaceful protest activity arranged by Occupy Cleveland, an offshoot of the Occupy Wall Street movement. Occupy Cleveland representatives stated that the would-be bombers "were in no way representing or acting on behalf of Occupy Cleveland."[97] An FBI sting operation led to the quintet's arrest.[98] Purportedly, the group relied on an undercover FBI employee to supply them with two inert bombs that the conspirators believed were functional.[99]

Criminal acts involving anarchist extremists do not have to be event-driven. For example, Eric G. King pled guilty to using explosive devices to commit arson in a failed 2014 attempt to ignite a fire at the Kansas City, MO, office of U.S. Representative Emanuel Cleaver II. The incident occurred when the office was unoccupied, but King had posted violent commentary regarding police to social media.[100]

DHS noted that anarchist extremists had set fires at urban development project sites in Vancouver, Canada, and Seattle, WA, in 2013. Anarchist extremists are also suspected in a similar incident that occurred in Grand Rapids, MI in 2011.[101] These attacks followed instances of what DHS characterized as "lower-level criminal activity or mischief involving anarchist or 'anti-gentrification statements.'"[102]

In another case that was not event-driven, Joseph Konopka, the self-dubbed "Dr. Chaos," allegedly led a group of boys he called "The Realm of Chaos" in a series of crimes involving vandalism to radio and cell phone towers in the late 1990s and early 2000s. In 2002, he was arrested in Chicago for storing more than a pound of deadly cyanide powder

[93] Pheifer, "Guilty Pleas."

[94] Ibid.

[95] Department of Justice, "Five Men Arrested in Plot to Bomb Ohio Bridge," press release, May 1, 2012. Hereinafter: Department of Justice, "Five Men." David Ariosto, "5 Arrested in Alleged Plot to Blow Up Cleveland-Area Bridge," *CNN*, May 1, 2012.

[96] Kim Palmer, "'Anarchist' Convicted in Ohio Bridge Bomb Plot," *Reuters*, June 13, 2013.

[97] Henry J. Gomez, "Bridge Bomb Plot: Suspects Were Active in Occupy Cleveland, Even As Movement Slowed to a Crawl," *Cleveland Plain Dealer*, May 2, 2012.

[98] Department of Justice, "Five Men."

[99] Ibid. Four of the conspirators pled guilty "to conspiracy to use weapons of mass destruction, attempted use of weapons of mass destruction, and malicious use of an explosive device to destroy property used in interstate commerce." See Department of Justice, "Three Men Sentenced to Prison for Roles in Plot to Bomb Ohio Bridge," press release, November 20, 2012. A fifth was "convicted of conspiracy to use a weapon of mass destruction and other charges." See Kim Palmer, "'Anarchist' Convicted in Ohio Bridge Bomb Plot," *Reuters*, June 13, 2013.

[100] Tony Rizzo, "Man Who Threw Molotov Cocktails at Rep. Emanuel Cleaver's KC Office Gets 10-Year Sentence," *Kansas City Star*, June 28, 2016; Department of Justice, "KC Man Pleads Guilty to Throwing Molotov Cocktails at Congressional Office," press release, March 3, 2016.

[101] Department of Homeland Security, "Self-Identified Anarchist Extremists Target Urban 'Gentrification' Sites with Arson," July 23, 2013.

[102] Ibid.

in a passageway in a Chicago Transit Authority subway tunnel.[103] He had obtained the material (potassium cyanide and sodium cyanide) from an abandoned warehouse.[104] In 2002, Konopka pled guilty in federal court to possessing chemical weapons, and in 2005 he pled guilty to 11 felonies, including conspiracy, arson, creating counterfeit software, and interfering with computers in Wisconsin.[105]

### White Supremacist Extremists

The term "white supremacist extremism" (WSE) describes people or groups who commit criminal acts in the name of white supremacist ideology. According to media sources, in May 2017, FBI and DHS released a joint intelligence bulletin reputedly stating that white supremacists "were responsible for 49 homicides in 26 attacks from 2000 to 2016 ... more than any other domestic extremist movement."[106]

At its core, white supremacist ideology purports that the white race ranks above all others. WSE draws on the constitutionally protected activities of a broad swath of racist hate-oriented groups active in the United States ranging from the Ku Klux Klan to racist skinheads. Some of these groups have elaborate organizational structures, dues-paying memberships, and media wings. Additionally, many individuals espouse extremist beliefs without having formal membership in any specific organization.

A large proportion of white supremacists dualistically divide the world between whites and all other peoples who are seen as enemies.[107] Particular animus is directed toward Jews and African Americans. In fact, a common racist and revisionist historical refrain is that the civil rights movement succeeded only because Jews orchestrated it behind the scenes.[108]

Scholars indicate that white supremacists believe in racial separation and that society discriminates against them. To them, whites have lost "ground to other groups and ... extreme measures are required to reverse the trend."[109] All of this has been encapsulated in a slogan known as the "Fourteen Words": "We must secure the existence of our race and a future for white children." This was coined by David Lane, a member of a

---

[103] Juliet Williams, Federal appeals Court Overturns Dr. Chaos Conviction," *Associated Press,* May 31, 2005; Mike Robinson, "Federal Prosecutors Want 'Dr. Chaos' to Remain Locked Up," *Associated Press,* March 13, 2002; Meg Jones and Jesse Garza, "'Anarchist' Charged Over Cache of Cyanide," *Milwaukee Journal Sentinel,* March 12, 2002.

[104] "Man Pleads Guilty to Storing Cyanide," *Associated Press,* November 21, 2002.

[105] "Judge Sentences 'Dr. Chaos' to Prison for Damage to Wisconsin Power Systems, *Associated Press,* November 30, 2005.

[106] Jana Winter, "FBI and DHS Warned of Growing Threat From White Supremacists Months Ago," *Foreign Policy.com,* August 14, 2017.

[107] Chip Berlet and Stanislav Vysotsky, "Overview of U.S. White Supremacist Groups," *Journal of Political and Military Sociology,* vol. 34, no. 1 (Summer 2006), p. 13. Hereinafter: Berlet and Vysotsky, "Overview."

[108] Leonard Zeskind, *Blood and Politics: The History of the White Nationalist Movement from the Margins to the Mainstream* (New York: Farrar, Straus, and Giroux, 2009), p. 40. Hereinafter: Zeskind, *Blood and Politics.*

[109] Rory McVeigh, "Structured Ignorance and Organized Racism in the United States," *Social Forces,* vol. 82, no. 3 (March 2004), pp. 898–899.

violent terrorist group active in the 1980s. The Fourteen Words have been described as "the most popular white supremacist slogan in the world."[110]

Neo-Nazism and its obsession with Adolph Hitler and Nazi Germany is also a prominent component of white supremacist extremism in the United States.[111] The father of American neo-Nazism, George Lincoln Rockwell, became publicly active in the late 1950s. According to one scholar, Rockwell laid down three concepts that have shaped neo-Nazism ever since. For his followers, he reconfigured the racial notion of "white," broadening it beyond "Aryan" to include people of Southern and Eastern European descent. Additionally, Rockwell denied the Holocaust. He also encouraged tying neo-Nazism to religion, and some of his followers took up the obscure creed of Christian Identity.[112]

### *Conflict and Conspiracy*

Aside from racial superiority, a dualistic view of the world, and neo-Nazism, at least two other broad concepts shape white supremacy in the United States. They are the inevitability of violent conflict, and a belief that conspiracies hostile to white supremacy shape the existing world.[113] It can be said that WSE broadly shares these concepts with the militia movement (discussed below).

The FBI has stated that white supremacists "commonly anticipate" waging war against their opponents.[114] For example, the inevitability of RAHOWA—an acronym for "racial holy war"—is a central tenet of the neo-Nazi Creativity Movement, which has its roots in the Church of the Creator, a racist group founded by Ben Klassen in 1973.[115] Klassen, who committed suicide in 1993, argued that whites had no choice but to wage war against non-whites.[116] Likewise, some white supremacists use racism to interpret

---

[110] Anti-Defamation League, *Guidebook,* p. 16. Lane died in 2007 while serving 190 years in prison for his involvement with a terrorist group named the Order. See "Founder of Terrorist Group Dies in Prison," *Terre Haute Tribune-Star,* May 29, 2007, http://tribstar.com/local/x1155692948/Founder-of-terrorist-group-dies-in-prison. Among other writings, Lane also drafted an influential racist ideological tract titled *The 88 Precepts.*

[111] Anti-Defamation League, *Guidebook,* p. 15.

[112] Fredrick J. Simonelli, "The Neo-Nazi Movement," Southern Poverty Law Center. See also Charles S. Clark, "An American Nazi's Rise and Fall," *American History,* vol. 40, no. 6 (February 2006), pp. 60–66; Simonelli, "The American Nazi Party," *Historian,* vol. 57, no. 3 (Spring 1995), pp. 553–566. A follower assassinated Rockwell in 1967. For information on Christian Identity, see Kevin Borgeson and Robin Valeri, *Terrorism in America* (Sudbury, MA: Jones and Bartlett, 2009), pp. 47–72; Martin Durham, "Christian Identity and the Politics of Religion," *Totalitarian Movements and Political Religions,* vol. 9, no. 1 (March 2008), pp. 79–91; Tanya Telfair Sharpe, "The Identity Christian Movement: Ideology of Domestic Terrorism," *Journal of Black Studies,* vol. 30, no. 4 (March 2000), pp. 604–623; Anti-Defamation League, "Christian Identity."

[113] Berlet and Vysotsky, "Overview," pp. 12–13 highlights dualism, conspiracism, and apocalypticism as key themes.

[114] The Bureau has noted that "warfare" is reflected in beliefs drawn from Christian Identity, the Creativity Movement, neo-Nazism, and Odinism. See Federal Bureau of Investigation, *White Supremacist Recruitment of Military Personnel since 9/11,* July 7, 2008, p. 4. Hereinafter: Federal Bureau of Investigation, *White Supremacist.*

[115] After Klassen's 1993 death, the Church of the Creator was revived in an altered form by Matt Hale. For more information see Dobratz, "The Role," p. 290; and Federal Bureau of Investigation, *White Supremacist,* p. 4.

[116] Ben Klassen, "RAHOWA: The Fighting Slogan of the White Race," *Racial Loyalty,* no. 32 (February 1986).

apocalyptic imagery from Norse mythology embodied in Odinism.[117] Most Odinists are not racists, however.[118]

Conspiracism has been defined as "the idea that most major historic events have been shaped by vast, long-term, secret conspiracies that benefit elite groups and individuals."[119] Conspiracy theories are not the province of a particular movement or group. Regardless, conspiracy theories can particularly shape the outlooks and actions of white supremacist extremists. Media sources have stated that Richard Poplawski—convicted of shooting and killing three Pittsburgh police officers in April 2009—believed that a Zionist conspiracy controlled government and major corporations in the United States.[120]

As in Poplawski's example, anti-Semitism plays a prominent role in the racist conspiracies of many white supremacists.[121] Many anti-Semites—as well as anti-government extremists—believe in something they call the Zionist Occupied Government (ZOG).[122] ZOG refers to the federal government, which adherents contend is "controlled or manipulated by international Jewish interests."[123] On its website, one WSE group sold versions of a video game titled "ZOG's Nightmare." Gameplay involves shooting non-whites while being chased by a police agency controlled by Jews.[124] Racists explain all sorts of personal or social grievances by invoking ZOG.[125] One scholar has described ZOG as

> an omnipresent and omnipotent cabal involving at its heart varying constellations of Jews, Illuminati, Freemasons, plutocrats, and multinational corporations. It operates through many social 'front' institutions, from the United Nations to Parent-Teacher Associations.... ZOG can be used to explain not only the existence of affirmative action, environmental pollution, and pornography but also why a certain individual made poor grades in school, lost his job, or seems unable to find a partner.[126]

---

[117] Federal Bureau of Investigation, *White Supremacist*, p. 4. Odinism has been defined as either a combination of old Norse religion and Christianity or a belief system that draws exclusively on Nordic mythology. See Jonathan White, "Political Eschatology: A Theology of Antigovernment Extremism," *The American Behavioral Scientist*, vol. 44, no. 6, (February 2001), p. 939.

[118] Berlet and Vysotsky, "Overview," p. 30.

[119] Berlet and Vysotsky, "Overview," p. 12. For more on conspiracy theories and terrorism see Jamie Bartlett and Carl Miller, *The Power of Unreason: Conspiracy Theories, Extremism, and Counter-Terrorism*, Demos, London, August 29, 2010. Barlett and Miller (p. 24.) suggest that conspiracy theories "are one of a number of factors that can lead to extremism, and can turn extremism to violence."

[120] Timothy McNulty, Paula Reed Ward and Sadie Gurman, "Jury Decides Poplawski Should Die for Killing 3 Officers," *Pittsburgh Post-Gazette*, June 28, 2011. Hereinafter: McNulty et al., "Jury Decides." See also Anti-Defamation League, "Richard Poplawski: The Making of a Lone Wolf," April 8, 2009. Hereinafter: Anti-Defamation League, "Richard Poplawski." Sean D. Hamill, "Man Accused in Pittsburgh Killings Voiced Racist Views Online," *New York Times*, April 7, 2009. Hereinafter: Hamill, "Man Accused."

[121] Berlet and Vysotsky, "Overview," p. 13.

[122] Also seen as "Zionist Occupation Government."

[123] Institute for Intergovernmental Research, *Investigating Terrorism*, p. 93; Mattias Gardell, *Gods of the Blood: The Pagan Revival and White Separatism* (Durham, NC: Duke University Press, 2003), pp. 11, 54, 68–69. Hereinafter: Gardell, *Gods*.

[124] Anti-Defamation League, *The National Socialist Movement*.

[125] Gardell, *Gods, p. 68.*

[126] Ibid.

According to adherents, ZOG is said to control the media, arts, religion, science, and education.[127]

### *Loss of Prominent Leaders and Decline of their Groups*

In the 1980s and 1990s, a small number of figures dominated white supremacist circles. They were intimately linked to their own relatively cohesive organizations. By the early 2000s, these groups fragmented as they lost their leaders.

Two particularly well-known white supremacist figures died in the early 2000s. William Pierce, head of the National Alliance, died in 2002. Richard Butler, leader of Aryan Nations, died in 2004. Both Pierce and Butler articulated clear ideologies that attracted followers and drew upon resources such as rural headquarters/compounds to sustain their organizations.[128] By the early 2000s, the National Alliance even had a substantial revenue stream estimated at $1 million annually generated from a publishing company and record labels it owned as well as dues.[129] The deaths of Butler and Pierce exacerbated the downfall of both organizations. The decline of these groups also resulted from a number of other forces, such as infighting among members and pressure from law enforcement and watchdog groups.[130] Other groups have emerged since to promote white supremacist ideas. Several movements espousing such views participated in the August 2017 rally in Charlottesville, VA, that led to violence mentioned earlier.[131]

Two prominent white supremacist movements are discussed below.

### *National Socialist Movement (NSM)*

One long-standing white supremacist organization active in the United States is the National Socialist Movement (NSM). It has benefitted from the decline of other groups as well as new leadership in the form of Jeff Schoep.[132] The NSM also capitalized on the expansion of the Internet in the early 2000s. The group, which emerged in 1974, is a descendant of the American Nazi Party, and until the 1990s and early 2000s "it operated only on the fringes of the neo-Nazi movement."[133] As of 2008, the group had around 500 members and close associates throughout the United States.[134] The NSM is flexible

---

[127] Ibid.

[128] Freilich, Chermak, and Caspi, "Critical Events," 511.

[129] Ibid., pp. 512, 513.

[130] Ibid., p. 516.

[131] Groups such as Vanguard America (started in 2014), Identity Evropa (founded in 2016), and the Traditionalist Worker Party (begun in 2015) reportedly participated. "Various Far-Right Extremist Groups Joined at Virginia Rally," *Associated Press*, August 15, 2017; Terence Cullen, "Vanguard America, Group Charlottesville Driver James Fields Jr. Marched with, Has Increasingly Become a Neo-Nazi Voice," *New York Daily News*, August 13, 2017; Hailey Branson-Potts, "In Diverse California, a Young White Supremacist Seeks to Convert Fellow College Students," *Los Angeles Times*, December 7, 2016; Ralph Ellis, At Least 7 People Injured at Sacramento Rally, Authorities Say," *CNN*, June 27, 2016.

[132] Anti-Defamation League, *American Stormtroopers: Inside the National Socialist Movement*, (2008), p. 3. Hereinafter: Anti-Defamation League, *American Stormtroopers*.

[133] Ibid.

[134] Ibid.

about membership, allowing its members to also participate in other white supremacist organizations.[135]

Individuals allegedly tied to the NSM at some point in their lives have run afoul of the law.

- In Minnesota in April 2012, Joseph Benjamin Thomas was indicted on drug-related charges, and Samuel James Johnson was indicted on weapons-related charges. Purportedly the two were tied to NSM—at one point Johnson had allegedly served as its leader in Minnesota. The duo had reportedly formed their own white supremacist group, gathering weapons and ammunition and planning to attack the government and other targets.[136] In June 2012, Johnson pled guilty to "one count of being a felon in possession of firearms."[137] In July 2012, Thomas pled guilty to "possession with intent to distribute more than 50 grams of high-purity methamphetamine."[138]
- William White, a onetime member of the NSM and founder of his own white supremacist organization, has faced charges in several criminal cases. In September 2014, he was found guilty on charges related to a December 2013 indictment that included "five counts of making threats in aid of extortion over the Internet and one count of the unlawful use of identification information in furtherance of those offenses."[139] He threatened a Florida judge, a state attorney, and an FBI agent, with kidnapping, torture, rape, and murder. According to DOJ, White included the families of these individuals in his threats. The officials that White threatened had been involved in prosecuting suspects tied to the American Front, a white supremacist organization in Florida. White apparently hoped that his threats would somehow secure the release of the American Front suspects.[140] In January 2011, White was convicted[141] of soliciting violence online against the jury foreman in *U.S. v. Matthew Hale*.[142] In April 2011, a federal judge reversed

[135] Southern Poverty Law Center, "National Socialist Movement."

[136] Department of Justice, "Mendota Heights Man Indicted for Distributing Methamphetamine," press release, April 27, 2012; Department of Justice, "Austin Felon Indicted for Possessing Firearms," press release, April 27, 2012; Amy Forliti, "Affidavit: 2 Men With Supremacist Ties Had Weapons," *Associated Press*, April 27, 2012.

[137] Department of Justice, "Austin Felon Pleads Guilty to Possessing an Assault Rifle," press release, June 6, 2012.

[138] Department of Justice, "Mendota Heights Man Pleads Guilty to Possessing Methamphetamine," press release, July 11, 2012.

[139] Department of Justice, "Neo-Nazi Sentenced for Sending Gruesome Threats to Florida Officials and Their Families," press release, November 21, 2014; Department of Justice, "White Supremacist Charged with Sending Online Threatening Communications to a Florida Judge, State Attorney, and Task Force Agent," press release, December 11, 2013.

[140] Ibid.

[141] Department of Justice, "Self-Proclaimed White Supremacist William White Convicted of Soliciting Violence Against Hale Jury Foreman," press release, January 5, 2011.

[142] Matthew Hale was convicted of soliciting the murder of U.S. District Judge Joan Humphrey Lefkow. In the mid 1990s, Hale revived the Church of the Creator fortunes. He changed the organization's name to the World Church of the Creator, and according to a watchdog group, by 2002 it had more chapters in the United States than any other neo-Nazi organization. Judge Lefkow had originally ruled in favor of Hale in a trademark infringement case involving the name "World Church of the Creator." Her ruling was reversed on appeal, and as a result, she had to enforce the higher court's reversal. Via email and during a conversation, Hale discussed with his security chief the idea of killing Lefkow. Hale did not know that

White's conviction. Upon appeal, the conviction was reinstated.[143] In an unrelated case, in December 2009, White was convicted of four counts of communicating threats in interstate commerce and one count of witness intimidation. One of the convictions for communicating threats in interstate commerce was later reversed.[144] The witness intimidation charges involved White reportedly attempting to "delay or prevent the testimony" of African Americans in a discrimination case.[145] According to publicly available information, in 2005 and 2006 White was involved with NSM, for a time serving as its national spokesman.[146] His activity with NSM ceased after he had a falling out with Schoep.[147]

### *Racist Skinheads*

In the United States, racist skinheads have a legacy stretching back to the 1980s.[148] However, skinhead culture originated in the United Kingdom in the late 1960s and today has a global reach.[149] Since the early 2000s, the movement in the United States has been characterized by a proliferation of regional groups or crews rather than a united core organization.[150] In law enforcement circles, racist skinheads have a reputation for violence. This is "reinforced by hate-filled white power music and literature." "[T]hey foster [their reputed toughness] through their appearance (shaved heads or close-cropped hair, white power tattoos) and dress (bomber jackets, 'braces' (suspenders), steel-toed boots)."[151]

---

his security chief was an FBI informant. In 2003, Hale was arrested for soliciting the murder of Judge Lefkow, and this, as well as his subsequent conviction on charges related to the case, hastened a downturn in fortune for his World Church of the Creator. Hale is serving a 40-year prison term. After another name change, the group—currently known simply as the Creativity Movement—shows signs of revival under new leadership. See Michael, *Theology of Hate*, pp. 120–133, 173–188; Chris Dettro, "Follow-Up File: White Supremacist Finds Quiet Life in Prison," *The State Journal-Register*, Springfield, IL, October 25, 2010; Federal Bureau of Investigation, "A Different Breed of Terrorist," June 6, 2004.

143 Department of Justice, "White Supremacist William White Sentenced to 42 Months in Prison for Soliciting Violence Against Hale Jury Foreman," press release, February 20, 2013; Laurence Hammack, "Judge Tosses William A. White Verdict," *The Roanoke Times*, April 20, 2011.

144 Department of Justice, "Roanoke, Virginia Neo-Nazi Sentenced for Threats, Witness Intimidation," press release, April 14, 2010.

145 Ibid. See also Laurence Hammack, "Former Neo-Nazi Leader Gets 3 More Months in Prison," October 23, 2012.

146 Laurence Hammack, "White's Life on Fringe Puts Him at Center of Storm," *The Roanoke Times*, July 26, 2009.

147 Ibid; Southern Poverty Law Center, "Bill White," 2011. For other cases involving individuals allegedly tied to NSM, see Department of Justice, "Valley Man Enters Guilty Plea for Possession and Transport of an Improvised Explosive Device," press release, September 27, 2011; Department of Justice, "Valley Man Indicted for Possessing and Transporting Improvised Explosive Devices," press release, January 26, 2011, http://phoenix.fbi.gov/dojpressrel/pressrel11/px012611.htm; Rudabeh Shahbazi, "Documents Show Apache Junction Man Planned To Take IEDs to the Border," *ABC 15*; Federal Bureau of Investigation, "Domestic Terrorism: Tip Leads to Sting, Prison for Plotter," November 29, 2006.

148 Serge F. Kovaleski, "American Skinheads: Fighting Minorities and Each Other," *Washington Post*, January 16, 1996; Southern Poverty Law Center, *Skinheads in America: Racists on the Rampage*, p. 3. Hereinafter: Southern Poverty Law Center, *Skinheads.*

149 Ibid.

150 Ibid., p. 13; Federal Bureau of Investigation, *Rage and Racism*, p. 8.

151 Federal Bureau of Investigation, *Rage and Racism*, pp. 5–6.

Skinheads emerged as a non-racist movement among British working-class youth in the late 1960s. These early skinheads rejected the hippie lifestyle and embraced elements of Jamaican culture, particularly reggae and ska music. As immigration from South Asia to the UK grew, some white British skinheads embraced racism and neo-Nazism. This racist skinhead variant of the subculture materialized in the U.S. Midwest and in Texas in the early 1980s.[152]

In the mid-1990s, many U.S.-based racist skinhead groups allied with one another to form the Hammerskin Nation (HSN). HSN eventually developed chapters throughout the United States and in Europe. It had its own annual meeting/concert called Hammerfest, ran a record label, and had a publishing company. In the early 2000s, other groups such as the Outlaw Hammerskins, Hoosier State Hammerskins, and Ohio State Skinheads challenged HSN for preeminence. These groups saw HSN as "elitist."[153]

In January 2010, the FBI released a bulletin that, among other things, emphasized that some racist skinheads formed the most violent segment of WSE adherents.[154] This supported the findings in a 2008 FBI assessment.[155] Between 2007 and 2009, skinheads were involved in 36 of the 53 violent incidents the FBI identified in the United States as being tied to WSE proponents.[156] The Bureau has stated that "violence is an integral part of the racist skinhead subculture."[157] Elements within the fractious movement even target one another.[158] These criminal acts are typically unrehearsed and opportunistic, targeting nonwhites and "other religious and social minorities."[159]

At least one exception involved greater levels of planning. One man was convicted and two others pled guilty in a Connecticut case that involved the illegal sale of firearms and homemade grenades. The scheme included multiple meetings between late 2008 and early 2010 to negotiate the transactions, prepare the firearms, and assemble the grenades. The trio was tied to a skinhead group known as Battalion 14 (originally called the Connecticut White Wolves). They sold the weapons to a convicted felon working as an FBI cooperating witness. The informant posed as a member of the Imperial Klans of America, a Ku Klux Klan organization. Two others in the case, including the leader of Battalion 14 and a man not tied to the group, were acquitted of charges.[160]

---

152 Michael R. Ronczkowski, *Terrorism and Organized Hate Crime: Intelligence Gathering, Analysis, and Investigations*, 2nd ed. (Boca Raton, FL: CRC Press, Taylor and Francis Group, 2007), pp. 40–41. Hereinafter: Ronczkowski, *Terrorism*. Southern Poverty Law Center, *Skinheads*, pp. 3–4.

153 Southern Poverty Law Center, *Skinheads*, p. 5.

154 Federal Bureau of Investigation, *White Supremacist Extremist Violence Possibly Decreases But Racist Skinheads Remain the Most Violent*, January 28, 2010. Hereinafter: Federal Bureau of Investigation, *White Supremacist Extremist Violence*.

155 Federal Bureau of Investigation, *Rage and Racism: Skinhead Violence on the Far Right*, December 10, 2008. Hereinafter: Federal Bureau of Investigation, *Rage and Racism*.

156 Federal Bureau of Investigation, *White Supremacist Extremist Violence*, p. 4.

157 Federal Bureau of Investigation, *Rage and Racism*, p. 5.

158 Southern Poverty Law Center, *Skinheads*, pp. 5, 16.

159 Federal Bureau of Investigation, *Rage and Racism*, p. 5.

160 Department of Justice, "Milford Man Sentenced to 10 Years in Prison for Making Grenades and Selling Guns Intended for White Supremacist Group," press release, May 5, 2011, http://newhaven.fbi.gov/dojpressrel/pressrel11/nh050511.htm; Michael P. Mayko, "Two Acquitted in White Wolves Conspiracy Case," *Connecticut Post*, December 2, 2010; Michael P. Mayko, "White Wolves Called 'Home Grown Terrorists,'" *Connecticut Post*, November 16, 2010; Anti-Defamation League, "Connecticut White Supremacists Indicted on Firearms and Explosives Charges," March 24, 2010. For another case allegedly involving racist

### Anti-Government Extremists

As mentioned above, DOJ considers both unauthorized militias and sovereign citizens as anti-government extremists. *Neither militia membership nor advocacy of sovereign citizen tenets makes one a terrorist or a criminal.* However, in some instances both militia members and sovereign citizens have committed crimes driven in part by their ideologies.[161]

#### *Militia Extremists*

The militia movement became prominent in the 1990s as a collection of armed, paramilitary groups formed to stave off what they perceived as intrusions of an invasive government.[162] Central to this is a fear of firearm confiscation by a federal government thought to be out of control. Some adherents also believe in anti-Semitic and racist ideologies.[163] Regardless, most militia members engage in constitutionally protected activity.

Militia groups typically coalesce around a specific leader. Groups can run training compounds where they rehearse paramilitary tactics, practice their survival skills, and receive weapons instruction and lessons in movement ideology. Some militia groups also maintain websites for recruitment and fundraising.[164] Extremists within the movement who run afoul of law enforcement "tend to stockpile illegal weapons and ammunition, trying illegally to get their hands on fully automatic firearms or attempting to convert weapons to fully automatic. They also try to buy or manufacture improvised explosive devices."[165]

Segments of the militia movement believe that the U.S. government is either run by some hidden conspiracy or is an overreaching sham. Some see a "New World Order" controlling U.S. institutions such as the media and the federal government. They contend that this is partly fostered by international organizations such as the United Nations. From this perspective, these organizations sap American sovereignty. Some militia supporters believe that agents of an unauthentic "Shadow Government" are interested in seizing lawfully owned firearms as part of a plan to undermine democracy.[166] Importantly, others in the militia movement hold that the federal government has overstepped its

---

skinheads, see Amy Pavuk and Henry Pierson Curtis, "Details Emerge in Osceola Skinhead Race-War Case," *Orlando Sentinel*, May 8, 2012.

161 The material in this section describes militia extremists and sovereign citizen extremists. On occasion more broadly anti-government extremists engage in violence but defy easy categorization. For example, in 2014, broadly anti-government extremists Jerad and Amanda Miller (husband and wife) shot and killed two Las Vegas, NV, Metropolitan Police Department officers. Police shot and killed the couple. Mark Berman, Las Vegas Shooters Had Expressed Anti-Government Views, Prepared for 'Lengthy Gun Battle,'" *Washington Post*, June 9, 2014.

162 Institute for Intergovernmental Research, *Investigating Terrorism and Criminal Extremism: Terms and Concepts*, Version 1.0, (Tallahassee, Florida: Institute for Intergovernmental Research, 2005), p. 49; Hereinafter: Institute for Intergovernmental Research, *Investigating Terrorism.*

163 Arizona Counter-Terrorism Information Center, "Sovereign Citizens and Militia Information," August 19, 2008, p. 1.

164 Lane Crothers, "The Cultural Foundations of the Modern Militia Movement," *New Political Science*, vol. 24, no. 2 (2002), p. 231. Hereinafter: Crothers, "The Cultural."

165 Federal Bureau of Investigation, "Domestic Terrorism: Focus on Militia Extremism," September 22, 2011.

166 Lane Crothers, *Rage on the Right: The American Militia Movement from Ruby Ridge to Homeland Security* (Lanham, MD: Rowman and Littlefield, 2003), p. 57. Hereinafter: Crothers, *Rage on the Right.*

constitutional bounds.[167] One scholar has noted that some militia members assert that they have "the right to organize, purchase and use firearms, and enforce the law against agents of the government who behave unconstitutionally."[168]

A small minority of Americans who held anti-government fears formed militias largely in response to two incidents in the early 1990s. These were confrontations between federal law enforcement and private citizens at Ruby Ridge, ID, and at a site near Waco, TX.[169] Both involved warrants related to firearms violations.

- In August 1992, Randy Weaver and his family were engaged in an 11-day standoff with federal law enforcement agents. Randy Weaver had failed to appear in court on firearms-related charges in 1991. Subsequently, an unsuccessful operation to arrest Weaver led to the death of his 14-year-old son and a U.S. Marshal. It also precipitated the standoff. During the standoff, Weaver and a friend were shot and wounded. An FBI sniper also shot and killed Weaver's wife, Vicki.[170] Weaver was eventually found guilty of failing to appear in court on the gun charges that played a role in the standoff. In October 1993, he was sentenced to 18 months in jail and a $10,000 fine. In 1995, Weaver received a $3.1 million settlement in a wrongful death suit filed against the U.S. government.[171] The events at Ruby Ridge helped precipitate the militia movement, whose members tend to view Randy Weaver as a hero and demonize the federal government.[172]
- The militia movement also emerged because of the 51-day standoff between federal law enforcement and a religious sect named the Branch Davidians near Waco.[173] On February 28, 1993, an unsuccessful attempt by Bureau of Alcohol Tobacco Firearms and Explosives (ATF) agents to arrest the sect's leader, David Koresh, initiated the events near Waco. He was wanted on suspicion of federal firearms and explosives violations.[174] Four ATF agents and six Branch Davidians died in a gunfight during the operation.[175] Protracted discussions followed between federal negotiators and Koresh. These failed. On April 19, federal agents assaulted the

[167] Crothers, "The Cultural," pp. 226–228.

[168] Ibid., p. 228.

[169] Ibid., pp. 230–231. See also Michael Barkun, "Appropriated Martyrs: The Branch Davidians and the Radical Right," *Terrorism and Political Violence*, vol. 19, no. 1 (2007), p. 120. Hereinafter: Barkun, "Appropriated Martyrs." See also Steven M. Chermak, *Searching for a Demon: The Media Construction of the Militia Movement*, (Boston: Northeastern University Press, 2002).

[170] Stuart A. Wright, *Patriots, Politics, and the Oklahoma City Bombing* (New York: Cambridge University Press, 2007), pp. 142–148. Hereinafter: Wright, *Patriots*. Weaver has been described as a survivalist who believed in the Christian Identity religion. See Barkun "Appropriated Martyrs," p. 118. He has also been described as holding white supremacist beliefs and was not a militia member. See Crothers, *Rage on the Right*, pp. 78–79.

[171] Crothers, *Rage on the Right*, p. 90.

[172] Wright, *Patriots*, pp. 149–152; Crothers, *Rage on the Right*, pp. 92–97; Barkun, "Appropriated Martyrs," pp. 120–121.

[173] Crothers, *Rage on the Right*, p. 104.

[174] Department of Justice, *Report to the Deputy Attorney General on the Events at Waco, Texas*, October 8, 1993. The Branch Davidian sect emerged from the Seventh-Day Adventist Church and was formed in 1929. The two severed official ties with one another in 1934. David Koresh was not a militia member. See Crothers, *Rage on the Right*, pp. 100–101.

[175] Crothers, *Rage on the Right*, p. 105.

Davidian compound, which caught on fire. At least 75 Branch Davidians perished in the assault.[176]

If the incidents involving the Weavers and the Branch Davidians helped form the militia movement, Timothy McVeigh's bombing of the Alfred P. Murrah Federal Building in Oklahoma City on April 19, 1995, helped usher in a temporary decline.[177] In the bombing's aftermath, militia groups received greater law enforcement scrutiny.[178] The bombing claimed 168 lives, and until 9/11 was the largest single act of terrorism on U.S. soil. The militia movement declined after the bombing.[179] Although McVeigh's bombing cannot fully account for a dip in militia activity, it affected the movement by causing some groups to temper their rhetoric while others grew more extreme, and militias became more marginalized.[180]

Observers have noted that the militia movement has experienced resurgence in the last decade, likely driven by growing antipathy toward the federal government.[181] A few individuals still draw inspiration from McVeigh. Jerry Drake Varnell was arrested in August 2017 after he allegedly intended to damage or destroy a bank in downtown Oklahoma City by reportedly attempting to detonate what he thought was a bomb in a van. But the inert explosive device was based on materials provided by an undercover FBI agent as part of an investigation that nabbed Varnell, who allegedly was inspired by the Timothy McVeigh's 1995 bombing. Varnell purportedly hewed to militia extremist beliefs and, according to investigators, expressed an interest in founding a small militia.[182]

Two widely reported incidents in recent years have attracted militia and other anti-government extremists.

- In 2014, multiple individuals led by Cliven Bundy engaged in an armed standoff with police officials at Bundy's ranch in Bunkerville, NV, preventing the execution of a court order related to a dispute involving the grazing of cattle on federal lands.[183] One individual involved was sentenced to 68 years in prison for a variety of crimes related to his involvement in the standoff.[184]

---

[176] Crothers, *Rage on the Right*, p. 110.

[177] McVeigh was not a militia member, but he interacted with others who were.

[178] Devlin Barrett and Eileen Sullivan, "FBI Sees Little Chance of Copycat Militia Plots," *Associated Press*, March 31, 2010.

[179] Andrew Wolfson, "The Execution: Militias Dwindle Since Oklahoma City Bombing," *USA Today*, June 20, 2001.

[180] Crothers, *Rage on the Right*, p. 138, 147.

[181] Max Strasser, "Fed Up with the Feds," *Newsweek*, May 2, 2014.

[182] Eli Watkins and Shimon Prokupecz, "FBI Arrests Man in Oklahoma Bombing Sting," *CNN*, August 14, 2017; United States v. Jerry Drake Varnell, criminal complaint, U.S. District Court, Western District of Oklahoma, August 13, 2017.

[183] "Federal Authorities Indict 19 in 2014 Range Standoff in Nevada," *Associated Press*, March 4, 2016; Department of Justice, "Fourteen Additional Defendants Charged for Felony Crimes Related to 2014 Standoff in Nevada," press release, March 3, 2016; United States v. Cliven Bundy, et al., superseding indictment, United States District Court, District of Nevada, March 2, 2016. This standoff is included in this memo's list of domestic terrorist/extremist incidents, because the superseding indictment in the federal criminal case related to the standoff describes it as "a massive armed assault against federal law enforcement officers."

[184] The charges included assault on a federal officer; threatening a federal law enforcement officer; obstruction of the due administration of justice; interference with interstate commerce by extortion; interstate

- For 41 days in late 2015 and early 2016, Ammon and Ryan Bundy (sons of Cliven Bundy) led numerous individuals in armed occupation of federal property at the Malheur National Wildlife Refuge in Oregon. Although the ringleaders of the broader occupation—including the Bundy brothers—were acquitted in federal court of many of the most serious charges levied against them, a violent incident occurred during the occupation. Oregon State Police officers fatally shot LaVoy Finicum. The shooting occurred after Finicum reportedly drove a pickup truck at high speed toward a police roadblock, reputedly endangering officers before careening into a nearby snowbank. According to law enforcement officials, Finicum subsequently left the vehicle, refusing to comply with police commands, and reached for a gun in his pocket before he was shot to death.[185] In the fallout related to the Malheur National Wildlife Refuge takeover, Cliven Bundy was arrested on charges tied to the 2014 Bunkerville standoff.

Several other examples highlight how some militia adherents have reportedly engaged in criminal activity since 9/11.

- Purportedly, Curtis Allen, Gavin Wright, and Patrick Eugene Stein conspired to detonate explosives at an apartment complex in Garden City, KS. Prosecutors allege Allen, Wright, and Stein hoped to target Somali immigrants living in the complex.[186] The trio was part of a small militia-style group dubbed the Crusaders. Underscoring the violent viewpoints the trio reputedly held, a larger militia organization in Kansas reportedly rejected Wright and Stein for membership because the larger group perceived the duo as too extreme.[187]
- In November 2011, the FBI arrested four retirees, Samuel J. Crump, Ray H. Adams, Dan Roberts, and Frederick W. Thomas, who allegedly formed a fringe militia group and planned violent attacks on government officials. The group, based in northern Georgia, purportedly had ties to an unnamed militia organization. According to DOJ, the quartet "discussed multiple criminal activities, ranging from murder; theft; manufacturing and using toxic agents; and assassinations in an effort to undermine federal and state government and to advance their interests."[188] Between June and November 2011, Roberts and Thomas met

travel in aid of extortion; and three counts of use and carry of a firearm in relation to a crime of violence. See Department of Justice, "Phoenix Man Sentenced to Over 68 Years in Prison for Threat and Assault of Federal Law Enforcement and Other Charges Related to 2014 Armed Standoff in Bunkerville," press release, July 26, 2017.

185 Patrik Jonsson, "After the Bundy Acquittal, Some Surprising Lessons of the Malheur Occupation," *Christian Science Monitor,* October 29, 2016; Hal Bernton, "Jury Acquits Leaders of Malheur Wildlife-Refuge Standoff," *Seattle Times,* October, 27, 2016. A second trial led to additional verdicts, see Department of Justice, "Jury Delivers Verdict in Second Oregon Standoff Trial," press release, March 10, 2017. Greg Botelho and Michael Martinez, "Shooting Death of LaVoy Finicum Justified, Necessary, Prosecutor Says," *CNN,* March 8, 2016. In 2017, an FBI agent involved in the Finicum shooting was federally indicted for his allegedly attempting to cover up his own involvement in the shooting. See Maxine Bernstein, "LaVoy Finicum Shooting: Indictment of Agent 'devastating' for FBI," *The Oregonian,* June 29, 2017.

186 Department of Justice, "Three Kansas Men Charged With Plotting a Bombing Attack Targeting the Local Somali Immigrant Community," press release, October 14, 2016.

187 Judy L. Thomas, "Kansas Militia Says It Spurned Alleged Terrorists Arrested in Garden City Case," *Kansas City Star,* November 2, 2016.

188 Department of Justice, "North Georgia Men Arrested, Charged in Plots to Purchase Explosives, Silencer and to Manufacture a Biological Toxin," press release, November 1, 2011.

with an FBI undercover agent to negotiate the purchase of matériel for the plot: "a silencer for a rifle and conversion parts to make a fully automatic rifle, as well as explosives."[189] In October, plotters reportedly discussed making ricin, a deadly poison derived from castor beans.[190] In April 2012, Roberts and Thomas pled guilty to conspiring to obtain an unregistered explosive device and silencer.[191] Crump and Adams were found guilty of "conspiring to make ricin to be used as a weapon in January 2014. Also, they were found guilty of one count each of possessing a biological toxin for use as a weapon." Adams was acquitted of "attempting to develop, produce and possess a biological toxin."[192]

- In June 2012, three individuals were found guilty in Anchorage, AK, of conspiracy and firearms charges related to a scheme purportedly led by Francis "Schaeffer" Cox.[193] He and his followers allegedly plotted "a potential retaliatory response to any attempt by law enforcement to arrest Cox, who had an outstanding bench warrant for not attending a trial over a misdemeanor weapons charge."[194] They were members of the Alaska Peacemaker's Militia based in Fairbanks, AK, and also held sovereign citizen beliefs. The plotters supposedly codenamed their plan "241 (two for one)," because they reputedly intended to kill two government officials for every militia member killed in the operation.[195]

The above activities are not necessarily indicative of trends toward violence in the larger militia movement, and in one prominent case, DOJ failed to convince the presiding judge of serious charges revolving around a purported violent plot. In March 2012, a federal judge acquitted members of a Michigan Militia group known as the Hutaree on charges of seditious conspiracy or rebellion against the United States and conspiring to use weapons of mass destruction. The judge also cleared the accused Hutaree members of weapons crimes related to the conspiracies.[196]

---

189 Ibid.

190 Craig Schneider, "Documents: Men with Castor Beans, Guns Worried about Getting Caught," *Atlanta Journal-Constitution*, November 6, 2011.

191 Department of Justice, "North Georgia Men Plead Guilty to Plot to Purchase Explosives and a Silencer," press release, April 10, 2012.

192 Kate Brumback, "Jury Finds 2 Georgia Men Guilty in Ricin Plot," *Associated Press*, January 17, 2014.

193 Department of Justice, "Guilty Verdicts in USA v. Cox, Barney, and Vernon," press release, June 19, 2012.

194 Department of Justice, "Superseding Indictment Returned by Federal Grand Jury Against Fairbanks-Area Men for Conspiracy to Kill Federal Officers," press release, January 23, 2012; Sam Friedman, "Details Emerge in Alleged Plot to Kill Alaska State Troopers, Judge," *Fairbanks Daily News-Miner*, March 3, 2011. Cox has also been described as a sovereign citizen (discussed below). See Sam Friedman, "The Schaeffer Cox File: The Trail of a Young Man," *Fairbanks Daily News-Miner*, April 10, 2011. For a related case see Department of Justice, "Salcha Couple Pleads Guilty to Conspiracy to Murder Federal Officials," press release, August 27, 2012; Department of Justice, "Couple Charged with Conspiracy to Murder Judge and Federal Firearms Crimes, Two Others Indicted for Conspiracy to Possess Destructive Devices and Illegal Weapons," press release, March 17, 2011.

195 For examples of other militia adherents involved in crime, see Meghann M. Cuniff, "Health Problems Reduce Militia Leader's Sentence," *The Spokesman-Review*, August 11, 2011; David Cole, "Militia Member Sentenced on Federal Firearms and Explosives Charges," *Coeur d'Alene Press*, August 9, 2011; Federal Bureau of Investigation, "Preventing Terrorist Attacks on U.S. Soil: The Case of the Wrong Package Falling into the Right Hands," April 9, 2004; Scott Gold, Case Yields Chilling Signs of Domestic Terror Plot," *Los Angeles Times*, January 7, 2004.

196 Ed White, "Michigan Militia Members Cleared of Conspiracy," *Associated Press*, March 27, 2012, http://abcnews.go.com/US/wireStory/critical-charges-dropped-michigan-militia-16013255?singlePage=true#.T3MB5kd_lLc. Hereinafter: White, "Michigan Militia."

The case garnered headlines in March 2010, when nine Hutaree members were indicted for allegedly preparing to violently confront U.S. law enforcement.[197] Their supposed plotting included the murder of a local law enforcement officer and an attack on fellow officers who gathered in Michigan for the funeral procession. According to DOJ, the Hutaree discussed the use of explosives against the funeral procession.[198] Audio recordings by an undercover FBI agent of reputed Hutaree leader David Brian Stone capture him discussing the New World Order and how, "it's time to strike and take our nation back so we will be free of tyranny.... The war will come whether we are ready or not."[199] According to DOJ, the group had a hit list that included federal judges, among others.[200] However, during the trial an Assistant U.S. Attorney acknowledged that the Hutaree had not formed a "specific plan" to attack government targets.[201] U.S. District Judge Victoria Roberts stated that, "The court is aware that protected speech and mere words can be sufficient to show a conspiracy. In this case, however, they do not rise to that level."[202] Three Hutaree members pled guilty to firearms charges.[203]

### *Sovereign Citizen Movement*

The FBI defines the sovereign citizen movement as "anti-government," involving people "who believe that even though they physically reside in this country, they are separate or 'sovereign' from the United States. As a result, they do not accept any government authority, including courts, taxing entities, motor vehicle departments, or law enforcement."[204] However, simply holding these views is not a criminal act, and numerous movement adherents solely exercise their beliefs via constitutionally protected activities.

The ideas behind the movement originated during the 1970s with a group known as the Posse Comitatus and enjoyed some popularity in extremist circles during the 1980s

[197] Department of Justice, "Nine Members of a Militia Group Charged with Seditious Conspiracy and Related Charges," press release, March 29, 2010.

[198] Ibid.

[199] Corey Williams and Jeff Karoub, "Prosecutor: Undercover FBI Agent Infiltrated Militia," *Associated Press*, March 31, 2010.

[200] Dan Harris, Emily Friedman, and Tahman Bradley, "Undercover Agent Key Witness Against Hutaree Militia Members," *ABC News*, April 1, 2010, http://abcnews.go.com/GMA/undercover-agent-credited-hutaree-militia-bust/story?id=10257584.

[201] Robert Snell and Christine Ferretti, "Key Charges Dropped Against Hutaree Militia," *Detroit News*, March 28, 2011.

[202] White, "Michigan Militia."

[203] See Department of Justice, "Members of the Hutaree Militia Plead Guilty to Weapons Charges," March 29, 2012; Matthew Dolan, "Defendant in Michigan Militia Case Changes Plea to Guilty," press release, December 6, 2011, http://online.wsj.com/article/SB10001424052970204083204577080630555077796.html?mod=googlenews_wsj. When the Hutaree suspects were arrested in the case, some militia members in Michigan did not support the group's alleged scheming. For example, a member of another militia group in Michigan provided information to authorities regarding the whereabouts of a fugitive Hutaree militia member. See Kirk Johnson, "Militia Draws Distinctions Between Groups," *New York Times*, March 31, 2010. Also, a militia leader from Michigan has said that the Hutaree case, "caused a rift in the militia movement about whether this is the sort of group we want to rally behind or if what they were doing was outside the scope of what's acceptable." See Robert Snell, "Militias Split over Defending Hutaree," *Detroit News*, March 31, 2011.

[204] Federal Bureau of Investigation, "Domestic Terrorism: The Sovereign Citizen Movement," April 13, 2010. Hereinafter: Federal Bureau of Investigation, "Sovereign Citizen."

and 1990s.[205] Early on, the movement featured white supremacist elements, but this has not kept some African Americans from subscribing to its ideals in recent years.[206] In the 1990s, the movement attracted 250,000 followers and was marked by the FBI's standoff with a group known as the Montana Freemen that lasted 81 days.[207] Estimates from 2011 suggested a membership of 300,000.[208] For the most part, the sovereign citizen movement is diffuse and includes few organized groups.[209] The FBI suggests that sovereigns "operate as individuals without established leadership and only come together in loosely affiliated groups to train, help each other with paperwork [critical to some of their schemes], or socialize and talk about their ideology."[210] The movement involves leaders described as "gurus" who proselytize online, in print publications, or via in-person seminars. These gurus rouse followers into believing a conspiracy theory in which the legitimate federal government has been replaced by a government designed to take away the rights of ordinary citizens.[211] This shares the same broad interplay between concepts of legitimate and illegitimate rule seen in the New World Order and WSE theories about ZOG. Gurus can also promote illegal techniques that individuals can use to supposedly cut their ties to the federal government or avoid its reach, particularly when it comes to taxation.[212]

Sovereign citizens reject the legitimacy of much of the U.S. legal system.[213] Many believe that the 14th Amendment "shifted the nation from its original common-law roots with states' rights to a federal corporation that legally enslaved everyone."[214] According to movement members, the amendment ushered in an illegitimate federal government by supposedly abrogating individual rights and replacing them with a system that

---

205 J.M. Berger, "Without Prejudice: What Sovereign Citizens Believe," *George Washington University Program on Extremism*, June 2016.

206 Sarah Netter, "Anti-Government Sovereign Citizens Taking Foreclosed Homes Using Phony Deeds, Authorities Say," *ABC News*, August 23, 2010, http://abcnews.go.com/US/georgia-battling-sovereign-citizens-squatting-foreclosed-homes/story?id=11445382. See Leah Nelson, "Sovereigns in Black," *Intelligence Report*, Southern Poverty Law Center, no. 143 (Fall 2011).

207 Patrik Jonsson, "'Sovereign citizens': Is Jared Loughner a sign of revived extremist threat?" *Christian Science Monitor*, March 9, 2011.

208 Ibid.

209 One sovereign citizens group is the "Republic for the united States of America" (RuSA) which is based in Alabama. RuSA is a successor to a group known as the Guardians of the Free Republics (GFR), which in 2010 mailed letters to the governors of all 50 U.S. states urging them to leave office. See Southern Poverty Law Center, "Sovereign President," *Intelligence Report*, Southern Poverty Law Center, no. 143 (Fall 2011). In March 2013, the group's self-proclaimed president was convicted of "conspiracy to defraud the United States, attempting to pay taxes with fictitious financial instruments, attempting to obstruct and impede the Internal Revenue Service (IRS), failing to file a 2009 federal income tax return, and falsely testifying under oath in a bankruptcy proceeding." See Department of Justice, "Self-Proclaimed President of Sovereign Citizen Nation Convicted in Alabama of Federal Tax Crimes," press release, March 25, 2013.

210 Federal Bureau of Investigation, Counterterrorism Analysis Section, "Sovereign Citizens: A Growing Domestic Threat to Law Enforcement," *FBI Law Enforcement Bulletin*, (September 2011). Hereinafter: FBI Counterterrorism Analysis Section, "Sovereign Citizens."

211 Anti-Defamation League, *The Lawless Ones: The Resurgence of the Sovereign Citizen Movement*, August 9, 2010, pp. 2–6. Hereinafter: Anti-Defamation League, *The Lawless*.

212 Ibid., p. 6.

213 However, this reportedly does not keep some sovereign citizen extremists from cashing government paychecks. See J.J. McNabb, "Working for the Man: Anti-Government Extremists Who Cash Government Paychecks," *Forbes*, March 5, 2012.

214 Tom Morton, "Sovereign Citizens Renounce First Sentence of 14th Amendment," *Casper Star-Tribune*, April 17, 2011, http://trib.com/news/local/casper/article_a5d0f966-7ed0-549f-a066-b1b2c91f9489.html.

"grant[ed] privileges through contracts such as marriage and driver's licenses, gun permits, and property codes."[215]

By ignoring all sorts of laws, avoiding taxes, disregarding permit requirements, and destroying government-issued identification documents, some sovereign citizens have tried to cut formal ties with what they perceive as an illegitimate regime.[216] Sovereigns have filed court documents stating that they are not U.S. citizens.[217] They have also created bogus financial documents to harass or defraud their enemies. (For more information, see the "Paper Terrorism": Liens, Frivolous Lawsuits, and Tax Schemes" section in this report.)

Sovereign citizens have in some instances created fictitious entities and used fake currency, passports, license plates, and driver licenses. In 2009, a federal jury found three men guilty of conspiring to use and sell fraudulent diplomatic credentials and license plates that they believed allowed "their customers [to] enjoy diplomatic immunity and [to] no longer ... pay taxes or be subject to being stopped, detained, or arrested by law enforcement personnel."[218] In 2003, Ronald K. Delorme developed the Pembina Nation Little Shell Band of North America[219] into a sovereign citizen group.[220] It is a sham Native American tribe that anyone can join to try and avoid taxes and government-imposed costs, such as auto registration fees. For example, news reports indicate that in June 2010, a sheriff's deputy in Florida pulled over John McCombs when the law enforcement official noticed a Pembina Nation Little Shell license plate on the motorcycle McCombs was driving. According to publicly available sources, McCombs presented a fraudulent letter of diplomatic immunity and an invalid Pembina Nation Little Shell vehicle registration.[221]

Some sovereign citizen fraud appears to be motivated by economic opportunism rather than ideology.[222] This includes "pyramid schemes, other investment schemes, bogus trust scams, real estate fraud, and various types of tax frauds [as well as] more esoteric scams ... ranging from immigration fraud to malpractice insurance fraud."[223] In November 2011, husband and wife Monty and Patricia Ervin were convicted in federal court of conspiring to defraud the United States as well as three counts of tax evasion. In addition, the federal jury convicted Patricia of structuring transactions to avoid bank reporting requirements.[224] The couple allegedly had not filed federal income tax

---

215 Ibid.

216 Anti-Defamation League, *The Lawless*, pp. 4–5.

217 Lance Griffin, "'Sovereigns' Gain Attention of Law Enforcement," *Dothan Eagle*, May 21, 2011.

218 Department of Justice, "Jury Convicts Three Men of Conspiracy To Use Fake Diplomatic Identification," press release, August 31, 2009.

219 The group is not a federally recognized tribe.

220 Anti-Defamation League, *The Lawless*; Chris Gerbasi, "Tribal Claims Causing Charlotte Controversy," *Sarasota Herald Tribune*, July 25, 2010; "Punta Gorda Man Arrested for Driving with Pembina Nation Plate," *WINK News*, June 1, 2010.

221 Ibid.

222 For a discussion of redemption as a scam, see Federal Bureau of Investigation, *Common Fraud Schemes*, http://www.fbi.gov/scams-safety/fraud.

223 Anti-Defamation League, *The Lawless*, p. 24.

224 Department of Justice, "Self-Proclaimed 'Governor' of Alabama and Wife Convicted of Tax Fraud," press release, November 4, 2011. Hereinafter: Department of Justice, "Self-Proclaimed."

returns between 2000 and 2008, denied their U.S. citizenship, and dubbed themselves "sovereign" when the IRS investigated.[225] The Ervins earned more than $9 million from investment properties they owned.[226] A group of self-proclaimed sovereign citizens in North Georgia was indicted in March 2011 for using sovereign schemes to allegedly steal millions of dollars worth of real estate.[227]

Some avowed sovereign citizens have been involved in violent altercations with law enforcement officers:

- In June 2016, Gavin Long shot and killed three police officers and wounded three others in Baton Rouge, LA, before police killed him. He had articulated sovereign citizen views online.[228]
- In May 2010, two self-professed sovereign citizens were involved in a violent confrontation with West Memphis, TN, police officers. During a traffic stop, Joe Kane fired an AK-47 assault rifle and killed two officers. Kane and his father Jerry fled the scene. Law enforcement sighted their vehicle in a nearby parking lot 90 minutes later. The duo died in the ensuing shootout, which also wounded two more officers.[229] The FBI had investigated Jerry Kane five years before the murders because he was allegedly traversing the United States peddling what the FBI termed a "debt elimination scheme."[230]

In June 2012, the FBI issued a bulletin suggesting that some sovereign extremists might move away from more spontaneous violence simply in *reaction* to encounters with police and are potentially preparing for conflict in advance, "making more specific plans to interfere with state and local law enforcement officers during traffic stops and, in some cases, intentionally initiating contact with law enforcement."[231] In August 2013, authorities in Las Vegas, NV, arrested two reputed Sovereigns, David Allen Brutsche and Devon Campbell Newman, after a local investigation uncovered the duo's purported schemes to kidnap and kill police officers. Reportedly, the Las Vegas Metropolitan Police Department ran an undercover investigation to nab the two after they encountered Brutsche in what has been characterized as a series of vehicle stops during which "Brutsche would espouse his Sovereign Citizen beliefs that he wasn't bound by the law Metro officers were enforcing."[232] Brutsche pled guilty to felony kidnapping conspiracy

[225] Ibid; *United States v. Patricia Ervin and Monty Ervin*, Superseding Indictment, 1:11-CR-07-MHT, District Court, Middle District of Alabama, February 17, 2011.

[226] Department of Justice, "Self-Proclaimed."

[227] Megan Matteucci, "12 'sovereign citizens' indicted," *Atlanta Journal-Constitution*, March 15, 2011.

[228] Joshua Berlinger, "Gavin Long: Who is Baton Rouge Cop Killer?" *CNN*, August 4, 2016.

[229] Cindy Wolff, "West Memphis Police Sued by Widow of Man Killed in Shootout," *The Commercial Appeal*, April 21, 2011; Kristina Goetz, Cindy Wolff, "Grieving West Memphis Chief Raises National Curtain on Sovereign Citizens," *The Commercial Appeal*, April 17, 2011.

[230] Scott Knoll, "The Warning That Never Came: What the FBI Knew About Jerry Kane," *WREG*, March 2, 2011.

[231] Federal Bureau of Investigation, *Recent Sovereign Citizen Extremist Targeting of Law Enforcement Highlights Potential for Violence during Traffic Stops*, June 1, 2012.

[232] Jackie Valley, "Metro Infiltrates Sovereign Citizens Movement, Uncovers Plots to 'Snatch,' Execute Officers," *Las Vegas Sun*, August 22, 2013.

in February 2014 after "prosecutors abandoned the two most serious charges—conspiracy to murder and attempted armed kidnapping."[233]

Other cases have garnered attention. For example, in July 2011 James M. Tesi allegedly shot at a local police officer trying to arrest him near Fort Worth, TX. Tesi was reportedly wounded in the altercation. Outstanding "arrest warrants for speeding, driving without a license in possession, and failure to appear" prompted the attempted apprehension.[234] Court documents described in news reporting noted that Tesi linked himself to a sovereign citizen group.[235] In February 2012, Tesi was found "guilty of aggravated assault on a public servant with a deadly weapon."[236] In June 2011, a police officer in Page, AZ, shot and killed William Foust while responding to a domestic violence 911 call. The shooting reportedly occurred during a physical struggle in which Foust attempted to "gain control of" the police officer's Taser.[237] According to a press account, Foust had declared his sovereign citizen status in court proceedings in Kanab, UT (about 75 miles from Page), related to a speeding ticket.[238]

### Black Separatist Extremists

DOJ includes black separatism in its list of movements that potentially spawn domestic terrorists.[239] However, most black separatists solely engage in constitutionally protected behavior. Since 9/11, there has been little public discussion of federal investigations involving black separatist extremists. One group exhibiting what can be described as black separatist views, the New Black Panther Party for Self Defense (NBPP), has received national attention over several incidents.

The NBPP emerged in the early 1990s, and it is not tied to the Black Panthers from the 1960s.[240] Watchdog groups have described the NBPP as "a virulently racist and anti-Semitic organization whose leaders have encouraged violence against whites, Jews, and law enforcement officers,"[241] as well as "the largest organized anti-Semitic and racist black militant group in America."[242] The NBPP, which denies that it is a hate group, engages in "high-profile" rhetoric at rallies or demonstrations intended to encourage confrontation with authorities. The group's actions occur "on behalf of the poor or dis-

---

233 Ken Ritter, "Man Takes Plea Deal in Las Vegas 'Sovereign Citizen' Case," *Associated Press*, February 7, 2014.

234 Domingo Ramirez Jr., "Man in 'Sovereign Citizen' Group is Wounded in Shootout," July 22, 2011.

235 Ibid.

236 Steve Norder, "'Sovereign Citizen' Gets 35 Years for Assault on Officer," *Fort Worth Star-Telegram*, February 1, 2012, http://www.star-telegram.com/2012/01/31/3702338/sovereign-citizen-found-guilty.html.

237 Todd Glasenapp and Larry Hendricks, "Page Officer Kills Man in DV Incident," *Arizona Daily Sun*, June 21, 2011, http://azdailysun.com/news/local/crime-and-courts/article_61e27d9d-6d47-5655-8a71-d28b846d8e3e.html.

238 Ibid. For other violent plots with alleged sovereign ties, see Alyssa Newcomb, "Suspects in Louisiana Cop Killings Linked to Sovereign Citizens Movement," *ABC News*, August 19, 2012, http://abcnews.go.com/US/alleged-louisiana-cop-shooters-linked-sovereign-citizen-movement/story?id=17038353#.UL4plddrq1g; J.J. MacNabb, "Sovereign Extremist Injured in Texas Bomb Explosion," *Forbes*, July 3, 2012.

239 Department of Justice, *White Paper*, p. 59.

240 D.J. Mulloy, "New Panthers, Old Panthers, and the Politics of Black Nationalism in the United States," *Patterns of Prejudice*, vol. 44, no. 3 (2010), pp. 217, 219, 229–236. Hereinafter: Mulloy: "New Panthers."

241 Southern Poverty Law Center, "New Black Panther Party."

242 Anti-Defamation League, "New Black Panther Party for Self Defense," June 1, 2011.

advantaged, involving the ready display of firearms."[243] As an example of the rhetoric the group uses, an NBPP representative characterized the March 2011 shooting death of a drug suspect in Jacksonville, FL, as "a violent act of terrorism" committed by police.[244] Soon after the shooting, the Jacksonville Sheriff's Office said that the confrontation involved undercover officers serving a search warrant at an apartment. Officers claimed that inside the apartment, the victim—an alleged drug dealer with a criminal record—was holding a firearm.[245] In an infamous recent incident, Micah Johnson shot and killed five police officers in Dallas, TX, in July 2015. He reportedly "liked" groups on Facebook tied to black separatism and may have been involved at some point with the NBPP in Houston.[246] Johnson purportedly told police that he wasn't affiliated with any groups at the time of the shooting.[247] He died in the altercation with police.

In 2008, the Philadelphia, PA, chapter of the NBPP was involved in a case that generated public controversy. A 2009 civil suit filed by DOJ claimed that two NBPP members wearing the group's paramilitary uniforms loitered around the entrance to a 2008 federal general election polling station in Philadelphia. One of the NBPP members allegedly carried a nightstick. According to DOJ, some poll watchers feared for their safety because of this activity. Philadelphia police officers responding to claims of voter intimidation removed the nightstick-wielding NBPP member and allowed the other to remain (the latter was a certified poll watcher). Police asked people at the polling station whether they had been threatened by the two individuals. All those questioned replied that they had not. However, at least one individual claimed that the presence of the two NBPP members had been intimidating.[248] The NBPP disavowed the actions of its two members.[249] In May 2009, DOJ voluntarily dismissed claims against defendants in the case, and a July 2009 letter from 10 Members of Congress to DOJ's Inspector General questioned the decision to do so. DOJ's Office of Professional Responsibility (OPR) investigated, and in March 2011, OPR issued a report which argued that DOJ officials did not act inappropriately regarding the matter.[250]

### Abortion Extremists

The vast majority of activists who either favor or oppose abortion engage in constitutionally protected activity. However, abortion extremism involves crimes committed based on such beliefs. Over the past two decades, most abortion-related violence

---

243 Mulloy: "New Panthers," pp. 223, 233.

244 "Black Panthers Protest Police Shooting," October 14, 2011; "Black Panthers Protest Police Shooting," *First Coast News*, March 19, 2011.

245 Ibid.

246 Melissa Jacobs, "Dallas Police Sniper Was Shunned by New Black Panthers, Says Group's Leader," *Fox News*, July 12, 2016. Brian Fung, "What You Need to Know about the Black Nationalists the Dallas Shooter Liked on Facebook," *Washington Post*, July 9, 2016; "Dallas Shooter Was Ex-Member of Houston's New Black Panther Party," *Click2Houston*, website of NBC affiliate station in Houston, TX, July 7, 2016.

247 Ibid.

248 Department of Justice, Office of Professional Responsibility, Report, *Investigation of Dismissal of Defendants in* United States v. New Black Panther Party for Self-Defense, Inc. et al., March 17, 2011, pp. 6–8. Hereinafter: DOJ, OPR, *Investigation of Dismissal*.

249 Mulloy: "New Panthers," pp. 217–218.

250 DOJ, OPR, *Investigation of Dismissal*, pp. 1–3.

appears to have targeted abortion providers.[251] Eighty-four instances of "extreme violence" targeting abortion providers and clinics occurred in the United States from 1997 through 2015, according to one group that supports abortion rights and tracks criminal activity intended to limit access to abortion services.[252] These cases involved shootings, bombings, arson incidents, and acid attacks.[253] Since 1993, eight clinic workers have been murdered by anti-abortion extremists in the United States.[254] Because of a wave of violence focused on abortion providers in the 1980s and early 1990s, Congress passed and President Clinton signed into law the Freedom of Access to Clinic Entrances Act (FACE Act) (18 U.S.C. §248) in 1994.[255] As with other types of domestic terrorism investigations, it is unclear exactly which incidents of violence perpetrated against abortion providers the FBI considers terrorist acts.

Two violent incidents have been prominent in recent years. In 2015, Robert Dear Jr., allegedly killed three people and wounded nine others in a shooting at a Planned Parenthood facility in Colorado Springs, CO.[256] The 2009 murder of George Tiller, an abortion provider, received significant public attention. On January 29, 2010, Scott Roeder was convicted of first-degree murder and two counts of aggravated assault for killing Tiller. Roeder shot Tiller while the latter was at church on May 31, 2009. Roeder was sentenced to "life in prison with no possibility of parole for 50 years."[257]

A number of other unrelated schemes targeting abortion clinics have been uncovered since Roeder's arrest. These incidents appear to involve individuals largely operating alone.

- In January 2012, Bobby Joe Rogers was charged in the firebombing of a Pensacola, FL, abortion clinic on New Year's Day 2012. The bombing destroyed the clinic,

[251] There also has been at least one incident involving violence reportedly by anti-abortion activists. See Philip Jankowski, "APD: Woman Threw Molotov Cocktail Near Anti-Abortion Protesters," *The American-Statesman,* (Austin, TX), March 24, 3015; "Woman Arrested for Throwing Molotov Cocktail in Front of Planned Parenthood," KXAN, NBC affiliate, Austin, TX, March 23, 2015.

[252] National Abortion Federation, "Clinic Violence," http://www.prochoice.org/about_abortion/violence/history_extreme.asp. See also "NAF Violence and Disruption Statistics," https://prochoice.org/education-and-advocacy/violence/violence-statistics-and-history/.

[253] Ibid.

[254] NARAL Pro-Choice America Foundation, "Anti-Choice Violence and Intimidation," press release.

[255] This is not a terrorism-related statute. In fact, DOJ's Civil Rights Division, prosecutes both criminal and civil cases involving the FACE Act. See http://www.justice.gov/crt/about/crm/overview.php; http://www.justice.gov/crt/about/spl/face.php. The FACE Act (18 U.S.C. §248), "protects the exercise of free choice in obtaining reproductive health services, and the exercise of First Amendment religious freedoms. Section 248 makes it unlawful for a person to use force, threat of force, or physical obstruction to intentionally injure or intimidate a person because he/she is or has been obtaining or providing reproductive health services. Section 248 also makes it unlawful for a person to use force, threat of force, or physical obstruction to intentionally injure or intimidate a person because he/she is lawfully exercising the right of religious freedom at a place of worship. Finally, Section 248 makes it unlawful for a person to intentionally damage or destroy the property of a facility because it provides reproductive health services, or because it is a place of worship. Section 248 also prohibits anyone from attempting to commit any of the above."

[256] Julie Turkewitz, et al., "Robert Dear, Suspect in Colorado Killings, 'Preferred to be Left Alone,' " *New York Times,* November 28, 2015. Dear was found mentally incompetent to stand trial. Lance Benzel, "Robert Dear Remains Mentally Incompetent to Stand Trial for Colorado Springs Planned Parenthood Attack," *Colorado Springs Gazette,* November 17, 2016.

[257] Ron Sylvester, "Scott Roeder Gets Hard 50 in Murder of Abortion Provider George Tiller," *Wichita Eagle,* April 1, 2010. Hereinafter: Sylvester, "Scott Roeder." Roeder reportedly also adhered to anti-government beliefs beginning in the 1990s. See Ron Sylvester, Abortion Issue Front and Center in Roeder Murder Trial," January 10, 2010, *Wichita Eagle.*

which had been targeted in the past.[258] In February 2012, a federal grand jury indicted him on two counts—arson and damaging a reproductive health facility.[259] He pled guilty to the charges in July 2012.[260]

- In May 2011, Ralph Lang was arrested after allegedly accidently firing his handgun through the door of a hotel room in Madison, WI. He was reportedly planning to kill abortion providers in the area.[261]

One underground network that supports attacks on abortion clinics is the Army of God (AOG).[262] The loosely structured organization openly promotes anti-abortion violence.[263] However, its members deny that they are terrorists. They also deny that attacks against clinics and abortion providers constitute violent activity, because they see it as "Godly work."[264] AOG first made headlines with the 1982 kidnapping of a doctor and his wife, both of whom ran an abortion clinic in Illinois. Three individuals who claimed membership in AOG were responsible.[265] The group disseminates a manual that "is a 'how to' for abortion clinic violence. It details methods for blockading entrances, attacking with butyric acid, arson, bomb making, and other illegal activities. The manual contains anti-abortion language as well as anti-government and anti-gay/lesbian language. The manual begins with a declaration of war on the abortion industry."[266] Eric Rudolph, who in the late 1990s bombed an abortion clinic near Atlanta, GA, and one in Birmingham, AL, "published his writings on the Army of God website."[267]

---

[258] "Man Indicted for Abortion Clinic Firebombing," *Associated Press*, February 23, 2012.

[259] Department of Justice, "Arson Indictment Returned Regarding American Family Planning Clinic," press release, February 23, 2012.

[260] Department of Justice, "Man Pleads Guilty to Arson of Reproductive Health Facility in Pensacola," press release, July 19, 2012.

[261] Kevin Murphy, Feds Mull Felony Charge for Suspect Ralph Lang of Marshfield in Abortion Clinic Shooting Plot," *Marshfield News*, May 28, 2011; Department of Justice, "Wisconsin Man Charged with FACE Act Violations," press release, May 26, 2011, http://www.justice.gov/opa/pr/2011/May/11-crt-695.html. For other examples of individuals involved in abortion-related violence, see Department of Justice, "Man Pleads Guilty to Civil Rights Violation in Connection with Arson at Planned Parenthood and Vandalism of Mosque in Madera, California," press release, October 7, 2011. Mower also threw a brick at a mosque in Madera. Ryan Seals, "Update: Concord Man Charged in Plot to Bomb Abortion Clinic," *Greensboro News and Record*, September 9, 2010; "Man Guilty of Bombing Plot Gets 30 Months," *Salisbury Post*, March 2, 2011.

[262] National Consortium for the Study of Terrorism and Responses to Terrorism (START), "Terrorist Organization Profile: Army of God." Hereinafter: START, "Army of God."

[263] Mireille Jacobson and Heather Royer, "Aftershocks: The Impact of Clinic Violence on Abortion Services," National Bureau of Economic Research, Working Paper No. 16603, (January 7, 2010), p. 6.

[264] Jennifer Jefferis, *Armed for Life: The Army of God and Anti-Abortion Terror in the United States* (Santa Barbara, CA: Praeger, 2011), p. xvi. Hereinafter: Jefferis, *Armed for Life.*

[265] Ibid., p. 23. The victims were released unharmed after eight days of captivity. See; "Abortion Opposition Stressed in Kidnapping Trial in Illinois," *New York Times*, January 26, 1983.

[266] START, "Army of God."

[267] Beau Seegmiller, "Radicalized Margins: Eric Rudolph and Religious Violence," *Terrorism and Political Violence*, vol. 19, no. 4 (October 2007), p. 524. The 1998 bombing in Birmingham killed a police officer and injured a nurse. On May 31, 2003, Rudolph was arrested and charged with the clinic bombings, bombing the Centennial Olympic Park during the 1996 summer Olympic games in Atlanta (claiming one life), and attacking a gay club—Atlanta's Otherside Lounge—in 1997. Rudolph admitted to the bombing spree in April 2005. He claimed that the 1996 attack at Centennial Olympic Park was intended to shame the U.S. government for what Rudolph saw as its support of abortion rights. See "Rudolph Pleads Guilty in Series of Bombings," *Associated Press* at *MSNBC*, April 13, 2005; "Rudolph Agrees to Plea Agreement,"

### Protected Activities vs. Terrorism—Divergent Perceptions of the ALF

*The boundary between constitutionally protected legitimate protest and terrorist activity has received much attention in public discussions of domestic terrorism. As an example of this, the next several sections of this report explore such considerations regarding the ALF.*

#### A Serious Domestic Concern or "Green Scare?"

U.S. law enforcement, some business groups, and some scientists—among others—have stressed that animal rights extremists (and ecoterrorists) are a security and law enforcement concern. In 2008, the FBI stated that animal rights extremists and ecoterrorists together posed a serious domestic terrorism threat for several reasons, including the number of crimes attributed to animal rights extremists and ecoterrorists (between 1,800 and 2,000 incidents accounting for more than $110 million[268] in damages from 1979 to early 2009), the broad pool of victims (such as large pharmaceutical corporations, scientific laboratories, ski resorts, automobile dealerships, individual researchers, and lumber companies), and the movement's rhetoric and destructive tactics.[269] In March 2012, the FBI suggested that the threat from ecoterrorists may be declining.[270]

As articulated by some scientific researchers, the monetary toll on legitimate businesses and laboratories in the United States exacted by animal rights and eco-extremists is compounded by less tangible issues. For example, animal rights extremists and ecoterrorists have impacted the work of scientists. In some cases, special equipment and research materials have been destroyed in attacks. The consequences of criminal activity in the name of movements such as the ALF can also be more personal. Two advocates of animal research conducted strictly according to federal regulations have noted that the actions of animal rights extremists have pushed some scientists to quit lab work involving animals. Often, this work relates to products and procedures that some maintain cannot feasibly be marketed without animal testing.[271] In 2006, a UCLA professor of behavioral neuroscience declared he was stopping his research on monkeys because

*CNN*, April 12, 2005, http://articles.cnn.com/2005-04-08/justice/rudolph.plea_1_emily-lyons-eric-robert-rudolph-atlanta-attacks?_s=PM:LAW.

268 ELF claims that it has caused over $150 million in damages, although the geographic range and timeframe for this figure are unknown. Earth Liberation Front.org, "What Is the Earth Liberation Front?" Hereinafter: ELF, "What Is the Earth?" See also http://www.animalliberationfront.com/ALFront/ELF/ELFPressOffice.htm.

269 There is some imprecision in the FBI's public statements regarding the number of crimes committed by animal rights extremists and ecoterrorists. In April 2009, the FBI estimated that "to date [animal rights and eco-] extremists have been responsible for more than 1,800 criminal acts." Ten months earlier, in June 2008, the FBI placed the number of criminal acts at "over 2,000 since 1979." See Michael J. Heimbach, Assistant Director, Counterterrorism Division, Federal Bureau of Investigation, press conference, April 21, 2009. Hereinafter: Heimbach, press conference. See also FBI, "Putting Intel." The $110 million figure remained the same in both publicly released documents.

270 Juliet Eilperin, "As Eco Terrorism Threat Wanes, Governments Keep Eyes on Activists," *Washington Post*, March 11, 2012. Hereinafter: Eilperin, "As Eco Terrorism."

271 Conn and Parker, *The Animal*, pp. xii, xvi. See also 21 C.F.R. §314.610 (regarding approval based on evidence of effectiveness from studies in animals).

of what he described as harassment by animal rights groups.[272] Additionally, animal rights extremists are said to be driving out students from research programs.[273]

Critics of U.S. efforts to fight animal rights extremism and ecoterrorism have suggested that the threat is overblown by law enforcement and that the government's pursuit of purported extremists perpetuates a "green scare," chilling the exercise of protected speech by protesters.[274] Some say that the government conflates property crime with terrorism.[275] Others add that people engaged in what the government describes as animal rights extremism or ecoterrorism do not deserve the terrorist label.

### *Animal Enterprise Terrorism Act* (P.L. 109-374)

The Animal Enterprise Terrorism Act ( P.L. 109-374; AETA) expanded the federal government's legal authority to combat animal rights extremists who engage in criminal activity. Signed into law in November 2006, it amended the 1992 Animal Enterprise Protection Act (P.L. 102-346; AEPA). Namely, the AETA

> Amends the federal criminal code to revise criminal prohibitions against damaging or interfering with the operations of an animal enterprise to include intentional damage or loss to any real or personal property and intentional threats of death or serious bodily injury against individuals (or their family members, spouses, or intimate partners) who are involved with animal enterprises.[276]

The AETA expanded the AEPA to include both successful and attempted conspiracies. It also prohibits intentionally placing a person in "reasonable fear" of death or serious bodily injury while damaging or interfering in the operations of an animal enterprise. The AETA revised and increased monetary and criminal penalties. It also stipulates that it does not prohibit First Amendment-protected activity.

DOJ successfully prosecuted individuals on charges relating to animal enterprise terrorism for the first time under the AEPA in 2006 (the case had been built before the AETA had been signed into law).[277] Six individuals were convicted for what DOJ described as "their roles in a campaign to terrorize officers, employees, and shareholders of HLS [Huntingdon Life Sciences, a research corporation that performs animal research and

[272] Samantha Henig, "UCLA Professor Halts Monkey Research," *Chronicle of Higher Education*, vol. 53, no. 2 (September 1, 2006), p. 21.

[273] Michael Conn and James Parker, "Winners and Losers in the Animal Research Wars," *American Scientist*, vol. 96, no. 3 (May–June 2008), p. 184.

[274] See Will Potter, *Green Is the New Red: An Insider's Account of a Social Movement Under Siege*, (San Francisco: City Lights Books, 2011), p. 61.

[275] Coalition to Abolish the AETA, "AETA v. AEPA: A Side-by-Side Comparison," October 16, 2008, http://abolishtheaeta.org/web/aeta-v-aepa-a-side-by-side-comparison/; Center for Constitutional Rights, factsheet, "The Animal Enterprise Terrorism Act (AETA)," http://ccrjustice.org/learn-more/faqs/factsheet%3A-animal-enterprise-terrorism-act-(aeta).

[276] P.L. 109-374, CRS summary. Instead of damage and interference, the AEPA focused on the "physical disruption to the functioning of an animal enterprise." According to AETA, "animal enterprise" means: "(A) a commercial or academic enterprise that uses or sells animals or animal products for profit, food or fiber production, agriculture, education, research, or testing; (B) a zoo, aquarium, animal shelter, pet store, breeder, furrier, circus, or rodeo, or other lawful competitive animal event; or (C) any fair or similar event intended to advance agricultural arts or sciences."

[277] Department of Justice, "Three Militant Animal Rights Activists Sentenced to Between Four and Six Years in Prison," press release, September 21, 2006.

has U.K. and U.S. facilities]."[278] These individuals belonged to an animal rights campaign named Stop Huntingdon Animal Cruelty (SHAC)[279] and the entity SHAC USA, Inc. SHAC involves both legal protests and criminal activity against HLS.

Reportedly, the six incited threats, harassment, and vandalism and on this basis were convicted of violating the AEPA.[280] DOJ has noted that SHAC's stated mission was to work "outside the confines of the legal system."[281] DOJ proved in court that the group managed websites that encouraged others "to direct their intimidation, harassment, and violence against HLS and its targeted employees, as well as secondary targets—companies and employees who did business with HLS."[282]

DOJ has also successfully applied the AETA. For example, on February 14, 2011, Scott DeMuth was sentenced to six months in prison on one count of misdemeanor conspiracy to commit animal enterprise terrorism. He was involved in a raid that released about 200 ferrets at a Minnesota farm in 2006. Activists had claimed the action in the name of the ALF.[283] In another case, William James Viehl and Alex Hall were sentenced to 24 months and 21 months in prison, respectively, under AETA. The duo had released 650 minks, destroyed breeding records, and vandalized structures at the McMullin Ranch in South Jordan, UT, in 2008.[284]

DOJ has experienced at least one setback in its application of the AETA. In February 2009, the FBI announced the arrests of what it described as "four animal rights extremists." The four (two women, two men, all in their 20s) allegedly violated the AETA by using "force, violence, or threats to interfere with the operation of the University of

278 Ibid. See also "The SHAC 7," http://www.shac7.com/case.htm.

279 An undercover British television report on the treatment of animals at a British company, Huntingdon Life Sciences (HLS), sparked the creation of Stop Huntingdon Animal Cruelty (SHAC) in the United Kingdom in 1999. Active in a number of countries around the world, including the United States, the campaign has tried to compel business and financial firms to cut ties to HLS. It has involved both legal protests and crime. John P. Martin, "Animal Rights and Wrongs," *Newark Star-Ledger*, November 28, 2004; Anti-Defamation League, *Ecoterrorism*. For more on SHAC from a movement perspective, see "History of the Animal Liberation Front," http://www.animalliberationfront.com/ALFront/Premise_History/ALF_History.htm. The SHAC campaign made its way to the United States in 2000. See Heimbach, press conference.

280 Four of the six were guilty of other charges related to the case as well. Department of Justice, "Militant Animal Rights Group, Six Members Convicted in Campaign to Terrorize Company, Employees, and Others," March 2, 2006. Hereinafter: Department of Justice, "Militant Animal Rights." Anti-Defamation League, "Animal Rights Group Sentenced for Inciting Violence and Stalking." Hereinafter: Anti-Defamation League, "Animal Rights Group."

281 Department of Justice, *White Paper*, p. 60.

282 Ibid. The convictions in the case were upheld by a federal appeals court in 2009. See Lisa Coryell, "Convictions of Animal Rights Activists Upheld," *Times of Trenton*, October 14, 2009. Subsequently, the U.S. Supreme Court refused to review the case. See Center for Constitutional Rights, "U.S. v. SHAC 7," http://ccrjustice.org/us-v-SHAC7; Will Potter, "Supreme Court Will Not Hear SHAC 7 Case," March 7, 2011, http://www.greenisthenewred.com/blog/shac-7-supreme-court/4447/.

283 Ryan J. Foley, "Minn. Man Gets 6 Months for Raid on Ferret Farm," *Associated Press*, February 14, 2011. Jennifer Kotila, "Minneapolis Man to Be Sentenced for Releasing HL Ferrets He Thought Were Mink," *Delano Herald Journal*, (Minnesota) December 20, 2010.

284 Dennis Romboy, "Man Who Raided South Jordan Mink Farm Sentenced," *Deseret News*, July 1, 2010; Department of Justice, "Viehl Pleads Guilty to Damaging, Interfering with Animal Enterprise in Connection with McMullin Mink Farm Incident," press release, September 3, 2009.

California."[285] The incidents leading to the indictment included protests at the houses of researchers from the University of California, Berkeley and University of California, Santa Cruz. According to the FBI's press release, in one instance, three of the indicted individuals tried to forcibly enter the home of a researcher, whose husband was hit by an object while confronting the protesters.[286] In July 2010, a federal judge dismissed the indictment against the four. According to the ruling, the indictment failed to specifically describe crimes allegedly committed by the defendants.[287] Opponents of the prosecution stress that the case involved over-broad application of AETA to First Amendment-protected behaviors.[288]

Criticisms of federal government efforts to counter animal rights extremists have focused on the AETA itself and First Amendment-related issues. Opponents of the AETA suggest that it expanded the AEPA too much by making it easier to prosecute individuals who wage protest campaigns against secondary or tertiary targets—companies or people (such as insurers) indirectly tied to an animal enterprise.[289] Opponents also take issue with the inclusion of "reasonable fear" in the AETA, suggesting that protected speech or activities may possibly be interpreted as provoking "reasonable fear" in some instances. Echoing critiques of the AETA, one observer emphasizes that while activities linked to U.S.-based animal rights extremists have caused significant property damage, none of these criminal acts has physically harmed people. This critic suggests that describing vandalism or arson as *terrorism* and not ordinary *crime* dampens constitutionally protected protest activity by people who support animal rights or radical environmentalism but do not engage in criminal activity.[290] In essence, this position argues that the U.S. government is encouraging a "green scare" by labeling the activity of movements such as the ALF and the ELF as terrorism or extremism.[291] After serving 40 months in prison for her involvement with SHAC USA, Lauren Gazzola argued that she was not a terrorist, claiming, "I hadn't hurt anyone or vandalized any property. In fact, the indictment didn't allege that I'd committed any independent crime at all, only that I'd 'conspired' to publish a website that advocated and reported on protest activity against a notorious animal testing lab in New Jersey."[292]

---

285 Federal Bureau of Investigation, "Four Extremists Arrested for Threats and Violence Against UC Researchers," press release, February 20, 2009, http://sanfrancisco.fbi.gov/pressrel/pressrel09/sf022009.htm.

286 Ibid.

287 "S.C. Animal Activists Won't Face Charges," *The Monterey County Herald*, July 14, 2010.

288 Will Potter, "Breaking: AETA 4 Case Dismissed, But Re-Indictment Possible," *GreenIstheNewRed.com*, July 12, 2010, http://www.greenisthenewred.com/blog/aeta-4-case-thrown-out-dismissed/3015/; Bill Quigley and Rachel Meeropol, "Victory for Animal Rights Dissent," *Huffington Post*, July 16, 2010. Hereinafter: Quigley and Meeropol, "Victory for Animal."

289 The AETA makes it illegal to damage or interfere with the operations of an animal enterprise. Presumably this covers tertiary targets.

290 Will Potter, "The Green Scare," *Vermont Law Review*, vol. 33, no. 4 (June 2009), pp. 672–673.

291 Ibid; Quigley and Meeropol, "Victory for Animal."

292 Lauren Gazzola, "Animal Rights Activists Like Me Aren't Terrorists," *EGP News*, January 12, 2012, http://egpnews.com/?p=33714.

The U.S. Code's definition of "domestic terrorism" has been seen by some as potentially chilling to legitimate animal rights and environmental protest activities.[293] As mentioned, the current delineation of domestic terrorism in the U.S. Code includes criminal acts "dangerous to human life" that appear to intend to intimidate or coerce a civilian population or influence governmental policy via intimidation or coercion. This line of reasoning suggests that the crimes committed by animal rights extremists and ecoterrorists cannot be compared to clearly violent attacks by groups such as Al Qaeda. An opposing commentary stresses that such discussion is irrelevant and

> miss[es] the mark. The ALF ideology encourages members to instill fear in those who engage in the activities that the ALF opposes: fear of harm to themselves and their families, and fear of personal and professional economic loss. Additionally, these arguments assume that "true terrorism" is fundamentally different from animal rights terrorism. While it is true that animal rights terrorism, as a whole, does not engage in the same scale of violence as other extremist groups, those working in academia, research, agriculture, and food service industries are no less fearful when their homes and workplaces are firebombed; violent tactics can instill fear even when they are used infrequently.[294]

## Assessing Domestic Terrorism's Significance

Domestic terrorist attacks have come nowhere near the devastation of 9/11. However, it is worth noting that (as mentioned above) Timothy McVeigh's bombing of the Alfred P. Murrah Federal Building in Oklahoma City on April 19, 1995, claimed 168 lives and injured more than 500 others. It ranks as the second-deadliest terrorist attack on U.S. soil, behind only the devastation wrought by Al Qaeda on 9/11. Domestic terrorists feature prominently among the concerns of some law enforcement officers. For example, Los Angeles Deputy Police Chief Michael P. Downing recently described violent Islamists such as Al Qaeda, Hezbollah, and Hamas as Los Angeles's main terrorist threats "along with three other terrorist categories: black separatists, white supremacist/sovereign citizen extremists, and animal rights terrorists."[295] A 2014 national survey of state and local law enforcement officers found that among terrorist threats, sovereign citizens were "the top concern."[296] In one 2008 study, state police agencies "overwhelmingly reported" dangerous domestic extremist groups present in their jurisdictions.[297] Of course, as one expert reminds us, most followers of extremist viewpoints pose no threat: "Most of them are not going to do anything but bore their relatives and friends with ridiculous papers and treatises."[298]

---

293 American Civil Liberties Union, "How the USA PATRIOT Act Redefines "Domestic Terrorism," December 6, 2002. For an additional view suggesting that the activities of movements such as the ALF and the ELF should not be treated as terrorism, see DeMond Shondell Miller, Jason David Rivera, and Joel C. Yelin, "Civil Liberties: The Line Dividing Environmental Protest and Ecoterrorists," *Journal for the Study of Radicalism*, vol. 2, no. 1 (2008), pp. 109–123.

294 Grubbs, "Saving Lives," pp. 364–365.

295 Bill Gertz, "L.A. Police Use Intel Networks Against Terror," *Washington Times*, April 11, 2011.

296 Jessica Rivinius, "Sovereign Citizen Movement Perceived as Top Terrorist Threat," National Consortium for the Study of Terrorism and Responses to Terrorism, July 30, 2014. For the report, see Carter, David, et al., "Understanding Law Enforcement Intelligence Processes," National Consortium for the Study of Terrorism and Responses to Terrorism, 2014.

297 "Far Right Domestic Terrorism on Par with Foreign Threat, Experts Say," CNN, July 25, 2011.

298 Ibid.

Four broad themes speak to the threat posed by domestic terrorists. First, domestic terrorists likely have been responsible for numerous incidents since 9/11. Second, a large number of those labeled as domestic terrorists do not necessarily use major terrorist tactics such as bombings or airplane hijackings. Third, domestic terrorists—much like their violent jihadist analogues—are often Internet savvy and use the medium as a resource for their operations. Fourth, domestic terrorism can be seen as a somewhat decentralized threat often involving lone wolves and movements operating under the model of leaderless resistance.

## Counting Incidents

The U.S. government does not keep a publicly available list of domestic terrorist incidents (foiled plots or attacks). This makes it especially challenging for anyone trying to develop a sense of this particularly diverse threat.[299] However, as of August 2017, the New America Foundation reportedly has found that people who can be characterized as domestic terrorists have killed 75 people in the United States since 9/11, whereas jihadist terrorists have killed 95.[300]

Some U.S. government sources suggest levels of domestic terrorist activity. Examples of such sources include the following:

- An unclassified 2008 DHS report includes a table that lists *selected* criminal acts perpetrated by people involved in the animal rights extremist and ecoterrorist movements. This list counts 74 criminal acts between 9/11 and March 2008.[301]
- As noted, the FBI estimated that animal rights extremist and ecoterrorists together committed between 1,800 and 2,000 criminal incidents accounting for more than $110 million in damages from 1979 to early 2009.[302] In 2012, the FBI also publicly discussed a decline in ecoterrorism, especially after a wave of successful prosecutions in 2007. The Bureau reportedly attributes the perceived dip to activists possibly viewing "a Democratic administration as more sympathetic to their goals and [thus] be less inclined to take radical steps."[303]
- An unclassified FBI intelligence bulletin estimates that 53 acts of violence were committed by what it calls "white supremacist extremists" between 2007 and

[299] From 2004 to early 2012, the National Counterterrorism Center's Worldwide Incidents Tracking System (WITS) publicly captured information on terrorist incidents (attacks) worldwide, including in the United States. It is no longer available. Prior to WITS, the FBI published regular reports of such activity. See https://www.fbi.gov/investigate/terrorism/publications.

[300] These figures are based on tallies available at the New America Foundation website. See https://www.newamerica.org/in-depth/terrorism-in-america/what-threat-united-states-today/. The figure for domestic terrorists combines the 67 people killed by "far right wing" terrorists as described by the New America Foundation study with 8 deaths since 9/11 attributed to "black separatist/nationalist/supremacist" actors tabulated in the same report.

[301] Department of Homeland Security, *Ecoterrorism: Environmental and Animal-Rights Militants in the United States*, Universal Adversary Dynamic Threat Assessment, May 7, 2008. Table 1 from the report is a "compilation of material from ALF and ELF communiqués and publications, media reports, and law enforcement" listing *selected* criminal acts perpetrated by the ALF and the ELF from 1984 to March 2008. Table 1 from the DHS report is not a comprehensive list of crimes tied to the ALF and the ELF. Hereinafter: Department of Homeland Security, *Ecoterrorism*.

[302] Heimbach, press conference; Federal Bureau of Investigation, "Putting Intel."

[303] Eilperin, "As Eco Terrorism."

2009 in the United States. Victims included other white supremacists, African Americans, and Latinos. Most of the incidents involved assaults. The bulletin bases these findings on law enforcement and media reporting.[304]

- In February 2012, the FBI announced that sovereign citizen convictions increased from 10 in 2009 to 18 in both 2010 and 2011.[305]

Additionally, a key caveat regarding estimates of domestic terrorist activity may be of importance. Many domestic terrorist incidents have been linked to either animal rights extremists or ecoterrorists. As highlighted elsewhere in this report, many animal rights extremists and ecoterrorists claim to avoid violent acts that directly target people. The attacks by these individuals can often be described as property crimes involving arson or vandalism.

### "Nonviolent" Strategies

While some terrorists engage in violence, others commit much different crimes that do not physically harm people. This latter group differs from their homegrown violent jihadist counterparts, who are often bent on killing or harming people. Two types of activities that avoid visiting violence upon people but are commonly associated with subjects of domestic terrorism investigations stand out. First, many animal rights extremists, ecoterrorists, and anarchist extremists believe in "direct action." This typically involves what movement members would characterize as *nonviolent but criminal* protest or resistance activities furthering the movement's ideology. While direct action has a long legacy among anarchists, in recent years the ALF and the ELF have played a large role in articulating its meaning. Second, "paper terrorism" is a term used to describe some of the *nonviolent* criminal activity committed by sovereign citizens involving the filing of fraudulent documents in the hopes of harassing enemies or bilking state or federal tax authorities.

### Direct Action

Anarchist extremists, animal liberation extremists, and environmental extremists refer to much of their operational activity as "direct action." This term has a long history, and it can be used to describe legitimate protest such as letter writing campaigns or work stoppages. However, this report uses "direct action" to describe criminal activities such as sabotage and arson.[306]

---

[304] Federal Bureau of Investigation, *White Supremacist Extremist Violence*, pp. 1–2. The FBI bulletin defines "acts of violence" to include "arson; assaults and murders; and acts designed to threaten or intimidate due to a person's ethnicity, religious beliefs, or lifestyle." See Federal Bureau of Investigation, *Rage and Racism* p. 5.

[305] Patrick Temple-West, "Anti-Government Extremists Opposed to Taxes and Regulations Pose a Growing Threat to Local Law Enforcement Officers in the United States, the FBI Warned on Monday," *Reuters*, February 6, 2012.

[306] According to the DOJ's Office of the Inspector General, the FBI "generally" defines "direct action" as, "criminal activity designed to cause economic loss or to destroy property or operations." See Department of Justice, Office of the Inspector General, Oversight and Review Division, *A Review of the FBI's Investigations of Certain Domestic Advocacy Groups*, (September 2010), p. 97; Darren Thurston, *The ALF Primer*, n.d. p. 4. DOJ believes Thurston authored the *Primer*, although he is not attributed as an author in the document. Hereinafter: Thurston, *The ALF Primer*. See also *Guide to Direct Action, 2010*, http://www.animalliberationfront.com/ALFront/Activist%20Tips/Direct_Action-Guide.htm; Earth

ALF and ELF members understand that criminality and direct action are one and the same. *The Animal Liberation Primer,* a movement resource, highlights criminality in the actions of supporters: "anyone working in the ALF is a criminal. You have to begin to think like a criminal." ALF and ELF members also generally view direct action as nonviolent and heroic. Using politically charged language, the ALF allegedly styles itself along the lines of the Underground Railroad, freedom fighters in Nazi Germany, anti-Apartheid protestors, U.S. civil rights activists, and Palestinian groups opposing Israel.[307] The ELF views constitutionally protected protest as "state sanctioned" and eschews such activity. The ELF, much like the ALF, also wraps itself in the mantle of reformers and describes itself as inheriting the spirit of Luddites, abolitionists, suffragists, and even the American revolutionary-era Boston Tea Party.[308]

### The ALF: "Live Liberations" and "Economic Sabotage"

The ALF frames its version of direct action as "economic sabotage" or "ethical vandalism." The ALF supports the destruction of property and intimidation of individuals and businesses considered by the movement to be involved in the exploitation of animals. Cells and individuals linked to the ALF also engage in trespassing and theft, or what they perceive as "live liberations" or "rescuing" animals from "the horrors of exploitation"[309] and human use[310] by stealing them from places such as legitimate research facilities or farms. Economic sabotage can be virtual. The North American Animal Liberation Press Office (NAALPO) has carried claims of cyber hacking incidents in the name of animal rights.[311] NAALPO is one of the web-based vehicles used by ALF supporters to publicize criminal activities claimed on behalf of the movement.

### The ELF: "Monkeywrenching"

Like the ALF, the ELF's discussions of direct action also revolve around economic sabotage. The ELF rejects legal protest tactics partly for what it views as pragmatic reasons—"because they have been proven not to work, especially on their own."[312] Economic sabotage in the name of environmentalism has a long history, perhaps stretching back to the 1950s,[313] and has been called "monkeywrenching," a term taken from a 1975 novel, *The Monkey Wrench Gang* by Edward Abbey. The book depicts such activity.[314] A

---

Liberation Front.org, "Earth Liberation Front Frequently Asked Questions," Hereinafter: ELF, "FAQs." See also http://www.animalliberationfront.com/ALFront/ELF/elf_faq.pdf.

[307] NAALPO, "History."

[308] ELF, "FAQs."

[309] NAALPO, "History." A section of *The ALF Primer* describes both economic sabotage and live liberation as legitimate strategies. See Thurston, *The ALF Primer,* p. 2.

[310] Conn and Parker, *The Animal,* p. xvii.

[311] See North American Animal Liberation Press Office, communiqué, July 13, 2007.

[312] ELF, "FAQs."

[313] Bron Taylor, "The Tributaries of Radical Environmentalism," *Journal for the Study of Radicalism,* vol. 2, no. 1 (2008), p. 45.

[314] Edward Abbey, *The Monkey Wrench Gang,* 3rd ed. (Salt Lake City, UT: Dream Garden Press, 1985).

guidebook that describes monkeywrenching offers what can be interpreted as a call to arms for would-be extremists:

> It is time for women and men, individually and in small groups to act heroically in the defense of the wild, to put a monkeywrench into the gears of the machine that is destroying natural diversity. Though illegal, this strategic monkeywrenching can be safe, easy, and—most important—effective.[315]

The guidebook also defines monkeywrenching as nonviolent by stressing that it should never target people or "other forms of life."[316]

### *Arson and Explosive Devices*

Federal officials are especially concerned about the use of incendiary devices and explosives by animal rights extremists and ecoterrorists. In congressional testimony from 2005, then-ATF Deputy Assistant Director Carson Carroll stated that the "most worrisome" trend regarding animal rights extremists and ecoterrorists was their "willingness to resort to incendiary and explosive devices."[317]

This pronouncement came on the heels of two related incidents that occurred near San Francisco, CA, and involved explosive devices. An entity called the Revolutionary Cells of the Animal Liberation Brigade claimed responsibility for both attacks, which the FBI has also linked to a man named Daniel San Diego. In August 2003, two ammonium nitrate pipe bombs exploded at the campus of the biotechnology firm Chiron but caused little damage and no injuries. In October 2003, a reputed 10-pound ammonium nitrate bomb damaged the offices of Shaklee, a health, beauty, and household product company. No one was injured. The perpetrator(s) believed that both companies did business with Huntingdon Life Sciences (the same firm targeted by SHAC and discussed above). A related communiqué stressed that, "all customers and their families are considered legitimate targets."[318]

One commentator has suggested that the combination of "fire" as a tactic and instilling "fear" as a goal ensures ecoterrorists will continue to warrant the terrorist label.[319] Both

---

315 Dave Foreman, "Strategic Monkeywrenching," in *Ecodefense: A Field Guide to Monkeywrenching*, ed. Dave Foreman and Bill Haywood, 3rd ed. (Chico, CA: Abzug Press, 1993), p. 8. Hereinafter: Foreman, "Strategic Monkeywrenching." Foreman was a founder of Earth First! See Anti-Defamation League, *Ecoterrorism*.

316 Dave Foreman, "Strategic Monkeywrenching," p. 9.

317 Statement of Carson Carroll, p. 43.

318 Stacy Finz, "Militants Say They Planted Shaklee Bomb," *San Francisco Chronicle*, October 1, 2003, http://articles.sfgate.com/2003-10-01/bay-area/17512148_1_pipe-bombs-shaklee-chiron; Stacy Finz, Bernadette Tansey, "2 Bombs Shatter Biotech Firm's Windows," August 29, 2003. The FBI assessed that the devices may have been intended to harm people. The second Chiron bomb was timed to explode after the first, "an apparent strike at first responders," while the Shaklee bomb was wrapped in nails, "to significantly increase its lethality to anyone in the area at the time of the detonation." See U.S. Congress, Senate Committee on Environment and Public Works, "Statement of John E. Lewis, Deputy Assistant Director, Counterterrorism Division, Federal Bureau of Investigation," *Eco-Terrorism Specifically Examining Stop Huntingdon Animal Cruelty ("SHAC")*, 109th Cong., 1st sess., October 26, 2005, 109-1005 (Washington: GPO, 2008), p. 7. In April 2009, the FBI placed Daniel San Diego on its Most Wanted Terrorists List for his involvement in the bombings. See Heimbach, press conference. The Bureau also tied him to SHAC. He had slipped away from FBI surveillance in October 2003. See Federal Bureau of Investigation, "New Most Wanted Terrorist," April 21, 2009. Hereinafter: FBI, "New Most Wanted"; "Daniel Andreas San Diego," *America's Most Wanted*.

319 Grubbs, "Saving Lives," p. 370.

animal rights extremists and ecoterrorists have histories of using incendiary devices to damage or destroy property—the Vail, CO, fire (mentioned elsewhere in this report) setting a prominent example for extremists. In fact, one of the hallmark publications circulated in extremist circles is a handbook on how to fashion incendiary devices titled *Arson Around with Auntie ALF.*[320] A recent example underscores this focus on arson.

- In January 2012, NAALPO issued a communiqué in which "unnamed activists" claimed responsibility for setting fires that damaged 14 tractor trailer rigs at the Harris Ranch, a cattle feedlot in Coalinga, CA. The perpetrators used containers of accelerant, kerosene-soaked rope, and digital timers to set the blazes. According to the communiqué, the fires apparently embodied a reaction to "the horrors and injustices of factory farming."[321]

Some ELF adherents have focused on targets they perceive as emblematic of urban sprawl[322] or the excesses of industrialized society. Since 2000, a number of ELF actions have involved the torching of housing developments as well as activities such as the damaging and destruction of sports utility vehicles and other emblems of industrialized society and urban sprawl.[323] Between August and October 2002, three individuals tied to the ELF damaged construction vehicles and sports utility vehicles, and vandalized fast food restaurants in Virginia. In one incident, these individuals vandalized two homes under construction, spray painting "sprawl" on one of the structures. In November 2005, the ELF claimed responsibility for fires set in five townhomes under construction in Hagerstown, MD.[324] Similar activity has occurred on the West Coast.[325]

### *Guidelines*

Both the ALF and the ELF have established guidelines and posted them on the web for cells or lone wolves to follow. The guidelines are straightforward and short for both movements (see **Figure 1**). A key point in the guidelines for both the ALF and the ELF

---

320 Auntie ALF, Uncle ELF, and the Anti-Copyright Gang, *Arson-Around with Auntie ALF: Your Guide for Putting the Heat on Animal Abusers Everywhere,* 2001. Hereinafter: *Arson-Around.*

321 See North American Animal Liberation Press Office, communiqué, January 10, 2012; Henry K. Lee, "14 Cattle Trucks Burned in Arson at Harris Ranch," *San Francisco Chronicle,* January 11, 2012. For other examples, see Peter Young, "Fire and Explosions Rock Oregon Mink Farm," July 28, 2010, North American Animal Liberation Press Office; J.M. Brown, "A Year after Firebombings, No Arrests, Though Awareness Remains among Scientists," *Santa Cruz Sentinel,* August 2, 2009; John Coté, "Firebombings Suggest New Tactic for Animal Activists," *San Francisco Chronicle,* August 5, 2008; Shanna McCord, "FBI to Take Over Santa Cruz Firebombs Case," *Monterey County Herald,* August 4, 2008; Anti-Defamation League, '"Justice Department' Claims Responsibility for Threats against UCLA Animal Researcher," December 3, 2010. Hereinafter: Anti-Defamation League, '"Justice Department.'"

322 Brad Knickerbocker, "Firebrands of 'Ecoterrorism' Set Sights on Urban Sprawl," *Christian Science Monitor,* August 6, 2003. Hereinafter: Knickerbocker, "Firebrands."

323 Anti-Defamation League, "Radical Environmentalist Group Suspected in San Diego Arson," August 8, 2003; Knickerbocker, "Firebrands"; Chris Dixon, "Arrest in Vandalism of S.U.V.s," *New York Times.*

324 Federal Bureau of Investigation, *Terrorism 2002–2005,* http://209.235.0.153/publications/terror/terrorism2002_2005.htm.

325 "Activists Topple Towers, Claim Dangers of AM Radio Waves," *CNN.com,* September 4, 2009, http://articles.cnn.com/2009-09-04/justice/washington.towers.terrorism_1_elf-radio-station-radio-waves?_s=PM:CRIME; "Officials: No Explosive Devices Found at Scene of Seattle-Area House Fires," *Fox News,* March 4, 2008; Debera Carlton Harrell, Aubrey Cohen, and Paul Shukovsky, "'Street of Dreams' Houses Torched; Eco-Terrorists Suspected," *Seattle Post-Intelligencer,* March 4, 2008; "Camano Island Mansion Fire Ruled Ecoterrorist Arson," KOMO News.Com, January 20, 2006.

is to avoid harming any animal, human and non-human.[326] The ALF also stipulates that individuals professing affiliation with the movement must be vegetarians or vegans.[327]

Interestingly, the ALF employs a number of caveats in its understanding of violence. On the one hand, it supports intimidation as a tactic. On the other, the movement does not see intimidation as potentially involving violence.[328] The ALF also views arson as "violence against property," not people.[329] Beyond this, ALF does not greatly elaborate on its notion of violence.

**Figure 1. ALF and ELF Guidelines**

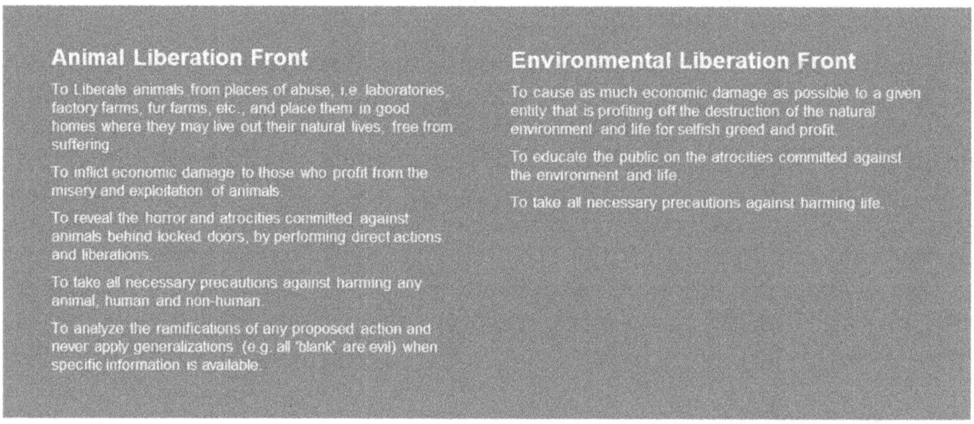


**Source:** CRS graphic based on ALF and ELF guidelines.

**Notes:** For ALF guidelines, see http://www.animalliberationfront.com/ALFront/alf_credo.htm. For ELF guidelines, see http://www.animalliberationfront.com/ALFront/ELF/elf_faq.pdf.

### *Exceptions*

Some animal rights extremists support violence. For example, in February 2012 Meredith Lowell was arrested for allegedly using a Facebook page she created (under an assumed name) to solicit a hit man to kill "someone who is wearing fur."[330] In the investigation, the FBI used an undercover employee to pose as a hit man and communicate with Lowell online. She was arrested before anyone could be harmed.[331]

---

[326] For ALF guidelines, see http://www.animalliberationfront.com/ALFront/alf_credo.htm. For ELF guidelines, see http://www.animalliberationfront.com/ALFront/ELF/elf_faq.pdf.

[327] Ibid.

[328] Ibid.

[329] See North American Animal Liberation Front, "Frequently Asked Questions about the North American Animal Liberation Press Office."

[330] James Ewinger, "Cleveland Heights Woman Charged with Using Facebook to Hire Killer," *Cleveland Plain Dealer,* February 21, 2012, http://blog.cleveland.com/metro/2012/02/heights_woman_charged_with_usi.html.

[331] Ibid.

An animal rights extremist entity named the "Justice Department" has argued for the efficacy of violence against humans.[332] Founded in the United Kingdom in 1993, the "Justice Department" has been described as an offshoot of the ALF.[333] In 1999, the first incident claimed in its name on U.S. soil involved the mailing of more than 80 envelopes containing razor blades allegedly positioned to cut recipients. Some of the razors may have been covered in rat poison. The letters were received by animal researchers, hunting guides, and others in the United States and Canada.[334] In November 2010, individuals asserting ties to the "Justice Department" mailed two communiqués to NAALPO. The missives claimed that "Justice Department" extremists had mailed AIDS-tainted razors to two scientists at the University of California, Los Angeles.[335] One of the communiqués read:

> We are the past generation of animal liberationists, but we will now be the future, striking at the heart of the vivisection industry, and if we have to go back to egg timers and insence [sic] sticks then we will. Mark our words, we will destroy all who fall into our focus.[336]

Presumably, allusion to egg timers and incense sticks suggested timing devices and fuses for explosive or incendiary devices.[337]

### "Paper Terrorism": Liens, Frivolous Lawsuits, and Tax Schemes

Sovereign citizens have committed nonviolent crimes based on their ideological underpinnings.[338] These are often bundled under the concept of "paper terrorism."[339] This concept can include forging documents (fake money orders and bad personal checks, for example), failing to pay taxes, phony tax filings, and presenting sham legal arguments in court. Sovereign citizens have filed fraudulent property liens against their foes.[340]

---

332 North American Animal Liberation Press Office, "Liberationist Group 'Justice Department' Increasingly Vocal on Animal Abuse," press release, November 23, 2010. Hereinafter: NAALPO, "Liberationist Group."

333 Anti-Defamation League, '"Justice Department.'"

334 Ibid; Southern Poverty Law Center, "Eco-Violence: The Record," *Intelligence Report*, Southern Poverty Law Center, no. 107 (Fall 2002).

335 NAALPO, "Liberationist Group."

336 Ibid.

337 *Arson-Around*, pp. 16–17 describes assembly of an incendiary device incorporating incense sticks as a fuse. Incense sticks have been used as fuses for incendiary devices by ELF and ALF activists. See Federal Bureau of Investigation, *Terrorism 2000–2001*, 2004, p. 4, for an example of an ELF incident. For additional examples involving the cell known as "The Family" active with both the ALF and the ELF, see *U.S. v. Dibee et al.* Kitchen timers are discussed in William Rodgers and Stanislas Meyerhoff, *Setting Fires with Electrical Timers: An Earth Liberation Front Guide*, May 2001, pp. 15–17. Although the document lists no authors, DOJ believes that Rodgers and Meyerhoff wrote it. They were members of "The Family" which also used kitchen timers in its incendiary devices. See *United States v. Joseph Dibee et al*, Indictment, CR 06-60011-AA, District Court, District of Oregon, January 19, 2006.

338 Department of Homeland Security and the Federal Bureau of Investigation, *Sovereign Citizen Group Calls for Removal of U.S. Governors*, March 29, 2010, p. 2. Hereinafter: *"Sovereign Citizen Group Calls."*

339 For an example of the use of this oft-used term, see Department of Justice, "Member of Anti-Government Movement Pleads Guilty to Laundering Money for FBI Undercover Agents," press release, March 25, 2011.

340 One source has defined a lien as "a claim encumbrance or charge on property for payment of a debt or obligation." Liens can be consensual or nonconsensual. They can be statutory or derive from common law. An example of a nonconsensual common law lien is "when a mechanic refuses to return a car until repairs are paid for." See Robert Chamberlain and Donald P. Haider-Markel, "'Lien on Me': State Policy

Some sovereigns hold illegal courts and target officials with fake criminal indictments. They can also "issue warrants for judges and police officers."[341]

### *Retaliatory Filings*

While these acts may not be violent, they are frequently "designed to intimidate or defraud targeted individuals, private institutions, or government entities."[342] Thus, some sovereigns saddle their opponents with time-consuming legal efforts to wipe out sham retaliatory court filings. As a result, sovereign foes incur court fees and their credit ratings potentially suffer. In some cases, these proceedings arise from what most citizens might consider fairly mundane run-ins with law enforcement authorities. Some sovereigns do not necessarily see violations like parking tickets and trespassing arrests as run-of-the-mill. They can react to such encounters with police by challenging the very authority and jurisdiction of U.S. law enforcement and by harassing officials with dubious liens, for example.

- In November 2011, Kenneth W. Leaming, from Spanaway, WA, was arrested for allegedly issuing billions of dollars in frivolous liens to intimidate public officials enforcing laws against sovereign citizens. Reportedly, he had been tied to other sovereign citizen adherents and groups. Also, he purportedly planned to harass the children of U.S. Supreme Court Chief Justice John Roberts.[343] In 2013, Leaming was convicted of "three counts of filing false liens against federal officials and one count of harboring federal fugitives and being a felon in possession of firearms."[344]

### *Redemption*

Sovereign citizen guru Roger Elvick is the reputed founder of "redemption,"[345] a concept that blurs the line between sovereign citizen ideology and pure scam. Redemption suggests that when the United States left the gold standard during the Great Depression, the nation found a way to monetize people. According to the theory, each child who is born

Innovation in Response to Paper Terrorism," *Political Research Quarterly*, vol. 58, no. 3 (September 2005), p. 450.

[341] Ibid.; Federal Bureau of Investigation, "Sovereign Citizen." See also Christopher A. Young, "Minnesota Has New Weapons in the Fight Against 'Paper Terrorism,'" *Hennepin Lawyer*, August 28, 2007, http://hennepin.timberlakepublishing.com/article.asp?article=1148.

[342] *"Sovereign Citizen Group Calls,"* p. 2.

[343] Levi Pulkkinen, "FBI: Spanaway 'Sovereign Citizen' Planned to Track Down Justice's Children," *Seattle Post-Intelligencer*, November 28, 2011; Anti-Defamation League, "Little Shell Pembina Band," http://www.adl.org/learn/ext_us/little_shell.asp?learn_cat=extremism&learn_subcat=extremism_in_america&xpicked=3&item=little_shell. For other examples, see Rick Montgomery, "Sovereign Citizens: Crackpots, Crooks, or Defenders of Liberty?" *Kansas City Star*, November 26, 2011. Hereinafter: Montgomery, "Sovereign Citizens."

[343] Marnie Eisenstadt, "Fringe Group Terrorizes Small-Town Officials with False Liens," *The Post Standard*, May 23, 2011; Montgomery, "Sovereign Citizens;" Marnie Eisenstadt, "Fringe Group Terrorizes Small-Town Officials with False Liens," *The Post Standard*, May 23, 2011; "Two Admit Scheme to Defraud Public Employees," *Daily Freeman*, January 14, 2011, http://www.dailyfreeman.com/articles/2011/01/14/blotter/doc4d2fb54d3189f270459164.txt; Michael Virtanen, "NY Man's Sentencing Put Off in Liens Case," *Associated Press*, July 12, 2011.

[344] Department of Justice, "Four Convicted in Sovereign Citizen Investigation," press release, March 7, 2013.

[345] "His 'Straw Man' Free, a Scammer Finds the Rest of Him Isn't," *Intelligence Report*, Southern Poverty Law Center, Issue 118, (Summer 2005). Hereinafter: Southern Poverty Law Center, "His Straw Man Free."

in the United States and has a birth certificate also has a U.S. Treasury account "valued from $630,000 to more than $3 million"[346] viewed as collateral against the nation's debts. Redemption supporters hold that by filing certain forms with state or federal authorities, people can draw money from these accounts. To do so, they occasionally attempt to pass bogus checks.[347]

On a broad level, redemption can be viewed as an ideologically driven tactic meant to illegally wrangle money from the U.S. government via the IRS. According to DOJ, in some instances this involves the filing of "a series of false IRS forms, including tax returns, amended returns, and Forms 1099 (including Form 1099-OID) or Forms W-2, to request fraudulent tax refunds based on phony claims of large income tax withholding."[348]

In addition, DOJ describes some redemption adherents as scammers who dupe customers into filing false IRS forms to redeem money via the purported secret accounts the government holds for its citizens.[349] One guru recently pled guilty to money laundering charges.[350] In another case, in December 2009 Audie Watson received a 14-year prison sentence for his involvement in an immigration benefit fraud scheme that sold membership in the Pembina Nation Little Shell Band to illegal aliens. Watson and co-conspirators charged individuals $1,500 and couples $2,000. They conned clients into believing that membership could be used to avoid removal from the United States.[351]

- In March 2011, DOJ announced that the U.S. District Court for the Western District of Missouri had permanently barred Gerald A Poynter "from preparing tax returns for others and from promoting" a redemption scam.[352] Poynter informed his customers that he could obtain tax refunds for them, charged them for his services, and then produced fraudulent IRS forms claiming $64 million in refunds for 165 customers.[353]

### The Internet and Domestic Terrorists

In the counterterrorism world, there has been much concern regarding violent jihadist use of the Internet and social media.[354] However, domestic terrorists also are computer

---

[346] FBI Counterterrorism Analysis Section, "Sovereign Citizens."

[347] Elvick promoted his ideas in the 1980s, and was jailed for much of the 1990s as well as in the next decade because of passing bad checks, forgery, extortion, and corruption. See Ibid.; Southern Poverty Law Center, "His Straw Man Free"; For a description of redemption, see Institute for Intergovernmental Research, *Investigating Terrorism*, pp. 70–71.

[348] Department of Justice, "Government Files Seven Lawsuits Nationwide to Block Alleged Scheme Involving Fraudulent Tax-Refund Claims," press release, October 28, 2009.

[349] Ibid.

[350] Carri Greer Thevenot, "Idaho Man Pleads Guilty to Money Laundering," *Las Vegas Review-Journal*, March 25, 2011.

[351] Immigration and Customs Enforcement, "South Florida Man Sentenced to 14 Years in Prison for Immigration Fraud," press release, December 8, 2009.

[352] Department of Justice, "Federal Court Shuts Down Missouri Tax Preparer Who Promoted Tax Scam," press release, March 28, 2011. For the injunction, see http://www.justice.gov/tax/Poynter_Injunction.pdf.

[353] Ibid.

[354] For example, see J.M. Berger, "The Social Apocalypse: A Forecast," *Intelwire*, August 31, 2016; Edna Erez, Gabriel Weimann, and A. Aaron Weisburd, "Jihad, Crime, and the Internet: Content Analysis of Jihadist Forum Discussions," October 31, 2011, Report submitted to the National Institute of Justice in fulfillment of requirements for Award Number 2006-IJ-CX-0038; Akil N. Awan, "The Virtual Jihad: An Increasingly

savvy and active online. A web presence may help extremist groups—some relatively small, with rosters in the 100s or fewer—educate their existing membership and forge a group identity. Also, in many instances they can use websites to focus on outsiders to propagandize, socialize, and recruit new adherents.[355] A few domestic terrorists also have exploited the web to harm their targets.

White supremacists have long been using computer technology to communicate and interact. As one study has suggested, white supremacists "were among the very early users of the electronic communication network that eventually evolved into the Internet."[356] Among a variety of findings, the study indicated that white supremacist extremist websites were possibly an effective recruiting tool that the groups exploited. Membership forms are available on some sites. Others exhibit multimedia material, and some actually retail items such as music and video games.[357] The Internet allows individuals and groups to connect with one another and to disseminate ideology.[358] It also enables groups to manage how others perceive them. Many white supremacist sites claim that their sponsoring groups are nonviolent and not even racist.[359]

Some white supremacists may be unwilling to affirm their views in public spaces such as work, school, or in street demonstrations. To them, the virtual realm is an important antidote. As one study has suggested, "free spaces" in both the real and virtual worlds—where conflict with non-believers will be minimized—are important for adherents. In them they can "meet, articulate, and support their views."[360] Supremacists can turn to virtual free spaces to receive indoctrination into movement culture, key narratives outlining movement grievances, adopt ideologies, and "talk of violence against 'racial enemies.' "[361] A 2016 study found that Americans espousing white supremacist ideals on the social-media platform Twitter outnumber the supporters of the foreign terrorist organization known as the Islamic State by many measures:

> On Twitter, ISIS's preferred social platform, American white nationalist movements have seen their followers grow by more than 600% since 2012. Today, they

---

Legitimate Form of Warfare," *CTC Sentinel*, vol. 3, no. 5 (May 2010), p. 11; Gilbert Ramsay, "Relocating the Virtual War," *Defence Against Terrorism Review*, vol. 2, no. 1 (Spring 2009), p. 34; Tim Stevens, "Regulating the 'Dark Web:' How a Two-Fold Approach Can Tackle Peer-to-Peer Radicalisation," *The RUSI Journal*, vol. 154, no. 2 (April 2009), p. 29; Gabriel Weimann, *Terror on the Internet: The New Arena, the New Challenge* (Washington, DC: United States Institute of Peace Press, 2006); Maura Conway, "Terrorism and Mass Communication: Nitro to the Net," *The World Today*, vol. 60, no. 8/9 (Aug/Sep 2004), pp. 19–22, http://doras.dcu.ie/513/1/nitro_to_net_2004.pdf.

355 Jeffrey Kaplan, Leonard Weinberg, and Ted Oleson, "Dreams and Realities in Cyberspace: White Aryan Resistance and the World Church of the Creator," *Patterns of Prejudice*, vol. 37, no. 2 (2003), pp. 149–150.

356 Phyllis B. Gerstenfeld, Diana R. Grant, Chau-Pu Chiang, "Hate Online: A Content Analysis of Extremist Internet Sites," *Analysis of Social Issues and Public Policy*, vol. 3, no. 1, (2003), p. 29. Hereinafter: Gerstenfeld et al., "Hate Online."

357 Ibid.

358 See Josh Adams and Vincent J. Roscigno, "White Supremacists, Oppositional Culture, and the World Wide Web," *Social Forces*, vol. 84, no. 2 (December 2005), pp. 759–778.

359 Gerstenfeld et al., "Hate Online," pp. 33–41.

360 Pete Simi, Robert Futrell, "Cyberculture and the Endurance of White Power Activism," *Journal of Political and Military Sociology*, vol. 34, no. 1 (Summer 2006), p. 117. Hereinafter: Simi and Futrell, "Endurance."

361 Ibid., 122-126, 131. Some free spaces exist in the real world. Examples include the privacy of the home, supremacist events such as conferences, isolated compounds or communities, and ideologically-focused musical concerts.

outperform ISIS in nearly every social metric, from follower counts to tweets per day.[362]

Much of this online ideological activity involves constitutionally protected speech. A number of examples stand out.

- The ALF and the ELF have their long-established guidelines posted on the web for independent groups or individuals to follow.[363] Movement websites virtually connect like-minded individuals. As mentioned elsewhere in this report, key ideological texts are also made available online.[364] The websites of animal rights extremists and ecoterrorists also post press releases publicizing crimes perpetrated on behalf of the movements.[365]
- Reverend Donald Spitz administers the Army of God's website.[366] Among other things, the site includes lists of people who support "violent opposition to abortion" as well as listing people incarcerated because of anti-abortion crimes they committed.[367]
- The National Socialist Movement sponsors its own social networking site, the "New Saxon Social Network."[368]

Some domestic terrorists also engage in cyberattacks. According to DOJ, an animal rights extremist cell (SHAC USA, Inc.) active between 2001 and 2004 listed online the personal information—names, addresses, phone numbers—of workers at a firm it was targeting. (The business uses animals in its research.) The extremist cell likely devised the list to help focus the activities of the group's online followers. In some cases, the published information included the names of spouses and children of employees, license plate numbers, churches attended by the employees, as well as the schools their children attended. The websites used by the extremist cell also posted suggestions for action by supporters—including what it described as the "top 20 terror tactics."[369] Supporters across the United States vandalized victims' homes and automobiles and engaged in

[362] J.M. Berger, "Nazis vs. ISIS on Twitter: A Comparative Study of White Nationalist and ISIS Online Social Media Networks," *George Washington University Program on Extremism*, September 2016.

[363] See http://www.animalliberationfront.com/ALFront/alf_credo.htm; ELF, "What Is the Earth?"

[364] Anti-Defamation League, *Ecoterrorism: Extremism in the Animal Rights and Environmentalist Movements*. Hereinafter: Anti-Defamation League, *Ecoterrorism*.

[365] See http://www.animalliberationfront.com/; http://www.animalliberationpressoffice.org/; and http://www.earthliberationfront.org/.

[366] Jefferis, *Armed for Life*, p. 53.

[367] Ibid., p. 77.

[368] See http://newsaxon.org/.

[369] Department of Justice, *White Paper*, p. 60; *United States v. Stop Huntingdon Animal Cruelty USA, Inc., et al*, Superseding Indictment, CR 04-373, District Court, District of New Jersey, n.d. Hereinafter: Department of Justice, *United States v. Stop Huntingdon*. The "top 20 terror tactics" included activity such as: "demonstrations at one's [a target's] home using a loudspeaker; abusive graffiti, posters and stickers on one's car and house; invading offices and, damaging property and stealing documents; chaining gates shut, and blocking gates; physical assault including spraying cleaning fluid into one's eyes; smashing the windows of one's house while the individual's family was at home; flooding one's home while the individual was away; vandalizing one's car; firebombing one's car; bomb hoaxes; threatening telephone calls and letters including threats to kill or injure one's partner or children; e-mail bombs in an attempt to crash computers; sending continuous black faxes causing fax machines to burn out; telephone blockades by repeated dialing to prevent the use of the telephone; and arranging for an undertaker to call to collect one's body."

cyberattacks against the research firms and other companies tied to it, among other activities.[370]

### A Decentralized Threat

Domestic terrorism can be described as a decentralized threat. As this report has already suggested, domestic terrorism suspects generally operate on their own or in small, independent cells. In other words, they do not necessarily belong to organizations with cohesive, well-articulated leadership structures or cadres.

However, independently acting domestic terrorism suspects are not necessarily isolated, adrift, and cut off from any outside contact or influence. Some take ideological cues from broader movements or groups espousing extremist ideas. These groups or movements publicly disavow violent criminal behavior and engage in constitutionally protected activities. This dynamic—the interplay between above-ground groups or movements proffering extremist dogma or ideology (protected speech) that is then consumed and acted upon by independent underground groups or cells who commit crimes—is a critical feature of domestic terrorism.

### Leaderless Resistance

Within the domestic terrorism realm, the notions of decentralized activity received attention in the 1980s and early 1990s when white supremacist Louis Beam circulated his theories of "leaderless resistance."[371] He saw leaderless resistance as a means to transform the white supremacy movement. Beam described it as a means of avoiding law enforcement infiltration of white supremacist groups, and he suggested *two levels* of leaderless movement activity. First, on an operational level, militant, underground, ideologically motivated cells or individuals (lone wolves) engage in movement-related illegal activity without any centralized direction or control from an organization that maintains traditional leadership positions and membership rosters. Second, on another level, the above-ground public face (the "political wing") of the movement propagandizes and disseminates ideology—engaging in protected speech. In this system, underground cells or lone wolves would be responsible for their own actions, and the public face of the movement would not be held accountable.[372]

---

[370] According to the superseding indictment in the case, the cell also placed reports of intimidation and vandalism on its websites to encourage its followers. See Department of Justice, *United States v. Stop Huntingdon.*

[371] He was a Ku Klux Klan (KKK) and Aryan Nations activist.

[372] Paul Joosse, "Leaderless Resistance and Ideological Inclusion: The Case of the Earth Liberation Front," *Terrorism and Political Violence*, vol. 19, no. 3 (September 2007), pp. 351–368. Hereinafter: Joosse, "Leaderless Resistance." Fred Burton, "The Challenge of the Lone Wolf," *STRATFOR*, May 30, 2007; Hereinafter: Burton, "The Challenge." Southern Poverty Law Center, "Louis Beam," http://www.splcenter.org/get-informed/intelligence-files/profiles/louis-beam; Anti-Defamation League, "Louis Beam," http://www.adl.org/learn/ext_us/beam.asp?xpicked=2&item=beam. Beam secretly discussed leaderless resistance among white supremacists and anti-government extremists as early as 1983. See Wright, *Patriots*, p. 87. Forms of leaderless resistance likely have a long history. For example, late-nineteenth-century anarchists can be seen as having engaged in a type of leaderless resistance in their rejection of organized authority. See Jean-Marc Flükiger, "The Radical Animal Liberation Movement: Some Reflections on Its Future," *Journal for the Study of Radicalism*, vol. 2, no. 2 (2009), pp. 112. Hereinafter: Flükiger, "The Radical." See also Ramón Spaaij, "The Enigma of Lone Wolf Terrorism: An Assessment," *Studies in Conflict and Terrorism*, vol. 33, no. 9 (2010), p. 859. Hereinafter: Spaaij, "The Enigma."

Online comments from the leadership of the neo-Nazi National Socialist Movement (NSM) offer a specific example of an above-ground movement avoiding violence and the terrorist label. The NSM's leader has posted the following statement on the group's website:

> I want it made perfectly clear to all of our members, supporters, prospective members, readers, etc. that the National Socialist Movement condemns illegal actions and in such we do not endorse any acts of violence or terrorism. The NSM is a White Civil Rights Movement that adheres to Political activism, and a legal means to restore America to its former glory. Acts of violence or terrorism against America, or its Citizens is unacceptable, and not tolerated within the ranks of the National Socialist Movement.[373]

### *"The Turner Diaries"*

One of the key texts read by neo-Nazis and anti-government extremists is *The Turner Diaries,* a 1978 novel by William Pierce, the deceased founder of the neo-Nazi group National Alliance.[374] This book can be seen as an above-ground product that motivates underground cells or individuals to commit crimes. The book has partly inspired a number of violent acts by white supremacist extremists and anti-government extremists.

*The Turner Diaries* predates the widespread acceptance of the "leaderless resistance" concept. However, its lasting place in the neo-Nazi and anti-government extremist movements highlights how leaderless resistance works. Pierce's book has been described as "the most widely read book among far-right extremists."[375] The novel reflects the author's own racist religious philosophies.[376] Perhaps 500,000 copies of the book have been sold.[377] In it, Pierce emphasized that the current racial order of things had to be cataclysmically destroyed and reborn in accordance with white supremacist ideals.[378] To convey this message, he devised his book as the edited diaries of neo-Nazi character Earl Turner. As such, Turner's story is annotated by a fictionalized editor, one Andrew Macdonald. The novel describes Turner leading a terrorist group whose actions trigger a race war that results in the overthrow of the government—controlled by Jews in Pierce's construction. Turner also initiates a nuclear war that wipes out earth's non-white human inhabitants. The atomic apocalypse allows for the rebirth of a revitalized white race.[379]

---

373 Jeff Schoep, "CDR Jeff Schoep Denounces Violence & Domestic Terrorism."

374 Renee Brodie, "The Aryan New Era: Apocalyptic Realizations in *The Turner Diaries,*" *Journal of American Culture,* vol. 21, no. 3, (fall 1998), pp. 13–22.

375 Anti-Defamation League, *"The Turner Diaries,"* 2005, http://www.adl.org/learn/Ext_US/turner_diaries.asp.

376 See Brad Whitsel, *"The Turner Diaries* and Cosmotheism: William Pierce's Theology," *Nova Religio: The Journal of Alternative and Emergent Religions,* vol. 1, no. 2 (April 1998), pp. 183–197. Hereinafter: Whitsel, *"The Turner Diaries."*

377 Freilich, Chermak, and Caspi, "Critical Events," p. 505. Another estimate dating back to 2001 places the number sold at 300,000. See Rob McAlear, "Hate, Narrative, and Propaganda in *The Turner Diaries," The Journal of American Culture,* vol. 32, no. 3 (September 2009), p. 192. Hereinafter: McAlear, "Hate, Narrative."

378 George Michael, "The Revolutionary Model of Dr. William L. Pierce," *Terrorism and Political Violence,* vol. 15, no. 3 (Autumn 2003), p. 75.

379 Whitsel, *"The Turner Diaries,"* p. 185; Terence Ball and Richard Dagger, *"The Turner Diaries*: Neo-Nazi Scripture," *PS: Political Science and Politics,* vol. 30, no. 4, (December 1997), pp. 717–718. McAlear, "Hate, Narrative," p. 196.

The book has informed the activities of domestic terrorists. In September 1983, white supremacist Robert Mathews formed a small underground group known as The Order. Its inspiration came from passages in *The Turner Diaries*. The group planned for and engaged in what it viewed as a revolution.[380] Over the next 15 months, The Order went on a violent crime spree. Among other crimes, it robbed banks, armored cars, electronic stores, a truck stop, and a video store, and allegedly gave some of the spoils to Richard Butler, who was at the time the leader of the WSE group Aryan Nations. The Order also bombed a synagogue and murdered a Jewish talk show host, Alan Berg, before it was dismantled by federal law enforcement.[381]

Anti-government extremist Timothy McVeigh, an avid reader of the book, had passages from the *Turner Diaries* with him when he was arrested. The 1995 bombing of the Alfred P. Murrah federal building in Oklahoma City mimicked one described in the novel and involved a small cell of underground conspirators.[382] Sales of the book allegedly rose after the bombing.[383]

### *The ALF, the ELF*

The concept of leaderless resistance has been mirrored by other extremist movements in the United States. Both the ALF and the ELF have rejected recognizable leadership structures or hierarchies and follow a leaderless resistance model instead, making their activities more difficult for law enforcement to investigate.[384] According to the model, above-ground elements in the movements provide guidelines and an ideological platform that underground individuals (lone wolves) or independent cells can draw upon to motivate their own criminal actions. Exercising First-Amendment rights, the above-ground components of the ALF and the ELF lawfully communicate shared identities largely via websites. As one scholar has suggested for the ELF, this possibly creates a broad consensus focused on a very specific cause and avoids internecine conflicts over ideological fine points.[385] Much like the NSM, the above-ground elements of the ALF take pains to distinguish themselves from criminal activity. For example, NAALPO states:

> Disclaimer: The Animal Liberation Press Officers do not engage in illegal activities, nor do they know any individuals who do. Rather, the Press Office receives and posts communiqués from anonymous parties and provides comment to the media.[386]

[380] Wright, *Patriots*, pp. 87–88; Anti-Defamation League, "Richard Scutari," http://www.adl.org/learn/ext_us/scutari.asp?xpicked=2&item=scutari. Hereinafter: Anti-Defamation League, "Scutari." Zeskind, *Blood and Politics*, pp. 96–100.

[381] Balch, "The Rise and Fall," 87, 109; Wright, *Patriots*, pp. 86–89.

[382] McAlear, "Hate, Narrative," p. 192; Wright, *Patriots*, pp. 6, 10.

[383] Freilich, Chermak, and Caspi, "Critical Events," p. 505.

[384] Ackerman, "Beyond Arson," p. 151.

[385] Joosse, "Leaderless Resistance," pp. 352, 354.

[386] NAALPO, "History."

Additionally, the above-ground literature of both the ALF and the ELF suggests that independent cells avoid communication with one another.[387] This leaderless format is followed to avoid law enforcement infiltration and is based on models used by other domestic terrorists. As one scholar has suggested, this parallels franchising in the business world.[388]

### Lone Wolves

Some domestic terrorists are "lone wolves." This can be seen as a form of leaderless resistance. One scholar has offered a succinct conceptualization:

> Lone wolf terrorism involves terrorist attacks carried out by persons who (a) operate individually, (b) do not belong to an organized terrorist group or network, and (c) whose modi operandi are conceived and directed by the individual without any direct outside command hierarchy.[389]

Lone wolves have committed crimes in the names of a number of domestic terrorism movements. For example, according to the FBI, when it comes to violence attributed to white supremacist extremism, lone wolves play a prominent role. Lone wolves filter in and out of WSE groups. They can either get dismissed from these groups because of their "violent tendencies" or voluntarily leave because they find the organizations too passive.[390] There is little research on the lone wolf phenomenon and no universally accepted definition of the term.[391]

The above definition stresses how lone wolves operate. Just as critical is what they believe. Lone wolves can hew to broader ideological causes and use them to justify their actions.[392] This suggests that lone wolves potentially adopt the ideas of broader terrorist movements while not claiming formal membership in them. Divining exactly what "formal membership" constitutes leads to debate regarding whether or not some individuals acted as lone wolves or part of larger movements. For example:

- On January 29, 2010, Scott Roeder (also discussed above) was convicted of first-degree murder and two counts of aggravated assault for killing abortion provider George Tiller.[393] Roeder allegedly had "connections with militant abortion foes but few formal ties with known groups."[394] Some supporters of abortion rights consider his contacts among anti-abortion adherents as evidence of possible

[387] Thurston, *The ALF Primer,* p. 1. See also *United States v. Joseph Dibee et al,* Indictment, CR 06-60011-AA, District Court, District of Oregon, January 19, 2006; Leader and Probst, "The Earth Liberation Front," pp. 37–58.

[388] Flükiger, "The Radical," pp. 111–119.

[389] Ibid., p. 856.

[390] Federal Bureau of Investigation, *Rage and Racism,* p. 8.

[391] Spaaij, "The Enigma," pp. 855–856.

[392] Ibid.

[393] Sylvester, "Scott Roeder."

[394] Judy L. Thomas, "Was Suspect in Tiller Case a Lone Wolf?" *The Kansas City Star,* June 14, 2009. Hereinafter: Thomas, "Was Suspect?"

conspiracy.[395] Meanwhile, some anti-abortion activists have stressed that Roeder was a lone wolf.[396] He remains the only person convicted in Tiller's murder.

- Described as a neo-Nazi and white supremacist, James von Brunn reportedly shot and killed a security guard at the U.S. Holocaust Memorial Museum in Washington, DC, in June 2009. In January 2010, the 89-year-old von Brunn died in federal prison before he could be tried.[397]

Because lone wolves are not plugged into terrorist organizations, distinguishing them from individuals who commit hate crimes can also be difficult.[398] In these cases, as mentioned above, the FBI likely attempts to determine whether the motives involved were personal (hate crime) and not focused on broader ideologies (domestic terrorism).

### *The Law Enforcement Challenges Posed by Lone Wolves*

Lone wolves present particular challenges to law enforcement. Because lone wolves, by definition, operate alone, it can be difficult for law enforcement to assess exactly which radicalized individuals intend to turn their beliefs into action and pursue terrorist activity. One former FBI counterterrorism official has said:

> The lone wolf is arguably one of the biggest challenges to American law enforcement. How do you get into the mind of a terrorist? The FBI does not have the capability to know when a person gets up in middle America and decides: "I'm taking my protest poster to Washington or I'm taking my gun."[399]

Aside from intent, it is also hard to assess the operational capability of potential lone wolf terrorists—knowledge of explosives, familiarity with firearms, or experience in surveillance, for example.[400] Lone wolves do not participate in terrorist networks or training camps that can be infiltrated or whose communications can be traced. They do not rehearse their schemes or practice their criminal skills with conspirators who can potentially act as cooperating witnesses. To attempt to overcome these issues, the FBI asserted in 2009 that it was "beginning an extensive study on identified lone offenders to come up with indicators and behavior predictors that investigators can use to assess suspects."[401]

Not all of the news for law enforcement regarding lone wolves is necessarily dire. They have weaknesses. Their lack of tradecraft may make it harder for lone wolves to engage in large-scale attacks. Likewise, lone wolves do not necessarily experience the

---

395 Amanda Robb, "Not a Lone Wolf," *Ms. Magazine*, vol. 20, no. 2 (Spring 2010), pp. 26–31.

396 Thomas, "Was Suspect?"

397 Anti-Defamation League, "James von Brunn: An ADL Backgrounder," http://www.adl.org/main_Extremism/von_brunn_background.htm.

398 Eric Boehlert, "Terrorism or Hate Crime?" *Salon.com*, April 17, 2003, http://dir.salon.com/story/news/feature/2003/04/17/terrorist_act/index.html.

399 Gary Fields and Evan Perez, "FBI Seeks to Target Lone Extremists," *Wall Street Journal*, June 15, 2009, http://online.wsj.com/article/SB124501849215613523.html.

400 Scott Stewart and Fred Burton, *Lone Wolf Lessons*, STRATFOR, June 3, 2009. Hereinafter: Stewart and Burton, *Lone Wolf*. See also Steven M. Chermak, Joshua D. Freilich & Joseph Simone Jr., "Surveying American State Police Agencies About Lone Wolves, Far-Right Criminality, and Far-Right and Islamic Jihadist Criminal Collaboration," *Studies in Conflict and Terrorism*, vol. 33 no. 11 (2010).

401 Federal Bureau of Investigation, "Domestic Terrorism."

reinforcement of a closely knit terrorist social network. They cannot rely on others to assist them in any type of complicated plot.[402]

Regardless, apparent lone wolf attacks can be lethal. For example, in March 2017, James Harris Jackson, allegedly acting alone, used a two-foot-long sword to stab to death Timothy Caughman, an African American individual who Jackson is said to have encountered while trolling New York City for victims. According to New York District Attorney Cyrus Vance Jr., Jackson "prowled the streets of New York for three days in search of a black person to assassinate in order to launch a campaign of terrorism...."[403] Jackson, who reportedly espoused white supremacist beliefs, faces state-level murder and terrorism charges.[404] Aside from the 2016 shooting by Gavin Long, the 2010 actions of Scott Roeder, and the 2009 shooting involving James von Brunn (described above), other evidence suggests the lethality of lone wolf violence:

- According to one scholarly examination, between 1990 and April 2009, "far-rightists" were responsible for the deaths of 42 law enforcement officers—most from state and local agencies in the United States. Most of the incidents involved firearms, *and most of the assailants acted alone.*[405]
- Richard Poplawski shot and killed three Pittsburgh police officers in April 2009. He has been described as a "white supremacist" lone wolf.[406] He had posted anti-government messages on racist websites.[407]
- On January 21, 2009, Keith Luke allegedly shot and killed two Cape Verdean immigrants and raped and shot a third. Police arrested him before he could attack a synagogue, as he planned.[408] Luke purportedly informed police that he had decided to go on his spree after reading about "the demise of the white race" on a neo-Nazi website.[409] He reputedly said that he was "fighting for a dying race" and that he had been planning the attack for six months.[410]

[402] Stewart and Burton, *Lone Wolf.*

[403] Daniella Silva, "White Supremacist James Harris Jackson Charged with Terrorism for Killing Black Man in NYC," *NBC News,* March 27, 2017.

[404] Ibid. See also Jean Marbella, "A Baltimore Man's Inexplicable Path from Quaker School to Army to Rikers Island Cell," *Baltimore Sun,* April 14, 2017; Ashley Southall, "White Suspect in Black Man's Killing Is Indicted on Terror Charges," *New York Times,* march 27, 2017; Colleen Long and Jennifer Peltz, "Police: White Sword Killer Went to NY to Attack Black People," *Associated Press,* March 22, 2017.

[405] START, "Background Information: Far-Right Attacks on U.S. Law Enforcement," press release, April 2009. The scholars who developed the information in the press release defined "far-right ideology" as "principles such as fierce nationalism, anti-globalization, suspicions of centralized Federal authority, support for conspiracy theories, and reverence for individual liberties (including gun ownership."

[406] McNulty et al., "Jury Decides." See also Anti-Defamation League, "Richard Poplawski."

[407] Hamill, "Man Accused."

[408] John Ellement, "DA Says Racism Drove Brockton Killings, Rape," *Boston Globe,* January 23, 2009.

[409] Phillip Martin, "Man Will Face Charges After Police Standoff," *WGBH,* April 4, 2011, http://wwe.wgbh.org/articles/-2503.

[410] Maureen Boyle, "Prosecutor: Suspect in double slaying in Brockton hatched an 'Evil Plan of Mass Murder and Rape,'" *Brockton Enterprise,* January 22, 2009, updated June 9, 2010. The shootings perpetrated by Roeder and von Brunn had been described by the federal government as terrorist acts. It is unclear whether the Poplawski and Luke cases are considered as such. Both von Brunn and Roeder were included in the National Counterterrorism Center's open-source Worldwide Incidents Tracking System (WITS) database (now unavailable) that compiled worldwide terrorist incidents between 2004 and early 2012. Poplawski and Luke were not.

Lone wolves do not necessarily have to focus on gun-related crimes. Kevin Harpham's case illustrates as much. On March 9, 2011, law enforcement officers arrested Kevin Harpham (discussed elsewhere) and charged him in connection to a bomb concealed in a backpack and placed along the route of a Martin Luther King Jr. Day March in Spokane, WA. In September 2011, Harpham pled guilty to committing a federal hate crime and attempting to use a weapon of mass destruction.[411] Media reports and watchdog groups have indicated that Harpham had ties to white supremacists. Allegedly, he was a member of the neo-Nazi National Alliance in 2004. The group denied that he was still a member. Harpham had also been in contact with Paul Mullet, leader of a white supremacist group active in Athol, ID. Mullet said that he and Harpham spoke many times but that the latter never joined Mullet's group.[412] Harpham reportedly made postings on white supremacist websites and read *The Turner Diaries*.[413]

Also, lone wolf activity is not solely the domain of purported white supremacists. Another case illustrates the kind of attack a domestic lone wolf animal rights extremist can commit:

- In November 2010, Walter Bond pled guilty to two felonies stemming from an April 2010 arson that destroyed a store known as the Sheepskin Factory in Glendale, CO.[414] Speaking from jail, Bond condemned the business, which sold sheepskin products, as engaging in "blood trade" and drawing profits "from the death and exploitation of suffering animals."[415] Bond worked alone. A web posting claimed the arson "in defense and retaliation for all the innocent animals that have died cruelly at the hands of human oppressors."[416] Apparently, Bond strongly identified with the notion of being a lone wolf. The ATF, working with a confidential informant, recorded Bond discussing the fire and the fact that he actually used the nickname "Lone Wolf."[417] In a jailhouse letter, Bond stated, "I used the name 'ALF Lone Wolf' in the media to convey to my ALF brothers and sisters worldwide (whoever they are) the power of acting alone."[418]

---

[411] Department of Justice, "Attempted Bomber Pleads Guilty to Federal Hate Crime and Weapons Charge," press release, September 7, 2011; Department of Justice, "Attempted Bomber Arrested," press release, March 9, 2011.

[412] See Southern Poverty Law Center, "Spokane Bombing Arrest Details Emerge," March 9, 2011. Hereinafter: Southern Poverty Law Center, "Spokane Bombing." Thomas Clouse and Meghann M. Cuniff, "White Supremacist Arrested in MLK Bomb Plot," *Spokesman-Review*, March 10, 2011. Hereinafter: Clouse and Cuniff, "White Supremacist." Joel Millman and Evan Perez, "Suspect Is Arrested in Spokane Bomb Case," *Wall Street Journal*, March 10, 2011. Hereinafter: Millman and Perez, "Suspect Is Arrested."

[413] Federal Bureau of Investigation, "MLK Parade Bomber," press release, January 13, 2012; Jessica Robinson, "Court Documents Reveal Evolution Of MLK Day Bomber's Racist Beliefs," *Northwest News Network*, December 1, 2011, http://kuow.org/northwestnews.php?storyID=143023416; Department of Justice, "Colville, Wash., Man Indicted for Federal Hate Crime in Attempted Bombing of the MLK Unity March," press release, April 21, 2011; "FBI: Bomb Found on MLK March Route," *MSNBC*, January 18, 2011.

[414] Yesenia Robles, "Vegan Activist Pleads Guilty to Torching Sheepskin Factory," *Denver Post*, November 19, 2010. Hereinafter: Robles, "Vegan Activist."

[415] "Suspect in Arson at Sheepskin Factory in Glendale Decries Animal 'Blood Trade,'" *Denver Post*, August 6, 2010.

[416] Robles, "Vegan Activist."

[417] *United States v. Walter Bond*, Criminal Complaint, MJ-01120-MJW, District Court, District of Colorado, July 23, 2010. Hereinafter: *U.S. v. Walter Bond*.

[418] Walter Bond, "I Am the ALF 'Lone Wolf,'" December 4, 2010, (North American Animal Liberation Press Office). He was also convicted for two other arsons. See "Walter Bond Sentenced to 7 years for

## Scoping the Threat Remains Difficult for Policymakers

As this report suggests, at least three factors may make it hard for policymakers to form a baseline evaluation of the domestic terrorism threat from publicly available information. First, federal agencies employ varying terminology to describe the threat. Second, the federal government lacks a public and official method for either designating specific domestic groups as terrorists or formally and openly describing particular extremist movements as threats. Finally, there is no clear sense of how many domestic terrorism plots and attacks the government has investigated in recent years.

### Terminology

The federal government has used broad conceptualizations to describe domestic terrorism. DOJ discusses the issue in terms of a handful of general "threats" such as animal rights extremists, ecoterrorists, anarchists, and anti-government extremists—not specific groups. Additionally, terms such as "terrorism" and "extremism" appear to be used interchangeably. Presumably, using the term "extremist" allows lawyers, policymakers, and investigators the flexibility to discuss terrorist-like activity without actually labeling it as "terrorism" and then having to prosecute it as such. However, this may lead to inconsistencies in the development and application of the law in the domestic terrorism arena. For example, policymakers may ponder why a specific terrorism statute covers ideologically motivated attacks against businesses that involve animals,[419] while there are no other domestic terrorism statutes as narrow in their purview covering a particular type of target and crime.

### Designating Domestic Terrorist Groups

The federal government lacks a process for publicly designating domestic terrorist organizations. In other words, there is no official open-source roster of domestic groups that the FBI or other federal agencies target as terrorist organizations. *The lack of such a designation may spring partly from First Amendment concerns.* Such a list might discourage speech and expression related to the ideologies underpinning the activities of named groups. Regardless, this stands in stark contrast to the world of international counterterrorism, where the United States maintains a well-established—legally and procedurally proscribed—regimen regarding the identification of foreign terrorist organizations (FTOs).[420]

Official FTO designation benefits counterterrorism efforts in a number of ways. Most importantly, it facilitates the prosecution of those who provide material support[421] to

two ALF Arsons," http://www.animalliberationfrontline.com/walter-bond-sentenced-to-7-years-for-animal-liberartion-front-arsons/; Scott Stewart, Escalating Violence from the Animal Liberation Front," STRATFOR, July 29, 2010. See also *U.S. v. Walter Bond.*

419 The Animal Enterprise Terrorism Act (P.L. 109-374).

420 Department of State, "Foreign Terrorist Organizations."

421 As described in U.S. Code, Title 18, Part I, Chapter 113B, 2339A and 2339B. For more information, see CRS Report R41333, *Terrorist Material Support: An Overview of 18 U.S.C. §2339A and §2339B*, by Charles Doyle. DOJ has used material support charges as a key component in its prosecutions against foreign terrorist organizations. See CRS Report R41416, *American Jihadist Terrorism: Combating a Complex Threat*, by Jerome P. Bjelopera, for a discussion of a number of these cases targeting homegrown jihadists.

listed foreign terrorist groups. Arguably, because there is no domestic terrorism equivalent of FTO designation, it is more difficult to press material support charges against domestic terrorists. In 2010, one scholar was unable to identify any material support cases involving "a domestic terrorist group or its supporters."[422] According to the Department of State, FTO designation has other effects. It

> 1. Supports [U.S.] efforts to curb terrorism financing and to encourage other nations to do the same. 2. Stigmatizes and isolates designated terrorist organizations internationally. 3. Deters donations or contributions to and economic transactions with named organizations. 4. Heightens public awareness and knowledge of terrorist organizations. 5. Signals to other governments our concern about named organizations.[423]

This description suggests that the absence of a designation regimen for domestic terrorist groups makes it harder for the federal government to discredit such groups and simultaneously strengthen public understanding of the domestic terrorist threat. Likewise, the lack of a list might make it more difficult for the federal government to communicate exactly what the threat is to its own agencies, let alone local or state entities.

While there is no official designation process for domestic terrorist *organizations*, as it stands, DOJ and the FBI have publicly named and discussed domestic terrorism *threats*—such as animal rights extremism or anarchist extremism—without illuminating exactly how they arrive at these categories. Federal lawmakers may opt to consider the feasibility of officially formalizing this process and/or opening it up to greater oversight. An attempt to render this process less bureaucratically opaque might simultaneously (1) enhance federal efforts to combat domestic terrorism and (2) help protect civil rights and civil liberties. For example, such a list may potentially offer agencies outside of DOJ—including relevant players at the state and local level—formal opportunities to provide input into ranking domestic terrorism threats while enshrining mechanisms by which individuals who believe in the philosophies undergirding a designated threat could petition to have that threat "de-listed."[424] On the other hand, making this process more open may take away the FBI's flexibility to rapidly adapt its domestic terrorism priorities, especially if threats quickly mutate.

### A Public Accounting of Plots and Incidents

A publicly available official accounting of domestic terrorist plots and incidents may help policymakers understand the scope of the threat in lieu of a regimen designed to name domestic terrorism organizations. However, the federal government does not produce such a document. The National Counterterrorism Center's (NCTC) Worldwide Incidents Tracking System (WITS) had provided an official record of terrorism incidents around the globe, including the United States. This was a publicly accessible database

[422] Heller, "Designating Domestic," p. 70. It may be possible to use 18 U.S.C. 2339A to prosecute an individual engaged in domestic terrorism. This statute "restricts aid to perpetrators of terrorism in general." See Benjamin Yaster, "Resetting *Scales:* An Examination of Due Process Rights in Material Support Prosecutions," *New York University Law Review,* vol. 83, no. 4 (October, 2008), p. 1364; and ibid.

[423] Department of State, "Foreign Terrorist Organizations," https://www.state.gov/j/ct/rls/other/des/123085.htm.

[424] The FTO designation process has such provisions. See ibid.

active from 2004 to early 2012. It included basic information regarding terrorist incidents. Prior to the advent of WITS, the FBI used to publish regular reports on terrorist activity in the United States.[425]

The lack of a publicly available federal accounting of domestic terrorism plots and attacks makes it especially difficult to determine the scope of this diverse threat, which, for example, can be investigated and prosecuted at the state, local, or federal level. Also, the lines between domestic terrorism and other forms of criminality such as tax fraud or hate crimes can be blurry. A fuller accounting of domestic terrorism plots and attacks may reveal the instances in which FBI *investigated* individuals as domestic terrorists but DOJ did not *prosecute* them as such. This could offer policymakers a clearer sense of the domestic terrorism threat.

### Better Sense of Scope May Assist Policymakers

A better sense of domestic terrorism's scope publicly proffered by the federal government may assist policymakers. It may be of policymaking value for executive branch agencies to release annual statistics on domestic terrorism prosecutions, naming individuals and movements involved. Congress may also consider requesting an even more detailed annual public report that counts and describes the domestic terrorist plots dismantled; the number of attacks investigated; and the federal, state, and local agencies involved. The lack of such an accounting makes it difficult for policymakers to exercise oversight by comparing the levels of domestic terrorist activity against items such as homegrown violent jihadist activity and other threats to the homeland. A regular public accounting could also help policymakers assess the effectiveness of the government's response to the domestic terrorist threat. It may also assist policymakers who wish to compare one domestic terrorist threat against another. It can help inform the allocation of resources to specific federal counterterrorism efforts, such as those designed to keep people from radicalizing and becoming violent extremists in the first place. Finally, without a clear, publicly available understanding of the domestic terrorist threat, it may be difficult to measure how much federal funding is allocated to this issue.

## Author Contact Information

Jerome P. Bjelopera
Specialist in Organized Crime and Terrorism
jbjelopera@crs.loc.gov, 7-0622

[425] For example, see http://www.fbi.gov/stats-services/publications/terrorism-2002-2005.

## DOCUMENT NO. 2

# ACROSS THE UNIVERSE? A COMPARATIVE ANALYSIS OF VIOLENT BEHAVIOR AND RADICALIZATION ACROSS THREE OFFENDER TYPES WITH IMPLICATIONS FOR CRIMINAL JUSTICE TRAINING AND EDUCATION

**Final Report**

**John G. Horgan, PhD**
Georgia State University

**Paul Gill, PhD**
University College, London

**Noemie Bouhana, PhD**
University College, London

**James Silver, JD, PhD**
Worcester State University

**Emily Corner, MSc**
University College, London

**Document No.: 249937**

Date Received: June 2016

## ABOUT THE REPORT

### ABOUT THE PROJECT

The content of this report was produced by John Horgan (Principal Investigator (PI)), Paul Gill (Co-PI), James Silver (Project Manager), Noemie Bouhana (Co-Investigator), and Emily Corner (Research Assistant). This research is supported by Award No. 2013-ZA-BX-0002, awarded by the National Institute of Justice, Office of Justice Programs, U.S. Department of Justice. The opinions, findings, and conclusions or recommendations expressed in this document are those of the authors and do not necessarily reflect those of the Department of Justice.



## PROJECT TEAM

**Research Team**
John Horgan—Georgia State University
Paul Gill—University College London
James Silver—Worcester State University
Emily Corner—University College London
Noemie Bouhana—University College London

**Data Collection Intern Team**
*University of Massachusetts Lowell*
Andrew Valcourt, Autumn Calbria, Cassaundra Pellerin, Christian Nambu, Christopher Park, Cristiana Federico, Dijana Djuric, Gregory Johnson, Hank Harrington, Jackson Kellog, James Russell, Jennifer Rogers, Jessica Botero-Rua, Katie Kacmarek, Kelsie Ferris, Kevin Kearney, LaDonya Buchanan, Lindsey Viera, Matthew Febles, Melissa Mejia, Oti Achamfour, Remilekun Ogunfowara, Sean Rogers, Stephen Lidell, Tom Arsenault, Wesley Boudreau, Zachary Miliano

*University College London*
Amy Lafferty, Jordana Clark, Linh Le, Matteo Pezella, Sarika Dewan, Sophie Preisendoerfer

## EXECUTIVE SUMMARY

- Lone actor terrorists (sometimes referred to as 'lone wolves') and mass murderers are more often than not assumed to be distinct, with little validity for comparison. Yet, both engage (or attempt to engage) in largely public and highly publicized acts of violence and often use similar weapons.
- Using a series of bivariate and multivariate statistical analyses, we compared demographic, psychological and offense-related behavioral variables across and between 71 lone actor terrorists and 115 solo mass murderers.
- Results indicate there is little to distinguish these offender types in terms of their socio-demographic profiles. However, their behaviors significantly differ with regards to (a) the degree to which they interact with co-conspirators (b) their antecedent event behaviors and (c) the degree to which they leak information prior to the attack.
- The fundamental distinction between the two groups—motivation—dictates different actuation points for violence. By definition, mass murderers lack an ideology

and, thus, cannot be said to engage in the decision and search activity involving calculations based on current political and security climates that characterizes the incipiency of lone actor and solo actor terrorist attacks. In fact, the majority of mass murderers (57%, N = 65) are concerned with personal feelings of having been wronged by a specific person and ultimately murder (or attempt to murder) the person whom they hold responsible for that wrong. Other mass murderers (16%, N = 18) have a grievance against a category of persons and attack representatives of that group (the remainder were either spontaneous attacks and/or any grievance is unknown). Nor do mass murderers typically concern themselves with post-event activity and strategic analysis as do lone actor and solo actor terrorists. Unlike lone and solo actor terrorists, some mass murders appear to be spontaneous incidents, arising from the physical or emotional conflicts immediately prior to the attack and in which the individual does not exhibit any meaningful planning behaviors related to the attack. While the percentage of mass murders that occur in these circumstances (N = 17, 15%) is relatively small, the apparent lack of predetermined intent and strategy sets at least these offenders apart from the terrorists in our dataset.

- Although still exploratory in nature, our examination of the 98 mass murderers in our dataset who do not engage in spontaneous violence reveals that they do *not* reliably follow the same "natural history from inception to completion" of the attack as lone actor and solo actor terrorists.
- As compared to the 1990–2005 period, the 2006–2013 period contains fewer offenders who (a) had previous military experience (b) made verbal statements to family/friends/wider audiences about their intent and beliefs (c) socialized face to face with members of a wider network (d) experienced being degraded or the target of an act of prejudice or unfairness (e) expressed a desire to hurt others (f) experienced a recent stressor. It is worth re-iterating that whilst prior military experience is often noted in media reports regarding the increase in mass murder events, the statistics suggest this factor only appears a third as much in the current era than it did in the 1990–2005 era which suggests that some so-called "risk factors" may have cohort-effects rather than having stable influences over time.
- One of the major implications of comparative analyses such as this could be to provide guidance or a framework to those tasked with responding to such phenomena. Given our counter-intuitive findings on the leakage of intent, this may be particularly relevant in terms of early disruption of plots. An understanding of this complexity and the multiplicity of potential factors could help inform how threat assessments of particular lone actors should be carried out. When we talk about 'threat', and the related concept of risk, we need to consider multiple, overlapping questions including issues related to identification of threats (e.g., threat of what precisely?), exposure (e.g., under what conditions are particular offences more likely?) and management (i.e., which interventions are likely to be effective in terms of mitigating either risk, broadly speaking, or a specific threat).
- The results suggest that both offenders are very similar in terms of their behaviors—this in turn suggests that similar threat and risk assessment frameworks may be applicable to both types of offenders.

## 1. Introduction

Current efforts to analyze violent extremism are hampered both by recurring conceptual errors and limited empirical support. To date, attempts to understand radicalization and/or terrorist motivation have largely tended toward generalist explanations that often border on explanatory fictions (Horgan, 2014). Furthermore, such explanations, be they theoretical models or descriptive analyses of large-n datasets, tend to treat group members as homogenous. Other analyses do distinguish offender types (e.g. lone wolf vs. al Qaeda-member) but these comparisons tend to be based on single case studies and devoid of crime prevention paradigms (for example, McCauley, Moskalenko and Van Son, 2013).

In the absence of useful comparison or, additionally, control groups (e.g. Merari, 2010), even unashamedly empirical analyses can at best offer largely descriptive (and as a result, partial) account of violent extremism. As LaFree (2013:60) notes, there has been a nascent research trend towards the development of "specialized data sets on specific subsets of terrorism cases" which represents the third major development in the empirical study of terrorism.[1]

This project report seeks to contribute to this trend by engaging in an inter-disciplinary and data-driven approach to understanding lone actor terrorists[2], and solo mass murderer attackers[3]. Instead of using the 'terrorist' or 'offender' as the dependent variable under investigation, we feel it may be more instructive to disaggregate and compare socio-demographic, psychological and behavioral features across and between these offender types.

The discipline of criminology has largely progressed through embracing disaggregated methods and this project report is amongst the first to apply such methods to the study of terrorist and or/extremist outcomes. We are aware of very little prior research that empirically compares terrorists and criminals in a rigorous manner. Cairns (1987) cites the works of Elliot and Lockhart (1980) and Curran (1984). The Elliot and Lockhart study compared forty juvenile terrorist offenders in Northern Ireland with a matched group of juvenile non-terrorist criminals. The terrorist sample was older, more intelligent, more socially outgoing, less likely to be truant from school or referred to a child psychiatrist. The Curran study focused upon a similar sample but required participants to self-report on 155 statements from the Jesness Inventory. The non-terrorist offenders scored higher on measures of aggression, autism, toughness and sensation seeking. Lyons and Harbinson (1986) compared 47 terrorists convicted of murder with 59 non-terrorist murderers. The non-terrorists were significantly more likely to be under the influence of alcohol during the offense and have a family history of personality disorder. Lankford (2012) compared the self-harming motivations and behaviors of 81

[1] The first being the development of international databases of terrorist attacks. The second being the collection of domestic international attacks.

[2] Defined as an individual who engages in ideologically-inspired violence in support of a broader group but absent of ties to or material support from that group.

[3] Defined as an individual who kills four or more people in one event over a relatively short period of time (within 24 hours). We exclude incidents that are state sponsored, gang/organized crime related, or solely domestic in nature.

suicide terrorists and rampage, workplace and school shooters in the U.S. from 1990 to 2010, finding only superficial differences across the groups.

Our report compares offender types whose violence appears similar yet whose motivational structure differs. We propose that there may be significant implications for improving investigative practice (at a variety of levels and stages) by understanding the relevant distinctions between offender types. In particular, we are interested in the differences between lone actor terrorists and solo mass murderer offenders. Both engage (or attempt to engage) in largely public and highly publicized acts of violence and often use similar weapons. So while their outcomes often share multiple features, we ask if the trajectories into violence followed by the respective actors may be equally similar.

Understanding the comparative nature of the development of extreme behavior with violent outcomes is important. From a disruption perspective, different kinds of guidance would effectively be tailored for offender-specific intervention policies. For example, what works for understanding and responding to a mass murderer may not necessarily be relevant for the management of a lone actor terrorist. Their behaviors, routines and proximity to other actors may differ substantially and as a result, give rise to different kinds of responses at whatever stage of the investigative process we are focused, be it prevention or disruption. From a criminal justice perspective, a greater understanding of offender types may help with targeted treatment policies and risk assessments (Tracy and Kempf-Leonard, 1996). From a research perspective, it will ultimately help with our understanding of who takes part in particular violent offenses, the nature of their involvement with others and ultimately how they desist or disengage from violent activities (Horgan, 2009). Investigating whether particular variables more closely correlate with particular offender types also concerns the very nature of how we theorize about terrorist involvement and whether general models of 'radicalization' or 'pathways' into terrorism are appropriate, It also highlights whether research on pathways into violence should be tailored for particular manifestations of terrorist or violent activity. Existing approaches therefore may miss the subtle psychological, behavioral, socio-demographic or organizational factors that may explain how and why some individuals are more likely to take part in particular violent activities than others.

Chapter two presents the results of a series of statistical tests to distinguish the differences between lone actor terrorists and solo mass murderers in terms of socio-demographic characteristics and behavioral traits prior and after their violent attack. The results highlight that whilst some differences are apparent, their behaviors and characteristics are similar.

Chapter three builds upon these findings and asks whether conceptualizing these types of offenders as an either/or classification is valid. It then quantifies and plots each offender according to the dimensional models previously theorized by Borum et al. (2011).

Chapter four focuses on the conceptual and methodological problem of low base rates and long observational periods.

Chapter five outlines 12 case studies, and utilizes crime scripting approaches to offer differing conceptual models of the violent radicalization and attack planning process across lone actor terrorists, solo terrorists and solo mass murderers.

## Data

We used open source data collection methods to develop a unique dataset that categorizes the socio-demographic, developmental antecedent attack, attack preparation and commission properties of 71 lone actor terrorists and 115 mass murderers. This addresses the paucity of data that has long been noted in the study of terrorists and mass murderers (Schmid & Jongman, 1988; Silke, 2001, 2004, 2013). To reduce bias in the sample, we limit our focus to United States-based offenders. Importantly, given the fact that lone actor terrorist attacks are still 'black-swan' type events (i.e., rare), the level of available behavioral data is consequently far higher than that of group-based offenders who operate on behalf of a prolific group. From experience of previous data-collection endeavors (e.g. Asal, et al. 2013; Gill and Horgan, 2013; Gill et al. 2014; Corner and Gill, 2015), it is very difficult to obtain much more than the very basic socio-demographic information of such group offenders from open sources (see Gill, 2015 for a longer discussion). Only two solo terrorists were identified. For the statistical comparative analyses, these two individuals are subsumed into the category of lone actor terrorist. We treat them as different offender types in the crime scripting analyses.

Despite the palpable rise in public anxiety following events such as Columbine, Aurora, and Sandy Hook, the fact remains that mass murder is a rare event in the U.S compared to homicides with fewer fatalities. From 1976 to 2000, the percentage of murders that involved more than one victim ranged from 3% to 4% of homicides per year (Fox & Zawitz, 2003). A review of the FBI's Supplementary Homicide Reports from 2000 to 2012 shows that the number of mass murders (four or more victims) was approximately *one-tenth of one percent* of all murders (excluding the 9/11 deaths). Nevertheless, perhaps because it occurs so infrequently but is so disturbing, there are few crimes that receive more news coverage than mass murder (Duwe, 2000).

Prior to data collection, academic literature on lone actor terrorism was examined and from there an actor dictionary was built. This actor dictionary encompassed a list of offenders fitting the above criteria. Further names were also sourced through tailored search strings developed and applied to the LexisNexis "All English News" option. More individuals were also identified through the Global Terrorism Database developed by the National Consortium for the Study of Terrorism and Responses to Terrorism (START) and lists of those convicted of terrorism-related offences in the United Kingdom and the United States. We also examined the academic literature on mass murderers and built an actor dictionary, producing a list of names that fit our criteria (see below). Next, we identified additional offenders through databases created by *Mother Jones, USA Today* and Mayors Against Illegal Guns. Finally, we conducted searches on Lexis/Nexis using specific terms and searched the Federal Bureau of Investigation's Uniform Crime Reports for each year of the relevant time period to find other offenders who meet our criteria. Our final sample comprises 115 mass murderers.

A pervasive problem with research on mass murder is the shifting definition of what exactly is a mass murder. Some criteria that have been considered include offender motive (Hempel, Meloy & Richards, 1999; Rappaport, 1998), the type of weapon used (Hempel et al., 1999) and the number of wounded (Dietz, 1986). Generally, these criteria are not relied upon in the literature, perhaps because they appear to be arbitrary. There is, however, general agreement that a mass murder involves multiple victims killed at one (or multiple but geographically close) locations over a relatively short period of time (Dietz, 1986: Holmes & Holmes, 1992; Hempel et al., 1999; Fox & Levin, 1998, 2003; Meloy & Felthous, 2004).

Nevertheless, there is less agreement about the minimum number of victims required to define a murder event as "mass". Some researchers use a threshold of two victims (Palermo & Ross, 1999), others use three (Dietz, 1986; Holmes & Holmes, 1992, 1994, 2001; Peete, Padget & York, 1997), and still others use four (Duwe, 2000; Fox & Levin, 1998, 2003). The definition used in this study is *four or more victims (not including the offender)* for the following reasons. First, four or more victims (not including the offender) is the demarcation line accepted by the Federal Bureau of Investigation in its 2005 report: *Serial Murder: Multi-Disciplinary Perspectives for Investigators,* released after a meeting of experts in various fields relevant to the study of multiple homicides. This definition of mass murder as involving four or more fatalities was the result of considered reflection by the leading academics (criminologists, psychologists, forensic psychiatrists), and practitioners (state and federal law enforcement officials and prosecutors) brought together by the FBI for the specific purpose of clarifying issues related to serial and mass murder.

Second, in studies such as the present one where data is collected via open source research methods, the number of victims is an important determinant of media coverage of multiple murder events. Research has suggested that media attention given to any mass murder is affected by certain factors, and high profile mass murders are significantly more likely to involve larger numbers of killed and wounded, stranger victims, public locations, assault weapons and workplace violence (Duwe, 2000, 2005).

Third, practical considerations necessitated a threshold of four victims instead of three. A review of the FBI's Supplementary Homicide Reports from 1976 to 1999 reveals that there are over three times as many cases of three victim homicides as there are four victim homicides (Duwe, 2004). Employing a mass murder definition of three or more victims would have necessitated reducing the time span of the study from approximately 24 years, to at most eight years. While that approach may be useful in future research, this study opts for the use of a greater time span which also matched the time span utilized in the previous lone actor terrorist data collection endeavors.

To facilitate comparison to lone actor terrorists who, by definition, act alone and without direction or support, the sample includes only mass murderers who acted alone. In keeping with that same principle, the study also excludes state-sponsored as well as gang and organized crime related incidents. Also, attacks that are solely domestic are excluded, as these are frequently treated separately in the literature and appear to have a distinct genesis (Aldridge & Brown, 2003; Campbell, Glass, Sharps, Laughon, & Bloom, 2007; Lankford, 2012).

The codebook used in this project was developed based on a review of literature on individuals who commit a wide range of violent and non-violent crimes, are victimized, and/or engage in high-risk behaviours as well as a review of other existing codebooks used in the construction of terrorism-related databases. The variables included in the codebook span socio-demographic information (e.g., age, gender, occupation, family characteristics, relationship status, occupation, employment, etc.), antecedent event behaviours (e.g., aspects of the individual's behaviours towards others and within their day-to-day routines), event specific behaviours (e.g., attack methods, who was targeted) and post-event behaviours and experiences (e.g., claims of responsibility, arrest/conviction details, etc.). Data were collected on demographic and background characteristics and antecedent event behaviours by examining and coding information contained in open source news reports, sworn affidavits and when possible, openly available first-hand accounts. The vast majority of sources came from tailored LexisNexis searches. Information was gleaned from relevant documents across online public record depositories such as documentcloud.org, biographies of a number of lone actors and all available scholarly articles. For a definition of different variables, see Gill et. al (2014).

Three independent coders coded each observation separately. After an observation was coded, the results were reconciled in two stages (coder A with coder B, and then coders A+B with C). In cases when three coders could not agree on particular variables, differences were resolved by a senior member of the research team based on an examination of the original sources that the coders relied upon to make their assessments. Such decisions factored in the comparative reliability and quality of the sources (e.g., reports that cover trial proceedings vs. reports issued in the immediate aftermath of the event) and the sources cited in the report.

## 2. Comparing Lone Actor Terrorists and Solo Mass Murderers

### Introduction

This chapter addresses whether similarities and/or dissimilarities are observable across lone actor terrorists and solo mass murderers and explores the implications for law-enforcement. Our expectation is that while the socio-demographic profiles will be similar between the two offender types, it is in the behavior and attack planning where many differences will emerge.

### Method

The results below are based upon a series of bivariate and multivariate analyses. The full significant results from the bivariate analyses (chi-square, Fisher's exact tests) are outlined in the next section. For the statistical analyses that follow, where possible, we do report or distinguish between missing data and 'no' answers, but it should be kept in mind that the likely result is that 'no' answers are substantially undercounted in the analysis. Unless otherwise stated, each of the figures reported below are of the whole sub-samples (n=71 lone actor terrorists and 115 mass murderers). There is precedent for this in previous research on attempted assassinations of public figures, fatal school shootings and targeted violence affecting institutions of higher education (Fein and Vossekuil, 1999; Vossekuil et al, 2002; Drysdale et al, 2010).

### Bivariate Analyses

Table 2.1 outlines the behaviors where there is a significant difference between the lone actor terrorists (LA) and the solo mass murderers (MM). The results are split into three types of variables: group-related activities, antecedent attack behaviors and leakage-related behaviors.

**Table 2.1: Results from the Bivariate Analyses**

| | | | | | | 95% CI | |
|---|---|---|---|---|---|---|---|
| **Variable** | **$X^2$** | **LA %** | **MM %** | **p** | **Odds Ratio** | **Lower** | **Upper** |
| **Group-Related Activities** | | | | | | | |
| Tried to Recruit Others | 20.822 | 23.9 | 2.6 | 0.000 | 0.085 | 0.024 | 0.303 |
| Interacted Face to Face with Members of a Wider Network | 35.690 | 43.7 | 7.0 | 0.000 | 0.096 | 0.041 | 0.228 |
| Interacted Virtually with Members of a Wider Network | 20.822 | 23.9 | 2.6 | 0.000 | 0.085 | 0.024 | 0.303 |
| Letters/Public Statements Prior to Attack | 46.045 | 59.2 | 12.2 | 0.000 | 0.096 | 0.046 | 0.199 |
| Recent Joined Wider Movement | 22.458 | 32.4 | 6.1 | 0.000 | 0.135 | 0.054 | 0.337 |
| **Antecedent Attack Behaviors** | | | | | | | |
| University Experience | 8.334 | 43.7 | 23.5 | 0.004 | 0.396 | 0.209 | 0.749 |
| Military Experience | 4.855 | 32.4 | 18.3 | 0.028 | 0.466 | 0.235 | 0.926 |
| Military at Incident | Fisher's | 8.5 | 0.9 | 0.008 | 0.095 | 0.011 | 0.807 |
| Combat Experience | Fisher's | 11.3 | 1.7 | 0.014 | | | |
| Criminal Convictions | 4.028 | 57.5 | 42.6 | 0.045 | 0.543 | 0.299 | 0.988 |
| Tipping Point | 6.006 | 62.0 | 43.5 | 0.014 | 0.472 | 0.258 | 0.864 |
| Changed Address | 14.238 | 67.6 | 39.1 | 0.000 | 0.308 | 0.165 | 0.574 |
| Live Alone | 7.561 | 43.7 | 24.3 | 0.006 | 0.415 | 0.220 | 0.782 |
| Substance Abuse | 5.785 | 26.8 | 44.3 | 0.016 | 2.181 | 1.148 | 4.142 |
| Socially Isolated | 11.620 | 50.7 | 26.1 | 0.001 | 0.343 | 0.184 | 0.641 |
| Dry Runs | 31.568 | 33.8 | 3.5 | 0.000 | 0.071 | 0.023 | 0.215 |
| Degraded | 10.206 | 16.9 | 39.1 | 0.001 | 3.161 | 1.531 | 6.525 |
| Ignored/Treated Poorly | 4.742 | 14.1 | 27.8 | 0.029 | 2.352 | 1.075 | 5.147 |
| Helpless Victim | 3.298 | 11.3 | 21.7 | 0.069 | 2.188 | 0.927 | 5.163 |
| Problems with Personal Relationship | 21.506 | 26.8 | 61.7 | 0.000 | 4.416 | 2.314 | 8.427 |
| Escalating Anger | 3.875 | 40.8 | 27.0 | 0.049 | 0.534 | 0.285 | 1.001 |
| Recent Stress | 5.126 | 39.4 | 56.5 | 0.024 | 1.996 | 1.093 | 3.645 |
| Chronic Stress | 22.575 | 26.8 | 62.6 | 0.000 | 4.583 | 2.399 | 8.753 |
| History with Event Location | 44.994 | 29.6 | 79.1 | 0.000 | 9.028 | 4.575 | 17.815 |

| | | | | | | 95% CI | |
|---|---|---|---|---|---|---|---|
| **Variable** | $X^2$ | **LA %** | **MM %** | **p** | **Odds Ratio** | **Lower** | **Upper** |
| Stockpile | 7.285 | 52.1 | 32.2 | 0.007 | 0.436 | 0.237 | 0.801 |
| **Leakage Related Behaviors** | | | | | | | |
| Verbalize Intent to Family/Friends | 13.984 | 59.2 | 31.3 | 0.000 | 0.315 | 0.170 | 0.582 |
| Verbalize Intent to Wider Audience | 6.021 | 49.3 | 31.3 | 0.014 | 0.469 | 0.255 | 0.862 |
| Aware Grievance | 21.241 | 80.3 | 46.1 | 0.000 | 0.210 | 0.105 | 0.419 |
| Desire to Hurt Others | 7.995 | 69.0 | 47.8 | 0.005 | 0.412 | 0.221 | 0.767 |
| Others Involved Procured Weaponry | 8.134 | 21.1 | 7.0 | 0.004 | 0.279 | 0.112 | 0.698 |
| Others Aware of Planning | 8.719 | 36.6 | 17.4 | 0.003 | 0.364 | 0.184 | 0.721 |

In terms of group-related activities, the results indicate that lone actor terrorists were significantly more likely to try to recruit others, interact face-to-face with members of a wider network, virtually interact with members of a wider network, produce letters and/or public statements prior to the attack and recently join a wider movement.

In terms of antecedent attack behaviors, lone actor terrorists were significantly more likely to have university experience, military experience, combat experience, criminal convictions, experience a tipping point in their pathway to violent extremism, change address prior to their attack, live alone, be socially isolated, engage in dry runs, demonstrate that their anger is escalating and possess a stockpile of weapons. Solo mass murderers, on the other hand, were significantly more likely to have a history of substance abuse, experience being degraded or treated poorly by others in the build-up to their violent event, experience being a helpless victim, have problems with personal relationships, experience both recent and chronic stress and have a history with the event location.

In terms of leakage related behaviors, lone actor terrorists were significantly more likely to verbalize intent to commit violence to friends/family/wider audiences, have others aware of their grievance, express a desire to hurt others, have others involved in procuring weaponry and have others aware of their attack planning. This has very important implications for detection prior to the event itself. Without leaking intent, it increases the chances that intelligence or policing services will be unaware of the plot (supposing the recipient of the leak reports it to the relevant authorities). The difference in prevalence highlights the increased difficulty in detecting mass murders in advance of time compared to lone actor terrorist offences and this should be reflected in any threat management protocols going forward. The following sections go into these findings in greater detail. Later, we conduct a series of regressions based on these variable types.

## The Offenders

Now we turn towards comparing both sets of offenders. The aim here is not to create an offender 'profile'. Given the broad spectrum of motivations and ideologies across a low base rate of lone actor terrorists (Gill, 2015; Gill, Horgan and Deckert, 2014) such an endeavor is conceptually and empirically problematic and also holds little practical relevance for investigative purposes. Instead, our goal is to provide better insight into what variables we see universally across all crimes and terrorist types, and what offender characteristics appear to be particularly prominent within one sample compared to the other.

### Age

Within criminology, there is a long established relationship between age and offending. A number of studies (across a wide range of crimes) illustrate that as individuals become older, they also become less likely first time offenders. The chances of becoming a first time offender "ascends rapidly during adolescence, peaks in early adulthood and falls thereafter" (Stolzenberg and D'Alessio, 2008:66). Hirschi and Gottfredson (1983:552) refer to this relationship as "one of the brute facts of criminology" (Hirschi and Gottfredson, 1983:552). Data from Gill and Horgan's (2013) study of 1240 Provisional Irish Republican Army members demonstrates a similar relationship (see figure 2.1). Here, the peak first-time offending years were between 17 and 21, followed by a slow decline until the age of 27 where there is a precipitous fall followed by a long slow decline.

**Figure 2.1—Age Crime Curve of 1240 PIRA Members**

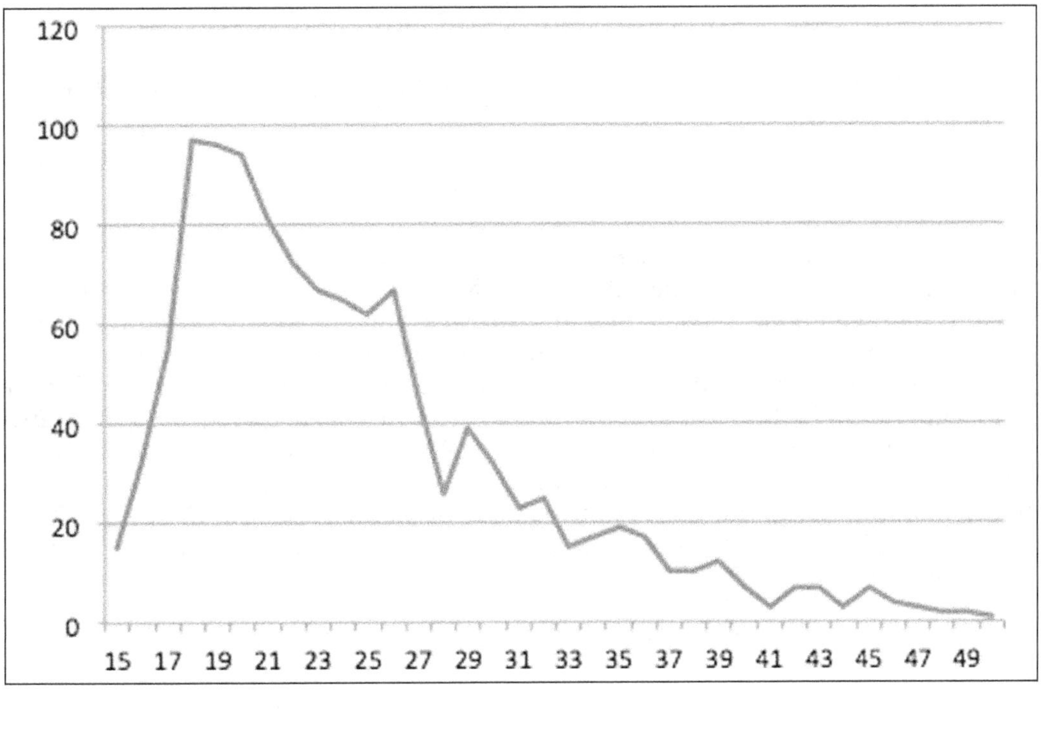

Both the lone actor terrorist sample and the mass murderer offender sample do not reflect "one of the brute facts of criminology" (Hirschi and Gottfredson, 1983:552). There was no significant difference between the two sub-samples and the average age of the whole sample was 34 years. Figure 2.2 illustrates no curvilinear relationship, with peak offending occurring in the early 20s, late 20s and mid-30s. The average age appears much higher than terrorist group-based studies previously highlighted. Florez-Morris' (2007) sample of Colombian terrorists (across three distinct groups, CRS, M-19 and the EPL) averaged 20 years of age. Both Gill and Horgan's (2013) sample of Provisional IRA members and Sageman's (2004) global jihadist sample averaged 25 years of age.

**Figure 2.2—Age Crime Curve of Lone Actor Terrorists and Mass Murderers Combined**

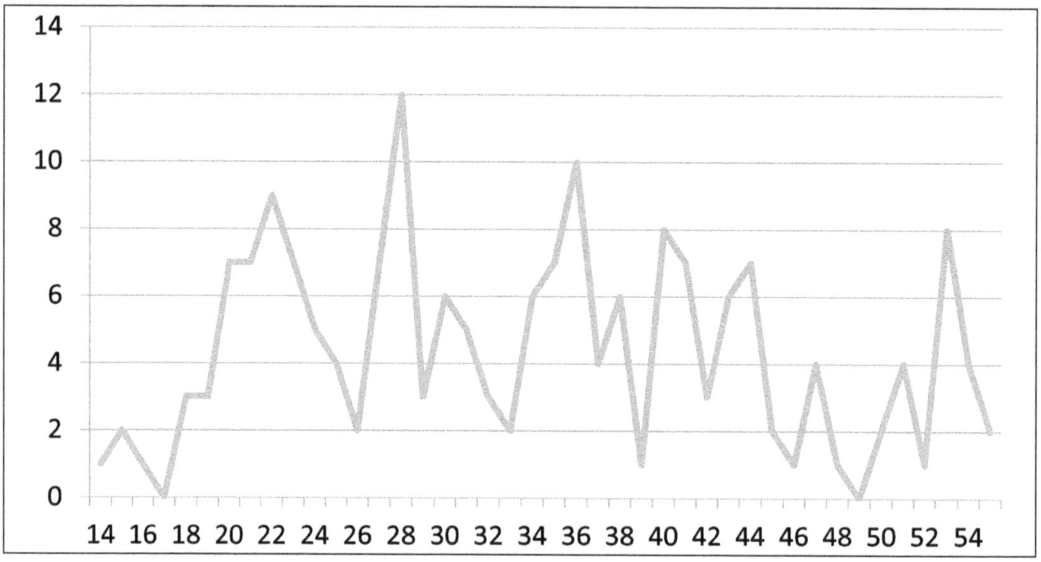


### Gender

Males heavily dominate both offence types. Only three females made the mass murderer offender dataset: in October 2006, Valerie Moore (by then an already convicted and released murderer) killed 12 and injured a further 31 after intentionally setting fire to a mattress outside the hotel room of an individual with whom she had recently argued. Also in 2006, Jennifer San Marco returned to her former workplace at a Postal Service office and shot and killed six before turning the gun on herself. During a February 2014 tribal meeting to discuss her possible eviction, Cherie Lash Rhoades fired from two handguns and wielded a butcher knife, killing four. Rachelle "Shelley" Shannon was the only female who made the lone actor terrorist dataset. She shot Dr. George Tiller (who survived but was later assassinated by lone actor Scott Roeder) outside his abortion clinic in Kansas in 1993.

These outliers are similarly reflected in gender representation within terrorist groups such as the Provisional Irish Republican Army (4.9%) and ETA (6.4%) (Gill and Horgan, 2013; Reinares, 2004). The wider crime literature also shows that males are also far more likely to engage in a wide range of violent and illegal behaviors (see Gill, 2015 for a full explanation). Indeed, males account for 93.2% of all sentenced prisoners in state or federal prisons according to a 2010 U.S. Department of Justice report (Guerine, Harrison, & Sabol, 2011). In effect, the relatively low preponderance of females in the sample is nothing extraordinary.

### Education, Employment & Relationship Status

Of those lone actor terrorists with available data (n=48), two-thirds took part in some form of university education with 21% possessing an undergraduate degree as their highest form of educational attainment, an additional 15% holding a masters and 4% holding an accredited Doctoral degree. Only 10% dropped out of secondary education. Generally speaking, the mean education level for this offender sample is impressive. The mass murderers were significantly less educated. Only 24% of the sample had some experience of university education, with 11% finishing an undergraduate degree, and 4% finishing some form of graduate degree.

However, the educational success of the lone actor terrorists did not translate into direct success in the job market. 38% were unemployed. 21% worked in the service or administrative sectors. Only 8% were active professionals. The general aggregate picture from the lone actor terrorist cohort is that of a well-educated sample but one who largely failed to translate this to real-world success. Despite the lower education attainment, only 28% of the mass murder offenders were unemployed, 33% worked in the service or administrative sectors and 5% were professionals.

There was no significant difference between the samples in terms of relationship status. A high percentage of both lone actors and mass murderers were single (37% and 43% respectively), smaller numbers were married (19% and 17%) or divorced (16% and 13%).

### Previous Criminal History

In 2007, Jason Roach published a research article called 'Those who do big bad things also usually do little bad things'. Roach promotes the concept of 'self-selection' to catch serious offenders. The basic idea is that serious offenders are often identified and captured by police after the commission of a lesser offence: "serious offenders are often crime versatile, committing an array of different crimes, including minor as well as serious offences. People who do big bad things, will not cavil at doing little bad things" (Roach, 2007:67). It should be no surprise therefore that much academic work on volume crime shows that a large predictor of future engagement with criminal and illicit behaviors is whether the individual has a previous history of criminal or illicit activities. Previous research has shown that offenders with prior convictions (including child molestation, robbery, or multiple probation sentences) are more likely to engage in a spree of homicidal offending (DeLisi, Hochstetler, Scherer, Purhmann, & Berg, 2008). Fein and Vossekuil's (1999) study of individuals who took part in or attempted to take part in an assassination of a public figure illustrated that 56% of the sample had one or more arrests for a non-violent offense while 20% had one or more arrests for a violent offense.

When we turn to the lone actor terrorist sample, we find similarly high figures. 58% had a previous criminal conviction. Of this sub-sample, 59% served time in prison indicating the seriousness and/or prolific nature of their offending. The corresponding figure for previous convictions amongst the mass murderers was lower, at 43%. However, a higher percentage of these individuals (67%) served time for their offence (suggesting they are more serious previous offenders). Offences across both sub-samples included non-violent activism, vehicle theft, counterfeiting, disorderly conduct, robbery, drink driving, concealed weapons conviction, counterfeiting, felony drugs convictions, assault, aggravated harassment, extortion, tax fraud, sexual assault, lewd conduct, arson, kidnapping, child pornography possession, firearms offences, grand larceny, and bank robbery. We therefore see a very wide range of illegal activities and certainly no concentration of one crime type that we can identify as an escalatory "trigger" for subsequent behavior into lone actor terrorism or mass murder.

### Other Distal Factors

There are a number of other behaviors logged within both datasets that provide an understanding of the offender's behavioral background. These are listed in Table 2. The results highlight the fact that lone actor terrorists were significantly more likely to be socially isolated, living alone at the time of their offense, and to have a history of military and combat experience. Mass murderers on the other hand were significantly more likely to have experienced long-term stress. Examples of this include: academic frustration stemming from learning disorders; difficulty maintaining employment and failure in business ventures; disabling injuries from automobile and work accidents; a range of mental health issues including depression, bi-polar disorder and post-traumatic stress disorder; an inability to establish appropriate social relationships; long-lasting discord in marriages and romantic relationships; and even being the main suspect in a double murder for over six years.

**Table 2.2 Prevalence of Distal Factors**

| Variable | Lone Actor Terrorists | Mass Murderers |
|---|---|---|
| Socially Isolated | 51%*** | 26% |
| History of Mental Illness | 39% | 48% |
| Lived Alone at Time of Event | 44%*** | 24% |
| Experience of Long-Term Stress | 27% | 63%*** |
| History of Substance Abuse | 27% | 44%** |
| Military Experience | 32%** | 18% |
| Combat Experience | 11%*** | 2% |

*** = $p < .001$, ** = $p < .01$, * = $p < .05$

Although there was no significant difference in terms of mental illness prevalence, Corner, Gill and Mason (2015) illustrated that the nature of the disorders themselves differed across actor types. Figure 2.3 presents these results. Lone actors show higher prevalence of psychotic disorders (those within the F20–F29 bracket of the ICD-10). Whereas mass murderers demonstrate higher prevalence of substance related disorders, major depressive disorder, personality disorders, disorders related to psychological development (F70–F79, F80–F89), and behavioral disorders with juvenile onset (F90–F98).

**Figure 2.3: Mental Disorder Prevalence across Actor Types**

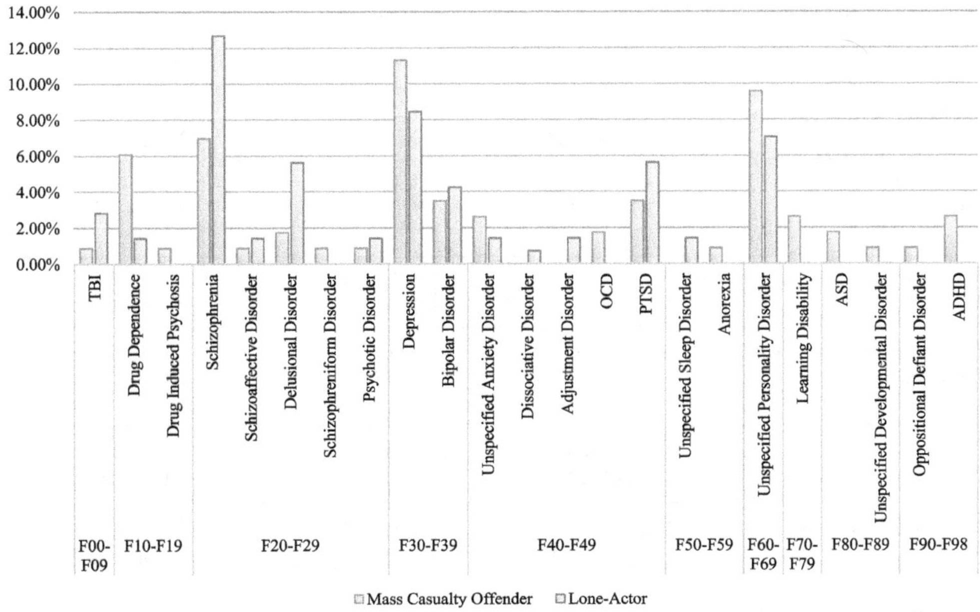


## Proximal Factors

This section provides an overview of the prevalence of behaviors the individual engaged in very near to the terrorist event or planned event. None of these behaviors are attack-related specifically, but again provide a more holistic view of the immediate life-situation various actors found themselves in just prior to planning their attack. The results again highlight the importance of short-term situational risk factors. Consistently across a number of variables, it appears that these short-term risk factors appear most commonly for mass murderers, particularly in the 6-month time frame prior to their eventual attack.

**Table 2.3. Prevalence of Proximal Behaviors**

| Variable | Occurred within 2 Years | Occurred within 1 Year | Occurred within 6 Months |
|---|---|---|---|
| | LA = Lone Actor MM = Mass Murderer | LA = Lone Actor MM = Mass Murderer | LA = Lone Actor MM = Mass Murderer |
| **Religious Beliefs Noticeably Intensified** | LA—6% MM—1% * | LA—4% MM—1% | LA—3% MM—1% |
| **Ideological Beliefs Noticeably Intensified** | LA—35% MM—1.7% *** | LA—28% MM—1.7% *** | LA—18% MM—1% *** |
| **Recently Unemployed** | LA—28% MM—30% | LA—22% MM—28% | LA—13% MM—24% |
| **Experienced Being Degraded** | LA—13% MM—31% ** | LA—11% MM—24% * | LA—6% MM—17% * |
| **Target of a Perceived Act of Prejudice** | LA—17% MM—24% | LA—14% MM—17% | LA—6% MM—10% |
| **Problems with Personal Relationships** | LA—17% MM—40% ** | LA—13% MM—37% *** | LA—7% MM—25% ** |
| **Financial Problems** | LA—24% MM—24% | LA—20% MM—24% | LA—13% MM—19% |
| **Elevated Level of Stress** | LA—32% MM—51% * | LA—27% MM—45% * | LA—17% MM—36% ** |

*** = $p < .001$, ** = $p < .01$, * = $p < .05$

## Attack Signaling

One of the most surprising behavioral trends was the extent to which the sample tended to leak information to others regarding their attack plan (See Table 4). Studies of similar actors have however found similar results. For example, Meloy et al.'s (2001) study of adolescent mass murderers in North America illustrated that 44% of the sample discussed the act of murder with at least one other person prior to the event itself. Also, 58% of the offenders in their study made threatening statements alluding to mass murder prior to the event and this was usually to a third-party audience. In 81% of Vossekuil et al.'s (2002) sample of U.S.-based school shooters, at least one other individual had known of the offender's intentions or specific plans for the school attack. In 59% of the cases, more than one non-attack related person had prior knowledge. Unlike Meloy et al.'s study, there was a lower rate of school shooters (17%) who provided specific pre-event warnings. Vossekuil et al. (2002:26) also found that although most of the offenses were committed by individuals, in 44% of the cases the solo offender was "influenced by other individuals in deciding to mount an attack, dared or encouraged by others to attack, or both". In some of these cases, others aided the solo offender in acquiring the weapon and/or ammunition. Finally, Fein and Vossekuil (1999) studied individuals who committed or attempted to commit assassinations of public figures in the United States. They illustrate that although specific pre-attack warnings are a rare-event, often others close to the offender were either aware of his/her interest in assassinations (44%), history of verbal/written communications about the eventual target (77%) or history of indirect, conditional or direct threats concerning the eventual target (63%).

The leaking of intent is therefore a key indicator to keep in mind with regards to developing a strategy to counter lone actor terrorism. However, this information cannot be acted upon if the recipient of the leaked information does not communicate with the relevant authorities. There could be clear barriers to this information being passed on. For example, Borum (2013:108) posits that "those with kinship bonds may not approve at all of the attacker's intent, but they may feel restrained from acting because of love and loyalty or concern about the consequences". Borum further outlines that research on such reporting mechanisms shows that factors such as the presence of multiple reporting channels, anonymity, accessibility, safety and credibility are key to successful transmission of this information. Of course, not all of the instances in which information is received about verbalized intent are viable threats or risks so instead of acting straight away, the logical next step is to engage in a risk assessment and look at the rest of the individual's behaviors with regard to their situation, capability, motivation and opportunity to act. The results in table 4 highlight the fact that lone actor terrorists engage in significantly more 'leaky' behaviors and this could be for a number of reasons. Lone actor terrorists may be less likely at the outset to actually want to be alone in the attack. This is evidenced in the contrasting findings with regard to their likelihood of trying to recruit others. Political grievances also may tend to have a wider audience than the deeply personal and idiosyncratic grievances of mass murderers. Hence, the opportunities to interact and leak intent may also be strengthened. Another possible reason may be that lone actors may be more likely to attack high profile targets which may lead to a longer attack planning and hence more time to leak intent. This lack of planning on a subset of the mass murderer sample may be indicated by the large number that consumed alcohol or drugs prior to their attack. Finally, it may be because of the 'lone actor terrorist dilemma' depicted by Gill (2015). Without leaking intent prior to the attack, the lone actor terrorist's actions may be depicted as the actions of a mad man rather than that of a rational terrorist. Without the ideological drivers being reported, the act cannot be an act of terrorism because it is 'message-less' for all intents and purposes.

**Table 2.4. Leakage & Group-Related Activities**

| Behavior | Lone Actor Terrorist | Mass Murderer |
|---|---|---|
| Other People Aware of the Individual's Grievance | 80%*** | 46% |
| Other People Aware of Individual's Extremist Ideology | 77% | N/A |
| Made Verbal Statements to Friends/Family about Intent or Belief | 59%*** | 31% |

| Behavior | Lone Actor Terrorist | Mass Murderer |
|---|---|---|
| Interacted Face to Face with Members of a Wider Network | 44%*** | 7% |
| At Least One Other Knew of the Individual's Research/Planning/Prep for an Attack | 37%** | 17% |
| Interacted Virtually with Members of a Wider Network | 24%*** | 3% |
| Received Help in Procuring Weaponry | 21%*** | 7% |
| Produced Public Statements Prior to the Event | 59%*** | 12% |
| Made a Pre-Event Warning | 26% | 19% |
| Sought Legitimization from Epistemic Authority Figures | 10%*** | 0% |
| Learnt Through Virtual Sources | 29%*** | 10% |
| Tried to Recruit Others | 24%*** | 3% |

*** = $p < .001$, ** = $p < .01$, * = $p < .05$

Finally, there are additional event related behaviors that produced interesting results. The mass murderer sample were significantly more likely to have familiarity of the attack location (79% vs. 30%) and this may account for why the lone actor terrorists were significantly more likely to engage in dry runs (34% vs. 4%). The mass murderers were also significantly more likely to consume drugs or alcohol just prior to the attack (20% vs. 4%).

## Regression Analysis

None of the above behaviors occur in isolation. The development of any of these individuals' behavior typically involves the crystallization in time and space of a number of factors. Because of this, we conducted a series of logistic regression analyses.[4]

The variables from Table 2.1 were entered into a series of regression analyses. Tables 2.5–2.7 outline these results. Model 1 analyses group-related behaviors using a logistic regression (mass murderers =1) (see table 5). The analysis showed that in combination, the independent variables significantly impacted upon whether the individual was a lone actor terrorist or a solo mass murderer ($X^2(5)=68.510$ $p<0.001$). Individuals who carry out both face to face and virtual interactions with co-ideologues, and those who produced letters after the event were significantly more likely to be lone actor terrorists, These results are not unexpected given the ideological motivations of lone actor terrorists versus the personal motivations of mass murderers, but do underscore ways in which these different impulses to action may affect offenders' willingness and/or need to interact with others both before and after the attack.

[4] For all the subsequent regression analyses, all assumptions for model were met (linearity of logit not relevant as all independent variables were categorical, no overdispersion was present), and diagnostics (including Collinearity) are presented in Appendix 1.

**Table 2.5—Logistic Regression Analysis of Group Related Behaviors**

| Variable | B(SE) | Sig. | Lower | Exp(B) | Upper |
|---|---|---|---|---|---|
| Recently Joined a Wider Group | –.431(.739) | .559 | .153 | .650 | 2.763 |
| Interacted Face to Face with Members of a Wider Network | –1.403(.665) | .035* | .067 | .246 | .906 |
| Interacted Virtually with Members of a Wider Network | –1.848(.740) | .013* | .037 | .158 | .672 |
| Tried to Recruit Others | –1.381(.774) | .074 | .055 | .251 | 1.145 |
| Produced Letters Post-Event | –2.270(.566) | .000*** | .034 | .103 | .314 |
| Constant | | .000 | | 4.375 | |

Model 2 analyses antecedent-event behaviors using a logistic regression (see table 2.6). The analysis showed that in combination, the independent variables significantly impacted upon whether the individual was a lone actor terrorist or a solo mass murderer ($X^2(19)=169.313$ $p<0.001$). A number of variables were significant predictors of actor type. Individuals who had university experience, military experience, a history of criminal convictions, experienced a recent change in address, experienced a recent tipping point, showed evidence of social isolation, showed evidence of escalating anger just prior to the event, and stockpiled weapons were significantly more likely to be lone actor terrorists. Individuals who had a history of substance abuse, problems with personal relationships, experienced a recent stressor, experienced chronic stress, and a history with the attack location were significantly more likely to be solo mass murderers.

Model 3 analyses leakage related behaviors using a logistic regression (see table 2.7). The analysis showed that in combination, the independent variables significantly impacted upon whether the individual was a lone actor terrorist or a solo mass murderer ($X^2(7)=61.558$ $p<0.001$). Only two of the variables remained significant. Individuals who produced letters prior to their attack, and those who had help in procuring weaponry for their attack were significantly more likely to be lone actor terrorists.

**Table 2.6—Logistic Regression Analysis of Antecedent Event Behaviors**

| Variable | B(SE) | Sig. | Lower | Exp(B) | Upper |
|---|---|---|---|---|---|
| University Experience | –2.836(.902) | .002** | .010 | .059 | 3.44 |
| Military Experience | –3.129(.952) | .001** | .007 | .044 | .283 |
| Criminal Conviction | –3.410(.955) | .000*** | .005 | .033 | .215 |
| Recent Address Change | –2.562(.815) | .002** | 0.16 | 0.77 | 3.81 |
| Tipping Point Experienced | –1.724(.770) | .025* | .039 | .178 | .807 |
| Lived Alone | .618(.778) | .427 | .404 | 1.856 | 8.531 |
| History of Substance Abuse | 3.593(1.003) | .000*** | 5.085 | 36.328 | 259.515 |
| Socially Isolated | –1.807(8.72) | .038* | .030 | .164 | .907 |

| Variable | B(SE) | Sig. | Lower | Exp(B) | Upper |
|---|---|---|---|---|---|
| Experienced Being Degraded | 2.207(8.58) | .010* | 1.689 | 9.084 | 48.857 |
| Experienced Having a Promise Broken | 3.050(2.963) | .303 | .064 | 21.120 | 7023.44 |
| Experienced Being Ignored | –.153(1.094) | .889 | .101 | .858 | .7321 |
| Experienced Others Not Caring For Them | 1.720(1.017) | .091 | .761 | 5.585 | 41.000 |
| Felt Helpless | –.783(1.019) | .442 | .062 | .457 | 3.368 |
| Problems with Personal Relationships | 1.877(.755) | .013* | 1.489 | 6.537 | 28.690 |
| Evidence Anger was Escalating | –2.964(1.035) | .004** | .007 | .052 | .393 |
| Experienced a Recent Stressor | 1.880(7.67) | .014* | 1.457 | 6.552 | 29.474 |
| Experienced Chronic Stress | 1.398(.633) | .027* | 1.170 | 4.045 | 13.986 |
| History with Attack Location | 3.570(.861) | .000*** | 6.570 | 35.533 | 192.181 |
| Stockpile of Weapons | –2.475(.849) | .004** | .016 | .084 | .444 |
| Constant | 2.328(1.025) | .023 | | 10.260 | |

**Table 2.7—Logistic Regression Analysis of Leakage Related Behaviors**

| Variable | B(SE) | Sig. | Lower | Exp(B) | Upper |
|---|---|---|---|---|---|
| Produced Letters Prior to the Attack | –2.253(.439) | .000*** | .044 | .105 | .248 |
| Made Verbal Statements to Family About Intent | –.634(.436) | .146 | .226 | .530 | 1.246 |
| Made Verbal Statements to Wider Audience | .556(.447) | .214 | .726 | 1.743 | 4.184 |
| Others Aware of Grievance | –.543(.473) | .251 | .230 | .581 | 1.467 |
| Expressed a Desire to Hurt Others | –.020(.423) | .962 | .428 | .980 | 2.244 |
| Other Individuals Helped Procure Weaponry | –1.274(.587) | .030* | .089 | .280 | .883 |
| Other Individuals Aware of Attack Planning | –.293(.469) | .532 | .297 | .746 | 1.871 |
| Constant | 1.881(.351) | .000 | | 6.559 | |

## Clustering Behaviors

In this section, we utilize multidimensional scaling techniques to assess the variables' relationships with one another rather than their relationship with pre-determined dimensions (e.g., lone actor vs. mass murderer).

The analysis below depicts a Smallest Space Analysis based on 16 supposed risk factors for engaging in lone actor events, be they inspired by ideology or personal grievance (or often both). The output (Figure 2.4) geometrically represents the levels of association between variables. The closer two variables are, the more often they co-occur and the less often each occurs in the absence of the other.

The output highlights a number of interesting findings:

1. Capability matters. Whilst much emphasis is placed upon motivations in various analyses, the below output highlights that capability should also be analyzed in as much detail. Whether the individual tried to recruit others (RECRUIT) and whether they had previous military experience (MILITARYEXP) are on opposite ends of the spectrum, meaning that they rarely co-occur. The reasons why individuals attempted to recruit others include issues such as not being prepared in terms of technical capability or individual psychology to go it alone. Military training may help negate such worries.

2. Many do not set out to be lone actors. The right hand side of the output illustrates a number of behaviors related to engagement with wider activist groups. They include whether the individual virtually interacted with members of a wider network (VIRTUALINTERACTION), interacted with members of a wider network face-to-face (F2F), tried to recruit others (RECRUIT), and whether others were aware of attack planning (OTHERSAWARE).

3. The most common co-occurring risk factors related to leakage and included whether the individual made verbal statements to friends and family about their intent (VERBALFAF), or verbal statements to wider audiences about their goals (VERBALWA), or grievance (AWAREGRIEVANCE).

4. Violent extremism is not an offline vs. online dichotomy. Our observations very often interacted with other members of a wider network in both virtual (VIRTUALINTERACTION) and real-world domains (F2F). This finding is presumably driven by the lone actor terrorist cohort.

5. Background factors mixed with short-term stressors are key to understanding many of the lone extremists. We included two variables related to recent stressors; stress (ELEVATEDSTRESS) and whether the individual experienced a tipping point prior to their violent radicalization (TIPPINGPOINT). These two proximal stressors are noticeably close to distal risk factors such as the experience of mental illness (MENTALILLNESS), substance abuse (SUBSTANCE ABUSE), previous military experience (MILITARYEXP), a history of criminality (CRIMINALCON) and a history of violent behavior (PREVVIOLENCE). This is particularly noticeable when the group-related behaviors outlined in finding 2, appear on the opposite side of the output.

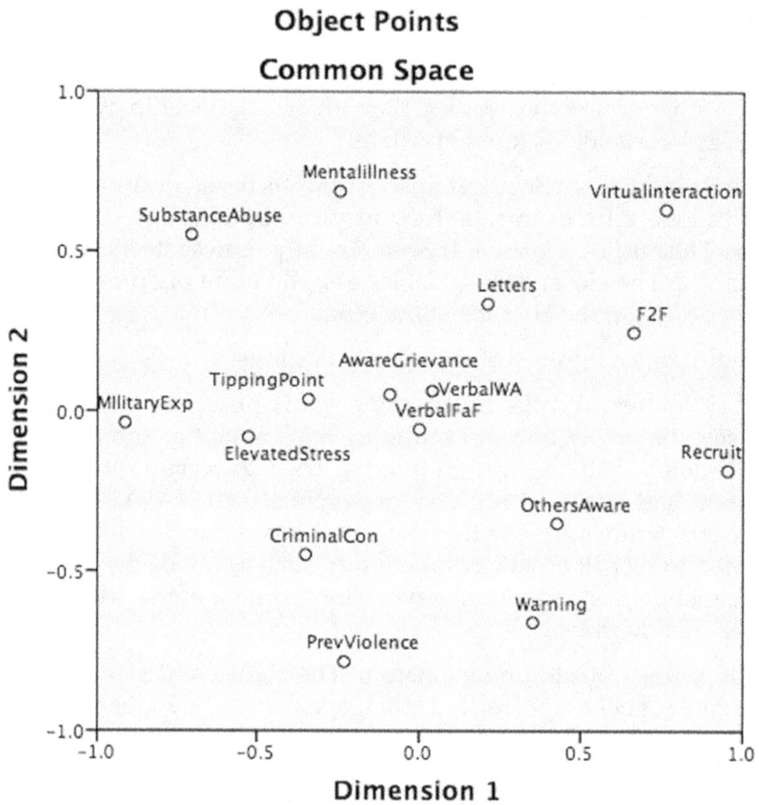


**Figure 2.4—Multidimensional Scaling Analysis of Behavior Clustering**

## Conclusion

What we see from the analysis we offer here is that lone actor terrorism and mass murderer attacks are (both) usually the culmination of a complex mix of personal, political and social drivers that crystalize at the same time to drive the individual down the path of violent action. Whether the violence comes to fruition is usually a combination of the availability and vulnerability of suitable targets that suit the heady mix of personal and political grievances and the individual's capability to engage in an attack from both a psychological and technical capability standpoint. Many individual cases share a mixture of personal life circumstances coupled with an intensification of beliefs that later developed into the idea to engage in violence. What differed was how these influences were sequenced. Sometimes personal problems led to a susceptibility to ideological influences. Sometimes long-held ideological influences became intensified after the experience of personal problems. This is why we should be wary of mono-causal 'master narratives' about how this process unfolds. The development of these behaviors is usually far more labyrinthine and dynamic. The chapters that follow seek to measure (a) whether, in light of these findings, a new continuum-based understanding of large-scale individual violent actors is realizable and (b) whether the temporal sequencing of these violent radicalization pathways differ. The conclusion considers the practical implications of these findings.

## 3. Rethinking Our Conceptualizations

Chapter two began with the assumption that lone actor terrorists and mass murderers are distinct categories of offender. The subsequent analysis highlighted that, in fact, they share more similarities than dissimilarities. The binary classification (lone actor terrorist versus mass murderer) is not so easy when we drill deeper into specific cases. Consider the cases of Jim David Adkisson (largely considered a terrorist) and Elliot Rodger (largely considered a mass murderer).

In 2008, Jim David Adkisson opened fire on a church congregation, killing two and injuring seven. Adkisson had a history of drug and alcohol problems and repeatedly lost jobs. The opening and concluding page of his four-page suicide note/claim of justification[5] outlines: "I guess you're wondering why I did this. Well let me explain in detail. Over the years I've had some good jobs, but I always got layed [sic] off. Now I'm 58 years old and I can't get a decent job. I'm told I'm 'overqualified', which is a codeword for 'too damned old'. Like I'm expected to age gracefully into poverty. No thanks! I'm done ... No one gets out of this world alive so I've chosen to skip the bad years of poverty. I know my life is going downhill fast from here. The future looks bleak. I'm sick and tired of being sick and tired. I'm absolutely fed up". In his initial police interrogation, Adkisson admits to anger and depression stemming from his unemployed status and lack of future prospects. His food stamps were also at risk of being revoked, which Adkisson had only just learnt about prior to the shooting. Adkisson further admits he channelled this anger out on the church and its congregation. With these details, Adkisson appears to be like a typical solo mass murderer,motivated by personal grievances and life-circumstances.

However, the contents of Adkisson's suicide note/claim of justification go into great detail on the political reasons for his actions. There, he calls the Democrat party an ally of the terrorists in the war on terror and labels liberalism "the worst problem America faces today". He accuses major news outlets of being the "propaganda arm" of the Democrats. The note also blames liberalism for ruining the country and its institutions "from the boy scouts up to the military, from education to religion". The church he targeted is framed as a "cult", ultra-liberal", "a den of un-American vipers", "a collection of sicko's, weirdo's, and homo's", that "embrace every pervert". He refers to his actions variously as a "hate crime", "political protest", and a "symbolic killing". He concludes the note: "So I thought I'd do something good for the country and kill Democrats 'til the cops kill me ... Tell the cop that killed me that I said, 'Thanks, I needed that.' I have no next of kin, no living relative. If you would take my sorry carcass to the body farm, or donate it to science, or just throw me in the Tennessee River".

With this information, we can now depict Adkisson as an example of an individual whose personal life circumstances led to a series of problems that he largely blamed

[5] The note can be found here http://web.knoxnews.com/pdf/021009church-manifesto.pdf.

upon wider political processes which after a period of time built up to the extent that he decided to act violently. He chose to attack a church that he felt was a mirror image of the decay he saw emanating from Washington D.C.

However, this was not just a random church. Adkisson had previous contact with this church. His ex-wife previously attended there. His marriage had not ended well by any measure. According to court documents, Adkisson had threatened to "blow" both of their "brains out". With that information, the landscape of Adkisson's motivation changes again. We now have an individual whose personal problems he blamed on the political and when he decided to act upon it found a target that reflected his political concerns but also housed an individual he had a previous and highly acrimonious relationship with. In effect, a mixture of personal and political reasons led to his decision to act violently in the first place, and to act in that location specifically.

Similarly, Elliot Rodger developed over time a justification for killing, but his grievance was rooted not in a movement, but rather in an increasing frustration at his own social and sexual isolation. On May 23, 2014 in the California college town of Isla Vista, 22-year-old Rodger stabbed to death three men in his apartment and then went on a shooting rampage, killing two women outside of a sorority house and one other man, injuring 14 more before taking his own life. Again, a number of interrelated factors appear to have culminated in the murderous attack. According to a New York Times article, Rodger (a) was emotionally disturbed as a youth (b) was deeply affected by the divorce of his parents when he was in the first grade, (c) was bullied and seen as an "oddball" throughout his school years (d) never had a romantic relationship and felt rejected by all women (e) became bitterly envious of his male and female peers who did have relationships, particularly sexual relationships (f) perceived himself to be under financial strain (g) had previously acted violently toward women for not paying attention to him (h) had made threats to kill people who aggrieved him. A detailed description by Lovett and Nagourney (2014) describes how before the attack, Rodger even mailed a lengthy testimonial ("My Twisted World") and posted a You Tube video ("Elliot Rodger's Retribution") just prior to his attack. The testimonial read like a political manifesto, just not a political stance that has much resonance outside of Elliot Rodger's world. He notes that he "expanded on the political and philosophical ideals I concocted when I was seventeen, and I soon became even more radical about them than I ever was before". Listed amongst his grievances are racial minorities and inter-racial couples. The video detailed his lonely suffering, his rage at girls who "gave their affection and sex and love to other men but never to me", and expressing his intent to punish all those who enjoyed the romantic and sexual success to which he aspired but never achieved (Lovett and Nagourney, 2014). In the final view, Rodger comes out a mass murderer and not a terrorist because the genesis of his action is found not in a movement or ideology but rather in personal agony.

Both Adkisson and Rodger experienced a range of personal, financial stressors coupled with social, political and personal grievances. Both experienced distal risk factors, had made threats of violence to others, had suicidal ideations and access to firearms. Their violent acts were very similar. One is treated as a terrorist, the other as a mass murderer. Is there a better way to categorize these types of offenders?

Borum, Fein and Vossekuil (2013) outline a dimensional approach to understanding lone actor terrorism. They the case that instead of debating definitions, it may be more useful to view (a) the degree of loneness the offender exhibited (b) the degree of external direction the offender received and (c) the depth of their political motivation, as continuums. "Analyzing cases by their features, rather than by their types, might better aid the investigative process, particularly if each dimension is linked to a key facet of the attack and tracked across the spectrum of attack-related activity from idea to action" (2013:104). They refer to these three such features as loneness, direction and motivation. Loneness measures independence of activity. The loneness continuum plots the degree to which offenders received assistance in initiating planning, preparing for and executing the attack. Direction measures the level of autonomy the lone actor displayed in decision-making. It plots the degree to which the offender received instruction or guidance on issues concerning whether to attack, what to target and the attack type to deploy. The motivation continuum plots the degree to which the action is ideologically or personally driven. Borum et al. (2013) make the case that very few offenders will be placed on the extremes of a continuum but are likely to be found somewhere between the polar opposites.

We put this theorizing to the test by plotting each of our lone actor terrorists and mass murderers on a three-dimensional continuums space. Each offender was assigned a score for each of the three continuums.

We adapted Borum et al.'s continuums slightly to make a finer distinction between the loneness and direction continuums. For the loneness continuum, we included behaviors related to the degree to which the individual had prior contact with members of a wider network prior to the plot's inception as well as whether others were aware a plot was being developed. Basically, the loneness continuum captures the degree to which bystanders may have noticed something in the individual's violent radicalization trajectory. We included behaviors such as whether or not the individual (a) raised finance for a wider movement (b) had recently joined a wider pressure group or movement (c) made verbal statements to others about their intent to commit violence (d) expressed intentions to hurt others (e) had other individuals in their close social network involved in violent activity for a group/cause (f) had a spouse involved in a wider group/cause (g) engaged in face to face interactions with members of a wider network (h) engaged in virtual interactions with members of a wider network (i) attempted to recruit others (j) was rejected from a wider group/movement. For each behavior carried out by the offender, they received one point. Those scoring high here are therefore not very lone, those scoring low are very lone up (until the point of plotting).

The direction continuum looks at the degree of external help/coordination/direction provided from the point of plot inception to the point of the attack (remember, to be included in this dataset they needed to carry out the attack alone). We included behaviors such as whether or not the individual (a) sought legitimization from epistemic authority figures for their attack (b) received training (c) learnt aspects of their attack from virtual sources (d) downloaded bomb-making manuals (e) other individuals procured the weaponry on their behalf (f) other individuals helped build the Improvised Explosive Device (IED) for them (g) others had knowledge about the attack planning

(h) displayed evidence of command and control links. For each behavior carried out by the offender, they received 1.25 points.

At one end of the motivation continuum are those individuals who are purely ideologically motivated. At the other end are those purely motivated out of personal grievances. We included behaviors such as whether they (a) directly communicated a stated ideology (b) wrote letters/publications espousing an ideology (c) made verbal statements to friends/family about their ideology (d) had other people be aware of their grievance (e) had other people be aware of their extremist ideology (f) consumed propaganda from a wider group/movement (g) claimed the attack on behalf of a group. The received 1.11 points if any of these behaviors were apparent. They were deducted 1.11 points if either of the following behaviors were apparent (a) a recent stressor or (b) chronic stress. The motivation scale therefore initially ran from –2.22 (personally motivated) to 7.77 (ideologically motivated).

We were then left with scores for each offender across each continuum. As an illustration, let's return to the cases of Adkisson and Rodger which opened this chapter. Adkisson scored 1 on loneness, 1.25 on direction and 5.55 on motivation. Rodger scored 3 on loneness, 1.25 on direction and 4.44 on motivation indicated he was less 'lone' and slightly more personally motivated. At a very aggregate level, there were significant differences between our lone actor terrorists and mass murderers across all three continuums. Lone actor terrorists were significantly higher up each continuum

- Motivation ($M = 4.11$ vs. $-.2$, $t(106.45) = -18.745$, $p < .001$)
- Direction ($M = 1.70$ vs $0.23$, $t(78.99) = -7.68$, $p < .001$)
- Loneness ($M = 2.97$ vs. $1.16$, $t(100.16) = -6.25$, $p < .001$)

In other words, on average, lone actor terrorists were less 'lone', more directed and more politically motivated. This is perhaps unsurprising given the different underpinnings of these two criminal offender types. However, once we plotted these scores on a three-dimensional space, some interesting results emerged.

For the below visualizations, we computed direction scores to resemble the 0–10 scale in the other two continuums. Figure 3.1. plots all mass murderers on the three dimensional space. They showed little variance in terms of the loneness continuum, with 33% scoring 0, a further 33% scoring 1 and a further 23% scoring 2. There was even less variance on the direction continuum, with 80% scoring 0 and 16.5% scoring 1. The remaining four offenders all scored 2. The motivation continuum received the greatest level of variance, with 42% scoring a combined figure of the two lowest scores, with 26% collecting scores closer toward the ideological end of the spectrum.

Figure 3.1. Plotting Mass Murderers Across Three Dimensions

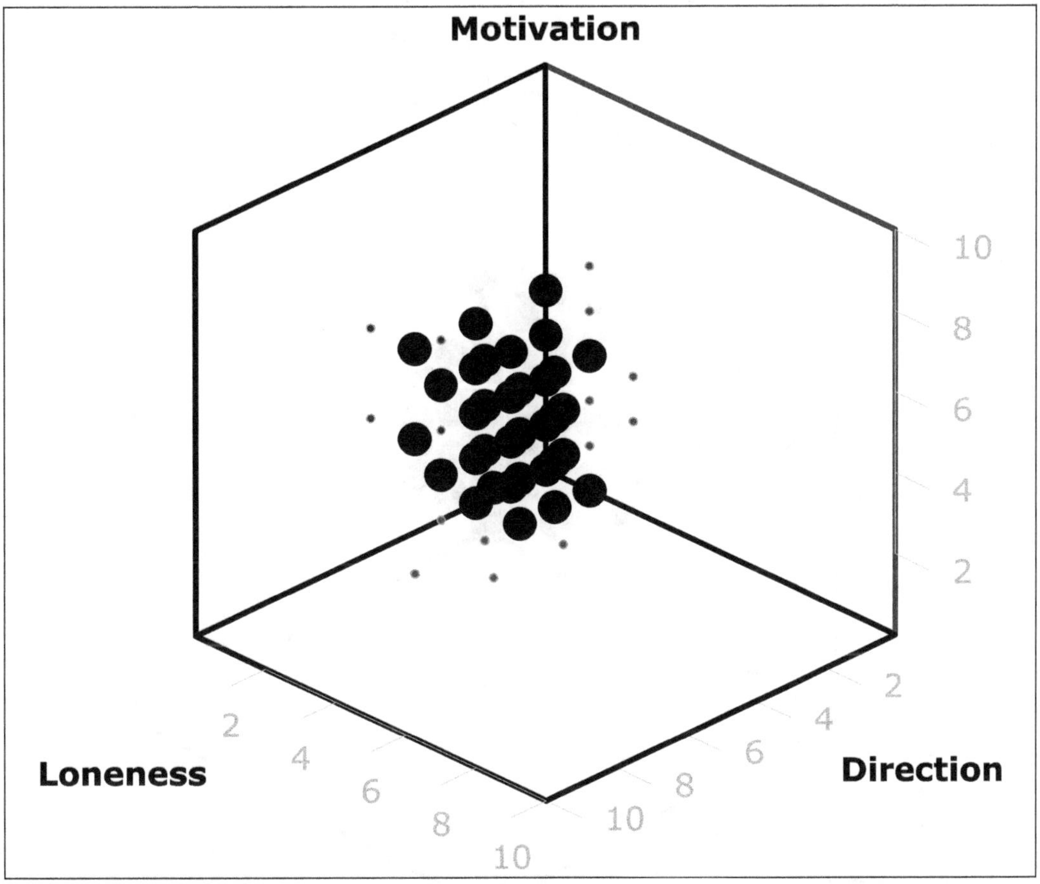


As you would expect from the comparison of means results, above, greater variation was apparent within the lone actor terrorists. Just under half of the offenders scored three or more points. A quarter scored five or more points. However, the other half of offenders scored similar points to 80%+ of the mass murderers (e.g. in the 0 to 2 range). In terms of the direction continuum, 30% scored two or more points, with five offenders scoring more than 5. 16% however scored 0, which is what the vast majority of mass murderers scored. In terms of motivational continuum, 75% scored three or more points. The results are displayed in Figure 3.2

Figure 3.2. Plotting Lone Actor Terrorists Across Three Dimensions

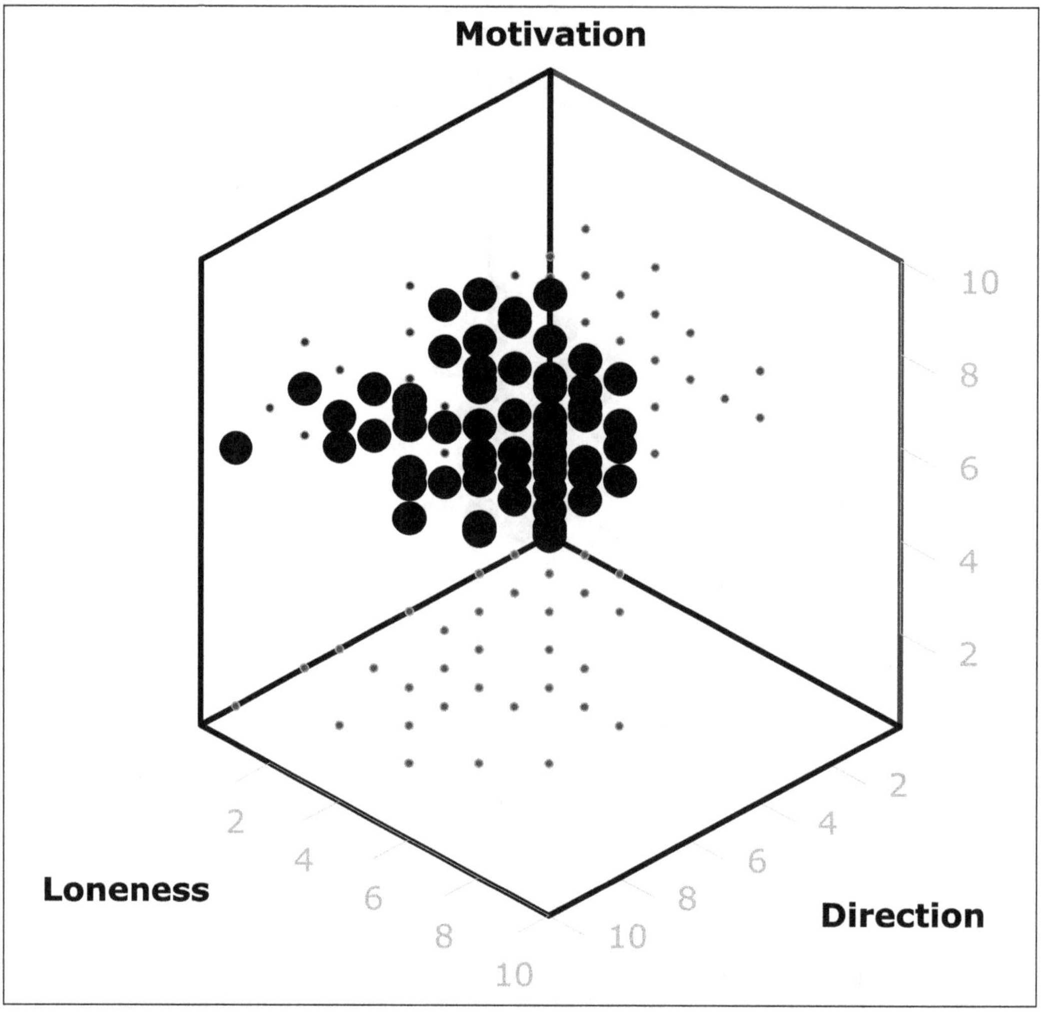


Finally, Figure 3.3 includes both lone actor terrorists (blue) and mass murderers (red). Although there is a clear demarcation between a large number of lone actor terrorists and all of the mass murderers the higher up the motivation continuum, it is evident also that very many lone actor terrorists inhabit similar areas that the vast majority of mass murderers are typically plotted. So whilst many lone actor terrorists are most definitely a different breed than mass murderers, many of them do appear exceptionally similar to mass murderers in these three regards.

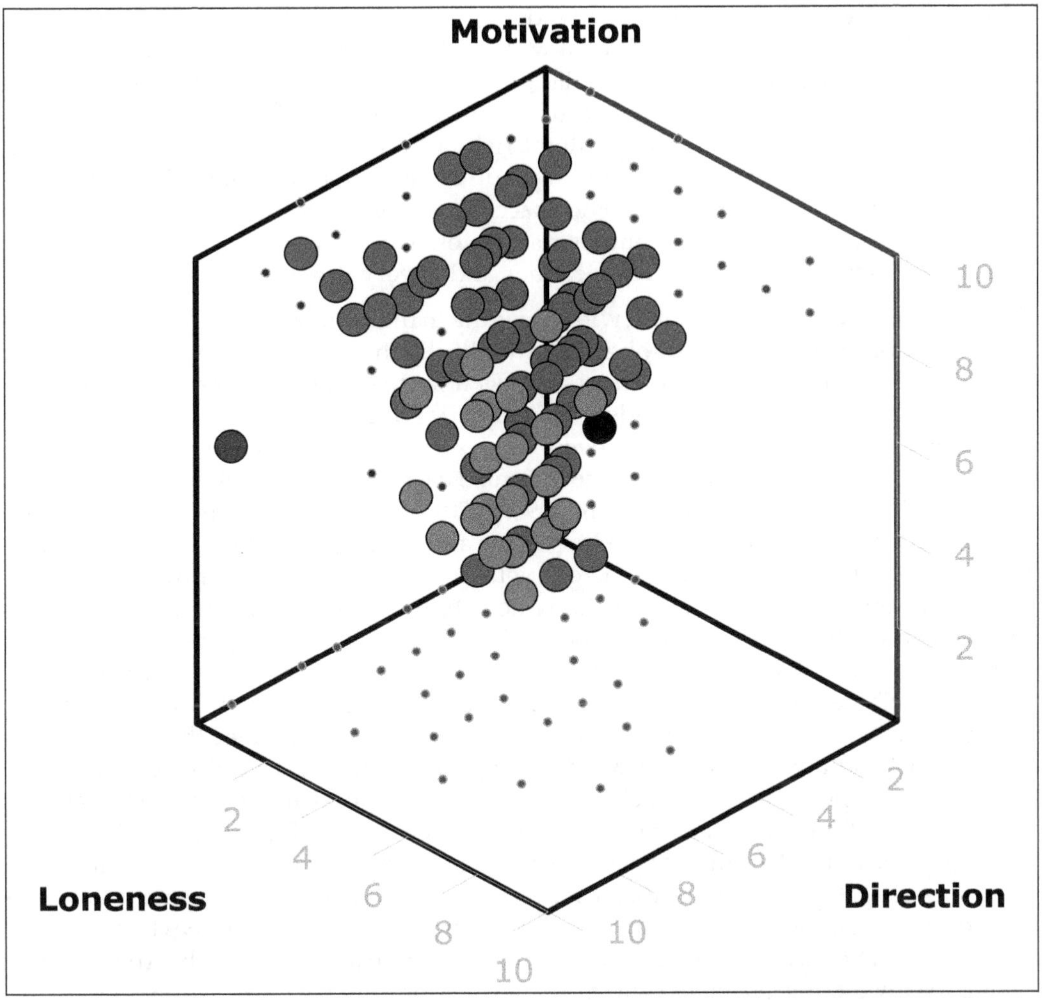


**Figure 3.3 Plotting Mass Murderers and Lone Actor Terrorists Across Three Dimensions**

### 4. 'Risk Factors' and Lone Actor Violent Events: The Problems of Low Base Rates & Long Observational Periods

Chapters two and three outlined a series of studies related to the prevalence and clustering of various indicators and risk factors potentially associated with lone actor terrorism and mass murder events. In terms of the methodological approaches taken and in terms of how the variables were treated, the chapters typified the wider study of school shooters (Langman, 2009), mass murderers (Bowers et al, 2010), lone actor terrorism (Gill et al, 2014) and spree shooters (Lankford, 2013). Such studies of low likelihood events build on the study of risk and high-volume crimes like arson and stalking. Whilst the burgeoning number and rigorous quality of data-driven approaches is to be welcomed, a key methodological factor differentiates these two types of crime studies, and it is one frequently overlooked by the former. Studies of high-likelihood, low-impact crimes typically utilize a sample of offenders that are highly clustered temporally. For example, they analyze offenders from a wider cohort born in the same year (and often in the same town) or they analyze similar offences that occurred in the same year. Such studies can afford to do so simply because of the high volume of observable offenders. Such approaches can potentially highlight risk factors that are relevant to that cohort or geographic space which are essentially outliers and not generalizable to offenders outside of that temporal or geographic space. However, given the comparative ease of conducting such studies, these outlier risk factors can be weeded out via replication studies conducted in very different locations and at very different times.

The study of risk factors associated with engaging in high-impact, low-likelihood violent events is afforded no such luxury because thankfully these crimes remain rare. Instead, these studies collect data on offenders across a large number of years. For example, Meloy et al. (2001) analyzed offender characteristics of 27 mass murderers (individuals who killed three or more in a single event) over a 41-year period. Hempel and Richard's (1999) analysis of mass murderers focuses on 30 cases spread over 50 years. Gill (2015) analyses 111 lone actor terrorists from 1990 to 2014. Finally, Fein and Vossekuil (1999) conducted a behavioral analysis of 83 assassins and (attempted) attackers over a 50-year period. Each study highlights risk factors, yet fails to consider whether these factors are driven by temporal-cohorts within the wider observation pool or are uniform across the expanses of time under consideration. We never know if the high prevalence of one factor in the overall sample due to it being universally present in a small time frame or is it distributed evenly across the time period. This is potentially most worrisome in those analyses where the number of years of study is far greater than the number of individuals analyzed. In other words, though the complete descriptive results may indicate a large propensity for a behavior to occur, a temporal analysis may indicate that the propensity for the behavior to occur actually decreases (or increases) over time. As a consequence, and unless this is specified, there may not exist the same implications for future investigations. This has major repercussions for how risk assessment protocols are developed going forward. A more useful approach is to determine which facets of offender behavior are increasing/decreasing across time and whether this trend (if any) is statistically distinguishable from random behavior.

This chapter compares a cohort of violent lone actors (composed of lone actor terrorists, and solo mass murderer attackers) from 1990–2005 with a cohort from 2006 to 2013. The latter period witnessed a step-change in the rate and intensity of lone actor mass violent events so a corollary to this exploration of whether risk factors differ across time is to try and identify factors that may help explain this recent increase in events.

### Do 'Risk Factors' Change Over Time? Learning from High-Likelihood, Low-Impact Crimes

In 1995, Kaplan lamented that studies have not demonstrated the association between risk factors and criminality for two different generational cohorts. Twenty years later, Farrington et al (2015:48) outlined that a "key issue in criminology is to what extent are risk factors for offending similar over time", yet the "question has rarely been investigated". As mentioned previously, the risk factor literature related to violent and frequent crime is typically unworried by this temporality/generalizability issue because the volume of such studies can distinguish between risk factors that are common or outliers.

The alternative to such approaches is to compare similar crimes in similar contexts, but in different temporal eras. We are aware of only four such studies, three of which have been published since 2013. This section briefly outlines these studies.

Farrington et al. (2015) investigated the extent to which a wide variety of risk factors can predict general offending across two generations. Utilizing the Cambridge Study in Delinquent Development they compared the original sample of 411 males from London with their children. Risk factors for both generational cohorts were positively correlated. Eleven risk factors were significant predictors for offending in both generations. They included a convicted father and mother, harsh discipline, poor parental supervision, a disrupted family, low family income, large family size, poor housing, low school attainment, daring/risk-taking and antisocial child behavior. The findings only distinctly differed on three factors: parental conflict, low social class and hyperactivity/attention problems (although this last risk factor was measured differently across the two generations). The risk factors were therefore generally very robust across generations with the author's concluding, "most of the findings in one generation were remarkably replicable in the next generation" (2015:60).

Menard and Johnson (2015) employed a similar research design to Farrington et al. (2015). They analyzed data from the National Youth Survey Family Study (NYSFS), which had an original sample of 2,360 youths aged between 11 and 17 in late 1976. Menard and Johnson compared the results of this original sample group with the sample group's children in 2003–2004. They found similar inter-generational risk factor robustness in terms of delinquent peer bonding and offending. Differences emerged in terms of gender as a predictor between generations 1 and 2 (e.g. being a male is less important), while the impact of school strain (e.g. poor grades and lower expectations of gaining a college education) became an important predictor in the later generation.

Johnson et al. (2015) utilizes the same data as Menard and Johnson (2015), but tests a different series of predictor variables. Seven of the nine predictors demonstrated the same significance scores and direction in relationship inter-generationally. The earlier generation was more heavily influenced by negative life events (for example parental divorce/separation), whilst the later generation was more influenced by delinquent peer association.

Farrington and Loeber (1999) came to similar conclusions in their comparative study of the 411 London males from the 1960s (mentioned above) with a replication study entitled the Pittsburgh Youth Study, which examined 508 males in the 1980s. The results indicated that the risk factors were not only temporally robust but also geographically robust.

The four studies therefore illustrate that risk factors associated with general offending and delinquency have proven to be quite robust across generational cohorts. In the next section, we conduct a series of analyses to investigate whether the same holds true for lone actor violent events.

## Method

We compared the prevalence of risk factors across two temporal domains within this combined sample of lone actor terrorists and solo mass murderers. We decided to split the sample from 1990–2005 and 2006–2013. This is because from 2006 onwards, there was a distinct scale shift in the number of actors per year: 1990–2005 averages 5 per year; the corresponding figure for 2006–2013 is 12.75.

We then used bivariate analyses to compare the prevalence of socio-demographic and behavioral differences. Variables displaying significant differences were then entered into a logistic regression to illustrate which factors held the most predictive power as to whether they occurred within the phase 1990–2005 (0) or 2006–2013 (1).

### Results

We found no significant differences in terms of socio-demographic variables across the two temporal periods. This included factors such as age, education, and socio-economic status. Table 4.1 outlines those variables with significant differences.

**Table 4.1: Bivariate Comparison of Behaviors between 1990–2005 and 2006–2013**

| | | | | | | 95% Confidence Interval | |
|---|---|---|---|---|---|---|---|
| Variable | $X^2$ | 1990–2005 (%) | 2006–2013 (%) | p | Odds Ratio | Lower | Upper |
| Military Experience | 15.590 | 38.0 | 13.1 | 0.001**** | 0.246 | 0.119 | 0.506 |
| Previous Imprisonment | 4.274 | 21.5 | 35.5 | 0.039*** | 2.009 | 1.031 | 3.913 |
| Verbalized Intent to Family | 4.266 | 50.6 | 35.5 | 0.039*** | 0.537 | 0.297 | 0.971 |
| Verbalized Intent to Wider Audience | 9.035 | 50.6 | 29.0 | 0.003*** | 0.398 | 0.217 | 0.730 |
| Others Aware of Grievance | 9.611 | 72.2 | 49.5 | 0.002*** | 0.379 | 0.204 | 0.705 |
| Experienced a Tipping Point | 12.835 | 65.8 | 39.3 | 0.001**** | 0.336 | 0.183 | 0.615 |
| Experienced being Degraded | 9.923 | 43.0 | 21.5 | 0.002*** | 0.362 | 0.191 | 0.688 |
| Target of Injustice | 13.246 | 45.6 | 20.6 | 0.001**** | 0.309 | 0.162 | 0.589 |
| Expressed Desire to Hurt Others | 3.032 | 63.3 | 50.5 | 0.082* | 0.591 | 0.326 | 1.070 |
| Experienced Recent Stressor | 4.951 | 59.5 | 43.0 | 0.026** | 0.513 | 0.285 | 0.926 |
| Substance Use Prior to Event | 2.991 | 8.9 | 17.8 | 0.084* | 2.221 | 0.884 | 5.577 |
| Multiple Attack Methods | 4.510 | 12.7 | 25.2 | 0.034** | 2.329 | 1.053 | 5.151 |
| Non-Discriminate Target | 5.309 | 26.6 | 43.0 | 0.021** | 2.083 | 1.110 | 3.907 |
| Face to Face Interaction | 9.449 | 31.6 | 13.1 | 0.002*** | 0.325 | 0.156 | 0.678 |

Overall, the results indicate that very few behaviors can be solely attributable to the upward scale shift in lone actor terrorist and mass murder incidents in the 2006–2013 period. Out of the vast number of behaviors tested, only five show a greater preponderance in the 2006–2013 era, and one is only marginally significant (substance use prior to attack). Perhaps it is no great surprise that offenders are now significantly more likely to make use of the Internet in their planning given its ubiquity in routine activities for the whole population but the percentage rise is still relatively small (17%) compared to the more than doubling of events in both time periods. The 2006–2013 cohort is also significantly more likely to have been previously imprisoned, engaged in multiple attack methods (e.g. a bombing and a shooting) and targeted ordinary citizens rather than a political or military target for example.

The results also indicate that the 2006–2013 period contains fewer offenders who (a) had previous military experience (b) made verbal statements to family/friends/wider audiences about their intent and beliefs (c) socialized face to face with members of a wider network (d) experienced being degraded or the target of an act of prejudice or unfairness (e) expressed a desire to hurt others (f) experienced a recent stressor. It is worth re-iterating that whilst prior military experience is often noted in media reports regarding the increase in mass murder events, the statistics suggest this factor only appears a third as much in the current era than it did in the 1990–2005 era which suggests that some so-called risk factors may have cohort-effects rather than having stable influences over time.

It suggests therefore that the crystallization of risk factors noted elsewhere in our research has perhaps become more diffuse in the 2006–2013 period. Future research may also investigate whether there is a greater clustering or copycat effect in the latter era.

The logistic regression shows that, in combination, the independent variables significantly impacted on temporal era, $X^2(14) = 54.965$, $p < 0.001$. The model correctly predicted 72.6% of responses. Specific individual variables were significant predictors of year of attack as shown in Table 4.2. Odds of greater than one indicate a positive relationship between the predictor and dependent variable.

Those individuals with military experience were more likely to carry out an attack in the years 1990–2005. Individuals who utilized multiple different weapons in an attack were more likely to carry out the attack in the years 2006–2013. Individuals who interacted with like-minded members of a wider network were more likely to carry out an attack in the years 1990–2005.

**Table 4.2: Logistic Regression of Behaviors between 1990–2005 and 2006–2013**

| | | | 95% CI for Odds Ratio | | |
|---|---|---|---|---|---|
| **Variable** | **B (SE)** | **Significance** | **Lower** | **Exp (B)** | **Upper** |
| **Military Experience** | –1.272(0.438) | 0.004*** | 0.119 | 0.280 | 0.662 |
| **Previous Imprisonment** | 0.616(0.407) | 0.129 | 0.835 | 1.852 | 4.109 |
| **Verbalized Intent to Family** | –0.283(0.417) | 0.497 | 0.333 | 0.754 | 1.706 |
| **Verbalized Intent to Wider Audience** | –0.345(0.426) | 0.419 | 0.307 | 0.708 | 1.633 |
| **Others Aware of Grievance** | 0.379(0.463) | 0.414 | 0.589 | 1.460 | 3.662 |
| **Experienced a Tipping Point** | –0.605(0.409) | 0.139 | 0.245 | 0.546 | 1.217 |
| **Experienced being Degraded** | –0.586(0.412) | 0.155 | 0.248 | 0.557 | 1.248 |
| **Target of Injustice** | –0.586(0.412) | 0.111 | 0.208 | 0.494 | 1.174 |

| Variable | B (SE) | Significance | 95% CI for Odds Ratio | | |
|---|---|---|---|---|---|
| | | | Lower | Exp (B) | Upper |
| Expressed Desire to Hurt Others | –0.705(0.442) | 0.595 | 0.369 | 0.808 | 1.771 |
| Experienced Recent Stressor | –0.408(0.382) | 0.286 | 0.315 | 0.665 | 1.406 |
| Substance Use Prior to Event | 0.218(0.577) | 0.705 | 0.402 | 1.244 | 3.851 |
| Multiple Attack Methods | 0.871(0.495) | 0.079* | 0.905 | 2.389 | 6.307 |
| Non-Discriminate Target | 0.442(0.398) | 0.267 | 0.713 | 1.556 | 3.395 |
| Face to Face Interaction | –1.137(0.484) | 0.019** | 0.124 | 0.321 | 0.829 |
| Constant | 1.426 | 0.003 | | 4.162 | |

Note: B= regression coefficient, Exp (B)= odds ratio

****=p<.001; ***=p<.01; **p=<.05; *p=<.1

## Conclusion

The results illustrate the importance of considering temporality with low-likelihood, high impact events such as these. Approximately 20% of the variables that were tested in a bivariate manner displayed demonstrably different prevalence rates across two eras. This has several implications. First, we should treat with caution some findings related to risk factors in studies of low-likelihood, high-impact events. This is especially the case for those studies where the years under consideration are greater (or even approximate to) the number of units of observation because there is likely a great variance within the sample. Because of this caution, studies should highlight this fact and draw some inferences about what variables are on the increase/decrease. Second, it also highlights the need for law enforcement and intelligence agencies to consistently update their threat assessment protocols because some factors that underpin risk may be dynamic in nature. Technological, societal and environmental changes can open a gateway for a new generation of offenders or act as a deterrent and hence the risk factors associated with these types of crimes can change. Relatedly, it calls for the need to continuous and systematic data collection procedures. Finally, this finding might necessitate moving away from examining risk factors in isolation. Instead, perhaps we should look at how factors cluster, sequence and crystalize and whether some risk factors act as substitutes in the absence of others (e.g. does the Internet replace the need for face-to-face interaction with members of a wider network). Through such endeavors we may come to realize a mechanism-based approach to understanding the factors that may signal low-likelihood, high-impact attacks.

## 5. Routine Activity Case Studies

Whilst chapter four was interested in whether the prevalence of risk factors and indicators changed over time, this chapter is interested in a different aspect of temporality and risk. More specifically, it is interested in how pre-attack behaviours are sequenced temporally within specific cases. This chapter draws heavily from established conceptual frameworks such as Situational Crime Prevention and Routine Activity Theory, in order to understand the behaviors that have underpinned previous successfully executed lone actor terrorist events. As noted by Horgan (2005:109), it is useful to view each terrorist offence as comprising of a series of stages "almost with a natural history from inception to completion." Through such a process, it may be possible to formulate phase-specific intervention strategies that seek to deter and disrupt future lone actor terrorist plots. In order to illustrate the applicability of routine activity theory to understanding terrorist events, this report provides five routine activity analyses of lone actor terrorist events.

Situational crime prevention (SCP) focuses upon crime events rather than criminality (for a full exploration of SCP in relation to terrorism see Clarke and Newman, 2006 and Freilich and Newman, 2009). Rather than focusing on individual characteristics of the criminal, situational crime prevention attempts to understand the *how* and *what* of crime: from an analysis of the offender to a greater consideration of the social and behavioral qualities of the offense. Though later analyses reduced the more overt emphasis on rational choice theory, such perspectives view offenders as a rational decision maker who evaluates the costs and benefit of committing or disregarding the crime (Carroll & Weaver, 1986; Cornish & Clarke, 1986). It has a specific focus upon the 'near causes' of crime, the situational aspects that make a crime more likely to occur or a potential victim more likely to be victimized. Opportunity therefore is seen to be an important cause of crimes and a focus for prevention. The attractiveness of SCP is that opportunity is often more malleable than an offender's internal disposition. We see SCP every day in relation to counter-terrorism, including target hardening of key buildings, the West Bank barrier, making fertilizer inert and therefore no use in the development of HME and airport security. All of these measures are in place to reduce the likelihood of a terrorist attack, not to prevent or disrupt the adoption of extremist ideologies or to alleviate perceived grievances. It is about the controlling the process of how terrorist attacks may be executed, rather than ameliorating the drivers behind why the attack is being planned in the first place. Rather than focusing upon identifiers of the individual's radicalization or general intelligence capabilities or potential to engage in terrorist activity, SCP approaches are much more interested in factors such as the routine decisions that underpin the actual act of violence.

Using the framework outlined in Horgan (2005), each of five lone actor case studies and two solo terrorist case studies below is disaggregated into four specific stages; (a) decision and search activity, (b) preparation, (c) event execution, and (d) post-event activity and strategic analysis. The decision and search activity phase includes endeavors such as target selection. Targeting is not a random exercise, but rather is usually the result of careful deliberation and can be affected by contemporary political and security climates as well as individual capabilities (Horgan, 2005:111).

The preparation phase addresses the operational, logistical and organizational issues affecting the violent event. Whereas the decision phase sets a broad strategic agenda, the preparation phase covers tactical concerns. Choosing the correct tactic for particular operations may be influenced by a number of issues, including technological feasibility, cost-effectiveness, deterrent value, the post-event image of the individual and his/her motives to wider constituents and supporters, the dangers of unwanted results (e.g. extreme repression by counter-terrorists or the possibility of the wrong people being killed) and the ability to overcome security measures (Dolnik and Bhattacharjee, 2002). The direct manifestation of violence may be a function of the individual's ability to procure or develop different types of weaponry or explosives. From a logistics standpoint, this phase usually sees organizational decision makers choosing individual(s) with the specific skillsets and experience to engage in the event and equipping the individual(s) with the weaponry to do so. With lone actor terrorists, however, the preparation phase may look different because they cannot rely upon routine activities that may be perfected by groups over time or a terrorist group's network of specialized talent. Surveillance of targets, building a bomb, testing the device, procuring weaponry and concealing or hiding physical evidence also fall within this phase. If present, these activities illustrate not only premeditation, but also other facets that concern the temporal and sequential flow of the preparation of a terrorist attack.

The event execution stage is the sole phase that the terrorist plays out in public. It may involve a number of discrete events, such as maintaining security pre-event (e.g. priming an IED in secrecy). Other events include the transport of the individual and/or IED to the location of the planned attack, or in the case of a shooting attack, storage of the offending weapon post-attack. It also includes aspects of decision-making that concern the time of day to commit the offence and considerations of risk and opportunity in the commissioning of a terrorist offence.

The final phase of post-event activity and strategic analysis includes ensuring that the lone actor can escape after the event without being arrested or killed as well as conducting a review of the whole attack. The adaptations present in follow-up attacks may reflect aspects of the offender's strategic analysis.

The case studies elaborated upon below include the attacks attributed to five lone actor terrorists, five mass murderers and two solo terrorists. These cases represent a good mixture of bombings, shootings and alternative attack types. They also represent a good spread of al-Qaeda inspired, left-wing and right-wing causes.

## Lone actor Terrorists

### Mohammed Reza Taheri-Azar

On March 3rd, 2006, Taheri-Azar attempted to 'run over' students attending University of North Carolina (UNC)—Chapel Hill with a vehicle. In total, he injured nine. There were no fatalities.

#### Decision and Search Activity Stage

Taheri-Azar's decision to turn to violence seems largely a response to U.S. foreign policy and developed over the course of two years. His letter of responsibility[6] claimed that "due to the killing of believing men and women under the direction of the United States government, I have decided to take advantage of my presence on United States soil … to take the lives of as many Americans and American sympathizers as I can in order to punish the United States for their immoral actions around the world". He cited religious justification for his actions: "In the Qur'an, Allah states that the believing men and women have permission to murder anyone responsible for the killing of other believing men and women. I know that the Qur'an is a legitimate and authoritative holy scripture

[6] Taheri-Azar left this letter in his apartment for police to find. The contents of which are widely available online.

since it is completely validated by modern science and also mathematically encoded with the number 19 beyond human ability. After extensive contemplation and reflection, I have made the decision to exercise the right of violent retaliation that Allah has given me to the fullest extent to which I am capable at present". Although Taheri-Azar did not manage to cause any fatalities through his attack, according to his letter of responsibility his intention was to "murder citizens and residents of the United States of America ... by running them over with my automobile and stabbing them with a knife if the opportunities are presented to me by Allah".

### Preparation Stage

Taheri-Azar began his preparations for the eventual attack two months prior to the attack. He initially wanted to join the U.S. military in order to use their weapons against a U.S. target. In a letter to a local media outlet following his arrest he stated, "ideally ... I wanted to fly an airplane over Washington, D.C. and drop a nuclear bomb on the city". As a part of this plan, he allegedly twice met Army recruiters at his office and applied to a number of clinical psychology graduate schools to prepare for a position as a fighter pilot. Within a month, this plan was abandoned.

By February of 2006, his second plan involved a shooting attack inside the Lenoir Dining Hall at the UNC—Chapel Hill campus. Taheri-Azar provides two different accounts of why this plan was abandoned. In his letter of responsibility he states that he applied for a permit for a handgun but "the process of receiving a permit for a handgun in this city is highly restricted and out of my reach at the present, most likely due to my foreign nationality". In a letter to local media after his arrest, however, Taheri-Azar states that although he visited a gun store in Raleigh, North Carolina, and obtained the necessary application documents for a gun permit from the Orange County Sheriff's Department in Hillsborough, he changed his mind "about attacking with a gun because they seem to jam very easily," or "malfunction and acquiring one would have attracted attention to me from the FBI in all likelihood".

Taheri-Azar finally decided to engage in a vehicular assault "by running over several people in a concentrated target zone". He also acquired two cans of pepper spray, a five-inch knife, and viewed Navy Seals training videos. All of these actions were geared towards aiding Taheri-Azar in the case of a physical confrontation immediately following the vehicular assault.

Taheri-Azar decided to attack students at the University of North Carolina because it was close to his home. He was also familiar with the location—he graduated from UNC the previous December. Taheri-Azar also chose to time his attack to coincide with lunch in order to maximize the number of potential fatalities and injuries. His letter of responsibility claimed that, "I have chosen the particular location on the University campus as my target since I know there is a high likelihood that I will kill several people before being killed myself or jailed and sent to prison if Allah wills".

Shortly before the attack, Taheri-Azar penned a letter claiming responsibility for the attacks. The day before the attack itself, Taheri-Azar rented a Jeep Cherokee for the specific purpose of using it in the attack. He chose this vehicle because it "runs things over and keeps going".

### Event Execution Stage

Between 11:30am and 11:53am, Taheri-Azar left his apartment and drove toward campus. At 11:53am Taheri-Azaar drove the rented Jeep Cherokee onto UNC Chapel Hill's campus. He drove toward "The Pit", a student hub, and accelerated aiming to hit nearby students. After his first attempt, he made a 90-degree turn around the dining hall and proceeded to try to assault more students. Taheri-Azar drove two more miles, near the University Mall, and then phoned a police dispatcher and turned himself in. Later, Taheri-Azar stated that he turned himself in "to assure the world that I wasn't some insane person who went on a killing rampage suddenly".

### Post-Event Activity and Strategic Analysis

Overall, Taheri-Azar was disappointed in the attack's outcome. He stated disappointment that "there weren't more people in the area". There is little other publicly available information on how Taheri-Azar analyzed his event after the fact.

## Timothy McVeigh

Executed by Timothy James McVeigh, on April 19th 1995, the Oklahoma City Bombing killed 168 people and injured over 500. This remained the deadliest terrorist act on American soil until the events of September 11th, 2001.

### Decision and Search Activity Stage

McVeigh had a long-standing interest in firearms. Trained to shoot by his grandfather from an early age, McVeigh would later consume many gun-related publications, and frequented military stores and gun shows talking to others about weaponry and gun rights. Over time, he became gradually more immersed in the survivalist movement and radical right-wing literature. He read *The Turner Diaries*[7] dozens of times, cajoled others into reading it and began to adopt its message.

In May 1988, McVeigh decided to join the army and participated in U.S. Army basic training at Fort Benning, Georgia. There, McVeigh formed a close bond with two of his later co-conspirators in the attack at Oklahoma City: Terry Nichols and Michael J. Fortier. McVeigh and Nichols, in particular, withdrew from others in their unit. McVeigh's interest in survivalism continued during his time in the army. After being transferred (alongside Nichols and Fortier) to Fort Riley, Kansas, McVeigh rented a storage unit which he stocked with 100 gallons of fresh water, weaponry, ammunition, rations and other supplies.

McVeigh was deployed during Operation Desert Storm. In battle he killed two Iraqi soldiers. In later interviews, McVeigh suggested these killings contributed to his suffering from post-traumatic stress. The underlying reasons behind the war and the depth of power asymmetry in the battle itself bothered him. He also became convinced the

[7] The day of the bombing, McVeigh was arrested. Inside his getaway vehicle, officers found an envelope with slips of paper McVeigh had clipped from books and newspapers. One such slip of paper contained a paragraph from the *Turner Diaries* that read "The real value of our attacks today lies in the psychological impact, not in the immediate casualties."

United Nations was planning to take over the world. Upon returning from Operation Desert Storm, McVeigh became a decorated soldier (Bronze Star, the Army Achievement Medal, the Southwest Asia Service Medal and the Kuwait Liberation Medal). He discharged from the Army in 1991, disillusioned by his failure to join the Army's Special Forces. This in turn led to a growing dislike of the U.S. government. After being discharged, McVeigh became increasingly paranoid that the government intended to take away his rights, especially the right to bear arms. McVeigh's anger toward the government increased following the FBI siege at Ruby Ridge during the summer of 1992, and grew further during the standoff between the U.S. Bureau of Alcohol, Tobacco, Firearms and Explosives (ATF) and the Branch Davidians in Waco, Texas (an event McVeigh drove to and witnessed first-hand). One month after witnessing the fatal raid and fire at Waco (alongside Nichols), McVeigh told Fortier and his wife it was time to act violently against the government.

Prior to the bombing, McVeigh corresponded with a Michigan woman who made the letters available to the FBI after the bombing. One letter reads:

> The people of this nation should have flocked to Waco with their guns and opened fire on the bastards! The streets of Waco should have run red with the blood of the tyrants, oppressors and traitors that have slaughtered our people. Every person responsible for this massacre deserves nothing less than to die. If we want to live in peace, then sometimes we must go to war ... If this is too extreme for you, then bow down, lick the hand of your master like a willing, complacent whore and shut your mouth. Take whatever is dealt to you and your children and do not dare to complain to me about your fate. I do not have the patience to listen to the whining of cowards. There will be future massacres because we allow them to occur (cited in Kaplan, 1997:93)

At McVeigh's trial, the prosecution's opening statement outlined that "Waco really sparked his anger; and as time passed, he became more and more and more outraged at the government, which he held responsible for the deaths.... And he told people that the federal government had intentionally murdered people at Waco.... He described the incident as the government's declaration of war against the American people. He wrote letters declaring that the government had drawn ... 'first blood' ... at Waco; and he predicted there would be a violent revolution against the American government. As he put it, blood would flow in the streets." While on death row, McVeigh confirmed the prosecution's arguments. In a letter to Fox News Correspondent Rita Cosby, McVeigh explains that "foremost, the bombing was a retaliatory strike, a counter attack, for the cumulative raids (and subsequent violence and damage) that federal agents had participated in over the preceding years (including, but not limited to Waco).... This bombing was also meant as a pre-emptive (or proactive) strike against these forces and their command and control centers within the federal building." In a separate letter shown to the *Observer* newspaper, McVeigh stated further that when the "branches of government concluded that the federal government had done nothing fundamentally wrong during the raid ... the system not only failed the victims who died during the siege but also failed the citizens of this country. This failure in effect left the door open for more Wacos." He then "reached the decision to go on the offensive—to put a check on government abuse of power, where others had failed in stopping the federal juggernaut running amok.... Borrowing a page from U.S. foreign policy, I decided to send a message to a government that was becoming increasingly hostile, by bombing a government building and the government employees within that building who represent that government."

### Preparation Stage

McVeigh's plan required more than 5,000 pounds of ammonium nitrate fertilizer, approximately 1,200 pounds of nitro methane racing fuel, 350 pounds of Tovex, and 16 55-gallon drums; this contributed to a total of 7,000 pounds. McVeigh realized this was far too much to assemble on his own, so he persuaded Fortier and Nichols to help him. At some point, McVeigh and Nichols experimented with smaller explosives on Nichols' farm in Michigan. Much of McVeigh's knowledge came from a mail order bomb-making manual entitled *Home Made C4*, which he purchased in the Spring of 1993. According to the prosecution, "This book provides essentially a step-by-step recipe as to how to put together your own fertilizer fuel-based bomb. And the book even provides helpful hints as to where to acquire the various ingredients, the components." The locations where McVeigh eventually purchased ammonium nitrate fertilizer and nitro methane were both suggested in this book.

On September 30th, 1994, McVeigh and Nichols purchased a ton of ammonium nitrate from the McPherson branch of the Mid-Kansas Co-op using the names "Mike Havens" and "Terry Havens." They needed two tons but feared such a large purchase would create suspicion. On October 2nd, McVeigh and Nichols stole explosives from the Martin Marietta Aggregates Rock Quarry in Kansas, near Nichols' home. In total, they stole more than 500 electric blasting caps, seven cases of Tovex explosives (which would later serve as a booster to help ignite the IED's main charge), and 80 spools of shock tube, or ignition cord.[8] Using his real name, McVeigh rented a storage locker in Kingman, Arizona on October 4th, 1994 for the stolen explosives. This was largely funded through McVeigh's actions on the gun show circuit, where he sold anti-government T-shirts, hats, bumper stickers, and guns (often illegally). On October 18th, Nichols bought the second ton of ammonium nitrate using the same pseudonym at the same store as the September 30th purchase. The ammonium nitrate was then kept at a rented storage unit in Herington, Kansas.

Originally, McVeigh wanted to use anhydrous hydrazine, a potent rocket fuel, to mix with the ammonium nitrate fertilizer. After making several calls to chemical companies using a phone card under the alias Daryl Bridges, McVeigh was unable to find a sufficient supply of anhydrous hydrazine at an affordable price. Realizing he could use a different chemical, McVeigh changed his plan to nitro methane, a motor-racing fuel. On October 21st, McVeigh attended a drag race in Dallas, Texas. There he met with Racing Fuels employee Tim Chambers, and asked for fuel so that he and his friends could ride motorcycles back home. McVeigh purchased three fifty-five-gallon drums of nitro methane for between $925 and $2,775 (dependent upon which source is used).

On November 5th, 1994, McVeigh convinced Terry Nichols to rob a gun dealer in Arkansas who had once been a friend of McVeigh. Nichols stole an estimated $60,000 in valuables and weapons from Roger Moore, justified by McVeigh as capital for the bomb

[8] McVeigh later cut the electric blasting caps from the plan because he felt the risk of static electricity accidentally setting off the bomb was too high.

expenses. Nichols stored the stolen guns in a locker in Council Grove, Kansas. Heavily influence by the attack on the J. Edgar Hoover FBI building in Earl Turner's *The Turner Diaries,* McVeigh decided to bomb a government building. Unlike Turner's location in Washington DC, McVeigh wanted to hit the heartland of America. His initial list included possible targets in Arkansas, Missouri, Oklahoma, Arizona, and Texas. Ultimately, he decided on the Alfred P. Murrah Federal Building in Oklahoma City because he understood that it held offices for the ATF, Drug Enforcement Administration, and Secret Service, thereby providing maximum federal government causalities. Additionally he believed the U-shaped glass building would be easily damaged with a bomb placed inside the "U." On December 15th, McVeigh and Fortier set out to Kansas to pick up the stolen guns from the locker in Council Grove. On the way there, they drove through Oklahoma City to scope out the Murrah building and surrounding area for suitable locations for the getaway car.

Now that McVeigh had chosen a location, he needed to choose a day. April 19th was chosen for two reasons. First and foremost, it was exactly two years to the day after the tragic incident at Waco. Secondly, it was exactly 220 years after the "shot heard round the world" at the Battle of Lexington and Concord, the first military battle between the Patriots and the Loyalists in the American Revolutionary War.

McVeigh needed a fake drivers license to rent the Ryder truck, which Michael Fortier's wife, Lori Fortier, helped him laminate. The alias on the license was Robert D. Kling, born April 19, 1972. On April 14, 1995 around 4pm, McVeigh checked into the Dreamland Motel in Junction City, Kansas; he used his real name but gave the Nichols' farm as his address. Since McVeigh was having problems with his current Pontiac station wagon, he decided to purchase a new getaway car. McVeigh purchased a 1977 Mercury Marquis from Tom Manning at the Firestone Service Center for $250 in Junction City, Kansas. McVeigh left Nichols' home address and telephone number on the bill. McVeigh then used his phone card to reserve a twenty-foot Ryder truck from Elliot's Truck Agency. During the phone call, McVeigh stated that he needed a vehicle capable of carrying 5,000 pounds. He used the alias "Bob Kling" for the one-way rental to Omaha, Nebraska. On April 15th, McVeigh completed the requisite paperwork for his truck rental and paid $280.32 in cash. He did not buy insurance. On April 16th, Nichols drove to Oklahoma City to meet McVeigh and help him with the getaway car. McVeigh parked the car in an alley very close to the Murrah Building and placed a sign that said, "Not abandoned. Please do not tow. Will move by April 23 (needs battery and cable)." Then McVeigh rode with Nichols back to Kansas. On April 17th, McVeigh picked up the Ryder truck at 4:20pm, and returned to the motel in Junction City.

On April 18th at 9am, McVeigh drove the truck to the storage unit at Geary Lake, Kansas, where he met Nichols. There the two men set to work creating the bomb. They mixed the nitro methane with each of the fifty-pound bags of ammonium nitrate fertilizer in the 55-gallon drums, using a bathroom scale for measuring. McVeigh placed the barrels in a "T" configuration so that he would not break an axle or flip the truck over. Once everything was mixed, McVeigh began working on the dual-fuse system. He drilled two sets of holes through the cab and the cargo box. Then he ran plastic fish-plank tubing through the holes, creating a two-minute fuse and a five-minute fuse as backup. At the end of each fuse, he placed non-electric blasting caps. He also placed blasting caps onto two lines of shock tube so that when the caps exploded they would instantly spark the Tovex, which was placed in the center drum at the intersection of the T. The bomb took over three hours to construct. At one point, work had to stop because there were passersby. McVeigh then made his way to Oklahoma City, disposing of the clothes he wore while mixing the explosives along the way. He stayed overnight in a roadside motel.

### Event Execution Stage

The bombing occurred the following morning, April 19th. The original plan was for the bomb to detonate at 11am. On the morning of the bombing, McVeigh decided that waiting that long was too risky, so he moved the time forward to 9am. McVeigh felt that by 9am, there would be a requisite number of bystanders who could be killed in the bombing. McVeigh's intention to maximize the number of killings came through in his alleged statement to his defense attorneys that he "would not have gotten the point across to the government" without a heavy casualty toll. At 7am, he left the motel where he had stayed overnight. He entered Oklahoma City at approximately 8:50am. Shortly after, he pulled his truck to the side to ignite the five-minute fuse. A block from the Murrah building, he stopped at a traffic light and lit the two-minute fuse. He accelerated slowly, fearing that sudden movement would prematurely detonate the bomb. The front parking area of the Murrah building was empty so he parked in front of the building, checked the fuses, locked the truck, and walked away.

McVeigh walked about 150 yards before he felt the explosion. The explosion created a crater twenty feet wide and eight feet deep. The bombing killed a total of 168 people: 163 were inside the building during the explosion. At least 500 people were injured.

### Post-Event Activity and Strategic Analysis

McVeigh made it to the Mercury Marquis and was on the road by 9:10am, eight minutes after the bombing. At approximately 10:20am, McVeigh was pulled over 80 miles north of the bombing by trooper Charles Hanger for driving without a license plate. Hanger searched the car and arrested McVeigh for carrying an unregistered gun. McVeigh was held at the Noble County Jail in Perry, Oklahoma. Meanwhile, the police had found the vehicle ID number from the Ryder truck's axle and traced it back to Robert Kling. Two days later, McVeigh was transferred to federal custody on federal bombing charges.

There is very little evidence of McVeigh's post-event strategic analysis. McVeigh's published letters, to a large extent, do not go into much detail about this issue. Operationally, he viewed the bombing as successful. Strategically, he was unsure of the long-lasting impact of the bombing. McVeigh felt that he left his fellow Americans with "the choice to try to learn from me or ... choose to remain ignorant, and suffer the consequences."

## Floyd Lee Corkins

On August 15th 2012, Corkins entered the offices of the conservative lobbying group, the Family Research Council (FRC) with the intention of "killing as many people as I could".[9] Corkins managed to injure a security guard before being overpowered and held at gun-point until the police arrived. A list found on Corkins suggested he also planned to target three other social conservative advocacy groups.

### Decision and Search Activity Stage

The government's sentencing memorandum highlights that Corkins acknowledged that he wanted to engage in violent activism for a long time. His parents told the FBI that he "has strong opinions with respect to those he believes do not treat homosexuals in a fair manner". It is also known that Corkins suffered with mental health issues (including major depressive disorders and psychotic features) throughout his adult life. Six months prior to his violent action, Corkins voluntarily committed himself to a mental hospital because he suffered from hallucinations and "thoughts of killing his parents and conservative right-wing Christians". He left a month later and continued counseling and medication. This is not to suggest however that there is a clear link between this illness and his decision to engage in violence. There are also no publicly available details on what helped transition Corkins from years of thinking about conducting violence, to actually preparing a violent act.

### Preparation Stage

Floyd Lee Corkins originally planned to conduct a bombing attack but told police he "didn't have the patience for it". The vast majority of planning and preparation occurred in the week prior to the attempted attack. On August 7th, while browsing online Corkins identified Blue Ridge Arsenal in Chantilly, Virginia as a suitable location to purchase firearms. On August 9th, Corkins perused for firearms at the Blue Ridge Arsenal. The following day he returned and purchased a semi-automatic pistol and received two-hours of free firearms training. On August 12th, he visited the Southern Poverty Law Center's website and identified the FRC as being anti-gay. He also visited the websites of the FRC and the other three advocacy groups. The FRC's website states that its mission is to "shape the public debate and formulate public policy that values human life and upholds the institutions of marriage and the family". He then printed MapQuest and Google map directions to the FRC and one of the other groups. Upon his later arrest Corkins made various statements like "I don't like the organization and what it stands for" and "I don't like these people, and I don't like what they stand for". On August 13th, he rehearsed the journey to the FRC. In his own words, he was "basically tying to go over exactly what I was gonna do" on the day of the attack. He managed to access the lobby of their office by telling the receptionist he was there to meet an FRC employee and provided a fake name. The receptionist checked the employee directory, failed to find someone with the provided name, informed Corkins and he, in turn, exited the lobby. On August 14th, Corkins visited a branch of Chick-fil-A and bought fifteen chicken sandwiches. He intended to smear these sandwiches in the face of his victims "to make a statement against the people who work in that building … and with their stance against gay rights and Chick-fil-A. They endorse Chick-fil-A and also Chick-fil-A

[9] Cited in the government's sentencing memorandum—http://msnbcmedia.msn.com/i/MSNBC/Sections/NEWS/z-pdf-archive/20130919_Corkins_Sentencing.pdf

came out against gay marriage so I was going to use that as a statement". A Chick-fil-A executive, two months earlier, had expressed his opposition to same-sex marriage. Later that day, Corkins purchased a black backpack at K-mart that was eventually used to conceal his firearm and ammunition on the day of the attack. On the evening of August 14th, Corkins returned to the Blue Ridge Arsenal and purchased and took part in another two hours of firearms training with the weapon he purchased days earlier. Later that night, he loaded three magazines for the violent event he planned to conduct the following day.

### Event Execution Stage

On the morning of August 15th, Corkins drove his family's car from his hometown of Herndon, Virginia to the East Falls Church Metro Station. There, he took the Metro into the District of Columbia. After departing the Gallery Place Metro stop, he loaded the Sig Sauer P229 semiautomatic he purchased six days prior. He then walked to the FRC's headquarters, arriving at 10.46am. He gained access to the building claiming to be there for an interview for an internship. Upon entering the building, an unarmed security guard seated at reception asked to see Corkins' identification. Corkins pulled a handgun from his backpack and pointed it at the security guard. The security guard rushed at Corkins and in the ensuing struggle Corkins shot three times, one of which hit the guard's arm. Despite this injury, the guard managed to overpower and subdue Corkins until the Metropolitan Police Department arrived. The police searched Corkins and found two fully loaded magazine clips, 50 rounds of 9mm ammunition, 15 Chik-fil-A chicken sandwiches and a handwritten list including the names of four organizations including the FRC that Corkins previously researched online.

### Post-Event Activity and Strategic Analysis

There is no publicly available information with regards to this stage.

## Abdulhakim Mujahid Muhammad

At 10.19am on June 1st 2009, Abdulhakim Mujahid Muhammad (formerly Carlos Bledsoe) conducted a drive-by shooting on soldiers outside of a U.S. military recruitment office in Little Rock, Arkansas, killing one and injuring one.

### Decision and Search Activity Stage

Muhammad acknowledges membership in a gang prior to his conversion to Islam in 2004 (http://www.commercialappeal.com/jihad/competency-evaluation/). He left school at 12th grade and experienced a number of suspensions previously because of fighting. Gartenstein-Ross' (2014) in-depth case study of Muhammad utilized police and court records that illustrated how Muhammad had previously come into contact with authorities in relation to (1) a 2002 fight with another former gang member (2) a 2002 altercation that involved a knife being pulled (3) a 2003 car crash to which Muhammad reacted by first running to the other driver's vehicle and "hitting the rear passenger window with chrome-plated brass knuckles. Muhammad yelled, 'Bitch I'm gonna kill you, get out, I'm going to kill you when I get your address" (Gartenstein-Ross, 2014:113) (4) a 2004 incident in which police found Muhammad in a car alongside a SKS assault rifle and a single-shot shotgun that Muhammad claimed he was selling to an individual who successfully fled from police. He was also found in possession of a bag of marijuana. All of these events occurred before he turned 20. He converted to Islam soon after being charged and receiving a 14-year suspended sentence for the unlawful weapons and drug possession offence.

In his justification statement, Muhammad states: "There's an all out war against Islam and Muslims in Afghanistan, Pakistan, Waziristan, Chechnya, Somalia, Palestine, Phillipines, Yemen etc. And Muslims have to fight back ... We believe in an eye for eye not turn the other cheek. Now it's all out war on American and I'm on the other side. The side of the Muslims—Yes! The side of Al-Qaeda—Yes! Taliban- Yes! Al-Shabaab—Yes! We are all brothers under the same banner. Fighting for the same cause which is to rid the Islamic world of Infidel and Apostate Hypocritic [sic] regimes and Crusader Invaders and re-establish the Caliphate, the Islamic Empire and Islamic Law as was ended officially in 1924 by the fall of the Ottomans" (cited in Gartenstein-Ross, 2014:118). Here, Muhammad not only aligns with and portrays himself as being the same as Al-Qaeda, the Taliban and Al-Shabaab, he also places himself in a long historical narrative of resistance that has been ongoing since 1924.

In September 2007, he left the U.S. for Yemen ostensibly to learn Arabic. During this time, he apparently radicalized further. He desired entry into Somalia to obtain militant training. Before he could leave, Yemeni authorities arrested him in October 2008. He returned to the U.S and to his hometown of Little Rock in January 2009.

### Preparation Stage

Upon his return to the U.S., Muhammad began planning an attack. He researched potential targets online including military facilities, Jewish centers, a post office, a Baptist church and a childcare center. These targets were geographically spread and included Little Rock, Memphis, Nashville, Florence, Kentucky, Philadelphia, Baltimore and Washington D.C

He claims the eventual attack "wasn't part of Plan A. Plan A was aborted because of failed attacks in Tennessee and Kentucky". In Nashville Tennessee, his attempt to firebomb a Rabbi's house failed when the Molotov Cocktail bounced harmlessly off the window rather than smashing through it. In Florence, Kentucky a drive-by shooting at an Army recruitment center was called off when he realized it was closed as he arrived.

So, the eventual attack at "the Crusader Center in Little Rock was Plan B. And compared to what I had planned originally, it was like a grain of sand. One crusader dead, one wounded, 15 terrorized, big deal. Nidal Malik is the real Islamic Warrior, and my plan A was on that scale. It included Little Rock, Memphis, Nashville, Florence KY, Philadelphia, Baltimore, and was supposed to end in DC." He also lamented his failure to obtain bomb-making training in Yemen or Somalia. "I wanted training in explosives, on how to make bombs and in particular, car bombs, and had I got this training my story would have ended a lot differently than it's going to end now. My drive-by would have been a drive-in, with none escaping the aftermath"[10].

He bought a series of firearms second-hand. Finally, he bought a .22 rifle "over the counter at Wal-Mart to test if I'd get caught or questioned". It was a "test to see if I was under surveillance". Once the new gun was purchased, he thought to himself "It's on ... Meaning, I'm not under surveillance. The FBI had not put a hold or checked" (http://www.commercialappeal.com/jihad/competency-evaluation/).

The night before his attack, he watched a number of jihadist videos online. Muhammad attributed one particular video as the sole reason for his shooting. "I started seeing more pictures of just women being raped you know, gang raped and you know it's one woman named Fatima, she's in a prison so she got raped more than nine times on one day and she was wanting to kill herself and you know it was just—it was a point of insanity, I ... I think is what happened and I just like blacked out you know. And ... and I just kind of went insane all of a sudden". This is a highly unlikely scenario given the extensive planning it took to become as equipped with firearms as Muhammad became.

### Event Execution Stage

On the morning of June 1st, Muhammad drove to the recruitment center at Little Rock and fired a semi-automatic rifle at two individuals having a cigarette outside the center. He shot both and continued firing at the center, hoping to hit at least some of the 15 individuals located inside. Muhammad fled the scene in his vehicle. Police apprehended him eight miles from the attack location. He was in possession of two rifles (one with a scope and laser sight), two handguns (one semi-automatic), 562 rounds of ammunition, homemade sound suppressors, and binoculars. Police also found Molotov Cocktails in his home.

### Post-Event Activity and Strategic Analysis

There is no publicly available information with regards to this stage. However, following his arrest, Muhammad's violence continued in jail. On one occasion he stabbed a fellow inmate, on another occasion the victim was a prison guard. He used a shank both times. Muhammad has also been associated with a number of threats against prison staff and repeatedly vandalizing his cell.

## Eric Rudolph

On July 26th 1996, Eric Rudolph committed a bombing attack at the 1996 Atlanta Olympics. The bombing killed one civilian and injured a 111.

### Decision and Search Activity Stage

Over the course of 18 months, Rudolph bombed two abortion clinics, the Atlanta Olympics and a lesbian bar. He carried out all of the planning, preparation and actions

[10] Scanned copies of these Muhammad's correspondence with Katrina Goetz can be found at http://www.commercialappeal.com/jihad/

alone. Yet, in his numerous writings throughout the bombing campaign, during his sentencing and while in prison, Rudolph depicts himself as part of a wider movement of anti-abortion activists. As noted by Seegmiller (2007), between 1973 (when abortion was legalized in the U.S.) and 2007, over 200 abortion clinics were bombed or set on fire and over 4000 acts of violence were carried out or threatened against abortion providers. Rudolph sees himself as just one component of what is a wider movement of committed action. He "frames his activism and identity as connected to an amorphous milieu of violent, radical anti-abortion activists who largely draw upon religious authority, biblical language, and apocalyptic narratives to frame and justify their activities" (Seegmiller, 2007: 521). Indeed, Rudolph's writings are hosted on the Army of God website including his 240 page autobiography which suggests they view him as one of their own also. The autobiography states that Rudolph's goal was to overthrow an illegitimate government but he acknowledges "Naturally, I couldn't do it alone. I had no delusions on that score. I had to somehow encourage others to help ... The hope was that my actions would push other pro-lifers and Patriots to bridge the gap between their rhetoric and their actions" (Rudolph, 2013:5-6). Rudolph had also grown quite skeptical of how effective the pro-life movement had become while it remained on a non-violent course. "The masters of the media have censored the pro-life movement out of the mainstream society. The protestors ... might as well be on the moon as far as most Americans are concerned. I was planning my own protest for the anniversary of Roe v. Wade. Unlike other protests, mine wouldn't be ignored. I planned to blow Northside Family Planning off the map" (Rudolph, 2013:27).

During the Spring of 1995, Rudolph decided to turn to violence. He decided to "carry out a series of high profile attacks against symbols of the regime: abortion mills, Sodomite organizations, left-wing interest groups, and agents of the Washington government ... These attacks were not part of some personal vendetta against abortionists, homosexuals, or government agents; they were acts of war aimed at damaging, undermining and ultimately, overthrowing the liberal establishment in America. When I heard they were bringing the Summer Olympics to Atlanta, I thought it would make the perfect target" (Rudolph, 2013:6).

On the Atlanta Olympics bombing, Rudolph's justification states:

> "In the summer of 1996, the world converged upon Atlanta for the Olympic Games. Under the protection and auspices of the regime in Washington millions of people came to celebrate the ideals of global socialism/Multinational corporations spent billions of dollars, and Washington organized an army of security to protect these best of all games. Even though the conception and purpose of the so-called Olympic movement is to promote the values of global socialism, as perfectly expressed in the song Imagine by John Lennon, which was the theme of the 1996 Games even though the purpose of the Olympics is to promote these ideals, the purpose of the attack on July 27 was to confound, anger and embarrass the Washington government in the eyes of the world for its abominable sanctioning of abortion on demand. The plan was to force the cancellation of the Games, or at least create a state of insecurity to empty the streets around the venues and thereby eat into the vast amounts of money invested."

The decision to act alone was simple. He outlined that he had "been around long enough to know the pitfalls of collaboration" (Rudolph, 2013:6). He later lamented the lack of help during his fourth bombing (the one that led to his capture): "Oh, how easy it would be if I had a partner ... Though working alone had its advantages, namely, there was nobody to rat me out, it also made a quick execution and getaway more difficult" (Rudolph, 2013:42). It also appears he was inspired by other lone actors. In his autobiography, Rudolph begins the Olympics bombing chapter with two paragraphs telling the story of Paul Hill. For Rudolph, Hill "seemed like a perfect anomaly, a genuine American hero in an age of cowardice. I'd read about such people in history books, but I didn't think they existed anymore. I knew then that the era of hot air was over. People were finally bridging the gap between their rhetoric and their actions. I knew then it was time for me to act as well" (Rudolph, 2013:3).

### Preparation Stage

In June 1996, Rudolph left his hometown and rented a trailer forty miles west. Rudolph initially wanted to bomb Atlanta's power grid during the Olympics rather than place a bomb at the Olympics itself. He dropped this plan because "making enough charges to disable Atlanta's power grid would take too much time and money. I had neither. The Olympics was fast approaching, and I needed to come up with a new plan" (Rudolph, 2013:7). Instead he turned to smaller pipe bombs. Rudolph "drove 100 miles to Gadsden, Alabama, where I bought pipes, alarm clocks, batteries, and circuit wire. Then I drove a little more, hoping to make my activities hard to track" (Rudolph, 2013:7). In total, he spent six weeks manufacturing and testing his IEDs. During this time Rudolph feared that his landlady, who searched his trailer on a number of occasions, could have rumbled his preparations. The opportunity to test these IEDs in the "remote hollows along the North Carolina-Tennessess border" undoubtedly helped Rudolph's plot develop from a technical standpoint (Rudolph, 2013:7).

A couple weeks prior to the eventual bombing, Rudolph surveilled security at the Olympics. For this task, he wore a light disguise. He noticed "there were no metal detectors, and bags were searched selectively. After sundown the crowds grew enormous. Upwards of a hundred thousand people packed into Five Points. Security at the park became overwhelmed. They stopped searching bags altogether, and the entrances flew wide open. I knew then that I could smuggle in a bomb" (Rudolph. 2013:10).

Rudolph pushed back the date of his initial IED attack on the Atlanta Olympics when his truck was broken into and a window was smashed in the process. Rudolph feared police pulling him over for the broken window so he fixed it before he could use the truck to transport his pipe bombs to the target site (Rudolph, 2013:11).

Rudolph also slept rough the nights before the bombing hoping to avoid the CCTVs installed at hotels.

Rudolph's last task before setting off to bomb the Atlanta Olympics was to bury an emergency cache in the woods that contained enough food, oil and camping equipment to allow him to survive for a year.

### Event Execution Stage

On the night of the bombing itself, a third-party took a picture of a water fountain at the Olympic Park. Rudolph was convinced he also was in the picture and in his autobiography admits that this was enough to engender "several tense moments of indecision" and the "strong urge to flee" without priming and detonating the IED (Rudolph, 2013:13-14). Rudolph claims the plan was to disrupt the Olympics, not for the bomb to detonate. After priming the device, he sought to leave a warning with police from a pay phone. Rudolph notes: "Quickly, I stuffed each nostril with wet toilet tissue and slipped on my pair of gloves and pulled a little plastic funnel from my pocket. The tissue and funnel should help distort my voice. 'Atlanta—nine—one—one' said the woman operator. 'Do you understand me?' I asked. 'Yah'. 'We defy your ...' suddenly the line went dead". Rudolph's attempt to provide a justification alongside the warning failed. Rudolph then left that scene and found another set of payphones close by "but the street was packed with people. Groups of tourists shuffled past me. I waited. Agonizing minutes were wasted. A break in the crowd developed. I faced the other way and found a phone. 'Make it quick; just a flat warning; no statement' I told myself" (Rudolph, 2013:14). Without leaving the justificatory message, Rudolph acknowledges that the bombing "sent the wrong message. Aimed at Washington and the corporate sponsors, the bombing came off as an indiscriminate attack on innocent civilians. I would see to it that never happened again. From now on I'd choose specific targets" (Rudolph, 2013:21).

### Post-Event Activity and Strategic Analysis

In his sentencing remarks for the Olympics bombing and in his autobiography, Rudolph refers to the victims as "innocent civilians" and that he felt "much remorse" because of the "fatal decision", "horrible mistake" and "dangerous tactic" of planting the bomb in a crowded area, calling in an advanced bomb warning, and hoping that the area would be cleared of civilians.

This 'mistake' did not dissuade Rudolph from violent action however. In the months preceding the Atlanta bombing, Rudolph also bombed two abortion clinics and a lesbian bar (which reflects with his theorizing that only specific targets should be hit in order for the violence not to be message-less like the Olympics bombing). The second abortion clinic bombing killed a security guard and critically injured a nurse. In his sentencing remarks for the abortion clinic fatalities, Rudolph commented "I did not target them for who they were—but for what they did. What they did was participate in the murder and dismemberment of upwards of 50 children a week". In Rudolph's eyes, these were legitimate targets.

Rudolph gave up on producing enough explosives for the main charge of his later IED attacks, stating that the effort was "not worth the cost in time, money and brain cells" (Rudolph, 2013:22). Instead, he turned to stealing commercial explosives from quarries and an explosives manufacturer.

### Scripting Lone actor Terrorist Events

Figure 5.1 below outlines a diagram of the lone actor terrorist event script. It highlights the complexity of the first two stages, particularly the preparation phase.

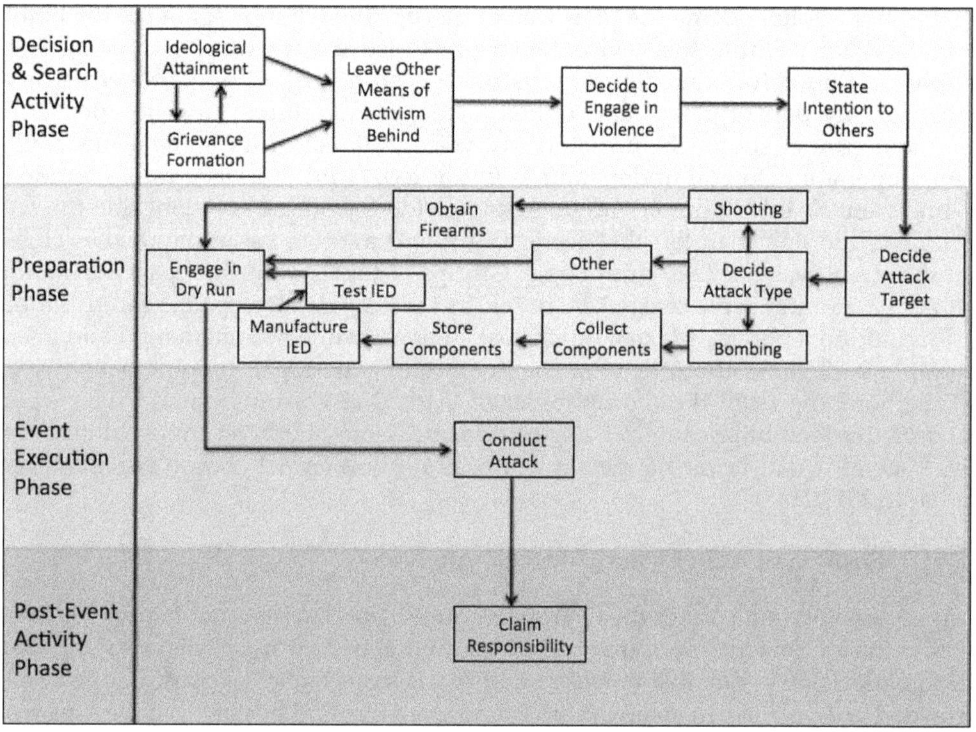


**Figure 5.1 Lone Actor Attack Script**

## Solo Terrorists

### Faisal Shahzad

On the evening of May 1, 2010, Faisal Shahzad, a 30 year-old U.S. citizen, drove an SUV rigged with an improvised explosive device (IED) into a still-crowded Times Square in New York City. He parked the vehicle, activated the bomb, and walked away. Police were alerted, the IED was safely dismantled, and there were no casualties.

#### Decision and Search Activity Stage

Born in Pakistan in 1979; his father is a retired Pakistani Air Force official who provided an upper middle-class lifestyle for his family, with chauffeurs and servants.

In January 1999, Shahzad was granted a student visa and came to the U.S., enrolling in college in Washington, D.C., and later transferring to the University of Bridgeport in Connecticut, from which he graduated with a Bachelor's degree in computer science.

In April, 2002, Shahzad received another three-year visa, and he started graduate studies at the University of Bridgeport. Here Shahzad worked toward an MBA alongside working in accounting at the global cosmetics firm Elizabeth Arden. Upon graduating Shahzad found work as an analyst at the financial marketing firm Affinion Group. During this time, Shahzad bought and sold a condominium in Norwalk, Connecticut and then bought a house in Shelton, Connecticut. In 2004, Shahzad married Huma Mian, a 23 year-old accountant from Denver, Colorado.

By 2006, friends noticed that Shahzad became more religious and distanced himself from what he considered the liberal 'elite' world of his father. He stopped drinking alcohol, prayed five times a day, and began frequenting Mosques in Stamford, Norwalk, and Bridgeport. In February 2006, Shahzad's ideological fervor was more open noticeable. In an email to a group of friends, Shahzad's distress regarding the wars in Iraq and Afghanistan, and the publication in Denmark of cartoons ridiculing the Prophet Mohammed was clearly evident:

> "It is with no doubt that we today Muslim, followers of Islam are attacked and occupied by foreign infidel forces. The crusade has already started against Islam and Muslims with cartoons of our beloved Prophet PBUH as War drums … Everyone knows how the Muslim country bows down to pressure from west [sic]. Everyone knows the kind of humiliation we are faced with around the globe."

In other e-mail messages, Shahzad argued that the West is at war with Islam, and that Muslims have strayed from their religious duty to fight back. The Internet messages of Anwar al-Awlaki reportedly inspired his devout, radical behaviors. During a visit to Pakistan in 2008, Shahzad asked his father for permission to fight in Afghanistan, a request his father denied.

In an April 2009 ceremony at the federal courthouse in Bridgeport, Connecticut, Shahzad became a U.S. citizen. It was around this time that Shahzad appeared to be struggling financially, complaining to a friend that he found it stressful to keep up with mortgage payments. Others noticed strains in his marriage. He pressured his wife to wear a hijab, and insisted that she should not work, despite their financial issues. In February 2009, Shahzad obtained a $65,000 equity loan. In June, Shahzad stopped paying his mortgage and other bills, and on 2nd June, 2009, he and his family left the U.S.

### Preparation Stage

After departing the U.S. for his hometown in Pakistan, Shahzad abruptly left his family on 9th December, 2009, and travelled to Taliban training camps in North Waziristan where he received bomb-making training from trainers affiliated with Tehrik-e-Taliban. It was during this time the plot was devised. Shahzad also met with a member of Lashkar-e-Taiba, the group responsible for the attacks on the Indian city of Mumbai in 2008. Shahzad requested money from Tehrik-e-Taliban, and received $4,000. Shahzad later claimed to have met with Taliban leader Hakimullan Mehsud and that the attack on Times Square was retribution for Mehsud's death in a drone strike.

On February 2nd 2010, Shahzad returned to the U.S. on a one-way ticket from Pakistan. Due to the recent "underwear bomber" scare in December 2009, he was subjected to extra screening by U.S. Customs. During this conversation, Shahzad stated to officials that he had been in Pakistan for five months, and he indicated that he intended to stay at a hotel in Connecticut whilst he arranged for more permanent work and living arrangements. Shahzad provided a telephone number (which belonged to a pre-paid mobile that was activated on 16th April 2010). Shahzad then spent three weeks looking for more permanent accommodation, where he could have privacy to carry out the preparation.

Shahzad received two monetary donations from a member of Tehrik-e-Taliban during the preparation stage. The first occurred on 25th February, 2010. Shahzad received $5,000 in cash in Massachusetts. The second occurred on 10th April, 2010, in Ronkonkoma, New York, and totaled $7,000. Shahzad admitted that these donations were for purchasing the components for the attack.

On 15th March, 2010, Shahzad purchased a semi-automatic 9 millimeter Kel-Tec rifle in Connecticut.

In mid-April, Shahzad used the pre-paid mobile to approach an individual selling a 1993 Nissan Pathfinder. During the initial conversation Shahzad arranged to meet with the seller on 24th April in a Supermarket car park in Connecticut. The pre-paid mobile was contacted four times on the morning on 24th April, 2010, by a number in Pakistan. These phone calls highlight the extent to which Shahzad acted under direction of a larger group. It was after these calls were made that Shahzad rang the seller of the Pathfinder twice. Shahzad met with the seller, and purchased the vehicle for $1,300 using cash on the afternoon of 24th April 2010. Shahzad changed the registration plates, and tinted the windows following the transaction. On 25th April 2010, Shahzad again used the mobile to contact a fireworks store on Pennsylvania. These calls were all made prior to 28th April 2010, when the phone was cut off.

During April, 2010, Shahzad also purchased the various constituent parts of the IED, and used a garage at his residence to store them. Shahzad also reportedly carried out a dry run in the Pathfinder on 28th April, 2010, driving around to seek out the most appropriate place for the event.

### Event Execution Stage

The IED consisted of three full propane tanks, two five-gallon gasoline canisters, several plastic bags containing fertilizer, 152 M-88 fireworks, and two alarm clocks connected to wiring.

Shahzad drove from Connecticut to New York on 1st May 2010. At 18:30 UTC, he attempted to detonate the IED in the Nissan Pathfinder vehicle at 45th Street and Seventh Avenue in Manhattan. He initiated the device, left the engine on, and walked to Grand Central Station, catching a train to Connecticut.

### Post Event Activity and Strategic Analysis

A member of the public informed a mounted police officer of the presence of the unoccupied Pathfinder. When the officer approached the car, he observed smoke emanating from it, and he summoned assistance. The entire area was evacuated, and the NYPD bomb squad and fire department responded to the scene. When law enforcement officers searched the Pathfinder, a number of keys were recovered, including the key to an Isuzu Rodeo vehicle, and his Connecticut residence.

A video was posted online on 2nd May 2010. This video showed Shahzad explaining his reasoning behind his decision to act. It was narrated by Qari Hussain Mehsud, a chief bomb maker, and claimed that the Taliban in Pakistan was responsible for the attack. Two subsequent follow up videos were also posted on 3rd May 2010, showing meetings between Shahzad and Hakimullah Mehsud, and threatened further attacks against the U.S. and NATO allies.

Shahzad was arrested on May 3rd 2010 at 23:45 UTC at John F. Kennedy International Airport, as he attempted to leave the U.S. on a flight to Dubai. Subsequent to his arrest, Shahzad admitted to officers that he had attempted to detonate the device in Times Square, he had received training in Waziristan and Pakistan, and that he had driven a car to the airport on 3rd May, 2010, and that there was a gun in this car. Officer's recovered this car on 4th May, 2010, and found the Kel-Tec rifle.

During detention, Shahzad repeatedly waived his Miranda rights. He provided agents with details regarding ongoing movements of subjects of investigation, which led to arrests. He also admitted that had he not been arrested, he would have detonated another bomb in New York City two weeks later. Shahzad was indicted in federal court; an excerpt of his underlying intentions is given below:

> THE COURT: "Last year. Didn't you swear allegiance to this country when you became an American citizen?"
>
> SHAHZAD: "I did swear, but I did not mean it."
>
> THE COURT: "I see. You took a false oath?"
>
> SHAHZAD: "Yes."
>
> THE COURT: "Very well. Is there anything else you want to tell me?"
>
> SHAHZAD: "Sure. I am ashamed that I belong to a slave country like Pakistan, who has accepted the slavery of the West from the day it was born. Bush had made already clear when he started the war on us, on Muslims, he said: You are either with us or against us. And so it's very clear for us Muslims, either we are with the mujahideen or we are with crusading losing Christians. There is no in between. Blessed be the immigrants and the leader Sheikh Osama Bin Laden, who will be known as no less than Saladin of the 21 century crusade and blessed be those who give him asylum."

On 21st June, 2010, Shahzad pled guilty to all charges, and was sentenced to life in prison. He repeatedly expressed his total lack of remorse, and his desire to repeat the crime, if he were given the opportunity.

At his sentencing hearing on 5th October, 2010, Shahzad requested to make a speech prior to any decision. This was granted:

> "In the name of Allah, the most gracious, the most merciful, this is but one life. If I am given a thousand lives, I will sacrifice them all for the sake of Allah fighting this cause, defending our lands, making the word of Allah supreme over any religion or system. We Muslims don't abide by human-made laws, because they are always corrupt ... The sentence the judge will not mean anything to me, for how can I be judged when the Court does not understand the suffering of my people. They don't understand my side of the story, where the Muslim life of is no value. Therefore, the only true judgment will be on the day of resurrection when Allah

> will judge between me and you as to who is fighting for the just cause. So decree whatever you desire to decree, for you can only decree regarding the life of this world. The crusading U.S. and NATO forces who have occupied the Muslim lands under the pretext of democracy and freedom for the last nine years and are saying with their mouths that they are fighting terrorism, I say to them, we don't accept your democracy nor your freedom, because we already have Sharia law and freedom. Furthermore, brace yourselves, because the war with Muslims has just begun. Consider me only a first droplet of the flood that will follow me ... So let's see how you can defeat your Creator, which you can never do. Therefore, the defeat of U.S. is imminent and will happen in the near future, inshallah, which will only give rise to much awaited Muslim caliphate, which is the only true universal world order ... We are only Muslims trying to defend our religion, people, honor, and land. But if you call us terrorists for doing that, then we are proud terrorists, and we will keep on terrorizing until you leave our land and people at peace. But if you don't, then I remind you that we have watches and we have time. We will defeat you with time."

### Umar Farouk Abdulmutallab

On 25th December 2009, Abdulmutallab boarded Northwest Airlines Flight 253 from Amsterdam to Detroit. He ignited an incendiary device shortly before arrival in Detroit in an attempt to destroy the plane, and 289 individuals on board. There were no fatalities or serious injuries.

#### Decision and Search Activity Stage

Abdulmutallab reportedly became very pious in his religion during his teenage years in Nigeria. He spent his free time reading the Quran, and earned the nickname "Alfa ". Over 300 Internet postings under the handle "farouk1986" were identified. Abdulmutallab spoke of love, his future ambitions, and his inner struggle between liberalism and extremist as a devout Muslim. In January 2005, Abdulmutallab confessed:

> "I am in a situation where I do not have a friend. I have no one to speak too, no one to consult, no one to support me and I feel depressed and lonely. I do not know what to do and then I think this loneliness leads me to other problems ... I get lonely sometimes because I have never found a true Muslim friend".

Abdulmutallab's postings display his gradual ideological changes towards more devout Islamic opinions and practices, and display his views of violence and extremism, without specific mention of his own choice to follow such behaviors.

However, when Abdulmutallab enrolled in mechanical engineering at University College London in September 2005, his religious beliefs began attracting attention. Abdulmutallab became head of the campus branch of the Islamic Society in 2006, inviting controversial speakers, and former Guantanamo Bay inmates to attend functions. He regularly attended prayers at London Mosques monitored by the British security services. He was seen 'reaching out' to known extremists, and was noted as being 'on the periphery' of various investigations. He was not, however, considered a threat by British counterintelligence.

In June 2008 Abdulmutallab graduated and was granted a multiple entry tourist visa to the United States (U.S.). In January 2009, Abdulmutallab enrolled at the University of Wollongong, Dubai to study a business course. In August 2009, Abdulmutallab dropped out and travelled to Yemen, studying at the Sana's Institute for Arabic Language. At this time Abdulmutallab attempted to return to England, but his student visa request was refused. Abdulmutallab later explained that he travelled to Yemen to meet radical Imam Anwar al-Awlaki, after studying his preachings. Whilst attending a Mosque in Yemen, Abdulmutallab was introduced to 'Abu-Tarak', who was allegedly a member of Al-Qaeda, and during daily discussions, they discussed various ways to attack the U.S. In October 2009, Abdulmutallab travelled to the Shabwa Province, and attended an Al-Qaeda training camp, purportedly under the direction of al-Awlaki. In November 2009, Abdulmutallab agreed to become involved in an aerial martyrdom attack against the U.S. It was also during this time that Abdulmutallab contacted his parents, and hinted at his involvement in a movement. His father contacted CIA officials at the United States embassy in Nigeria, expressing concerns for his son.

### Preparation Stage

Abdulmutallab claimed to have met the bomb maker, a Saudi Arabian individual, whilst in Yemen. The device, consisting of Pentaerythritol Tetranitrate (PEIN) and Triacetone Triperoxide (TATP), weighed approximately 200g. The device had no metal parts, and therefore would not alert airport security. Detonation was to be achieved by injecting liquid acid into the PEIN and TATP at a time of choosing. The device was designed to be part of Abdulmutallab's underwear. Prior to leaving Yemen, Abdulmutallab recorded a video. The video showed Abdulmutallab at a desert training camp shooting at targets including a Jewish star, the British Union Jack flag, and the initials "UN". Abdulmutallab's statement was only a portion of the video:

> "Oh, ye who believe, take not the Jews and the Christians for your allies and protectors. They are but allies and protectors to each other and he amongst you that turns to them is of them. Verily, Allah guides not a wrongdoing people ... My Muslim brothers in the Arabian Peninsula, you have to answer the call of jihad because the enemy is in your land along with their Jewish and Christian armies. Allah, the most high ... unless you go forth ... He [Allah] will punish you with a grievous penalty and put others in your place. But him ... you would not harm in the least."

Abdulmutallab was instructed to destroy a U.S. aircraft over U.S. territory, however he was given complete control over which airliner, and which flight. This highlights that he networked with others in an organization, yet acted alone. In December 2009, Abdulmutallab left Yemen, and flew then to Ghana, then Nigeria, then Amsterdam. Abdulmutallab wore the device in his underwear continuously from leaving Yemen. In the Netherlands, Abdulmutallab boarded Northwest Airlines flight 253 to Detroit on 25th December 2009. Abdulmutallab had attempted to book onto flights to Houston, Chicago, and California, and told travel agencies numerous false scenarios in order to secure a flight. Whilst passing through U.S. preclearance Abdulmutallab provided false information and details to customs officers. When Abdulmutallab boarded the plane, he engaged in rituals, he fasted and spent an extended period of time in the airplane toilet, purifying himself.

### Event Execution Stage

Abdulmutallab returned to his seat, explained to his neighboring passenger that he felt unwell, and covered himself with a blanket. At 11:44 EDT, Abdulmutallab pressed a button to detonate the device. Several passengers reported hearing a loud pop, which reportedly sounded like a firecracker. The TATP in the device did explode, but the PETN failed to ignite, the result of which was a small fire, which engulfed Abdulmutallab's groin area, and spread to the carpet, walls, and seat. Passengers restrained Abdulmutallab, and removed him from seat 19A (a window seat on the wing), walked him down the plane, and placed him in seat 1G, where he could be monitored. Abdulmutallab's clothing and shoes were removed, and he was given a blanket to cover himself with. The captain was informed of a fire, and brought Flight 253 into a steep descent, and landed the plane at 11:49 EDT.

### Post Event Activity and Strategic Analysis

Whilst the plane was being brought into Detroit airport, Abdulmutallab spoke to a passenger and a steward who sat with him to ensure he would carry out no further disruption. Abdulmutallab explained that he had triggered an explosive device on his person. Abdulmutallab proceeds to tell each individual he came into contact with what his actions were. The conversation with the U.S. customs officer is detailed below:

Officer Steigerwald: "What is going on? What were your intentions on the flight?"

Abdulmutallab: "To bring down the airplane."

Officer Steigerwald: "Who are you involved with?"

Abdulmutallab: "Al-Qaeda."

Officer Steigerwald: "Where did you get the device?"

Abdulmutallab: "Yemen, in the Middle East."

Officer Steigerwald: "Who are you involved with?"

Abdulmutallab: "I'm with al-Qaeda."

Officer Steigerwald: "What kind of device was it?"

Abdulmutallab: "A bomb."

Officer Steigerwald: "What were your intentions?"

Abdulmutallab: "To bring the plane down over U.S. soil."

Officer Steigerwald: "Where did you have the device?"

Abdulmutallab: "In my underwear."

Abdulmutallab is then transported to the University of Michigan Hospital, during transportation he has a conversation with a paramedic:

Jessica Worsley: "Where's that powder from?"

Abdulmutallab: "There was a syringe and they told me to push the syringe in the stitching of my clothing"

Jessica Worsley: "Who is they?" ... "Were you trying to commit suicide or harm yourself?"

Abdulmutallab: "Yes"

Abdulmutallab arrives at the Hospital at 12:25 EDT. A conversation Abdulmutallab had with a nurse between 14:30 and 15:00 EDT was also recorded:

> Julia Longenecker: "Have you ever thought about harming yourself or others?"
>
> Abdulmutallab: "No"
>
> Julia Longenecker: "Well, what about what happened on the plane today? Didn't you try to harm yourself or others?"
>
> Abdulmutallab: "That was martyrdom."

At the hospital, Abdulmutallab has a converses with Dr. James Pribble. He describes how the bomb worked, and that he injected a syringe into powder, and it triggered the explosion. Abdulmutallab also requested that Christmas music playing throughout the hospital to be turned off.

At 15:35 EDT, when Abdulmutallab had been sufficiently treated at the Hospital, two FBI agents, Special Agent Peissig, and Timothy Waters interviewed him. The interview lasted between 45 and 50 minutes, during which Abdulmutallab explained the entire plot. Abdulmutallab told the agents that he went to Yemen in order to become involved in the jihad against the U.S. He explained that he tracked down and found Al-Qaeda, he explained his introduction to Abu-Tarak, and their daily conversations regarding plans to attack the U.S. Abdulmutallab went on to explain how the suggestion to target a U.S. plane was put into action. He spoke at length of meeting with the Saudi Arabian bomb maker, and the engineering behind the device. Abdulmutallab then detailed his travel from Yemen to the U.S.

The martyrdom video—titled "America and the Final Trap"—that Abdulmutallab recorded prior to leaving Yemen was released following the attack. In the video, Al-Qaeda claimed responsibility for the attack, explaining how the bomb defeated Western airport security, and why Abdulmutallab turned to jihad.

During forensic testing of what remained of the device, officials found fingerprints on the underside of the tape that held the bomb together. The fingerprints were not Abdulmutallab's, and it was concluded they were left by another individual who assembled the device. This corroborates Abdulmutallab's statements regarding the Saudi Arabian bomb maker. Forensic experts also found an encryption code for communication with Al Qaeda written on a slip of paper, in Abdulmutallab's shoe. It was purported that Abdulmutallab used this encryption code to communicate with someone just prior to boarding the plane.

Abdulmutallab's initial court appearance was 26th December 2009, he agreed to be represented by the Federal Public Defender's Office. However, on 13th September 2010, Abdulmutallab informed the pre-trial hearing that he wished to represent himself, as he believed representation appointed to him by the American district court would not be in his best interests. The conversation went as follows:

> The Court: "Mr Abdulmutallab, I must advise you that in my opinion you would be far better defended by a trained lawyer than you can be by yourself. I think it is unwise of you to try to represent yourself. You're not familiar with the law, you are not familiar with court procedure, you're not familiar with the rules of evidence, and I would strongly urge you not to try to represent yourself. Now, in light of the penalty that you might suffer if you are found guilty, and in light of all the difficulties

of representing yourself, is it still your desire to go forward and represent yourself without giving another try to having an attorney represent you, just even over the next month or two, to see if perhaps we can appoint an attorney who would have what you believe to be your best interests in mind?"

Abdulmutallab: "Yeah, I don't want that, no."

The Court: "You don't want another attorney?"

Abdulmutallab: "No."

The Court: "Is your decision entirely voluntary on your part?"

Abdulmutallab: "Yeah."

The Court: "All right. I find that the defendant has knowingly and voluntarily waived his right to counsel, and I will permit him to represent himself. However, I am going to appoint standby counsel, which I would always do in the case of trial, but I believe this case demands that we have standby counsel available for you to consult with for any questions that you might have as you prepare to represent yourself at the trial in this matter."

On 5th August 2011, Abdulmutallab's standby counsel filed a motion to suppress the statements Abdulmutallab made at the Hospital, and a motion for a competency hearing under seal. Abdulmutallab claimed that the witness statements from the Hospital should be suppressed, as he was not given a Miranda warning prior to making the statements, and he was under the influence of the pain-relief medication Fentanyl at this time. This was rejected.

On 12th October 2011, Abdulmutallab pled guilty to all eight counts against him, and released this statement, which highlights the degree of the command and control links with others in Al Qaeda:

"In the name of Allah, the most merciful, if I were to say I the father did not do it, but my son did it and he conspired with the holy spirit to do it, or if I said I did it but the American people are guilty of the sin, and Obama should pay for the crime, the Court wouldn't accept that from me or anyone else. In late 2009 in fulfillment of a religious obligation, I decided to participate in jihad against the United States. The Koran obliges every able Muslim to participate in jihad and fight in the way of Allah, those who fight you, and kill them wherever you find them, some parts of the Koran say, an eye for an eye, a tooth for a tooth. I had an agreement with at least one person to attack the United States in retaliation for U.S. support of Israel and in retaliation of the killing of innocent and civilian Muslim populations in Palestine, especially in the blockade of Gaza, and in retaliation for the killing of innocent and civilian Muslim populations in Yemen, Iraq, Somalia, Afghanistan and beyond, most of them women, children, and non-combatants. As a result, I travelled to Yemen and eventually to the United States, and I agreed with at least one person to carry an explosive device onto an aircraft and attempt to kill those on board and wreck the aircraft as an act of jihad against the United States for the U.S. killing of my Muslim brothers and sisters around the world. I was greatly inspired to participate in jihad by the lectures of the great and rightly guided mujahedeen who is alive, Sheikh Anwar al-Awlaki, may Allah preserve him and his family and give them victory, Amin, and Allah knows best. Participation in jihad against the United States is considered among the most virtuous of deeds in Islam and is highly encouraged in the Koran; however, according to U.S. law, which is unjust and oppressive according to the Koran, my actions make me guilty of a crime in the United States, in particular, the following counts in my indictment ... The United States—The United States should be warned that if they continue and persist in promoting the blasphemy of Muhammad and the prophets, peace be upon them all, and the U.S. continues to kill and support those who kill innocent Muslims, then the U.S. should await a great calamity that will befall them through the hands of the mujahideen soon by God's willing permission. Or God will strike them directly with a great calamity soon by his will, Amin. If you laugh at us now, we will laugh at you later in this life and on the day of judgment by God's will, and our final call is all praise to Allah, the lord of the universe, Allahu Akbar ... The mujahedeen are proud to kill in the name of God, and that is exactly what God told us to do in the Koran."

### Scripting Solo Terrorist Events

The solo terrorist script (Figure 5.2) appears similar to that of the lone actor terrorist script (Figure 5.1) except for the preparation phase which is ultimately simplified here through the pooling of social, technical and financial capital typically found within larger organizations.

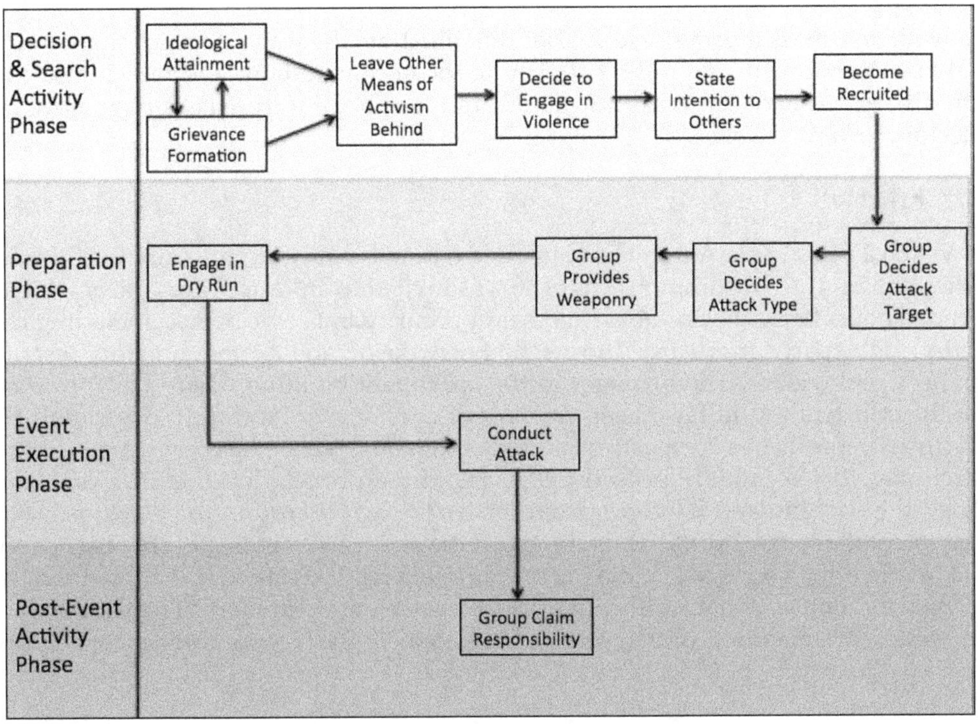


**Figure 5.2 Solo Actor Attack Script**

## Mass Murderers

We now turn to a comparison group of offenders, mass murderers[11], who like terrorists, engage (or attempt to engage in) largely public acts of violence and who often use similar weapons, but who are commonly distinguished from terrorists based on the absence of ideology. Our analysis of the 115 mass murderers in our unique dataset reveals that these offenders also differ from lone actor and solo actor terrorists in certain behaviors that typify their trajectory into violence.

In the first place, unlike lone and solo actor terrorist attacks, some mass murders appear to be spontaneous incidents, arising from the physical or emotional conflicts immediately prior to the attack and in which the individual does not exhibit any meaningful planning behaviors prior to the attack. While the percentage of mass murders that occur in these circumstances (N = 17, 15%) is relatively small, the apparent lack of predetermined intent and strategy sets at least these offenders apart from lone actor and solo actor terrorists.

Nevertheless, like lone actor and solo actor terrorists, the majority of mass murderers (83%, N = 98) engage in a series of discreet, sequential behaviors that culminate in a planned attack. In other words, most mass murders are the result of a process comprising a series of recognizable stages. A reasonable question, then, is whether the "script" that mass murderers follow is the same as the four-stage process we identified above for lone and solo terrorists.

Below are five mass murder case studies that illustrate the ways in which mass murder might be described through the pathway to violence paradigm and which also highlight differences between mass murderers and lone actor terrorists as they move on a trajectory toward violence.

### Kyle Huff

On March 25, 2006 Kyle Aaron Huff attended a "zombie rave" in the Capitol Hill neighborhood in Seattle, Washington. There he was invited to an "after-rave" party which he attended hours later. The rave itself had heavy security, but some people, including Huff, continued the party afterward. Those who knew the 6'5 and 270-pound Huff described him as a gentle giant. The manager of the apartment building where Huff lived said that the murders would have been "so far out of character" for Huff, describing Huff and his twin brother as "respectful" and good tenants. But in the early morning of that March day, this seemingly peaceful 28-year-old man briefly left the after-rave party, retrieved a shotgun and handgun from his truck parked around the block, paused to spray-paint the word "NOW" three times on the sidewalk, and began shooting as soon as he reached the house where the party was being held. He then walked methodically through the house, shooting through locked doors, and shouted "There's plenty for everyone" (or something to that effect). He killed six partygoers (four males and two

[11] Defined as an individual who kills four or more people in one event over a relatively short period of time (within 24 hours), excluding state sponsored or organized crime related events, or events that are solely domestic in nature.

females) who ranged in age from 14 to 32, and seriously wounded two others. As the police arrived, Huff committed suicide.

Huff had moved to Seattle from Whitefish, Montana with his twin brother approximately four years before the mass murder. He had attended college but did not graduate, had been unemployed for several months before the event after several short stints as a pizza delivery driver, and was single. He had no known history of a diagnosed mental illness, and his criminal record was limited, with only a conviction for criminal mischief while he was living in Montana.

### Grievance

At first, there was little evidence pointing to a motive for this seemingly random attack. The police were not able to establish any connection between Huff and any of the victims (other than attendance at the rave event) or between Huff and anyone who owned the private house where the shooting occurred. Further, the police did not uncover evidence of a dispute of any kind between Huff and anyone at the party, let alone the type of serious confrontation that might conceivably lead someone to feel the need to resort to deadly violence.

Then, nearly a month after the murders and in a completely unrelated matter, the Seattle police responded to a report of a suspicious package found in a dumpster approximately a block from where Huff had lived in Seattle. The package itself was actually harmless, but what the police found in a fast-food bag in the dumpster shed new light on Huff's mass murder. In the bag was a suicide note written by Huff two days before the attack. In the letter, addressed to his twin brother with whom he lived, Huff explained his motivation—defending society from the dangers of the rave-culture that he perceived as dangerous and promiscuous. Huff wrote: "this is something I feel I have to do, my life would always feel in complete otherwise. I can't let them get away with what theyre doing, kids like me and you are seriously dying over this shit. I hate this world of sex that they are striving to make." The presence of the letter in the dumpster has never been explained.

Some have speculated that the spray-painted words "NOW" may have been in reference to the "now, now, now, now" refrain from a popular song by the Seattle based band Nirvana, which was one of Huff's favorite groups. Whether this was intended to provide a measure of insight into the motivation for the attack or was merely a troubled man paying homage a favorite group remains unknown.

### Ideation

It is not possible to determine at what point Huff decided that mass murder was a reasonable approach to address his grievance. Neither his brother nor any of his friends in Montana or in Seattle can recall any signs that Huff would act violently and even those at the party that early morning had no indication that Huff was about to launch his attack. Huff is clear about his violent intent when he writes the suicide note, but the note does not provide any meaningful clues as to when he came to this violent ideation. It may have been as long as weeks before as he began attending rave parties, or at some even earlier time, although likely after he moved to Seattle.

### Research and Planning

Subsequent to the finding of the suicide letter, the police investigation revealed that Huff had probably been planning the mass murder for longer than two days before the attack when he penned the suicide note. Apparently, Huff had been conducting surveillance on the rave community in Seattle for weeks. Some witnesses said that they saw Huff in his truck watching a rave in the beginning of February, nearly seven weeks before the murders. When the police searched Huff's computer, they found searches related to the rave culture and a limited number of searches regarding a variety of hate groups. These searches do not seem to have been directly related to the planning of the mass murder.

Since he was invited to the party only once he was actually at the rave, it is not clear that Huff's original plan had been to attack at that particular after-party. Based on the amount of ammunition he had with him in the truck, it could be that he intended to start shooting at the rave itself where there were many more potential targets. However, there were four guards at the rave checking for drugs and weapons, which might have discouraged Huff from attacking that site.

### Preparation

While it is unclear exactly why Huff chose this particular party for his attack, it is clear that he was well-prepared for the event. Seattle Deputy Police Chief Clark Kimerer said that the slayings were definitely pre-meditated, noting that Huff had loaded his truck with weapons and over 300 rounds of ammunition. Upon leaving the party, Huff retrieved a Winchester pump action 12-gauge shotgun and a Ruger P-94 handgun, two bandoliers full of shotgun ammunition, and a tactical ammunition pouch holding AR-15 ammunition, even though he did not carry the AR-15 rifle back to the house, leaving it in the truck. Huff also left a machete and "flex-cuffs" in the truck, although it is not known if these items were related to the attack plan.

### Breach

The breach in this case was both deadly and effective. Had he chosen to conceal his weaponry in some fashion, Huff likely could have simply walked back into the party he had voluntarily left moments earlier. Nevertheless, Huff took a more forceful approach, openly carrying his weapons through the street to the house. As he neared the front porch of the house, Huff immediately shot two of the victims, one of whom fell through the front doorway, which had an unintended effect on the breach. Several party-goers who heard the gunfire and had seen the two victims fall tried to push shut the front door but were unable to do so because the body of one of the victims was physically blocking the doorway. This allowed Huff to simple shove open the door and step over the victim's body as he continued firing.

### Attack

Somewhat curiously, Huff launched his attack as the party was winding down and many of the approximately 50 people who had attended the party had either left or were in the process of leaving. Had he began shooting a few hours before, he would likely have had even more targets to attack.

In any event, Huff was able to gain entry by shooting his way in. While his shooting pattern does show some evidence of disorganization, Huff had some measure of control as he began; noticing that the first two victims that he shot with the shotgun were still alive, he pulled out the pistol and shot each again. He went upstairs, came back downstairs, and then went into the basement. Along the way he discarded or dropped one bandolier, and when he stopped shooting, he walked back out the front door. The attack ended when Huff saw the police and shot himself in the head.

### Michael McDermott

On December 26, 2000 Michael McDermott went to work at Edgewater Technologies in Wakefield, Massachusetts where he was a software tester, talked for some time with his co-workers, and then took out a semiautomatic rifle and shotgun and killed seven co-workers (four women and three men). Most of the victims worked in the human resources and accounting department of Edgewater Technologies. McDermott was apprehended on site and subsequently went to trial for the murders. His defense was that he was psychotic during the attack, believed that he had traveled back in time following instructions from God, and was actually shooting Nazis in Adolph Hitler's bunker during 1940. He was convicted and sentenced to life in prison without the possibility of parole.

At the time, McDermott, who often went by "Mucko" (a nickname bestowed on him by his young nephews who could not pronounce his name), was 6′2, weighed over 300 pounds, and had long, bushy beard. People at work thought he was reasonably amiable, but a bit peculiar. He lived by himself, and spent some of his free time posting on Internet bulletin boards, where he was known to have some expertise regarding explosives, although he did not make threatening posts or any that were considered politically volatile.

He had served six years in the United States Navy and was honorably discharged, never attended college, had no criminal convictions and no arrests prior to the mass murder. By 2000, he had been divorced for four years and lived alone. At trial, he presented evidence that as a young child a neighbor raped him repeatedly, and that he had attempted suicide several times as a teenager and as an adult. Approximately four years before the attack, McDermott was diagnosed with recurrent major depression, a mixed character disorder, and obsessive-compulsive personality. In the weeks before the mass murder, McDermott's work performance suffered and he frequently showed up late for work.

#### Grievance

McDermott's grievance—his belief that he was being treated unfairly by the human resources and accounting department at Edgewater—stemmed directly from the intersection of his mounting financial debts and efforts of the Internal Revenue Service to collect back-taxes. While a neighbor who lived upstairs from McDermott said that McDermott never mentioned any financial difficulties, McDermott was, in fact, continually in debt and was facing particularly acute financial stress around the time of the attack. In the months and years before the attack, McDermott was frequently late with his rent, and one landlord stated that McDermott moved out without paying over $1,600 in rent (which he never repaid).

The police investigation revealed that sometime in the month before the murders, the Internal Revenue Service contacted Edgewater Technologies and requested that they garnish McDermott's wages. McDermott was upset about the company's plan to comply with the IRS request. Additionally, on December 21st, just days before the shooting, McDermott learned that his car was going to be repossessed if he did not make his payments.

### Ideation

When employees in the accounting and human services department informed him of the planned garnishment, McDermott became explosively angry. It may have been at this time that McDermott settled on violence as a means of redress for what he considered unjust treatment. Additional evidence that McDermott settled on violence as a course of action is that at on December 22nd, four days before the event, McDermott asked several co-workers to sign as witnesses to a will he had prepared. This end-of-life planning, particularly since it was done at work, would seem to indicate that McDermott was at least contemplating a violent end for himself at approximately the same time that he was informed of the latest and most severe consequences of his financial instability—the garnishment of his wages and the potential loss of his car.

### Research and Planning

McDermott's research and planning phase comprises two distinct areas. He not only carefully planned the attack, but he just as carefully planned his defense at trial. Knowing that surprise would be the key to killing as many of his targets as possible, McDermott stashed most of his weaponry in his work space the evening before (which was Christmas), when he stopped by Edgewater for a brief time (18 minutes) even though the offices were closed for the holiday. As for his claim at trial of psychosis, the prosecution countered by producing evidence that McDermott had used his personal computer to conduct research about how to fake mental illness. A record of his Internet searches showed that he had been constructing his legal defense at the same time that he was planning his mass murder.

### Preparation

McDermott was well prepared for his assault. He test-fired his shotgun and semiautomatic rifle two days before the attack, and dropped off weapons and ammunition in his work locker the day before the mass murder. On the day of the event, McDermott used a duffel bag to conceal the additional shotgun shells and cartridge boxes he was carrying. When police later searched his apartment, they found bomb-making materials, blasting caps, and three gallons of nitric acid, which can be used to make nitroglycerine. The investigation did not reveal any indication that McDermott intended to use those chemicals for any violent purpose.

### Breach

McDermott's breach was only that in the most technical sense, as he simply walked into work at his usual time and as expected. He chose to attack at a place where he knew the physical layout of the site and was confident that there would be no security measures that could defeat his intent. The targets he chose were also well known to him, as were their work schedules and their exact locations in the building. Thus, there was no need for him to use violence or deceit of any kind on the morning of the attack; in fact, any efforts to do so might have given his targets a warning of some kind and an opportunity to escape.

### Attack

Part of McDermott's method of attack was to rely on the usual routine of Edgewater. He arrived at work at 9:00 am and went about his normal activities. At 10:30 am he was in the company kitchen speaking with several co-workers. Those who were there recall that McDermott appeared to be unusually sociable, but that ceased when one of the co-workers began staring at the duffel bag McDermott was carrying. At approximately 11:07 am, McDermott received a telephone call from the repossession company about his car, and he stated that he no longer needed it and the repossession company could pick it up at the Edgewater garage. He also spoke by telephone with his mother.

After the calls, McDermott returned to the lobby reception area carrying his duffel bag. When asked by the receptionist what he was doing, McDermott replied that he needed to see someone in human resources, and began firing, killing the receptionist and another co-worker. McDermott then walked to the accounting and human resources offices, bypassing several potential targets, and killing four more people as he went. In total, he fired more than three-dozen rounds from the semiautomatic rifle and shotgun.

When the police arrived, they found McDermott sitting silently in the lobby with his loaded weapons within reach. The defendant did not respond to police commands initially, stating: "I don't speak German." The police then arrested McDermott without incident.

### Jeffrey Weise

On March 21, 2005 16-year-old Weise killed his grandfather, who was a tribal law enforcement officer on the reservation where they lived, and his grandfather's girlfriend, then drove to his school and opened fire at students and teachers in the hallways. He eventually killed nine people and wounded seven others. When law enforcement officers arrived, Weise engaged in a shootout before eventually retreating to a nearby classroom and killing himself. It appears that the victims at Red Lake High School were random. He did not leave a suicide note.

### Grievance

It is difficult to pinpoint what exactly motivated Weise to commit the murders, although is clear that he was troubled for many years before the murders. Jeffrey Weise had a difficult life from the time he was very young. Before Jeffrey was sixteen, his father had committed suicide and his mother was in a nursing home after suffering traumatic injuries in a car accident. After moving several times in his youth, he eventually moved in with his grandfather on the Red Lake Reservation in Minnesota. He was also a loner who was reportedly bullied at school, although apparently not to an extreme degree. By the time he was in high school he had been diagnosed with depression and had been prescribed increasingly higher doses of Prozac.

An examination of his online posts show Weise admired Hitler, disapproved of "racial mixing", and sometimes referred to himself online as the "Angel of Death" in German on various websites and chat rooms. He often drew comic books featuring images of people shooting each other and his sketch of a skeleton playing guitar accompanied by the words: "March to the death song 'til your boots fill with blood" was displayed in his English classroom. Approximately 17 months prior to the mass murder, Weise pulled the eraser from a pencil and used the exposed metal edge to gouge his arm. Just a few months before the attack, he was reprimanded by a teacher at school and confined to a cubicle in the suspension room where he again gouged his arm. He was eventually expelled from school for violating rules, and at the time of the attack was in a program that provided tutoring at home. It may be that the accumulation of loss (of his father), rejection (by his peers), and his inability to connect with his mother (in a nursing home) propelled Weise toward extreme violence.

### Ideation

There is no clear indication of when Weise came to the decision to murder both family members and fellow students. Surviving family members believe that at least part of the explanation for Weise's actions can be traced to a change in medication he was taking. The summer before the attack, Weise had attempted suicide, and afterward was put on a higher dose of the anti-depressant Prozac than he had been on before the attempt. Weise's fascination with Nazis, seen in his computer searches and online postings and chats, indicate some attraction to violence as a solution to problems. And, he clearly seemed to understand that he was an angry and potentially dangerous person; in a profile page on an Internet site, Weise he described himself as "16 years of accumulated rage suppressed by nothing more than brief glimpses of hope, which have all but faded to black." So, it appears that aside from being depressed and suicidal for years before the attack, Weise was also masking powerful feelings of anger (presumably) toward others whom he may have held responsible for his lot in life—including members of his family as well as his peers.

### Research and Planning

Another teenager was arrested in connection with the mass murder, and is believed to have helped Weise plan the assault and reportedly also considered being part of the rampage. Both because Weise died in the attack and because of the status of both Weise and his alleged co-conspirator as minors, not all information regarding the planning of the attack has been made public. After a review of his emails though, law enforcement authorities concluded that Weise's assault was not spontaneous and that he (and perhaps others) planned the event well in advance.

### Preparation

Weise was able to prepare for the mass murder in short order. He had everything he needed in his grandfather's house—guns, ammunition, body armor, and transportation. Once he killed his grandfather and his grandfather's girlfriend, he was fully prepared for his extensive assault on Red Lake High School. He would have known that he was barred from the school and that the (unarmed) security guard at the front door would challenge him. Weise was prepared for this circumstance, as he was armed and ready to shoot as he arrived at the school

### Breach

Weise did not breach the first site of his attack, as he killed his grandfather and his grandfather's girlfriend in the home that they all shared. Weise's breach at Red Lake High school was violent and efficient. As he entered the school through a doorway with a metal detector he simply shot and killed the unarmed security guard who confronted him. Weise was then free to roam the hallways.

### Attack

After killing his grandfather, who was a member of the tribal police force, Weise armed himself with his grandfather's police-issued .40 caliber handgun, a 12-gauge shotgun, and his grandfather's body armor vest before driving to the school in his grandfather's police cruiser.

After killing the unarmed guard and gaining entry to the school lobby, Weise proceeded down a connected hallway. As he walked, Weise fired at a teacher and some students, who immediately fled into a classroom. Weise followed them into the classroom, killing the teacher and several of the students. He then continued down the hallway, apparently firing at random victims.

Four armed police officers entered the school and Weise fired on them as well. At least one officer returned fire, although it is not known if Weise was injured in that exchange. Shortly after this confrontation, Weise went into a classroom and shot himself in the head. During his attack, Weise fired 45 times, killing all of his victims at the school in less than three minutes, although he continued to wander the hallways shooting at random for approximately another six minutes.

## Robert Hawkins

On December 5, 2007 19-year-old Robert Hawkins walked into the Von Maur department store at the Westroads mall in Omaha, Nebraska and started firing at shoppers with an AK-47-style semiautomatic rifle. He killed five women and three men, and injured two others. Finally, he killed himself. Hawkins had no known connection to any of the people he killed or wounded, and had no particular association with the mall itself (although it was only 20 miles from where he lived at the time and he had likely been there previously).

Hawkins had a long history of drug use and troubling behavior, including a voluntary admission to a psychiatric treatment center after threatening to kill his stepmother when he was fourteen years old. While at this facility, Hawkins received private psychotherapy and drug counseling and eventually became a ward of the state when his family's health insurance did not cover his continuing treatment. Hawkins lived in a variety of foster homes over the next several years, and was hospitalized at least twice more for psychiatric problems. He was eventually diagnosed with attention-deficit disorder, oppositional defiant disorder, and mood disorder.

At the time of the event, the state had terminated its custody, and Hawkins lived with the family of a friend after having been asked to leave the home of his latest foster parents. He was a high school dropout and his criminal record included being a minor in possession of an open container of alcohol, assault after a fight in high school, and possession with the intent to deliver drugs, and weeks before the mass murder he had been ticketed on suspicion of contributing to the delinquency of a minor and two alcohol charges. He had recently been fired from his job at a fast-food restaurant and broken up with his girlfriend.

### Grievance

Hawkins had no known grievance with the people he killed or that mall where he attacked; his grievance appears to have been a more global one, driven both by his psychiatric and family history as well as by recent failures in his life. Since he committed suicide at the scene, the potentially complex ways in which these factors intersected and may have pushed Hawkins toward his murderous rampage will never be known with certainty.

Hours before the shooting, Hawkins called the house where he had been staying, speaking both with his friend and his friend's mother and telling them that he was sorry and that they wouldn't have to worry about him anymore. During that phone call, Hawkins revealed that he had just been fired from his job at McDonald's, having been accused of stealing money from his till. After that phone call, the friend and the friend's mother were worried that Hawkins was suicidal and they checked his room, discovering two suicide notes. The pair then called Hawkins's biological mother, who came and picked up the notes and took them to the police.

Hawkins wrote one note to his family:

> Family, I'm so sorry for what I've put you through. I never meant to hurt all of you so much and I don't blame any one of you for disowning me I just can't be a burden to you and my friends any longer. You are all better off without me. I'm so sorry for this.
>
> I've just snapped I can't take this meaningless existence anymore I've been a constant disappointment and that trend would have continued. just remember the good times we had together.

That note ends with Hawkins expressing his love for his parents and various friends. There is no mention in the note of the attack at the mall.

The second note, which ends with a short will, is addressed to his friends, and begins much like the first note, expressing remorse for having caused trouble for his friends, having been a burden, and states that "this is the only option." But, after requesting that his friends recall the many good times they managed to share, Hawkins writes something entirely different: *Just think tho I'm gonna be fuckin famous.* Approximately 40 minutes before the attack, Hawkins also texted a former girlfriend and said that he wanted to shoot a lot of people at a mall and then kill himself.

### Ideation

Well before the mass murder Hawkins had revealed his violent ideation, not only threatening to kill his stepmother as a 14-year-old, but much more recently telling a friend that he would kill her and her family and burn their house down because he suspected her of stealing a CD player from his car. In addition to these specific instances of threatening murder, friends also say that Hawkins had been fixated on death for years and talked about it frequently.

As shown in the suicide note addressed to his friends, Hawkins saw violence not only as a means to address the frustration and despair that he was feeling, but also as a means to achieve a more general goal that had eluded him so far in his life—to become famous. Hawkins used mass murder as a means of forcing others to pay attention to him.

### Research and Planning

It is not possible to know how much time Hawkins spent planning his attack, but there is clear evidence that he did at least some minimal amount of research and planning. Even though he writes in his suicide notes that he "just snapped", he obviously didn't, as one of the notes shows that he had planned to kill not only himself, but also many others, at least enough to make him "famous." It is unclear when Hawkins wrote the notes, but given his goal, it seems likely that Hawkins did at least enough research to know how many people he would have to kill in order to obtain the amount of media coverage that would qualify him, at least in his mind, as a famous person. Hawkins was also likely very much aware of the intense media coverage that Seung-Hui Cho received after the Virginia Tech shootings earlier that year. It is probable that he chose a location—the mall—precisely because it would be filled with holiday shoppers and would present a substantial number of targets, thereby increasing his chances of reaching his goal.

### Preparation

Hawkins did not have to invest significant time in preparing. He simply stole the rifle and ammunition from his stepfather. The day before the mass murder, Hawkins actually showed the rifle to the family with whom he was staying at the time. They did not think much of the weapon (which was apparently not in very good condition), and assumed that Hawkins was only going to target shoot or hunt, which would not have been unusual for him.

### Breach

While Hawkins had access to the mall during normal business hours, his method of entry was somewhat unusual and actually could have derailed his plan. Security video released by law enforcement shows Hawkins, wearing a hooded sweatshirt, entering the mall and looking around for a few moments before walking out and then coming back in the same door minutes later. This second time, he appears to be carrying something or have something hidden under his sweatshirt. He is then seen getting on an elevator. This unusual activity drew the attention of the unarmed mall security guards. It is unclear what actions the security guards took, but by the time police officers arrived minutes later in response to the shooting, Hawkins had already killed eight others and himself.

### Attack

Although the shooting actually began in the children's department where Hawkins fired his rifle straight up in the ceiling, security photographs released by law enforcement show Hawkins standing on the balcony of the third floor of the mall, his sweatshirt unzipped and aiming the rifle at unseen targets. Hawkins then walked to the atrium where he leaned over an escalator railing and shot one man in the head. Hawkins next fired on people in front of a customer service counter, eventually walking around to fire at those hiding behind the counter. He did not appear to target either specific people or a specific type of person; witnesses said it appeared that Hawkins was shooting at random targets, although he appeared to be aiming at people and not simply randomly shooting. The entire attack took only minutes, and was over by the time the first police officers arrived at the mall a little over five minutes after the first 911 call. Sounds of gunfire can be heard in the background of the call. The attack ended with Hawkins committing suicide.

## Gang Lu

On November 1, 1991 Gang Lu went on a shooting rampage at two separate buildings at the University of Iowa campus in Iowa City. Lu, who had recently earned his doctorate in physics from the school, killed four people and critically wounded two others before shooting himself in the head.

A 28-year-old native of the People's Republic of China, Lu was by all accounts a brilliant student who excelled in the study of physics. For six years, he had been one of the most gifted students in the nationally recognized department, specializing in space plasma theory. But he was also a loner, and others from the department who knew him said he lacked social skills and was isolated from his colleagues, including those from his native country who were also studying at the University of Iowa. He was single and had no known criminal record or mental health history. According to acquaintances, since graduation Lu had seemingly been under a greater than usual amount of pressure, most of it self-imposed.

### Grievance

Although many who succeed academically in competitive graduate departments are ambitious and hard-working, former professors described Lu as being extremely competitive; he was seen as someone who drove himself relentlessly toward academic achievement during his entire time at the university. Certain faculty members and fellow students also saw him as temperamental and easily agitated. A doctoral candidate who had been a roommate of Lu said that Lu "had a very bad temper and saw himself as No. 1. He had a psychological problem with being challenged." This apparent need to be the best and to be perceived as the best led to Lu's grievance aimed at the university.

Although his dissertation regarding computer calculations of the properties of ionized glass impressed the faculty, Lu was extremely upset that he did not win an academic award for his dissertation. The prestigious Spriesterbach Dissertation Prize and the $2,500 that went with it were instead awarded to another student who had previously been Lu's roommate. Ultimately, that student was one of the persons Lu specifically targeted and killed.

Subsequent to the attack, investigators recovered five letters written by Lu in which he reportedly identified his targets. None of the letters (four written in English and one in Chinese) were mailed before the attack. Lu had actually entrusted the letters to an acquaintance who was to mail them, but the acquaintance turned the letters over to the authorities after learning of the mass murder. Authorities said the letters described Lu's grievance and outlined his detailed plans to kill even more university employees than he eventually did. The letters, though, make it clear that Lu's grievance was primarily motivated by what he perceived to be slights to his academic reputation which he perceived would tar his professional reputation and prospects.

### Ideation

After failing to receive the dissertation award, Lu did not turn to violence immediately as a solution to his grievance. Instead, he first wrote a series of letters to the university appealing the departmental decision concerning the award of the dissertation prize. None of these appeals succeeded, and Lu eventually dropped this non-violent approach. As indicated in his letters later recovered by the police, at some point after his written appeals were rejected, he consciously and deliberately decided to kill those he held responsible for his unjust treatment.

### Research and Planning

The attack Lu carried out did not require extensive research or planning. At most, he needed to know where his targets would be on campus and he was likely able to establish their locations in advance of his attack. In addition, he attacked in locations with which he was very familiar and to which he had unfettered access. The department meeting was a scheduled event and Lu would certainly have known that many, although not all, of his targets would be present. He also knew that he would be able to carry his handguns into the meeting, as there were no special security measures at this routine academic gathering. Once he was finished shooting at the meeting, Lu also knew exactly which other building on campus he needed to access in order to complete his task. He would have known how far the second building was from the first and how long it would take to walk from one to the next. In short, based on familiarity with the university and its personnel and procedures, Lu would have had little reason to conduct surveillance of any kind or commit time or resources to researching his targets and their schedules.

### Preparation

Lu applied for a permit to buy a firearm in Iowa on May 21st, over five months before the mass murder. After showing his visa and Chinese passport, he was granted the permit three days later (although he legally owned the weapons, Lu did not have a permit to carry them). In addition to acquiring the means to carry out the attack, Lu also engaged in end-of life activities. Aside from giving letters explaining his actions to an acquaintance, Lu also mailed a package of personal belongings to his parents in China just an hour before the attack. When police searched his apartment, they concluded that Lu had taken the time to put his financial and personal affairs in order and had been preparing for the attack for some time.

### Breach

Lu had no difficulty gaining entrance to the campus buildings for his attack. Although he was no longer a student at the University, he continued to work in a physics lab on campus as he sought employment. Thus, he had unfettered access to both buildings where he attacked, and his presence would have been unnoticed at the department meeting where he began the assault.

### Attack

The shootings began at approximately 3:40 pm when Lu stood up during a scheduled meeting in his department and shot and killed four men. He did not say a word during the assault. The entire attack lasted less than 10 minutes, during which time Lu moved from the building where the meeting was being held to a nearby building where he continued firing. He appeared to specifically target certain people, shooting each victim at close range using a .38 caliber revolver. He also carried with him a .22 caliber handgun that he did not fire. Once inside the second building, Lu eventually shot himself in the head, but was alive when police found him minutes after he fired his last shot.

In addition to murdering the student who received the dissertation award, Lu also killed three professors who were on his dissertation committee, including the chairman of the department. After walking the few block to the second building, he shot the vice president of academic affairs and her receptionist. After this, he walked upstairs to another floor where he shot himself. Lu eventually died from this self-inflicted gunshot.

### Scripting Mass Murder Events

Although still exploratory in nature, our examination of the 98 mass murderers in our dataset who do not engage in spontaneous violence reveals that they do *not* reliably follow the same "natural history from inception to completion" of the attack as lone actor and solo actor terrorists.

Indeed, the fundamental distinction between the two groups—motivation—dictates different actuation points for violence. By definition mass murderers lack an ideology and, thus, cannot be said to engage in the **decision and search activity** involving calculations based on current "political and security climates" that characterizes the incipiency of lone actor and solo actor terrorist attacks. Most mass murderers (57%, N = 65) are concerned with personal feelings of having been wronged by a specific person and ultimately murder (or attempt to murder) the person whom they hold responsible for that wrong. Other mass murderers (16%, N = 18) have a grievance against a category of persons and attack representatives of that group (the remainder were either spontaneous attacks and/or any grievance is unknown).

Nor do mass murderers typically concern themselves with **post-event activity and strategic analysis** as do lone actor and solo actor terrorists. The majority of mass murderer events are resolved when the offender commits suicide at the scene (43%, N = 50) or is killed by the police at the scene (10%, N = 12), and even those who survive appear not to have planned much beyond their homicidal attack. Very few displayed any evidence of having planned an escape (17%, N = 19) or having any intent to commit another attack (14%, N = 16). In short, it seems as if most mass murderers give very little attention to post-attack planning or strategizing of any kind.

It is reasonable, then, to ask whether mass murderers follow a different "script" than do lone actor and solo actor terrorists. A model that may better describe the script of a mass murder has its origins in a behavioral pathway model conceptualized in two US Secret Service studies, one involving assassinations of public figures and the other school shootings (Fein & Vossekuil, 1999; Vossekuil et al., 2002). These and following studies theorized a route from idea to action comprising ideation, planning, preparation and implementation. These same phases were subsequently incorporated into an expanded model of a *pathway to violence* (Calhoun & Weston, 2003), which proposes the following six milestones:

**Grievance** (the cause of the individual's distress or resentment, often based on a perception—whether based in reality or not—of having been wronged or treated unfairly or inappropriately; resulting in a desire, even a sense of mission, to right the wrong and achieve a measure of deserved justice);

**Ideation** (the point at which the individual realizes and accepts that violence is the appropriate and necessary means to address the grievance; the stage where the conscious choice is made to cause harm to others);

**Research and Planning** (at least a minimal amount of research and planning takes place once violence is adopted as the means to address the grievance, even if only to identify when an where the attack should take place; amount of research and planning can vary widely);

**Preparation** (after a plan, however rudimentary is developed, the individual must acquire the means to carry out the plan; even if already possessing the weapon to be use, the person may need to acquire more or special ammunition, arrange transportation, etc.);

**Breach** (the step immediately prior to the attack in which the individual positions himself or herself for the assault and defeats any security measures in place, however minimal they might be); and

**Attack** (the final stage where the intended plan for violence is enacted).

The five cases above provide illustrations of the pathway to violence paradigm, but they by no means cover the universe of experiences of those on a trajectory to perpetrate mass murder. Below, Table 5.1 outlines other examples taken from our unique dataset of 115 mass murderers of the behaviors for the six stages along the pathway to violence:

**Table 5.1 Stages within the Pathway of Violence**

| | |
|---|---|
| Grievance | • Sense of being treated unfairly at work<br>• Desire for revenge for being bullied at school<br>• Belief in being unjustly denied fame<br>• Lack of success in forming romantic relationships<br>• Belief that a failing grade in high school resulted in adult unemployment<br>• Sense of being targeted for harassment by acquaintances and family |

| | |
|---|---|
| **Ideation** | • Communicating to third-parties the desire to harm others<br>• Dropping non-violent alternatives (appeals, lawsuits) to resolving grievance<br>• Identifying with Columbine murderers<br>• Contextually inappropriate use of firearms<br>• Fixation on militaristic gear and paraphernalia<br>• Generation of violent written content and images |
| **Research & Planning** | • Stalking<br>• Surveillance of potential attack sites<br>• Practice approaches<br>• Keeping a log of thoughts and information concerning the grievance |
| **Preparation** | • Acquiring weapons and/or ammunition<br>• Modifying weapons for ease of concealment or use<br>• Acquiring/arranging transportation<br>• Relatively minor "practice" aggressive acts |
| **Breach** | • Using a hostage to demand entry to attack site<br>• Shooting out doors/windows of a business<br>• Entering the lobby of a shopping mall<br>• Hiding a handgun in a backpack carried into work<br>• Dressing as a FedEx worker to gain entry to a home |
| **Attack** | • Taking children hostage at a schoolhouse<br>• Randomly shooting at shoppers in mall<br>• Walking into work and attacking co-workers<br>• Setting fire to a crowded nightclub<br>• Killing a former spouse and bystanders at her place of work |

This exploratory analysis suggests that mass murderers follow a different "script" than lone actor and solo actor terrorists as they move toward and through violence, and that the *pathway to violence* model offer a means of conceptualizing the process. We recognize that the *pathway to violence* model is just that—a model—and that there may be other relevant variables (such as the time between stages) that may have explanatory power. We do, though, see the model as a useful tool to integrate for further study the behaviors that typically compose the phenomenon of mass murder.

## 6. Conclusion

On the surface, both lone actor terrorism and mass murder attacks seem to defy explanation. The immediate aftermath of both phenomena is marked by drama, panic and an inevitable search for simple answers. In particular, there is an unerring tendency to reach for mono-causal master narrative explanations. We can consider President Obama's words on lone actors as an illustration:

> The biggest concern we have right now is not the launching of a major terrorist operation ... the risk that we're especially concerned over right now is the lone wolf terrorist, somebody with a single weapon being able to carry out wide-scale massacres ... You know, when you've got one person *who is deranged or driven by a hateful ideology*, they can do a lot of damage (emphasis added—http://security.blogs.cnn.com/2011/08/16/obama-biggest-terror-fear-is-the-lone-wolf/)

"Deranged or driven by a hateful ideology" is a perfect example of two master narratives that are often proffered and treated as being mutually exclusive. The individual actor is either deranged, unbalanced, unhinged, disturbed, mad, crazy, nuts and unstable, or he/she is driven by a hateful ideology, radicalized, politically focused, inspired by some foreign 'entity', or determined to effect some social or political upheaval or policy change. In the days that follow an event such as these, the framing of the individual's motivation usually takes on one of these two narratives. The chosen narrative depends upon the easy availability of information regarding their ideological content, mental health history or personal background details.

Yet what we see from the analysis we offer here, lone actor terrorism and mass murderer attacks are (both) usually the culmination of a complex mix of personal, political and social drivers that crystalize at the same time to drive the individual down the path of violent action. Whether the violence comes to fruition is usually a combination of the availability and vulnerability of suitable targets that suit the heady mix of personal and political grievances and the individual's capability to engage in an attack from both a psychological and technical capability standpoint. Many individual cases share a mixture of unfortunate personal life circumstances coupled with an intensification of beliefs that later developed into the idea to engage in violence. What differed was how these influences were sequenced. Sometimes personal problems led to a susceptibility to ideological influences. Sometimes long-held ideological influences became intensified after the experience of personal problems. This is why we should be wary of mono-causal master narratives. The development of these behaviors is usually far more labyrinthine and dynamic.

One of the major implications of comparative analyses such as this could be to provide guidance or a framework to those tasked with responding to such phenomena. Given our counter-intuitive findings on the leakage of intent, this may be particularly relevant in terms of early disruption of plots. An understanding of this complexity and the multiplicity of potential factors could help inform how threat assessments of particular lone actors should be carried out. When we talk about 'threat', and the related concept of risk, we need to consider multiple, overlapping questions including issues related to identification of threats (e.g. threat of what precisely?), exposure (e.g. under what conditions are particular offences more likely?) and management (i.e. which interventions are likely to be effective in terms of mitigating either risk, broadly speaking, or a specific threat) (Borum, 1999). The illustrations highlight that the target and/or target location of the violence was usually associated with something to do with the individual's personal grievance. This may help give us a sense of what Borum calls the 'scenarios of exposure' or the conditions under which a particular individual become a threat. The temporal issues also highlight the fact that we need to view risk dynamically. Given a set of circumstances and conditions an individual may appear to be no or low risk. However, small changes in their life-course, personal circumstances or opportunity to offend can have a force-multiplier effect and propel the individual into a higher category of risk. These issues are explored in detail by Monahan (2012) who warns however, of the need for comparison samples (including control groups) in order to scientifically validate many of the otherwise working assumptions relevant to risk assessment.

From the analysis presented in this paper, however, the actual violence conducted by lone actors and mass murderers looks very similar. We sought to examine whether their 'radicalization' trajectory toward this act of violence was also similar. The analyses suggest that they share a lot in common but significant differences persist. This has a multiplicity of implications for early detection, threat management and possibly disruption. The job of intelligence analysts (be it for the police or intelligence communities) often involves assessing the scale of an individual's threat based on often fragmentary information. The analyses above do not point toward one single behavioral profile from which risk assessments can be built. They do however, help frame the types of questions that intelligence analysts can ask to get a fuller picture of the threat. In a later deliverable for this project, we return to this issue by examining how behaviors cluster together across a sizeable number of individuals (both lone actors and mass murderers). The results also highlight the fact that (a) in most cases there tends to be long-held risk factors but (b) they tend to be enabled in a force multiplier effect by much more recent situational stressors and that (c) the trajectory into violence tends to be a lengthy process. Phases may be identifiable on this process, from grievance formation to fixation to capacity building to attack planning. If an individual is identified ahead of time (say for example after leaking key information), the individual's position in this pathway can be plotted, and a range of disruption/prevention tools can be implemented from there.

In terms of indicators, the vast majority of lone actor terrorists each demonstrated elements concerning (a) their grievance, (b) an escalation in their intent to act, (c) gaining capability—both psychologically and technically and (d) attack planning (see Figure) 6.1.

Finally, the routine activity studies also provided much insight from a disruption and prevention perspective. Much of the anxiety concerning the threat of lone actor terrorism stems from concerns regarding the ability to detect and intercept lone actor terrorist events before they occur. Traditional methods employed against formal terrorist organizations and loosely connected terrorist networks (such as counter-intelligence, HUMINT, interception of communications, surveillance of persons, targeted killing etc.) may not be as readily applicable against the threat of lone actor terrorists. Strategies aimed at countering radicalization in the community may have no reference point in identifying lone at-risk individuals. Deterrence measures also may prove problematic for countering lone actor terrorism. Because prediction and identification are difficult, it might be better to instead guard against future lone actor terrorists by making the actual undertaking of a terrorist attack more difficult. For example, it might be easier and more cost-efficient to deter a budding lone actor terrorist by making it more difficult to acquire the necessary bomb-making materials than by convincing him/her of counter-narratives.

**Figure 6.1: Threat Assessment Framework**

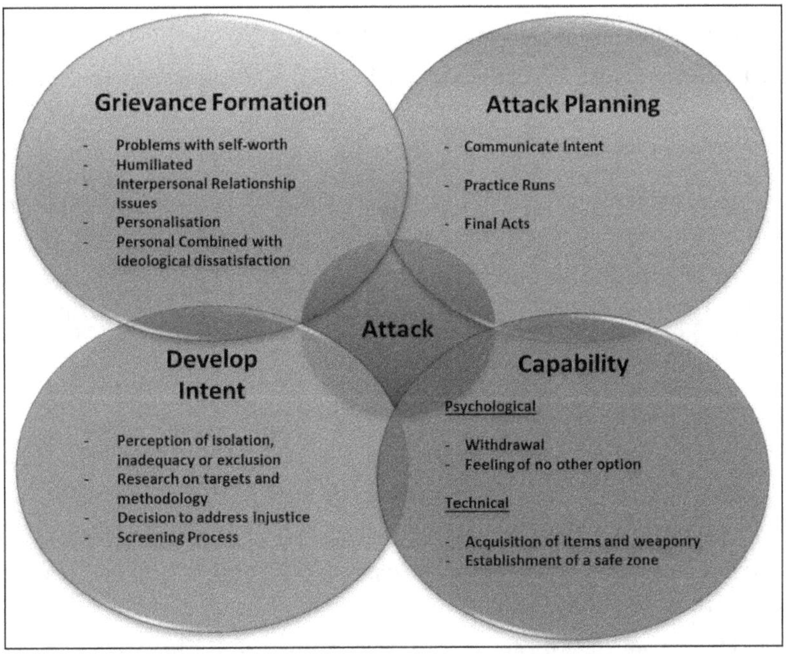


In terms of future research, there are a myriad number of ways to improve our understanding. First, there has been next to no rigorous research involving interviews with lone actor terrorists or mass murderers. We are therefore lacking in a particularly rich source of information, not only on radicalization, attack planning and attack commission, but also issues surrounding deradicalization and disengagement. Second, on only a couple of the key factors do we have a sense of societal base rates. An ambitious program of work is needed to assess how different prevalence rates of risk factors and their co-occurrence are against the rates found within wider society. Third, sequencing analysis like those used in chapter five do not necessarily have to involve thick qualitative case studies but can utilize quantitative approaches (like State Transition Diagrams). What has held the field back for so long is the lack of data but that is becoming increasingly less of an issue. Finally, this study (and most of the associated field) is reliant upon open-source data. Closer collaboration between academics and law enforcement agencies tasked with responding to these threats is needed. This relationship is not necessarily uni-directional (e.g. academics help practitioners) but can be a two way process where practitioners actively relay the operational difficulties they face and the practical questions they feel need addressing.

## References

A. (2013, October 3.) Jeffrey James "Jeff" Wesise-Red Lake. *Native News Today.*

Asal, V., Gill, P., Rethemeyer, R. K., & Horgan, J. (2013). Killing Range Explaining Lethality Variance within a Terrorist Organization. *Journal of Conflict Resolution*, 0022002713508927.

Bernton, H., & Carter, M. (2006, April 2). Kyle Huff's journey. *The Seattle Times.*

Borum, R. (2013). Informing Lone-Offender Investigations. *Criminology & Public Policy, 12*(1), 103–112.

Boweden, M. (1995, June 11). On social matters, eastern and western points of view news coverage of a campus killing in Iowa provided a context for studying cultural differences. *The Philadelphia Inquirer*, p. E03.

Bowers, T. G., Holmes, E. S., & Rhom, A. (2010). The nature of mass murder and autogenic massacre. *Journal of Police and Criminal Psychology, 25*(2), 59–66.

Cairns, E. (1987). *Caught in crossfire: Children and the Northern Ireland conflict.* Syracuse University Press.

Calhoun, F.S. & Weston, S.W. (2003). *Contemporary Threat management: A Guide for Identifying, Assessing, and Managing Individuals of Violent Intent.* San Diego, CA: Specialized Training Services.

Cole, R. (2007, December 6). Shooter lost his job Wednesday. *Omaha World-Herald*, p. 01A.

Commonwealth v. Michael McDermott, 448 Mass. 750, 864 N.E.2d 471 (Supreme Judicial Court of Massachusetts, 2007).

Connor, T. (2007, December 6). Very troubled' teen snapped after breakup with girlfriend & losing job. *Daily News*, p. 2.

Corner, E., & Gill, P. (2015). A false dichotomy? Mental illness and lone actor terrorism. *Law and human behavior, 39*(1), 23.

Curran, D. (1984). Juvenile offending, civil disturbance and political terrorism: A psychological perspective. *unpublished paper.*

Davey, M., & Harris, G. (2005, March 26). Family wonders if Prozac prompted school shootings. *New York Times.*

DeLisi, M., Hochstetler, A., Scherer, A. M., Purhmann, A., & Berg, M. T. (2008). The Starkweather Syndrome: exploring criminal history antecedents of homicidal crime sprees 1. *Criminal Justice Studies, 21*(1), 37–47.

DePalma, A. (1992, April 8). Iowa city journal; town faces its ghosts without anger. *The New York Times*, p. 17.

Drysdale, D. A. (2010). *Campus attacks: Targeted violence affecting institutions of higher education.* DIANE Publishing.

Duwe, G. (2000). Body-Count Journalism The Presentation of Mass Murder in the News Media. *Homicide Studies, 4*(4), 364–399.

Eggen, D., & Hedgpeth, D. (2005, March 29). Juvenile arrested in Minn. Shootings; Suspect might be charged as adult. *The Washington Post*, p. A01.

Elliot, R., & Lockhart, W. H. (1980). Characteristics of scheduled offenders and juvenile delinquents'. *A Society Under Stress: Children and Young People in Northern Ireland.*

Emery, T. (2000, December 27). Seven slain inside office; co-worker in custody. *South Bend Tribune,* p. A1.

Farrington, D. P., & Loeber, R. (1999). Transatlantic replicability of risk factors in the development of delinquency. *Historical and geographical influences on psychopathology,* 299–329.

Farrington, D. P., Ttofi, M. M., Crago, R. V., & Coid, J. W. (2015). Intergenerational Similarities in Risk Factors for Offending. *Journal of Developmental and Life-Course Criminology, 1*(1), 48–62.

Fein, R. & Vossekuil, B. (1999). Assassination in the United States: An operational study of recent assassins, attackers, and near-lethal approachers. *Journal of Forensic Sciences, 44,* 321–333.

Fein, R. A., & Vossekuil, B. (1999). Assassination in the United States: an operational study of recent assassins, attackers, and near-lethal approachers. *Journal of Forensic Sciences, 44*(2), 321–333.;

Fein, R. A., & Vossekuil, B. (1999). Assassination in the United States: an operational study of recent assassins, attackers, and near-lethal approachers. *Journal of Forensic Sciences, 44*(2), 321–333.

Florez-Morris, M. (2007). Joining guerrilla groups in Colombia: Individual motivations and processes for entering a violent organization. *Studies in Conflict & Terrorism, 30*(7), 615–634.

Forliti, A. (2005, March 23). An obsession with death; Teen shooter's story was one of 'devastation and loss.' *Hamilton Spectator,* p. A15.

Fox, J. A., and M. W. Zawitz. 2007. *Homicide trends in the United States.* Washington, DC: Bureau of Justice Statistics. http://bjs.gov/content/pub/pdf/htius.pdf

Fox, J. A., Burgess, A. W., Levin, J., & Wong, M. (2006, July 17). Panel report on the March 25, 2006 Capitol Hill shooting.

Getlin, J. (2000, December 28). If anyone, 'it would be him'; Michael McDermott was a self-taught computer whiz. The quiet, hulking man 'schmoozed' with colleagues minutes before the shooting. *Hamilton Spectator,* p. B03.

Gill, P. (2015). *Lone actor Terrorists: A Behavioural Analysis.* Routledge.

Gill, P., & Horgan, J. (2013). Who Were the Volunteers? 1 The Shifting Sociological and Operational Profile of 1240 Provisional Irish Republican Army Members. *Terrorism and Political Violence, 25*(3), 435–456.

Gill, P., Horgan, J., & Deckert, P. (2014). Bombing Alone: Tracing the Motivations and Antecedent Behaviors of Lone-Actor Terrorists. *Journal of forensic sciences, 59*(2), 425–435.

Goldberg, C. (2000, December 27). 7 die in rampage at company; co-worker of victims arrested. *The New York Times,* p. 1.

Guerino, P., Harrison, P. M., & Sabol, W. J. (2011). Prisoners in 2010. *Bureau of Justice Statistics, Washington, DC.*

Gunderson, D. (2005, March 23). Who was Jeff Weise? *Minnesota Public Radio.* Retrieved from http://news.minnesota.publicradio.org/features/2005/03/22_ap_redlakesuspect/

Haga, C. (2005, March 26). Shattered relatives seek answers; Teen gunman in school shooting had been on Prozac for depression, family members say. *The Globe and Mail,* p. A13.

Hanners, D. (2005, March 22). School-shooting suspect admired Hitler. *Pioneer Press.*

Hanners, D. (2005, March 23). FBI to examine traits of teen gunman. *Pioneer Press.*

Hedgpeth, D. (2005, March 27). Tribe responds to killings with grief rather than anger. *The Washington Post,* p. A03.

Hempel, A. G., & Richards, T. C. (1999). Offender and offense characteristics of a non-random sample of mass murderers. *Journal of the American Academy of Psychiatry and the Law Online, 27*(2), 213–225.

Hirschi, T., & Gottfredson, M. (1983). Age and the explanation of crime. *American journal of sociology,* 552–584.

Horgan, J. (2009). *Walking away from terrorism: accounts of disengagement from radical and extremist movements.* Routledge.

Horgan, J. (2014) *The Psychology of Terrorism 2nd Edition.* London: Routledge

Horgan, J. (2014) The Psychology of Terrorism. 2nd Edition. London: Routledge

Huffstutter, P. J. (2005, March 29). 2nd teen is linked to school shooting. *Los Angeles Times*

Hughes, A. (2005, April 18). Feds: Assault at Red Lake over in nine minutes. *Minnesota Public Radio.* Retrieved from http://news.minnesota.publicradio.org/features/2005/04/18_hughesa_redlakeupdate/

Johnson, K. (2000, December 28). In wake of killings, strands of suspect's life. *The New York Times,* p. 1.

Johnson, M. C., Morris, R. G., & Menard, S. (2012). Historical invariance in delinquency causation: a test of equivalent models of delinquency for two generations of adolescents. *Crime & Delinquency,* 0011128712446051.

K. Huff, personal communication, March 23, 2006.

Kasindorf, M. (2006, March 30). Rave scene not to blame, says Seattle mayor; 'Disturbed' man, not techno music, blamed in killings. *USA Today,* p. 3A.

Konigsber, E. (2007, December 8). From 'troubled' to 'killer,' despite many efforts. *The New York Times,* p. 1.

LaFree, G. (2013). Lone- Offender Terrorists. *Criminology & Public Policy, 12*(1), 59–62.

Langman, P. (2009). Rampage school shooters: A typology. *Aggression and Violent behavior, 14*(1), 79–86.Lankford, A. (2013). A comparative analysis of suicide terrorists and rampage, workplace, and school shooters in the United States from 1990 to 2010. *Homicide studies, 17*(3), 255–274.

Lankford, A. (2012). A comparative analysis of suicide terrorists and rampage, workplace and school shooters in the United States from 1990 to 2010. *Homicide Studies, 17*(3), 255–274.

Lee, J. R. (2005, July 24). Shooter's motive remains a mystery; months later, those close to 16–year-old Jeffrey Weise still find his actions hard to believe: Red Lake shooting. *Wisconsin State Journal*, p. A1.

Lovett, I., Nagourney, A. (2014). 'Deadly rampage in college town after video rant', New York Times. 25 May.

Lyons, H. A., & Harbinson, H. J. (1986). A comparison of political and non-political murderers in Northern Ireland, 1974–84. *Medicine, Science and the Law, 26*(3), 193–198.

MacQuarrie, B., & Klein, R. (2000, December 28). Seven victims were methodically targeted, court told: bomb-making equipment found in accused's apartment. *Edmonton Journal*, p. A4.

Marriott, M. (1991, November 3). Gunman in Iowa wrote of plans in five letters. *The New York Times, p. 26.*

Marriott, M. (1991, November 4). Iowa gunman was torn by academic challenge. *The New York Times.*

Marshall, S. & Bullard, C. (1991, November 4). Killer coveted award // Iowa Ph.D called 'cold blooded.' *USA Today*, p. 2A.

McCauley, C., Moskalenko, S., & Van Son, B. (2013). Characteristics of lone-wolf violent offenders: A comparison of assassins and school attackers. *Perspectives on Terrorism, 7*(1).

McPhee, M., Saltonstall, D., & Goldiner, D. (2000, December 27). Man slays 7 in web office biz was to hold his wages to IRS. *The Patriot Ledger*, p. 3.

Meloy, J. R., Hempel, A. G., Mohandie, K., Shiva, A. A., & Gray, B. T. (2001). Offender and offense characteristics of a nonrandom sample of adolescent mass murderers. *Journal of the American Academy of Child & Adolescent Psychiatry, 40*(6), 719–728.

Meloy, J. R., Hempel, A. G., Mohandie, K., Shiva, A. A., & Gray, B. T. (2001). Offender and offense characteristics of a nonrandom sample of adolescent mass murderers. *Journal of the American Academy of Child & Adolescent Psychiatry, 40*(6), 719–728.

Menard, S., & Johnson, M. C. (2015). An intergenerational test of integrated theory. *Deviant Behavior, 36*(2), 87–100.

Merari, A. (2010). *Driven to death: Psychological and social aspects of suicide terrorism.* Oxford University Press.

Monahan, J. (2012). The individual risk assessment of terrorism. *Psychology, Public Policy, and Law, 18*(2), 167.

Montero, D., & Connor, T. (2000, December 28). Gruesome details of a 'methodical' spree; police: gunman blew away door to reach victims. *The New York Post*, p. 004.

Morales, T. (2005, April 12). Red Lake massacre took 3 minutes. *CBS.*

Myers, S. L. (1991, November 2). Student opens fire at U. of Iowa, killing 4 before shooting himself. *The New York Times*, p. 8.

Newman, M. (2006, March 28). Settle police and partygoers still puzzle over attack. *The New York Times*, p. 10.

Nichols, A. (2007, December 8). After penning rambling suicide letter ... camera catch final act of Neb. gunner. *Daily News*, p. 5.

Overbye, D. (2007, March 27). A tale of power and intrigue in the lab, based on real life. *The New York Times*, p. 3.

Postman, D., Sullivan, J., & Carter, M. (2006, March 26). North Seattle man is suspected shooter. *The Seattle Times.*

Rave, J. (2005, July 10). Why did Jeffrey do it? *Lincoln Journal Star*, p. 1.

Reinares, F. (2004). Who are the terrorists? Analyzing changes in sociological profile among members of ETA. *Studies in Conflict and Terrorism, 27*(6), 465–488.

Roach, J. (2007). Those who do big bad things also usually do little bad things: Identifying active serious offenders using offender self-selection. *International Journal of Police Science & Management, 9*(1), 66–79.

Roberts, N. (2006, March 28). Party killer was polite-landlord never saw guns. *The Daily Telegraph*, p. 15.

Roe, A., Krishnan, S., & Siderius, C. (2007, December 27). Suspects arrested in slayings near Seattle; The victims were killed on Christmas Eve but their bodies were not found until Boxing Day morning. *The Vancouver Sun*, p. A4.

Rosario, R. (2013, November 26). Weise planned a far more lethal assault. *Pioneer Press.*

Safranek, L. (2007, December 7). Gun seen on videotape Von Maur's cameras show Robert Hawkins toting an AK-47. *Omaha World-Herald*, p. 01A.

Sageman, M. (2004). Understanding terror networks.

Saulny, S. (2007, December 8). In photos and notes, new details on shootings. *The New York Times.*

Schmidt, A. P., & Jongman, A. I. (1988). Political terrorism. *A Research Guide to Concepts, Theories, Databases and Literature, Amsterdam and New Brunswick.*

Silke, A. (2001). The devil you know: Continuing problems with research on terrorism. *Terrorism and Political Violence, 13*(4), 1–14.

Silke, A. (2004). The road less travelled: recent trends in terrorism research. *Research on terrorism: trends, achievements and failures*, 186–213.

Sims, P. (2005, March 24). School killer's cartoon predicted massacre. *The Evening Standard*, p. 19.

Spencer, K. (2007, December 6). Six deadly minutes in the end, Hawkins made good on threats. *Omaha World-Herald*, p.01A.

Stolzenberg, L., & D'Alessio, S. J. (2008). Co-offending and the age-crime curve. *Journal of Research in Crime and Delinquency, 45*(1), 65–86.

Tracy, P. E., & Kempf-Leonard, K. (1996). *Continuity and discontinuity in criminal careers.* Springer Science & Business Media.

United States Department of Justice. Federal Bureau of Investigation. Uniform Crime Reporting Program Data: Supplementary Homicide Reports, 2000–2012.

Unnamed Author (1991, November 4). Campus shooting planned in detail by angry student. *Hamilton Spectator*, p. A8.

Unnamed Author (2005, March 23). School gunman stole police pistol, vest student killed 9 before turning weapon on himself. *CNN*.

Unnamed Author (2005, March 23). Shooter obsessed with violence. *Fox News*.

Unnamed Author (2007, April 14). Conviction upheld in killing of 7 in Wakefield; Former Marshfield man loses appeal to high court. *The Patriot Ledger*, p. 16.

Unnamed Author (2007, December 5). Gunshots, screams and 8 slain in Omaha. *St. Paul Pioneer Press*, p. A1.

Unnamed Author (2007, December 6). 'It happened to us' AK-47-style semiautomatic assault rifle. *Omaha World-Herald*.

Unnamed Author (2007, December 6). 'Very troubled' teen just fired from job and fixated on death, pals say. *Daily News*.

Unnamed Author (2007, December 6). 8 dead in mall massacre-madman picks off holiday shoppers. *The New York Post*.

Unnamed Author (2007, December 6). Holiday horror. *Daily News*.

Unnamed Author (2007, December 6). Police investigation begins police search crime scene, gunman's residence. *Omaha World-Herald*.

Unnamed Author (2007, December 6). The Nebraska gunman: Robert Hawkins. *Guardian Unlimited*

Unnamed Author (2007, December 7). Police: nine killed in shooting at Omaha mall, including gunman. *CNN*.

Unnamed Author (2007, December 8). Police release Hawkins' two suicide notes and a will. *Omaha World-Herald*.

Vossekuil, B., Fein, R. A., Reddy, M., Borum, R., & Modzeleski, W. (2002). The final report and findings of the Safe School Initiative. *US Secret Service and* [sic]

Vossekuil, B., Fein, R., Reddy, M., Borum, R., & Modzeleski, W. (2002). *The Final Report and Findings of the Safe School Initiative: Implications for the Prevention of School Attacks in the United States*. Washington, DC: U.S. Department of Education and U.S. Secret Service.

Zeleny, J., & Konigsber, E. (2007, December 7). Searching for clues to a young killer's motivation. *The New York Times*, p. 24.

# DOCUMENT NO. 3

# SIFTING DOMESTIC TERRORISM FROM HATE CRIME AND HOMEGROWN VIOLENT EXTREMISM

## CRS INSIGHT

August 14, 2017 (IN10299)

Jerome P. Bjelopera, Specialist in Organized Crime and Terrorism
(jbjelopera@crs.loc.gov, 7-0622)

*In light of the violence related to protests in Charlottesville, VA, on August 12, 2017, policymakers may be interested in how the concepts of domestic terrorism, hate crime, and homegrown violent extremism compare with one another. They are fairly distinct ideas that federal law enforcement agencies use to categorize key types of criminals whose illegal activities are at least partly ideologically motivated. Specifically, these terms may be part of public discussion regarding a widely reported incident involving James Alex Fields, who according to witnesses drove his car into a group of people protesting a rally featuring white supremacists in Charlottesville on August 12. Fields allegedly killed 1 person and injured 19 others. The Department of Justice has opened a civil rights investigation into the incident, presumably pursuing possible hate crime charges. Additionally, Attorney General Jeff Sessions has publicly stated that terrorism investigators are involved in investigating the incident, ostensibly exploring the possibility of characterizing it as an act of domestic terrorism rather than a hate crime.*

### Domestic Terrorism

Domestic terrorism cases differ from ordinary criminal activity in key ways. Most importantly, unlike ordinary criminals—who are often driven by self-centered motives such as profit and tend to opportunistically seek easy prey—domestic terrorists are driven by a cause or ideology. If the motives involved eventually align with the definition laid out in 18 U.S.C. §2331(5), presumably the case becomes a domestic terrorist investigation.

- The Federal Bureau of Investigation (FBI) has defined domestic terrorism as "acts of violence that [violate] the criminal laws of the United States or any state, committed by individuals or groups without any foreign direction, and appear to be intended to intimidate or coerce a civilian population, or influence the policy of a government by intimidation or coercion, and occur primarily within the territorial jurisdiction of the United States."

Domestic terrorists are a widely divergent lot, drawing from many philosophies and worldviews to justify their illegal acts. They can be motivated to commit crimes in the name of ideas such as animal rights, environmental rights, white supremacy, anti-government beliefs, and anarchism, for example. Importantly, the expression of these worldviews—minus the commission of crimes—involves constitutionally protected activity. As such, individuals and movements openly and *legally* espousing such beliefs distance themselves from terrorists who use the ideas to justify their own criminal actions.

The FBI safeguards against cases focused solely on constitutionally protected activities. All FBI investigations have to be conducted for an authorized national security, criminal, or foreign intelligence collection purpose. Investigations may not solely monitor the exercise of First Amendment rights. Finally, the Department of Justice and the FBI conceptualize domestic terrorism in terms of threats, not named or designated groups or actors.

## Hate Crime

Current federal law defines hate crimes to include any crime against either person or property in which the offender intentionally selects the victim because of the victim's actual or perceived race, color, religion, national origin, gender, gender identity, disability, or sexual orientation. Hate crimes may appear to involve ideological issues. However, as described by one FBI official, a "hate crime" "generally involve[s] acts of personal malice directed at individuals" and is missing the broader motivations driving acts of domestic terrorism. For investigators, distinguishing between "personal malice" and ideologically motivated actions may be difficult in specific cases. This suggests that sorting domestic terrorism from hate crimes depends on the degree of a suspect's intent. Did the suspect articulate an ideology, belong to a domestic terrorist group, or follow an extremist movement? The grey area between domestic terrorism and hate crime suggests that in some instances, suspects with links to domestic terrorist movements or ideologies supporting domestic terrorism may be charged with hate crimes. It is unclear to what extent this influences how the government understands the threat posed by extremist movements that hold racist beliefs. If some individuals of this ilk commit crimes against police or judges, for example, is the government more apt to label this activity as terrorism while individuals sharing these same racist motivations but targeting ordinary citizens based on race, religion, disability, ethnic origin, or sexual orientation are charged with hate crimes?

## The Harpham Case

The FBI's public description of the case of confessed would-be bomber Kevin Harpham exemplifies how difficult it may be to characterize acts as domestic terrorism. Initially the FBI viewed the case as domestic terrorism. In 2011, Harpham, allegedly motivated by white supremacist ideology, left a bomb—which never detonated—along the route of a parade in Spokane, WA, honoring Dr. Martin Luther King Jr. The FBI's Northwest Joint Terrorism Task Force led the investigation. In prepared public remarks framing the "current state of the terrorism threat" from April 2011, the then-FBI assistant director for the Counterterrorism Division noted that Harpham's case was one of "several recent domestic terrorism incidents [that] demonstrate the scope of the threat." Harpham eventually pled guilty to committing a federal hate crime and attempting to use a weapon of mass destruction. Thereafter, the bureau described the case as the successful prevention of a "horrific hate crime."

## Homegrown Violent Extremism

The FBI and DHS have popularized the phrase "homegrown violent extremist" (HVE). It divides domestic terrorists from U.S.-based terrorists motivated by the ideologies of foreign terrorist organizations. Reportedly, according to DHS and the FBI, an HVE is "a person of any citizenship who has lived and/or operated primarily in the United States or its territories who advocates, is engaged in, or is preparing to engage in ideologically-motivated terrorist activities (including providing support to terrorism) in furtherance of political or social objectives promoted by a foreign terrorist organization, but is acting independently of direction by a foreign terrorist organization." They also assert that an HVE is not a domestic terrorist—these are two distinct categories of terrorist actors.

**Figure 1. Who Are Domestic Terrorists?**

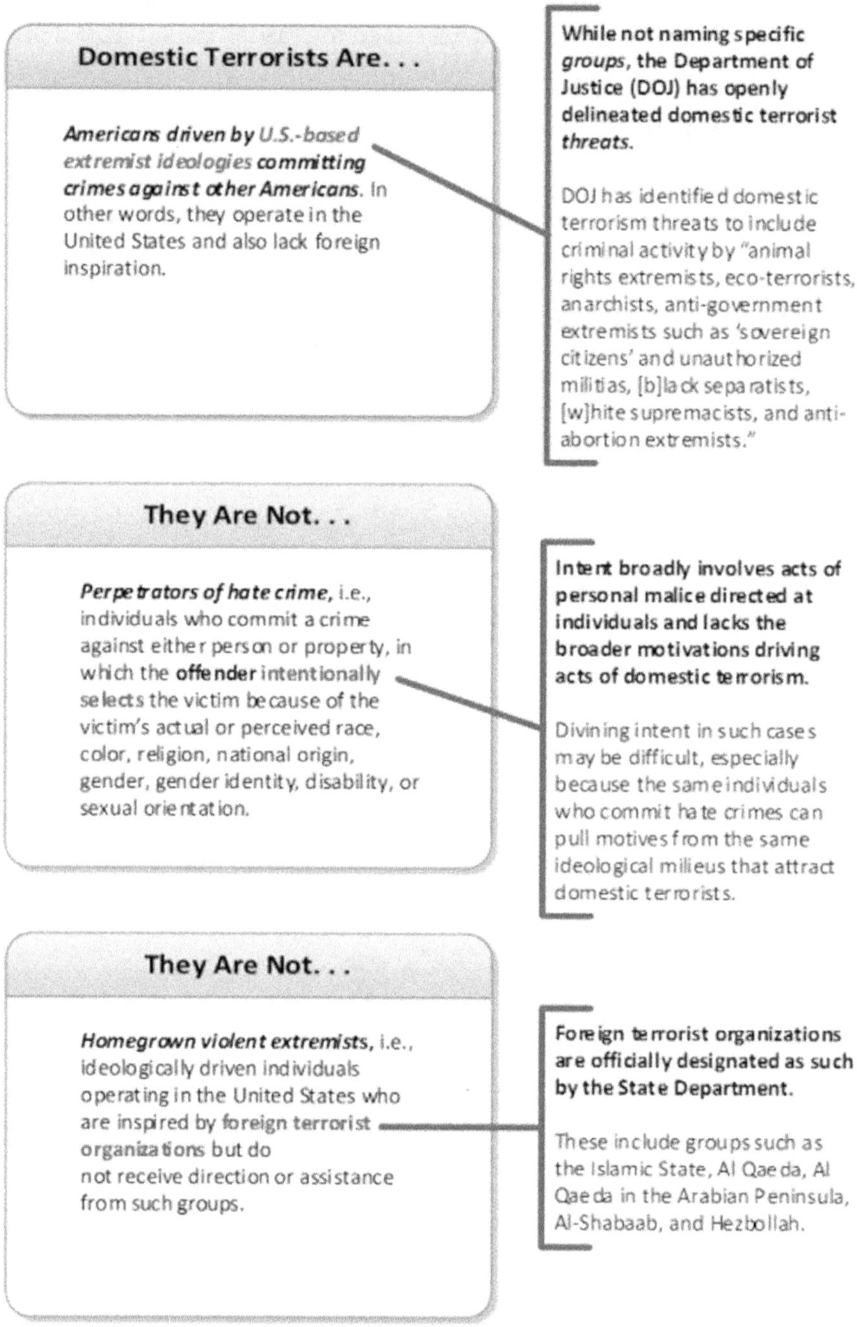


**Source:** CRS graphic derived from information in https://www.fbi.gov/about-us/investigate/civilrights/hate_crimes/overview; https://www.fbi.gov/news/testimony/animal-rights-extremism-andecoterrorism; Department of Justice, Counterterrorism White Paper; https://www.fbi.gov/news/stories/2009/september/domterror_090709.

# DOCUMENT NO. 4

# REPORT: LONE WOLF TERRORISM


**Prepared by**
**Security Studies Program**
**National Security Critical Issue Task Force**

June 27, 2015

Lydia Alfaro-Gonzalez, RJ Barthelmes, Christina Bartol, Michael Boyden, Thomas Calderwood, Daniel Doyle, Jacob Green, Erin Herro, Taylor Johnson, Katelyn Lawrenz, Katharine McMaster, Margaret Nencheck, Neil Noronha, Lee Smith, Kathleen Walsh, Letitia Wu, Kaila Yee

*GEORGETOWN UNIVERSITY*

Professors Jeffrey Connor & Carol Rollie Flynn




## Abbreviations

| | |
|---|---|
| AQ | Al-Qa'ida |
| AQAP | Al-Qa'ida in the Arabian Peninsula |
| CT | Counterterrorism |
| CVE | Countering Violent Extremism |
| DHS | Department of Homeland Security |
| DOJ | Department of Justice |
| DOS | Department of State |
| ELF | Earth Liberation Front |
| FBI | Federal Bureau of Investigation |
| IC | Intelligence Community |
| ISIL | Islamic State of Iraq and the Levant |

| | |
|---|---|
| NCTC | National Counter Terrorism Center |
| NSCITF | National Security Critical Issue Task Force |
| LE | Law Enforcement |
| LEO | Law Enforcement Officer |
| LWT | Lone Wolf Terrorist |
| OPSEC | Operational Security |
| US | United States |
| USG | United States Government |

## Executive Summary

The United States (US) is the primary target among western states for lone wolf terrorist (LWT) attacks, and the frequency of attacks continues to increase. Even though LWT attacks remain less common and precipitate fewer casualties than terrorist attacks conducted by organizations, the US must continue to focus counterterrorism resources and encourage further research to combat this threat to national security. In this assessment, the Georgetown National Security Critical Issue Task Force (NSCITF) hopes to inform key stakeholders about the most critical lone wolf terrorism issues and spark new policy discussions on how to address the problem.

The NSCITF articulates eight findings that inform the collective understanding of lone wolf terrorism and offers three actionable recommendations to address those findings. First, the NSCITF finds that no single USG definition on lone wolf terrorism exists. Second, the NSCITF identifies the following four current trends in domestic LWT attacks, each of which highlight multiple issues that US policymakers must consider when drafting counterterrorism policies directed at LWTs:

1) Increased targeting of law enforcement (LE) and military personnel;

2) Overwhelming use firearms to conduct attacks, compared to LWTs in other western countries who rely on hijackings or bombs;

3) Increased radicalization via the Internet, extremist media, and the civilian workplace; and,

4) Proclamation of an individual ideology instead of claiming affinity to specific, organized extremist groups.

Third, despite the presence of overarching trends among domestic LWTs, the NSCITF determines that profiling fails to target potential LWTs effectively. Consequently, in the fourth finding, the NSCITF provides a framework to understand how an individual becomes a LWT and to identify possible intervention points. Fifth, the NSCITF develops a typology that organizes lone wolves in terms of their ideological autonomy and social competence to explicate why lone wolves operate alone, a key gap in the extant literature on terrorism.

The final three findings address US federal and local law enforcement policies to prevent LWT attacks. In the sixth finding, the NSCITF identifies the challenges of using traditional law enforcement tactics to identify and stop LWTs. Specifically, the NSCITF highlights how the expansion of the Internet and social media offers individuals an ability to become radicalized without physically interacting with others and research various attack methodologies undetected. The seventh finding demonstrates that aggressive law enforcement tactics—namely, surveillance and monitoring of targeted individuals—risk community mistrust because of perceived infringements on civil liberties and privacy rights. In the final finding, the NSCITF notes that the US lacks a comprehensive, "whole of government" approach that coherently and systematically organizes the federal, local, and state efforts to combat lone wolf terrorism.

Based on the above findings, the NSCITF offers three recommendations. First, the USG should adopt a standard definition of lone wolf terrorism. Second, the USG should appoint clear leadership over the problem of lone wolf terrorism to streamline future policy responses and improve governmental coordination at the federal, state, and local levels. Finally, the USG should emphasize the prevention and short-circuiting of the radicalization process. Each recommendation will help the USG streamline future policy responses and improve governmental coordination at the federal, state, and local levels to prevent future LWT attacks.

## Methodology and Scope

The NSCITF developed the findings and recommendations outlined in this report through substantial research into the existing open source literature on LWTs. The NSCITF supplemented this research by conducting interviews with subject matter experts, USG policymakers, attorneys, and academics.

This assessment relies extensively on two datasets (Spaaij 2012 and Hamm & Spaaij 2015) to analyze the scope of the problem and the trends in domestic attacks. The authors in both datasets require that an individual threaten or commit violence alone to constitute "lone wolf terrorism," as opposed to violence committed by pairs or trios. Thus, the datasets remain consistent with the NSCITF's definition of lone wolf terrorism.

In addition, although recent academic literature and open source reports have addressed the possible threat of lone wolf cyber terrorists, this assessment will not address the use of computer network attacks as a methodology for terrorist attacks.[1] The NSCITF believes that the most immediate and concerning method used by LWTs as it relates to US national security is the use of violence targeting human lives and property; currently, there are no examples of domestic lone wolf terrorists launching cyber terrorist attacks that precipitate casualties or property destruction. However, the definition does *not* exclude the possibility that lone wolf cyber attacks could constitute terrorism, and the potential of lone wolf cyber terrorism warrants future study.

[1] Computer network attacks include actions taken through computer networks to disrupt, deny, degrade, or destroy the information within computers and computer networks and/or the computer/networks themselves.

## Finding 1: There Is No Single USG Definition of LWT

A review of existing definitions from government, private organizations, media reporting, and academic literature reveals little uniformity in the definition of the expression "lone wolf terrorism." For this report, the NSCITF defines it as: *The deliberate creation and exploitation of fear through violence or threat of violence committed by a single actor who pursues political change linked to a formulated ideology, whether his own or that of a larger organization, and who does not receive orders, direction, or material support from outside sources.* Absent violence or the threat of violence, the individual may hold extremist or radicalized views, but he or she is not a terrorist. Absent political motivation, an attack would more closely resemble traditional forms of crime, organized violence, or hate crimes. Absent the individual acting alone, the attack would fall under the traditional definition of terrorism that encompasses violence conducted by organized terrorist groups.

Clearly defining lone wolf terrorism is critical for research and policy purposes. Precision enables methodical analysis of the problem and potential solutions, revealing components of a problem that can be addressed separately or together. It also provides a clear definition of the problem to assist in forming solutions, some of which will ultimately require very specific analyses of targets. Finally, the division of the definition into precise elements is useful for data collection and organization, as well as the analyses and study of trends.

## Finding 2: Four Measurable Trends in Lone Wolf Terrorism

### Frequency of Lone Wolf Terrorist Attacks Increasing

LWT attacks remain relatively rare; however, their frequency has increased between 1968 and 2010 in the US and other western countries. In that time, lone wolf attacks constituted 1.8 percent of all terrorist attacks, increasing from thirty attacks in the 1970s to seventy-three in the 2000s, a growth of 143 percent.[2,3] As Figure 1 shows, the US has experienced a sixteen-fold increase in the number of attacks since the mid-twentieth century, from two attacks during the 1950s to thirty-two attacks during the 2000s.[4] It is important to note, however, that while the frequency of attacks is increasing, the rate of casualties has remained constant.[5]

In addition, the US remains the primary target among western states for LWT attacks. Of the 198 LWT attacks carried out between 1968 and 2010 across the US and fourteen other predominantly western countries, 113 occurred in the United States, representing fifty-seven percent of all attacks.[6] Terrorism in the United States "differs from terrorism in other countries in that a significant portion of terrorist attacks have been carried out

---

[2] Ramon Spaaij, "The Enigma of Lone Wolf Terrorism An Assessment," *Studies in Conflict and Terrorism* 33, no. 9 (2010), 858.

[3] Ramon Spaaij, *Understanding Lone Wolf Terrorism: Global Patterns, Motivations, and Prevention,* (New York: Springer, 2012), 27.

[4] Spaaij, *Understanding Lone Wolf Terrorism*, 32.

[5] Ibid, 30.

[6] Ibid.

by unaffiliated individuals rather than by members of terrorist organizations."[7,8] This recent increase in domestic LWT attacks suggests that these attacks may be poised to increasingly replace group-actor terrorist attacks for the foreseeable future.[9]

**Figure 1: Number of Domestic Lone Wolf Terrorist Attacks from 1950–2009[10]**

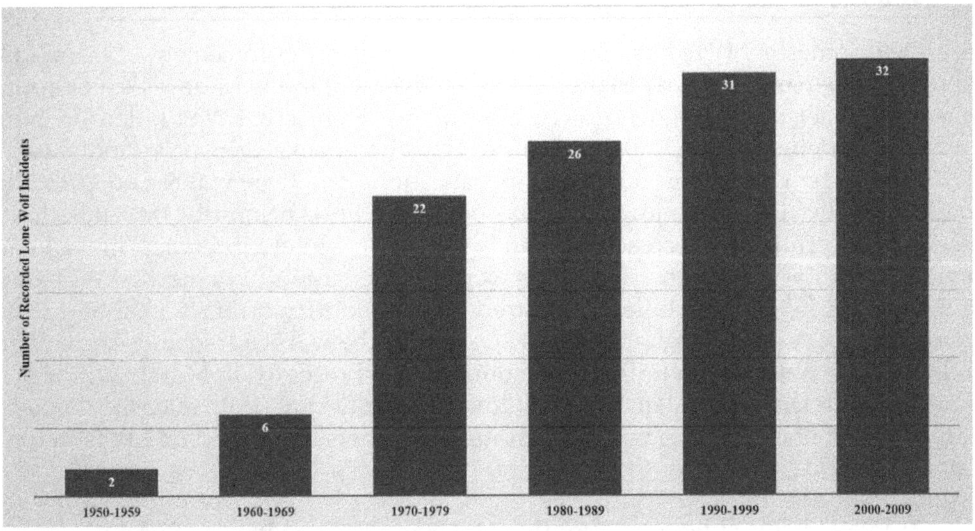


## Four Main Trends in US LWT Attacks

This assessment identifies four prominent trends in domestic LWT attacks since 2001. Domestic LWTs:

1) Increasingly target law enforcement (LE) and military personnel;

2) Overwhelmingly use firearms to conduct attacks, compared to LWTs in other western countries who rely on hijackings or bombs;

3) Increasingly become radicalized via the Internet, extremist media, and the civilian workplace; and,

---

[7] The countries chosen for this study other than the United States include the United Kingdom, Germany, France, Spain, Italy, Poland, The Netherlands, Denmark, Sweden, Czech Republic, Portugal, Russia, Australia, and Canada; Ramon Spaaij, *Understanding Lone Wolf Terrorism*, 27.

[8] Christopher Hewitt, *Understanding Terrorism in America: From the Klan to al Qaeda*, (New York: Routledge, 2003), 78.

[9] Lars Erik Berntzen and Sveinung Sandberg, "The Collective Nature of Lone Wolf Terrorism: Anders Behring Breivik and the Anti-Islamic Social Movement," *Terrorism and Political Violence* 26, no. 5 (2014): 759–779, doi: 10.1080/09546553.2013.767245.

[10] Mark Hamm and Ramon Spaaij, "Lone Wolf Terrorism in America: Using Knowledge of Radicalization Pathways to Forge Prevention Strategies," *National Criminal Justice Reference Service*, February 2015, accessed June 8, 2015, https://www.ncjrs.gov/pdffiles1/nij/grants/248691.pdf.

4) Proclaim an individual ideology instead of claiming affinity to specific, organized extremist groups.

These overall trends highlight multiple issues that US policymakers must consider when drafting counterterrorism policies directed at LWTs.

### 1) Increased Targeting of Law Enforcement and Military Personnel

Since 2009, domestic LWTs have increasingly targeted law enforcement officers (LEOs) and military personnel, either to protest US involvement in the Middle East or support white supremacist or anti-government movements. Domestic LWTs killed or injured twelve LEOs between the 1940s and mid-2000s, the attacks primarily "motivated by black power, the Palestinian question, and abortion."[11] Between 2009 and 2013 alone, domestic LWTs killed or injured twenty-four law LEOs, primarily in retaliation for perceived government overreach and in support of white supremacy movements.[12] Previously, military personnel and bases were not the targets of domestic LWT attacks, but since 2009, LWTs have killed or injured more than fifty military members.[13] With few exceptions, "al-Qaeda sympathizers angry over the wars in Iraq and Afghanistan" conducted those attacks on military personnel.[14] Most recently, in March 2015, a group claiming affiliation to the Islamic State of Iraq and the Levant (ISIL) released the names, addresses, and photos of one hundred military members and called on LWTs in the US to attack them.[15]

### 2) Increased Incidents of Shootings Instead of Hijackings or Bombs

Since the late 1990s, LWTs in the US have typically used firearms as their method of attack, unlike in other western countries where the primary methods are hijackings or bombings. Before 2001, LWT bombings killed or injured over 230 individuals in the US, "a phenomenon undoubtedly related to the bombing campaigns of terrorist groups during much of the period."[16] Between 2001 and 2010, these bombings in the United States only killed or injured eight people.[17,18] Conversely, during this same period, 80 percent of LWTs in the US used firearms to attack, compared to only 23.8 percent in other western countries, and no LWTs in the US have attempted armed hijackings.[19,20] Terrorism scholars conclude that the difficulties of acquiring bomb-making materials following the 1995 Oklahoma City bombing coupled with the relative simplicity of

[11] Hamm and Spaaij, "Lone Wolf Terrorism in America," 5.

[12] Ibid.

[13] Ibid.

[14] Ibid, 6.

[15] Will Dunham and Eric Beech, "Islamic State Calls on Backers to Kill 100 US Military Personnel," *Reuters*, March 21, 2015, accessed June 8, 2015, http://reut.rs/1EE5fZW.

[16] Hamm and Spaaij, "Lone Wolf Terrorism in America," 6.

[17] Ibid.

[18] Spaaij, *Understanding Lone wolf Terrorism*, 115.

[19] Ibid, 859.

[20] Ibid, 864.

acquiring firearms in the US have made shootings the most popular method for conducting domestic LWT attacks.[21]

### 3) The Internet and Civilian Workplaces Becoming the Loci of Radicalization

A growing number of domestic LWTs after the September 11, 2001, attacks have radicalized via the Internet or at their civilian workplaces. Prior to 2001, the primary locus of radicalization "was an extremist group that the lone wolves may have belonged to but had since abandoned."[22] As Figure 2 illustrates, interacting with fellow extremists online or watching extremist media previously radicalized only three percent of domestic LWTs. Today, interactions facilitated by the Internet have become one of the most powerful radicalization tools for domestic lone wolves. Interactive terrorist "chat rooms," in particular, have helped reinforce individuals' extremist views and "are among the most influential aspects of the Internet for inspiring terrorist attacks by those who might otherwise never consider going to such extremes."[23] Civilian workplaces have also become a prominent place for individuals to radicalize, especially if they work with individuals who share a similar ideology.[24]

**Figure 2: Loci of Domestic Lone Wolf Terrorist Radicalization Before and After 9/11[25]**

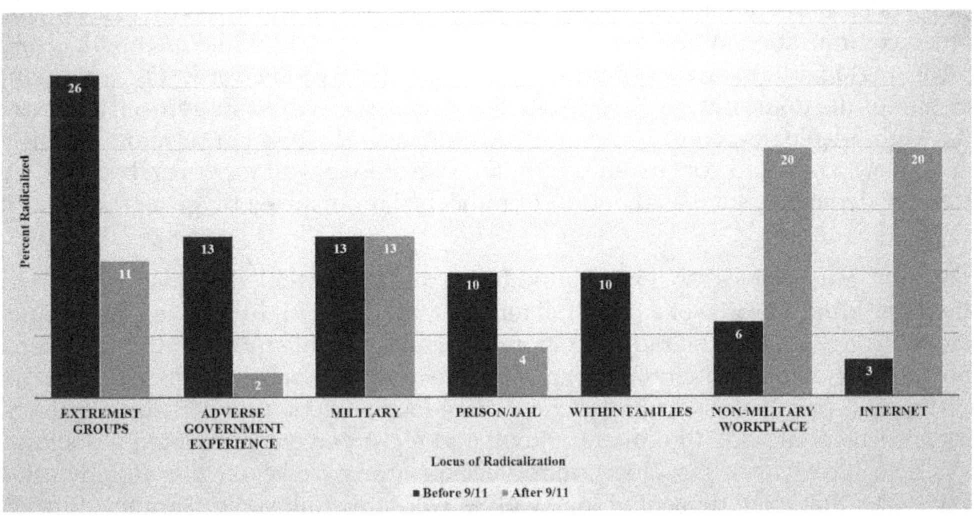


[21] Hamm and Spaaij, "Lone Wolf Terrorism in America," 6.

[22] Ibid, 7.

[23] Jeffrey Simon, *Lone Wolf Terrorism: Understanding the Growing Threat,* (New York: Prometheus Books, 2013), 203–204.

[24] Hamm and Spaaij, "Lone Wolf Terrorism in America," 7.

[25] Ibid, 25. Figure 3 is a combination of two figures within Hamm and Spaaij's article.

### 4) Declining Affinity toward Specific, Organized Extremist Groups

Since the early 2000s, fewer domestic LWTs publicly support or express sympathy for specific extremist organizations; instead, they self-proclaim and publicize a personal ideology or grievance. Between the 1960s and late 1990s, sixty-three percent of domestic LWTs affiliated with the ideological causes of specific groups, namely the neo-Nazi and anti-abortion organizations.[26] Since then, only forty-two percent of domestic lone wolves sympathize with a specific group, such as al-Qa'ida (AQ) or the neo-Nazi National Alliance.[27] The twenty-one percent decline in affinity correlates with the Internet becoming the primary locus of radicalization. Now, "lone wolves may be seeking direction through venues other than organizations: namely, via networks of like-minded activists found online or on cable television."[28] In addition, the expansion of mass media and social networking has enabled LWTs to proclaim their individual extremist views without attaching themselves to preexisting groups. For example, Joseph Stack, who did not express affinity toward a specific organization, posted his personal three-thousand-word, anti-government manifesto online before crashing a plane into the Internal Revenue Service building in Austin, Texas in February 2010.[29]

## Finding 3: Profiling Lone Wolf Terrorists is Ineffective

Despite some frequent demographic commonalities, there is no clear or set profile of a likely LWT, and attempting to develop one may lead to resentment of LEOs among profiled communities. While the majority of LWTs are single, white men with criminal records, these patterns are too broad to develop a clear profile for LEOs. For example, over half of the domestic LWTs have acted in support of white supremacist or extremist far-right ideologies, contributing to the frequency of white perpetrators.[30] This pattern is likely to shift in concurrence with the rise of lone wolf terrorism based in other extremist ideologies, such as the form of radical Islam inspired by groups such as ISIL and AQ.

Examining lone wolves' socioeconomic backgrounds further demonstrates the difficulty in building a profile of a potential terrorist, though it highlights the importance of personal grievances on the radicalization process. A recent study of 119 LWTs demonstrates a diversity of educational backgrounds: twenty-five percent of lone wolves' highest education completed was high school, fifty-four percent attended some university, thirteen percent attended graduate school, and eight percent completed a doctorate.[31] LWTs also have varying socioeconomic backgrounds; however, the aforementioned study found that forty percent of lone wolves were unemployed when they attacked.[32] The inability to gain employment, coupled with relatively high education levels, suggests that a perception of having been slighted by society contributes to a feeling of

[26] Hamm and Spaaij, "Lone Wolf Terrorism in America," 8.

[27] Ibid.

[28] Ibid.

[29] Simon, *Lone Wolf Terrorism*, 202.

[30] Hamm and Spaaij, "Lone Wolf Terrorism in America," 7.

[31] Paul Gill, John Horgan, and Paige Deckert, "Bombing Alone: Tracing the Motivations and Antecedent Behaviors of Lone-Lone Actor Terrorists," *Journal of Forensic Science* 59, no. 2, (2014): 428.

[32] Gill, Horgan, and Deckert, "Bombing Alone," 429.

relative deprivation.[33] These personal grievances and distorted perceptions of fairness influence an individual's susceptibility for extremist ideology.

While developing a suspect profile is part of standard LE work, the government must be wary of unfairly targeting certain populations. International media and US government officials continue to depict homegrown radical Islamic terrorism as one of the most significant threats to public safety. However, an examination of terrorism cases and LE reports over the last five years suggests this is not the case.[34,35] From 2009 to 2012, the number of Muslim-American terrorism cases and perpetrators declined each year, reaching fourteen cases in 2012. While this same number increased each year from 2012 to 2014, that trend included the spike in individuals joining Islamic terrorist organizations abroad.[36] Joining a foreign terrorist organization does not necessarily lead to homegrown terrorist acts, lone wolf or otherwise: since 2011, there has been a decline in the number of cases where Muslim-Americans plotted or engaged in violence inside the United States. Furthermore, a University of Maryland study found that, while radical Islamic terrorism in the United States has increased since the attacks on September 11, 2001, there has also been a continued, if not greater, increase in individual radicalization from the far right.[37] Overall, homegrown radical Islamic terrorism poses no greater threat to the public than other forms of domestic radicalization, but by unfairly focusing on the Muslim community, the USG risks inciting further divisions.[38] "American Muslims' view of their treatment also has led to a growing guardedness in their relationship with [law enforcement agencies] (LEAs),"[39] which in turn yields mistrust and reluctance to cooperate with LEAs.

### Finding 4: Lone Wolves Follow a Similar Radicalization and Mobilization Path

The radicalization process described below applies to both LWTs and group actors. Terrorists generally share a similar radicalization process: each starts with a personal, social, or political grievance that creates a receptive point. However, terrorists often experience a crisis event that exacerbates these grievances and leads them to adopt a radical ideology. After the radical ideology resonates, they go through anger projection and moral outrage simultaneously with escalating irritation by the initial grievance.

33 Fathali M. Moghaddam, "The Staircase to Terrorism: A Psychological Exploration," *American Psychologist* 60, no. 2 (2005): 163.

34 Martin Pengelly, "Eric Holder Says US 'At War' With 'Lone Wolf' Terrorists After Paris Attacks," *The Guardian*, January 11, 2015, accessed June 25, 2015, http://www.theguardian.com/world/2015/jan/11/eric-holder-paris-unity-rally-war-against-terrorists.

35 Scott Shane, "Homegrown Radicals More Deadly than Jihadists in US," *The New York Times*, June 24, 2015, accessed June 24, 2015, http://www.nytimes.com/2015/06/25/us/tally-of-attacks-in-us-challenges-perceptions-of-top-terror-threat.html?_r=0.

36 Charles Kurzman, "Terrorism Cases Involving Muslim-Americans, 2014," *Triangle Center on Terrorism and Homeland Security at Duke University*, February 9, 2015, accessed June 10, 2015, http://sites.duke.edu/tcths/files/2013/06/Kurzman_Terrorism_Cases_Involving_Muslim-Americans_2014.pdf.

37 Michael Jensen, Patrick James, and Herbert Tinsley. "Profiles of Individual Radicalization in the United States: Preliminary Findings," *Study of Terrorism and Response to Terrorism*, January 2015, accessed June 10, 2015, https://www.start.umd.edu/pubs/PIRUS%20Research%20Brief_Jan%202015.pdf.

38 Amy Julia Harris, "Islam Judged More Harshly Than Other Religions in Terrorist Attacks," *Reveal News*, January 16, 2015, accessed June 24, 2015, https://www.revealnews.org/article/islam-judged-more-harshly-than-other-religions-in-terrorist-attacks/

39 Faiza Patel, *Rethinking Radicalization* (New York: Brennan Center for Justice, 2011), 23.

As this cycle of anger continues, the terrorist eventually reaches a trigger point where they determine it is time to act. This point is when they decide to act alone or with a group, and this decision is significantly influenced by social competence and ideological autonomy, which is discussed in the following finding on lone wolf typologies. The LWT will then continue to mobilize and take action.

### A Framework for Radicalization

The NSCITF develops a framework for LWT radicalization and mobilization to assist LEOs, members of the intelligence community (IC), and policymakers in developing effective and targeted counterterrorism strategies. Understanding an individual's progression from believing in an extremist ideology to committing violence provides actionable opportunities for intervention and prevention.

**Figure 3: Framework for Lone Wolf Radicalization and Mobilization**

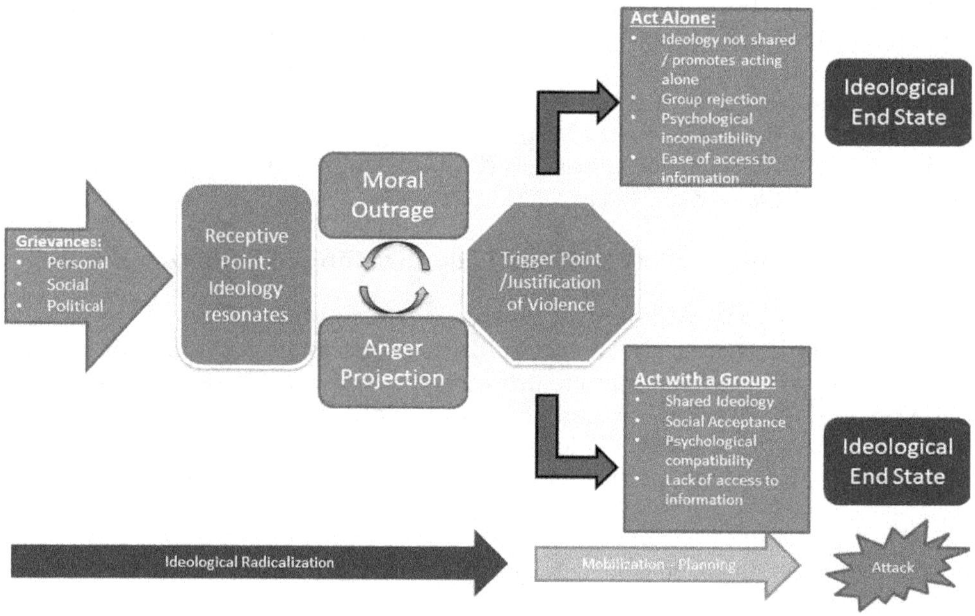


The framework in Figure 3 illustrates this process, demonstrating how personal, social, and political grievances increase susceptibility to extremist ideology, influence an individual's worldview, and ultimately justify violence as a tool for political change. While personal grievances are acute at the beginning of the LWT's radicalization, their influence diminishes over time as the LWT focuses anger on a societal, rather than individual, level. Furthermore, this framework distinguishes the crucial decision point where an individual determines whether they can best achieve their ideological end state by working with a group or acting alone.

## Receptive Point to Extremist Ideology

The receptive point, otherwise known as a "cognitive opening," occurs when internal or external factors shake certainty in the individual's previously accepted beliefs, rendering him or her receptive to alternative views and perspectives."[40] These factors include personal grievances, frustration at political or social circumstances, and psychological tendencies. In addition, the Internet's discussion forums, chat rooms, and messaging applications can facilitate radicalization by enabling individuals at the receptive point to explore extremist ideologies.

Critical events in the LWT's life, especially those leaving the LWT feeling personally wronged, are fundamental to radicalization. Thus, many LWTs adopt extremist ideologies as a means "to channel their own personal frustrations and assign blame to others."[41] For example, Olympic Park bomber Eric Rudolph's troubled childhood, father's death, and mother's transient lifestyle made him disgruntled and frustrated, increasing his susceptibility to extremism.

Frustration at social or political circumstances can further augment an extremist ideology's resonance with an individual. Often these grievances are linked to either personal or vicarious connections to perceived victims. Nidal Malik Hassan, for example, became increasingly angry at what he saw as American foreign policy targeting and killing fellow Muslims in the Middle East, enabling a radical jihadist ideology to take root.

While psychological dynamics underlie the entire radicalization process, certain mental issues are especially pronounced at the receptive point. Most LWTs are likely to suffer from some psychological disturbance, increasing the likelihood of extremist ideologies resonating.[42] An individual who has suffered trauma may disassociate himself or herself from his identity and seek alternative worldviews to replace this loss.[43] These new extreme ideologies are frequently grounded in a religion that gives meaning to pain, provides a community and sense of self, and offers a system of behavior and identity, particularly appealing to psychologically traumatized individuals.[44]

## Moral Outrage and Anger Projection

Terrorists frequently express outrage that the world is morally or physically in decline and project their anger on a particular group, blaming them for society's perilous state. As motivations and ideological narratives differ, the reason and cause for the world's decay will vary among LWTs. In addition, a LWT's personal and sociopolitical grievances influence the selection of his or her enemy. For example, LWTs who ascribe to hate-based ideologies rooted in the white supremacy and neo-Nazi movements blame minorities for the world's decline. David Copeland, the London nail bomber, blamed

---

[40] Quintan Wiktorowicz, "Joining The Cause: Al-Muhajiroun and Radical Islam," accessed June 7, 2015, http://insct. syr. edu/wp-content/uploads/2013/03/Wiktorowicz.Joining-the-Cause.pdf.

[41] Joel A. Capellan, "Lone Wolf Terrorist or Deranged Shooter? A Study of Ideological Active Shooter Events in the US, 1970–2014," *Studies in Conflict & Terrorism* 38, no.6 (2015): 398.

[42] Spaaij, *Understanding Lone Wolf Terrorism*, 50.

[43] Anne Speckhard, "Lone Wolf Terrorism," (presentation, Georgetown Security Studies Program, Washington, D.C., May 30, 2015).

[44] Ibid.

his inability to obtain employment on immigrants, leading him to believe that it was necessary to "trigger a race war."[45]

In addition, most religiously motivated LWTs are involved with a formal religious institution early on in the radicalization process that helps them target their moral outrage toward non-believers or other groups of wrongdoers and sinners. Extreme interpretations of religions that hold bifurcated views of the world consider non-believers to be the enemy, providing what they see as canonized rationale for projecting anger to a certain population.[46]

### Trigger Point and Justification of Violence

Once an individual has adopted an extremist ideology and identified the cause of their anger, there can be trigger point when an individual believes that mobilization and immediate action is required to halt the perceived decline of society. It is important to note that the vast majority of radicalized individuals do not experience a trigger point but will remain radicalized. Personal trauma or the suffering of others often drives LWTs to action.[47] Just as specific trigger points will vary among individuals, personal differences can cause those with shared extremist ideologies to react differently to the same event. Once an individual reaches this critical juncture and determines that violence is the only means to achieve their ultimate ends, they become a potential LWT. For example, Ted Kaczynski, the "Unabomber," was enraged when foresters destroyed the woods surrounding the cabin where he lived in self-imposed exile. Following this crucial trigger point, Kaczynski saw reform as impossible and believed that violence was the only way to destroy the industrial system, stating: "The only way we will get rid of it is if it breaks down and collapses."[48]

> ***Religiously motivated terrorism accounts for 43 percent of lone wolf attacks in the United States, and continues to rise post-9/11.***[13] [*sic*]

After determining that violence is necessary to restore world order, the terrorist dehumanizes the enemy, weakening his or her psychological barriers to committing violent acts.[49] This step is evident in many terrorist manifestos, as the LWTs justify violence as necessary to protect an oppressed or abused population, achieve ideological end goals, or cleanse society. Eric Rudolph's manifesto decried those who failed to stop the "wholesale slaughter of children" and described his attacks against abortion clinics as

[45] "Operation Marathon: Interviews with David Copeland," *Metropolitan Police Department.*

[46] US government subject matter expert, "Lone Wolf Terrorism," (presentation, Georgetown Security Studies Program, Washington, D.C., June 06, 2015).

[47] J. Ried Meloy and Jessica Yakeley, "The Violent True Believer as a 'Lone Wolf'—Psychoanalytic Perspectives on Terrorism," *Behavioral Sciences & the Law* 23, no. 3 (2014): 359.

[48] "Interview with Ted Kaczynski, Administrative Maximum Facility Prison, Florence, Colorado, USA," *Earth First Journal,* June 1999.

[49] Spaaij, *Understanding Lone Wolf Terrorism,* 54.

the "fundamental duty for a moral citizen."[50] Furthermore, religiously motivated terrorists might point to scripture that they believe sanctifies violence against the non-believer or enemy. In white supremacist and other racist ideologies, the "us" vs. "them" narrative allows the LWT to separate himself or herself from the enemy target population, allowing the LWT to then dehumanize others.[51] For example, Wade Page justified his fatal shooting of six people at a Sikh temple in Wisconsin by reducing minorities to what he considered "dirt people."[52] This psychological step is essential to enabling an individual to conduct an attack without hesitation or moral quandary.

## Choosing the Lone Wolf Path

The decision whether to join a terrorist group or become a LWT is influenced by social, psychological, and ideological characteristics. Social isolation and frequent psychological disturbances in LWTs lead to either failed and rejected attempts to join a group, or a tendency to avoid social interaction all together. Moreover, ideological differences also may influence an individual's decision to become a LWT rather than act with a group, as was the case for Anders Brievek.

Social alienation and interpersonal ineffectiveness can lead to an individual's decision to become a LWT and act alone possibly to avoid rejection.[53] Most LWTs tend to be socially isolated and unmarried, and one study notes that thirty-seven percent of far-right lone wolves lived alone at the time of attack.[54] The lack of a reliable social structure can create an environment lacking in rational feedback, allowing a continued downward spiral into radicalization. For example, Kaczynski recalled not fitting in with his classmates and being the subject of verbal abuse and bullying, and Rudolph was described as "different, a loner who didn't make a whole lot of friends."[55] Furthermore, some LWTs can attempt to join organized groups and later chose to operate alone after determining that their fellow members were not sufficiently violent or extreme.[56] David Copeland, for example, joined and later abandoned the British National Party because it did not advocate violence.

Individuals with mental illness are significantly more likely to embrace lone wolf terrorism rather than join terrorist groups because those groups may reject psychologically unstable recruits who present logistical and security threats.[57] While LWTs frequently exhibit symptoms of psychological disorders, their psychopathologies are

[50] "Full Text of Eric Rudolph's Statement," *National Public Radio*, April 12, 2005, accessed June 10, 2015, http://www.npr.org/templates/story/story.php?storyId=4600480.

[51] Nick Haslam, "Dehumanization: An integrative review," *Personality And Social Psychology Review* 10, no. 3 (2006): 252–264.

[52] Marilyn Elias, "Sikh Temple Killer Wade Michael Page Radicalized in Army," *Intelligence Report* 148 (2012), accessed June 7, 2015, http://www.splcenter.org/get-informed/intelligence-report/browse-all-issues/2012/winter/massacre-in-wisconsin. Report is a product of the Southern Poverty Law Center.

[53] Spaaij, *Understanding Lone Wolf Terrorism*, 50.

[54] Jeff Gruenewald, Steven Chermak, and Joshua D. Freilich, "Distinguishing "Loner" Attacks From Other Domestic Extremist Violence," *Criminology & Public Policy 12*, no. 1, (2013): 65–91, 70.

[55] Southern Poverty Law Center, "Tim and Sarah Gayman Discuss Growing Up in the Anti-Semitic Christian Identity Movement," *Intelligence Report* 102 (2001), accessed June 10, 2015, http://www.splcenter.org/get-informed/intelligence-report/browse-all-issues/2001/summer/coming-out.

[56] Spaaij, *Understanding Lone Wolf Terrorism*, 52.

[57] Speckhard, "Lone Wolf Terrorism," 2015.

generally insufficient to cause psychotic behavior or cognitive disorganization.[58] As a result, many LWTs remain mentally and physically capable of functioning in society and carrying out attacks.

While some individuals align their extremist views with an existing group's narrative, others build a self-constructed and unique ideology. For example, Breivik believed in a unique ideology combining elements of "Islamophobia, cultural conservative nationalism, anti-feminism ... white supremacy ... right-wing Christian-fundamentalist, and national-romantic temple-order traditions."[59] Breivik was unable to find a group that shared all of his various beliefs and decided to act alone.

Religiously motivated LWTs choose to act alone rather than with a group usually following a break from their congregation, often because of the terrorist's increasing radicalization and support for violence. Furthermore, organized terrorist groups such as ISIL and the Earth Liberation Front (ELF) have encouraged individuals to conduct lone wolf attacks throughout the world.[60] This tactic resembles the call for "leaderless resistance," a decentralized violence strategy executed by individual actors in the Christian Identity movement.[61] To encourage individual attacks, organizations like ELF and ISIL are increasingly using online magazines and videos to publicly venerate successful attackers, demonstrating the rewards and sense of belonging achievable and inspiring other vulnerable, radicalized individuals to follow in their footsteps.

### Ideological End State

Similar to members of organized terrorist groups, LWTs believe that violence will lead to their desired ideological and sociopolitical end states and oftentimes their personal goals. As extremist ideologies consider the world to be in a state of moral decline, the various end states feature the restoration of world order. Though terrorist organizations aim to bring about their political and ideological end states, LWTs frequently envision themselves singularly capable of healing society. For example, Wade Page believed that it was his duty to "stand up for [his] race ... and land."[62] Particularly in societies that value individual contributions and widely accept that "one person can change the world," LWTs may feel especially encouraged that their lone act will be successful in bringing about their desired end state.

---

[58] Liah Greenfeld, "The Making of a Lone Wolf Terrorist," *Psychology Today,* October 26, 2014, accessed June 6, 2015, https://www.psychologytoday.com/blog/the-modern-mind/201410/the-making-lone-wolf-terrorist.

[59] Siri Merethe Neset, Daniel Heradstveit, and G. Matthew Bonham. "The Lone Wolf behind the Norwegian Tragedy: The Ideological Foundations of Anders Behring Breivik," Paper presented at International Society of Political Psychology, Annual Convention, July 2012, accessed June 06, 2015, http://faculty.maxwell.syr.edu/gmbonham/The_Lone_Wolf.pdf.

[60] Michael Steinbach, "Statement Before the House Judiciary Committee, Subcommittee on Crime, Terrorism, Homeland Security, and Investigations," *ISIL in America: Domestic Terror and Radicalization,* Hearing, February 26, 2015, (Serial No. 114-6), Washington: Government Priniting Office, 2015, accessed June 09, 2015, http://judiciary.house.gov/_cache/files/121d6120-6f86-4b4e-a39b-7076fa8c7825/114-6-93527.pdf

[61] "Press Release: Operation Lone Wolf," *Federal Bureau of Investigation, San Diego Division,* n.d., accessed June 25, 2015, https://www.fbi.gov/sandiego/about-us/history/operation-lone-wolf.

[62] Chris McGreal, "Wade Michael Page's Acquaintances Recall A Troubled Man Guided By Hate," *The Guardian,* August 7, 2012, accessed June 29, 2015, http://www.theguardian.com/world/2012/aug/07/wade-michael-page-wisconsin-shooting.

## Finding 5: Existing Typologies Fail to Explain Why Lone Wolves Act Alone

Scholars have developed a number of typologies for LWTs that employ unique methodologies and offer distinct insights, but the extant literature fails to provide a simple and accessible method for evaluating why LWTs act alone. Therefore, this report proposes a typology that helps to describe the decision to act as a LWT, and the typology organizes LWTs in terms of their ideological autonomy—the extent to which they espouse their own ideology or the ideology of an existing organization, and social competence—a psychological construct that describes an individual's ability to create and maintain relationships.

Phillips and Pohl (2012) apply economic theories of rational choice to profile LWTs, the results of which yield two main categories for LWTs: risk-aversive and risk-seeking.[63] Phillips and Pohl describe members of the risk-aversive group as part-time terrorists who alternately engage in a series of terrorist acts along with legitimate activities, while risk-seeking LWTs place a higher value on the expected returns from their attack than the potential threat of capture.[64] This model remains a useful tool for explaining what types of activities a LWT may undertake (i.e. why LWTs choose serial, low impact attacks versus single incident, spectacular attacks), but it does not explain why the individual would choose to act alone rather than join with or recruit a group.

Conversely, Pantucci creates four discrete categories of lone Islamist terrorists, which he derives from a review of case studies.[65] Pantucci differentiates LWTs based on such factors as means and nature of radicalization, motive, and tactical circumstances. The first category is the loner, an "isolated individual who seek[s] to carry out an act of terrorism using some form of extremist ideology as their justification" but lacks clear connections to a greater network.[66] The second category is the lone wolf, an individual motivated by an extremist ideology who possesses connections to broader extremist networks but does not exist within an organization's command and control structure.[67] The third category is the lone wolf pack, a group of lone wolves who operate together but remain independent of formal command and control structures.[68] The fourth and final category is the lone attacker, an individual who operates alone but possesses clear command and control ties to existing organizations.[69] Pantucci's typology is descriptive in nature and successfully achieves its goal of describing the strategic scope of lone wolf terrorism. However, the inclusion of lone wolf packs and lone wolf attackers blurs the lines between traditional LWTs and other manifestations of the terrorist phenomenon and still does not address why an individual chooses to act alone.

[63] Rodger A. Bates, "Dancing With Wolves: Today's Lone Wolf Terrorists," *The Journal of Public and Professional Sociology* 4, no. 1 (2012): 7, accessed June 9, 2015, http://digitalcommons.kennesaw.edu/cgi/viewcontent.cgi?article=1023&context=jpps.

[64] Ibid.

[65] Raffaello Pantucci, "A Typology of Lone Wolves: Preliminary Analysis of Lone Islamist Terrorists," *The International Centre for the Study of Radicalization and Political Violence,* March 2011, 4, accessed June 9, 2015, http://www.trackingterrorism.org/sites/default/files/chatter/1302002992ICSRPaper_ATypologyofLoneWolves_Pan tucci.pdf.

[66] Pantucci, "A Typology of Lone Wolves," 19.

[67] Ibid, 20.

[68] Ibid, 24.

[69] Ibid, 29.

Building on Pantucci's typology, Rodger Bates evaluates LWTs along continuums on four dimensions. As Figure 4 shows, Bates' first dimension evaluates the extent to which a LWT is self-radicalized or radicalized by a group.[70] Second, Bates offers a method to determine whether a lone wolf's motivation for violence is political and ideological (altruistic) or derived from personal grievances (egoistic).[71] Bates' final two dimensions mimic Phillips and Pohl's evaluation on whether LWTs are risk-seeking or risk-averse and serial offenders (form-career) or one time offenders (form-chaos).[72]

**Figure 4: Bates' General Model of Lone Wolf Terrorism**

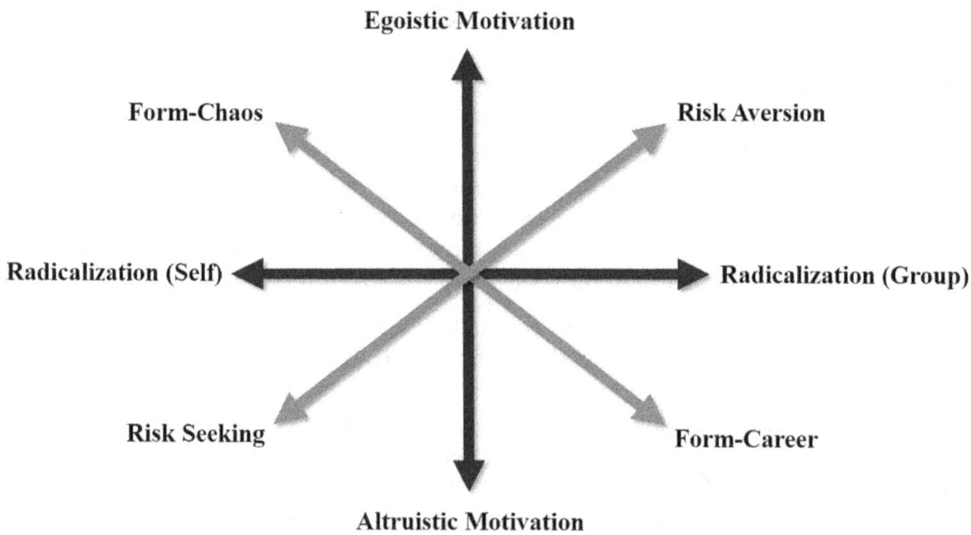


Bates' detailed typology sacrifices simplicity for accuracy, and Bates himself admits that "a model with this many possibilities is too complex for normal use, but the four dimensions contribute to a more complete understanding."[73] However, Bates' model is more comprehensive than either Phillips and Pohl or Pantucci and begins to explain why an individual might choose to act alone.

### A New Lone Wolf Typology: Social Competence and Ideological Autonomy

The NSCITF offers a new typology on LWTs. To develop a simple, practical typology to elucidate why LWTs act alone, a logical starting point is to examine two common themes distinguishing lone wolves from other group-oriented terrorists: social competence and ideological autonomy. First, LWTs have higher rates of psychopathology and social alienation than both the general population and group actor terrorists.[74] Even

[70] Bates, "Dancing With Wolves: Today's Lone Wolf Terrorists," 8.

[71] Ibid, 9.

[72] Ibid.

[73] Ibid. 10.

[74] Spaaij, *Understanding Lone Wolf Terrorism*, 50.

in the absence of diagnosable mental illness, Ramon Spaaij finds a "degree of social ineffectiveness and social alienation" that often limits LWTs' ability to participate in larger groups.[75] While social inadequacy is not sufficient to explain why individuals become LWTs, its prevalence suggests it is necessary to explain LWTs.

Considerable psychological research on interpersonal relationships and social ability has focused on the construct of social competence, which can provide a broad measure for LWTs' social ability. Social competence is defined as "all the factors within an individual that influence relationship quality and are necessary for recruiting and maintaining supportive close personal relationships."[76] A wide variety of interrelated factors, including social skills, disposition, early family experiences, social support, and psychopathology contribute to one's social competence.[77] Notably, many of the deficits that LWTs display in their ability to interact with society may be measurable as deficits in social competence. For example, Kaczynski argued that skipping a grade in elementary school marked a critical point on his journey towards terrorism because it led to an underdevelopment of his social skills, later compounded by his self-exile from society.[78] Relationships are a necessary part of group participation, regardless of the purpose of the organization. LWTs may choose to operate alone to improve their operational security (OPSEC) and avoid detection; however, they may also feel *obligated* to operate alone because they lack the necessary social competence to gain acceptance or mobilize others to their cause.

In addition to social competence concerns, a second distinctive characteristic of LWTs is the confusing myriad motivations behind their violence. Ultimately, "assigning clear-cut motive or ideology to solo actor terrorists is often a problematic exercise."[79] The problems here are twofold: LWTs tend to mix personal grievances with ideological causes,[80] and it is often difficult to discern the degree to which a LWT acts on behalf of his own idiosyncratic ideology or if he assumes the ideology of an existing organization. Evaluating LWTs' ideological autonomy can provide rich insights into why they choose to operate alone and how they interact with elements of a broader terrorist movement.

## Evaluating by Social Competence and Ideological Autonomy

The importance of social competence and ideological autonomy as key characteristics of LWTs suggests the possibility of creating a typology using these dimensions. As Figure 5 illustrates, the permutations of this typology generate four possible subcategories of LWTs. These categories should be understood as simplified classifications: not all LWTs will fall neatly into a single category. This assessment uses four case studies to demonstrate the utility of this typology in evaluating why the LWT operates alone.

---

[75] Ibid.

[76] B. Mallinckrodt, "Attachment, Social Competencies, Social Support, and Interpersonal Process in Psychotherapy," *Psychotherapy Research* 10, no.3 (2010): 243, accessed June 9, 2015, http://dx.doi.org/10.1093/ptr/10.3.239.

[77] B. Mallinckrodt, "Attachment, Social Competencies, Social Support, and Interpersonal Process in Psychotherapy," 241.

[78] Ramon Spaaij, *Understanding Lone Wolf Terrorism*, 53.

[79] Ibid, 39.

[80] Ibid, 38.

**Figure 5: Typology of Lone Wolf Terrorists by Social Competence and Ideological Autonomy**

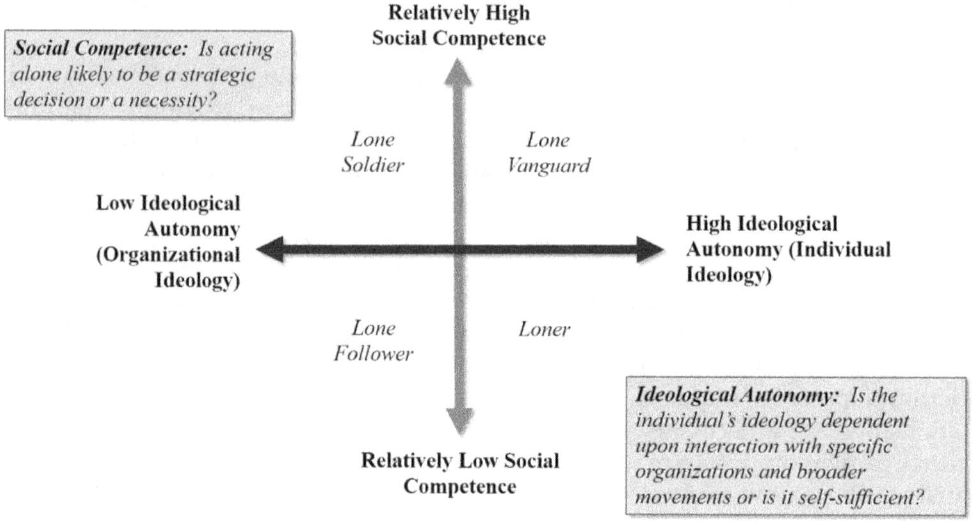


### Case Study 1: Lone Soldiers

The first category is *lone soldiers,* or individuals who demonstrate high levels of social competence and low levels of ideological autonomy. Individuals in this category will act alone for strategic purposes to advance the ideological and political objectives of a larger terrorist organization. Their adherence to a specific organization's ideology suggests they are more likely to attempt contact with terrorist networks. The lone soldier possesses comparatively higher social competence in relation to other LWTs and can function as a member of society. The Fort Hood shooter Nidal Hasan displays several of the characteristics of the lone soldier, for example.

Hasan embraced aspects of AQ ideology, objected to US policies in the Middle East, and sought contact with the Al-Qai'da in the Arabian Peninsula (AQAP) imam Anwar al-Awlaki.[81] Although he displayed questionable social skills and was noted for poor relationships with his patients, Hasan was socially adept enough to attain the rank of Major in the US Army.[82] The US military documented Hasan's grievances concerning US policies in the Middle East prior to the attack, lending credence to the notion that Hasan's lone wolf attack emulated's ideology.[83]

---

[81] Taylor Schmaltz, "Killings at Fort Hood," *Terrorism Since 9/11: The American Cases,* ed. John Mueller (Columbus: Mershon Center, 2015): 3,8, accessed June 9, 2015, http://politicalscience.osu.edu/faculty/jmueller/32HOOD7.pdf.

[82] Schmaltz, "Killings at Fort Hood," 8–9.

[83] Ibid, 5.

### Case Study 2: Lone Vanguards

The second category is *lone vanguards,* or individuals who demonstrate high levels of social competence and ideological autonomy. This type of LWT chooses to act alone to advance his individual ideology, which makes him or her less likely to possess ties to formal terrorist organizations though he or she has the requisite social skills to form relationships. This describes Norwegian LWT Breivik: prior to his two-stage terror attack in Norway, Breivik created a 1,500-page manifesto detailing his extremist views. While he derives many of his ideas from right-wing extremist literature, his ideology represents a departure from the established ideologies of any existing organization or movement.[84] Breivik initially joined Norway's conservative Progress Party but left of his own accord after concluding the party did not advance its policies far enough.[85] Although Breivik often shunned visitors and displayed socially alienating behaviors, he functioned as a mildly successful business entrepreneur at a young age.[86] In his compendium, Breivik specifically identified lone wolf plots as ideally suited for the OPSEC necessary to conduct his own attack.[87]

### Case Study 3: Loners

The third category is *loners,* or individuals who demonstrate low levels of social competence and high levels of ideological autonomy. Individuals in this category act alone to advance the goals of their individualized ideology, but their low social competence suggests they may also lack the ability to build relationships with peers or mobilize others to their cause. Loners are likely to be among the most isolated LWTs because they struggle to interact with others and do not rely on others for ideological motivation. The Unabomber, Kaczynski, typifies the loner. Akin to Breivik, Kaczynski believed his unique message warranted a manifesto, a 35,000-word diatribe against modernity entitled "Industrial Society and Its Future."[88] Kaczynski's manifesto draws inspiration from anarchism, environmentalism, and Luddism, but defies classification into any individual category. Kaczynski also struggled with psychopathology throughout his life, seeking psychiatric help while studying at the University of Michigan and describing periodic battles with depression.[89] Kaczynski's crippling social anxiety and resulting isolation likely left him no choice but to operate alone.

### Case Study 4: Lone Followers

The final category is *lone followers,* or individuals who demonstrate low levels of social competence and ideological autonomy. Individuals in this category seize the ideology of an existing organization but lack the social competence needed to gain acceptance into the group. Low social competence and the adoption of a group's ideology suggest that

[84] Spaaij, *Understanding Lone Wolf Terrorism,* 39.

[85] Ibid, 19.

[86] Jacob Aasland Ravndal, "A Post-Trial Profile of Anders Behring Breivik," *CTC Sentinel* 5, no. 10 (20120: 16–19, accessed June 9, 2015, https://www.ctc.usma.edu/posts/a-post-trial-profile-of-anders-behring-breivik.

[87] Rafaello Pantucci, "What Have We Learned about Lone Wolves from Anders Behring Breivik?" *Perspectives on Terrorism* 5, no. 5–6 (2011): 35.

[88] Spaaij, *Understanding Lone Wolf Terrorism,* 40.

[89] Ibid, 51.

personal grievances may strongly motivate lone followers, prompting questions about whether the attack constitutes terrorism. Michael Zehaf-Bibeau conforms to the general typology of the lone follower. Prior to his shooting spree in Ottawa, Zehaf-Bibeau lived on the margins of society—in the decade prior to his October 2014 attack, he was homeless and unable to hold a steady job.[90] In the video message recorded before his attack, Zehaf-Bibeau justified his actions as a response to Canadian atrocities against Muslims in the Middle East.[91] Although he did not specifically reference a terrorist organization during his martyrdom video, residents at homeless shelters in the weeks prior to the attack reported Zehaf-Bibeau became increasingly vocal in his support for ISIL.[92] His inability to secure a passport for travel to the Middle East sparked his decision to attack. Despite his increasing adherence to ISIL's ideology, Zehaf-Bibeau's attack appears to have been a spontaneous response to a personal crisis rather than a strategic attack in support of deeply held extremist beliefs.

### Importance and Scope of New Typology

It is important to note that the lone wolf terrorism typology proposed in this assessment does not attempt to describe or explain every feature of LWTs; rather, it provides a simple way to organize insights as to why LWTs operate alone. Measuring ideological autonomy and social competence yields numerous insights. First, the construct of social competence offers a meaningful and measurable way to encompass the spectrum of social and psychological concerns seen in LWTs. Second, the possibility that LWT violence is at least partly explained by social competence raises the prospect that a mental health or social work model may be efficacious in the prevention of some LWTs. Third, the synthesis of ideological autonomy and social competence offers insights into how LWTs relate to established terrorist organizations and broader extremist movements and may help investigators anticipate the types of communications a prospective LWTs may have with larger networks, such as seeking ideological sustenance.

## Finding 6: Challenges in Identifying Lone Wolves Using Traditional Law Enforcement Tactics

Established LE tactics, specifically those intended for counterterrorism (CT) operations, often focus on detecting threats and thwarting attacks via suspicious activity reports and communications monitoring. While those tactics have some applicability to preventing lone wolf terrorism, they require modifications to be more effective for combating the unique threat posed by lone wolf actors.

### Community Reporting Often Provides Crucial Information

LE has enhanced efforts to increase community awareness of the warning signs of radicalization. Many government agencies—including the Department of State (DOS),

[90] Michael Friscolanti, "Uncovering a Killer: Addict, Drifter, Walking Contradiction," *Macleans*, October 30, 2014, accessed June 9, 2015, http://www.macleans.ca/news/canada/michael-zehaf-bibeau-addict-drifter-walking-contradiction/.

[91] "Transcript of Michael Zehaf-Bibeau's Message," *Ottawa Citizen*, March 6, 2015, accessed June 9, 2015, http://ottawacitizen.com/news/national/transcript-of-michael-zehaf-bibeaus-final-message.

[92] Friscolanti, "Uncovering a Killer."

National Counter Terrorism Center (NCTC), and the Federal Bureau of Investigation (FBI)—have created community engagement teams for this specific purpose, teaching community groups (e.g. schools, neighborhoods, and religious groups) the consequences of LWT attacks and the importance of early reporting.

Given the high probability that at least one individual with prior knowledge regarding an attack or attacker, community engagement programs are essential cornerstones of lone wolf identification. One study concludes that "in sixty-three percent of the cases, family and friends were aware of the individual's intent to engage in terrorism-related activities because the offender verbally told them."[93] The FBI has incorporated tip lines and websites in all fifty-six national field offices, increased community outreach programs, and developed the Guardian Threat Management system, which allows coordination of terrorism-related tips with other federal, state, and local LE partners.

In addition, the FBI's Countering Violent Extremism (CVE) Office is developing a strategic messaging plan to encourage the identification of radicalized individuals with a scheduled release by September 2015. This plan will outline ways in which the FBI can provide training and education to community members, particularly in schools for grades nine through twelve. The FBI is also creating a website to educate students on the threat of violent extremist narratives, although this project has been delayed due to funding restrictions.[94]

### Human Source Reporting

Traditional LE undercover sources in radicalized groups or criminal enterprisers can provide information about individual members at varying stages of the radicalization process. LE sources may also be able to provide group or neighborhood dynamics, including crucial insight regarding which individual may be a potential threat. LEOs can then engage traditional investigative and interview techniques to determine the extent of radicalization and potential for mobilization, and respond as needed.

Indonesia's de-radicalization program, for example, has not led directly to the capture of Jemaah Islamiyah militants or leaders, but it has opened channels of communication between Indonesian police, current militants, and ex-radicals. The program's current value is as a source of intelligence and non-stigmatizing connections with radicals and their families, and as a mechanism to identify future sources.[95]

### Communications Monitoring

The Internet provides much of the radicalization material for those who become LWTs—and, therefore, to the LE organizations working to identify potential lone actors. LE can monitor social media platforms such as Twitter and Facebook, along with websites and chat rooms known to profess extremist views. Reviewing search histories can provide useful leads and evidence of extremist activity, focusing their attention on individuals who have already been identified as potential threats. In the case of suspected terrorist

[93] Gill, Horgan, and Deckert, *Bombing Alone.*

[94] Countering Violent Extremism Office, Federal Bureau of Investigation, Interview with Georgetown University National Security Critical Task Force, Personal interview, Washington D.C., June 4th, 2015.

[95] Kathleen E. Schulze, "Indonesia's Approach to Jihadist Deradicalization," *CTC Sentinel* 1, no. 8, (2008): 9.

Sohiel Omar Kabir, the Department of Justice (DOJ) used his Facebook activity to identify his involvement in terrorist activity. Kabir had posted propaganda and "liked" a variety of extremist pages.[96] Recent advances in data analytics could provide faster and more accurate identification techniques of online behavior associated with lone wolves.

CT and counter-radicalization experts also engage potentially violent individuals in online conversation, working with specialists to attempt de-radicalization. This last strategy has had mixed results. ISIL, for example, is known for its aggressive social media campaigns, but there have been successful counter-messaging efforts by Islamic ideology experts.[97] However, the DOS counter-messaging attempt against ISIL has fallen short of its intended target audience.[98] Its efficacy is also limited since the messages are sent from an official government source, a poor point of origin for those who are opposed to the US government. A well-planned and executed counter-messaging campaign is a useful tactic, but respected community leaders and experts should spearhead this campaign, rather than the USG.

### The Internet and Countering Radicalization

Until the growth of social media and the Internet, radicalization occurred via person-to-person interaction, which allowed LE to track known groups with standard surveillance and investigative tools. As use of the Internet increases, so does the availability of extremist material, thus facilitating the radicalization and mobilization processes. AQAP, for instance, has produced thirteen online issues of its English-language magazine *Inspire* to date.[99] The Internet reduces the need for face-to-face recruitment, enabling terrorist organizations to amass a global following.[100] Online information provides potential LWTs with instructions on obtaining weapons, building explosive devices from easily-obtained materials, and names and descriptions of potential US-owned targets."[101]

The importance of the Internet in shaping the US government's CVE response is well documented. In a 2010 Senate hearing, Garry Reid outlined the challenge of the Internet in the promotion of extremist ideology and radicalization, but US government programs have failed to produce effective counter-messaging strategies five years later. At the same hearing, Ambassador Daniel Benjamin, Coordinator for the Department of State

96 *United States v. Sohiel Omar Kabir, et al.*, Criminal Complaint, United States District Court for the Central District of California, November 16, 2012 (unsealed November 19, 2012).

97 Harry Bruinius, "Muslim youth counter Islamic State with #NotInMyName Twitter campaign," *Christian Science Monitor*, September 22, 2014, accessed June 12, 2015, http://www.csmonitor.com/World/Europe/2014/0922/Muslim-youths-counter-Islamic-State-with-NotInMyName-Twitter-campaign.

98 Rita Katz, "The State Department's Twitter War with ISIS is Embarrassing," *Time*, December 16, 2014, accessed June 24, 2015, http://time.com/3387065/isis-twitter-war-state-department/.

99 U.S. Senate, "U.S. Government Efforts to Counter Violent Extremism," hearing before the Subcommittee on Emerging Threats and Capabilities of the Committee on Armed Services, One Hundred Eleventh Congress, March 10, 2010, accessed June 25, 2015. http://www.gpo.gov/fdsys/pkg/CHRG-111shrg63687/html/CHRG-111shrg63687.htm.

100 Ibid.

101 Steve Hopkins, "Al-Qaeda Published Recipe For Easy-To-Make Bomb That Would Evade Airport Check That 'Any Determined Muslim Can Prepare,'" *Daily Mail*, December 2014, accessed June 9, 2015, http://www.dailymail.co.uk/news/article-2905276/Al-Qaeda-publishes-recipe-easy-make-bomb-evade-airport-check-determined-Muslim-prepare.html.

Counterterrorism Bureau, addressed DOS' CVE efforts. Using partnerships with host countries and local nongovernmental organizations in foreign nations, it has worked to make ideologies that counter extremist views available on the web.[102] Benjamin noted, "If you look at the history of terrorism, the Internet is probably the most important technological innovation since dynamite, and it's enormously difficult to deal with all the different aspects."[103]

Easily accessible websites provide much of the same radical ideology that previously relied on in-person contact. LE should therefore be prepared for a potential increase of lone wolf actors who would not otherwise have reached radical extremes, due to either a lack of resources or an unwillingness to interact with other radicalized individuals, both of which the Internet easily circumvents. Conversely, the increased prominence of online radicalization can provide extra opportunities for LE, who can track websites and monitor online communications to pinpoint radicalized individuals.

> *"Enabled by 21st century technology, extremists have optimized the use of Internet chat rooms, Web sites, and email chains to spread their virulent messages and reach a global audience of potential recruits. What was once a lengthy process of establishing contact, exchanging ideas, arranging meetings, providing training, and developing attack plans can now be condensed into a much shorter timeline, across multiple international boundaries, and beyond the reach of any single law enforcement agency or military task force."*
>
> *—Garry Reid, Deputy Assistant Secretary for Defense for Special Operations and Combating Terrorism, hearing to the Senate Committee for Armed Services*[29 [sic]]

## Finding 7: Law Enforcement Responses Can Result in Community Mistrust

### Surveillance and Civil Liberties

The USG must strike the appropriate balance between monitoring potential LWTs and protection civil liberties. In response to the September 11, 2001 attacks, the US Congress passed legislation authorizing LEAs previously serving an investigative role to undertake intelligence-gathering missions.[104] Collectors and consumers of intelligence derived from these programs assert the data's value in thwarting terrorist (lone wolf included) plots, but other studies question that assessment. For instance, a December 2013 report by the President's Review Group on Intelligence and Communications Technologies stated: "Information contributed to terrorist investigations by the use of telephone metadata was not essential to preventing attacks and could readily have been obtained in a timely manner using conventional court orders."[105]

---

[102] U.S. Senate, "U.S. Government Efforts to Counter Violent Extremism," hearing.

[103] Ibid.

[104] USA PATRIOT Act (U.S. H.R. 3162, Public Law 107-56).

[105] Richard Clarke, Michael Morell, Geoffrey Stone, Cass Sunstein, and Peter Swire, Swire, ell, Geoome-Twitter-campaignntext=jp*Review Group on Intelligence and Communications Technologies,* December 12,

### Tracking Identified Individuals

The Antiterrorism and Effective Death Penalty Act of 1996 and the Intelligence Reform and Terrorism Prevention Act of 2004 for surveillance of suspected LWTs have offered the USG new legal means to combat lone wolf terrorism.[106] The US Congress passed the former law following Eric Rudolph's 1996 bombing at Atlanta's Centennial Olympic Park and allocated one billion dollars to "enhance federal LE capacity to deter, investigate, and prosecute terrorism."[107] The latter allows authorities to track non-US nationals suspected of being LWTs, even if they have no confirmed ties to terrorist groups. This provision corresponds to the surveillance authority provided to the USG in the USA PATRIOT Act that passed after September 11, 2001.

In January 2015, the New American Foundation conducted a study that concluded that NSA telephonic collection efforts were only useful in approximately 7.5 percent of terrorism cases.[108] While these studies examined the efficacy of the phone data in terrorism cases generally, Lone Wolf Terrorism is a subset of terrorism in general. As such, if the mass of data was only useful in 7.5 percent of all terrorism cases, we can expect an even lower success rate against LWT. These studies likely will bolster public scrutiny of these programs.[109]

### The Limitations of Sting Operations

Sting operations are another successful, albeit controversial, LE tactic. After identifying an individual who appears likely to commit a violent act, LE establishes a relationship with the individual and engages in dialogue to determine how far the suspect is willing to go down the path of mobilization. By the time the suspect is ready to act, LE has a complete picture of the person's motivations, connections, and sufficient evidence for prosecution. As the events preceding the attack are controlled by LE, there is no risk of an actual attack.

Sting operations are sometimes criticized as entrapment, potentially pushing a suspect further than they would have gone alone by offering otherwise unobtainable financial, intellectual, or material support[110]. Even so, those resources are available from legitimately violent sources, and it is difficult to determine if sting operations add to the radicalization process rather than just substituting the source of the support. Despite

---

2013, 104, accessed on June 9, 2015, https://www.whitehouse.gov/sites/default/files/docs/2013-12-12_rg_final_report.pdf.

[106] Elizabeth B Bazan, "Intelligence Reform and Terrorism Prevention Act of 2004: 'Lone Wolf' Amendment to the Foreign Intelligence Surveillance Act," *CRS Report for Congress*, 2004, accessed June 10, 2015, http://fas.org/irp/crs/RS22011.pdf.

[107] Spaaij, *Understanding Lone Wolf Terrorism*, 78.

[108] Bailey Cahall, David Sterman, Emily Schneider, and Peter Bergen. "Do NSA's Bulk Surveillance Programs Stop Terrorists?" New American Foundation, January 13, 2014, accessed June 9, 2015, https://www.newamerica.org/international-security/do-nsas-bulk-surveillance-programs-stop-terrorists/.

[109] George Gao, "What Americans Think about NSA surveillance, national security and privacy," *Pew Research Center*, May 29, 2015, accessed June 10, 2015, http://www.pewresearch.org/fact-tank/2015/05/29/what-americans-think-about-nsa-surveillance-national-security-and-privacy/.

[110] "Illusion of Justice: Human Rights Abuses in U.S. Terrorism Prosecutions," Human Rights Watch in partnership with Human Rights Institute at Colombia University Law School, July 2014, accessed June 10, 2015, http://www.hrw.org/sites/default/files/reports/usterrorism0714_ForUpload_1_0.pdf.

the controversy, the operations are generally successful at preventing attacks, since they are managed at every step.

## Finding 8: The US Lacks a "Whole of Government" Approach

### Lack of Lead Agency/Organizer

LEAs and the IC are not organizationally suited to address LWTs, and they face considerable bureaucratic and legal constraints. Many agencies and departments are addressing different facets of the problem, but there is no designated coordinator or lead agency. The current "to each their own" approach limits both programmatic and geographic efficacy. Departments have developed duplicate programs, which are at best a waste of funding and resources, and at worst may exacerbate the issue by highlighting government inefficiency, biases, or sending overlapping messages to the public, all of which risk further aggrieving a radicalized individual.[111] Creating metrics for analyzing program efficacy is also difficult: success against radical ideologies is reflected in changing attitudes and behaviors, which are difficult to measure, and since each agency's focus is different, their measures of success may vary, too. However, we could track some progress by number of radicalized individuals arrested or rate of successful incidents.

### Scattered Responses

The most commonly applied initiatives for LWT prevention are aimed at countering the propagation of violence. A number of US and international programs attempt to defeat ideological narratives and violent extremism, and while all of them contain elements applicable to LWTs, they have not been fully applied or implemented.

It seeks to "empower ... state, local, and community partners to assist in this effort,"[112] focusing primarily on Islamic extremism and deployed in only three cities: Boston, Minneapolis, and Los Angeles.[113] Despite establishing a full-time CVE Coordinator at the Department of Homeland Security (DHS),[114] the absence of federal LE—including the FBI Director—at the White House's February 2015 three-day CVE summit is a clear indication of the lack of federal planning coordination.[115]

---

[111] Jerome P. Bjelopera, "Countering Violent Extremism in the United States," *Congressional Research Service* February 19, 2014, 27–28, accessed on June 9, 2015, available at http://fas.org/sgp/crs/homesec/R42553.pdf.

[112] Robert Mueller, Statement Before the Senate Judiciary Committee, *Oversight of the Federal Bureau of Investigation,* Hearing, May 16, 2012, (Serial No. J–112–76), Washington: Government Printing Office, 2012, accessed June 10, 2015, http://www. judiciary.senate.gov/mwg-internal/de5fs23hu73ds/progress?id=IJPY jIfojXMGCNSpCpo5fFR0dqdQk2S7msrNhT35ypk.

[113] FBI National Security Branch, "A New Approach to Countering Violent Extremism: Sharing Expertise and Empowering Local Communities," *Federal Bureau of Investigation,* October 7, 2014, accessed June 27, 2015, http://leb.fbi.gov/2014/october/a-new-approach-to-countering-violent-extremism-sharing-expertise-and-empowering-local-communities.

[114] Office of the Press Secretary, "White House Countering Violent Extremism Fact Sheet," *The White House,* February 18, 2015, accessed June 4, 2015, https://www.whitehouse. gov/the-press-office/2015/02/18/fact-sheet-white-house-summit-countering-violent-extremism.

[115] Michael S. Schmidt, "FBI Chief Not Invited to Meeting on Countering Violent Extremism," *The New York Times,* February 19, 2015, accessed June 15, 2015, http://www.nytimes.com/2015/02/20/us/politics/fbi-chief-not-invited-to-meeting-on-extremists.html.

## US Attempts to Defeat Ideological Narratives

The US government has historically focused on the identification and interdiction of violent actors through traditional LE methods; however, in 2011, it modified its policy to focus on the prevention and identification of violent extremists.[116] Broad policy objectives encourage the use of numerous existing programs originally designed to counter other national issues, such as drugs and gang activity. The DOJ's Comprehensive Gang Model, providing community-led alternatives to youth targeted for gang recruitment, is an example.[117] Such programs are primarily targeted toward youth. Thus far, the programs are only in their initial stages and have produced limited visible effects,[118] but today's programs build off historical US experiences in LE and government, attempting to reform criminals or counter ideology.

Other US programs include a joint DOJ/DHS effort, the Building Communities of Trust Initiative. This seeks to increase dialogue and transparency between federal, state, and local LE, communities, and civil liberty groups, highlighting the importance of meaningful information sharing, responding to community concerns, and distinguishing between cultural behaviors and indicators of legitimate terrorist activity.[119] By engaging in dialogue with communities and transparently disclosing the aims and activities of LE, extremist groups have difficulty proving to their would-be members that authorities are "evil" or "wrong" and must also compete with pre-established counter-narratives of unity and inclusion.

DOJ runs another joint program with the Department of Education and the Department of Health and Human Services: the Safe Schools and Healthy Students initiative, which resulted from studies undertaken post-Columbine. Providing grants for individually developed programs to schools working with local LEOs and mental health professionals allows them the flexibility to combat a variety of radicalization factors, and initial results suggest a decrease in school violence.[120] The FBI has developed community outreach programs, providing radicalization briefings at the request of community leadership, local LEOs, and schools—while effective, the number of requests outstrips the number of agents, resulting in considerable backlog.[121]

## Foreign Responses to LWT

Indonesia's program, run by the country's national police's Bomb Task Force, is founded on the premise that a moderate community leader will have limited credibility with

[116] National Security Council, "Empowering Local Partners to Prevent Violent Extremism in the United States," *The White House,* August 2011, accessed June 4, 2015, https://www.whitehouse.gov/sites/default/files/empowering_local_partners.pdf.

[117] Ibid.

[118] U.S. Army Brigadier General Russell D. Howard, Interview with Georgetown University National Security Critical Task Force, Personal Interview, Washington, D.C., June 9th, 2015.

[119] National Security Council, "Empowering Local Partners."

[120] "Findings from the National Evaluation of the Safe Schools/Healthy Students Initiative: Program Overview and Update—2013," *Substance Abuse and Mental Health Services Administration,* n.d., accessed June 5, 2015, http://www.samhsa.gov/safe-schools-healthy-students/national-evaluation.

[121] Countering Violent Extremism Office, Federal Bureau of Investigation, Personal interview, June 4, 2015.

extremists,[122] and reformed radicals should therefore be the primary spokespersons of de-radicalization programs. This program is specific to radical Islam and focuses primarily on de-radicalizing the jihadist mindset regarding "the killing of civilians, and the "need" for an Islamic state."[123] However, this program's success is dependent on a supply of de-radicalized people who are willing to speak out. Since the United States has not introduced any formal de-radicalization programs, it would be difficult to identify any de-radicalized individuals who could participate in an initiative like Indonesia's. This finding suggests that the United States should consider implementing de-radicalization programs, which would not only provide alternatives ways to address threats from radicalized individuals but would also identify potential participants for a spokesperson position.

Saudi Arabia uses a six-week prison program with a combination of counseling and societal reintegration assistance, under the guidance of religious clerics, psychologists, and security officers.[124] The program has included four thousand prisoners and has expanded to include repatriated Guantanamo Bay detainees, but the primary challenge lies in determining its effectiveness. Its most notable result is the establishment of a government-funded halfway house dedicated to assisting parolees with societal integration, as well as concentrated re-education targeting radical beliefs and the misinterpretation of scripture.

This program is consistent with most US criminal reintegration assistance programs, which could in turn apply to developing US programs. Current criminal programs incorporate vocational rehabilitation and regular visits by social workers have reduced rates of recidivism and risk of re-exposure to the individual's previous criminal lifestyle.[125,126] Disengaging from a community supportive of detrimental behavior is critical to maintaining good behavior in other released inmates, and providing radicals—operating alone or in groups—with that opportunity appears to have had a parallel effect in maintaining de-radicalization. Ultimately, Saudi Arabia's results indicate altering an existing US program to address LWTs is a suitable option, and Minneapolis may be an unintentional pilot city. While Abdullahi Yusuf failed to obtain a passport to travel to Syria awaits sentencing, the federal judge has remanded him to a halfway house to see if reintegration is possible.[127] If this is successful, it could establish a precedent for more thorough programs designed to provide the psychological and lifestyle assistance necessary to redirect radical thinking.

In the United Kingdom, the PREVENT program, a coordinated, comprehensive approach to countering violent extremism and stopping individual actors, hopes to

[122] Schulze, "Indonesia's Approach to Jihadist Deradicalization," 8.

[123] Ibid, 9.

[124] Marisa Porges, "The Saudi Deradicalization Experiment," *The Council on Foreign Relations,* January 22, 2010, accessed June 08, 2015, http://www.cfr.org/radicalization-and-extremism/saudi-deradicalization-experiment/p21292.

[125] Richard P. Seiter and Karen R. Kadela, "Prisoner Reentry: What Works, What Does Not, and What Is Promising," *Crime and Delinquency* 49, no. 3 (2003), 373.

[126] Seiter and Kadela, "Prisoner Reentry," 378.

[127] John G. Horgan, "De-radicalization Programs Offer Hope in Countering Terrorism," *Los Angeles Times,* February 13, 2015, accessed June 5, 2015, http://www.latimes.com/opinion/op-ed/la-oe-0215-horgan-terrorist-deradicalization-20150215-story.html.

eliminate or minimize virtually all radicalization factors and directly combats extremist ideologies through collaboration and logical argument on a national scale.[128] Its success has yet to be determined, and the relationship between NGOs and the government has been strained, preventing many of the community-based programs from developing dialogue between the communities and the authorities.[129] Even so, its focus on youth, disrupting those who promote violent extremism, and increasing LE engagement both parallel some U.S. attempts and highlight what the United States still needs to accomplish.

Violent extremism that leads to lone wolf terrorism is an international issue, and the countries mentioned here are only some of those that have implemented de-radicalization programs. While their applicability in the United States has not been tested, each carries important lessons.

## Recommendations for the Future

### Recommandation [*sic*] One: Adopt a Standard Definition

The NSCITF recommends the adoption of the definition: *Lone wolf terrorism is the deliberate creation and exploitation of fear through violence or threat of violence committed by a single actor who pursues political change linked to a formulated ideology, whether his own or that of a larger organization, and who does not receive orders, direction, or material support from outside sources.*

### Recommendation Two: Appoint Clear Leadership over Lone Wolf Terrorism

The USG should name a single individual to coordinate strategy and planning for lone wolf terrorism. This individual should ideally report to the White House. The organization within which the mission leader resides is not determined here, although Recommendation Six of the Congressionally mandated report—"The FBI—Protecting the Homeland in the Twenty-first Century"—recommends that CVE efforts be moved from the FBI to DHS or distributed to other agencies.[130]

### Recommendation Three: Emphasize Preventing and Short Circuiting Radicalization

Effectively addressing lone wolf terrorism requires a broader campaign that must include engaging with and strengthening the informal community, focusing on early childhood education, building resilience in childhood and adolescence, and instituting effective law enforcement practices. Unfortunately, CVE programs do not currently have effective ways to complete this range of requirements.

---

[128] "Preventing Violent Extremism: A Strategy for Delivery," *Government of the United Kingdom,* May 2008, accessed June 7, 2015, http://www.northants.police.uk/files/linked/terrorism/Preventing%20Violent%20Extremism.pdf.

[129] "Countering Violent Extremism: The Counter-Narrative Study," *Qatar International Academy for Security Studies,* September 9, 2013, accessed June 08, 2015, http://qiass.org/test/.

[130] Bruce Hoffman, Edwin Meese III, Timothy J. Roemer, "The FBI—Protecting the Homeland in the 21st Century," *Report of the 9/11 Review Commission,* March 2015, accessed June 27, 2015, https://www.fbi.gov/stats-services/publications/protecting-the-homeland-in-the-21st-century.

There are crises and decision points along the continuum of radicalization that can change directions, for better or worse. Of course, the earliest intervention possible can prevent the individual from getting on the continuum from the start. Early in the radicalization process, the close community of family, friends, schools and the informal network of neighbors and service providers begin to notice questionable behavior. The family, friends, and peers may not consider the individual a future terrorist at this point; rather, the individual appears odd. The current CVE educational efforts should be brought together under the mission leader to be strengthened and new ideas developed by including the best innovative thinkers from the film and music industry, sports, social media, and game developers.

As troubling behaviors escalate and the individual becomes more estranged from his or her community, the NSCITF finds that the resources available to assist the individual are minimal. It is often at this point that family members, friends, and peers face a difficult decision: ignore the behavior or call the police. Both responses are often not effective because the behavior is too important to ignore but likely not yet a law enforcement issue because the individual has not committed a crime. The mission leader will need to engage the education and social service network to enhance those programs that have been or could become effective alternatives to making the issue one of law enforcement at this point.

In the NSCIFT radicalization model, the aforementioned timeline precedes and includes the receptive point. Social support can provide an effective alternative if it is specifically tailored to the need and readily available. Unfortunately, even in the best environment with adequate social support, individuals may still adopt radical extremism as their solution to personal or social grievances. Therefore, the focus now shifts to law enforcement—specifically, the monitoring, surveillance, and potential arrest of the individual.

In addition to the focus on the individual, the mission leader will need to develop more effective counter messaging capabilities. Currently, the sophistication of extremist messaging for recruitment is exceeding that of our counter messaging approaches. The White House's CVE summit earlier this year proposed a joint NCTC-Hollywood workshop to develop counter-extremist films, which holds potential for more effective media productions, along with a "CVE Hub," a non-governmental organization to lead community involvement in countering violent extremist narratives.[131] Messages must be insightful, realistic, and interesting, and DOS' coordination of US approaches to combating Islamic extremist ideology could benefit from widening its mission to combat general extremist ideology.

---

[131] National Security Council, "White House Countering Violent Extremism Fact Sheet."

## Bibliography


Agarwal, Adesh and Ashok Kumar Saxena. *Psychological Perspectives in Environmental and Developmental* Issues. New Delhi: Concept Publishing Co, 2003.

Ahmed, Saeed and Greg Botelho. "Who is Michael Zehaf-Bibeau, the man behind the deadly Ottawa attack?" *CNN,* October 23, 2014. Accessed June 10, 2015. http://www.cnn.com/2014/10/22/world/canada-shooter/.

"Andrew McCabe Named Assistant Director of the Counterterrorism Division." *Federal Bureau of Investigation,* May 09, 2012. Accessed June 13, 2015. http://www.fbi.gov/news/pressrel/press-releases/andrew-mccabe-named-assistant-director-of-counterterrorism-division.

Bakker, Edwin and Beatrice de Graff. "Preventing Lone Wolf Terrorism: Some CT Approaches Addressed." *Perspectives on Terrorism,* 2011. Accessed June 10, 2015. http://www.terrorismanalysts.com/pt/index.php/pot/article/view/preventing-lone-wolf/html.

Barnes, Beau D. "Confronting the One-Man Wolf Pack: Adapting Law Enforcement and Prosecution Responses to the Threat of Lone Wolf Terrorism." *Boston University Law Review* 92.1 (2012): 1613–1662. Accessed June 11, 2015. http://www.bu.edu/law/central/jd/organizations/journals/bulr/volume92n4/documents/BARNES.pdf.

Bates, Rodger A. "Dancing with Wolves: Today's Lone Wolf Terrorists." *The Journal of Public and Professional Sociology* 4, no.1 (2012): 1-12. Accessed June 9, 2015. http://digitalcommons.kennesaw.edu/cgi/viewcontent.cgi?article=1023&context=jpps.

Bazan, Elizabeth B. "Intelligence Reform and Terrorism Prevention Act of 2004: 'Lone Wolf' Amendment to the Foreign Intelligence Surveillance Act." *CRS Report for Congress,* December 29, 2004. Accessed June 10, 2015. http://fas.org/irp/crs/RS22011.pdf.

Beam, Louis. "Leaderless Resistance." *The Seditionist* 12 (1992). Accessed June 9, 2015. http://www.louisbeam.com/leaderless.htm.

Berntzen, Lars Erik and Sveinung Sandberg. "The Collective Nature of Lone Wolf Terrorism: Anders Behring Breivik and the Anti-Islamic Social Movement." *Terrorism and Political Violence* 26, no. 5 (2014): 759–779. doi: 10.1080/09546553.2013.767245.

Bjelopera, Jerome P. "Countering Violent Extremism in the United States." *Congressional Research Service,* February 19, 2014. Accessed June 9, 2015. http://fas.org/sgp/crs/homesec/R42553.pdf.

Breivik, Anders Behring. "2083—A European Declaration of Independence." 2011. Accessed May 31, 2015. https://info.publicintelligence.net/AndersBehringBreivik Manifesto.pdf.

Brooks, Risa A. "Muslim 'Homegrown' Terrorism in the United States" *International Security* 36, no.2 (2011): 7-47. Accessed June 12, 2015. http://belfercenter.ksg.harvard.edu/files/Muslim%20Homegrown%20Terrorism%20in%2 0the%20United%20States.pdf.

Bruinius, Harry. "Muslim youth counter Islamic State with #NotInMyName Twitter campaign." *Christian Science Monitor,* September 22, 2014. Accessed June 6, 2015. http://www.csmonitor.com/World/Europe/2014/0922/Muslim-youths-counter-Islamic-State-with-NotInMyName-Twitter-campaign.

Buerkle, Tom. "22-Year-Old Man Held for 3 Murders as Officials Hope Terror Is Ended: London Bombing Suspect is Charged." *The New York Times*, May 3, 1999. Accessed June 08, 2015. http://www.nytimes.com/1999/05/03/news/03iht-london.2.t.html.

US Department of State Bureau of Counterterrorism. "Foreign Terrorist Organizations," *US Department of State*. Accessed June 14, 2015. http://www.state.gov/j/ct/rls/other/des/123085.htm.

Byman. Daniel. *A High Price: The Triumphs and Failures of Israeli Counterterrorism*. Oxford: Oxford University Press, 2011.

Cahall, Bailey, David Sterman, Emily Schneider, and Peter Bergen. "Do NSA's Bulk Surveillance Programs Stop Terrorists?" *New American Foundation*, January 13, 2014. Accessed June 9, 2015. https://www.newamerica.org/international-security/do-nsas-bulk-surveillance-programs-stop-terrorists/.

Capellan, Joel A. "Lone Wolf Terrorist or Deranged Shooter? A Study of Ideological Active Shooter Events in the US, 1970–2014." *Studies in Conflict & Terrorism* 38, no.6 (2015): 395–413. Accessed June 10, 2015. http://www.tandfonline.com/doi/abs/10.1080/1057610X.2015.1008341?tab=permissions.

Carmichael, Callie "Anti-government Extremist Groups Reach Record Levels, Say Experts," *CNN*, March 6, 2013. Accessed June 19, 2015. http://www.cnn.com/2013/03/05/us/splc-extremist-groups-report/.

Clarke, Richard, Michael Morell, Geoffrey Stone, Cass Sunstein, and Peter Swire. "Liberty and Security in a Changing World." *Review Group on Intelligence and Communications Technologies*, December 12, 2013. Accessed June 9, 2015. https://www.whitehouse.gov/sites/default/files/docs/2013-12-12_rg_final_report.pdf.

"Countering Violent Extremism: The Counter-Narrative Study." *Qatar International Academy for Security Studies*, September 9, 2013 (released). Accessed June 08, 2015. http://qiass.org/test/.

Croft, Stuart and Cerwyn Moore. "The Evolution of Threat Narratives in the Age of Terror: Understanding terrorist threats in Britain." *International Affairs* 86, no.4 (2010): 821–835. doi: 10.1111/j.1468-2346.2010.00914.x.

Drake, Bruce. "Divide between blacks and whites on police runs deep." *Pew Research Center*, April 28, 2015. Accessed June 26, 2015. http://www.pewresearch.org/fact-tank/2015/04/28/blacks-whites-police/.

Dickey, Christopher. "Most Suicide Bombers Have Three Things in Common." *Newsweek*, September 29, 2009. Accessed June 10, 2015. http://www.newsweek.com/most-suicide-bombers-have-three-things-common-christopher-dickey-79525.

Donohue, Lacey. "What We Know about Alleged LAX Gunman Paul Ciancia." *Gawker*. November 3, 2013. Accessed June 10, 2015. http://gawker.com/what-we-know-about-alleged-lax-gunman-paul-ciancia-1457862009.

Dunham, Will and Eric Beech. "Islamic State Calls on Backers to Kill 100 U.S. Military Personnel." *Reuters*, March 21, 2015. Accessed June 8, 2015. http://reut.rs/1EE5fZW.

Elias, Marilyn. "Sikh Temple Killer Wade Michael Page Radicalized in Army." *Intelligence Report* 148 (2012). Accessed June 7, 2015. http://www.splcenter.org/get-informed/intelligence-report/browse-all-issues/2012/winter/massacre-in-wisconsin.

Federal Bureau of Investigation and the U.S. Department of Homeland Security. "Use of Small Arms: Examining Lone Shooters and Small-Unit Tactics." *Joint Intelligence Bulletin,* August 16, 2011. Accessed June 13, 2015. http://www.cbsnews.com/htdocs/pdf/JIB_Use_of_Small_Arms_Examining_Lone_Shooters.pdf.

Federal Bureau of Investigation, Countering Violent Extremism Office. Interview with Georgetown University Security Studies National Security Critical Task Force. *Georgetown University.* Washington, D.C. June 4, 2015.

Federal Bureau of Investigation, National Security Branch. "A New Approach to Countering Violent Extremism: Sharing Expertise and Empowering Local Communities." *Federal Bureau of Investigation,* October 7, 2014. Accessed June 7, 2015. http://leb.fbi.gov/2014/october/a-new-approach-to-countering-violent-extremism-sharing-expertise-and-empowering-local-communities.

"Findings from the National Evaluation of the Safe Schools/Healthy Students Initiative: Program Overview and Update—2013." *Substance Abuse and Mental Health Services Administration,* n.d. Accessed June 5, 2015. http://www.samhsa.gov/safe-schools-healthy-students/national-evaluation.

Friscolanti, Michael. "Uncovering a Killer: Addict, Drifter, Walking Contradiction." *Macleans,* October 30, 2014. Accessed June 9, 2015. http://www.macleans.ca/news/canada/michael-zehaf-bibeau-addict-drifter-walking-contradiction/.

"Full Text of Eric Rudolph's Statement." *National Public Radio,* April 12, 2005. Accessed June 10, 2015. http://www.npr.org/templates/story/story.php?storyId=4600480.

Gao, George. "What Americans Think about NSA surveillance, national security and privacy." *Pew Research Center,* May 29, 2015. http://www.pewresearch.org/fact-tank/2015/05/29/what-americans-think-about-nsa-surveillance-national-security-and-privacy/.

Georgetown Professor. Interview by Georgetown University Security Studies National Security Critical Task Force. *Georgetown University.* Washington, D.C. June 17, 2015.

Gill, Paul, John Horgan, and Paige Deckert. "Bombing Alone: Tracing the Motivations and Antecedent Behaviors of Lone-Lone Actor Terrorists." *Journal of Forensic Sciences.* 59, no. 2 (2014): 425–435. doi: 10.1111/1556-4029.12312.

Greenfeld, Liah. "The Making of a Lone Wolf Terrorist." *Psychology Today.* October 26, 2014. Accessed June 6, 2015. https://www.psychologytoday.com/blog/the-modern-mind/201410/the-making-lone-wolf-terrorist.

Gruenewald, Jeff, Steven Chermak, and Joshua D. Freilich. "Distinguishing 'loner' attacks from other domestic extremist violence." *Criminology & Public Policy* 12, no.1 (2013): 65–91. doi: 10.1111/1745-9133.12008.

Hamm, Mark S. and Ramon Spaaij. "Lone Wolf Terrorism in America: Using Knowledge of Radicalization Pathways to Forget Prevention Strategies." *National Criminal Justice Reference Service,* February 2015. Accessed June 8, 2015. https://www.ncjrs.gov/pdffiles1/nij/grants/248691.pdf.

Harris, Amy Julia. "Islam Judged More Harshly Than Other Religions in Terrorist Attacks" *Reveal News,* January 16, 2015. Accessed June 24, 2015. https://www.revealnews.org/article/islam-judged-more-harshly-than-other-religions-in-terrorist-attacks/.

Harwood, Matthew. "The Lone-Wolf Terror Trap: Why the Cure Will Be Worse Than the Disease." *American Civil Liberties Union,* February 5, 2015. Accessed June 08, 2015. https://www.aclu.org/blog/lone-wolf-terror-trap-why-cure-will-be-worse-disease.

Haslam, Nick. "Dehumanization: An integrative review." *Personality and Social Psychology Review* 10, no.3 (2006): 252–264. doi: 10.1207/s15327957pspr1003_4.

Hewitt, Christopher. *Understanding Terrorism in America: From the Klan to al Qaeda.* New York: Routledge, 2003.

Hoffman, Bruce, Edwin Meese III, and Timothy J. Roemer. "The FBI—Protecting the Homeland in the 21st Century." *Report of the 9/11 Review Commission,* March 2015. Accessed June 27, 2015. https://www.fbi.gov/stats-services/publications/protecting-the-homeland-in-the-21st-century.

Hoffman, Bruce. *Inside Terrorism.* New York: Columbia University Press, 2006.

Hopkins, Steve. "Al-Qaeda published recipe for easy-to-make bomb that would evade airport check that 'any determined Muslim can prepare'." *Daily* Mail.com, December 2014. Accessed June 9, 2015. http://www.dailymail.co.uk/news/article-2905276/Al-Qaeda-publishes-recipe-easy-make-bomb-evade-airport-check-determined-Muslim-prepare.html.

Horgan, John G. "De-radicalization Programs Offer Hope in Countering Terrorism." *Los Angeles Times,* February 13, 2015. Accessed June 5, 2015. http://www.latimes.com/opinion/op-ed/la-oe-0215-horgan-terrorist-deradicalization-20150215-story.html.

Hoskinson, Charles. "Ideology, social media keep 'lone wolf' terror attacks coming." *The Washington Examiner.* October 24, 2014. Accessed June 10, 2015. http://www.washingtonexaminer.com/ideology-keeps-lone-wolf-attacks-coming/article/2555218.

Huit, Gavin Chua Hearn. "Singapore's Approach to Counterterrorism." *Combating Terrorism Center West Point Sentinel,* December 3, 2009. Accessed June 14, 2015. https://www.ctc.usma.edu/posts/singapore's-approach-to-counterterrorism.

"Illusion of Justice: Human Rights Abuses in U.S. Terrorism Prosecutions." *Columbia Law School, Human Rights Institute. Human Rights Watch,* July 2014. Accessed June 10, 2015. http://www.hrw.org/sites/default/files/reports/usterrorism0714_ForUpload_1_0.pdf.

"Interview with Ted Kaczynski." Administrative Maximum Facility Prison. Florence, Colorado." *Earth First Journal.* June 1999.

Jensen, Michael, Patrick James, and Herbert Tinsley. "Profiles of Individual Radicalization in the United States: Preliminary Findings." *Study of Terrorism and Response to Terrorism,* January 2015. Accessed June 10, 2015. https://www.start.umd.edu/pubs/PIRUS%20Research%20Brief_Jan%202015.pdf.

Jensen, Richard Bach. "The Pre-1914 Anarchist 'Lone Wolf Terrorism and Governmental Response." *Terrorism and Political Violence* 26, no. 1 (2014): 86–94. doi: 10.1080/09546553.2014.849919.

Jenkins, Brian Michael, Andrew Liepman, and Henry H Willis. *Identifying Enemies among Us: Evolving Terrorist Threats and the Continuing Challenges of Domestic Intelligence Collection and Information Sharing.* Santa Monica: RAND Corporation, 2014. http://www.rand.org/pubs/conf__proceedings/CF317.

Johnston, Amanda K. *Assessing the Effectiveness of Deradicalization Programs on Islamist Extremists.* Thesis. Naval Postgraduate School, Monterey, 2009. Accessed June 6, 2015. http://www.dtic.mil/dtic/tr/fulltext/u2/a514433.pdf.

"Judgment of Anders Behring Breivik 2012-08-24." *The Breivik Archive,* 2012. Accessed June 13, 2015. https://sites.google.com/site/breivikreport/documents/judgment-of-anders- behring-breivik-2012-08-24.

Kaplan, Jeffrey. "Leaderless Resistance." *Terrorism and Political Violence* 9.3 (1997): 80–95.

Katz, Rita. "The State Department's Twitter War with ISIS is Embarrassing." *Time,* September 16, 2014. Accessed June 15, 2015. http://time.com/3387065/isis-twitter-war-state-department/.

King, Colbert I. "You Can't Fight Terrorism with Racism." *The Washington Post,* July 30, 2005. Accessed June 06, 2015. http://www.washingtonpost.com/wp-dyn/content/article/2005/07/29/AR2005072901626.html.

Kurzman, Charles. "Terrorism Cases Involving Muslim-Americans, 2014." *Triangle Center on Terrorism and Homeland Security,* February 9, 2015. Accessed June 10, 2015. http://sites.duke.edu/tcths/files/2013/06/Kurzman_Terrorism_Cases_Involving_Muslim-Americans_2014.pdf.

LaFree, Gary and Laura Dugan. "Integrated United States Security Database (IUSSD): Data on the Terrorist Attacks in the United States Homeland, 1970 to 2011." *Study of Terrorism and Response to Terrorism,* December 2012. Accessed June 8, 2015. http://www.start.umd.edu/sites/default/files/files/publications/START_IUSSDDataTerrorist AttacksUS_1970-2011.pdf.

Lawless, Jill. "Can Identifying Mental Illness Stop Terror Attacks?" *New York Times,* December 15, 2014. Accessed June 6, 2015. http://www.nytimes.com/aponline/2014/12/15/world/europe/ap-eu-terrorism-and-mental-illness.html?_r=1.

Los Angeles Interagency Coordination Group. "Los Angeles Framework for Countering Violent Extremism." *U.S. Department of Homeland Security,* February 2015. Accessed June 6, 2015. http://www.dhs.gov/sites/default/files/publications/Los%20Angeles%20Framework%20for%20CVE-Full%20Report.pdf.

Mallinckrodt B. "Attachment, Social Competencies, Social Support, and Interpersonal Process in Psychotherapy." *Psychotherapy Research,* 10, no. 3 (2010): 239–266. Accessed June 9, 2015. http://dx.doi.org/10.1093/ptr/10.3.239.

"Man Haron Monis: 'Damaged' and 'Unstable'." *BBC,* December 16, 2014. Accessed June 10, 2015. http://www.bbc.com/news/world-australia-30484419.

McCann, Joseph. *Terrorism on American Soil: A Concise History of Plots and Perpetrators from the Famous to the Forgotten.* Boulder: Sentient Publications, 2006.

McGreal, Chris. "Wade Michael Page's acquaintances recall a troubled man guided by hate." *The Guardian,* August 7, 2012. Accessed June 9, 2015. http://www.theguardian.com/world/2012/aug/07/wade-michael-page-wisconsin-shooting.

Meloy, J. Reid Dr. and Dr. Jessica Yakeley. "The Violent True Believer as a "Lone Wolf"—Psychoanalytic Perspectives on Terrorism." *Behavioral Sciences & the Law* 32, no. 3 (2014): 347–365. doi: 10.1002/bsl.2109.

*Mir Aimal Kasi v. Commonwealth of Virginia.* Opinion by Justice A. Christian Compton. Record numbers 980797, 980798. Circuit Court of Fairfax County 1998. Accessed June 4, 2015. http://www.courts.state.va.us/opinions/opnscvwp/1980797.pdf.

Moghaddam, F. M. "The Staircase to Terrorism: A Psychological Exploration." *American Psychologist* 60, no.2 (2005): 161–169. doi: 10.1037/0003-066X.60.2.161.

Mueller, Robert. Statement Before the Senate Judiciary Committee. *Oversight of the Federal Bureau of Investigation,* Hearing, May 16, 2012. (Serial No. J–112–76). Washington: Government Printing Office, 2012. Accessed June 10, 2015. http://www.judiciary.senate.gov/mwg-internal/de5fs23hu73ds/progress?id=IJPYjIfojXMGCNSpCpo5fFR0dqdQk2S7msrNhT35ypk.

National Security Council. "Empowering Local Partners to Prevent Violent Extremism in the United States." *The White House,* August 2011. Accessed June 4, 2015. https://www.whitehouse.gov/sites/default/files/empowering_local_partners.pdf.

Neset, Siri Merethe, Daniel Heradstveit, and G Matthew Bonham. *The Lone Wolf behind the Norwegian Tragedy: The Ideological Foundations of Anders Behring Breivik.* Paper presented at International Society of Political Psychology, Annual Convention, July 2012. Accessed June 06, 2015. http://faculty.maxwell.syr.edu/gmbonham/The_Lone_Wolf.pdf.

Neumann, Peter R. and Brooke Rogers. "Recruitment and Mobilisation for the Islamist Militant Movement in Europe." *The International Centre For The Study Of Radicalisation And Political Violence.* December 2007. Accessed June 10, 2015. http://icsr.info/wp-content/uploads/2012/10/1234516791ICSREUResearchReport_Proof1.pdf.

Office of Intelligence and Analysis. "Rightwing Extremists: Current Economic and Political Climate Fueling Resurgence in Radicalization and Recruitment." *Department of Homeland Security* April 7, 2009. Accessed June 10, 2015. http://fas.org/irp/eprint/rightwing.pdf.

Office of Juvenile Justice and Deliquency Program (OJJDP). "Best Practices To Address Community Gang Problems: OJJDP's Comprehensive Gang Model (Second Edition)." *U.S. Department of Justice,* October 2010. Accessed June 5, 2015. https://www.ncjrs.gov/pdffiles1/ojjdp/231200.pdf.

Office of the Press Secretary. "White House Countering Violent Extremism Fact Sheet." *The White House,* February 18, 2015. Accessed June 4, 2015. https://www.whitehouse.gov/the-press-office/2015/02/18/fact-sheet-white-house-summit-countering-violent-extremism.

"Operation Marathon: Interviews with David Copeland," *Metropolitan Police Department.*

O'Toole, Dr. Mary Ellen. "The School Shooter: A Threat Assessment Perspective." *Federal Bureau of Investigation,* n.d. Accessed June 7, 2015. https://www.fbi.gov/stats-services/publications/school-shooter.

Pantucci, Raffaello. "A Typology of Lone Wolves: Preliminary Analysis of Lone Islamist Terrorists." *The International Centre for the Study of Radicalization and Political Violence,* March 2011. Accessed June 9, 2015. http://www.trackingterrorism.org/sites/default/files/chatter/1302002992ICSRPaper_ATypologyofLoneWolves_Pantucci.pdf.

Pantucci, Rafaello. "What Have We Learned about Lone Wolves from Anders Behring Breivik?" *Perspectives on Terrorism* 5, no. 5–6 (2011). Accessed June 10, 2015. http://www.terrorismanalysts.com/pt/index.php/pot/article/view/what-we-have-learned/html.

Patel, Faiza. *Rethinking Radicalization.* New York: Brennan Center for Justice, 2011.

Pengelly, Martin. "Eric Holder says US 'at war' with 'lone wolf' terrorists after Paris attacks." *The Guardian,* January 11, 2015. Accessed June 08, 2015. http://www.theguardian.com/world/2015/jan/11/eric-holder-paris-unity-rally-war-against-terrorists.

Pisani, Anthony. "Emotion Regulation Difficulties, Youth-Adult Relationships, and Suicide Attempts among High School Students in Underserved Communities." *Journal of Youth and Adolescence* 42, no.6 (2013): 807–820. doi: 10.1007/s10964-012-9884-2.

Porges, Marisa. "The Saudi Deradicalization Experiment." *The Council on Foreign Relations,* January 22, 2010. Accessed June 5, 2015. http://www.cfr.org/radicalization-and-extremism/saudi-deradicalization-experiment/p21292.

"Press Release: Operation Lone Wolf." *Federal Bureau of Investigation,* n.d. Accessed June 10, 2015. https://www.fbi.gov/sandiego/about-us/history/operation-lone-wolf.

"Preventing Violent Extremism: A Strategy for Delivery." *Government of the United Kingdom* May 2008. Accessed June 7, 2015. http://www.northants.police.uk/files/linked/terrorism/Preventing%20Violent%20Extremism.pdf.

"Profile: Copeland the killer." *BBC,* June 30, 2000. Accessed June 10, 2015. http://news.bbc.co.uk/2/hi/uk_news/781755.stm.

Ramde, Dinesh. "Gunman had Criminal Record." *Salon.* August 6, 2012. Accessed June 10, 2015. http://www.salon.com/2012/08/06/gunman_in_sikh_temple_attack_was_white_supremacist/.

Rapaport, David C. "The Four Waves in Modern Terrorism." *Attacking Terrorism: Elements of a Grand Strategy,* ed. Audrey Kurth Cronin and James. M. Ludes. Washington D.C.: Georgetown University Press, 2004.

Ravndal, Jacob Aasland. "A Post-Trial Profile of Anders Behring Breivik." *CTC Sentinel* 5.10 (2012): 16–19. Accessed June 9, 2015. https://www.ctc.usma.edu/posts/a-post-trial-profile-of-anders-behring-breivik.

Riffkin, Rebecca. "Mentions of Terrorism Rise as U.S. Most Important Problem." *Gallup,* February 18, 2015. Accessed June 10, 2015. http://www.gallup.com/poll/181619/mentions-terrorism-rise-important-problem.aspx?utm_source=position6&utm_medium=related&utm_campaign=tiles.

Schmaltz, Taylor. "Killings at Fort Hood." *Terrorism Since 9/11: The American Cases,* ed. John Mueller. Columbus: Mershon Center, 2015. Accessed June 9, 2015. http://politicalscience.osu.edu/faculty/jmueller/32HOOD7.pdf.

Schmidt, Michael S. "FBI Chief Not Invited to Meeting on Countering Violent Extremism." *The New York Times,* February 19, 2015. Accessed June 09, 2015. http://www.nytimes.com/2015/02/20/us/politics/fbi-chief-not-invited-to-meeting-on-extremists.html.

Schmitt, Eric. "U.S. Intensifies Effort to Blunt ISIS' Message." *The New York Times,* February 16, 2015. Accessed June 9, 2015. http://www.nytimes.com/2015/02/17/world/middleeast/us-intensifies-effort-to-blunt-isis-message.html.

Schulze, Kathleen E. "Indonesia's Approach to Jihadist Deradicalization." *CTC Sentinel* 1.8 (2008): 8–10. Accessed June 7, 2015. https://www.ctc.usma.edu/posts/indonesia%e2%80%99s-approach-to-jihadist-deradicalization.

Scwartz, Mattathias, "How Dangerous Is a Man with a Knife? *New Yorker*, June 9, 2015.

Accessed June 14, 2015. http://www.newyorker.com/news/news-desk/how-dangerous-is-a-man-with-a-knife.

Seiter, Richard P. and Karen R. Kadela. "Prisoner Reentry: What Works, What Does Not, and What Is Promising." *Crime and Delinquency* 49.3 (2003): 360–388. Accessed June 10, 2015. http://canatx.org/rrt_new/professionals/articles/SEITER-WHAT%20WORKS.pdf.

Shane, Scott, "Homegrown Radicals More Deadly than Jihadists in U.S." *The New York Times*, June 24, 2015. Accessed June 24, 2015. http://www.nytimes.com/2015/06/25/us/tally-of-attacks-in-us-challenges-perceptions-of-top-terror-threat.html?_r=0.

Simon, Jeffrey. *Lone Wolf Terrorism: Understanding the Growing Threat.* New York: Prometheus Books, 2013.

Southern Poverty Law Center. "Tim and Sarah Gayman Discuss Growing Up in the Anti-Semitic Christian Identity Movement." *Intelligence Report* 102 (2001). Accessed June 10, 2015. http://www.splcenter.org/get-informed/intelligence-report/browse-all-issues/2001/summer/coming-out.

Spaaij, Ramon. "The Enigma of Lone Wolf Terrorism An Assessment." *Studies in Conflict and Terrorism* 33.9 (2010): 854–870. Accessed June 06, 2015. http://ramonspaaij.nl/wordpress/wp-content/uploads/Spaaij-Lone-Wolf-Terrorism.pdf

Spaaij, Ramón. *Understanding Lone Wolf Terrorism: Global Patterns, Motivations and Prevention.* New York: Springer, 2012.

Speckhard, Anne. *Lone Wolf Terrorism.* Speech presented at Georgetown University to Georgetown University Security Studies National Security Critical Task Force, May 2015.

Steinbach, Michael. Statement Before the House Judiciary Committee, Subcommittee on Crime, Terrorism, Homeland Security, and Investigations. *ISIL in America: Domestic Terror and Radicalization,* Hearing, February 26, 2015. (Serial No. 114-6). Washington: Government Priniting Office, 2015. Accessed June 09, 2015. http://judiciary.house.gov/_cache/files/121d6120-6f86-4b4e-a39b-7076fa8c7825/114-6-93527.pdf

Stephenson, Will. "The Story of Jason Woodring the Arkansas Power Grid Vandal." *Arkansas Times,* July 12, 2014. Accessed June 10, 2015. http://www.arktimes.com/arkansas/the-story-of-jason-woodring-the-arkansas-power-grid-vandal/Content?oid=3334926.

Thomas Pierre, Mike Levine, Jack Date, and Jack Cloherty. "EXCLUSIVE: How the FBI Foiled a 2012 Plot to Bomb the US Capitol." *ABC News,* January 15, 2015. Accessed June 17, 2015. http://abcnews.go.com/Politics/exclusive-inside-mind-homegrown-terrorist/story?id=28255276.

Thompson, Mark. "The Danger of the Lone-Wolf Terrorist." *Time,* February 27, 2013. Accessed June 08, 2015. http://nation.time.com/2013/02/27/the-danger-of-the-lone-wolf-terrrorist/.

"Transcript of Michael Zehaf-Bibeau's Message." *Ottawa Citizen,* March 6, 2015. Accessed June 9, 2015. http://ottawacitizen.com/news/national/transcript-of-michael-zehaf-bibeaus-final-message.

*United States v. Sohiel Omar Kabir, et al.* Criminal Complaint. United States District Court for the Central District of California. November 16, 2012. Unsealed November 19, 2012.

Uniting and Strengthening America by Providing Appropriate Tools Required to Intercept and Obstruct Terrorism Act of 2001 (USA PATRIOT Act), U.S. House of Representatives Resolution 3162, Public Law 107-56.

"Untreated mental health problems may hinder workplace productivity." *Harvard Health Publications,* n.d. Accessed June 9, 2015. http://www.health.harvard.edu/press_releases/untreated-mental-health-problems-may-hinder-workplace-productivity.

U.S. Army Brigadier General Russell D. Howard, interview by Georgetown University Security Studies National Security Critical Task Force. *Georgetown University,* June 9, 2015.

U.S. Government subject matter expert (2015, June). *Lone Wolf Terrorism.* Speech presented at Georgetown University to Georgetown University Security Studies National Security Critical Task Force, Washington, D.C.

Usher, Barbara Plett. "The US state department's Youtube 'digital jihad." *BBC,* November 28, 2014. Accessed June 7, 2015. http://www.bbc.com/news/magazine-30045038.

U.S. Senate. Committee of Armed Services. Subcommittee on Emerging Threats and Capabilities. *U.S. Government Efforts to Counter Violent Extremism,* Hearing, March 10, 2010. 111th Congress. 2nd Session. Washington: Government Printing Office, 2010. Accessed June 10, 2015. http://www.gpo.gov/fdsys/pkg/CHRG-111shrg63687/pdf/CHRG-111shrg63687.pdf.

Visconti, Luke. "Why Are Police Losing Credibility, and What Does Diversity Have to Do With It?" *DiversityInc,* February 19, 2015. Accessed June 5th, 2015. http://www.diversityinc.com/ask-the-white-guy/ask-white-guy-police-losing-credibility-diversity/.

Vossekuil, Bryan, Dr. Robert A. Fein, Dr. Marisa Reddy, Dr. Randy Borum, and William Modzeleski. "The Final Report and Findings of the Safe School Initiative: Implications for the Prevention of School Attacks in the United States." *United States Secret Service and United States Department of Education,* May 2002. Accessed June 6, 2015. http://www.secretservice.gov/ntac/ssi_final_report.pdf.

Wallheiser, Mark. "Alabama Hostage Standoff: Jimmy Lee Dykes Seized Boy to Gain Attention." *The Daily Beast,* February 6, 2013. Accessed June 10, 2015. http://www.thedailybeast.com/articles/2013/02/06/alabama-hostage-standoff-jimmy-lee-dykes-seized-boy-to-gain-attention.html.

Wiktorowicz, Quintan. "Joining The Cause: Al-Muhajiroun and Radical Islam." Accessed June 7, 2015. http://insct.syr.edu/wp-content/uploads/2013/03/Wiktorowicz.Joining-the-Cause.pdf.

# DOCUMENT NO. 5

# LONE WOLF TERRORISM IN AMERICA: USING KNOWLEDGE OF RADICALIZATION PATHWAYS TO FORGE PREVENTION STRATEGIES


| | |
|---|---|
| **Author(s):** | **Mark Hamm and Ramon Spaa[i]j** |
| **Document No.:** | **248691** |
| **Date Received:** | **February 2015** |
| **Award Number:** | **2012-ZA-BX-0001** |

**This report has not been published by the U.S. Department of Justice.**




## Lone Wolf Terrorism in America: Using Knowledge of Radicalization Pathways to Forge Prevention Strategies


Principle Investigators: Mark S. Hamm and Ramon Spaaij
Indiana State University


#2012-ZA-BX-0001
FINAL SUMMARY OVERVIEW


## Abstract


This research offers the largest and most comprehensive database ever created on lone wolf terrorism, along with a theory-informed case study component based on direct contact with imprisoned lone wolf terrorists, and a comparative analysis distinguishing lone wolves from those who undergo radicalization in a group setting. Strictly in terms of lethality, the data indicate that *lone wolf terrorism in America is not on the rise.* Although lone wolf terrorism may not be increasing, it is undergoing two important changes in modus operandi. First, uniformed police and military personnel have become the primary target of lone wolf terrorists. Second, consistent with the relaxation of U.S. gun laws since the 1990s and the recent trend in mass shootings, the lone wolf's preferred weaponry is now a staggering range of high-velocity firearms. While there is no standard profile of the lone wolf terrorist, most of them are unemployed, single white males with a criminal record. Compared to members of terrorist groups, lone wolves are older, less educated and more prone to mental illness.

The study validates a series of commonalities associated with pathways to radicalization for lone wolf terrorists. The radicalization model indicates that lone wolf terrorism begins with a combination of *personal and political grievances* which form the basis for an *affinity with online sympathizers.* This is followed by the identification of an *enabler,* followed by the *broadcasting of terrorist intent.* The final commonality is a *triggering event,* or the catalyst for terrorism. The ability of law enforcement and intelligence communities to detect and prevent lone wolf terrorism demands a clear understanding of these radicalization processes. Such insight may provide investigators with a sort of detection system, or "signatures"—as minimal as they may appear—that an individual with a terrorist intent will demonstrate in preparing for an attack. Crucial to this understanding is the broadcasting of intent. While lone wolves physically isolate from society, at the same time they seek recognition for their causes through spoken statements and threats, manifestos, e-mail messages, texting and videotaped proclamations. Focusing on this kind of immediate objective of radicalization among lone wolves, rather than on their underlying grievances, may sharpen our focus on the dangers posed by lone wolf terrorism.

**Purpose of the project:** The purposes of this research were to create a database of lone wolf terrorism in America, along with a theory-informed case study component based on direct contact with incarcerated lone wolf terrorists, and a comparative analysis seeking to distinguish lone wolves from those who undergo radicalization in a group setting (See Appendix 1). The objective of the study was to test the validity of a series of empirically-based commonalities associated with pathways to radicalization for lone wolves.

**Project subjects:** See Appendix 2 for a discussion of methods used to recruit subjects.

**Project design and methods:** To be included in the database and case studies, a case was required to meet the following definition: Lone wolf terrorism is political violence perpetrated by individuals who act alone; who do not belong to an organized terrorist group or network; who act without the direct influence of a leader or hierarchy; and whose tactics and methods are conceived and directed by the individual without any direct outside command or direction.

We discovered 98 cases fitting this definition between 1940 and 2013—representing all known cases of American lone wolf terrorism for the period (see Appendix 3 for a list of cases). Information on the 98 cases was gathered from an extensive review of previous research, biographies and memoirs, journalistic sources, government reports, court documents, encyclopedias and documentary films. The database catalogues the 98 cases across 21 different variables, generating 2,058 original data points. (Binary coding was used by a three-person team of raters who examined the variables.) It is the largest and most comprehensive database ever created on lone wolf terrorism.

Of the 98 cases in the database, 38 cases occurred before the terrorist attacks of 9/11 and 60 took place after 9/11. Of the 60 lone wolf cases after 9/11, however, 15 cases were law enforcement sting operations involving confidential informants and undercover agents; hence, they do not qualify as *authentic* lone wolf cases since more than one individual was involved. The sting cases were nevertheless included in the database because stings against standalone extremists have become a major counterterrorism strategy since 9/11. Indeed, they have recently been employed by the FBI to identify Americans with an interest in becoming foreign fighters, including those who have attempted to join ISIS. The following analysis of post-9/11 cases *excludes* the 15 stings and concentrates only on the authentic cases.

In summary, the database includes 38 lone wolf terrorists between 1940 and 2000 and 45 (authentic) lone wolves between 2001 and 2013, for a total of 83 cases. By comparing the pre-9/11 cases with the post- 9/11 cases across the full spectrum of 21 variables, we identify trends in lone wolf terrorism and their underlying causes and potential control strategies for law enforcement.

**Data analysis:** Based upon a descriptive analysis of the data, the major research conclusions are as follows.

*Trends in Lone Wolf Terrorism:* From 1940 through 2000, the 38 lone wolf terrorists committed 171 attacks, claiming 98 lives and injuring another 305. An array of firearms and homemade bombs were used in the attacks. Roughly 60% of the lone wolves committed a single attack and 40% committed multiple attacks, including such prolific terrorists as Unabomber Theodore Kaczynski who committed 16 bombings over a 17-year period, the racist serial killer Joseph Paul Franklin responsible for an estimated 23 attacks over four years, and Muharem Kurbegovic, the "Alphabet Bomber," who launched ten attacks in two years.

From 2001 through 2013, the 45 lone wolves committed 45 attacks, killing 55 people and injuring another 126. These attacks involved not only firearms and bombs but also airplanes, biological weapons, knives and construction equipment. In short, lone wolves have expanded their arsenal of weaponry in the post-9/11 era. While the multiple attackers were prominent in the pre-9/11 era, the single attacker rose to prominence after 9/11. They include such lone mass-murderers as Nidal Hasan who killed 13 and injured 30 in the 2009 Fort Hood shooting, Jared Laughner who killed six and wounded 13 in the Tucson shooting of 2011, and Wade Page who killed six and wounded four in the 2012 shooting at the Sikh temple in Oak Creek, Wisconsin.

Strictly in terms of lethality, the data indicate that *lone wolf terrorism in America is not on the rise.* Moreover, no decade has been bloodier than the 1990s when lone wolves left 212 victims, killing 30 and wounding 182 others.

*Modus Operandi:* Although lone wolf terrorism may not be increasing in the United States, it is undergoing dramatic changes in terms of modus operandi. The most significant change involves the targeting of uniformed police and military officers. Twelve law enforcement officers were killed or wounded by lone wolf terrorists in the 60 years preceding 9/11. This figure doubled in the first 13 years following 9/11 when the number of law enforcement personnel killed or wounded by lone wolves rose to 24. All of these attacks were bracketed by the years 2009 through 2013—the years coinciding with the Barack Obama presidency. Lone wolf attacks against police before 9/11 were motivated by black power, the Palestinian question and abortion. With one exception, since 9/11 attacks on law enforcement have been motivated by anti-government and white supremacy anger over the election of the nation's first African American president.

Not a single member of the U.S. military was targeted by lone wolf terrorists prior to 9/11. Since 9/11, lone wolves have killed or wounded 47 members of the military. Lone wolves have also attacked military bases or have been arrested in thwarted attacks against military installations. All of these terrorist attacks and plots were bracketed by the years 2009 to 2011. In every case but one, they were conducted by al-Qaeda sympathizers angry over the wars in Iraq and Afghanistan.

*Weaponry:* Prior to 9/11, a total of 234 victims were killed or wounded in bombings perpetrated by lone wolf terrorists—a phenomenon undoubtedly related to the bombing campaigns of terrorist groups during much of the period. Since 9/11, there have been only six victims of lone wolf bombings. This decline may reflect the stringent government controls on the purchase of bomb-making materials enacted in the aftermath of Oklahoma City. Consistent with the relaxation of U.S. gun laws since the 1990s and the recent trend in mass shootings, the lone wolf's preferred weaponry is now a staggering range of high-velocity firearms. Not only has the lethality of firearms increased by an order of magnitude, but lone wolf attacks have also become more personal.

*Copycat Attacks:* Even though we were not anticipating it, the database shows evidence of a copycat phenomenon in a third of the lone wolf cases.

*Diversity of Lone Wolf Terrorism:* Lone wolf terrorism is a multi-faceted crime. In addition to the 171 attacks committed by lone wolves in the pre-9/11 era, they were also responsible for at least 34 threats or aborted attacks. Due to technological advances, the post-9/11 era has shown a greater number of threats and aborted attacks. These have included anthrax hoaxes against abortion clinics and a presidential candidate, the aborted assassination attempt on President Obama with a radioactive bomb, and the downing of an electrical power grid, representing an *innovation* in American terrorism.

*Background Factors:* While there is no standard profile of the American lone wolf terrorist, the evidence indicates that most of them are unemployed, single white males with a criminal record. Compared to members of terrorist groups, lone wolves are older, less educated and more prone to mental illness. When compared to members of al-Qaeda, American lone wolf terrorists are more likely to be unmoored from society. The findings imply that lone wolf terrorism is caused by relative deprivation. In their social exclusion, lone individuals feel deprived of what they perceive as values to which they are entitled, and form grievances against the government responsible for their unemployment, discrimination and injustices. Their violence is a deviant adaptation to this gap between means and goals. One reason for this relatively high level of alienation is that more than half of the lone wolves embraced right-wing or anti-government ideologies. Nationalistic movements—such as American white supremacy movements—have tended to produce terrorists from the lower classes, while religious terrorists like al-Qaeda come from all classes.

## Pathways to Radicalization

*Loci of Radicalization:* Identifying the locus (or place) of radicalization is important because it draws attention to the social institution or means by which an individual is radicalized into violent extremism. Loci of radicalization are displayed in Appendix 4. The Appendix shows that the most common locus of radicalization in the pre-9/11 era was an extremist group that the lone wolves may have belonged to but had since abandoned. For lone wolf terrorists of the post-9/11 period, traditional loci of radicalization have been replaced by informal online social networks, the civilian workplace, and mass media.

*Motives:* Lone wolves tend to combine personal grievances with political grievances. Personal and political grievances are important because they go to the crucial question of motive. To validate the commonality, there must be evidence of *both* a personal and political grievance for any given case. For the pre-9/11 lone wolves, evidence of both themes was found in 30 of the 38 cases, or roughly 80% of the cases. For lone wolves of the post-9/11 era, evidence of both themes was found in 36 of the 45 cases: again, representing 80% of the cases indicating that the commonality is a *signature* of lone wolf terrorism that distinguishes loners from organized terrorists who share collective grievances. The end result of radicalization is the same, however. For both lone wolves and organized terrorists, violence is considered the only alternative to an unjust system

*Affinity with Extremist Groups:* Affinity implies that lone wolf terrorists are in sympathy with extremist groups; that their beliefs are in accordance with a clearly-defined organizational entity. The analysis shows that 63% of the pre-9/11 lone wolves had an affinity with organized extremists, including Southern segregationist and neo-Nazi groups, Palestinian movements; and anti-abortion groups. *Affinity for extremist groups is declining.* Only 42% of the post-9/11 lone wolves were found to have an affinity with extremist organizations, including al-Qaeda, Tea Party Patriots, and the neo-Nazi National Alliance. Yet the overall finding implies that lone wolves may be seeking direction through venues other than organizations: namely, via networks of like-minded activists found online or on cable television. This finding is consistent with radicalization patterns among recent organized terrorists.

*Enablers*: Lone wolves are enabled through either *direct* means in the form of people who unwittingly assist in planning attacks, or *indirectly* by people who provide inspiration for terrorism. Whereas affinity for extremist groups is a vicarious experience best understood as ideological validation of beliefs, an enabler is best understood at a personal level as someone who either unknowingly performs tasks that make an attack possible, or someone who indirectly encourages terrorism by example. Enablers are also common among group actors.

During the pre-9/11 era, 57% of the lone wolf terrorists were enabled by others. In the post-9/11 era, the figure rose to 67%. Nearly all of the enabling was indirect. For jihadists of the post-9/11 years, the most frequent enablers were Osama bin Laden and Anwar al-Awlaki. For white supremacists anti-government extremists of the post-9/11 period, the most frequent enablers were William Pierce, National Alliance founder and author of *The Turner Diaries*; and Internet personality Alex Jones.

*Broadcasting Intent:* While lone wolves physically isolate from society, at the same time they communicate with outsiders through spoken statements, threats, letters, manifestos and videotaped proclamations, similar to the jihadist martyrdom videos uploaded to the Internet by members of al-Qaeda and ISIS. Broadcasting intent can explicitly refer to an upcoming attack, or it can imply that an attack is imminent. Broadcasting intent may occur in the weeks, days and even hours before an attack. Broadcasting intent may be the most important commonality from the standpoint of prevention: If lone wolves announce their violent intentions beforehand, then presumably steps can be taken to stop them.

Broadcasting intent is pervasive among lone wolf terrorists. Evidence of broadcasting can be found in 84% of the pre-9/11 cases, including some the most crucial cases (the Unabomber, Eric Rudolph, Joseph Paul Franklin, and Leroy Moody). Among the post-9/11 lone wolf terrorists, 76% broadcasted their intent, often more than once. The broadcastings were made through e-mails, text messages, Facebook postings and Twitter feeds, PowerPoint presentations and Podcasts. It was done through television appearances; in statements to friends, family members, and mental health providers, transportation workers and police officers; in letters to lovers and newspaper editors; in town hall meetings and at protest rallies; and even in letters to Congress and the President of the United States. No case of broadcasting intent shows the potential for preventing a lone wolf attack better than Paul Ciancia's.

On the morning of his November 1, 2013 mass shooting at Los Angeles International Airport, killing and wounding three TSA officers and five bystanders, Ciancia ran into his roommate's bedroom and demanded a ride to LAX immediately. Around the same time, Ciancia sent text messages to his brother in Pennsville, New Jersey. One suggested that Ciancia was about to commit suicide. Alarmed, Ciancia's father called local police; who in turn called the Los Angeles Police Department. The call came in to the LAPD switchboard at 10:06 a.m. LAPD officers arrived at Ciancia's apartment six minutes later, but too late to prevent the shootings which had begun a mere 45 minutes earlier. On balance, Ciancia's rampage was nearly averted through a police response to the broadcasting of intent. Focusing on this kind of immediate objective of radicalization among lone wolves, rather than on their underlying grievances, may sharpen our focus on the dangers posed by lone wolf terrorism.

*Triggering Event:* The triggering event is a catalyst for lone wolf terrorism and such events are common among terrorist group members. For lone wolves, triggering events may be personal or political or some combination of the two. Triggering events are sometimes "sharp" or immediate. Other times events slowly accumulate over time (through a series of "escalation thresholds") until the lone wolf snaps under the pressure, triggering the act of terrorism. Evidence of a triggering event was found in 84% of the pre-9/11cases and in 71% of the post-9/11 cases.

*The Commonalities of Lone Wolf Terrorism: A Summary*: The commonalities form a radicalization model indicating that lone wolf terrorism begins with *personal and political grievances* which become the basis for an *affinity with an extremist group*. This is followed by the identification of an *enabler*, followed by *broadcasting of intent*. The final commonality is a *triggering event*, or the catalyst for terrorism. The research validates the model, except for the facet relating to the affinity with extremist groups during the post-9/11 era. This aspect of radicalization has changed over time and is not as important as it once was.

Four out of every 10 post-9/11 lone wolves demonstrated an affinity with extremist organizations, but affinities are an exception to the rule that lone wolf terrorists are becoming increasingly independent. At the root of this change is technology. With the rise of Internet chat rooms, conspiracy websites, Facebook and Twitter, online activists can connect scattered people who are worried about everything from drone strikes to a one-world government and the pending imposition of martial law in the United States and tell them that they do not worry in isolation. Moreover, radicalization is caused by an *affinity with online sympathizers.*

This new development in lone wolf terrorism is incorporated into the radicalization model presented in Appendix 5. Yet the model also includes affinity with extremist groups, even though this commonality of radicalization may be declining. The overarching point is this: Virtually all lone wolves demonstrate affinity with some person, community, or group, be it online or in the real world. This is a significant finding because it contests the policy assumption that lone wolf terrorists do not communicate or interact with others. They clearly do.

*Implications for Traveling to Syria:* The research applies the radicalization model to the 15 sting operations. The model effectively explains the sting cases in the same way that it explains authentic lone wolf cases. A case study based on open sources shows how the radicalization model may be used to explain lone wolves with the potential for traveling to Syria and joining ISIS.

## Paradigmatic Case Studies

The process of violent radicalization is so complex that a coherent government policy to halt lone wolf terrorism has yet to emerge. What is missing from security policy is a theoretical guidepost for understanding the lone wolves' criminal thinking styles and the specific circumstances that set them on the pathway to violent extremism. Criminological life-course theory can therefore be used to identify the sequence of individual trajectories leading to terrorism and the extent to which those turning points are embedded in the commonalities of radicalization. The theory can also be used to discern whether one commonality is more important than another. But life course theory can tell us much more.

The emergence of a turning point in life opens up the possibility for an individual to "knife off"—to completely amputate—the past from the present. Freed from personal history, the individual can invest in new relationships (real or virtual) that both foster social support for radicalization and encourage activities centered on violence. At this point, conditions exist for the individual to perform an identity transformation into an armed warrior.

We take on the challenge of applying life course theory to lone wolf terrorism by drilling down on two paradigmatic cases of police and military ambushing based on direct contact with the lone wolves who committed the assassinations. The cases also address the complex issues of gun control and the effects of mental illness on radicalization. One case reveals that the *triggering event* superseded the importance of all other facets of radicalization because it fused the loner's personal proclivity for anger and violence together with his political grievance over the abuse of Muslims by U.S. military forces. This defining event of radicalization allowed the subject to dehumanize his victims while elevating himself to a position of moral sanctity whereby he self-identified as a holy warrior. The second case reveals a series of escalation thresholds influenced by a combination of personal grievances over a lack of employment prospects and an intensification of the loner's paranoid political beliefs through his affinity with online sympathizers. Along this pathway the loner experienced a number of turning point, none more essential than his administrative discharge from military service which *triggered* his self-identification as an armed warrior, precipitating the assassination.

### Implications for Counterterrorism

The ability of law enforcement and intelligence communities to detect and prevent lone wolf terrorism demands a clear understanding of the radicalization process that lone wolves go through prior to their attacks. Insight into these processes may provide investigators with a sort of detection system, or "signatures"—as minimal as they may appear—that an individual with a terrorist intent will demonstrate in preparing for an attack.

Such signatures include the combining of personal and political grievances, broadcasting of terrorist intent, an affinity with online sympathizers/or extremist groups, the reliance on enablers, and triggering events. When fused with intelligence assembled by area specialists (religious scholars, psychologists, communications experts, explosive specialists and the like), these signatures could identify indicators of how lone wolf attacks are formulated. Equally important, investigators must have an understanding of counterterrorism efforts that have proven successful in the past, and the extent to which these successes have derived from an operational understanding of the radicalization process.

### List of Scholarly Products Produced or in Process

Hamm, Mark S. and Ramon Spaaij (under review) "Case Studies and Ethnography in Terrorism Research." In *Handbook on the Criminology of Terrorism*, edited by Joshua Frelich and Gary LaFree. New York: Wiley.

Spaaij, Ramon and Mark S. Hamm (in press) "Key Issues and Research Agendas in Lone Wolf Terrorism: A Rejoinder to Becker." *Studies in Conflict and Terrorism.*

Hamm, Mark S. and Ramon Spaaij *The Age of Lone Wolf Terrorism* (working title for a forthcoming book).

Hamm, Mark S. (2012) Review of *Understanding Lone Wolf Terrorism: Global Patterns, Motivations and Prevention* by Ramon Spaaij. *Perspectives on Terrorism*, 6 (3).

## Appendix 1
## Sources for of the Comparative Analysis

Bakker, Edward (2007) *Jihadi Terrorists in Europe: Their Characteristics and the Circumstances in Which They Joined the Jihad: An Exploratory Study.* The Hague: Clingendael Institute.

Hamm, Mark S. (2007) *Terrorism as Crime: From Oklahoma City to Al-Qaeda and* Beyond. New York: New York University Press.

Hamm, Mark S. (1993) *American Skinheads: The Criminology and Control of Hate Crime.* Westport, CT: Praeger.

Sageman, Marc (2008) *Leaderless Jihad: Terror Networks in the Twenty-First Century.* Philadelphia: University of Pennsylvania Press.

Sageman, Marc (2004) *Understanding Terror Networks.* Philadelphia: University of Pennsylvania Press.

Simi, Pete and Robert Futrell (2010) *American Swastika: Inside the White Power Movement's Hidden Spaces of Hate.* Lanham, MD: Rowman & Littlefield.

Smith, Brent L. (1994) *Terrorism in America: Pipe Bombs and Pipe Dreams.* Albany, NY: SUNY Press.

## Appendix 2
## Correspondence and Interviews with Terrorist Inmates: Challenges, Opportunities and a Recommendation for the Justice Department

Terrorism is arguably the most studied crime in the world today. Since 9/11, a thousand new books have been added to the terrorism literature each year. An average of four new books on terrorism is published each day; one book appears every six hours. Yet, it is estimated that less than percent of these studies have involved direct contact with terrorists.[1]

In this study, we were granted unprecedented access to terrorist inmates in American prisons. It is one of the rare "1%ers" of terrorism studies to contain direct contact with terrorists, providing a gold mine of original data on the process of violent radicalization. We offer the following account of our experiences in an effort to help future researchers navigate the difficult process of establishing direct contact with terrorist inmates. One cause of this difficulty can be traced to the academy itself. As one observer notes, "academia is currently ill-equipped to handle social science research activities that occur in high-risk areas."[2]

### The Grant

In early October of 2012, we received notification from NIJ that our grant had been approved, with one condition: We would not receive funding until full IRB approval for human subjects had been obtained along with approval from the various prisons where we would conduct interviews and mail correspondence with the lone wolf terrorists selected for the study.

We submitted an application to the Indiana State University Institutional Review Board (IRB) on October 19. Revisions were requested and revisions were submitted to the IRB in early January, 2013. Still, questions remained about human-subjects protection involving sensitive personal matters: How could we assure that prisoners would not experience psychological distress when asked questions about bombings and shootings that resulted in the death and wounding of others?

The IRB asked for further revisions on January 23. This time we were required to clarify the meaning of such terms as "custody" and "prison yard" and to explain the difference between trust and rapport. The third revision was submitted on February 22, but the IRB requested another revision addressing the security implications of sending inmates a postage stamp for return mailing of correspondence. A fourth revision was rejected for minor reasons on March 6, and a fifth revision was rejected on April 8 before the application was finally approved by the IRB on April 22. It had taken six months. The next stop was approvals at the prison level.

[1] Silke, Andrew (2008) "Research on Terrorism: A Review of the Impact of 9/11 and the Global War on Terrorism." In Chen, H. et al. (eds.) *Terrorism Infomatics: Knowledge Management and Data Mining for Homeland Security*, pp. 27–50; Post-2008 figures confirmed by e-mail from Andrew Silke to Mark Hamm, March 30, 2014.

[2] Taarnby, Michael (2013) "Professionalizing High-Risk Field Research in Academia." In Adam Dolnik (ed.), *Conducting Terrorism Field Research: A Guide*. New York: Routledge, p. 206.

## Terrorist Inmates

There are not hundreds or even tens of lone wolf terrorists incarcerated in the United States but only about 20. The IRB stipulated that we were prohibited from studying prisoners with severe mental illnesses, which eliminated roughly half of the 20 inmates. The final list of inmate subjects included:

> Islamic extremist Carlos Bledsoe (Abdulhakim Mohammad) imprisoned for life in the Arkansas Department of Corrections in connection with the fatal 2009 drive-by shooting attack on the Little Rock Army recruiting center.
>
> White supremacist Richard Poplawski imprisoned on death row in the Pennsylvania Department of Corrections for the killing of three Pittsburgh police officers in 2009.
>
> Islamic extremist Yonathan Melaku imprisoned for 25 years in the Federal Bureau of Prisons (BOP) for a series of firearm attacks on Northern Virginia military installations in 2010 and the 2011 attempted bombing of Arlington National Cemetery.
>
> Sami Hassoun imprisoned for 23 years in the BOP for an al-Qaeda related attempted bombing of a Chicago bar.
>
> White supremacist Kevin Harpham imprisoned for 32 years in the BOP in connection with the attempted bombing of a Martin Luther King Day parade in Spokane, Washington, in 2011.
>
> Islamic extremist Amine el Khalifi imprisoned for 30 years in the BOP in connection with an attempted suicide bombing at the United States Capitol in 2012.
>
> Islamic extremist Quazi Nafis imprisoned for 30 years in the BOP in connection with the attempted bombing of the Federal Reserve Bank in 2012.

Permissions to study these inmates were required from the research divisions of the Arkansas and Pennsylvania Departments of Corrections and the BOP. This was another extended process. Terrorist inmates are different from conventional criminals in terms of security concerns, so each of the inmates required vetting by counterintelligence and security officials. Each also required vetting by psychologists to assure that they did not suffer from severe mental illness. The prison approval process that began in late April of 2013 was completed on September 13, 2013.

Yet two more IRB approvals were required before the grant funds would be released. One was at the Department of Justice and the other was at the Australian Ethics Board, to cover the work of Ramon Spaaij, a faculty member at Victoria University in Melbourne, Australia.

Altogether, we were required to have a total of eight IRB/correctional agency approvals to study seven terrorist inmates. All of these approvals were completed by October, 2013 and the funds were released in November, 2013. All told, it took more than a year to gain full approval to conduct the research. And then the real work began.

## Correspondence and Interviews

Terrorist inmates typically demonstrate contempt for state authority (contempt for government is by definition a core terrorist value) and that includes researchers sponsored by the government. One inmate failed to return our introductory letters to him.

Two others refused to participate, fearing that it would jeopardize their ongoing legal appeals.

Yet something unexpected also transpired. We exchanged a total of 20 letters with two of the inmates during our recruitment phase. Both inmates asked a series of questions about their participation in the project and we answered all of them. Even though they had not signed the IRB-approved Informed Consent statement, in these letters the inmates voluntarily revealed details about their violent radicalization within al-Qaeda and the American white supremacy movement. *We did not solicit this information.* Rather, the inmates freely offered the information on their own accord. They did so—again—without signing the Informed Consent statement. Despite this, both inmates eventually refused to participate in the research; one would agree to participate only if NIJ could assure him of a release from prison and extradition to a Third World country. The other inmate gave no reason. These circumstances pose a dilemma for the academic study of terrorism.

On one hand, these inmates were not trifling figures in the history of American lone wolf terrorism. Instead, their crimes are representative of significant changes in the modus operandi of lone wolf terrorists. They willingly divulged information about their radicalization to us in a series of letters. Such information is rare and it can be used to achieve the primary goal of this project and any other on the subject: To explain how people *evolve* into lone wolf terrorists. Without an understanding of the trajectories radicalized individuals have followed, our ability to counter violent radicalization will be severely limited.

On the other hand, researchers are ethically bound to obtain a subject's consent before correspondence can be used for research purposes.

This dilemma is resolved in the following way: No material contained in the two subjects' correspondence with the authors is used this report, nor will it be used in subsequent publications. That material will remain confidential. Only publicly available open source material is used or will be used in writing about these two subjects. However, the correspondence is employed as a sort of survey instrument to detect those aspects of the subjects' life stories that appear to be most important to them, thereby allowing for new insight into the process of radicalization that goes far beyond open source information.

## The Contradiction

Two other BOP subjects signed the Informed Consent (let's call them inmate A and inmate B for brevity) and a series of letters was exchanged with them. Inmate A sent three letters followed by a six-hour interview with him at the U.S. Penitentiary, Leavenworth. Inmate B sent a 6-page letter detailing his background and the social pressures leading to his radicalization. But inmate B stopped short of agreeing to an interview based upon an apparent contradiction in the meaning of research confidentiality. This situation raises an issue worthy of consideration for the Department of Justice because it has implications for future investigators who attempt to conduct primary research on terrorist inmates within the BOP. The contradiction is as follows.

The terms of confidentiality assured in our Informed Consent statement, approved by the BOP, stipulates that: "The letters and interview notes will be used *for research purposes and no other purpose* without your consent." Our introductory letter to all inmates explicitly stated that we were researchers, and not members of the media or law enforcement. Inmate B signed the Informed Consent based upon his understanding of these assurances.

Then, prior to his interview, inmate B was asked by prison staff to sign the BOP's News Interview Authorization form which contains a different assurance:

> "I do hereby authorize the news media represented by this person [researcher Mark Hamm who had already stated to the inmate that he did *not* represent the media] to use any information gathered about me during this interview for any legitimate purpose. I further authorize the Bureau of Prisons and the Department of Justice, and their authorized representatives, to release to representatives of the news media *any documents or information* relating to allegations or comments made by me in this interview."[3]

Researchers are required to follow IRB regulations. Media representatives are not bound by these requirements. Our Informed Consent says that the interview will be conducted for research only, and no other purpose. The Informed Consent further assures that, "We will not ask to see your prison record during the research study." This language is inconsistent with the BOP News Media form which states that not only will interview information be used for purposes other than research (i.e., for the purpose of news making) but it also allows for a review of documents or information relating to "allegations or comments" made by the prisoner. Hence, the inmate is required to agree to two different terms of confidentiality: one for research purposes and another for media purposes.

This contradiction can be resolved by the creation and implementation of another BOP form expressly designed for researchers working within the constraints of human-subjects protection.

[3] U.S. Department of Justice, Federal Bureau of Pisons, News Interview Authorization, BP-A0233, JUN 10.

## Appendix 3
## List of Cases

| Year | Name | Terrorist Event | Source |
|---|---|---|---|
| 1) 1940–56 | George Metesky | New York bombings | Spaaij |
| 2) 1958 | Izola Curry | King Assassination attempt | Hamm |
| 3) 1960 | Richard Pavlick | Kennedy assassination attempt | Hamm |
| 4) 1963 | Floyd Simpson | Alabama civil rights murder | Hewitt |
| 5) 1963 | Byron de la Beckwith | Evers assassination | Hewitt/Spaaij |
| 6) 1968 | James Earl Ray | King assassination | Hewitt |
| 7) 1968 | Valorie Solanas | Warhol assassination attempt | Hamm |
| 8) 1968 | Sirhan Sirhan | R. Kennedy assassination | Spaaij/Hewitt |
| 9) 1970–75 | Neal Long | Dayton murder spree | Spaaij/Hewitt |
| 10) 1972–73 | Mark Essex | New Orleans police killings | Spaaij/Hewitt |
| 11) 1973–74 | Muharem Kurbegovic | LA airport killings/nerve gas threat | Spaaij |
| 12) 1974 | Samuel Byck | Nixon assassination attempt | Hamm |
| 13) 1975 | Lynnette Fromme | Ford assassination attempt | Hamm |
| 14) 1975 | Sara Jane Moore | Ford assassination attempt | Hamm |
| 15) 1976–80 | Joseph Paul Franklin | Murder, bombing spree | Spaaij/Hewitt |
| 16) 1978–95 | Theodore Kaczynski | Bombing campaign | Spaaij |
| 17) 1978 | Dan White | Moscone/Milk assassinations | Hamm |
| 18) 1980 | Joseph Christopher | Buffalo killing spree | Spaaij/Hewitt |
| 19) 1981 | Claude Dallas | Idaho game warden killings | Hamm |
| 20) 1982 | Frank Spisak | Cleveland killing spree | Spaaij/Hewitt |
| 21) 1982 | Norman Mayer | Washington bomb plot | Spaaij |
| 22) 1983 | Hussein Kholya | Texas plane hijacking | Spaaij |
| 23) 1989 | Leroy Moody | Southeastern mail bombings | Spaaij/Hewitt |
| 24) 1992–93 | Rachelle Shannon | Western abortion attacks | Spaaij |
| 25) 1993 | Mir Aimal Kansi | CIA shootings | Spaaij/Hewitt |
| 26) 1993 | Michael Griffin | Pensacola abortion killing | Spaaij/Hewitt |
| 27) 1993 | Colin Ferguson | Long Island train shootings | Spaaij |
| 28) 1994 | Rashid Baz | New York shooting | Spaaij |
| 29) 1994 | Paul Hill | Pensacola abortion killing | Spaaij/Hewitt |
| 30) 1994 | John Salvi | Boston abortion killing | Spaaij/Hewitt |

| Year | Name | Terrorist Event | Source |
|---|---|---|---|
| 31) 1996 | Larry Shoemake | Mississippi shootings | Spaaij |
| 32) 1996–98 | Eric Rudolph | Southern bombing spree | Spaaij/Hewitt |
| 33) 1997 | Ali Abu Kamal | New York shooting | Spaaij |
| 34) 1998 | James Kopp | New York abortion killing | Spaaij |
| 35) 1999 | Benjamin Smith | Midwestern killing spree | Hewitt |
| 36) 1999 | Buford Furrow | Los Angeles shootings | Spaaij/Hewitt |
| 37) 2000 | Ronald Taylor | Pennsylvania shootings | Spaaij |
| 38) 2000 | Rich Baumhammers | Pittsburgh killing spree | Spaaij |
| 39) 2001 | Bruce Ivins | Anthrax attacks | Hamm |
| 40) 2001 | Clayton Waagner | Anthrax hoaxes | Spaaij |
| 41) 2002 | Luke Helder | Midwestern mail bombings | Spaaij |
| 42) 2002 | Hesham Hadayet | Los Angeles airport killings | Spaaij |
| 43) 2002 | Steve Kim | United Nations shooting | Spaaij |
| 44) 2002 | Charles Bishop | Florida plane attack | Spaaij |
| 45) 2003 | Dwight Watson | Lincoln Memorial bomb plot | Spaaij |
| 46) 2004 | Van Crocker* | Tennessee ricin plot | Hamm |
| 47) 2006 | M. Taheri-azar | Chapel Hill auto attack | Spaaij |
| 48) 2006 | Naveed Haq | Seattle shootings | Spaaij |
| 49) 2007 | Paul Evans | Austin abortion bombing | Spaaij |
| 50) 2008 | Marc Ramsey | McCain anthrax hoax | Hamm |
| 51) 2008 | Jim David Adkisson | Knoxville church shootings | Hamm |
| 52) 2008 | James Cummings | Maine dirty bomb plot | Drake |
| 53) 2009 | Scott Roeder | Wichita abortion killing | Spaaij |
| 54) 2009 | Carlos Bledsoe | Little Rock military shooting | Spaaij/Hamm |
| 55) 2009 | Michael Finton* | Springfield bomb plot | Hamm |
| 56) 2009 | Nidal Hasan | Fort Hood shooting | Spaaij |
| 57) 2009 | Richard Poplawski | Pittsburgh police killings | Hamm |
| 58) 2009 | Joshua Cartwright | Florida police killings | Hamm |
| 59) 2009 | James von Brunn | Washington Holocaust killing | Hamm |
| 60) 2009 | Keith Luke | Massachusetts killing spree | Hamm |
| 61) 2009 | Hosam Smadi* | Dallas bomb plot | Hamm |
| 62) 2010 | Joseph Stack | Austin IRS plane attack | Spaaij |
| 63) 2010 | M Mohamud* | Portland bomb plot | Hamm |

| Year | Name | Terrorist Event | Source |
|---|---|---|---|
| 64) 2010 | James Lee | DC Discovery Channel attack | Drake |
| 65) 2010 | Yonathan Melaku | N. Virginia military shooting | Drake |
| 66) 2010 | Sandlin Smith | Florida mosque bombing | Hamm |
| 67) 2010 | Justin Moose* | N. Carolina abortion bombing | Hamm |
| 68) 2010 | Byron Williams | California police shootout | Hamm |
| 69) 2010 | John Bedell | Pentagon police shooting | Hamm |
| 70) 2010 | Casey Brezik | Missouri assassination attempt | Hamm |
| 71) 2010 | Antonio Martinez* | Maryland military bomb plot | Hamm |
| 72) 2010 | Farooque Ahmed* | Washington metro bomb plot | Spaaij |
| 73) 2010 | Sami Hassoun* | Chicago bomb plot | Hamm |
| 74) 2011 | Khalid Aldawsari | Bush bomb plot | Hamm |
| 75) 2011 | Rezwan Ferdaus* | Pentagon bomb plot | Hamm |
| 76) 2011 | Jared Loughner | Tucson Giffords shootings | Hamm |
| 77) 2011 | Kevin Harpham | Spokane MLK bombing | Hamm |
| 78) 2011 | Jose Pimentel* | New York subway bomb plot | Hamm |
| 79) 2011 | Ralph Lang | Wisconsin abortion clinic attack | Hamm |
| 80) 2011 | Naser Jason | Abdo Fort Hood bomb plot | Hamm |
| 81) 2011 | O.R.O-Hernandez | Obama assassination plot | Drake |
| 82) 2012 | Sami Osmakac* | Tampa bomb plot | Spaaij |
| 83) 2012 | Amine el Khalifi* | Capitol suicide bomb plot | Hamm |
| 84) 2012 | Wade Page | Milwaukee Sikh shootings | Hamm |
| 85) 2012 | Thomas Caffall | Texas A&M shootings | Hamm |
| 86) 2012 | Floyd Corkins | Washington DC shooting | Hamm |
| 87) 2012 | Adel Daoud* | Chicago bomb plot | Hamm |
| 88) 2012 | Francis Grady | Wisconsin abortion clinic arson | Hamm |
| 89) 2012 | Gregory Weiler | Oklahoma church bomb plot | Hamm |
| 90) 2012 | Quazi Nafis* | Federal Reserve bomb plot | Hamm |
| 91) 2012 | Raulie Casteel | Michigan highway shootings | Hamm |
| 92) 2013 | Derek Shrout | Alabama school bomb plot | Hamm |
| 93) 2013 | Jimmy Lee Dykes | Alabama kidnaping | Hamm |
| 94) 2013 | Christopher Dorner | Los Angeles shootings | Hamm |
| 95) 2013 | Matthew Buquet | Spokane ricin plot | Hamm |
| 96) 2013 | Jason Woodring | Arkansas power grid attack | Hamm |

| Year | Name | Terrorist Event | Source |
|---|---|---|---|
| 97) 2013 | Paul Ciancia | LA Airport shooting | Hamm |
| 98) 2013 | Terry Loewen* | Wichita bomb plot | Hamm |

* FBI sting operation (except for Jose Pimentel, case 78, NYPD sting).

**Summary:**

98 cases
38 pre-9/11 cases (all authentic lone wolf cases)
 60 post-9/11 cases
 15 post-9/11 stings (not to be included in authentic lone wolf cases)
45 authentic lone wolf post-9/11 cases

Primary Sources: Hewitt, Christopher (2003) *Understanding Terrorism in America: From the Klan to Al-Qaeda*. New York: Routledge; Spaaij, Ramon (2012) *Understanding Lone Wolf Terrorism: Global Patterns, Motivations and Prevention*. New York: Springer.

## Appendix 4
## Loci of Radicalization for Lone Wolf Terrorists

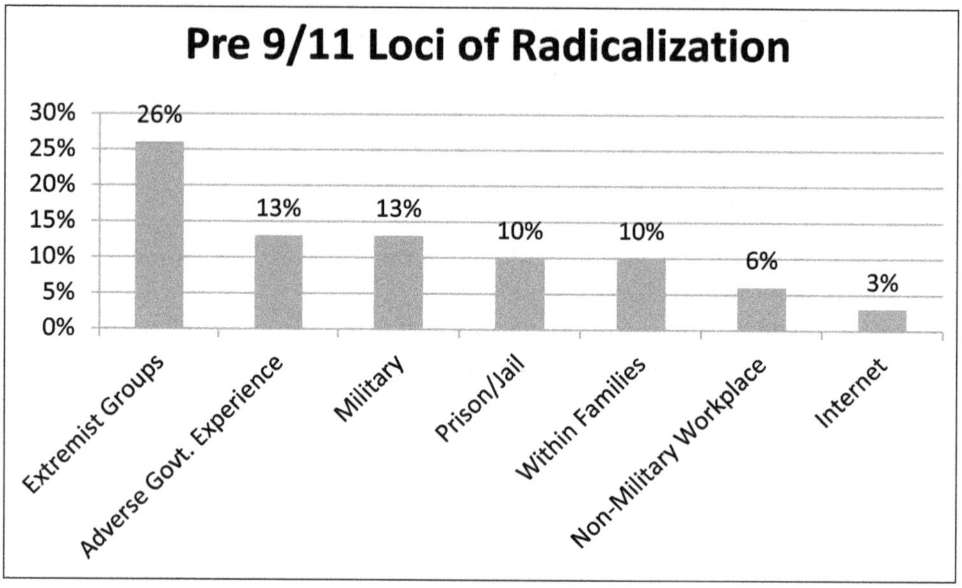


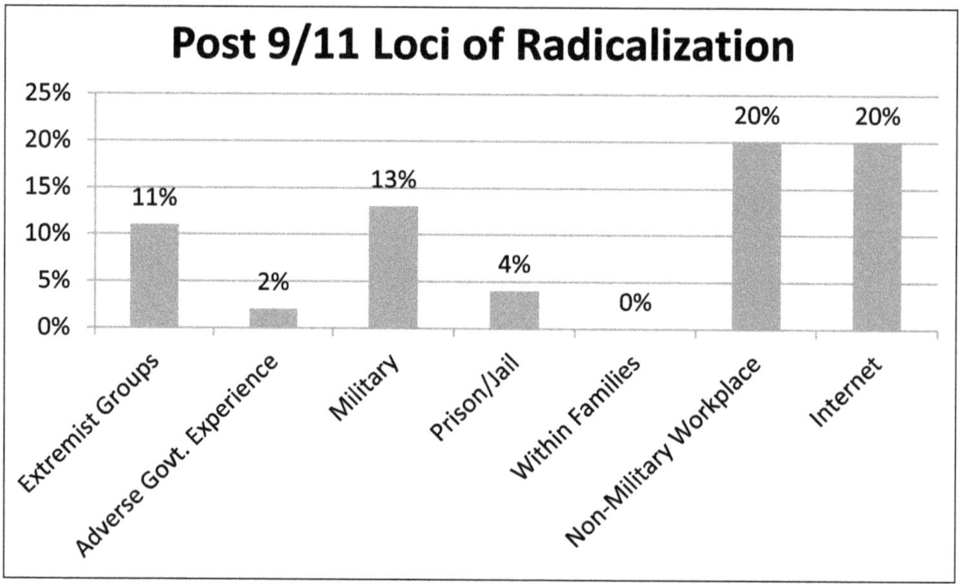

## Appendix 5
## The Radicalization Model of Lone Wolf Terrorism

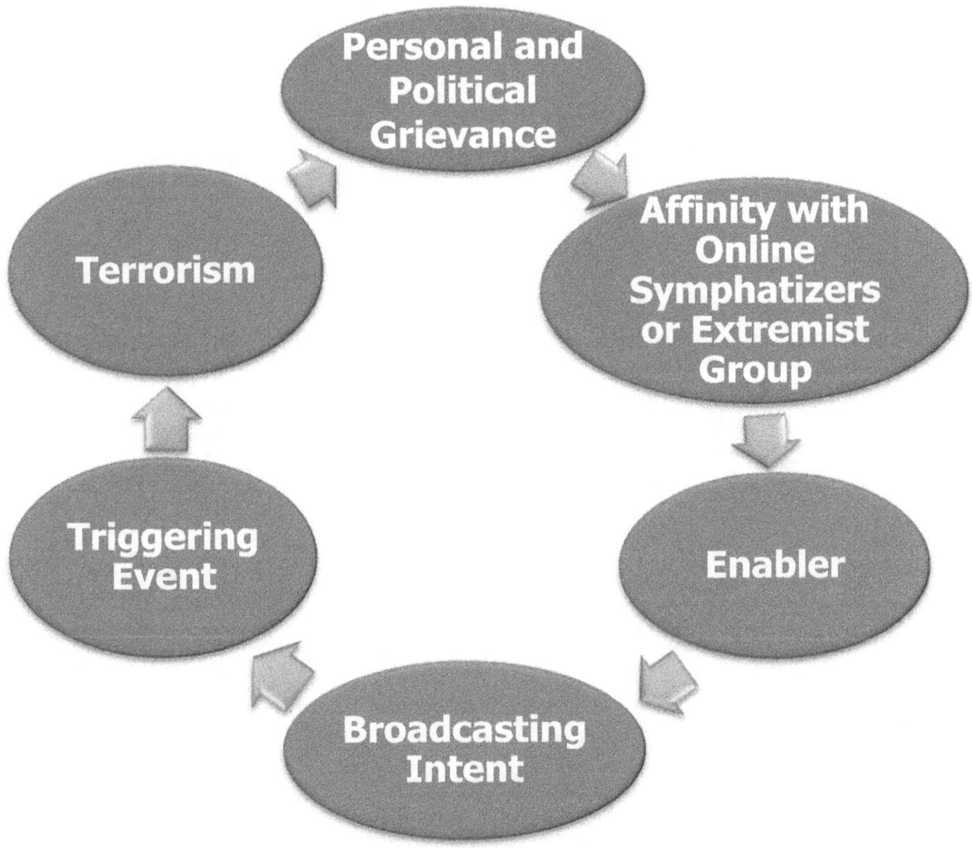

# B. PREVENTING LONE WOLF TERRORISM

## COMMENTARY

by
**Douglas C. Lovelace, Jr.**

Section B of this volume presents four documents that describe measures taken to thwart terrorism, including lone wolf terrorism. This volume focuses mainly on understanding, identifying, and preventing the acts of lone wolf terrorists. However, we begin Section B with a document that addresses how the U.S. government can mitigate acts of terrorism and help communities and victims recover. *Stafford Act Assistance and Acts of Terrorism* is a Congressional Research Service report that addresses difficulties with using the Act's provisions to address the harm wrought by certain types of terrorism. While the Act clearly applies to disasters caused by terrorist bombings, it has not been brought to bear on incidents of terrorism that did not involve explosions or widespread damage to infrastructure. Terrorist acts that resulted in large loss of life but little structural damage, such as those using firearms or vehicles as weapons, have not fallen under the purview of the Act.

The report cogently presents the arguments for and against amendment of the Act. Those in favor of amendment argue that communities that have suffered large losses of human life as a result of terrorist acts are as deserving and in need of federal assistance as those attempting recovery from terrorist acts that produce physical damage to infrastructure. They support their argument further by the observation that the amount of federal aid required to mitigate the cost of loss of life from terrorist attacks is so much less than that needed to replace damaged infrastructure that attacks in which significant damage to infrastructure has not occurred should also be covered by the Act.

Those who oppose amendment of the Act to allow it to compensate for the loss of life make several counterarguments. First, they claim that the Act, as written, is sufficiently flexible to provide the assistance states and families need in the aftermath of "large loss of life" terrorist attacks. The report's authors astutely assess that the extent to which the Act will be interpreted to cover such loss will depend not only on the potential cost to the federal government, but also on determinations of the respective roles of federal and state government in assisting surviving family members in coping with the loss of life. Amendment opponents contend that revising the Act so that it covers "large loss of life" attacks improperly shifts the burden of compensating victims' families from the states to the federal government.

Amendment proponents might be willing to accept revision that authorizes the federal government to provide assistance only when a state does not have the resources to provide adequate compensation. However, that position is problematic, in that the states would not be predisposed to maintain adequate victims' compensation funds if they knew that the federal government would step in as a back-up. While the report's authors do not take a position in the debate, their discussion of the issue and the competing views is uniquely informative, when considering how to deal with the aftermath of a "large loss of life" lone wolf terrorist attack.

The second document offered in this section is a report by the Committee on Homeland Security of the U.S. House of Representatives entitled *Preventing Another Boston Marathon Bombing*. The report is a follow-up to the Committee's March 2014 report resulting from its investigation of the bombing. In that report, the Committee concluded that cooperation between federal and local law enforcement, travel screening policy, information sharing, and capabilities to mitigate terrorist threats required improvement. To that end, the present report addresses U.S. government interagency actions to make the required improvements.

While the assessment is generally positive, the report does offer recommendations for additional improvement. The theme of the most important recommendations, unsurprisingly, is the need to continue to improve the sharing of information vertically and horizontally throughout the levels and agencies of government. Of course, access to classified information must be regulated to protect sources and methods and to avoid compromises that could thwart law enforcement efforts and even place law enforcement personnel in additional danger. The most important goal outlined in the report is the recognition by all levels of government of the importance of identifying, assessing, and promulgating lessons learned from successful as well as attempted attacks. It is only through a continual learning process that the federal, state, and local governments will be able to work together synergistically to prevent terrorist attacks and, when preventive efforts fail, to mitigate the effects of the attacks.

The third document presented in Section B addresses the formulation of strategy to counter violent extremists and the assessment of the efficacy of that strategy. *Countering Violent Extremism* is a Government Accountability Office (GAO) report on a study undertaken to review U.S. government efforts to prevent domestic occurrences of violent extremism. Defining violent extremism as ideologically, religiously, or politically motivated acts of violence, the GAO assessed U.S. government efforts to counter violent extremism by examining the extent to which the Department of Homeland Security (DHS), Department of Justice (DoJ), Federal Bureau of Investigation (FBI), and National Counterterrorism Center (NCTC) have implemented the tasks set forth in the 2011 Strategic Implementation Plan (SIP).

The GAO's findings are disturbing. As of December 2016, fewer than half of the tasks had been accomplished, with 23 underway and two not even initiated. Moreover, the GAO found that the federal government has no cohesive strategy or process for determining whether the actions accomplished to date have made the United States any safer from violent extremists. Without a strategy and an assessment process, the U.S. government has no way to determine where future resources should be devoted and what the funding priorities should be. The only explanation for the lack of emphasis placed on developing an effective strategy with measurable objectives is that violent extremism is still not seen as a serious threat to the security of Americans. However, with Omar Mateen's slaughter of 49 people in Orlando and Stephen Paddock's massacre of 58 in Las Vegas, the public's concern over violent extremism is on the rise. The GAO's admonitions to the DHS and DoJ are well-timed.

The final document we present in Section B discusses a primary tool used by the U.S. government to prevent terrorist attacks. *The Terrorist Screening Database and Preventing Terrorist Travel* is a CRS report that provides an updated description of the Terrorist Screening Database (TSDB) to include how it is used by the U.S. government in its attempts to identify potential terrorists and prevent them from mounting attacks. A major use of the TSDB is to screen foreign nationals traveling to the United States through either visa request screening or port of entry or pre–port of entry screening.

Some apparently uninformed commentators argue that the efficacy of visa screening is compromised significantly by the Visa Waiver Program (VWP), which allows vast numbers of foreign nationals to enter the United States for temporary periods without going through the visa application process. The CRS report points out that any foreign national entering the United States through the VWP will be vetted against the TSDB, through the Electronic System for Travel Authorization (ESTA). Customs and Border Protection (CBP) officers conduct additional screening at ports of entry using the TSDB as well. Additionally, the CRS report points out that foreigners entering the United States by commercial air are vetted through the Secure Flight Program of the Transportation Security Administration (TSA) and that the TSA manages risk through its TSA Pre-Check program.

A reading of the CRS report leaves the reader justifiably reassured that commercial carrier passengers entering the United States are being adequately screened. However, it leaves one less confident that the U.S. government has adequately reduced the risk of terrorists entering the United States by other means or that it has significantly improved its ability to identify and interdict lone wolf domestic terrorists before they act.

# DOCUMENT NO. 6

# STAFFORD ACT ASSISTANCE AND ACTS OF TERRORISM


**CRS Report R44801**

**Bruce R. Lindsay**
Analyst in American National Government


June 2, 2017


## Summary

The Robert T. Stafford Disaster Relief and Emergency Assistance Act (the Stafford Act) authorizes the President to issue two types of declarations that could potentially provide federal assistance to states and localities in response to a terrorist attack: a "major disaster declaration" or an "emergency declaration." Major disaster declarations authorize a wide range of federal assistance to states, local governments, tribal nations, individuals and households, and certain nonprofit organizations to recover from a catastrophic event. Major disaster declarations also make Small Business Administration (SBA) disaster loans available to eligible businesses and households. Emergency declarations authorize a more limited range of federal assistance to protect property and public health and safety, and to lessen or avert the threat of a major disaster. Only private nonprofit organizations are eligible for disaster loans under an emergency declaration.

The Stafford Act has been used to provide assistance in response to terrorist attacks in the past including the 1995 bombing of the Alfred P. Murrah Building in Oklahoma City, the September 11, 2001, attacks, and the 2013 Boston Marathon attack. Nevertheless, the tactics used in recent incidents such as the 2015 San Bernardino, CA, and the 2016 Orlando, FL, mass shootings, and the 2016 Ohio State University vehicular and knife attack, have brought to light two main challenges that might prevent certain types of terrorist incidents from receiving the wider assistance provided under a major disaster declaration:

- the major disaster definition lists specific incident types that are eligible for federal assistance. Past terrorist incidents were considered major disasters, in part, because they resulted in fires and explosions. Incidents without a fire or an explosion may not meet the definition of a major disaster; and

- the Federal Emergency Management Agency's (FEMA) recommendation to the President to issue a major disaster declaration is mainly based on damage amounts to public infrastructure compared to the state's population. Terrorist incidents with a large loss of life but limited damage to public infrastructure may not meet this criterion.

Some may argue that terrorist incidents warrant the wider range of assistance provided by a major disaster declaration, and advocate for changes to the Stafford Act and FEMA policies to make all acts of terrorism eligible for major disaster assistance. Others may disagree and argue that Stafford Act should not be altered for the following reasons:

- regardless of cause, state and local governments should be the main source of assistance if damages are limited;
- if the incident does not qualify for major disaster assistance, it could still be eligible for limited assistance under an emergency declaration.

Advocates of changing the Stafford Act may argue that emergency declaration assistance is too limited. For example, parts of FEMA's Individual Assistance (IA) program, which provides various forms of help for families and individuals, are not available without a major disaster declaration. Another concern is the limited availability of SBA disaster loans under an emergency declaration. Advocates might therefore argue that changes to the Stafford Act are needed to make it easier for certain terror attacks to qualify for major disaster assistance. These include

- expanding the major disaster definition to include terror incidents that do not involve fires and explosions;
- requiring FEMA to use additional metrics when making major disaster recommendations; and/or
- extending the availability of certain IA programs and SBA disaster loans under an emergency declaration.

This report provides an overview of emergency and major disaster declarations and explains how they might be used in the aftermath of a terrorist incident that does not involve a fire or an explosion, such as high casualty mass shootings or chemical gas attacks. This report also provides an overview of Stafford Act assistance provided for past terrorist incidents.

This report will be updated as events warrant.

## Background

Congress has been interested in disaster relief since the earliest days of the republic. On February 19, 1803, the 7th Congress passed the first known federal disaster assistance legislation, providing debt relief to the residents of Portsmouth, NH, following a December 26, 1802, fire that burned down most of the town ("A Bill for the Relief of the Sufferers by Fire, in the Town of Portsmouth," commonly known as the Congressional Act of 1803).[1]

[1] Acts of the 7th Congress, A Bill for the Relief of the Sufferers by fire, in the Town of Portsmouth, New Hampshire, 2 Stat. 201 "... all persons who, being indebted to the United States, for duties on merchandise,

Over the years, Congress has authorized the expansion of federal disaster assistance to individuals, businesses, and places (both for humanitarian reasons and as a means to enhance interstate commerce). For example

- During the 1930s, Congress passed legislation authorizing the Reconstruction Finance Corporation to make disaster loans for the repair and reconstruction of certain public facilities following an earthquake, and later, other types of disasters;[2] and the Bureau of Public Roads to provide funding for highways and bridges damaged by natural disasters.[3]
- During the 1950s, Congress passed legislation authorizing the President to respond to major disasters.[4]
- During the 1960s, Congress passed legislation expanding the U.S. Army Corps of Engineers' authority to implement flood control projects.[5]
- During the 1970s, Congress passed legislation authorizing federal loans and tax assistance to individuals affected by disasters, as well as federal funding for the repair and replacement of public facilities;[6] and the establishment of the presidential disaster declaration process.[7]
- During the 1980s, Congress passed legislation authorizing numerous changes to federal disaster assistance programs administered by the Federal Emergency Management Agency (FEMA), which had been created by Executive Order 12127 on March 31, 1979, to, among other activities, coordinate federal disaster relief efforts.[8]

Since the 1980s, Congress has focused on the oversight of FEMA's implementation of federal disaster relief efforts and assessing the Robert T. Stafford Disaster Relief and Emergency Assistance Act (of 1988), hereinafter the Stafford Act, as amended (42 U.S.C.

have given bond therefor, with one or more sureties, payable to the collector for the district of Portsmouth, and who have suffered a loss of property by the late conflagration, at that place, shall be, and they hereby are allowed to take up, or have cancelled, all bonds heretofore given for duties as aforesaid, upon giving to the said collector new bonds, with one or more sureties, to the satisfaction of said collector, for the sums of their former bonds respectively, payable in twelve months from and after the day of payment specified in the bonds to be taken up or cancelled as aforesaid; and the said collector is hereby authorized and directed, to give up or cancel, all such bonds upon the receipt of others as described in this act...."

114 buildings were reportedly "lost to the flames." See Portsmouth Athenaeum, "Portsmouth Fire Relief Papers, 1802-1803," at http://www.portsmouthathenaeum.org/findingaids/ms071.htm.

2 P.L. 72-2, the Reconstruction Finance Corporation Act of 1932, 47 Stat. 5.

3 P.L. 73-393, To increase employment by authorizing an appropriation to provide for emergency construction of public highways an related projects, and to amend P.L. 64-156, the Federal Aid Road Act, as amended and supplemented, and for other purposes, 48 Stat. 993.

4 P.L. 81-875, An Act to authorize federal assistance to states and local governments in major disasters, and for other purposes, 64 Stat. 1109.

5 P.L. 89-298, the Flood Control Act of 1965, 79 Stat. 1073.

6 P.L. 91-606, the Disaster Relief Act of 1970, 84 Stat. 1744.

7 P.L. 93-288, the Disaster Relief Act of 1974, 88 Stat. 143.

8 P.L. 100-707, the Disaster Relief and Emergency Assistance Amendments of 1988 (renaming the Disaster Relief Act of 1974 the Robert T. Stafford Disaster Relief and Emergency Assistance Act), 102 Stat. 4689; and Office of the President (Carter), "Executive Order 12127 of March 31, 1979, Federal Emergency Management Agency," 44 *Federal Register* 19367-19368, April 3, 1979.

5721 et seq.) to determine if its provisions meet current needs. One such potential need is providing disaster assistance following a terrorist attack.

### Stafford Act Assistance in Response to Terrorism

The Stafford Act authorizes the President to issue two types of declarations that could potentially provide federal assistance to states and localities in response to a terrorist attack: a "major disaster declaration" or an "emergency declaration."[9] Major disaster declarations authorize a wide-range of federal assistance to states, local governments, tribal nations, individuals and households, and certain nonprofit organizations to aid recovery from a catastrophic event. Major disaster declarations must be requested by the state governor or tribal leader. Emergency declarations authorize a more limited range of federal assistance and are issued by the President to protect property and public health and safety and to lessen or avert the threat of a major disaster.[10] In most cases, the state governor or tribal leader must request an emergency declaration; however, under 501(b) of the Stafford Act, the President has authority to issue an emergency declaration without a gubernatorial or tribal request under specified conditions.[11] Examples of these types of emergency declarations with respect to terrorist incidents include the April 19, 1995, bombing of the Alfred P. Murrah Building in Oklahoma City, and the September 11, 2001, attack on the Pentagon.[12] In each instance, the emergency declaration was followed by a major disaster declaration.

While the Stafford Act has been used to provide assistance in response to terrorist attacks in the past, recent incidents such as the mass shootings that occurred in 2015 and 2016 in San Bernardino, CA, and Orlando, FL, respectively, and the 2016 vehicular attacks in Nice, France, and Ohio State University may have brought to light some potential shortcomings in the Stafford Act. That is, certain terror attacks may not meet the criteria of a major disaster for two reasons. First, depending on the mechanism used in the attack, certain terror incidents may not meet the legal definition of a major disaster. Of interest here, the Stafford Act defines a major disaster as "any natural catastrophe (including any hurricane, tornado, storm, high water, wind-driven water, tidal wave, tsunami, earthquake, volcanic eruption, landslide, mudslide, snowstorm, or drought), or, regardless of cause, any fire, flood, or explosion, in any part of the United States, which in the determination of the President causes damage of sufficient severity and magnitude to warrant major disaster assistance."[13] The list of incidents that qualify for a major disaster declaration is specifically limited, and it is not clear if a terror attack would meet the legal definition of a major disaster if the incident involved something other than a fire or explosion.

---

[9] For more information on Stafford Act declarations see CRS Report R43784, *FEMA's Disaster Declaration Process: A Primer,* by Francis X. McCarthy; and CRS Report R42702, *Stafford Act Declarations 1953–2015: Trends, Analyses, and Implications for Congress,* by Bruce R. Lindsay and Francis X. McCarthy.

[10] Emergency declarations can be issued before an incident when a threat is detected (for example, before a hurricane makes landfall) to supplement and coordinate local and state efforts such as evacuations and the protection of public assets.

[11] P.L. 93-288, 42 U.S.C. Sec. 5191.

[12] The attack on the World Trade Center in New York was immediately declared a major disaster on September 11 and did not receive an emergency declaration designation.

[13] P.L. 93-288, 42 U.S.C. §5122.

Meeting the definition of a major disaster is a necessary but insufficient condition for the receipt of major disaster assistance. The incident's cost must also be beyond the capacity of the state and local government. When an incident occurs, FEMA meets with the state to assess damage costs to affected homes and public infrastructure. Damages to public infrastructure are particularly important because this amount is compared to the state's population. This comparison is called the "per capita threshold." FEMA uses the threshold to assess state and local government capacity. In general, FEMA will recommend that the President declare a major disaster if the incident meets or exceeds the per capita threshold. It is conceivable that a terrorist incident could cause substantial loss of life but cause little or no damage to homes and public infrastructure. This lack of damage (to public infrastructure) may disqualify these incidents from receiving the wider range of assistance provided under a major disaster declaration.

With respect to terrorism, some may view the Stafford Act's current framework adequate and oppose efforts to alter it. Their reasons are twofold. First, while terrorist incidents such as mass shootings can be devastating in terms of loss of life and impact on national morale, some argue that a major disaster should not be declared for terrorist incidents that do not cause enough damage to public infrastructure to warrant federal assistance. State and local governments, as well as insurance coverage, they say, should be the main sources of assistance if damages are limited. Second, they may argue that terror incidents that do not meet the criteria of a major disaster could be eligible for Stafford Act assistance under an emergency declaration. In contrast to the prescribed definition of incidents that qualify as a major disaster, an emergency is defined more broadly to include "any occasion or instance for which, in the determination of the President, federal assistance is needed to supplement State and local efforts and capabilities to save lives and to protect property and public health and safety, or to lessen or avert the threat of a catastrophe in any part of the United States."[14]

Some might argue that an emergency declaration would provide adequate assistance to individuals and households after a terrorist incident. For example, as outlined in Section 502 of the Stafford Act, an emergency declaration may include Section 408 assistance. Some examples of Section 408 assistance include

- FEMA's Individuals and Household Program (IHP), which provides housing and grants to individuals and families; and
- Other Needs Assistance (ONA) grants, which is part of the IHP program in the form of grants to families and individuals. These grants can cover items including medical and dental expenses caused by the incident as well as funeral expenses. ONA grants may also cover certain necessary expenses such as the replacement of personal property and other expenses.

Others may argue that most acts of terrorism warrant the wide range of assistance provided by a major disaster declaration. They would argue that the assistance provided under an emergency declaration is too limited. For example, the Crisis Counseling program is not provided under an emergency declaration.[15] The Crisis Counseling program

[14] Ibid.

[15] P.L. 93-288, 42 U.S.C. §5183.

may seem especially appropriate to a terrorist incident given the assistance it provides for what is likely a wrenching event for those involved.

In addition, the type of declaration determines what types of Small Business Administration (SBA) disaster loans are available. In general, homeowners, renters, businesses, and nonprofit organizations become eligible for disaster loans under a major disaster declaration. In contrast, typically only private nonprofit organizations are eligible for disaster loans under an emergency declaration. Finally, beyond the monetary assistance provided by a major disaster declaration, some would argue that major disaster declarations are important symbolic gestures of federal support to states and localities.

## Declaration Procedure

The Stafford Act requires that all major disaster declaration requests be made by state governors or tribal leaders. Such requests must be made on the basis that the incident is of such severity and magnitude that effective response is beyond the capability of the affected state and local government. The request for a declaration begins with a letter to the President from the governor or tribal leader. Included with the letter are supplemental material and any relevant information about the incident.[16] The letter also describes what types of federal assistance is being requested. In the case of a request for a major disaster declaration, a particularly important piece of information accompanying the letter is the Preliminary Damage Assessment (PDA). PDAs provide public infrastructure damage estimates (as well as estimated damage to households). By regulation, FEMA compares this damage estimate against the state's population.[17] In general, FEMA will make a recommendation to the President that a major disaster be declared if public infrastructure damages exceed $1.42 per capita. This formula is known as the "per capita threshold."[18]

A request for an emergency declaration follows the same basic regulatory procedures highlighted above for major disasters with some nuances. Similar to a request for a major disaster declaration, the basis for an emergency declaration is that the incident is of such severity and magnitude that effective response is beyond the capability of the affected state and local government. FEMA, however, does not apply any formulas—including the per capita threshold—in regulations to make emergency declaration recommendations to the President.

While there are differences between the two types of declarations, the ultimate decision to declare and grant federal assistance for emergencies and major disasters rests solely with the President.

[16] For additional discussion, see CRS Report R43784, *FEMA's Disaster Declaration Process: A Primer*, by Francis X. McCarthy.

[17] C.F.R. §206.48(a)(1).

[18] The per capita threshold is only used for making recommendations. Section 320 of the Stafford Act prohibits the use of formulas or sliding scales based on income or population to make declaration determinations.

### Major Disaster Declaration Criteria

In general, an incident must meet three criteria to be eligible for a major disaster declaration: (1) definition, (2) unmet need, and (3) state action.

#### Definition

The Stafford Act defines a major disaster as

> any natural catastrophe (including any hurricane, tornado, storm, high water, wind-driven water, tidal wave, tsunami, earthquake, volcanic eruption, landslide, mudslide, snowstorm, or drought), or, regardless of cause, any fire, flood, or explosion, in any part of the United States, which in the determination of the President causes damage of sufficient severity and magnitude to warrant major disaster assistance under this chapter to supplement the efforts and available resources of states, local governments, and disaster relief organizations in alleviating the damage, loss, hardship, or suffering caused thereby.[19]

The definition of a major disaster can be applied in several ways. The definition could be applied prescriptively. In this view, the definition would be considered as an itemized list of incidents eligible for federal assistance under the Stafford Act. As a result, certain incidents are not eligible for assistance because the definition is taken as verbatim and all inclusive. Another approach is to consider the definition as open to interpretation. In this view, the list of incidents is seen as providing examples of some of the incidents that could be considered a major disaster. Alternatively, the definition could be seen as a blend of the two approaches. The list of natural disasters might be seen as open-ended whereas human caused incidents are limited to the itemized list of "fire, flood, or explosion." Depending on the interpretation, the definition may limit certain incidents from receiving federal assistance.

The discussion regarding whether an incident would be denied assistance due to definitional limitations is hypothetical. There have been incidents denied for definitional reasons (such as the Flint water contamination incident) but thus far a Governor has not requested a major disaster for a *terrorist* incident and denied assistance based on the definition of a major disaster. It is unclear if the definition would be fatal to a request for a major disaster declaration. Ultimately, the President has the discretion to determine what incidents that meet this definition are eligible for a major disaster declaration.

#### Unmet Need

In addition to meeting the definition of a major disaster, the incident must result in damages significant enough to exceed the capabilities and resources of state and local governments. Exceeding state and local capabilities and resources is generally considered as the state's unmet need. Under the Stafford Act:

> All requests for a declaration by the President that a major disaster exists shall be made by the Governor of the affected state. Such a request shall be based on a finding that the disaster is of such severity and magnitude that effective response

[19] P.L. 93-288, 42 U.S.C. §5122.

> is beyond the capabilities of the state and the affected local governments and that federal assistance is necessary.[20]

In general, FEMA assesses the degree of damage for an incident to help determine unmet need. FEMA considers six general areas:

- estimated cost of the assistance;
- localized impacts;
- insurance coverage;
- hazard mitigation;
- recent multiple disasters; and
- other federal assistance programs.

While all of these factors are considered when assessing an incident's worthiness for federal assistance, the estimated cost of assistance is perhaps the most critical because it contains the per capita threshold mentioned earlier in this report, as well as the unmet needs of families and individuals. Attacks such as the 2016 Pulse nightclub shooting in Florida and the 2015 San Bernardino, CA, shooting had a high number of fatalities with relatively low damages to public infrastructure. Limited public infrastructure damages may make the per capita threshold difficult to reach—particularly for highly populated states.

### State Action

The state or tribal nation must implement its emergency plan, dedicate sufficient resources to respond to the incident, and agree to cost-sharing requirements, as follows:

> As part of such request, and as a prerequisite to major disaster assistance under this chapter, the Governor shall take appropriate response action under state law and direct execution of the state's emergency plan. The Governor shall furnish information on the nature and amount of State and local resources which have been or will be committed to alleviating the results of the disaster, and shall certify that, for the current disaster, state and local government obligations and expenditures (of which state commitments must be a significant proportion) will comply with all applicable cost-sharing requirements of this chapter.[21]

As conceptualized in **Figure 1**, an incident is eligible for a disaster declaration if all three criteria intersect. An incident that does not meet the definition of a major disaster, and/or does not have unmet need would not have intersecting criteria and may have more difficulty receiving a major disaster declaration.

---

[20] P.L. 93-288, 42 U.S.C. §5170.

[21] Ibid.

**Figure 1. Major Disaster Declaration Criteria**
Definition, Unmet Need, and State Action

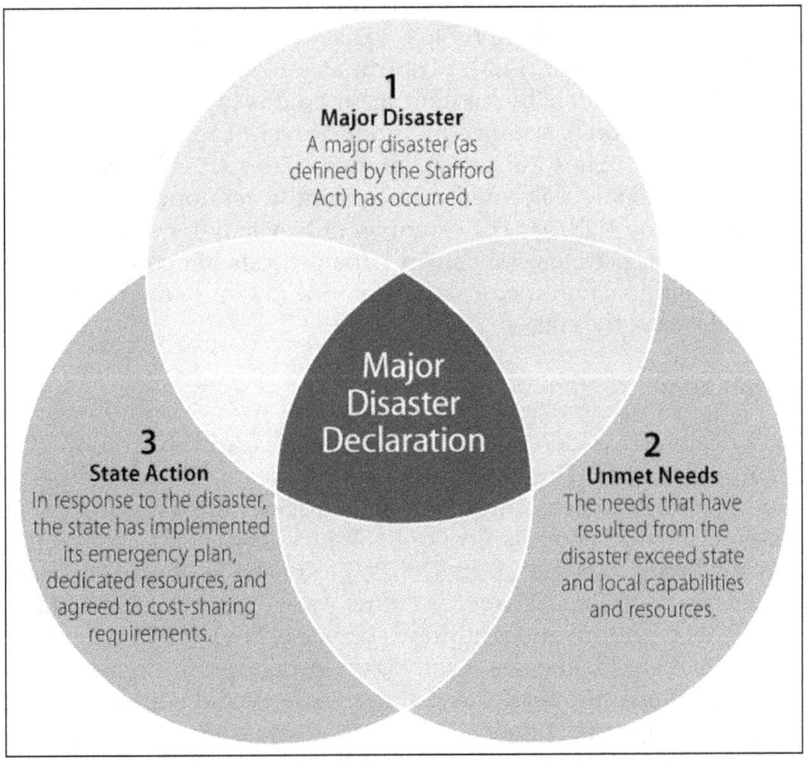


**Source:** Based on CRS analysis of Sections 102(2) and 401 of the Stafford Act.

## Major Disaster Assistance

### FEMA Assistance

The assistance provided for a major disaster declaration generally takes three forms: Public Assistance (PA), Individual Assistance (IA), and Hazard Mitigation Assistance (HMA). PA addresses the state or tribe's essential needs but concentrates on repairing damage to infrastructure (public roads, buildings, etc.).[22] IA helps families and individuals. IA can be in the form of temporary housing assistance and grants to address post-disaster needs (such as replacing furniture, clothing and other items). It may also include crisis counseling and disaster unemployment benefit. HMA provides grant funding to the state for mitigation projects. HMA does not necessarily need to mitigate risks from the type of disaster that was declared. Rather, HMA can be used for mitigation projects identified before the declaration was issued.

[22] For more information on FEMA's PA program see CRS Report *R43990, FEMA's Public Assistance Grant Program: Background and Considerations for Congress,* by Jared T. Brown and Daniel J. Richardson.

FEMA, however, does not exclusively perform all disaster response and recovery operations for the federal government. The President has the authority to direct any federal agency to use its authorities and resources to support state and local response and recovery efforts, primarily through Sections 402, 403, and 502 of the Stafford Act. In general, when a declaration is declared, FEMA coordinates federal entities and organizations that are involved in the incident by "assigning" missions to relevant agencies to address a state's request for federal assistance or support overall federal operations pursuant to, or in anticipation of, a Stafford Act declaration.[23] The activities carried out by other agencies through Mission Assignments are generally reimbursed by FEMA through the Disaster Relief Fund (DRF).[24] For example, FEMA may request the Department of Health and Human Services to establish and operate a shelter co-located with a federal medical station to support non-medical caregivers and family members accompanying patients being treated at the station.

### SBA Disaster Loan Program

Major disaster declarations also put the Small Business Administration (SBA) Disaster Loan Program into effect.[25] The loan program provides three main types of loans for disaster-related losses: (1) Home and Personal Property Disaster Loans, (2) Business Physical Disaster Loans, and (3) Economic Injury Disaster Loans (EIDL).[26] Home Physical Disaster Loans provide up to $200,000 to repair or replace disaster-damaged primary residences.[27] Personal Property Loans provide up to $40,000 to replace personal items such as furniture and clothing.[28] Business Physical Disaster Loans provide up to $2 million to help businesses of all sizes and nonprofit organizations repair or replace disaster-damaged property, including inventory and supplies.[29] EIDLs provide up to $2 million to help meet financial obligations and operating expenses that could have been met had the disaster not occurred.[30] Loan proceeds can only be used for working capital necessary to enable the business or organization to alleviate the specific economic injury and to resume normal operations.[31] Loan amounts for EIDLs are based on actual economic injury and financial needs, regardless of whether the business suffered any property damage.

---

[23] Federal Emergency Management Agency, *FEMA Mission Assignment (MA) Policy*, FP 104-010-2, November 6, 2015, p. 4, at https://www.fema.gov/media-library-data/1450099364660-fd855ba68f3189d974966ea259a2641a/Mission_Assignment_Policy.pdf.

[24] The DRF is FEMA's primary funding source for response and recovery projects. Funds from the DRF are not available for activities undertaken under other authorities or agency missions, or for non-Stafford Act incidents requiring a coordinated federal response.

[25] C.F.R. §123.3. For more information on the SBA Disaster Loan Program see CRS Report R41309, *The SBA Disaster Loan Program: Overview and Possible Issues for Congress*, by Bruce R. Lindsay; and CRS Report R44412, *SBA Disaster Loan Program: Frequently Asked Questions*, by Bruce R. Lindsay.

[26] While the type of declaration may determine what types of loans are made available, declaration type has no bearing on loan terms or loan caps.

[27] 13 C.F.R. §123.105(a)(2).

[28] 13 C.F.R. §123.105(a)(1).

[29] 13 C.F.R. §123.202(a).

[30] 13 C.F.R. §123.506.

[31] 13 C.F.R. §123.604(a).

Major disaster declarations that include both IA and PA make all three loan types available. Only private non-profit organizations are eligible for SBA physical disaster loans and EIDL, if the major disaster declaration only provides PA.

It is important to note that SBA disaster loans are usually the only type of federal assistance available to businesses after a terror attack because FEMA does not provide assistance to the private sector.

## Emergency Declaration Criteria

The three criteria for an incident to be eligible for an emergency disaster declaration include (1) definition, (2) unmet need, and (3) state action.

### Definition

The Stafford Act defines an emergency as

> any occasion or instance for which, in the determination of the President, federal assistance is needed to supplement State and local efforts and capabilities to save lives and to protect property and public health and safety, or to lessen or avert the threat of a catastrophe in any part of the United States.[32]

While the definition of a major disaster includes a list of incidents that could be considered a major disaster, emergencies are defined more broadly. Consequently, a terrorist attack such as a mass shooting or other nontraditional attack (such as using a vehicle as a weapon) under consideration as an "emergency" would likely not face the definitional challenge posed by the "major disaster" definition.

### Federal Responsibility

The Stafford Act procedure for an emergency declaration can be particularly useful when a terrorist incident involves federal property or a federal program is Section 501(b) of the act:

> The President may exercise any authority vested in him by section 502 or section 503 with respect to an emergency when he determines that an emergency exists for which the primary responsibility for response rests with the United States, because the emergency involves a subject area for which, under the Constitution or laws of the United States, the United States exercises exclusive or preeminent responsibility and authority. In determining whether or not such an emergency exists, the President shall consult the Governor of any affected state, if practicable. The President's determination may be made without regard to subsection (a).[33]

While Presidents have rarely invoked this authority, it could provide a path for rapid action and certain forms of terrorism might be easily and justly defined as a federal responsibility. And as noted previously, emergency declarations can later be converted to major disaster declarations. The use of Section 501(b) is infrequent and has been invoked on three occasions: (1) the Alfred P. Murrah Federal Building bombing in

[32] P.L. 93-288, 42 U.S.C. §5122.

[33] P.L. 93-288, 42 U.S.C. §5191.

Oklahoma City in 1995, (2) the 2003 Space Shuttle Columbia explosion,[34] and (3) the terrorist attack on the Pentagon on September 11, 2001.

It could be argued that the usefulness of 501(b) would be limited to certain situations that involve areas of federal responsibility (e.g., federal properties or programs). It could be further argued that that the use of Section 501(b) would be inappropriate, if the incident occurred in a business setting or an area of state and local jurisdiction. Others might disagree and argue that all terrorist incidents are a federal responsibility regardless of where they occur in the United States. According to this view, the 501(b) authority could be useful in the initial stages of a terrorist event since it provides the President with the discretion to act quickly without having to wait for a gubernatorial request for assistance. Others might be concerned that Section 501(b) might be invoked too often if applied to any situation that involved terrorism. For example, they may argue that it could lead to an expansion of federal assistance if routinely used in terror-related mass shootings.

### Unmet Need

In general, similar to a major disaster, an incident must result in damages significant enough to exceed the capabilities and resources of state and local governments. Under the Stafford Act

> All requests for a declaration by the President that an emergency exists shall be made by the Governor of the affected state. Such a request shall be based on a finding that the situation is of such severity and magnitude that effective response is beyond the capabilities of the state and the affected local governments and that federal assistance is necessary.[35]

As mentioned previously, the President has the authority to issue an emergency declaration in certain circumstances without a gubernatorial or tribal request. Thus, in certain circumstances, the response does not need to be beyond the capabilities of state and local governments since the response could be considered a uniquely federal responsibility.

### State Action

As with a major disaster, the state or tribal nation must implement its emergency plan, dedicate sufficient resources to respond to the incident, and agree to cost-sharing requirements, as follows:

> As a part of such request, and as a prerequisite to emergency assistance under this act, the Governor shall take appropriate action under State law and direct execution of the State's emergency plan. The Governor shall furnish information describing the state and local efforts and resources which have been or will be used to alleviate the emergency, and will define the type and extent of federal aid

[34] The Space Shuttle Columbia fell in parts across Texas and Louisiana in 2003. Since this was a federal activity and required work across two states, the President declared the emergencies as uniquely federal responsibilities.

[35] P.L. 93-288, 42 U.S.C. §5191.

required. Based upon such Governor's request, the President may declare that an emergency exists.[36]

As illustrated in **Figure 2**, an incident is eligible for an emergency declaration if all three criteria intersect. An incident that does not meet the definition of a major disaster, or does not have unmet need would not have intersecting criteria and may have more difficulty receiving a major disaster declaration.

**Figure 2. Emergency Declaration Criteria**
Definition, Unmet Need, and State Action

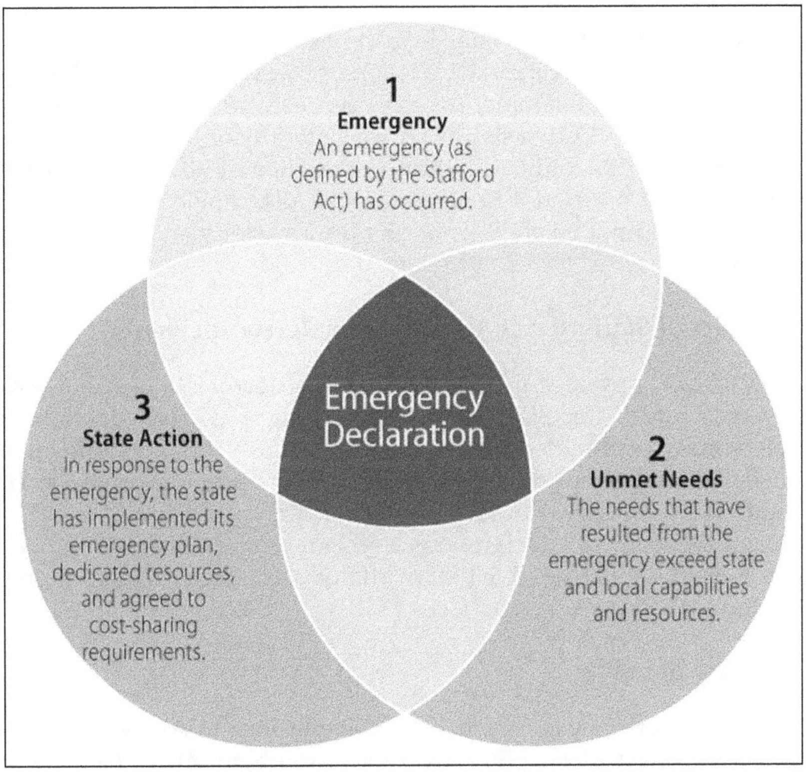


**Source:** Based on CRS analysis of Sections 102(1) and 501(a) of the Stafford Act.

## Emergency Declaration Assistance

### FEMA Assistance

Emergency declarations authorize activities that can help states and communities carry out essential services and activities that might reduce the threat of future damage. Emergency declarations authorize less assistance than a major disaster. Emergency declarations do not provide assistance for repairs and replacement of public infrastructure

[36] Ibid.

or nonprofit facilities. However, they do provide emergency services under the Stafford Act and other actions that might lessen the threat of a major disaster.

As with major disaster declarations, the President has the authority under an emergency declaration to direct any federal agency to use its authorities and resources in support of state and local response and recovery efforts under 502 of the Stafford Act. Also, the emergency authority includes Section 408 which means that housing assistance and grants for individuals and families could be provided under an emergency declaration.

### SBA Disaster Loan Program

Emergency declarations also trigger the SBA Disaster Loan Program, albeit usually on a limited basis. All three SBA disaster loan types are available when the emergency declaration includes IA. Emergency declarations, however, rarely provide IA. Typically, limited PA is provided. For example, 281 emergences were declared from 1990 to 2015. Of these, 18 included IA. SBA disaster loans are generally only available to private, nonprofit organizations for "PA-only" declarations. Some may see this as a limitation. For example, if an incident affected a business (e.g., malls, movie theaters, or nightclubs), those businesses would not be eligible for an SBA disaster loan under a PA-only emergency declaration.

## Selected Examples of Stafford Act Assistance for Terror Incidents

The following section provides information on past terror attacks that have received federal assistance under the Stafford Act, including a general description of what types of assistance was provided for the incident. It also provides information on the Orlando Pulse nightclub shooting. It is included in this discussion because the governor requested Stafford Act assistance. The San Bernardino and Ohio State attacks are not included because Stafford Act declarations were not requested. **Table 1** provides a comparison of each incident. It is notable that in all but one case, the declaration was issued on the same day as the attack.

### Oklahoma City Bombing

An emergency declaration was issued to Oklahoma for the Alfred P. Murrah Federal Building Bombing on April 19, 1995—the day of the bombing.[37] The emergency declaration permitted FEMA to take vital actions necessary just hours following the tragedy. This principally involved bringing in FEMA's Urban Search and Rescue (USAR) teams.[38] USAR Task Forces began arriving in Oklahoma City the afternoon of April 19, 1995.[39] In addition, the emergency declaration also provided the sources that allowed the debris removal process to begin. Debris removal, however, was a challenging operation since the area to be cleared was also a Federal Bureau of Investigation (FBI) crime

[37] FEMA, Emergency Declaration, EM 3115. For further information see https://www.fema.gov/disaster/3115.

[38] For more information on USAR, see CRS Report R43560, *Deployable Federal Assets Supporting Domestic Disaster Response Operations: Summary and Considerations for Congress,* coordinated by Jared T. Brown.

[39] City of Oklahoma City Final Report—Alfred P. Murrah Federal Building Bombing, April 19, 1995 (Fire Protection Publications: Stillwater, OK, 1996), p. 37.

scene and new protocols were needed to accomplish response operations in that unique environment. As then-FEMA Director James Lee Witt explained:

> Here were two earnest, dedicated, well-trained groups working as hard as they could—and yet there was an inherent conflict between them. In clearing out the debris, the search and rescue people needed to proceed slowly, carefully. The FBI wanted to pick up the pace, to get their hands on crime evidence immediately—and they wanted that evidence not to be contaminated. Each group was under tremendous pressure.[40]

A major disaster declaration was later issued for the incident on April 26, 1995. This action permitted, at the request of the governor, the activation of the Crisis Counseling program.[41] This program provides funding to state and local mental health authorities to provide service to survivors affected by a disaster incident. Since the great majority of damage was to federal facilities, FEMA's expenditures were limited for this event since FEMA aid under the Stafford Act is directed toward the losses of state, tribal and local governments. Aid to families and individuals (which includes crisis counseling) was the largest program expenditure at $5.5 million.

SBA approved 163 disaster loans for $7.3 million. This included 71 approved home disaster loans for $452,700 and 92 business disaster loans for $6.8 million.[42]

### September 11th Terrorist Attacks

Following the attacks on the Twin Towers, a major disaster declaration was issued on September 11, 2001 for the state of New York.[43] The following day an emergency was declared for Virginia, site of the Pentagon attack. Later, on September 21, 2001, a major disaster was declared for Virginia with September 11th identified as the beginning of the incident period.[44]

The scope of the New York attacks, along with the President's declaration, resulted in legislation that appropriated $40 billion to address not only recovery for these events but security concerns, including transportation safety and initiating counter measures against terrorism. Half of the appropriated amount ($20 billion) was devoted by law (P.L. 107-38) to recovery and assistance efforts in New York, Virginia, and Pennsylvania. FEMA's work involved urban search and rescue teams, debris removal, crisis counseling, and housing aid for displaced residents. FEMA's DRF expenditures in New York alone surpassed $8.7 billion.[45]

---

[40] James Lee Witt and James Morgan, *Stronger in the Broken Places* (New York: Times Books), p. 109.

[41] 42 U.S.C. §5183.

[42] Not all approved applicants accept the loans.

[43] FEMA, Major Disaster Declaration, DR-1391. For further information see https://www.fema.gov/disaster/1391.

[44] FEMA, Major Disaster Declaration, DR-1392. For further information see https://www.fema.gov/disaster/1392.

[45] The DRF is the main account used by FEMA to fund a wide variety of disaster assistance programs that provide grants and other forms of support to assist state, local, and tribal governments, as well as certain nonprofit entities during disaster recovery. For further information see CRS Report R43537, *FEMA's Disaster Relief Fund: Overview and Selected Issues,* by Bruce R. Lindsay.

In the case of Virginia, the largest expenditures were for aid to families and individuals. More than $14.5 million was provided for these programs (including crisis counseling), while nearly $5 million was provided for emergency work and debris clearance.

The two disaster declarations triggered the SBA Disaster Loan Program. For New York, SBA approved 6,384 loans for roughly $551 million. This included 412 approved home loans for roughly $6.0 million, 566 approved business loans for $37 million, and 5,406 approved EIDL loans for $507 million. For Virginia, SBA approved 256 loans for roughly $31 million. This included one approved business loan for $125,500, and 255 approved EIDL loans for approximately $31 million.[46]

### Boston Marathon Bombing

An emergency declaration was issued to Massachusetts on April 17, 2013, for the Boston Marathon Bombing—two days after the incident.[47] The Boston bombing was a unique situation that resulted in a large man-hunt, the shutdown of a major city, and the eventual capture of one perpetrator and the killing of the other in a shootout with the police.

Unlike some other terrorism-related incidents, this event stretched out over several days. In addition to the damage caused at the blast site, it also tested the resources of state and local first responders throughout the area. FEMA's Deputy Administrator explained FEMA's post-incident role:

> FEMA was authorized to provide Category B emergency protective measures to include items such as police personnel, search and rescue, and removal of health and safety hazards. FEMA also provided Public Assistance to include funding for shelters and emergency care for Norfolk and Suffolk counties, which was primarily used for residents whose homes had been impacted during the blast or could benefit from crisis counseling.[48]

Eventually, the incident period was extended, beginning on April 15, 2013, and concluding on April 22, 2013, to capture the eligible costs expended by public safety and other response personnel throughout the region. FEMA's portion of those costs (75% of the eligible amount) totaled just over $6 million. Additionally, FEMA "authorized state and local agencies in Massachusetts to use existing preparedness grant funding to support law enforcement and first responder overtime costs resulting from investigation support activities or heightened security measures."[49]

SBA approved four EIDL loans for $214,300 in the aftermath of the Boston Marathon Bombing.[50] Other SBA disaster loan types were not available because the incident was declared an emergency (as opposed to a major disaster).

---

[46] Not all approved applicants accept the loans.

[47] FEMA, Emergency Declaration, EM-3362. For further information see https://www.fema.gov/disaster/3362.

[48] Testimony of Richard Serino, Deputy Administrator, Federal Emergency Management Agency, before the Senate Homeland Security and Governmental Affairs Committee, U.S. Senate, Washington, DC, "Lessons Learned from the Boston Marathon Bombing: Preparing for and Responding to the Attack," p. 9, at http://www.fema.gov/media-library-data/20130726-1923-25045-1176/lessons_learned_from_the_boston_marathon_bombings_preparing_for_and_responding_to_the_attack.pdf.

[49] Ibid.

[50] Not all approved applicants accept the loans.

### Orlando Pulse Nightclub Shooting

On June 13, 2016, Florida Governor Rick Scott made a request to the President to issue an emergency declaration in response to the mass shooting at Pulse nightclub in Orlando, FL, on June 12, 2016. The governor's request is the first known Stafford Act request in response to a mass shooting incident. The governor requested $5 million for emergency protective measures (Category B) under the Public Assistance program. The assistance was intended to address health and safety measures, and assistance for management, control, and reduction of immediate threats to public health and safety.

According to FEMA Administrator Craig Fugate, the President denied the request for assistance partly because the Governor could not satisfactorily demonstrate that the response to the incident was beyond the capacity of the state and local governments. According to the denial letter sent by FEMA Administrator Craig Fugate to Governor Rick Scott:

> a presidential emergency declaration under the Stafford Act applies when federal assistance is needed to supplement state and local efforts and capabilities to save lives and to protect property and public health and safety, or to lessen or avert the threat of a catastrophe. Because your request did not demonstrate how the emergency response associated with this situation is beyond the capability of the state and affected local governments or identify any direct federal assistance needed to save lives or protect property, an emergency declaration is not appropriate for this incident.[51]

The request was also denied because other forms of federal assistance would be provided for the incident. The letter further states:

> although the Stafford Act is not the appropriate source of funding for those activities and this situation, several federal agencies, including the Department of Justice, the Federal Bureau of Investigation, and FEMA have resources that may help support the response to this incident absent an emergency declaration under the Stafford Act. We will work closely with you and your staff to identify these additional capabilities.[52]

Although the request for an emergency declaration was denied, FEMA approved a request from Florida to reallocate $253,000 in unspent money from the Homeland Security Grant Program to help pay for overtime costs in the wake of the shooting.[53]

SBA only provided EIDL for the attack and related investigation. This included five approved loans for $353,400.[54]

---

[51] Letter from W. Craig Fugate, FEMA Administrator, to Rick Scott, Governor of Florida, June 20, 2016, at http://www.flgov.com/wp-content/uploads/pdfs/FEDDENIAL.pdf.

[52] Ibid.

[53] U.S. Congress, House Committee on Oversight and Government Reform, Subcommittee on Transportation and Public Assets; Subcommittee on National Security, *Oversight of the Urban Area Security Initiative Grant Program*, Brian E. Kamoie Hearing Statement, 114th Cong., 2nd sess., July 15, 2016, p. 4.

[54] Not all approved applicants accept the loans.

**Table 1. Selected Examples of Domestic Terror Incidents**
A Comparison

| | Oklahoma City Bombing April 19, 1995 | September 11th Terrorist Attacks September 11, 2001 | Boston Marathon Bombing April 15, 2013 | Orlando Pulse Nightclub Shooting June 12, 2016 |
|---|---|---|---|---|
| Emergency Declaration number and Date | EM-3115 April 19, 1995 | Virginia: EM-3168 September 12, 2001<br>New Jersey: EM-3169 September 19, 2001 | EM-3362 April 17, 2013 | Request Denied |
| Major Disaster Declaration number and Date | DR-1048 April 26, 1995 | New York: DR-1391 September 11, 2001<br>Virginia: DR-1392 September 21, 2001 | N/A | N/A |
| Total FEMA Projected Obligations | $33,017,023 | New York: $8,703,240,139<br>Virginia: $28,326,526<br>New Jersey: $89,273,429 | $6,567,942 | N/A |
| Public Assistance | Yes | New York: Yes<br>Virginia: Yes<br>New Jersey: Yes | Yes | N/A |
| Individual Assistance | Yes | New York: Yes<br>Virginia: Yes<br>New Jersey: No | No | N/A |
| SBA Declaration Date and Loan Type | Program Automatically Triggered by Major Disaster Declaration | Program Automatically Triggered by Major Disaster Declaration | April 26, 2013<br>EIDL Only | June 23, 2016<br>EIDL Only |
| SBA Home Disaster Loan Amount | $453,000 | New York: $6,100,000<br>Virginia: N/A | N/A | N/A |
| SBA Business Disaster Loan Amount | $6,800,000 | New York: $37,500,000<br>Virginia: $125,500 | N/A | N/A |
| SBA EIDL Amount | N/A | New York: $507,000,000<br>Virginia: $31,400,000 | $214,000 | $353,000 |

**Sources:** Based on CRS analysis of funding data provided by FEMA and SBA. Declaration information was derived from https://www.fema.gov/disasters and https://www.sba.gov/loans-grants/see-what-sba-offers/sba-loan-programs/disaster-loans/current-disaster-declarations.

**Note:** Dollar amounts have been rounded.

## Policy Considerations

It is generally agreed that the government should help victims of terrorism in times of need, but the proper scope of that assistance with respect to the Stafford Act is subject to debate. Some might question whether the fiscal responsibility resides primarily with the federal or the state government. The debate may be further complicated if the incident does not clearly meet the definition of a major disaster or does not meet certain thresholds, or both. The selected approach will likely be influenced by how policymakers view the role of the federal government in response to terrorism. Some may argue that Stafford Act assistance is warranted for all or most acts of terrorism. Others might argue that Stafford Act assistance should only be provided in cases where the incident meets the existing framework of definitions and unmet need.

### Major Disaster Definition

As mentioned previously, the definition of a major disaster contains a list of incidents that can be considered a major disaster. One hypothetical concern is, as currently defined, certain acts of terror may not meet the definition of a major disaster. The following discussion demonstrates how Congress designed the definition to address natural disasters and human-caused incidents.

The term "major disaster" was originally defined in the Federal Disaster Relief Act of 1950 as

> any flood, drought, fire, hurricane, earthquake, storm, or other catastrophe in any part of the United States which, in the determination of the President, is or threatens to be of sufficient severity and magnitude to warrant disaster assistance by the federal government to supplement the efforts and available resources of states and local governments in alleviating the damage, hardship, or suffering caused thereby, and respecting which the governor of any State (or the Board of Commissioners of the District of Columbia) in which such catastrophe may occur or threaten certifies the need for disaster assistance under this Act, and shall give assurance of expenditure of a reasonable amount of the funds of the government of such state, local governments therein, or other agencies, for the same or similar purposes with respect to such catastrophe.[55]

Congress expanded on the list of specific incidents when it amended the definition in the Disaster Relief Act of 1974 which defined a major disaster as

> any hurricane, tornado, storm, flood, high water, wind-driven water, tidal wave, tsunami, earthquake, volcanic eruption, landslide, mudslide, snowstorm, drought, fire, explosion, or other catastrophe in any part of the United States which, in the determination of the President, causes damage of sufficient severity and magnitude to warrant major disaster assistance under this Act, above and beyond emergency services by the federal government, to supplement the efforts and available resources of States, local governments, and disaster relief organizations in alleviating the damage, loss, hardship, or suffering caused thereby.[56]

[55] P.L. 81-875.

[56] P.L. 93-288.

It is notable that the Senate report on the bill indicated that a major disaster is defined as "any damage caused by *these hazards* determined by the President to be of sufficient severity and magnitude to warrant federal assistance" to supplement state and local efforts.[57] To some, this would support the argument that the definition should be prescriptively viewed as a list of eligible incidents.

Congress amended the definition again in 1988—the year the Stafford Act was enacted. Congress designed the new definition with a subtle change in wording to limit human-caused incidents from receiving major disaster declarations. As shown in **Figure 3**, Congress removed "or other catastrophe" from the definition of a major disaster and inserted "or, regardless of cause."

**Figure 3. Major Disaster Definition**
Comparison of Disaster Relief Act and the Stafford Act

*from the*
Disaster Relief Act (1974)

"Major disaster" means any hurricane, tornado, storm, flood, high water, wind-driven water, tidal wave, tsunami, earthquake, volcanic eruption, landslide, mudslide, snowstorm, drought, fire, explosion, or other catastrophe in any part of the United States which, in the determination of the President, causes damage of sufficient severity and magnitude to warrant major disaster assistance under this Act, above and beyond emergency services by the Federal Government, to supplement the efforts and available resources of States, local governments, and disaster relief organizations in alleviating the damage, loss, hardship, or suffering caused thereby.

*from the*
Stafford Act (1988)

"Major disaster" means any natural catastrophe (including any hurricane, tornado, storm, high water, winddriven water, tidal wave, tsunami, earthquake, volcanic eruption, landslide, mudslide, snowstorm, or drought), or, regardless of cause, any fire, flood, or explosion, in any part of the United States, which in the determination of the President causes damage of sufficient severity and magnitude to warrant major disaster assistance under this Act to supplement the efforts and available resources of States, local governments, and disaster relief organizations in alleviating the damage, loss, hardship, or suffering caused thereby.

**Source:** 42 U.S.C. §5122.

**Note:** Highlights added to demonstrate definition differences. "Above and beyond emergency services by the federal government" was removed altogether from the definition.

According to the Senate report accompanying the bill, Congress removed "other catastrophe" because it had been broadly interpreted to justify federal assistance to humanly caused incidents. According to the Senate report

> Congress intended the [the Disaster Relief Act of 1974] to alleviate state and local conditions caused by natural catastrophes. Although non-natural catastrophes are not specifically enumerated by Section 102 of the act, the phrase

[57] U.S. Congress, Senate Committee on Public Works, *Disaster Relief Act Amendments of 1974*, 93rd Cong., 2nd sess., S. Rept. 93-778 (Washington: GPO, 1974), p. 11. Emphasis added.

> "other catastrophes" has been broadly interpreted to justify federal assistance in response to humanly caused traumatic events. The expansion of legislative intent in the administration of the Disaster Relief Act has provoked recent congressional concern.[58]

The report further states that

> Broadening the scope of the act to cover both natural and non-natural catastrophes has strained the capacity of programs designed to respond only to natural catastrophes. Within its intended context the act has functioned relatively well. It is comprehensive and flexible legislation, well-suited to handle the full range of natural disasters for which it was designed. It was not written, however, to respond to the occasionally catastrophic consequences of social, economic, or political activity and establishes no administrative or programmatic mechanisms to do so.[59]

As demonstrated above, it appears that Congress sought to prevent the Stafford Act from being used to address an array of social issues and the specificity of the amended definition may have precluded some incidents from being declared a major disaster. For example, Michigan Governor Rick Snyder's request for a major disaster declaration for the Flint water contamination incident was denied based on the grounds that it did not meet the definition of a major disaster. The denial letter sent from the FEMA Administrator to the governor (see **Appendix**) stated the incident did not meet the legal definition of a major disaster because it was "not a result of a natural disaster, nor was it caused by fire, flood, or explosion."[60]

Another potential issue related to the definition's strict enumeration of human-caused incidents is that it is hypothetically conceivable that two incidents with equal damages and loss of life with different mechanisms of destruction would be treated differently in terms of eligibility. For example, an explosion that kills 50 people could be eligible for a major disaster (if there are sufficient damages to public infrastructure) whereas if a vehicle (similar to the 2016 Nice, France, attack) was used to kill 50 people it could arguably be considered ineligible. A similar argument could be made about a sarin gas attack or a cybersecurity attack that do not involve an explosion or result in fire.

Others may argue that the definition's specificity would not preclude terror incidents from being declared major disasters if the consequences merited a major disaster declaration—regardless of the mechanism. They may further argue that an incident could be recast with some ingenuity to make the incident conform to the definition. For instance, they may argue that, broadly interpreted, firing a gun or releasing gas involves a type of explosion. An arguable example of recasting incident was attempted

---

[58] U.S. Congress, Senate Committee on Environment and Public Works, *Disaster Relief Act Amendments of 1988,* 100th Cong., 2nd sess., September 22, S. Rept. 100-524, p. 2.

[59] Ibid.

[60] Letter from W. Craig Fugate, FEMA Administrator, to Rick Snyder, Governor of Michigan, January 16, 2016. A copy of the letter can be located in **Figure A-1** of this report. The President issued an emergency declaration for the incident on April 25, 2016 (EM-3375). See https://www.fema.gov/disaster/3375.

in the unsuccessful appeal of Flint water contamination incident. The appeal letter stated that

> Respectfully, I appeal the determination that the event "does not meet the legal definition of a major disaster under 42 U.S.C. §5122." This unique disaster poses imminent and long-term threat to the citizens of Flint. Its severity warrants special consideration for all categories of the Individual and Public Assistance Programs, as well as the Hazard Mitigation program in order to facilitate recovery. While the definition under 44 C.F.R. §206.2(17) provides examples of what might constitute a natural disaster, I submit that this disaster is analogous to the flood category, given that the qualities within the water, over a long term, flooded and damaged the city's infrastructure in ways that were not immediately or easily detectable. This disaster is a natural catastrophe in the sense that lead contamination into water is a natural process.[61]

One concern that could emerge from broad interpretations of the definition is that it could lead to "declaration creep" wherein marginal incidents are increasingly considered major disasters. They may also argue that incidents without fire or explosions would likely not create significant damages and would therefore not warrant a major disaster declaration. An emergency declaration would be more appropriate according to this view.

If Congress is concerned that the definition of a major disaster might preclude some incidents from receiving federal assistance, it could consider amending the definition to explicitly include terrorism. Since FEMA is a component agency of the Department of Homeland Security (DHS) it might be assumed that a potential definition would be the one used by DHS. There are, however, multiple definitions used by the federal government and there is no consensus on the definition of terrorism. As demonstrated in **Table 2**, several U.S. governmental agencies have different definitions of terrorism. In some definitions, such as the one used by the Department of State, the act must be politically motivated whereas in other definitions it does not need to be a factor (such as the one used by the Federal Bureau of Investigation and DHS). Some might argue that definitions that rely on motivation are problematic if applied to Stafford Act assistance because they are based on the intentionality of the act rather than the act's consequences. For example, a mass shooting that is motivated by hate or brought about by mental illness might not be considered an act of terrorism while a similar incident that is politically motivated might.

Perhaps an alternative approach would be expanding the types of assistance available under an emergency declaration rather than amending the definition. For example, Congress could make crisis counseling and SBA disaster loans for businesses and households available under emergency declarations. This would arguably help to address events where there is great loss of life but relatively little damage to public infrastructure. These measures may also provide a boost for public morale in such a situation as well as an assurance to state and local governments that they may receive some supplemental help.

[61] Letter from Rick Snyder, Governor of Michigan, to Barack Obama, President, United States, January 20, 2016.

## Table 2. Examples of Terrorism Definitions

| | |
|---|---|
| **Department of Homeland Security**<br>*6 USC 101* | (16) The term "terrorism" means any activity that—<br>(A) involves an act that—<br>(i) is dangerous to human life or potentially destructive of critical infrastructure or key resources; and<br>(ii) is a violation of the criminal laws of the United States or of any State or other subdivision of the United States; and<br>(B) appears to be intended—<br>(i) to intimidate or coerce a civilian population;<br>(ii) to influence the policy of a government by intimidation or coercion; or<br>(iii) to affect the conduct of a government by mass destruction, assassination, or kidnapping. |
| **Federal Bureau of Investigation**<br>*28 CFR .85 (l)* | "Terrorism includes the unlawful use of force and violence against persons or property to intimidate or coerce a government, the civilian population, or any segment thereof, in furtherance of political or social objectives." |
| **Department of State**<br>*22 USC 2656f(d)(2)* | "the term 'terrorism' means premeditated, politically motivated violence perpetrated against noncombatant targets by subnational groups or clandestine agents" |
| **U.S. Code**<br>*18 USC 2331* | (1) the term "international terrorism" means activities that—<br>(A) involve violent acts or acts dangerous to human life that are a violation of the criminal laws of the United States or of any State, or that would be a criminal violation if committed within the jurisdiction of the United States or of any State;<br>(B) appear to be intended—<br>(i) to intimidate or coerce a civilian population;<br>(ii) to influence the policy of a government by intimidation or coercion; or<br>(iii) to affect the conduct of a government by mass destruction, assassination, or kidnapping; and<br>(C) occur primarily outside the territorial jurisdiction of the United States, or transcend national boundaries in terms of the means by which they are accomplished, the persons they appear intended to intimidate or coerce, or the locale in which their perpetrators operate or seek asylum;<br>(2) the term "national of the United States" has the meaning given such term in section 101(a)(22) of the Immigration and Nationality Act;<br>(3) the term "person" means any individual or entity capable of holding a legal or beneficial interest in property;<br>(4) the term "act of war" means any act occurring in the course of—<br>(A) declared war;<br>(B) armed conflict, whether or not war has been declared, between two or more nations; or<br>(C) armed conflict between military forces of any origin; and |

| | (5) the term "domestic terrorism" means activities that—<br>(A) involve acts dangerous to human life that are a violation of the criminal laws of the United States or of any State;<br>(B) appear to be intended—<br>(i) to intimidate or coerce a civilian population;<br>(ii) to influence the policy of a government by intimidation or coercion; or<br>(iii) to affect the conduct of a government by mass destruction, assassination, or kidnapping; and<br>(C) occur primarily within the territorial jurisdiction of the United States. |
|---|---|

**Source:** CRS analysis of statutory and regulatory definitions of terrorism.

### Per Capita Threshold

Some may be concerned that FEMA might not recommend a major disaster declaration to the President for an act of terrorism because the incident does not meet or exceed the $1.42 per capita threshold. Using this threshold, FEMA may not recommend a declaration for an incident with a high number of casualties but limited damage to public infrastructure. For example, the Orlando Pulse nightclub attack killed 49 people but caused little damage to public property. Almost all of the damage was to the nightclub.[62] In addition, damages to businesses are generally not considered when formulating the per capita threshold which is based on public sector damage.

Even if there is substantial damage to public infrastructure, some populous states may have difficulty meeting the per capita threshold. For example, in 2013 Illinois communities were denied federal assistance after a string of tornados devastated rural communities of the state. The storms caused significant damages to the rural communities but, given the state's large population, there was not enough damage to meet the per capita threshold.[63]

Some might argue that loss of life should play a larger role when FEMA makes declaration recommendations. Others might question whether terror attacks with limited public infrastructure damage—while devastating in their own right in terms of loss of life and the impact they can have on national morale—cause enough damage to warrant a major disaster declaration.

If Congress is concerned that the per capita threshold may prevent state and local governments from receiving a major disaster declaration for a terror attack, Congress could require FEMA to consider factors beyond damages to public infrastructure when formulating its recommendation to the President. One potential assessment tool is the value of statistical life (VSL) which assigns a monetary value to each fatality caused by

---

[62] In addition, FEMA assistance is not provided to private entities.

[63] Dick Durbin, "Illinois Members Renew Bipartisan, Bicameral Effort to Bring Fairness to FEMA Disaster Declaration Process," press release, March 26, 2015, at http://www.durbin.senate.gov/newsroom/press-releases/illinois-members-renew-bipartisan-bicameral-effort-to-bring-fairness-to-fema-disaster-declaration-process-.

the given incident. For example, the U.S. Department of Transportation uses $9.1 million as the VSL when evaluating risk reduction.[64] If this VSL amount was applied to the Orlando attack, the 49 fatalities would amount to roughly $446 million in damages.

Proponents might argue that evaluating a terror attack with VSL would provide objective criteria for making recommendations as to whether an incident warranted federal assistance. Others might question if altering the per capita threshold is necessary. They may point out that the per capita threshold is used solely by FEMA to make recommendations. Also, FEMA already considers damage to homes and rental properties. As noted previously, the ultimate decision to grant federal assistance for a major disaster rests solely with the President.

Furthermore, the per capita threshold is designed to evaluate a state's capacity to respond to an incident. It could be argued that highly populated states should be able to fund their recovery without federal assistance because they have a higher tax base on which to draw. According to this view, adjusting the per capita threshold or applying additional factors would be unnecessary.

### Emergency Declarations for Acts of Terrorism

Whereas Congress sought to limit the President's authority to issue major disaster declarations for human-caused incidents under the Stafford Act, the inverse might be said about emergency declarations. As demonstrated by **Figure 4**, the definition of an emergency in the Disaster Relief Act of 1974 included a specific list of incidents eligible for an emergency declaration. The amended definition eliminated the list and defined emergency more broadly.

**Figure 4. Emergency Definition**

Comparison of Disaster Relief Act and the Stafford Act

| *from the* Disaster Relief Act (1974) | *from the* Stafford Act (1988) |
|---|---|
| "Emergency" means any hurricane, tornado, storm, flood, high water, wind-driven water, tidal wave, tsunami, earthquake, volcanic eruption, landslide, mudslide, snowstorm, drought, fire, explosion, or other catastrophe in any part of the United States which requires federal emergency assistance to supplement state and local efforts to save lives and protect property, public health and safety or to avert or lessen the threat of a disaster. | "Emergency" means any occasion or instance for which, in the determination of the President, federal assistance is needed to supplement state and local efforts and capabilities to save lives and to protect property and public health and safety, or to lessen or avert the threat of a catastrophe in any part of the United States. |

**Source:** 42 U.S.C. §5122.

[64] U.S. Department of Transportation, *Economic Values Used in Analyses*, August 18, 2015, at https://www.transportation.gov/regulations/economic-values-used-in-analysis. The U.S. Department of Transportation defines VSL as the additional cost that individuals would be willing to bear for improvements in safety (i.e., reductions in risks) that, in the aggregate, reduce the expected number of fatalities by one.

It could be argued that the amended definition provides the President with a great deal of discretion to issue an emergency declaration in response to acts of terrorism. And as mentioned previously, FEMA does not use the per capita threshold formula to make emergency declaration recommendations to the President. To some, the broad definition and lack of a per capita formula make emergency declarations more suitable for certain types of terror attacks such as mass shootings.

Consequently, some may argue that there is no need to change the Stafford Act to make it easier for "soft target" attacks to receive a major disaster declaration because it is relatively easier to obtain an emergency declaration.[65]

Even so, some might see the decision to issue an emergency declaration as arbitrary and question how state capacity is determined. For example, in a news release in response to the denied emergency declaration for the Orlando shooting, Governor Rick Scott stated

> It is incredibly disappointing that the Obama Administration denied our request for an emergency declaration. Last week, a terrorist killed 49 people, and wounded many others, which was the deadliest shooting in U.S. history. It is unthinkable that President Obama does not define this as an emergency. We are committing every state resource possible to help the victims and the community heal and we expect the same from the federal government.[66]

The press release also provided links to other incidents that were approved for emergency declarations, including President Obama's 2009 inauguration, the 2016 Flint Water crisis, the Massachusetts water main break in 2010, and the 2013 Boston Marathon bombing , among others. Some might question why these incidents warranted emergency declarations but the Pulse nightclub shooting did not.

Proponents of changing the Stafford Act may also argue that, even if an incident receives an emergency declaration, the scope of the assistance is limited compared to a major disaster. For one, assistance is primarily provided to governmental entities under an emergency declaration. Individuals may receive some temporary housing assistance (which may not be applicable if the incident does not impact people's homes) and other forms of assistance such as Other Needs Assistance, which is a grant to households for necessary items damaged or destroyed by the incident, under Section 408 of the Stafford Act. But assistance to those experiencing mental health problems, generally addressed by FEMA's Crisis Counseling program, is not available under an emergency declaration. Further, as mentioned previously, SBA disaster loans are generally only available to private non-profit organizations under an emergency declaration.

If Congress is concerned that emergency declarations would not provide enough assistance in response to certain types of terror attacks, it could consider expanding the

[65] "Hard targets" may have several layers of perimeter security. Hard targets include government facilities, private corporations, manufacturing plants, military facilities, and most critical infrastructure sites. In contrast, soft targets are areas that are open to the public with limited or no security. Soft targets include most retail locations, hotels, restaurants, as well as other buildings open to the public. See Department of Homeland Security, *Active Shooter Workshop Module 3*, available at http://www.dhs.gov/xlibrary/assets/nppd/active-shooter-preparedness-workshop-module3-low-508.pptx.

[66] Rick Scott, 45th Governor of Florida, "Gov. Scott: Disappointing [sic] the Obama Administration Denied Request for Emergency Declaration Following Terror Attack," press release, June 20, 2016, at http://www.flgov.com/2016/06/20/gov-scott-disappointing-the-obama-administration-denied-request-for-emergency-declaration-following-terror-attack/.

types of assistance potentially available for these incidents. The expanded assistance could be tied to all emergency declarations, or designed exclusively for acts of terror. In addition, Congress could require the SBA to provide the full range of disaster loans if an emergency were declared for an act of terror.

### SBA Disaster Loans and CDBG Disaster Assistance

#### SBA Disaster Loan Program

This section examines how the SBA Disaster Loan programs might be used to assist businesses, individuals, and households following a terrorist attack. The section also examines a potential alternative source of federal funding that has been used to assist businesses negatively impacted by a terror attack.

As previously mentioned, SBA disaster loans are usually the only type of federal assistance available to businesses affected by a terror attack. There are potentially four scenarios where the SBA Disaster Loan Program could be used to support business recovery activities following a terror attack. These include two types of presidential declarations as authorized by the Stafford Act, and two types of SBA declarations authorized by the Small Business Act.[67] In addition to providing disaster loans for businesses, some of these declarations also make disaster loans available to individuals and households. As demonstrated below, the type of declaration determines what loans types are made available:

- **Major Disaster or Emergency Declaration Authorizing PA and IA.** The President issues a major disaster declaration, or an emergency declaration, and authorizes *both* IA and PA under the authority of the Stafford Act. When the President issues such declarations, Home and Personal Property Disaster Loans, and Business Physical Disaster Loans become available to homeowners, renters, businesses of all sizes, and nonprofit organizations located within the disaster area. Home and Personal Property Disaster Loans, and Business Physical Disaster Loans can be used to repair and replace items and structures damaged by an attack. EIDL may also be made available under this declaration to provide loans to businesses that suffered substantial economic injury as a result of the incident.
- **Major Disaster or Emergency Declaration Authorizing PA Only.** The President makes a major disaster declaration or emergency declaration that only provides the state with PA. In such a case, a private nonprofit entity located within the disaster area that provides noncritical services may be eligible for a SBA physical disaster loan and EIDL.[68]

  Disaster loans would not available to renters and homeowners under this type of declaration. In addition, Business Physical Disaster Loans, and EIDLs are generally not made available to businesses (unless they are a private nonprofit entity) when the declaration only provides PA.

[67] P.L. 85-536, Section 7(b) 72 Stat. 387, as amended.

[68] To receive FEMA grant assistance, these entities must first have applied for an SBA disaster loan and must have been deemed ineligible or must have received the maximum amount of assistance from SBA before seeking grant assistance from FEMA.

As mentioned previously, there are two scenarios under which SBA disaster loans could be provided in response to a terror attack without the issuance of presidential disaster declaration:

- **Gubernatorial Request for Assistance.** Under this scenario, the SBA Administrator issues a physical disaster declaration in response to a gubernatorial request for assistance.[69] Under this type of declaration, SBA disaster loans would be available to eligible homeowners, renters, businesses of all sizes, and nonprofit organizations within the disaster area or contiguous counties and other political subdivisions. EIDL would also be available under this type of declaration.
- **Gubernatorial Certification of Substantial Economic Injury.** The SBA Administrator may issue an EIDL declaration when SBA receives a certification from a governor that at least five small businesses have suffered substantial economic injury as a result of a disaster. This declaration may be offered only when other viable forms of financial assistance are unavailable. Small agricultural cooperatives and most private nonprofit organizations located within the disaster area or contiguous counties and other political subdivisions are eligible for SBA disaster loans when the SBA Administrator issues an EIDL declaration.

  These types of loans, however, may not be used to repair damages resulting from a terror attack. Rather, loan proceeds can only be used for working capital necessary to enable the business or organization to alleviate the specific economic injury and to resume normal operations. For example, a business may suffer a dramatic decline in its business operations and revenue stream or have difficulty obtaining materials as a result of a terror attack.

As illustrated above, the type of loans that are made available to individuals, homeowners, and businesses largely depends on declaration type.[70] Some observers might be concerned that certain disaster loans may not be available following a terrorist attack. In the view of those observers, Congress could consider amending existing programs by making all SBA disaster loan types available following a terror attack for certain declarations. For example, Congress might make EIDL, home and business disaster loans available for major disaster and emergencies that only provide PA.

### Community Development Block Grants[71]

Another source of potential assistance to businesses is Department of Housing and Urban Development's (HUD's) Community Development Block Grant (CDBG) program. The CDBG program provides grants to states and localities to assist their recovery efforts following a presidentially declared disaster. Generally, grantees must use at least half of these funds for activities that principally benefit low- and moderate-income

[69] The criteria used to determine whether to issue a declaration include a minimum amount of uninsured physical damage to buildings, machinery, inventory, homes, and other property. Generally, this minimum is at least 25 homes or businesses (or some combination of the two) that have sustained uninsured losses of 40% or more in any county or other smaller political subdivision of a state or U.S. possession. See 13 C.F.R. §123.3(3)(ii) and 13 C.F.R. §123.3(3)(iii).

[70] The declaration type has no bearing on loan terms or loan caps.

[71] This section is coauthored by Eugene Boyd, Analyst in Federalism and Economic Development Policy, Government and Finance Division.

persons or areas. The program is designed to help communities and neighborhoods that otherwise might not recover due to limited resources. While the SBA Disaster Loan Program is automatically triggered by a presidential disaster declaration, CDBG is not. Instead, Congress has occasionally addressed unmet disaster needs by providing supplemental disaster-related appropriations for the CDBG program. Consequently, CDBG is not provided for all major disasters, but only at the discretion of Congress.

Congress has authorized supplemental appropriations of funds in response to terror attacks through CDBG. For example

- In 1995, following the Alfred P. Murrah Federal Building attack in Oklahoma City, OK, Congress appropriated $12 million in supplemental CDBG funding to the City of Oklahoma City. Funds were to be used to establish a revolving loan fund only for the purposes of making loans to carry out economic development activities that would primarily benefit a designated area in the city impacted by the bombing.
- On November 26, 2001, two months following the terror attacks of September 11, 2001, Congress appropriated $700 million in CDBG supplemental funding to the state of New York for assistance to properties and businesses damaged by, and for economic revitalization related to the terror attack.[72]
- On January 10, 2002, Congress followed that initial appropriation with a second appropriation of $2 billion in CDBG assistance to the Lower Manhattan Development Corporation (LMDC) to be used to, among other things, reimburse businesses and persons for economic losses, including funds to reimburse tourism areas adversely impacted by the attacks.[73]
- On August 2, 2002, Congress appropriated an additional $783 million to the state of New York through the LMDC in cooperation with the City of New York in support of the city's economic recovery efforts. Funds were used to provide financial assistance to properties and businesses, including the redevelopment of infrastructure, and for economic revitalization activities.[74]

Most federal disaster assistance programs are funded through annual appropriations. This generally ensures that the programs have funds available when an incident occurs. As a result, these programs can provide assistance in a relatively short period of time. For example, a July 2015 SBA Office of Inspector General (OIG) study found that SBA's processing time for home disaster loans averaged 18.7 days and application processing times for business disaster loans averaged 43.3 days.[75]

CDBG disaster assistance, on the other hand, is funded through supplemental funding. In general, Congress only provides supplemental funding when disaster needs exceed the amount available through annual appropriations. This typically only occurs when a large incident takes place, such as Hurricanes Katrina and Sandy. This is because

[72] P.L. 107-73, 115 Stat. 699.

[73] P.L. 107-117, 115 Stat. 2236.

[74] P.L. 107-206, 116 Stat. 889.

[75] U.S. Small Business Administration, Office of Inspector General, Hurricane Sandy Expedited Loan Processes, Audit Report No. 15–13, July 13, 2015, p. 4, at https://www.sba.gov/sites/default/files/oig/Audit_Report_15-13_Sandy_Expedited_Processes.pdf.

Congress must debate and pass supplemental funding. Additionally, funding for CDBG disaster assistance is not available for all incidents.

Some might argue the necessity for supplemental funding would preclude smaller terror incidents from receiving CDBG disaster assistance. Others might be concerned that assistance is not timely. For example, an appropriation for CDBG disaster assistance was enacted on June 3, 2008. The allocation date for the CDBG disaster assistance was September 11, 2008—three months after the enacted appropriation.

One potential option would be to fund CDBG disaster assistance through annual appropriations. Doing so would create an account with funds that could be made immediately available to help expedite CDBG disaster assistance. Congress could examine strategies to make CDBG disaster assistance available to businesses that suffered damage as a result of a terrorist incident. The assistance could be triggered by a major disaster declaration, an emergency declaration, or both.

Critics of the above policy option might argue that if this approach were used, it would be necessary to determine under what situations CDBG disaster assistance would be released. Critics may also argue that determinations for CDBG disaster assistance are made by Congress. Changing the process to one based on annual appropriation might shift the determination to a (relevant) federal agency. Similarly, as mentioned previously, CDBG disaster assistance is typically only available for large-scale incidents. Creating a permanent CDBG program for disaster assistance might provide a gateway for smaller incidents to receive CDBG disaster assistance. This, in turn, might lead to increased federal expenditures for disaster assistance.

### Expanded FEMA Assistance

Some may question whether the Stafford Act is the appropriate authority for providing assistance to terror incidents with high number of casualties and limited damage. The assistance provided under the Stafford Act is primarily for recovery purposes (i.e., repairing and replacing damaged buildings and infrastructure). Under the existing Stafford Act authorities the assistance FEMA might provide would be the Other Needs Assistance (ONA) grant program that can be used to pay funeral expenses. And even in those cases, there may be private insurance already meeting those needs. Arguably, ONA could be expanded to begin to cover other costs following a death in the family and an expansion of FEMA coverage of related emergency health care costs might be helpful to the uninsured affected by a terrorist event. Similarly, a terrorist event could also be the trigger for expanded Disaster Unemployment Assistance benefits. But beyond those areas, little of the FEMA catalogue of assistance would apply beyond the programs already being employed.

## Concluding Observations

This report has outlined several different approaches, both definitional and administrative, that could fill in perceived gaps that have been forecast based on possible events juxtaposed against current policy parameters. One view argues that the Stafford Act should be amended to assure that terrorist attacks are eligible for major disaster assistance. Another view is that the Stafford Act is a flexible instrument that has assisted states and families and individuals through a myriad of unanticipated situations.

According to this view, the Stafford Act's existing structure is sufficient to meet the potential terrorism challenges that may lie ahead.

The selected approach will likely be influenced by two factors: (1) impact on federal costs, and (2) personal views concerning the appropriate nature of the federal government's role in addressing terrorism. Some might be concerned that amending the Stafford Act to assure that soft target and nonconventional terror attacks are eligible for major disaster assistance might, in their view, inappropriately shift the primary financial burden for addressing terrorism costs from the states to the federal government. Others might see these costs as minimal, particularly compared to the costs of natural disasters, such as those from major hurricanes. With respect to the appropriate role for the federal government in addressing terrorism costs, some might argue that the federal government should provide assistance for all instances of terrorism, even if those costs could be adequately handled by the state. Others might argue that federal assistance should be provided only in those cases where state and local government financial capacity is lacking.

## Appendix. Examples of Request and Denial Letters

### Figure A-1. FEMA Denial Letter: Flint Water Contamination Incident

January 16, 2016

U.S. Department of Homeland Security
500 C Street, SW
Washington, DC 20472

FEMA

JAN 16 2016

The Honorable Rick Snyder
Governor of Michigan
111 South Capitol Avenue
Lansing, Michigan 48909

Dear Governor Snyder:

This is in response to your January 14, 2016, request for an expedited major disaster declaration for the State of Michigan as a result of water contamination described in your request as beginning on April 25, 2014, and continuing. You specifically requested Individual Assistance and Public Assistance, including direct federal assistance for Genesee County and Hazard Mitigation statewide.

Based on our review of all of the information available, a major disaster declaration under the Stafford Act is not appropriate. The request does not meet the legal definition of a "major disaster" under 42 U.S.C. § 5122, as implemented at 44 C.F.R. §§ 206.2(17). The incident was not a result of a natural catastrophe, nor was it caused by a fire, flood, or explosion.

This denial may be appealed within 30 days after the date of this letter. Any appeal pursuant to 44 CFR § 206.46, along with additional information justifying the appeal, should be submitted to the President through Andrew Velasquez III, Regional Administrator, FEMA Region V, located at 536 South Clark Street, Chicago, Illinois 60605.

Sincerely,

W. Craig Fugate
Administrator

www.fema.gov

**Source:** Letter from W. Craig Fugate, FEMA Administrator, to Rick Snyder, Governor of Michigan, January 16, 2016.

**Figure A-2. Governor Scott Emergency Declaration Request: Pulse Nightclub Shooting**
June 13, 2016

RICK SCOTT
GOVERNOR

June 13, 2016

The Honorable Barack H. Obama
President of the United States
The White House
1600 Pennsylvania Avenue, NW
Washington, D.C. 20500

Through: Gracia Szczech, Regional Administrator
FEMA Region IV
Atlanta, GA 30341

RE: Request for Emergency Declaration
Orlando Terrorism Attack

Dear Mr. President:

Under the provisions of Section 501 of the Robert T. Stafford Disaster Relief and Emergency Assistance Act, 42 U.S.C. §§ 5121-5207 (Stafford Act), as implemented by 44 C.F.R. § 206.35, I request that you declare an emergency for the State of Florida due to the "horrific massacre" committed by a terrorist in Orlando, Florida.

During a June 12, 2016 press conference, you accurately characterized the terrorist attack as a "horrific massacre." I urge you to declare an emergency under the Stafford Act so that "the full resources of the federal government" can be made available for the individuals, families, and communities impacted by this "horrific massacre."

This request is timely under the five-day deadline established in 44 C.F.R. § 206.35(a).

As authorized by 44 CFR §206.66, I request the following forms of emergency assistance:

- Provision of health and safety measures; and
- Management, control, and reduction of immediate threats to public health and safety.

THE CAPITOL
TALLAHASSEE, FLORIDA 32399 • (850) 488-2272 • FAX (850) 922-4292

The Honorable Barack H. Obama
June 13, 2016
Page Two

I will keep you informed of any additional requests we may have for emergency assistance, including additional funds beyond the initial $5,000,000.00.

I have designated the Commissioner of the Florida Department of Law Enforcement, as the State Coordinating Officer for this emergency. He is authorized to provide any further information, assurances, requests, or justification on my behalf.

Sincerely,

Rick Scott
Governor

Enclosure:

A. OMB No. 1660-0009/FEMA Form 010-0-13

**Source:** http://www.flgov.com/wp-content/uploads/pdfs/OTA.pdf.

## Figure A-3. FEMA Denial Letter: Pulse Nightclub Shooting
June 20, 2016

U.S. Department of Homeland Security
500 C Street, SW
Washington, DC 20472

FEMA

June 20, 2016

The Honorable Rick Scott
Governor of Florida
State Capitol
Tallahassee, Florida 32399

Dear Governor Scott:

This is in response to your June 13, 2016, request for an emergency declaration for the State of Florida as a result of the mass shooting that occurred on June 12, 2016. You specifically requested emergency protective measures (Category B) under the Public Assistance program.

A Presidential emergency declaration under the Stafford Act applies when Federal assistance is needed to supplement State and local efforts and capabilities to save lives and to protect property and public health and safety, or to lessen or avert the threat of a catastrophe. Because your request did not demonstrate how the emergency response associated with this situation is beyond the capability of the State and affected local governments or identify any direct federal assistance needed to save lives or protect property, an emergency declaration is not appropriate for this incident. Therefore, I must inform you that your request for an emergency declaration is denied.

Although the Stafford Act is not the appropriate source of funding for those activities in this situation, several Federal agencies, including the Department of Justice, the Federal Bureau of Investigation, and FEMA have resources that may help support the response to this incident absent an emergency declaration under the Stafford Act. We will work closely with you and your staff to identify these additional capabilities.

This denial may be appealed within 30 days after the date of this letter. Any appeal pursuant to 44 CFR § 206.46, along with additional information justifying the appeal, should be submitted to the President through Gracia B. Szczech, Regional Administrator, FEMA Region IV, located at 3003 Chamblee Tucker Road, Atlanta, Georgia 30341.

Sincerely,

W. Craig Fugate
Administrator

www.fema.gov

**Source:** http://www.flgov.com/wp-content/uploads/pdfs/FEDDENIAL.pdf.

## Author Contact Information

Bruce R. Lindsay
Analyst in American National Government
blindsay@crs.loc.gov, 7-3752

## Acknowledgments

Robert Dilger, Senior Specialist, Government and Finance Division, assisted with editorial comments and suggestions; and Amber Wilhelm, Graphics Specialist, Publishing and Editorial Resources Section, assisted with figures in this report.

# DOCUMENT NO. 7

# PREVENTING ANOTHER BOSTON MARATHON BOMBING: REVIEWING THE LESSONS LEARNED FROM THE 2013 TERROR ATTACK

## HOUSE HOMELAND SECURITY COMMITTEE REPORT

U.S. HOUSE OF REPRESENTATIVES
COMMITTEE ON HOMELAND SECURITY
REP. MICHAEL McCAUL, CHAIRMAN

APRIL 2015

Prepared by the Majority Staff of the Committee on Homeland Security

## EXECUTIVE SUMMARY

In March 2014, the Committee on Homeland Security completed its investigation of the Boston Marathon bombing, which occurred on April 15, 2013, and released a report entitled "The Road to Boston: Counterterrorism Challenges and Lessons from the Marathon Bombings". The report identified four key areas needing improvement and issued seven recommendations to help strengthen the Federal government's counterterrorism efforts.

Since the report was released the Committee has continued to monitor the progress of the Federal government in closing the gaps that contributed to the tragic events in Boston. The Committee has actively exercised its oversight responsibility, and engaged with the Executive Branch, State and local officials, and outside experts in a robust dialogue to monitor progress in the four areas identified for improvement, which include:

### Key Areas of Improvement

- Cooperation between Federal and local law enforcement can be improved
- Policy surrounding the use of travel records and the screening of international travelers can be refined
- There is room for more thorough information sharing with regard to various terror/travel watch lists at the federal level

- Over the long-term, more sophisticated efforts are required to mitigate terrorist threats

In this report, the Committee will provide our impressions on the interagency's efforts to address the issues listed above, and will detail what we have learned with respect to progress made toward several of our specific recommendations.

The Committee is pleased to note that since the report was released, the Federal government, particularly the Department of Homeland Security (DHS), Federal Bureau of Investigation (FBI), and the National Counterterrorism Center (NCTC), have taken specific actions to address each of the four areas outlined in the initial report. This report explores some of those changes, but also details areas where further improvements can and should be made. Finally, in this report the Committee offers some additional recommendations based on its discussions with stakeholders at the Federal, State and local level that it hopes will build on the progress already made in addressing the areas of concern identified in the 2014 report.

As part of this review, Committee staff traveled to New York City, Austin and Boston to learn how State and local law enforcement agencies participating on Federal Joint Terrorism Task Forces (JTTF) viewed their relationships with their Federal partners in the aftermath of Boston, and how the Committee's report recommendations had been implemented.

Staff met with representatives from the following law enforcement agencies and fusion centers:

- New York City Police Department (NYPD)
- Austin Police Department (APD)
- Texas Department of Public Safety (TxDPS)
- University of Texas at Austin Police Department
- Massachusetts State Police (MSP)
- Boston Police Department (BPD)
- Austin Regional Intelligence Center (ARIC)
- Boston Regional Intelligence Center (BRIC)

The feedback provided by State and local agencies pertaining to information sharing within the JTTF and relationships with DHS, the FBI, and other federal agencies following the Boston Marathon bombing indicated that positive progress had been made. The Committee commends the efforts of DHS Secretary Johnson, FBI Director Comey, NCTC Director Rasmussen, and their agencies leadership in the field for the time they have invested to strengthen relationships with State and local partners. This commitment has had a notable effect on making State and local agencies feel that they are trusted, valued partners in the fight against terrorism.

While the progress made since the Boston Marathon bombing appears to have had an effect on enhancing collaboration on counterterrorism investigations, the Committee remains concerned about the continued reliance of personal relationships for information sharing in the field. Throughout the Committee's follow-up, State and local law enforcement articulated their concern about the rate of rotational leadership changes at

FBI and DHS field offices, and the effect they could have on cooperation in their region. Several of the Committee's additional recommendations seek to institutionalize structures for facilitating information sharing that can serve as a complement to the personal relationships that exist between organizations.

DHS, NCTC the FBI, and their partners must explore ways to share information with their State and local partners that go beyond traditional briefings, to ensure that pertinent information is disseminated to all the relevant consumers within the State or local organizations. The Committee looks forward to working with DHS, FBI and NCTC to identify ways to make information from closed threat assessments and preliminary investigations accessible to State and local partners for analysis based on their authorities and investigative priorities.[1]

When properly trained and informed, State and local law enforcement officers, analysts, and first responders can be a powerful force multiplier to Federal counterterrorism efforts. Now more than ever, as the threat from terrorism shifts from sophisticated global plots to small groups of Islamist extremists, radicalized on the internet, the Federal government must find ways to maximize the unique knowledge and relationships that State and local agencies have with their communities, to ensure it has a holistic view of the threat environment.

Since its creation more than a decade ago, the Committee on Homeland Security has worked to oversee and strengthen the nation's counterterrorism programs and policies. It is the Committee's duty to continually assess the government's strengths and weaknesses in counterterrorism—measuring both success and failure. The Committee aims to provide the necessary oversight and guidance to address any deficiencies, and to work with those agencies to ensure the United States homeland is secure. We owe that cooperation and commitment to the victims of the Boston Marathon bombing and their families. The Committee will continue to emphasize information sharing between Federal, State and local agencies, and will monitor DHS and the FBI's progress during the 114th Congress. We stand ready to partner with DHS and the FBI to further strengthen their counterterrorism and homeland security missions to ensure that Americans remain safe.

**MICHAEL T. McCAUL**
Chairman
Committee on Homeland Security

**WILLIAM R. KEATING**
Representative
Committee on Homeland Security

[1] Several partners in this Committee's review have acknowledged the utility of this effort, while raising the need for necessary privacy protections with regard to US persons. The Committee agrees, and is committed to helping the interagency build an information sharing system that is both effective and respects the privacy and civil liberties of Americans.

## SECTION I
## COOPERATION BETWEEN FEDERAL AND LOCAL LAW ENFORCEMENT CAN BE IMPROVED

### Recommendation 1:
### Greater information sharing with local law enforcement, and expanded access to the classified Guardian system at State and local fusion centers

The Committee's first recommendation addressed a troubling gap exposed by the Boston Marathon bombing in the relationship between State and local law enforcement, and their Federal law enforcement and intelligence partners on counterterrorism investigations. The Committee's report identified areas where Boston and Massachusetts State law enforcement agencies should have been better informed by the Boston JTTF and other Federal agencies about information collected on the Tsarnaev brothers. The Committee is also aware of the perception that Federal agencies do not always share pertinent investigative information with their State and local partners. While there are justifiable legal guidelines that limit the distribution of sensitive and classified information in some cases, the Federal government's lack of transparency, and poor communication with its partners, has contributed to this perception, and degraded the level of trust between organizations crucial to successfully conducting complex joint investigations.

Based on its discussions with State and local agencies, the Committee believes that work is being done to actively close this gap. Officials in Boston and Austin reported that the current Federal leadership in both cities, particularly at the JTTF and the FBI, had increased their level of engagement with State and local agencies since the Boston Marathon bombing, as exhibited by two recent developments:

1. *Quarterly Executive Briefings:* FBI Field Office JTTF leadership brief priority counterterrorism cases to executives from State and local law enforcement agencies participating on the JTTF.

2. *Weekly Case Scrubs:* State and local agencies also provided positive feedback about weekly "scrubs" of active counterterrorism investigations conducted by JTTF supervisors with JTTF personnel. Agency leadership indicated that all open cases were discussed at this meeting.

#### Recommendation 1-1:

The Quarterly Executive Briefings and Weekly Case Scrubs should be institutionalized at all JTTFs nationwide. The Committee urges the FBI to brief closed investigations and assessments at these meetings so that State and local partners are fully aware of the status of all JTTF investigations within their jurisdiction.

Throughout this review, the Committee found that both law enforcement officials and outside experts shared our view that these improvements need to be institutionalized. State and local leaders consistently registered their concern that due to leadership turnover, future FBI and JTTF executives may have different views about working with State and local law enforcement, which could lead to a degradation of information sharing.

A recently published report by Business Executives for National Security (BENS) titled, "Domestic Security: Confronting a Changing Threat to Ensure Public Safety and Civil

Liberties" further confirmed the Committee's findings on improving cooperation, and recommended that JTTF's should be directed by the FBI to "Notify in real time their State and local partners of the status of current terrorism cases within the jurisdiction of those partners."[2] The Committee agrees that this thoughtful recommendation should be further explored with the FBI.

**Recommendation 1-2:**

DHS and the FBI should continue to evaluate structures to formalize the methods and protocols for disseminating intelligence to relevant consumers up and downstream.

*Guardian Access and Training*

In the 2014 report, the Committee recommended expanding access to the Guardian system, which "serves as the primary database for setting leads to other Field Offices and JTTFs to open new terrorism related assessments of investigations"[3].

As the Committee recommended, the BENS report also endorses expanding access to counterterrorism databases, adding that the "FBI and DHS should encourage access to classified counterterrorism information systems by appropriate security-cleared State and local personnel without the need for on-site presence of FBI or DHS personnel."[4]

While it is not the FBI's responsibility to search databases for State and local law enforcement, it is the Bureau's responsibility to ensure that Task Force Officers (TFOs)[5] are adequately trained to leverage the Guardian database. The Committee understands that JTTF TFOs undergo two weeks of training at the FBI Academy where they receive Guardian training.

**Recommendation 1-3:**

Survey TFOs after the training, and annually conduct a brief check of their proficiency and level of confidence using Guardian. The FBI and its JTTF partners should also examine how TFOs use Guardian compared to FBI Agents assigned to the JTTF.

While the FBI has correctly pointed out that TFOs have full access to the classified Guardian system, and are free to search the database at anytime, the Committee believes that performing Guardian queries on behalf of his or her agency is at best a secondary priority for a TFO, whose job is to conduct multiple active, open investigations in a case agent or co-case agent capacity. Analysts are far better suited and trained for this work. Providing analysts assigned to a Fusion Center, or to the State or local agency, access to

[2] Business Executives for National Security (BENS) "Domestic Security: Confronting a Changing Threat to Ensure Public Safety and Civil Liberties", January 2015

[3] Hon. William H. Webster. Douglas E. Winter, Adrian L. Steel, Jr. William M. Baker, Russell J. Bruemmer, and Kenneth L. Wainstein, "Final Report of the William H. Webster Commission of the Federal Bureau of Investigation, Counterterrorism Intelligence, and the Events at Fort Hood, Texas, on November 5, 2009," *the William H. Webster Commission*, July 19, 2012. (Available at: http://www.fbi.gov/news/pressrel/press-releases/judge-webster-delivers-webster-commission-report-on-fort-hood)

[4] Business Executives for National Security (BENS) "Domestic Security: Confronting a Changing Threat to Ensure Public Safety and Civil Liberties", January 2015

[5] A Task Force is a collaborative effort between federal, State and local law enforcement, designed to target a particular criminal activity including terrorism, and often in a particular geographical area.

limited, unclassified information on pending and closed JTTF investigations through eGuardian or a separate system would significantly reduce the risk that potentially pertinent information from open and closed cases, or assessments are reviewed by a State or local agency, and do not slip through the cracks.

The FBI told the Committee that no information regarding the 2011 assessment of Tamerlan Tsarnaev was ever placed into eGuardian.[6] The FBI stated that current authorities prevented it from doing so.

Most terrorism related information that is presently shared between State and locals and the JTTF flows upstream to the federal partners. The Suspicious Activity Report (SAR) program is primarily designed to inform the JTTF and federal terrorism investigations. As we have learned from the Boston Marathon bombing there is value to having information from Federal terrorism assessments and investigations available for analysis at the State and local level. Using the Tsarnaev case as a model, the Committee believes that derogatory information provided by a foreign partner would constitute information that should be populated into eGuardian.

**Recommendation 1-4:**

The Committee believes that an enterprise tool, such as eGuardian, or another database that contains limited information on closed JTTF cases and assessments, should be accessible for analysis by State and local law enforcement, and fusion centers. The benefits could be numerous:

- It improves State and local officials' knowledge of the threat picture within their jurisdictions;
- Decision makers have more information to determine whether to open investigations, consistent with their authorities and priorities; and
- The quality of information flowing to federal partners is enhanced by further connecting derogatory information obtained at the local level to a terrorism investigation or assessment.

*Measuring Information Sharing*

In a briefing to Committee staff, the FBI explained that its Performance Appraisal Reports (PARs) for senior leadership at its Field Offices includes a rating for information sharing with partners. The FBI explained that much of the information used to evaluate senior leadership and grade them in this area is obtained through its Office of Partner Engagement.[7]

**Recommendation 1-5:**

The fact that the FBI is rating its Assistant Directors in Charge (ADICs), Special Agents-in-Charge (SACs) and Assistant Special Agents-in-Charge (ASACs) on information sharing with State and local partners indicates the serious level of attention

[6] FBI Brief to Committee on Homeland Security Staff, March 17, 2015

[7] Ibid

this matter is receiving at the FBI. The Committee recommends that the FBI ask its partners to complete brief surveys that capture the partner's views of the current information sharing relationship in a quantitative format that can be statistically analyzed and compared across the entire FBI. The Office of Partner Engagement could then conduct outreach to agencies where surveys returned low scores, and develop best practices where the relationship is found to be mutually advantageous to both sides.

*Homeland Security Information Network (HSIN)*

In follow up sessions with State and local fusion centers in Austin and Boston, Committee staff heard a number of comments about the user-friendliness, and the lack of information posted to HSIN[8] by DHS Component agencies. A number of agencies attributed the lack of information on the HSIN-Intel network to over-classification issues. Since many law enforcement agencies and fusion centers have limited personnel with Top-Secret level clearances, they are not able to view potentially relevant products.

DHS responded to this feedback in a letter to the Committee where it stated that it continues to increase information sharing through the Intelligence Community of Interest, to include: "targeted outreach to build DHS Component-specific Network webpages, identifying DHS Component points of contact responsible for managing these webpages and posting products, and providing tutorials on how to use and upload products. Recent platform improvements, including the creation of 'partner product pages', along with single sign-on relationships with key State and location information systems like the Regional Information Sharing System (RISS), have enhanced our ability to share information."[9]

While this is encouraging, the Committee is concerned, by the following statement in the letter: "While the Community of Interest represents an important means to share products and information with fusion centers, it is important to recognize that some DHS Components also leverage other platforms or mechanisms to share this information in accordance with their product handling and dissemination policies."[10]

**Recommendation 1-6:**

DHS needs to develop the proper incentives and hold all Components accountable for ensuring that the HSIN network is the primary DHS portal for sharing relevant sensitive but unclassified information with State and local authorities.

The Committee will remain engaged with DHS to ensure that HSIN is fully leveraged by the Department and its Components, and matures into the trusted network that State, local, tribal and territorial (SLTT) partners can rely on to manage homeland

[8] The Homeland Security Information Network (HSIN) is the trusted network for homeland security mission operations to share Sensitive But Unclassified information. Federal, State, Local, Territorial, Tribal, International and Private Sector homeland security partners use HSIN to manage operations, analyze data, send alerts and notices, and in general, share the information they need to do their jobs

[9] Department of Homeland Security letter to U.S. House of Representatives Committee on Homeland Security, December 12, 2014

[10] Ibid

security related operations. The Committee will also conduct oversight going forward to ensure the Department is doing its best to de-classify information through the use of tear-lines and other methods so that action can be taken at the State and local level.

**Recommendation 2:**
**The Memoranda of Understandings (MOU) between the Joint Terrorism Task Forces (JTTF) and State and local entities should be amended to allow for sharing information with State and local law enforcement without seeking supervisor approval. Equally important, leadership of all law agencies on the JTTFs should constantly encourage collaboration and sharing between members**

In our initial report, the Committee identified the MOU between the FBI and partner agencies with personnel assigned to JTTFs as contributing to Boston JTTF TFO's reluctance to share information with their parent agencies. The Committee recommended amending the MOU to encourage information sharing with State and local law enforcement by clarifying the supervisory approval process. The BENS report contained a similar recommendation further confirming the Committee's recommendation to amend the FBI's MOU with State, local, tribal and territorial agencies governing information sharing.[11]

In a June 29, 2014 letter to the Committee, the FBI stated that, "in response to input from our partners, we revised the language in the MOU and reiterated to each of our Assistant Directors and Special Agents in Charge (SACs) that the provision of the MOU that requires a supervisor's approval for the dissemination of information is not meant to discourage the sharing of information."[12] In a footnote to that statement, the FBI wrote, "The revised MOU language makes clear that Supervisory Special Agent approval to share FBI held information applies to both FBI Agents and TFOs. This requirement exists to ensure compliance with requirements including FISA minimization rules, protection of sources and methods, and the need to prevent inappropriate disclosure of information originating and controlled by other intelligence services."[13] Many agencies that the Committee spoke with in Boston and Austin were unaware of any changes to the MOU, and some reported to the Committee as of August 2014 that no change to the MOU had been made. As the FBI recently clarified, these changes are reflected in new MOUs being executed going forward, but that they were not revising or re-executing existing MOUs with partners unless it was requested by the partner agency. Representatives of the FBI insisted that the Bureau is fully prepared and willing to re-execute existing MOUs with any agency interested in doing so to reflect these changes.[14]

**Recommendation 2-1:**

The Committee strongly encourages all State and local law enforcement agencies and Federal agencies with personnel assigned to FBI JTTFs to consider re-executing their MOUs in order to institutionalize the progress it has made enhancing and standardizing information sharing with State and local partners across all the JTTFs.

[11] Ibid

[12] Stephen Kelly, Assistant Director, FBI Office of Congressional Affairs, letter to U.S. House of Representatives Committee on Homeland Security, June 29, 2014

[13] Ibid

[14] FBI Brief to Committee on Homeland Security Staff, March 17, 2015

Additionally, the FBI also sent an Electronic Communication (EC) to its Field Offices articulating as it reported to the Committee, that the spirit of the MOU is not meant to discourage sharing. In a brief to Committee staff, the FBI explained to the Committee that Director Comey and Deputy Director Giuliano have repeatedly instructed ADICs and SACs to ensure that this message is conveyed to their State and local partners at every Field Office.

**Recommendation 2-2:**

While the Committee notes the progress the FBI has made in collaborating with State and local agencies, and appreciates its willingness to re-execute the MOU, the FBI should take proactive steps to communicate to all its partners about the opportunity to re-execute the MOU. The Committee will continue to survey State and local agencies to obtain their views on the state of their information sharing relationship with the JTTF as part of its oversight responsibilities—and encourage them to re-execute their MOU if it is useful and feasible from a resource perspective.

## SECTION II
## POLICY SURROUNDING THE USE OF TRAVEL RECORDS AND THE SCREENING OF INTERNATIONAL TRAVELERS CAN BE REFINED

As noted in the Committee's Report, Customs and Border Protection's (CBP) failed to place Tamerlan Tsarnaev into secondary screening upon exiting and re-entering the United States. Additionally, it is unclear as to whether a CBP JTTF Task Force Officer notified the FBI Agent who had conducted the Tamerlan Tsarnaev assessment regarding his travel. These incidents are frustrating examples of unclear policies regarding travel records potentially contributing to catastrophe. Related to these policy concerns, the Committee also expressed concern with the vacancies in leadership positions at CBP, as an impediment to CBP's ability to evolve into a more agile and effective agency. The Committee notes that since the report was issued, R. Gil Kerlikowske was confirmed by the Senate on March 6, 2014 to be the new Commissioner of U.S. Customs and Border Protection.

### Recommendation 3:
### The records of each traveler of concern should be properly screened

In a letter to the Committee dated July 18, 2014 Secretary Johnson addressed the Report's third recommendation, "Secondary Examinations", stating that, "in April 2013 DHS' U.S. Customs and Border Protection (CBP) had updated its policy and corresponding guidance to stress the importance of continual monitoring and review to ensure prompt identification of high risk travelers departing the United States to promote timely coordination of examinations. Additionally, in June 2013, CBP implemented system enhancements to refine the identification of potential high risk travelers and facilitate review of the associated derogatory information."[15]

[15] Secretary Jeh Charles Johnson, Letter to the Honorable Michael T. McCaul, Chairman, U.S. House of Representatives Committee on Homeland Security, July 18, 2014

With regards to notifications of travel, DHS informed the Committee that it had implemented a policy requiring CBP JTTF officers to pass notifications to JTTF Case Agents via federal email systems.[16] This is an improvement to the previous process. However, many agencies the Committee met with recommended further enhancing the system to fully automate the process, and mitigate the possibility of human error to ensure important data does not fall through the cracks.

The Committee is pleased to note that DHS has reported that CBP and the FBI are in the process of concluding an interagency agreement to automatically correlate FBI-provided subject data with CBP travel records, and that the correlation will generate an automated notification to both the FBI and CBP when international travel into or out of the country is identified for these subjects.[17] The Committee has requested that DHS notifies the Committee when this agreement is completed, and provide details on how it will be implemented.

### Recommendation 4:
### The sharing of alerts and notifications should be documented electronically among members of the JTTFs and within member agencies

A number of State and local agencies asked for greater access to TECs, the law enforcement system used by CBP, so they would not be dependent on a single CBP point of contact to pass relevant inbound and outbound traveler data. DHS addressed this feedback and stated that, "State and local law enforcement agencies can receive relevant information from federal agencies that have access to the TECS system, such as U.S. Immigration and Customs Enforcement (ICE). Direct access to TECS is limited to ensure system integrity is maintained."[18] The Committee will continue to solicit feedback from State, local, tribal and territorial (SLTT) agencies on the need for direct access to TECS, and work with DHS as it completes its TECS modernization project, to ensure that a process exists for agencies to log requests for alerts and receive notifications in a timely manner when necessary.

## SECTION III
## THERE IS ROOM FOR INFORMATION SHARING WITH REGARD TO VARIOUS TERROR TRAVEL WATCH LISTS AT THE FEDERAL LEVEL

### Recommendation 5:
### The Committee recommends agencies provide all the information available to them in their nominations to terror watch lists and other databases

In its initial report, the Committee noted that inaccurate and incomplete data in the Terrorist Screening Database (TSDB) contributed to missed opportunities to engage with Tamerlan Tsarnaev when he traveled to Russia, and later returned to the U.S. The

[16] Secretary Jeh Charles Johnson, Letter to the Honorable Michael T. McCaul, Chairman, U.S. House of Representatives Committee on Homeland Security, December 12, 2014

[17] Ibid

[18] Ibid

Committee is pleased to note that NCTC detailed a number of steps that have been taken by the U.S. Intelligence Community to implement the Committee's recommendations.[19]

In its letter, NCTC described the progress that has been made to ensure that all relevant agencies comply with NCTC's requirements for sponsoring agencies to include all identifying information in their nominations, and set the requirement that a third-party agency with information on an individual in the TSDB proactively share corrections or additional information as they become available. The Committee is encouraged by this development and will continue to review its implementation.

## SECTION IV
## OVER THE LONG TERM MORE SOPHISTICATED EFFORTS ARE REQUIRED TO MITIGATE TERRORIST THREATS

### Recommendation 6:
### Efforts to educate the public on the terrorist threat (such as the See Something, Say Something campaign) need to be refined and evaluated

As the Committee's report pointed out, it was not until Tamerlan Tsarnaev's fingerprints were scanned nearly three and a half days after the marathon bombing that the identity of the attackers became known to authorities, nine hours after pictures of the suspects had been publicly distributed by the FBI in a plea for assistance. In that time, no associate of Tamerlan or Dzhokhar Tsarnaev identified them to the authorities. Had someone who knew either of the Tsarnaevs stepped forward and contacted police, MIT Police Officer Sean Collier might be alive today.

As this Committee has often highlighted, the public can be a powerful ally in identifying potential terrorist activity. Law enforcement's ability to build a strong partnership with the public, based on trust and transparency is crucial to obtaining information that will prevent violent attacks like Boston in the future. In order for the community to assist in preventing terrorist attacks, it is incumbent upon the federal government to provide the public with mechanisms to facilitate communication with law enforcement and to educate them on the threat posed by homegrown violent extremists.

The Committee reviewed efforts that DHS has taken to enhance its "If You See Something, Say Something" campaign. Shortly before the attack in Boston, the National Consortium for the Study of Terrorism and Responses to Terrorism (START) at the DHS Center of Excellence located at the University of Maryland released a report that found that 56% of the country had never heard of the campaign.[20] In a letter to the Committee, DHS reported that the campaign had added eight states as full partners, bringing the total to 32 states, and those 70 new partnerships with local city and county governments

[19] NCTC classified letter to U.S. House of Representatives Committee on Homeland Security, August, 25 2014

[20] National Consortium for the Study of Terrorism and Responses to Terrorism, "U.S. Attitudes Toward Terrorism and Counterterrorism", April 11, 2013, available at: http://www.start.umd.edu/sites/default/files/files/publications/research_briefs/START_USAttitudesTowardTerrorismandCounterterrorism_ResearchBrief_March2013.pdf

had been established. DHS also reported that it was planning to promote the campaign with students using social media as they returned to school in the fall.[21]

Feedback from State and local agencies about "See Something, Say Something" was generally positive, and there was widespread agreement that the potential of the program was substantial. Agencies did raise a concern that the program was limited to one point of contact for the public per local jurisdiction or statewide (i.e. a local 911 system). In a letter to the Committee in December 2014, Secretary Johnson stated that, "The campaign works with each partner to determine a proper reporting mechanism for the public, which is listed on the materials created specifically for each partner. Should any additional reporting mechanisms be established by our partners, the campaign will update or create new materials for the partner at any time they request."[22]

**Recommendation 6-1:**

DHS should re-communicate and conduct outreach with State and local entities to review and expand the number of outlets, if necessary, available to the public to provide information.

In its report, the Committee also recommended evaluating the efficacy of DHS' Countering Violent Extremism (CVE) strategy.[23] Boston authorities acknowledged taking part in DHS' sponsored Building Communities of Trust roundtable, and that it was a valuable event. They recommended conducting additional events, and expanding the participant list to include a broader array of represented groups.

A number of sources Committee staff spoke with commented on the need for DHS and the federal government to expand outreach efforts beyond the groups with whom the FBI or DHS traditionally engage.

In a response to this feedback, DHS reported that the Building Communities of Trust initiative has been implemented in over 15 urban areas across the Nation, and that more roundtables were planned for fiscal year 2015.[24]

The Department also stated that it is working with a broad range of government and civilian partners to counter violent extremism, and that supporting communities and local law enforcement through collaboration, information sharing, and outreach efforts such as the "See Something, Say Something" and the Building Communities of Trust program were essential to this effort. DHS stated that it aims to enhance incident preparedness through a "whole community" approach by providing training, products and resources to a broad range of stakeholders on issues such as terrorism and violent extremism.[25]

[21] Secretary Jeh Charles Johnson, Letter to the Honorable Michael T. McCaul, Chairman, U.S. House of Representatives Committee on Homeland Security, July 18, 2014

[22] Secretary Jeh Charles Johnson, Letter to the Honorable Michael T. McCaul, Chairman, U.S. House of Representatives Committee on Homeland Security, December 12, 2014

[23] The Committee is currently engaged in a separate review of the CVE efforts across the federal government, and will provide a more detailed discussion of some of these issues when the results of that effort become available.

[24] Secretary Jeh Charles Johnson, Letter to the Honorable Michael T. McCaul, Chairman, U.S. House of Representatives Committee on Homeland Security, December 12, 2014

[25] Ibid

DHS remarked that it has, "designed an approach to counter violent extremism that applies to all forms of violent extremism, regardless of ideology, which focuses on preventing violent attacks, and that it is working with communities to challenge violent extremist narratives used to recruit young Americans."[26]

**Recommendation 6-2:**

The Committee agrees that it is important to acknowledge a diverse and evolving threat landscape, but that particular emphasis should be placed on countering violent Islamist extremism—the ideology behind the Boston Marathon bombing as well as numerous other attacks in the United States Homeland, and also behind the rise of the Islamic State of Iraq and Syria (ISIS) and al Qaeda.

The Committee was encouraged to learn that in the wake of the Boston Marathon bombing, and the increased flow of foreign terrorist fighters to Syria, the Department has created a more targeted plan aimed at expanding engagement to relevant groups and communities.[27] DHS stated that it had developed a specific set of tools to engage with stakeholders while highlighting the relevant threats to their communities. DHS has cooperated with the National Counterterrorism Center to develop and implement a number of CVE initiatives including the Community Awareness Briefing, which is designed to share unclassified information with communities regarding the threat of violent extremism, and the Development of Community Resiliency exercise series which consists of half-day exercises to improve communication between law enforcement and communities.[28]

According to the Department, it has evolved its CVE strategy over recent months to become a more comprehensive prevention model that allows it to work with communities and recognize at-risk individuals before violent extremism takes root. A pilot program has been developed that encourages local partners to develop mechanisms for engaging various resources including the private sector and social service providers.[29]

The Committee is eager to continue its oversight of these and other CVE programs, and to help develop the most effective programs possible to keep the Homeland secure.

## Recommendation 7:
## Continually finding new ways to proactively improve our homeland security

The Committee's final recommendation in its 2014 report—that "investigators, analysts, intelligence and law enforcement professionals, and all those charged with guarding the nation's security continually find new ways to proactively improve our homeland security"—is among the most important for the long-term national security of the United States, but also recognized as the most challenging to implement. While there is still significant progress to be made in meeting this goal, the Committee is

---

[26] Ibid

[27] The Committee continues to examine the details of this and related efforts as part of its separate review of Federal CVE efforts

[28] Secretary Jeh Charles Johnson, Letter to the Honorable Michael T. McCaul, Chairman, U.S. House of Representatives Committee on Homeland Security, December 12, 2014

[29] Ibid

encouraged by the work of the current leadership at DHS, the FBI, and NCTC to tackle this challenge. Each has expressed support for greater transparency and worked with the Committee on multiple issues, demonstrating a renewed willingness to identify and mitigate weaknesses. As one small example, FBI Director Comey testified before the Committee on September 17, 2014. This hearing also included testimony from Secretary of homeland Security Jeh Johnson and NCTC Director Olsen, and was the first time in the Committee's history that the Bureau's Director had provided formal testimony for an oversight hearing. Events like these serve to demonstrate the partnership between this Committee and the stakeholder agencies spearheading our nation's counterterrorism efforts.

## CONCLUSION

As terrorism has evolved since 9/11, intelligence and law enforcement agencies at the Federal, State and local levels need to constantly evaluate and improve their efforts to investigate and mitigate threats. The statement by the FBI's Assistant Director for Counterterrorism at a February 2015 Committee on Homeland Security hearing regarding the number of foreign fighters leaving the U.S. and Europe to join the fight in Syria and Iraq illustrated the challenge facing the government. "We don't have it under control," said Assistant Director Mr. Michael Steinback, "Absolutely, we're doing the best we can. If I were to say that we had it under control, then I would say I know of every single individual traveling. I don't. And I don't know every person there and I don't know everyone coming back. So it's not even close to being under control."[30]

The threat to the Homeland from abroad and from homegrown self-inspired radicals calls for agility, and strengthening the web of relationships that exists between State, local and Federal partners to form a nationwide enterprise where State and locals collaborate and complement Federal counterterrorism capacity. The Committee is pleased with the progress that has been made since the Boston Marathon tragedy. It will continue its robust oversight of the information sharing process to ensure gaps are addressed as this dynamic threat changes. It stands ready to partner with the Executive Branch to ensure the requisite agencies have the authorities they need to carry out this critical mission.

[30] FBI AD Michael Steinback, testifying before the Committee on Homeland Security, February 11, 2015

## DOCUMENT NO. 8

# COUNTERING VIOLENT EXTREMISM: ACTIONS NEEDED TO DEFINE STRATEGY AND ASSESS PROGRESS OF FEDERAL EFFORTS

**United States Government Accountability Office**

**Report to Congressional Requesters**

April 2017

GAO-17-300

**COUNTERING VIOLENT EXTREMISM**

**Actions Needed to Define Strategy and Assess Progress of Federal Efforts**

## GAO Highlights

Highlights of GAO-17-300, a report to Congressional requesters

### Why GAO Did This Study

Violent extremism—generally defined as ideologically, religious, or politically-motivated acts of violence—has been perpetrated in the United States by white supremacists, anti-government groups, and radical Islamist entities, among others. In 2011, the U.S. government developed a national strategy and SIP for CVE aimed at providing information and resources to communities. In 2016, an interagency CVE Task Force led by DHS and DOJ was created to coordinate CVE efforts.

GAO was asked to review domestic federal CVE efforts. This report addresses the extent to which (1) DHS, DOJ, and other key stakeholders tasked with CVE in the United States have implemented the 2011 SIP and (2) the federal government has developed a strategy to implement CVE activities, and the CVE Task Force has assessed progress. GAO assessed the status of activities in the 2011 SIP; interviewed officials from agencies leading CVE efforts and a non-generalizable group of community-based entities selected from cities with CVE frameworks; and compared Task Force activities to selected best practices for multi-agency efforts.

### What GAO Recommends

GAO recommends that DHS and DOJ direct the CVE Task Force to (1) develop a cohesive strategy with measurable outcomes and (2) establish a process to assess the overall progress of CVE efforts. DHS and DOJ concurred with both recommendations and DHS described the CVE Task Force's planned actions for implementation.

For more information, contact Diana Maurer at (202) 512-8777 or maurerd@gao.gov.

## What GAO Found

As of December 2016, the Department of Homeland Security (DHS), Department of Justice (DOJ), Federal Bureau of Investigation, and National Counterterrorism Center had implemented 19 of the 44 domestically-focused tasks identified in the 2011 Strategic Implementation Plan (SIP) for countering violent extremism (CVE) in the United States. Twenty-three tasks were in progress and no action had yet been taken on 2 tasks. The 44 tasks aim to address three core CVE objectives: community outreach, research and training, and capacity building. Implemented tasks include, for example, DOJ conducting CVE outreach meetings to communities targeted by violent extremism and DHS integrating CVE content into law enforcement counterterrorism training. Tasks in progress include, for example, DHS building relationships with the social media industry and increasing training available to communities to counter violent extremists online. Tasks that had not yet been addressed include, implementing CVE activities in prisons and learning from former violent extremists. Federal CVE efforts aim to educate and prevent radicalization before a crime or terrorist act transpires, and differ from counterterrorism efforts such as collecting evidence and making arrests before an event has occurred.

**Figure: Countering Violent Extremism is Different from Counterterrorism**

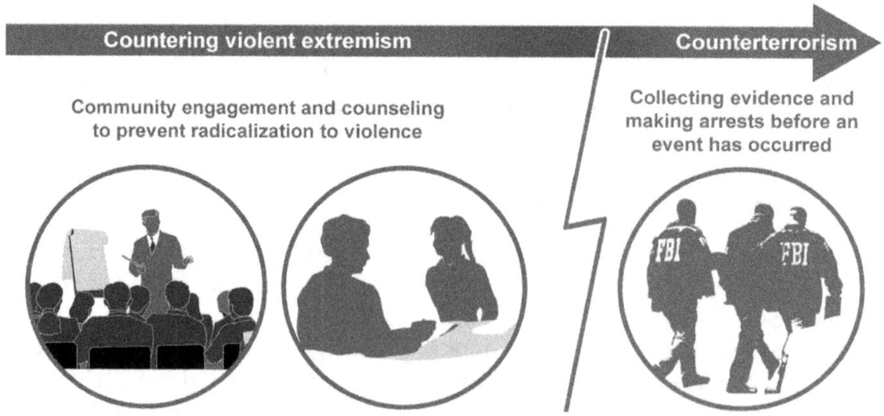


Source: GAO analysis of information from the White House, the Federal Bureau of Investigation (FBI), and the Department of Homeland Security (DHS); FBI (adapted photographs); Art Explosion (clip art). | GAO-17-300

The federal government does not have a cohesive strategy or process for assessing the overall CVE effort. Although GAO was able to determine the status of the 44 CVE tasks, it was not able to determine if the United States is better off today than it was in 2011 as a result of these tasks. This is because no cohesive strategy with measurable outcomes has been established to guide the multi-agency CVE effort. Such a strategy could help ensure that the individual actions of stakeholder agencies are measureable and contributing to the overall goals of the federal government's CVE effort. The federal government also has not established a process by which to evaluate the effectiveness of the collective CVE effort. The CVE Task Force was established in part to evaluate and assess CVE efforts across the federal government, but has not established a process for doing so. Evaluating the progress and effectiveness of the overall federal CVE effort could better help identify successes, gaps, and resource needs across stakeholder agencies.

### Abbreviations

| | |
|---|---|
| CAB | Community Awareness Briefings |
| CREX | Community Resilience Exercises |
| CVE | Countering Violent Extremism |
| DOD | Department of Defense |
| DHS | Department of Homeland Security |
| DOJ | Department of Justice |
| State | Department of State |
| ECDB | United States Extremist Crime Database |
| FBI | Federal Bureau of Investigation |
| FEMA | Federal Emergency Management Agency |
| FLETC | Federal Law Enforcement Training Center |
| ISIS | Islamic State of Iraq and Syria |
| NCTC | National Counterterrorism Center |
| OCP | Office of Community Partnerships |
| SLATT | State and Local Anti-Terrorism Training |
| SIP | Strategic Implementation Plan |
| START | Study of Terrorism and Responses to Terrorism |
| WORDE | World Organization for Resource Development and Education |

## U.S. GOVERNMENT ACCOUNTABILITY OFFICE

GAO
441 G St. N.W.
Washington, DC 20548

April 6, 2017

Congressional Requesters

Violent extremism—generally defined as supporting or committing violent acts to achieve political, ideological, religious, or social goals—has been perpetrated and promoted by a broad range of groups in the United States for decades. Such groups include white supremacists, anti-government groups, and groups with extreme views on abortion, animal rights, the environment, and federal ownership of public lands; and radical Islamist entities, such as the Islamic State of Iraq and Syria (ISIS), among others.[1] The September 11, 2001, attacks account for the largest number of fatalities in the United States resulting from violent extremism. According to the U.S. Extremist Crime Database (ECDB), since the September 11 attacks, 85 attacks in the United States by violent extremists—associated with both radical Islamist and far right ideologies—have resulted in 225 fatalities.[2]

In response to this threat, in 2011, the U.S. government developed a national strategy and a Strategic Implementation Plan (SIP) for countering violent extremism (CVE).[3] Primarily led by the Departments of Homeland Security (DHS) and Justice (DOJ) through an interagency task force, the federal government's leadership in CVE is aimed at educating and providing resources to communities for preventing violent extremist acts.[4] Specifically, CVE activities outlined in the 2011 SIP and updated in the 2016 SIP are aimed at enhancing the ability of local police and community organizations—including religious, educational, and non-profit entities—to provide information and resources to communities targeted by violent extremists and individuals who may have started down a road to violent extremism. These activities generally aim to provide alternative

[1] The organization referred to as the Islamic State of Iraq and Syria is alternatively known as the Islamic State of Iraq and the Levant, the Islamic State, and occasionally, "Daesh." Radical Islamist entities incorporate a militant ideology aimed at creating a worldwide community, or caliphate, of Muslim believers by any means necessary, including violence. Radical Islamist extremist groups include al-Qa'ida and ISIS, among others.

[2] The U.S. ECDB is maintained by the University of Maryland National Consortium for the Study of Terrorism and Responses to Terrorism (START). The ECDB is a database of the attacks committed by far rightists, radical Islamists and animal and environmental rights extremists in the United States since 1990. It includes the names of perpetrators and victims and the date and location of each incident, among other types of data. The 225 fatalities cited are victims and not perpetrators who may have died during the incident. START defines far right extremism as that which is motivated by a variety of far right ideologies and beliefs, generally favoring social hierarchy and seeking an idealized future favoring a particular group. Far right extremist groups include white supremacists and antigovernment militias, among others. START defines far left extremists as including those with extreme views on animal rights and the environment.

[3] In August 2011, The White House issued *The National Strategy for Empowering Local Partners to Prevent Violent Extremism in the United States* followed by *The National Strategy for Empowering Local Partners to Prevent Violent Extremism in the United States, Strategic Implementation Plan* in December 2011. The Strategic Implementation Plan was replaced by a new version in October 2016.

[4] The following departments and agencies have responsibility for implementing the 2016 SIP: DHS, DOJ, the Departments of State (State), Defense (DOD), Education, Health and Human Services, and Labor, as well as the Federal Bureau of Investigation (FBI), U.S. Agency for International Development, and National Counterterrorism Center (NCTC).

messages and options to terrorist or violent extremist recruitment and radicalization efforts through civic engagement.

Given the broad scope of activities associated with CVE and the importance of effective programs to address domestic threats, you asked us to review the implementation and organization of CVE efforts. This report addresses the extent to which (1) DHS, DOJ, and other key stakeholders tasked with CVE in the United States implemented the 2011 SIP and (2) the federal government has developed a strategy to implement CVE activities, and the CVE Task Force has developed a process for assessing overall progress.

To assess the extent to which DHS, DOJ, and other key stakeholders tasked with CVE in the United States implemented the 2011 SIP, we collected information from each agency responsible for leading 44 domestically related tasks in the 2011 SIP. Specifically, we asked for information—including, for example, program descriptions, internal progress reports, and materials distributed to the public—from each agency on the status of actions taken to address their assigned activities between December 2011 and December 2016. We assessed the information to determine whether each task had been implemented, was still in progress, or had not yet been addressed.

To determine the extent to which the federal government has developed a strategy to implement CVE activities and the CVE Task Force has developed a process for assessing overall progress, we reviewed the 2011 *National Strategy for Empowering Local Partners to Prevent Violent Extremism in the United States* (National Strategy), the 2011 and 2016 Strategic Implementation Plans for the strategy, and other documents related to the creation and activities of the CVE Task Force. Specifically, we reviewed these documents to identify whether measurable outcomes and associated metrics had been defined, and compared this information against practices for creating effective interagency collaborative efforts and managing cross-cutting issues. We interviewed officials from the stakeholder agencies including DHS, DOJ, the Department of Education, the Department of Health and Human Services, the Federal Bureau of Investigation (FBI), and the National Counterterrorism Center (NCTC) to discuss their approaches to CVE and their roles and responsibilities as part of the federal CVE effort. A detailed description of our scope and methodology can be found in appendix I.

We conducted this performance audit from October 2015 to April 2017 in accordance with generally accepted government auditing standards. Those standards require that we plan and perform the audit to obtain sufficient, appropriate evidence to provide a reasonable basis for our findings and conclusions based on our audit objectives. We believe that the evidence obtained provides a reasonable basis for our findings and conclusions based on our audit objectives.

## Background

### Violent Extremists in the United States

White supremacists, anti-government extremists, radical Islamist extremists, and other ideologically inspired domestic violent extremists have been active in the United States for decades. Examples of attacks include the 1993 World Trade Center bombing by radical Islamists, in which 6 persons were killed; and the 1995 Oklahoma City bombing of the Alfred P. Murrah federal building by anti-government far right individuals, in which 168 lives were lost. The September 11, 2001, attacks account for the largest number of fatalities in the United States in a single or closely-related attack resulting from violent extremism in recent decades. While the September 11, 2001, attacks were perpetrated by foreign violent extremists, from September 12, 2001 through December 31, 2016, attacks by domestic or "homegrown" violent extremists in the United States resulted in 225 fatalities, according to the ECDB. Of these, 106 were killed by far right violent extremists in 62 separate incidents, and 119 were victims of radical Islamist violent extremists in 23 separate incidents. Figure 1 shows the locations and number of fatalities involved in these incidents. A detailed list of the incidents can be found in appendix II. According to the ECDB, activities of far left wing violent extremist groups did not result in any fatalities during this period.

**Figure 1: Attacks in the United States by Domestic Violent Extremists from September 12, 2001 through December 31, 2016 that Resulted in Fatalities**

Source: U.S. Extremist Crime Database (ECDB) of the University of Maryland National Consortium for the Study of Terrorism and Responses to Terrorism (START); MapInfo (map) | GAO-17-300.

Note: Each circle or octagon represents a single attack with the size measuring the number of fatalities. The ECDB is a database that includes information on publicly known violent crimes committed in the United States by radical Islamist violent extremists, the violent far right, and far left violent extremists from 1990 through 2015. For 2016, attacks resulting in homicides by ideological violent extremists in the United States were provided to us by email updates from ECDB researchers. The ECDB includes information on the incidents themselves, as well as their perpetrators, related organizations, and victims. There were no attacks since 1990 by persons associated with extreme leftist ideologies that resulted in fatalities to non-perpetrators.

Since September 12, 2001, the number of fatalities caused by domestic violent extremists has ranged from 1 to 49 in a given year. As shown in figure 2, fatalities resulting from attacks by far right wing violet extremists have exceeded those caused by radical Islamist violent extremists in 10 of the 15 years, and were the same in 3 of the years since September 12, 2001. Of the 85 violent extremist incidents that resulted in death since

September 12, 2001, far right wing violent extremist groups were responsible for 62 (73 percent) while radical Islamist violent extremists were responsible for 23 (27 percent). The total number of fatalities is about the same for far right wing violent extremists and radical Islamist violent extremists over the approximately 15-year period (106 and 119, respectively). However, 41 percent of the deaths attributable to radical Islamist violent extremists occurred in a single event—an attack at an Orlando, Florida night club in 2016 (see fig. 2). Details on the locations and dates of the attacks can be found in appendix II.

**Figure 2: Number of Violent Extremist-linked Incidents and Resulting Fatalities in the United States from September 12, 2001 through December 31, 2016**

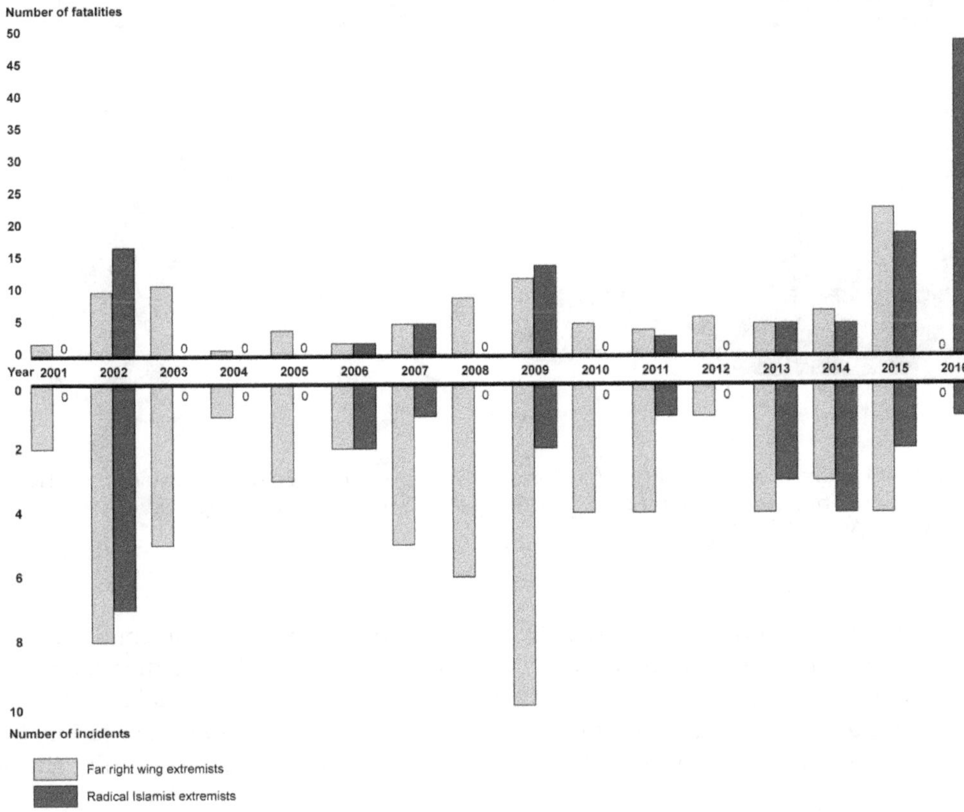


Source: U.S. Extremist Crime Database (ECDB) of the University of Maryland National Consortium for the Study of Terrorism and Responses to Terrorism (START). | GAO-17-300.

## The U.S. Approach to Countering Domestic Violent Extremism

In October 2016, the federal government defined the U.S. approach to countering violent extremism as proactive actions to counter efforts by extremists to recruit, radicalize, and mobilize followers to violence. The three parts of the U.S. approach to CVE efforts are: (1) empowering communities and civil society; (2) messaging and counter–messaging;

and (3) addressing causes and driving factors. CVE activities are different from traditional counterterrorism efforts, such as collecting intelligence, gathering evidence, making arrests, and responding to incidents, in that they generally focus on preventing an individual from finding or acting out on a motive for committing a crime, as shown in figure 3. In February 2015, the White House released a fact sheet stating that CVE encompasses the preventative aspects of counterterrorism as well as interventions to undermine the attraction of violent extremist movements and ideologies that seek to promote violence.

**Figure 3: Countering Violent Extremism is Different from Counterterrorism**

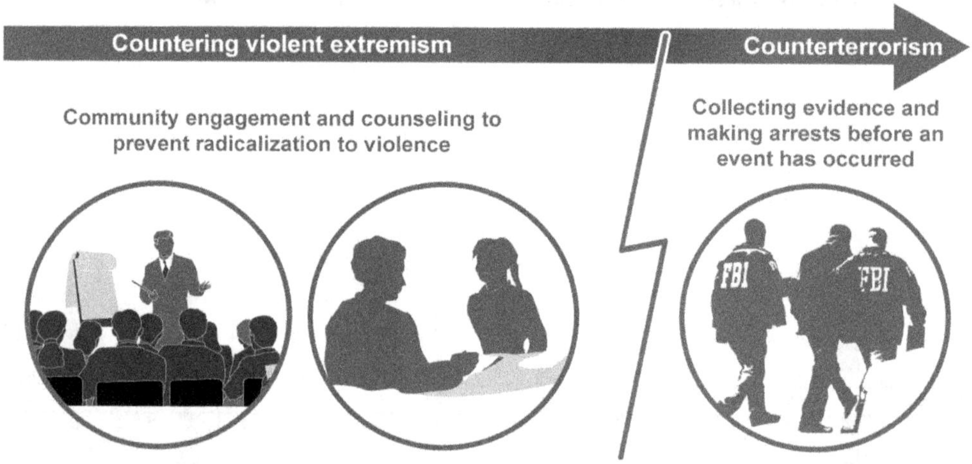


Source: GAO analysis of information from the White House, the Federal Bureau of Investigation (FBI), and the Department of Homeland Security (DHS); FBI (adapted photographs); Art Explosion (clip art). | GAO-17-300.

According to the national strategy, CVE actions intend to address the conditions and reduce the factors that most likely contribute to recruitment and radicalization by violent extremists. CVE efforts, as defined by the White House, are not to include gathering intelligence or performing investigations for the purpose of criminal prosecution. CVE efforts aim to address the root causes of violent extremism through community engagement, including:

- Building awareness—through briefings on the drivers and indicators of radicalization and recruitment to violence. For example, U.S. Attorney's and DHS offices host community outreach meetings in which they provide information on identifying suspicious activity.
- Countering violent extremist narratives—directly addressing and countering violent extremist recruitment messages, such as encouraging alternative messages from community groups online. For example, DOJ partnered with the International Association of Chiefs of Police to produce awareness briefs on countering online radicalization.

- Emphasizing community led intervention—supporting community efforts to disrupt the radicalization process before an individual engages in criminal activity. For example, the FBI aims to provide tools and resources to communities to help them identify social workers and mental health professionals who can help support at-risk individuals and prevent them from becoming radicalized.

Recognizing that most CVE activities occur at the community level, DHS and DOJ officials leading the CVE Task Force describe the federal role in CVE as a combination of providing research funding and training materials, and educating the public through activities such as DHS or DOJ hosted community briefings in which specific threats and warning signs of violent extremism are shared. According to FBI officials, these outreach efforts also provide an opportunity to build relationships in the community and help clarify the FBI's role in engaging community organizations. According to DHS officials, DHS also conducts regular community engagement roundtables in multiple cities that provide a forum for communities to comment on and hear information about Department activities, including CVE. In addition to community meetings, education of the public is to occur through a multiplicity of outreach channels, including websites, social media, conferences, and communications to state and local governments, including law enforcement entities.

### Organization of CVE Programs and Initiatives Have Undergone Recent Changes

Since 2010, federal agencies have initiated several steps towards countering violent extremism. In November 2010, a National Engagement Task Force, led by DHS and DOJ, was established to help coordinate community engagement efforts to counter violent extremism. The task force was to include all departments and agencies involved in relevant community engagement efforts and focus on compiling local, national, and international best practices and disseminating these out to the field, especially to U.S. Attorneys' Offices. The task force was also responsible for connecting field-based federal components involved in community engagement to maximize partnerships, coordination, and resource-sharing. According to DHS officials, the National Engagement Task Force disbanded in 2013.

In September 2015, DHS recognized that its CVE efforts were scattered across a number of components and lacked specific goals and tangible measures of success. DHS created the Office of Community Partnerships (OCP) to consolidate its programs, foster greater involvement of the technology sector and philanthropic efforts to support private CVE efforts, and to enhance DHS grant-making in the area. At the same time, federal agencies involved in CVE recognized that the CVE landscape had changed since the issuance of the national strategy and SIP in late 2011. According to DHS and DOJ officials, ISIS had emerged as a threat, and an increase in internet recruiting by violent extremist groups since 2011 required an update to the SIP. In 2015, NCTC led a review to ensure that the federal government was optimally organized to carry out the CVE mission. According to DOJ and DHS officials leading CVE activities, the review validated the objectives of the 2011 strategy, but identified gaps in its implementation. Specifically, representatives from 10 departments and agencies contributing to CVE efforts identified four needs: infrastructure to coordinate and prioritize CVE activities across the federal government and with stakeholders; clear responsibility, accountability, and communication internally and with the public; broad participation of departments and agencies outside national security lanes; and a process to assess, prioritize, and allocate resources to maximize impact.

In response, in January 2016, a new CVE task force was created to coordinate government efforts and partnerships to prevent violent extremism in the United States. The CVE Task Force is a permanent interagency task force hosted by DHS with overall leadership provided by DHS and DOJ. Staffing is to be provided by representatives from DHS, DOJ, FBI, NCTC, and other supporting departments and agencies. The Task Force is administratively housed at DHS and is to rotate leadership between DHS and DOJ bi-annually. The interagency CVE Task Force was established to: (1) synchronize and integrate whole-of-government CVE programs and activities; (2) conduct ongoing strategic planning; and (3) assess and evaluate CVE efforts.

In October 2016, the Task Force, through the White House, issued an updated SIP for the 2011 national strategy. The 2016 SIP outlines the general lines of effort that partnering agencies will aim to undertake to guide their coordination of federal efforts and implement the national strategy. These lines of effort include:

- *Research and Analysis:* The Task Force is to coordinate federal support for ongoing and future CVE research. Since 2011, DHS has funded 98 CVE related research projects and DOJ has funded 25. Coordination through this line of effort aims to prevent overlap and duplication while identifying guidelines for future evaluations. This line of effort also aims to identify and share guidelines for designing, implementing, and evaluating CVE programs.
- *Engagements and Technical Assistance:* The Task Force is to coordinate federal outreach to and engagement with communities. DHS, FBI, U.S. Attorneys, and other departments regularly provide information to local community and law enforcement leaders. To date, much of the information provided has been from the individual perspective of each agency and its mission rather than a coordinated CVE mission. This line of effort aims to coordinate these outreach efforts to synchronize the messages that are reaching the communities.
- *Interventions:* This line of effort aims to develop intervention options to include alternative pathways or "off-ramps" for individuals who appear to be moving toward violent action but who have not yet engaged in criminal activity. Law enforcement officials are looking for ways to support community led programs, particularly when they focus on juveniles and others who have the potential to be redirected away from violence. The CVE Task Force, in coordination with DOJ and the FBI, aim to support local multidisciplinary intervention approaches.
- *Communications and Digital Strategy:* Recognizing that general CVE information and resources are not easily accessible by stakeholders, the CVE Task Force aims to create a new online platform, including a public website, to ensure stakeholders around the country are able to quickly and easily understand national CVE efforts. This platform aims to serve as the national digital CVE clearinghouse by centralizing and streamlining access to training; research, analysis, and lessons learned; financial resources and grant information; networks and communities of interest; and intervention resources.

According to the 2016 SIP, the lines of effort were developed to align with the three priority action areas outlined in the 2011 national strategy and SIP: (1) enhancing engagement with and support to local communities; (2) building government and law enforcement expertise for preventing violent extremism; and (3) countering violent extremist propaganda while promoting our ideals. Also in October 2016, DHS issued its own strategy outlining the specific actions it aims to take to meet its CVE mission. Figure 4 shows a timeline of federal CVE milestones and activities.

**Figure 4: Timeline of Federal Countering Violent Extremism Milestones and Activities**

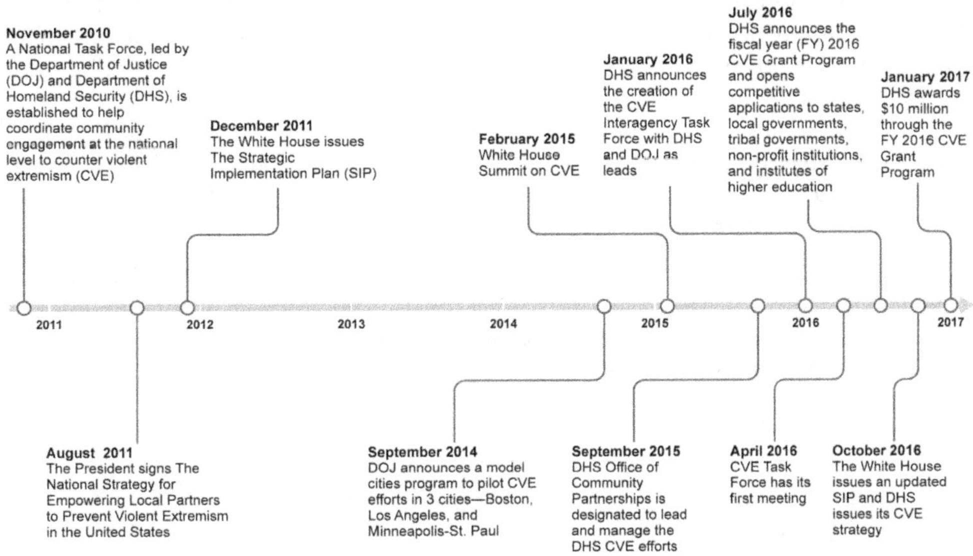


Source: GAO analysis based on Department of Homeland Security, Department of Justice, and White House documents. | GAO-17-300.

## CVE Funding

Consistent with direction in the 2011 National Strategy, federal CVE efforts have generally been initiated by leveraging existing programs and without a specific CVE budget. For example, activities that address violence in schools or hate crimes in communities may be relevant to constraining or averting violent extremism, but receive funding as part of a different program. In fiscal year 2016, the DHS Office of Community Partnerships operated with a $3.1 million budget and focused on raising awareness of violent extremists' threats in communities, building relationships with community organizations that are conducting CVE efforts, and coordinating CVE efforts within DHS. Additionally, DHS's fiscal year 2016 appropriation included $50 million to address emergent threats from violent extremism and from complex, coordinated terrorist attacks.[5] Of the $50 million,

[5] See Pub. L. No. 114-113, div. F, § 543, 129 Stat. 2242, 2518-19 (2015) (providing further that the Secretary may transfer funds made available for emerging threats between appropriations for the same purpose, notwithstanding other enacted provisions that affect the Secretary's authority to transfer funds).

- DHS awarded $10 million through a competitive grant program specific to CVE;
- DHS designated $1 million for a Joint Counterterrorism Workshop; and
- DHS designated the remaining $39 million to be competitively awarded under the existing Homeland Security Grant Program.

### Almost Half of Planned 2011 CVE Tasks Were Implemented, but Work Remains

Developed to help execute the 2011 National Strategy for Empowering Local Partners to Prevent Violent Extremism in the United States, the 2011 SIP detailed federal agency roles and responsibilities for current and future CVE efforts. The SIP outlined 44 tasks to address CVE domestically and called for the creation of an Assessment Working Group to measure CVE's progress and effectiveness.[6] From our analysis of agency documentation and other evidence as to whether tasks had been implemented, we determined that agencies implemented almost half of the 44 domestically-focused tasks identified in the 2011 SIP.[7] Specifically, from December 2011 through December 2016, federal agencies implemented 19 tasks, had 23 tasks in progress, and had not yet taken action on 2 tasks (see fig. 5 below and app. III for additional details).

While progress was made in implementing the tasks, the Assessment Working Group was never formed according to DHS and DOJ officials responsible for implementing the SIP. Moreover, as of December 2016, there had been no comprehensive assessment of the federal government's CVE efforts' effectiveness.

[6] The SIP included 47 tasks and designated federal agency lead(s) responsible for ensuring each task was implemented. We analyzed implementation of tasks that were led by DHS, DOJ, FBI, and NCTC. These four agencies are responsible for domestic CVE and were collectively responsible for implementing 44 of the 47 tasks in the SIP. We did not analyze the implementation of 3 of the 47 tasks because they were international in scope or led by an agency outside of the four agencies responsible for domestic CVE. Specifically, we did not analyze the Department of Treasury's efforts to address terrorism financing, the Department of Defense's effort to provide training to military personnel, and the State Department's international exchange program. We did not assess the quality of efforts taken related to the 44 tasks.

[7] For the 44 tasks identified in the SIP, DHS, DOJ, FBI and NCTC provided information on the status of actions taken on the tasks for which they were the lead agencies. Some tasks listed multiple agencies as co-leads responsible for completion. Some agency responses showed their actions substantially addressed the task, while others only took some action for the same task. DHS, DOJ, and FBI provided technical comments on our assessment which we incorporated as appropriate and officials from NCTC met with us to discuss the information it provided.

**Figure 5: Status of 2011 Strategic Implementation Plan's 44 Domestically-Focused Tasks**

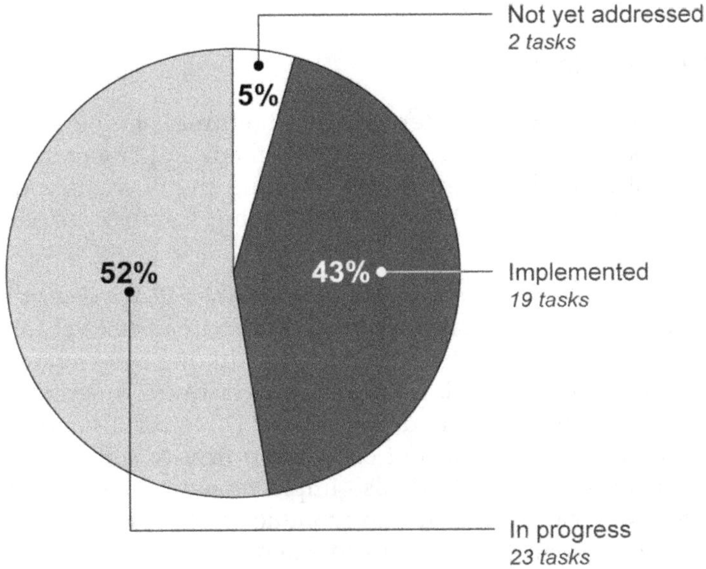


Source: GAO analysis of Department of Homeland Security, Department of Justice, Federal Bureau of Investigation and National Counterterrorism Center documents. | GAO-17-300.

The 44 domestically-oriented tasks identified in the 2011 SIP were focused on addressing three core CVE objectives: community outreach, research and training, and capacity building. Below is a description of progress made and challenges remaining by core CVE objective.

### Community Outreach

Community outreach aims to enhance federal engagement and support to local communities that may be targeted by violent extremism. For example, community outreach might include expanding relationships with local business and communities to identify or prevent violent extremism or integrating CVE activities into community-oriented policing efforts.

Of the 17 community outreach tasks in the SIP, we determined that agencies implemented 8 tasks and 9 remain in progress. In general, agencies implemented tasks focused on expanding CVE efforts in local communities and identifying ways to increase funding for CVE activities, among other things. For example, DOJ expanded CVE activities to communities targeted by violent extremism through a series of outreach meetings led by the U.S. Attorney's offices. Further, both DHS and DOJ identified funding within existing appropriations to incorporate CVE into eligible public safety and community resilience grants.

However, community outreach tasks that remained in progress include tasks related to reaching communities in the digital environment. For example, DHS aims to build relationships with the high-tech and social media industry and continues to meet with officials to discuss how to address violent extremism online. In providing a status update on such activities, DHS recognized this as an area that continues to need attention.

### Research and Training

Research and training relates to understanding the threat of violent extremism, sharing information, and leveraging it to train government and law enforcement officials. For example, activities under research and training might include funding or conducting analysis on CVE-related topics or developing training curriculums for CVE stakeholders.

Of the 19 research and training tasks we assessed in the SIP, we determined that agencies implemented 9 tasks, had 9 tasks in progress, and had not yet taken action on 1 task. Agencies implemented activities related to continuing research on CVE and integrating CVE training into federal law enforcement training, among other things. For example, DHS, through its Science and Technology Directorate, continued its research and reporting on violent extremist root causes and funded an open source database on terrorism as stated in the SIP. DHS also implemented a task related to integrating CVE content into counter-terrorism training conducted at the Federal Law Enforcement Training Center. Additionally, NCTC implemented tasks related to expanding awareness briefings to state and local law enforcement, and developing and reviewing guidance on CVE training, while the FBI implemented a task regarding the completion of a CVE coordination office.

Further, tasks related to training non-security federal partners to incorporate CVE training remain in progress. For example, DHS was given responsibility for collaborating with non-security federal partners to build CVE training modules that can be incorporated into existing programs related to public safety, violence prevention, and resilience. DHS acknowledged this task needs attention and noted that, while initial steps were taken, the interagency effort needs to better define roles and opportunities for future collaborations. However, agencies have not yet taken action on implementing CVE in federal prisons.

### Capacity Building

Capacity building tasks relate to investments of resources into communities to enhance the effectiveness and future sustainability of their CVE efforts. Capacity building might, for example, include expanding the use of informational briefings to a wider audience or outreach to former violent extremists to counter violent narratives.

Of the 8 capacity building tasks we assessed in the SIP, we determined that agencies implemented 2 tasks, 5 tasks were in progress, and action had not yet been taken on 1 task. For example, one of the implemented capacity building tasks included providing regular briefings on CVE to Congress and others. In implementing this task, DHS participated in over two dozen briefings and hearings for Congress.

Capacity building tasks that were in progress included brokering connections with the private sector and building a public website on community resilience and CVE, among others. DHS had, for example, taken steps to broker connections with the private sector. DHS officials also noted making initial progress with YouTube and the Los Angeles

Police Department in developing campaigns against violent extremism, but recognized this as an area that continues to need attention. Despite progress in 7 of 8 capacity building tasks, action had not yet been taken on a task related to learning from former violent extremists to directly challenge violent extremist narratives. According to DHS officials, legal issues regarding access to former violent extremists are being explored and DOJ will lead this task moving forward.

## The Federal CVE Effort Lacks a Cohesive Strategy with Measureable Outcomes and a Process for Assessing Progress

### A Cohesive CVE Strategy with Measurable Outcomes Has Not Been Established

Although we were able to determine the status of the 44 domestically focused CVE tasks from the 2011 SIP, we could not determine the extent to which the United States is better off today as a result of its CVE effort than it was in 2011. That is because no cohesive strategy with measurable outcomes has been established to guide the multi-agency CVE effort towards its goals.[8]

Neither the 2011 SIP nor its 2016 update provides a cohesive strategy—one that sets forth a coordinated and collaborative effort among partner agencies—that includes measurable outcomes. For example, the 2016 SIP includes a task on strengthening collaboration with the private sector and academia to pursue CVE-relevant communications tools and capabilities. The task describes the benefits of such collaboration, but does not include any information on how the task will be implemented, timeframes for implementation, desired outcomes, or indicators for measuring progress towards those outcomes. Similarly, the 2016 SIP includes a task on identifying and supporting the development of disengagement and rehabilitation programs. While the SIP describes research conducted in partnership with one such program that provides pathways out of violent extremism, it does not include any information on how the federal government will identify other groups and what kind of support they might provide. Absent defined measureable outcomes, it is unclear how these tasks will be implemented and how they will measurably contribute to achieving the federal CVE goals.

Consistent with the GPRA Modernization Act of 2010, establishing a cohesive strategy that includes measurable outcomes can provide agencies with a clear direction for successful implementation of activities in multi-agency cross-cutting efforts.[9] Participants in multi-agency efforts each bring different views, organizational cultures, missions, and ways of operating. They may even disagree on the nature of the problem or issue being addressed. As such, developing a mutually agreed-upon cohesive strategy with

[8] The National Strategy identifies the goal of CVE as, *"preventing violent extremists and their supporters from inspiring, radicalizing, financing, or recruiting individuals or groups in the United States to commit acts of violence."* It also describes priority action areas for CVE activities under the categories of: (1) enhancing engagement with and support to local communities that may be targeted by violent extremists; (2) building government and law enforcement expertise for preventing violent extremism; and (3) countering violent extremist propaganda while promoting our ideals.

[9] GAO, *Managing for Results: OMB Improved Implementation of Cross-Agency Priority Goals, But Could Be More Transparent About Measuring Progress*, GAO-16-509 (Washington, D.C.: May 20, 2016). The GPRA Modernization Act of 2010, Pub. L. No. 111-352, 124 Stat. 3866 (2011), updated the Government Performance and results Act of 1993 (GPRA), Pub. L. No. 103-62, 107 Stat. 285.

measureable outcomes can strengthen agencies' commitment to working collaboratively and enhance the effectiveness of the CVE effort while keeping stakeholders engaged and invested.[10]

Absent a cohesive strategy with defined measureable outcomes, CVE partner agencies have been left to develop and take their own individual actions without a clear understanding of whether and to what extent their actions will reduce violent extremism in the United States. For example, agencies such as the Department of Education and the Department of Health and Human Services are listed in the SIP as two of the agencies with responsibility for implementing the 2016 SIP.[11] However, the tasks for which they are listed as partners do not include measurable outcomes to guide implementation. As another example, in 2016 DHS issued its own CVE strategy for the department intended to align with the 2016 SIP.[12] It is specific to DHS components and programs, establishes goals, outcomes, and milestones, and states that DHS will assess progress. However, DHS's CVE strategy does not demonstrate how these activities will integrate with the overall federal CVE effort. Further, it establishes goals and outcomes for only one of the many departments responsible for CVE. DHS and DOJ officials speaking on behalf of the CVE Task Force stated that, as of November 2016, they had not determined if other stakeholder agencies, such as DOJ, the Department of Education, or the Department of Health and Human Services, would be developing similar strategies.

In January 2016, the CVE Task Force was established as the multi-agency body charged with coordinating government efforts and partnerships to prevent violent extremism in the United States.[13] As such, it is best positioned to work with federal stakeholders in developing a cohesive strategy with measureable outcomes. More details on the CVE Task Force are provided in the following section. Our previous work has shown that agencies across the federal government have benefited from applying such strategies to cross cutting programs.[14] By developing a cohesive strategy with measurable outcomes, CVE stakeholders will be better able to guide their efforts to ensure measurable progress is made in CVE.

---

[10] GAO, *Managing for Results: Key Considerations for Implementing Interagency Collaborative Mechanisms*, GAO-12-1022 (Washington, D.C.: Sept. 27, 2012).

[11] In April 2016, CVE Task Force leaders told us that they were working to establish a charter outlining specific roles of stakeholder agencies but, as of December 2016, had not completed it.

[12] *Department of Homeland Security Strategy for Countering Violent Extremism*, Oct. 28, 2016.

[13] In 2015, NCTC led a multi-agency effort to identify gaps and needs remaining to be fulfilled in CVE. Specifically, the effort considered the 2011 CVE National Strategy and SIP, and agency-reported efforts at that time to address CVE concerns. The assessment identified four needs: infrastructure to coordinate and prioritize CVE activities across the federal government and with stakeholders; clear responsibility, accountability, and communication internally and with the public; broad participation of departments and agencies outside national security lanes; and a process to assess, prioritize, and allocate resources to maximize impact. Following the 2015 assessment, the CVE Task Force was created in January 2016 to coordinate federal agencies in fulfilling the CVE effort. The gaps and needs identified in the 2015 assessment have been an important basis for creating and defining the CVE Task Force's first steps as a multi-agency collaborative effort.

[14] GAO, *Managing for Results: Practices for Effective Agency Strategic Reviews*, GAO-15-602 (Washington, D.C.: July 29, 2015).

## No Process for Assessing Overall CVE Progress Is In Place

The CVE Task Force has not established a process for assessing whether the federal government's CVE efforts are working. Establishing a process for assessing progress is a consistent practice of successful multi-agency collaborative efforts we have previously reviewed.

Moreover, such assessments can help identify successful implementation and gaps across agencies.[15]

Recognizing the need for assessing the effects of CVE activities, the 2011 SIP described a process in which departments and agencies were to be responsible for assessing their specific activities in coordination with an Assessment Working Group. Agencies were to develop a process for identifying gaps, areas of limited progress, resource needs, and any additional factors resulting from new information on the dynamics of radicalization to violence. Further, the progress of the participating agencies was to be evaluated and reported annually to the President. However, according to DHS and DOJ officials, the Assessment Working Group was never created and the process described in the SIP was not developed. As a result, no process or method for assessing the federal CVE effort's progress and holding stakeholders accountable was established.

Absent a mechanism for assessing the federal CVE effort, in 2015 NCTC, along with 10 federal agencies, including DHS and DOJ, undertook an effort to review progress agencies had made in implementing their CVE responsibilities. According to DHS and DOJ officials, the review, along with those of the supporting agencies, helped identify areas for continued focus and improvement in fulfilling the CVE effort. Specifically, the review team identified the need for clear responsibility and accountability across the government and with the public. It also identified the need for a process to assess, prioritize, and allocate resources to maximize impact, among other needs.

Informed by these efforts, in January 2016 the CVE Task Force was established as a permanent interagency task force with overall leadership provided by DHS and DOJ. As previously described, the task force was charged with coordinating government efforts and partnerships to prevent violent extremism in the United States. Moreover, the CVE Task Force was assigned responsibility for synchronizing and integrating CVE programs and activities and assessing and evaluating them. The CVE Task Force worked with its partner agencies to develop the 2016 SIP but did not identify a process or method for assessing whether the overall CVE effort is working. Instead, the SIP states that it will use prior evaluations of individual programs to develop guidelines for departments and agencies to evaluate their own programs. Moreover, according to CVE Task Force officials, they do not believe that assessing the overall effectiveness of the federal CVE effort is their responsibility.

Moving forward with the approach identified in the 2016 SIP is likely to continue to limit the federal government's understanding of progress made in CVE efforts to that of individual activities rather than the entirety of the federal CVE effort. Agencies have conducted assessments of the effectiveness of some individual CVE programs. However,

[15] See for example GAO, *Managing for Results: Implementation Approaches Used to Enhance Collaboration in Interagency Groups*, GAO-14-220 (Washington, D.C.: Feb 14, 2014). Also see GAO-06-15 and GAO-12-1022.

those assessments do not address the overarching effectiveness of the CVE effort. In addition, efforts to evaluate individual CVE initiatives alone will not provide an overall assessment of progress made in the federal CVE effort. For example, DOJ funded an evaluation of a community-based CVE programming effort led by the World Organization for Resource Development and Education (WORDE). The evaluation assessed WORDE's effectiveness in promoting positive social integration and encouraging public safety in Montgomery County, Maryland. The evaluation looked at community-based participation in CVE programs, community awareness of risk factors of radicalization to violent extremism, and the community's natural inclinations in response to these factors. The evaluation provides some insights into how WORDE's program worked in Montgomery County, Maryland, but not the overall federal CVE effort.

Absent a consistent process for assessing the federal CVE effort as a whole, the federal government lacks the information needed to truly assess the extent to which the WORDE effort and others have countered violent extremism. Further, stakeholders will be limited in their efforts to identify successes and gaps and allocate or leverage resources effectively. Given that the CVE Task Force, as a permanent interagency body, is charged with synchronizing and integrating CVE programs and activities and assessing and evaluating them, the CVE Task Force should establish a process for assessing overall progress in CVE, including its effectiveness.

## Conclusions

Combatting violent extremism is of critical importance for the United States. Extremist attacks of all kinds can have perilous effects on the perceived safety of our nation. It is therefore imperative that the United States employ effective means for preventing and deterring violent extremism and related attacks. To help confront this critical need, in 2011 the President issued a CVE strategy and corresponding implementation plan. However, over 5 years have passed and the federal government has not developed a cohesive strategy among stakeholder agencies that provides measurable outcomes to guide the collaborative implementation of CVE activities. While the CVE Task Force provided a forum for coordination and led the effort to develop a new SIP, the plan does not provide stakeholder agencies with specific direction and measures to identify successes and gaps in the implementation of their activities. In the absence of a cohesive strategy, DHS has developed its own strategy, while no such roadmap is in place for the collaborative implementation of activities by all stakeholder agencies. As the entity responsible for the synchronization and integration of CVE programs across the government, the CVE Task Force is well positioned to develop a cohesive strategy that provides all stakeholder agencies with a clear path forward in achieving the federal CVE effort's desired outcomes.

The CVE Task Force, established in part to assess and evaluate CVE programs, has also not established an approach for assessing overall progress. Without consistent measures and methodologies for evaluating CVE as a whole, the federal government lacks the necessary information needed to assess the extent to which stakeholder agencies are achieving their goals. Without this information, stakeholders will not be able to identify successes and gaps and allocate or leverage resources effectively. When dealing with programs and activities that are designed to keep Americans safe from the threat of violent extremism, agency leaders and policy makers need to be able to know how well the federal government is doing in implementing these activities. Establishing an approach for assessing progress of the overall CVE effort can help the CVE Task Force enhance understanding of progress made as a result of CVE.

## Recommendations

To help identify what domestic CVE efforts are to achieve and the extent to which investments in CVE result in measureable success, the Secretary of Homeland Security and the Attorney General—as heads of the two lead agencies responsible for coordinating CVE efforts—should direct the CVE Task Force to:

1. Develop a cohesive strategy that includes measurable outcomes for CVE activities; and

2. Establish and implement a process to assess overall progress in CVE, including its effectiveness.

## Agency Comments and Our Evaluation

We provided a draft of this report to the Departments of Education, Health and Human Services, Homeland Security (DHS), and Justice (DOJ) and the Office of the Director of National Intelligence (ODNI). In its written comments, reproduced in appendix IV, DHS concurred with both of our recommendations. In comments provided in an email from the DOJ Audit Liaison, DOJ also concurred with both recommendations. In addition, DHS, DOJ, and ODNI provided technical comments which we incorporated as appropriate. The Departments of Education and Health and Human Services did not comment on the report.

DHS, in its letter, concurred with our recommendation to develop a cohesive strategy that includes outcomes for CVE activities. DHS also recognized that additional strategic-level performance documentation will improve coordination and collaboration tasks among partner agencies, as well as define how cross-cutting tasks will be implemented and how they will measurably contribute to achieving federal CVE goals. DHS noted that the CVE Task Force is developing measurable outcomes to support and guide the development of performance, effectiveness, and benchmarks for federally sponsored CVE efforts. DHS stated that the CVE Task Force plans to report on the progress of implementing the 2016 Strategic Implementation Plan in January 2018. DOJ also concurred with the recommendation in comments received by email.

DHS also concurred with our recommendation to establish and implement a process to assess overall progress in CVE, including its effectiveness. DHS, in its comment letter, recognized that such a process will drive an understanding of the contributions of individual activities in the federal CVE effort. In DHS's response, the department maintained that the CVE Task Force will not be engaged in specific evaluations of its members or partners, but instead will develop resource guides on methodologies and measures that federal and non-government partners can use in evaluating their own CVE efforts. As noted in our report, the CVE Task Force's approach of providing guidance on evaluations might enhance the evaluation efforts of individual programs, but establishing a process that assesses progress and effectiveness across the federal

CVE effort can provide better insight into the successes and gaps within this multi-agency collaborative effort. DOJ also concurred with the recommendation in comments received by email.

We are sending copies of this report to Secretary of Education, the Secretary of Health and Human Services, the Secretary of Homeland Security, the Attorney General, the Director of the Office of National Intelligence and appropriate congressional committees and members, and other interested parties. In addition, this report is available at no charge on GAO's website at http://www.gao.gov.

If you or your staff have any questions, please contact Diana Maurer at (202) 512-8777 or maurerd@gao.gov. Contact points for our Offices of Congressional Relations and Public Affairs may be found on the last page of this report. GAO staff that made significant contributions to this report are listed in appendix IV.

[Signature]

Diana Maurer
Director, Homeland Security and Justice Issues

*List of Congressional Requesters*

The Honorable Ron Johnson
Chairman
The Honorable Claire McCaskill
Ranking Member
Committee on Homeland Security and Governmental Affairs
United States Senate

The Honorable Bennie G. Thompson
Ranking Member
Committee on Homeland Security
House of Representatives

The Honorable Nanette Barragán
House of Representatives

The Honorable Jose Luis Correa
House of Representatives

The Honorable Valdez Demings
House of Representatives

The Honorable Brian Higgins
House of Representatives

The Honorable Sheila Jackson-Lee
House of Representatives

The Honorable Bill Keating
House of Representatives

The Honorable Jim Langevin
House of Representatives

The Honorable Donald M. Payne
House of Representatives

The Honorable Kathleen M. Rice
House of Representatives

The Honorable Cedric L. Richmond
House of Representatives

The Honorable Norma J. Torres
House of Representatives

The Honorable Filemon Vela
House of Representatives

The Honorable Bonnie Watson Coleman
House of Representatives

## Appendix I
## Objectives, Scope, and Methodology

This report addresses the extent to which (1) the Department of Homeland Security (DHS), the Department of Justice (DOJ), and other key stakeholders tasked with Countering Violent Extremism (CVE) in the United States have implemented the 2011 Strategic Implementation Plan (SIP) and (2) the federal government has developed a strategy to implement CVE activities, and the CVE Task Force has developed a process for assessing overall progress.

To assess the extent to which DHS, DOJ, and other key stakeholders tasked with CVE in the United States implemented the 2011 SIP, we collected and analyzed information from each agency responsible for leading a task in the 2011 SIP, which included DHS, DOJ, the Federal Bureau of Investigation (FBI), and the National Counterterrorism Center (NCTC). The FBI was treated as a lead agency for reporting purposes because it was listed as a lead agency in the SIP. These four agencies were responsible for domestic CVE activities and were collectively responsible for implementing 44 out of the 47 tasks in the SIP. We did not analyze the implementation of 3 of the 47 tasks because they were international in scope and led by an agency outside of the four agencies responsible for domestic CVE. Specifically, we did not analyze the Department of Treasury's efforts to address terrorism financing, the Department of Defense's effort to provide training to military personnel, and the State Department's international exchange program. GAO asked for information from each lead agency on actions taken from December 2011 through December 2016 to address their assigned activities in the 2011 SIP. Based on information provided, one analyst analyzed each agency's action(s) to determine whether each task in the SIP had been implemented, was still in progress, or had not been addressed. A separate analyst independently reviewed each assessment and narrative. If there was disagreement on a rating, a third analyst reviewed that information and made a determination on the final rating. Upon preliminary completion of the appendix table, GAO sent the table to DHS, DOJ, FBI, and NCTC and incorporated technical comments as appropriate. The results of this assessment are shown in appendix III.

To determine the extent to which the federal government has developed a strategy to implement CVE activities and the CVE Task Force has developed a process for assessing overall progress, we reviewed the *National Strategy for Empowering Local Partners to Prevent Violent Extremism in the United States*, the 2011 and 2016 Strategic Implementation Plans for the strategy, and other documents related to the creation and activities of the CVE Task Force. Specifically, we reviewed these documents to identify whether measurable outcomes and associated metrics had been defined. We interviewed officials from the stakeholder agencies including DHS, DOJ, the Department of Education, the Department of Health and Human Services, FBI, and NCTC to discuss their approaches to CVE and their roles and responsibilities as part of the federal CVE effort. We compared the practices of the Task Force to selected leading practices of multi-agency collaborative efforts identified in prior GAO work as well as selected practices in the GPRA Modernization Act of 2010.[1] Practices were selected for comparison based on

[1] The GPRA Modernization Act of 2010, Pub. L. No. 111-352, 124 Stat. 3866 (2011), updated the Government Performance and results Act of 1993 (GPRA), Pub. L. No. 103-62, 107 Stat. 285.

their applicability to the CVE Task Force. For context and perspectives on how CVE activities were implemented in local areas we interviewed a non-generalizable group of community organizations selected based on their location in the three pilot cities that have adopted CVE frameworks: Los Angeles, California; Boston, Massachusetts; and Minneapolis-St. Paul, Minnesota.

We conducted this performance audit from October 2015 to April 2017 in accordance with generally accepted government auditing standards. Those standards require that we plan and perform the audit to obtain sufficient, appropriate evidence to provide a reasonable basis for our findings and conclusions based on our audit objectives. We believe that the evidence obtained provides a reasonable basis for our findings and conclusions based on our audit objectives.

## Appendix II
## Violent Extremist Attacks in the United States that Resulted in Fatalities, September 12, 2001 through December 31, 2016

This appendix provides details on the violent extremist attacks in the United States based on the U.S. Extremist Crime Database (ECDB) data and as described in the background section of this report. Specifically, tables 1 and 2 show a description, date, location and number of victim fatalities for each far right and radical Islamist attack between September 12, 2001 and December 31, 2016. During this period, no persons in the United States were killed in attacks carried out by persons believed to be motivated by extremist environmental beliefs, extremist "animal liberation" beliefs, or extremist far left beliefs. The information on these attacks, including the motivations of the attackers, is from the ECDB, maintained by National Consortium for the Study of Terrorism and Responses to Terrorism (START), at the University of Maryland. START is a Department of Homeland Security (DHS) Center of Excellence. The ECDB tracks violent extremist incidents in the United States since 1990. For our analysis, we included the time period from September 12, 2001 through December 31, 2016, to show violent extremist attacks that have occurred since the September 11, 2001 attacks. We assessed the reliability of this data source through review of database documentation and interviews with the ECDB principle investigators. We discussed cases with the ECDB investigators to clarify details as needed. We determined that this data source was sufficiently reliable for providing background information on the problem of violent extremism in the United States, including the number of attacks and fatalities by ideological motivation (far right or radical Islamist), year and location.

Far right violent extremist attackers are characterized by ECDB as having beliefs that include some or all of the following:

- Fiercely nationalistic (as opposed to universal and international in orientation);
- Anti-global;
- Suspicious of centralized federal authority;
- Reverent of individual liberty (especially right to own guns; be free of taxes);
- Belief in conspiracy theories that involve a grave threat to national sovereignty and/or personal liberty;
- Belief that one's personal and/or national "way of life" is under attack and is either already lost or that the threat is imminent; and
- Belief in the need to be prepared for an attack either by participating in or supporting the need for paramilitary preparations and training or survivalism.

In addition, according to the ECDB, many persons having violent extreme far right views express support for some version of white supremacy, the Ku Klux Klan, and neo-Nazism.

According to the ECDB, attackers with violent radical Islamist beliefs were generally those who professed some form of belief in or allegiance to the Islamic State of Iraq and Syria (ISIS), al-Qa'ida, or other (radical) Islamist-associated terrorist entities. ECDB's determination of these beliefs are based on statements made by attackers prior to, during, or after their attacks that showed a belief in violent extremist interpretations of Islam, or evidence gathered by police and other sources about the attackers.

According to the ECDB, all information in the database is collected from publicly available sources, including mass media reports. ECDB analyzes this information using a standardized and consistent methodology to characterize each attack in terms of the ideological motivation. In addition, ECDB rates the confidence in this assessment of ideological motivations using standard definitions of the factors that lead a confidence level on a scale from 0 to 4, where 0 is the lowest level of confidence and 4 is the highest level of confidence. During our reliability assessment, it was determined that the far right-motivated attacks included 12 incidents where there was unclear evidence about the motivation of the attacker; these 12 were excluded from our analysis.

**Table 1: Far Right Violent Extremist-Motivated Attacks that Resulted in Fatalities, September 12, 2001 through December 31, 2016, as reported in the U.S. Extremist Crime Database (ECDB)**

| Summary of ECDB Incident Description | Date | City | State | Number of Victim Deaths |
|---|---|---|---|---|
| White Supremacist member of Aryan Brotherhood killed a man | 9/15/2001 | Mesquite | Texas | 1 |
| Same white supremacist as previous case but another victim a few weeks later | 10/4/2001 | Mesquite | Texas | 1 |
| White supremacist murdered an African American | 3/21/2002 | Portland | Oregon | 1 |
| White supremacist skinhead murdered a transgender person | 4/10/2002 | El Paso | Texas | 1 |
| Far right violent extremists murdered 3 fast food workers (one Native American and two Hispanic) | 5/19/2002 | Mesa | Arizona | 3 |
| Neo-Nazi murdered a gay man | 6/12/2002 | Tucson | Arizona | 1 |
| Anti-government "Sovereign Citizen" murdered an Ohio police officer | 8/2/2002 | Massillon | Ohio | 1 |

| Summary of ECDB Incident Description | Date | City | State | Number of Victim Deaths |
|---|---|---|---|---|
| Two white supremacist skinheads murdered a man | 8/30/2002 | Las Vegas | Nevada | 1 |
| White supremacist skinhead beat a man to death outside a diner | 9/1/2002 | St. Louis | Missouri | 1 |
| White supremacist murdered bisexual man | 12/14/2002 | Salinas | California | 1 |
| White supremacist gang murdered a homeless man as part of a gang initiation | 3/23/2003 | Tacoma | Washington | 1 |
| Anti-government militiaman shot and killed a Michigan state trooper | 7/7/2003 | Fremont | Michigan | 1 |
| White supremacist shot and killed 6 co-workers at Lockheed Martin Plant | 7/8/2003 | Meridian | Mississippi | 6 |
| Neo-Nazi killed sex-offender priest | 8/23/2003 | Shirley | Massachusetts | 1 |
| Anti-government "constitutionalist" killed 2 in standoff over land | 12/8/2003 | Abbeville | South Carolina | 2 |
| White supremacist killed a man while "hunting down Mexicans" | 1/9/2004 | Dateland | Arizona | 1 |
| White supremacists murdered two homeless men | 4/15/2005 | Hingham | Massachusetts | 2 |
| Six white supremacist inmates beat another prisoner to death | 10/14/2005 | Kingman | Arizona | 1 |
| White supremacist skinhead murdered an African American woman | 12/16/2005 | Mays Landing | New Jersey | 1 |
| Neo-Nazi murdered a gay man | 3/23/2006 | New Port Richey | Florida | 1 |
| White supremacist inmate killed his African American cellmate | 11/13/2006 | Chipley | Florida | 1 |
| White supremacist murders Hispanic man in convenience store after argument | 7/2/2007 | Lubbock | Texas | 1 |

| Summary of ECDB Incident Description | Date | City | State | Number of Victim Deaths |
|---|---|---|---|---|
| White supremacist murdered Lubbock, TX police officer | 8/15/2007 | Brandon | Florida | 1 |
| Two white supremacists murdered a homeless man | 9/3/2007 | Reno | Nevada | 1 |
| Two white supremacists murdered a gay man as gang initiation rite | 10/26/2007 | Goldsby | Oklahoma | 1 |
| Skinhead gang murdered an Hispanic man | 12/4/2007 | Yucaipa | California | 1 |
| Middle school skinhead student shot and killed gay peer | 2/12/2008 | Oxnard | California | 1 |
| White supremacist teens beat a Hispanic man to death | 7/12/2008 | Shenandoah | Pennsylvania | 1 |
| Anti-government violent extremist killed 2 at Tennessee Valley Unitarian Universalist Church | 7/27/2008 | Knoxville | Tennessee | 2 |
| White man obsessed with Nazism murdered an African American man and a Hispanic man | 8/1/2008 | Bristol | Pennsylvania | 2 |
| White supremacist teens murdered an Ecuadorian immigrant | 11/8/2008 | Patchogue | New York | 1 |
| Two anti-government violent extremists planted a bomb inside a bank, killing 2 | 12/12/2008 | Woodburn | Oregon | 2 |
| Far rightist murdered a homeless man | 1/19/2009 | Woodstock | Illinois | 1 |
| White supremacist killed 2 immigrants | 1/21/2009 | Brockton | Massachusetts | 1 |
| Same perpetrator as previous case in Brockton, MA killed a homeless man later the same day | 1/21/2009 | Brockton | Massachusetts | 1 |
| Neo-Nazi murdered Wesleyan University Jewish student | 5/6/2009 | Middleton | Connecticut | 1 |

| Summary of ECDB Incident Description | Date | City | State | Number of Victim Deaths |
|---|---|---|---|---|
| White supremacists murdered 2 immigrants in home invasion | 5/30/2009 | Arivaca | Arizona | 2 |
| Anti-government Sovereign Citizen murdered abortion provider Dr. George Tiller | 5/31/2009 | Wichita | Kansas | 1 |
| White supremacist killed Holocaust museum guard | 6/10/2009 | Washington | District of Colombia | 1 |
| White supremacist and associate killed a child molester | 6/30/2009 | Carmichael | California | 1 |
| White supremacist murdered his stepfather to gain "street cred" | 7/28/2009 | Paradise | California | 1 |
| White supremacist murdered a convicted sex offender | 8/28/2009 | N. Palm Springs | California | 1 |
| Two white supremacist skinheads shoot at interracial couple and killed female | 10/3/2009 | Phoenix | Arizona | 1 |
| Anti-government violent extremist flew a small plane into an Austin, TX office building with U.S. Internal Revenue Service (IRS) office in it to protest the IRS and the government | 2/18/2010 | Austin | Texas | 1 |
| Neo-Nazi killed an African American man | 3/29/2010 | South Huntington | Pennsylvania | 1 |
| White supremacist shot and wounded 4 women then killed a man | 4/20/2010 | Wichita Falls | Texas | 1 |
| Two Sovereign Citizen members killed two police officers | 5/21/2010 | West Memphis | Arkansas | 2 |
| Prison gang white supremacists murdered another inmate for not objecting to having an African American cellmate | 3/1/2011 | Atlanta | Georgia | 1 |

| Summary of ECDB Incident Description | Date | City | State | Number of Victim Deaths |
|---|---|---|---|---|
| White supremacist teenagers run over and kill an African American man in a motel parking lot | 6/26/2011 | Jackson | Mississippi | 1 |
| Two white supremacists murdered a 53-year old African American man | 10/4/2011 | Eureka | California | 1 |
| Same perpetrators as previous case in Eureka, CA; perpetrators killed a teenager they thought was Jewish | 10/7/2011 | Corvallis | Oregon | 1 |
| Neo-Nazi killed 6 at a Sikh temple in Wisconsin | 8/5/2012 | Oak Creek | Wisconsin | 6 |
| Two neo-Nazis and a third associate murdered a local drug-dealer | 1/9/2013 | Verona | Kentucky | 1 |
| Anti-government "survivalist" boarded a school bus with a gun and demanded a student be given to him; he then shot and killed the bus driver | 1/29/2013 | Midland City | Alabama | 1 |
| Two white supremacists killed a husband and wife because the husband was a sex offender | 7/21/2013 | Jonesville | South Carolina | 2 |
| Anti-government extremist kills Transportation Security Administration officer at Los Angeles International Airport | 11/1/2013 | Los Angeles | California | 1 |
| White supremacist shot and killed 2 at a Jewish Community Center | 4/13/2014 | Overland Park | Kansas | 2 |
| Same perpetrator as previous attack in Overland Park; perpetrator murdered another person at a Jewish retirement center later the same day | 4/13/2014 | Leawood | Kansas | 1 |

| Summary of ECDB Incident Description | Date | City | State | Number of Victim Deaths |
|---|---|---|---|---|
| Anti-government married couple killed 2 officers during shooting rampage on Las Vegas strip | 6/8/2014 | Las Vegas | Nevada | 2 |
| Same perpetrators as previous attack in Las Vegas; perpetrators murdered another person later the same day | 6/8/2014 | Las Vegas | Nevada | 1 |
| Anti-government extremist Eric Frein murdered a state trooper. | 9/12/2014 | White Haven | Pennsylvania | 1 |
| White supremacist Dylann Roof shot and killed 9 African Americans in a shooting at an African American church in Charleston, SC | 6/17/2015 | Charleston | South Carolina | 9 |
| Right-wing extremist opened fire and killed 2 young women among patrons during an Amy Schumer movie | 7/23/2015 | Lafayette | Louisiana | 2 |
| White supremacist shot and killed 9 at his community college | 10/1/2015 | Roseburg | Oregon | 9 |
| Anti-government survivalist extremist killed 3 at Planned Parenthood clinic including a responding police officer | 11/27/2015 | Colorado Springs | Colorado | 3 |
| **Number of incidents: 62** | | | | **Total victims: 106** |

Source: U.S. Extremist Crime Database (ECDB) maintained by START at the University of Maryland. | GAO-17-300.

Note: Attacks committed by the same perpetrators on the same day and in proximate locations and time were counted as one attack.

**Table 2: Radical Islamist Violent Extremist-Motivated Attacks that Resulted in Fatalities, September 12, 2001 through December 31, 2016, as reported in the U.S. Extremist Crime Database (ECDB)**

| Summary of ECDB Incident Description | Date | City | State | Number of Victim Deaths |
|---|---|---|---|---|
| Washington, D.C. Beltway sniper attack prior to D.C. attacks; shot and killed 1 person in state of Washington | 2/16/2002 | Tacoma | Washington | 1 |
| Washington, D.C. Beltway sniper attack prior to D.C. attacks; shot and killed 1 person in Arizona | 3/19/2002 | Tucson | Arizona | 1 |
| Radical Islamist violent extremist killed 2 at Los Angeles International Airport El Al ticket counter | 7/4/2002 | Los Angeles | California | 2 |
| Washington, D.C. Beltway sniper attack prior to D.C. attacks; shot and killed 1 person in Atlanta, GA | 9/21/2002 | Atlanta | Georgia | 1 |
| Washington, D.C. Beltway sniper attack prior to D.C. attacks; shot and killed 1 person in Montgomery, AL, 19 hours after attack in Atlanta, GA | 9/21/2002 | Montgomery | Alabama | 1 |
| Washington, D.C. Beltway sniper attack prior to D.C. attacks; shot and killed 1 person in Baton Rouge, LA | 9/23/2002 | Baton Rouge | Louisiana | 1 |
| Washington, D.C. Beltway sniper attack | 10/2/2002 | Wheaton | Maryland | 1 |
| Washington, D.C. Beltway sniper attack | 10/3/2002 | Rockville | Maryland | 1 |
| Washington, D.C. Beltway sniper attack | 10/3/2002 | Aspen Hill | Maryland | 1 |
| Washington, D.C. Beltway sniper attack | 10/3/2002 | Silver Spring | Maryland | 1 |
| Washington, D.C. Beltway sniper attack | 10/3/2002 | Kensington | Maryland | 1 |
| Washington, D.C. Beltway sniper attack | 10/3/2002 | Washington | District of Columbia | 1 |

| Summary of ECDB Incident Description | Date | City | State | Number of Victim Deaths |
|---|---|---|---|---|
| Washington, D.C. Beltway sniper attack | 10/9/2002 | Manassas | Virginia | 1 |
| Washington, D.C. Beltway sniper attack | 10/11/2002 | Spotsylvania County | Virginia | 1 |
| Washington, D.C. Beltway sniper attack | 10/14/2002 | Fairfax County | Virginia | 1 |
| Washington, D.C. Beltway sniper attack | 10/22/2002 | Aspen Hill | Maryland | 1 |
| Perpetrator kills 1 at the Jewish Federation of Greater Seattle | 7/28/2006 | Seattle | Washington | 1 |
| Perpetrator kills 1 and injures 18 in hit-and-run driving spree in San Francisco and Fremont, CA | 8/29/2006 | Fremont | California | 1 |
| Salt Lake City, UT Trolley Square Shooting | 2/12/2007 | Salt Lake City | Utah | 5 |
| Perpetrator killed one army solider outside of a military recruiting center in Little Rock, AR | 6/1/2009 | Little Rock | Arkansas | 1 |
| Nidal Malik Hasan kills 12 soldiers and 1 civilian at Fort Hood, TX | 11/5/2009 | Fort Hood | Texas | 13 |
| Boston bomber Tamerlan Tsarnaev helped murder 3 persons four years before Boston bombing | 9/11/2011 | Waltham | Massachusetts | 3 |
| Reshad Riddle, a convert to Islam, murdered his father | 3/24/2013 | Ashtabula | Ohio | 1 |
| Boston bomber brothers Tamerlan Tsarnaev and Dzhokhar Tsarnaev planted two bombs at the Boston Marathon, killing 3 | 4/15/2013 | Boston | Massachusetts | 3 |
| Tsarnaev brothers shot and killed a Massachusetts Institute of Technology security officer | 4/18/2013 | Cambridge | Massachusetts | 1 |

| Summary of ECDB Incident Description | Date | City | State | Number of Victim Deaths |
|---|---|---|---|---|
| Incident 1 in a series of related murders: perpetrator shot and killed a man in a drive by shooting | 4/27/2014 | Seattle | Washington | 1 |
| Incident 2 in a series of related murders: perpetrator shot and killed 2 men in Seattle leaving a gay club | 6/1/2014 | Seattle | Washington | 2 |
| Incident 3 in a series of related murders: perpetrator shot and killed a man in a drive by shooting and killed a college student | 6/25/2014 | West Orange | New Jersey | 1 |
| Justin Nojan Sullivan, a convert to Islam, murdered his neighbor | 12/18/2014 | Morganton | North Carolina | 1 |
| Perpetrator opened fire on two military installations in Chattanooga, TN, killing 5 | 7/16/2015 | Chattanooga | Tennessee | 5 |
| San Bernardino, CA shooting spree: Syed Farook and Tashfeen Malik shoot up office party, killing 14 and injuring 22 | 12/2/2015 | San Bernardino | California | 14 |
| Orlando Night Club shooting. Omar Mateen killed 49 | 6/12/2016 | Orlando | Florida | 49 |
| **Number of Incidents: 23** | | | | **Total Victims: 119** |

Source: U.S. Extremist Crime Database (ECDB) maintained by START at the University of Maryland. | GAO-17-300

Note: All 10 attacks by the Washington, D.C. beltway sniper that occurred in the Washington, D.C. region are counted as 1 incident. All 5 attacks by the Washington, D.C. beltway sniper that occurred in the months before the Washington, D.C. attacks are counted as individual attacks.

## Appendix III
## Implementation of Tasks in the 2011 Strategic Implementation Plan

In August 2011, the White House issued the *National Strategy for Empowering Local Partners to Prevent Violent Extremism in the United States* followed by *The National Strategy for Empowering Local Partners to Prevent Violent Extremism in the United States, Strategic Implementation Plan* (SIP) in December 2011. The SIP designated the Department of Homeland Security (DHS), the Department of Justice (DOJ), the Federal Bureau of Investigation (FBI), and the National Counterterrorism Center (NCTC) as leads or partners for the 44 domestically-focused tasks identified in the 2011 SIP.[1] From December 2011 through December 2016, federal agencies implemented 19 tasks, had 23 tasks in progress, and had not yet taken action on 2 tasks. The tasks fall under three categories: community outreach, research and training, and capacity building.

The SIP identified 18 community outreach tasks to be implemented by federal agencies. Community outreach aims to enhance federal engagement and support to local communities that may be targeted by violent extremism. For example, community outreach might include expanding relationships with local business and communities to identify or prevent violent extremism or integrating CVE activities into community-oriented policing efforts.

### Table 3: Assessment of Community Outreach Tasks in the 2011 Strategic Implementation Plan (SIP) as of December 2016

| | |
|---|---|
| ✔ | Implemented |
| ⊃ | In Progress |
| ✖ | Not yet addressed |
| - | Not a lead agency |

| Tasks in SIP | | Lead Agency | Task | DHS | DOJ | FBI | NCTC | Status Summary |
|---|---|---|---|---|---|---|---|---|
| 1 | The Department of Justice (DOJ) will incorporate more U.S. Attorney's Offices as engagement leads in the field building on the initial U.S. Attorney-led effort. | DOJ | ✔ | - | ✔ | - | - | DOJ officials stated that they increased the number of U.S. Attorney's Offices as engagement leads within their districts and their activities with respect to violent extremism. |

[1] For the 44 tasks identified in the SIP, DHS, DOJ, FBI and NCTC provided information on the status of actions taken on the tasks for which they were the lead agencies. Some tasks listed multiple agencies as co-leads responsible for implementation. Some agency responses showed their actions substantially addressed the task, while others only took some action for the same task. DHS, DOJ, and FBI provided technical comments on our assessment which we incorporated as appropriate and officials from NCTC met with us to discuss the information it provided.

| Tasks in SIP | | Lead Agency | Task | DHS | DOJ | FBI | NCTC | Status Summary |
|---|---|---|---|---|---|---|---|---|
| 2 | The National Task Force will (1) disseminate regular reports on best practices in community engagement to local government officials, law enforcement, U.S. Attorneys, and fusion centers; (2) work with departments and agencies to increase support to U.S. Attorney-led engagement efforts in the field; and (3) closely coordinate federal engagement efforts with communities targeted by violent extremism radicalization. | **DOJ & DHS** | ➲ | ➲ | ✔ | - | - | While the National Task Force, led by the Department of Homeland Security (DHS) and DOJ, dissolved in 2013, agencies demonstrated that they worked with other federal partners to increase their support of U.S. Attorney-led engagement efforts and coordinated federal efforts with communities targeted by violent extremism as described in the task. The National Engagement Task Force drafted best practices for community engagement which was not disseminated. |
| 3 | In consultation with federal and local partners, the National Task Force and U.S. Attorney's Offices will facilitate, where appropriate, the inclusion of communities that may be targeted by violent extremist radicalization into broader engagement forums and programs that involve other communities. | **DOJ & DHS** | ➲ | ➲ | ✔ | - | - | DHS stated without continued inter-agency support the National Task Force dissolved in 2013; however, individual agencies have continued their inclusion of communities that may be targeted by violent extremist radicalization efforts. For example, the DHS Civil Rights Civil Liberties Office expanded its engagement to other communities before the National Task Force dissolved. DOJ increased outreach and inclusion |

| | Tasks in SIP | Lead Agency | Task | DHS | DOJ | FBI | NCTC | Status Summary |
|---|---|---|---|---|---|---|---|---|
| | | | | | | | | efforts by U.S. Attorney's Offices participation in cross-cultural events such as hosting an Interfaith Community Group and a Hate Crimes Outreach Summit, as well as a cooperative agreement with the World Organization for Resource Development and Education in Montgomery County Maryland. |
| 4 | U.S. Attorneys will coordinate closely with local government officials, law enforcement, communities, and civil society to enhance outreach events and initiatives. | **DOJ** | ✔ | - | ✔ | - | - | Through their participation in developing Countering Violent Extremism (CVE) frameworks in three pilot cities, DOJ coordinated with federal, state, local, and community partners to enhance outreach events and initiatives. |
| 5 | In fiscal year (FY) 2012, DHS Office for Civil Rights and Civil Liberties (CRCL) CRCL plans on expanding its quarterly community engagement roundtables to a total of 16. CRCL is also in the process of implementing a campus youth community engagement plan, through which it will engage with young adults on the topic of violent extremism. | **DHS** | ✔ | ✔ | - | - | - | DHS's CRCL, expanded youth specific engagement programs and implemented Syrian and Somali American engagement plans. |

| Tasks in SIP | | Lead Agency | Task | DHS | DOJ | FBI | NCTC | Status Summary |
|---|---|---|---|---|---|---|---|---|
| 6 | Depending on local circumstances, and in consultation with the Federal Bureau of Investigation (FBI) and other agencies as appropriate, U.S. Attorneys will coordinate any expanded engagement specific to CVE with communities that may be targeted by violent extremist radicalization. | DOJ | ✔ | - | ✔ | - | - | U.S. Attorneys coordinated expanded CVE activities to communities that may be targeted by violent extremism. These efforts include hosting or coordinating events such as a town hall meeting with Muslim and Arab leaders, and hosting a roundtable with the Somali community. |
| 7 | A FBI CVE Coordination Office will be established and, as part of its activities, will coordinate with the National Task Force on CVE-specific education and awareness modules. These modules will be developed and implemented, in part, by leveraging some of the FBI's existing programs and initiatives. | FBI | ⊃ | - | - | ⊃ | - | The FBI established and staffed the CVE office in 2012 and assigned the office to the Counterterrorism Division in 2013. FBI CVE products were jointly prepared with the National Task Force partner agencies or distributed for their comment. |
| 8 | DHS will oversee an online portal to support engagement by government officials and law enforcement with communities targeted by violent extremist radicalization, which will be used to share relevant information and build a community of interest. The portal will be accessible to | DHS | ✔ | ✔ | - | - | - | DHS launched a web portal in 2012 that has almost 4,900 users as of March 2016 and that is accessible to government and law enforcement officials involved in overseas and domestic CVE and community engagement efforts. |

| Tasks in SIP | | Lead Agency | Task | DHS | DOJ | FBI | NCTC | Status Summary |
|---|---|---|---|---|---|---|---|---|
| | government officials and law enforcement involved in overseas and domestic CVE and community engagement efforts to share best practices. | | | | | | | |
| 9 | DOJ will expand the efforts of the Building Communities of Trust (BCOT) initiative to help facilitate trust between law enforcement and community leaders. This dialogue could include local issues, as well as CVE. | **DOJ** | ✔ | - | ✖ | - | - | DOJ deferred responsibility of this task to DHS. DHS expanded the BCOT initiative through 21 separate events nationwide from December 2011 through February 2016. |
| 10 | The United States Government will build a digital engagement capacity in order to expand, deepen, and intensify our engagement efforts. Where possible, virtual engagement will build on real world engagement activities and programs. | **DHS** | ⊃ | ⊃ | - | - | - | DHS is continuing to build relationships with the high-tech and social media industry including recent meetings with senior administration officials and support of a government sponsored university competition designed to counter violent extremist narratives, but recognized this as an area that needs attention. |
| 11 | The federal government will help broker agreements on partnerships to counter violent extremism between communities and | **DHS** | ⊃ | ⊃ | - | - | - | DHS collaborated with local stakeholders in three cities to develop frameworks that aim to address issues facing their |

| Tasks in SIP | | Lead Agency | Task | DHS | DOJ | FBI | NCTC | Status Summary |
|---|---|---|---|---|---|---|---|---|
| | local government and law enforcement to help institutionalize this locally focused approach. | | | | | | | communities. While not leads for this activity, DOJ, FBI, and the National Counterterrorism Center (NCTC) helped partnerships through their participation in the three city pilot program. |
| **12** | DHS and DOJ will work to increase support for local, community-led programs and initiatives to counter violent extremism, predominantly by identifying opportunities within existing appropriations for incorporating CVE as an eligible area of work for public safety, violence prevention, and community resilience grants. | **DHS & DOJ** | ✔ | ✔ | ✔ | - | - | DHS updated its grant language to include CVE activities and has awarded training grants in FY13, FY14, and FY15. U.S. Attorney's Offices have researched ways to increase funding for CVE including funding for community summits and events, youth programs, research partners, and written materials or brochures.<br><br>Additionally, DOJ has partnered with the Virginia Center for Policing Innovation to develop and deliver a national training program providing law enforcement officers with the knowledge and skills necessary to effectively integrate community policing into their homeland security efforts. |

| | Tasks in SIP | Lead Agency | Task | DHS | DOJ | FBI | NCTC | Status Summary |
|---|---|---|---|---|---|---|---|---|
| 13 | DHS is working to increase funding available to integrate CVE into existing community-oriented policing efforts through FY12 grants. | **DHS** | ✔ | ✔ | - | - | - | DHS expanded its grant language to support law enforcement CVE efforts under Urban Area Security Initiative grants. |
| 14 | DHS is establishing a Homeland Security Advisory Committee Faith-Based Community Information Sharing Working Group to determine how the Department can: (1) better share information with faith communities; and (2) support the development of faith-based community information sharing networks. | **DHS** | ⊃ | ⊃ | - | - | - | DHS established a faith-based advisory committee in 2012, and is working with agencies within the department to determine new tasks. |
| 15 | DHS is developing its Hometown Security webpage to include resources such as training guidance, workshop reports, and information on CVE for both the general public and law enforcement. | **DHS** | ⊃ | ⊃ | - | - | - | DHS created a webpage with information on training guidance, pilot city information and other relevant CVE information, however, this content is not housed on the Hometown Security Webpage as stated in the SIP. |
| 16 | The Treasury will expand its community outreach regarding terrorism financing issues. | **Treasury** | N/A | - | - | - | - | |

| Tasks in SIP | | Lead Agency | Task | DHS | DOJ | FBI | NCTC | Status Summary |
|---|---|---|---|---|---|---|---|---|
| 17 | Depending on local circumstances and in consultation with the FBI, U.S. Attorneys will coordinate, as appropriate, any efforts to expand connections and partnerships at the local level for CVE, supported by the National Task Force where needed. | DOJ | ➲ | - | ➲ | - | - | DOJ expanded partnerships with local stakeholders for CVE by expanding local U.S. Attorney's Office participation in the three city pilot program. |
| 18 | Departments and agencies will expand engagement with the business community by educating companies about the threat of violent extremism and by connecting them to community civic activists focused on developing CVE programs and initiatives. | DHS | ➲ | ➲ | - | - | - | DHS highlighted one successful partnership between YouTube and the City of Los Angeles, CA. They also stated efforts are ongoing to include the high-tech sector and philanthropic community. |

Source: GAO analysis of information provided by the Department of Homeland Security, the Department of Justice, the Federal Bureau of Investigation, and the National Counterterrorism Center. | GAO-17-300.

The SIP identified 20 research and training tasks to be implemented by federal agencies. Research and training relates to understanding the threat of violent extremism, sharing information, and leveraging it to train government and law enforcement officials. We analyzed implementation of 19 research and training tasks in the SIP to determine the extent they had been implemented by the responsible agency(s).

**Table 4: Assessment of Research and Training Tasks in the 2011 Strategic Implementation Plan (SIP) as of December 2016**

| | |
|---|---|
| ✔ | Implemented |
| ➲ | In Progress |
| ✖ | Not yet addressed |
| - | Not a lead agency |

| Tasks in SIP | | Lead Agency | Task | DHS | DOJ | FBI | NCTC | Status Summary |
|---|---|---|---|---|---|---|---|---|
| 1 | Expand analysis in five priority areas<br>1. The role of the Internet in radicalization to violence and how virtual space can be leveraged to counter violent extremism.<br>2. Single-actor terrorism (so called "lone wolves"), including lessons learned from similar phenomena such as a school shooters.<br>3. Disengagement from terrorism and violent extremism.<br>4. Non-al-Qa'ida related radicalization to violence and anticipated future violent extremist threats.<br>5. Preoperational indicators and analysis of known case studies of extremist violence in the United States. | **DHS, FBI, NCTC, State** | ⊃ | ⊃ | - | ⊃ | ✔ | The Department of Homeland Security (DHS) expanded analysis in most areas; and has a program in progress to address the role of the Internet in radicalization to violence and how virtual space can be leveraged to counter violent extremism. The Federal Bureau of Investigation (FBI) expanded analysis in some areas of this task, including the creation of behavioral indicator cards, which depict mobilization and disengagement however there is no information on how the FBI expanded analysis on single-actor terrorism. The National Counterterrorism Center (NCTC) expanded their analysis in all areas. While not a lead for this task, the Department of Justice (DOJ) supported these efforts through research funded by the National Institute of Justice. While the Department of State (State) was also a lead for this activity, we did not request a response from the department because it is outside the scope of this review. |

| Tasks in SIP | | Lead Agency | Task | DHS | DOJ | FBI | NCTC | Status Summary |
|---|---|---|---|---|---|---|---|---|
| 2 | Continue DHS Science & Technology Directorate's (S&T) support for research on countering the threat of extremist violence. | DHS | ✔ | ✔ | - | - | - | DHS has a research program on Countering Violent Extremism (CVE) related topics and has released numerous reports on violent extremist root causes, and funded an open source databases on terrorism. For example DHS S&T funded the U.S. Extremist Crime Database (ECDB) which tracks extremist activity in the U.S. and released a report in 2012 regarding the hot spots of terrorism and other crimes. |
| 3 | Continue DHS collaboration with the FBI, the Bureau of Prisons, and NCTC to: (1) improve awareness of the risk of violent extremism in correctional systems; (2) enhance screening of new inmates to detect individuals associated with violent extremist organizations; (3) improve detection of recruitment efforts within the correctional environment; and (4) increase information sharing, as appropriate, with federal, state, and local law enforcement about inmates who may have adopted violent extremist beliefs and are being released. | DHS | ✖ | ✖ | - | - | - | DHS piloted a course related to violent extremism in prisons with the Orange County Sheriff's Office; however no additional information was identified to determine if specific elements of this task were met. DHS recognized this task as an area that needs attention. |

| Tasks in SIP | | Lead Agency | Task | DHS | DOJ | FBI | NCTC | Status Summary |
|---|---|---|---|---|---|---|---|---|
| 4 | Complete the creation of the FBI CVE Coordination Office to help assess and leverage existing Bureau efforts to better understand and counter violent extremism. | **FBI** | ✔ | - | - | ✔ | - | The FBI established and staffed the CVE Office in 2012 and assigned the office to the Counterterrorism Division in 2013. In 2015 the FBI realigned the CVE Office and changed from an office to a Section which now resides directly under the Deputy Director to have a broader cross-programmatic impact within the FBI. |
| 5 | Build lines of research specifically to support non-security federal partners. | **DHS/ NCTC** | ⊃ | ⊃ | - | - | ✔ | DHS completed one report and one additional report is in progress. However, DHS did not provide information on how these efforts are supporting non-security partners as stated in the SIP. NCTC supports non-federal security partners by publishing CVE related material in a variety of formats including a magazine and weekly unclassified document that gets sent to non-federal security partners. While not a lead for this task, DOJ supported these efforts by research funded by the National Institute of Justice. |

| Tasks in SIP | | Lead Agency | Task | DHS | DOJ | FBI | NCTC | Status Summary |
|---|---|---|---|---|---|---|---|---|
| 6 | Development of an analytic team focused on supporting local government and law enforcement CVE practitioners and increased production of analysis at appropriate classification levels. | **DHS** | ✔ | ✔ | - | - | - | DHS assembled a team and participates in multiple inter-agency efforts to share relevant CVE information. Additionally a team within DHS produces CVE information at all classification levels and provides briefings to non-traditional CVE stakeholders, state and local law enforcement, and DHS senior leadership. |
| 7 | Development of practitioner-friendly summaries of current research and literature reviews about the motivations and behaviors associated with single-actor terrorism and disengagement from violent extremism. | **DHS** | ✔ | ✔ | - | - | - | DHS S&T developed over 70 CVE projects including those related to single-actor terrorism. |
| 8 | Review of information-sharing protocols to identify ways of increasing dissemination of products to state, local, and tribal authorities. | **DHS, DOJ, FBI, NCTC** | ⊃ | ⊃ | ⊃ | ✔ | ✔ | DHS reviewed its information sharing protocols and shares products and other reports with fusion centers and local officials. DOJ participated in a review of the State and Local Anti-Terrorism Training (SLATT) Program and the effectiveness of the SLATT website. While the SLATT website is an important mechanism to disseminate |

| Tasks in SIP | | Lead Agency | Task | DHS | DOJ | FBI | NCTC | Status Summary |
|---|---|---|---|---|---|---|---|---|
| | | | | | | | | information, a review of the program found that a review of the website would be important to determine outreach and usage. The FBI reviewed information sharing practices and moved its CVE office to an office within the FBI whose primary mission is to improve the quality and timeliness of information to state, local, tribal, and territorial law enforcement. An office in NCTC focuses solely on dissemination of products at lower classification levels and produces a weekly article with relevant CVE information. |
| 9 | Expansion of briefings and information sharing about violent extremism with state and local law enforcement and government. | **DHS/ FBI, NCTC** | ⊃ | ⊃ | - | ✔ | ✔ | DHS reported their efforts as "in progress" and have increased the number of unclassified products. Additionally they have coordinated and facilitated national-level communication and outreach efforts with state, local, tribal, and territorial partners. The FBI hosted local and federal officials to learn about CVE policy and hosted a CVE conference. They also briefed |

| | Tasks in SIP | Lead Agency | Task | DHS | DOJ | FBI | NCTC | Status Summary |
|---|---|---|---|---|---|---|---|---|
| | | | | | | | | more than a dozen police departments and numerous police organizations including the Major County Sheriff's Association, Major City Chiefs Association, and the International Association of Chiefs of Police among others. NCTC participated in awareness briefings with government officials as well as educators and community members. |
| 10 | Departments and agencies are taking steps to identify training materials that may not meet internal standards and to improve processes for creating and reviewing such materials. Some departments are consulting with outside experts with established reputations to evaluate the content and training review process. Guidance on CVE-related training is being developed and will be issued, both across the organizations and to field components. Some departments may issue this as part of broader training guidance. | ALL | ✔ | ✔ | ✔ | ✔ | ✔ | Agencies took steps to develop and review guidance on CVE training. DHS completed an internal review and issued CVE training guidance in 2011. Additionally DHS hired two contractors to solicit feedback from internal and external stakeholders and to gather and create an hour training session. DOJ senior leadership sent information to U.S. Attorneys containing five overarching principles to guide DOJ's training efforts and to ensure that the communities DOJ serves are respected. The FBI reached out to prominent academics, researchers and others to solicit |

| Tasks in SIP | | Lead Agency | Task | DHS | DOJ | FBI | NCTC | Status Summary |
|---|---|---|---|---|---|---|---|---|
| | | | | | | | | feedback on FBI goals and strategies. NCTC co-led an inter-agency working group on training which reviewed all CVE related training throughout the government. |
| 11 | DHS, via the Federal Law Enforcement Training Center, (FLETC) is in the process of developing a CVE curriculum to be integrated into existing training programs for federal law enforcement. The curriculum will give federal law enforcement a better understanding of CVE and how to more effectively leverage existing local partnerships. | DHS | ✔ | ✔ | - | - | - | DHS reported that FLETC integrated CVE content into their counter terrorism training |
| 12 | DHS is in the process of establishing an internal committee to review all directly funded and issued DHS training on cultural competency, engagement, CVE, and counterterrorism. The committee will be responsible for reviewing any new content, evaluating experts, and establishing quality control. The Federal Emergency Management Agency (FEMA) | DHS | ✔ | ✔ | - | - | - | DHS completed an internal review and issued CVE training development guidance in 2011. A sub-Interagency Policy Committee on CVE training was established. Members of the group coordinated, among other things, training guidance, events, and grants to ensure inter-agency cohesion and quality control. |

| | Tasks in SIP | Lead Agency | Task | DHS | DOJ | FBI | NCTC | Status Summary |
|---|---|---|---|---|---|---|---|---|
| | will incorporate the recently released Informational Bulletin and training guidance into FY12 grant guidance and will also leverage existing mechanisms to hold grantees and sub-grantees accountable. | | | | | | | |
| 13 | DHS, in partnership with the Los Angeles Police Department and the National Consortium for Advanced Policing, is developing a CVE curriculum that includes a 16-hour continuing education module for executive and frontline officers, as well as a 30-minute module that will be introduced at police academies. Both will be certified by the Police Officers Standards and Training Council. In October 2011 the Major Cities Chiefs Association passed a motion to adopt and implement the DHS CVE curriculum, which will be piloted with state and local law enforcement in San Diego by the end of 2011. By 2013, DHS seeks to: (1) implement the curriculum across the country on a regional basis; (2) develop a national | **DHS** | ⊃ | ⊃ | - | - | - | DHS launched a CVE pilot program that aimed to develop CVE curriculum for local stakeholders in 2012 and shared curriculum via a DHS-FBI web portal. The program was not implemented across the country and a national network of trainers was not established. |

| Tasks in SIP | | Lead Agency | Task | DHS | DOJ | FBI | NCTC | Status Summary |
|---|---|---|---|---|---|---|---|---|
| | network of trainers and subject matter experts who can administer the training and keep it current; and (3) build an online component for the curriculum. | | | | | | | |
| 14 | DHS, via FLETC, will update current federal training programs to integrate the CVE curriculum for federal law enforcement in the coming year. | DHS | ✔ | ✔ | - | - | - | DHS updated its counter-terrorism training to include CVE specific modules. |
| 15 | DHS is working with European law enforcement partners to share best practices and case studies to improve training, community policing, and operational information sharing. | DHS | ⊃ | ⊃ | - | - | - | DHS states this task is ongoing and been reprioritized under the SIP. Additionally DHS developed joint products with international law-enforcement and collaborated with bilateral and multilateral efforts such as in the Global Counterterrorism Forum and eight international summits. Participation and findings were reported regularly to the DHS CVE Working group; however, DHS did not provide information on how these efforts improve training, community policing, and operational information sharing as stated in the SIP. |

| Tasks in SIP | | Lead Agency | Task | DHS | DOJ | FBI | NCTC | Status Summary |
|---|---|---|---|---|---|---|---|---|
| 16 | DHS Civil Rights and Civil Liberties is expanding and institutionalizing its CVE and cultural competence training curricula to further enhance the material and its effectiveness. | DHS | ✔ | ✔ | - | - | - | DHS expanded training efforts utilizing tools such as the Community Awareness Briefings (CAB) and Community Resilience Exercises (CREX) which are tools designed to help communities build awareness and understanding of violent extremism and to catalyze community efforts to respond to them. |
| 17 | The Interagency Working Group on Training will facilitate a "train the trainer program" to increase the reach of CVE training. | DHS, NCTC | ⊃ | ⊃ | - | - | ✔ | As of February 2016, DHS has been working to develop train-the-trainers curricula to enable law enforcement partners to deliver Community Awareness Briefings to law enforcement audiences. DHS acknowledged this task was in progress. NCTC co-led the train-the trainer program. |
| 18 | The Interagency Working Group on Training will facilitate the development of an online training program that provides professional development credit for a broad range of professions, particularly those involved with public safety, violence prevention, and resilience. This will help build a basic understanding of CVE among a broad cross-section | DHS, NCTC | ⊃ | ✖ | - | - | ✔ | DHS has several online CVE training efforts under development as a result of the Interagency Working Group including a web-based awareness level training for state, local and tribal territory law enforcement line officers, supervisors, and training academy directors. These efforts are currently under development and outside the scope of our review. |

| Tasks in SIP | | Lead Agency | Task | DHS | DOJ | FBI | NCTC | Status Summary |
|---|---|---|---|---|---|---|---|---|
| | of stakeholders who have related mandates. | | | | | | | NCTC participated in the creation and review of this online training that occurred under the auspices of the interagency Working Group on Training, before the establishment of the Task Force. |
| **19** | The Interagency Working Group on Training will collaborate with non-security partners, such as the Department of Education, to build CVE training modules that can be incorporated, as appropriate, into existing programs related to public safety, violence prevention, and resilience. These modules will be crafted in a way that is relevant to the specific audiences and their missions. Only trainers who have undergone CVE-specific training will deliver training programs that include CVE modules. | **DHS** | ⊃ | ⊃ | - | - | - | DHS recognized this task as needing attention and that while initial steps were made in the 3-pilot cities the interagency effort needs to better define roles and opportunities for future collaborations. No additional action to address this activity was identified. |
| **20** | The Department of Defense's (DOD) training programs and curricula will be informed by the work of the Interagency Working Group on Training, as appropriate. Additionally, DOD is conducting a | **DOD** | N/A | - | - | - | - | |

| Tasks in SIP | | Lead Agency | Task | DHS | DOJ | FBI | NCTC | Status Summary |
|---|---|---|---|---|---|---|---|---|
| | review of CVE-related curricula and will make revisions and adjustments as necessary. | | | | | | | |

Source: GAO analysis of information provided by the Department of Homeland Security, the Department of Justice, the Federal Bureau of Investigation, and the National Counterterrorism Center. | GAO-17-300.

The SIP identified 9 capacity building tasks to be implemented by federal agencies. Capacity building might include outreach to former violent extremists to counter violent narratives. We analyzed the implementation of 8 capacity building tasks in the SIP to determine the extent to which they had been implemented by the responsible agency(s).

### Table 5: Assessment of Capacity Building Tasks in the 2011 Strategic Implementation Plan (SIP) as of December 2016

| | |
|---|---|
| ✔ | Implemented |
| ➲ | In Progress |
| ✖ | Not yet addressed |
| - | Not a lead agency |

| Tasks in SIP | | Lead Agency | Task | DHS | DOJ | FBI | NCTC | Status Summary |
|---|---|---|---|---|---|---|---|---|
| 1 | Expanding efforts to raise community awareness about the threat of radicalization to violence, building from the experience of the Community Awareness Briefing (CAB), and adapting those materials for different audiences where appropriate. | **DHS DOJ, FBI, NCTC** | ✔ | ✔ | ✔ | ✔ | ✔ | The Department of Homeland Security (DHS) updated the CAB and adapted the briefings to different audiences. Department of Justice (DOJ) officials stated that the U.S. Attorneys have hosted several briefings and two U.S. Attorneys have developed their own community awareness briefings over |

| Tasks in SIP | | Lead Agency | Task | DHS | DOJ | FBI | NCTC | Status Summary |
|---|---|---|---|---|---|---|---|---|
| | | | | | | | | 2 years. The Federal Bureau of Investigation (FBI) met with more than 100 non-federal groups and briefed them on their proposed critical thinking tools and educational resources. The FBI incorporated feedback and launched Countering Violent Extremism (CVE) awareness tools for public use tailored to focus on foreign fighter recruitment and use of social media. The National Counterterrorism Center (NCTC) stated the CAB has been tailored to focus on foreign fighter recruitment and use of social media. |
| 2 | Learning from former violent extremists, specifically those who can speak credibly to counter violent narratives, provide insights to government, and potentially catalyze activities to directly challenge violent extremist narratives. | DHS | ✖ | ✖ | - | - | - | DHS stated this task needed attention and that DOJ is now responsible for the task. DOJ did not provide a response to this task at the time of our review. In March 2017, DOJ noted that it has worked with cooperating defendants, including those |

| Tasks in SIP | | Lead Agency | Task | DHS | DOJ | FBI | NCTC | Status Summary |
|---|---|---|---|---|---|---|---|---|
| | | | | | | | | who have traveled to or attempted to travel to join ISIS, in order to learn from their experiences and is exploring whether there may be appropriate opportunities for these individuals to speak publicly, as well as circumstances in which such defendants may offer their assistance toward CVE efforts. |
| 3 | Providing grants to counter violent extremist narratives and ideologies, within authorities and relevant legal parameters, by reprioritizing or increasing the flexibility of existing funding. | DHS | ↄ | ↄ | - | - | - | DHS recognized this task needed attention and in 2016 DHS developed a grant program. As of December 2016, award notices for these grants had not been issued. |
| 4 | Brokering connections between private sector actors, civil society, and communities interested in countering violent extremist narratives. | DHS | ↄ | ↄ | - | - | - | DHS noted initial progress with YouTube and the Los Angeles Police Department sponsorship of a university challenge where students develop campaigns against violent extremism. DHS recognized this task needed attention and that these efforts can be expanded. |

| Tasks in SIP | | Lead Agency | Task | DHS | DOJ | FBI | NCTC | Status Summary |
|---|---|---|---|---|---|---|---|---|
| 5 | Promoting international exchange programs to build expertise for countering violent extremist narratives. | **State** | N/A | - | - | - | - | |
| 6 | Increasing technical training to empower communities to counter violent extremists online, including the development of training for bloggers. | **DHS** | ⊃ | ⊃ | - | - | - | DHS reported that it expanded a public-private partnership to establish a university student challenge to develop online campaigns. DHS recognized this task as needing attention and that these efforts can be expanded. |
| 7 | Providing regular briefings to Congress, think tanks, and members of the media. | **DHS** | ✔ | ✔ | - | - | - | DHS has expanded briefings and hearings and delivered over two dozen briefings and hearings to Congress. |
| 8 | Creating programs to directly engage the public on the issue. | **ALL** | ⊃ | ⊃ | ⊃ | ✔ | ✔ | DHS reported that they have held dozens of events to discuss CVE, but a direct DHS-wide CVE public engagement campaign is needed. DHS recognized this task as needing attention and considered this to be an ongoing task. DOJ highlighted a CVE summit that brought members |

| Tasks in SIP | | Lead Agency | Task | DHS | DOJ | FBI | NCTC | Status Summary |
|---|---|---|---|---|---|---|---|---|
| | | | | | | | | of the SIP Pilot sites to discuss CVE issues with members of the community. The FBI hosts forums that open dialogue, outline their mission and activities, and create awareness of threats that may impact the community. NCTC stated the CAB is presented to a wide range of audiences. |
| 9 | Building a public website on community resilience and CVE. | **DHS** | Ↄ | Ↄ | - | - | - | DHS stated the CVE website was launched in 2012 and updated in 2015 but recognized that an online platform that encourages stakeholder interaction is still needed. According to DHS, the CVE Task Force launched the CVE Task Force website (www.dhs.gov/cve) in 2017 to bring together publicly-available information on the U.S. Government's response to violent extremism. |

Source: GAO analysis of information provided by the Department of Homeland Security, the Department of Justice, the Federal Bureau of Investigation, and the National Counterterrorism Center. | GAO-17-300.

# Appendix IV
# Comments from the Department of Homeland Security

U.S. Department of Homeland Security
Washington, DC 20528

Homeland Security

March 10, 2017

Diana Maurer
Director, Homeland Security and Justice Issues
U.S. Government Accountability Office
441 G Street, NW
Washington, DC 20548

Re: Management's Response to Draft Report GAO-17-300, "COUNTERING VIOLENT EXTREMISM: Actions Needed to Define Strategy and Assess Progress of Federal Efforts"

Dear Ms. Maurer:

Thank you for the opportunity to review and comment on this draft report. The U.S. Department of Homeland Security (DHS) appreciates the U.S. Government Accountability Office's (GAO) work in planning and conducting its review and issuing this report.

The Department is pleased to note GAO's positive recognition of DHS' countering violent extremist (CVE) efforts, particularly the threat posed by a range of violent ideologies in the United States, including white supremacists, militia extremists, and ISIL-inspired violent extremists, among others. In particular, GAO found that the Department's initiatives to partner with the social media industry and efforts to improve community outreach and law enforcement CVE-focused training were on track to meet the aims of the national CVE strategy and domestically-focused tasks identified in the 2011 Strategic Implementation Plan (SIP) for CVE in the United States.

In partnership with the Department of Justice (DOJ), DHS guides domestic CVE efforts for the Federal Government to implement the overall national strategy goal to prevent violent extremists and their supporters from inspiring, radicalizing, financing, or recruiting individuals or groups in the United States to commit acts of violence. The updated *Strategic Implementation Plan for Empowering Local Partners to Prevent Violent Extremism in the United States*, released in October 2016, responds to the current dynamics of violent extremism and reflects experience and knowledge acquired since publication of the national strategy. GAO notes that, as of December 2016, involved agencies have implemented tasks focused on expanding CVE efforts in local communities and identifying ways to increase funding for CVE activities. DHS has led or participated in thirty-seven of the forty-four 2011domestic-focused CVE tasks. Both DHS and DOJ identified funding within existing appropriations to incorporate CVE into eligible public safety and community resilience grants.

In accordance with the *2016 Department of Homeland Security Strategy for Countering Violent Extremism*, DHS remains committed to ensuring communities possess the information, resources, and tools to effectively counter radicalization and recruitment to violence, without regard to motivation; and will continue to partner with DOJ in leading non-security federal partners to build CVE programs across the nation.

The draft report contained two recommendations with which the Department concurs. Attached find our detailed response to each recommendation.

Again, thank you for the opportunity to review and comment on this draft report. Technical comments were provided under separate cover. Please feel free to contact me if you have any questions. We look forward to working with you again in the future.

Sincerely,

JIM H. CRUMPACKER, CIA, CFE
Director
Departmental GAO-OIG Liaison Office

Attachment

2

**Attachment: DHS Management Response to Recommendations Contained in GAO-17-300**

GAO recommended that the Secretary of Homeland Security and the Attorney General – as heads of the two lead agencies responsible for coordinating CVE efforts – should direct the CVE Task Force to:

**Recommendation 1:** Develop a cohesive strategy that includes measurable outcomes for CVE activities.

**Response:** Concur. DHS, in partnership with the DOJ, leads domestic CVE efforts across the Federal Government through the CVE Task Force. In October 2016, the White House issued an updated SIP that responds to the current dynamics of violent extremism and reflects experiences and knowledge acquired since the 2011 release of the national strategy and corresponding SIP. The 2016 SIP provides specific objectives and the multi-tiered actions of Federal departments and agencies to synchronize and integrate whole-of-government CVE programs and activities. The CVE Task Force and DHS recognize that additional strategic-level performance documentation will improve coordination and collaboration tasks among partner agencies; define how cross-cutting tasks will be implemented, and how they will measurably contribute to achieving the federal CVE goals. The CVE Task Force is currently developing measurable outcomes to support and guide the development of performance, effectiveness, and benchmarks for federally sponsored CVE efforts.

The CVE Task Force plans to report on the implementation progress of the 2016 SIP to the White House Homeland Security Advisor in January 2018. Estimated Completion Date (ECD): January 31, 2018.

**Recommendation 2:** Establish and implement a process to assess overall progress in CVE, including its effectiveness.

**Response:** Concur. The CVE Task Force and DHS recognize that establishing a process for assessing overall strategy success will drive an understanding of the contributions of individual activities in the federal CVE effort. While the Task Force will not be engaged in specific evaluation projects of its members or partners, the Task Force will support and guide the development of measures of performance, effectiveness, and benchmarks for federally sponsored CVE efforts. To develop a set of standard guidelines for CVE measurement and evaluation, the Task Force will consult with departments and agencies that have already invested in CVE program assessment, namely the Department of State, the U.S. Agency for International Development, the DOJ National Institute of Justice, and the DHS Science and Technology Directorate. Some of the CVE evaluation efforts undertaken by these agencies are still underway, but interim findings have been shared with the CVE Task Force regarding methodology and general areas of measurement. Based on this information, the CVE Task Force Research and Analysis team will develop and distribute summaries and resource guides to our federal and non-government partners. Overall, the long-term goal of the Task Force's engagement on CVE metrics is to develop an evidence based system in order to provide a meta-

3

assessment of CVE programs, similar to other rigorous federal efforts to evaluate gang prevention programs or community policing initiatives.

As the current agency lead for the CVE Task Force, DHS is working with DOJ to synchronize and integrate CVE programs and activities to ensure successful implementation of this multi-agency collaborative effort.

The CVE Task Force plans to report on the implementation progress of the 2016 SIP to the White House Homeland Security Advisor in January 2018. ECD: January 31, 2018.

4

## Appendix V
## GAO Contact and Staff Acknowledgments

### GAO Contact

Diana Maurer, (202) 512-8777 or maurerd@gao.gov

### Staff Acknowledgments

In addition to the individual named above, Joseph Cruz (Assistant Director), Eric Hauswirth, Kevin Heinz, Tyler Kent, Thomas Lombardi, Jonathan Tumin, Amber Sinclair, and Adam Vogt made significant contributions to the report.

# DOCUMENT NO. 9

# THE TERRORIST SCREENING DATABASE AND PREVENTING TERRORIST TRAVEL

**CRS Report R44678**

**Jerome P. Bjelopera**
Specialist in Organized Crime and Terrorism

**Bart Elias**
Specialist in Aviation Policy

**Alison Siskin**
Specialist in Immigration Policy

November 7, 2016

## Summary

After the terrorist attacks of September 11, 2001, the federal government developed a unified regimen to identify and list known or suspected terrorists. The regimen has received repeated congressional attention, and this report briefly discusses for congressional policymakers how the U.S. government fashions and uses the Terrorist Screening Database (TSDB) to achieve such an end. It also discusses how the federal government engages in two travel-related screening processes—visa screening and air passenger screening. Both processes involve subsets of the Terrorist Screening Database.

### The Terrorist Screening Database (TSDB)

The TSDB lies at the heart of federal efforts to identify and share information among U.S. law enforcement about identified people who may pose terrorism-related threats to the United States. It is managed by the Terrorist Screening Center (TSC), a multi-agency organization created by presidential directive in 2003 and administered by the Federal Bureau of Investigation (FBI). The TSDB includes biographic identifiers for those known either to have or be suspected of having ties to terrorism. In some instances it also includes biometric information on such people. It stores hundreds of thousands of unique identities. Portions of the TSDB are exported to data systems in federal agencies that perform screening activities such as background checks, reviewing the records of passport and visa applicants, official encounters with travelers at U.S. border crossings, and air passenger screening.

### Foreign Nationals Traveling to the United States

Two broad classes of foreign nationals are issued visas under the Immigration and Nationality Act (INA): immigrants and nonimmigrants. Many visitors, however, enter the United States without visas through the Visa Waiver Program (VWP). Under the VWP, foreign nationals from 38 countries with agreements with the United States—including most countries in the European Union—do not need visas to enter the United States for short-term business or tourism and are instead vetted using biographic information to authenticate and screen individuals.

### Screening Aliens

Department of State (DOS) consular officers check the background of all visa applicants in "lookout" databases that draw on TSDB information and other counterterrorism information such as the material housed in the National Counterterrorism Center's Terrorist Identities Datamart Environment. DOS specifically uses the Consular Lookout and Support System (CLASS) database, which surpassed 42.5 million records in 2012. Aliens entering through the VWP have been vetted through the Electronic System for Travel Authorization (ESTA), which checks them against the TSDB. In addition, before an international flight bound for the United States departs from a foreign airport, Customs and Border Protection (CBP) officers screen the passenger manifest. CBP inspectors also perform background checks and admissibility reviews at the ports of entry that draw on information from the TSDB.

### Screening at the Transportation Security Administration

The Transportation Security Administration (TSA) has initiated a number of risk-based screening initiatives to focus its resources and apply directed measures based on intelligence-driven assessments of security risk. A cornerstone of TSA's risk-based initiatives is the PreCheck program. PreCheck is TSA's latest version of a trusted traveler program that has been modeled after CBP programs. Under the PreCheck regimen, participants are vetted through a background check process (including screening against terrorist watchlist information). At selected airports, they are processed through expedited screening lanes, where they can keep shoes on and keep liquids and laptops inside carry-on bags.

All passengers flying to or from U.S. airports are vetted using the TSA's Secure Flight program. Secure Flight involves information from the TSDB housed in the No Fly List, Selectee List, and Expanded Selectee List to vet passenger name records. The No Fly List includes identities of individuals who may present a threat to civil aviation and national security. Listed individuals are not allowed to board a commercial aircraft flying into, out of, over, or within U.S. airspace; this also includes point-to-point international flights operated by U.S. carriers. The Selectee List includes individuals who must undergo additional security screening before being allowed to board a commercial aircraft. The Expanded Selectee List was created as an extra security measure in response to a failed attempt to trigger an explosive by a foreign terrorist onboard a U.S.-bound flight on December 25, 2009. It screens against all TSDB records that include a person's first and last name and date of birth that are not already on the No Fly or Selectee lists.

---

After the terrorist attacks of September 11, 2001, the federal government developed a unified regimen to identify and list known or suspected terrorists. The regimen has received repeated congressional attention, and this report briefly discusses for congressional policymakers how the U.S. government fashions and uses the Terrorist Screening Database (TSDB) to achieve such an end.[1] It also discusses how the federal government engages in two travel-related screening processes—visa screening and air passenger screening. Both processes involve subsets of the Terrorist Screening Database.

*The TSDB as well as terrorist watchlisting and screening efforts are of keen congressional interest. This report endeavors to offer policymakers an overview of these issues to help in the development of policy and oversight. The material herein is drawn from publicly available information released by federal agencies as well as other open source material. The report does not evaluate the TSDB or federal programs designed to prevent terrorist travel.*

## The Terrorist Screening Database

The Terrorist Screening Database (TSDB, commonly referred to as the terrorist watchlist)[2] lies at the heart of federal efforts to collect and share information with U.S. law enforcement and security agencies about identified people who may pose terrorism-related threats to the United States.[3] It is managed by the Terrorist Screening Center (TSC) and includes biographic identifiers for those known either to have or be suspected of having ties to terrorism. In some instances it also includes biometric information on such people.[4] It stores hundreds of thousands of unique identities.[5] Portions of the TSDB are exported to data systems in federal agencies that perform screening activities such as

[1] For an example, see U.S. Congress, House Committee on Homeland Security, Subcommittee on Transportation Security, *Safeguarding Privacy and Civil Liberties while Keeping Our Skies Safe,* hearing, 113th Cong., 2nd sess., September 18, 2014.

[2] CRS Report R44529, *The Terrorist Screening Database: Background Information,* by Jerome P. Bjelopera.

[3] Testimony of Christopher M. Piehota, Director, Terrorist Screening Center, Federal Bureau of Investigation, in U.S. Congress, House Committee on Homeland Security, Subcommittee on Transportation Security, *Safeguarding Privacy and Civil Liberties while Keeping Our Skies Safe,* hearing transcript, 113th Cong., 2nd sess., September 18, 2014 (Hereinafter: Piehota, Testimony).

[4] Testimony of Timothy J. Healy, (former) Director, Terrorist Screening Center, Federal Bureau of Investigation, in U.S. Congress, House Committee on the Judiciary, *Sharing and Analyzing Information to Prevent Terrorism,* hearing transcript, March 24, 2010. Jeremy Scahill, Ryan Devereaux, "Watch Commander: Barak Obama's Secret Terrorist- Tracking System, by the Numbers," *The Intercept,* August 5, 2014 (Hereinafter: Scahill and Devereaux, "Watch Commander").

[5] Department of Justice, Office of Inspector General, "Audit of the Federal Bureau of Investigation's Management of Terrorist Watchlist Nominations," March 2014, footnote 10, p. 2 (Hereinafter: Department of Justice, Office of Inspector General, "Audit").

background checks, reviewing the records of passport and visa applicants, and official encounters with travelers at U.S. border crossings.[6]

### The Terrorist Screening Center, the Hub of Watchlisting

The TSC, a multi-agency organization administered by the Federal Bureau of Investigation (FBI), maintains the TSDB.[7] The TSC was created by presidential directive in 2003 in response to the terrorist attacks of September 11, 2001.[8] Before the TSC consolidated federal watchlisting efforts, numerous separate watchlists were maintained by different federal agencies. The information in these lists was not necessarily shared or compared.[9]

The efforts that surround the federal watchlisting regimen can be divided into three broad processes centered on the TSDB:

- Nomination, which involves the identification of known or suspected terrorists via intelligence collection or law enforcement investigations. The U.S. government has a formal watchlist nomination process.[10]
- Verification of identities for the TSDB and export of data to screening systems, which involves managing records in the TSDB, as well as the compiling and export of special TSDB subsets for various intelligence or law enforcement end users (screeners).
- Screening, which involves end users—screeners—checking individuals or identities they encounter against information from the TSDB that is exported to screening databases.[11] These databases[12] include the No Fly List and the Selectee and Expanded Selectee lists for airline passenger screening; the Department of State's Consular Lookout and Support System (CLASS); the FBI's National Crime Information Center (NCIC); the TECS (not an acronym) system for border and port of entry screening; and the military base access and screening system. (In FY2011, there were "more than 1.2 billion queries against [the TSDB].")[13] The screening and vetting processes can yield more information on particular subjects that may be fed back into the TSDB.[14]

(See **Figure 1** for a visual depiction of the federal agencies involved in watchlisting.)

---

[6] Ibid. p. 4.

[7] See https://www.fbi.gov/about-us/nsb/tsc/about-the-terrorist-screening-center.

[8] Ibid. The TSC and the TSDB stem from *Homeland Security Presidential Directive/HSPD-6—Directive on Integration and Use of Screening Information to Protect against Terrorism*, September 16, 2003. In HSPD-6, the entity described as the Terrorist Threat Integration Center became the TSC.

[9] Federal Bureau of Investigation, "Ten Years After: The FBI since 9/11, Terrorist Screening Center," 2011.

[10] Federal Bureau of Investigation, "Terrorist Screening Center: Frequently Asked Questions," September 25, 2015.

[11] Department of Justice, Office of Inspector General, "Audit," p. 1.

[12] For a brief discussion of such databases, see the "Export" and the "National Security and Public Safety Reviews" sections of this report.

[13] Department of Justice, Office of Inspector General, "Audit," p. 2.

[14] For brief descriptions of CLASS and TECS, see "National Security and Public Safety Reviews" and "Export" sections of this report.

**Figure 1. U.S. Counterterrorism Watchlisting Regimen**

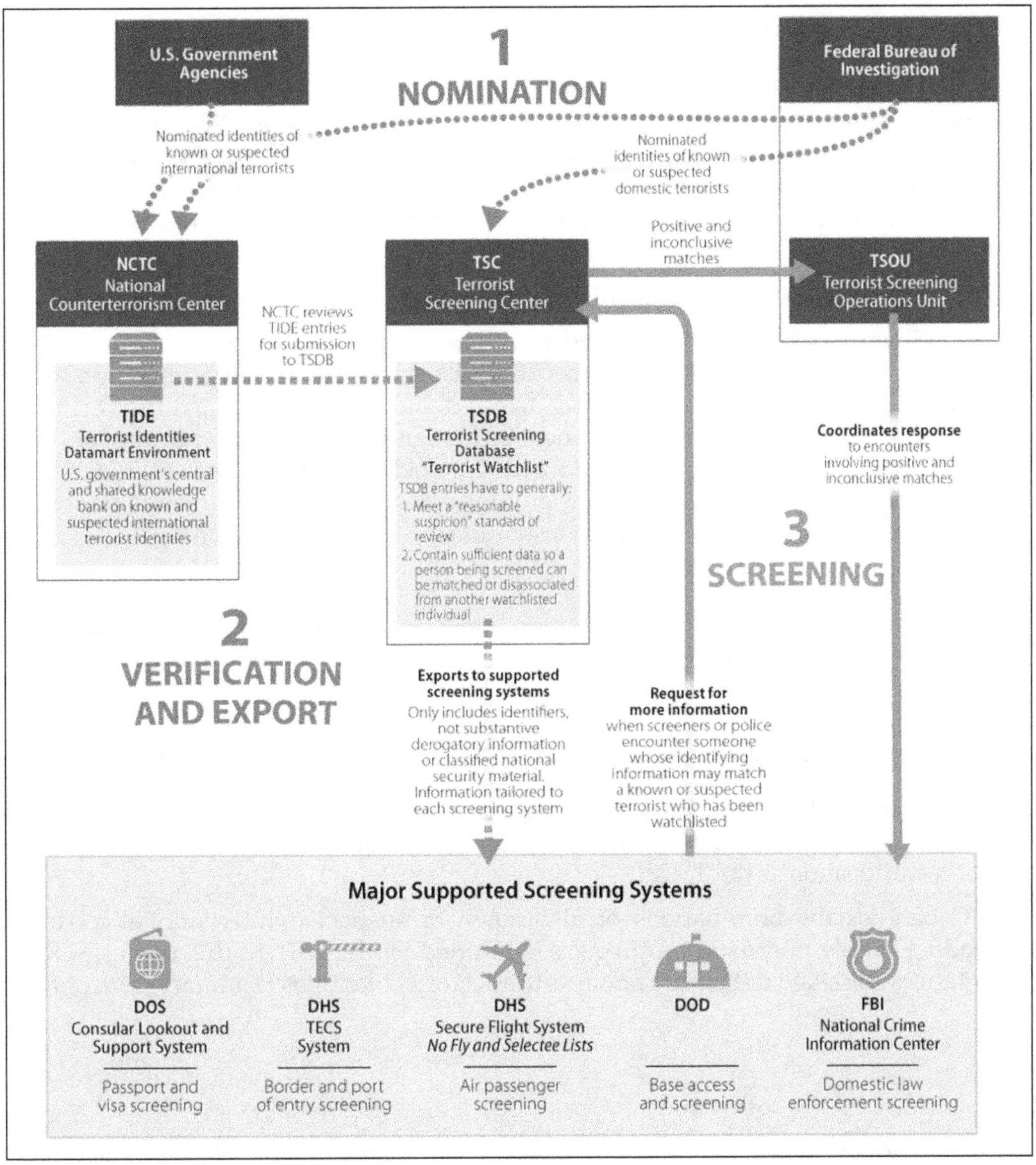


**Source:** Based on CRS analysis of Federal Bureau of Investigation, "Terrorist Screening Center: Frequently Asked Questions," September 25, 2015; Christopher M. Piehota, Director, Terrorist Screening Center, Federal Bureau of Investigation, statement before the House Homeland Security Committee, Subcommittee on Transportation Security, Hearing: "Safeguarding Privacy and Civil Liberties While Keeping our Skies Safe," September 18, 2014; National Counterterrorism Center, "Terrorist Identities Datamart Environment (TIDE)," August 1, 2014; Department of Justice, Office of Inspector General, "Audit of the Federal Bureau of Investigation's Management of Terrorist Watchlist Nominations," March 2014.

### Nominations

The first step toward adding identities to the TSDB is the nomination process. In their daily work poring over raw information or case files, staff at U.S. government agencies—dubbed "originators" in the watchlisting process—uncover the possible identities of people suspected of involvement in terrorist activity. Such identities can be nominated for addition to the TSDB. Originators can work in places such as intelligence and law enforcement agencies or U.S embassies and consulates. The nominations they initiate include people who are classed together in the watchlisting regimen as "known or suspected terrorists" (KSTs).

For the federal government's watchlisting regimen, a "known terrorist" is

> an individual whom the U.S. government knows is engaged, has been engaged, or who intends to engage in terrorism and/or terrorist activity, including an individual (a) who has been charged, arrested, indicted, or convicted for a crime related to terrorism by U.S. government or foreign government authorities; or (b) identified as a terrorist or member of a designated foreign terrorist organization pursuant to statute, Executive Order, or international legal obligation pursuant to a United Nations Security Council Resolution.[15]

A "suspected terrorist" is

> an individual who is reasonably suspected to be, or has been, engaged in conduct constituting, in preparation for, in aid of, or related to terrorism and/or terrorist activities based on an articulable and reasonable suspicion.[16]

### Verification of Identities for the TSDB and Export to Federal Data Systems

All nominated identities of known or suspected terrorists for the TSDB are vetted by analysts at either the National Counterterrorism Center (NCTC) or the FBI and then undergo verification at the TSC.[17]

NCTC handles the nominations of all known or suspected international terrorists (including purely international suspects submitted by the FBI). In this process, NCTC maintains a classified database known as the Terrorist Identities Datamart Environment

---

[15] Federal Bureau of Investigation, "Terrorist Screening Center: Frequently Asked Questions," September 25, 2015. See also Piehota, Testimony.

[16] Ibid.

[17] Federal Bureau of Investigation, "Terrorist Screening Center: Frequently Asked Questions," September 25, 2015; Department of Justice, Office of Inspector General, "Audit," p. 3. The nomination process is governed by watchlist procedures described in "Watchlisting Guidance" developed by the "watchlisting community." The community includes the Office of the Director of National Intelligence, the Central Intelligence Agency, the National Geospatial Intelligence Agency, the National Security Agency, the National Reconnaissance Office, the Department of Justice, the Department of Defense, the Department of State, the Department of the Treasury, the Department of Homeland Security, and the Department of Energy.

(TIDE). TIDE is the U.S. government's "central repository of information on international terrorist identities."[18] TIDE includes:

> to the extent permitted by law, all information the [U.S. government] possesses related to the identities of individuals known or appropriately suspected to be or to have been involved in activities constituting, in preparation for, in aid of, or related to terrorism (with the exception of purely domestic terrorism information).[19]

In late 2013, TIDE contained the identities of approximately 1.1 million people. Of this number, about 25,000 were U.S. citizens and lawful permanent residents[20] linked to international terrorist organizations.[21] Not all of the entries in TIDE get into the TSDB, which according to the FBI held approximately 800,000 identities in November 2014.[22] NCTC analysts constantly work on updating identities in TIDE, and NCTC exports a subset of its TIDE data holdings for the TSDB.[23] TSC analysts perform a final verification of identities before they become a part of the TSDB. (For more about the concepts involved, see "Making the TSDB Cut.") TIDE is also an important resource on its own, used by counterterrorism professionals throughout the U.S. intelligence community[24] in daily counterterrorism analytical work.

FBI analysts in its Terrorist Review and Examination Unit process FBI nominations to the TSDB.[25] These nominations often spring from FBI investigative work. The unit forwards international nominations to NCTC for inclusion in TIDE, where the data in the nomination is reviewed before release to the TSC.[26] The FBI also forwards nominations of purely domestic terrorists and "domestic terrorists that may have connections to international terrorism" *directly to* the TSC for review.[27]

### Making the TSDB Cut

To make it into the TSDB, a nomination vetted by either NCTC or the FBI has to (1) meet the "reasonable suspicion watchlisting standard" *and* (2) have sufficient identifiers. TSC

---

[18] TIDE is the "central and shared knowledge bank on known and suspected terrorists and international terror groups" mandated by the Intelligence Reform and Terrorism Prevention Act of 2004 (P.L. 108-458). See National Counterterrorism Center, "Terrorist Identities Datamart Environment (TIDE)," August 1, 2014.

[19] Ibid.

[20] A lawful permanent resident (LPR) refers to a foreign national who has been admitted to the United States to live and work indefinitely. It is synonymous with immigrant or legal permanent resident.

[21] Ibid.

[22] U.S. Congress, House Committee on Homeland Security, Subcommittee on Transportation Security, *Safeguarding Privacy and Civil Liberties while Keeping Our Skies Safe*, hearing transcript, 113th Cong., 2nd sess., September 18, 2014, p. 25. In 2013, there were 700,000. Also see Jeremy Scahill, Ryan Devereaux, "Watch Commander: Barak Obama's Secret Terrorist-Tracking System, by the Numbers," *The Intercept*, August 5, 2014 (Hereinafter: Scahill and Devereaux, "Watch Commander").

[23] Ibid.

[24] For a description, see http://www.dni.gov/index.php.

[25] Department of Justice, Office of Inspector General, "Audit," pp. 3–8.

[26] Ibid, p. 9.

[27] Piehota, Testimony.

personnel verify that each nomination that makes it into the TSDB meets both of these criteria.[28] The TSDB is a sensitive but unclassified dataset, and each record created by TSC personnel for the TSDB includes only an individual's identifiers and no "substantive derogatory information or classified national security" material.[29]

### *Reasonable Suspicion*

Articulable facts form the building blocks of the reasonable suspicion standard undergirding the nomination of suspected terrorists. Sometimes the facts involved in identifying an individual as a possible terrorist are not enough on their own to develop a solid foundation for a nomination. In such cases, investigators and intelligence analysts make rational inferences regarding potential nominees.[30] The TSC vets all nominations, and when it concludes that the facts, bound with rational inferences, hold together to form a reasonable determination that the person is suspected of having ties to terrorist activity, the person is included in the TSDB.[31] In the nomination process, guesses or hunches alone are not supposed to lead to reasonable suspicion. Likewise, one is not supposed to be designated a known or suspected terrorist based solely on activity protected by the First Amendment or race, ethnicity, national origin, and religious affiliation.[32]

### *Identifiers*

Once the reasonable suspicion standard is met, analysts must have the ability to distinguish a specific terrorist's identity from others. Thus, minimum biographic criteria must exist. At the very least, for inclusion in the TSDB a record must have a last name "and at least one additional piece of identifying information (for example a first name or date of birth)."[33]

Most nominations appear to make the TSDB cut. From FY2009 to FY2013, approximately 1.6 million individuals were nominated and only about 1% (just over 14,000) were rejected. (See **Figure 2**.)

---

[28] Federal Bureau of Investigation, "Terrorist Screening Center: Frequently Asked Questions," September 25, 2015.

[29] Piehota, Testimony.

[30] Exceptions to the reasonable suspicion threshold exist, and some people are placed in the TSDB "to support immigration and border screening by the Department of State and the Department of Homeland Security." See Piehota, Testimony. Presumably, an example of this was the reported watchlisting of the father of one of the shooters implicated in the San Bernardino shooting incident in December 2015. See also Paula Mejia, "Here's How You End up on the U.S. Watchlist for Terrorists," *Newsweek*, July 25, 2014. The FBI "generally requires" that subjects of closed terrorism investigations be removed from the TSDB. Limited exceptions exist. Department of Justice, Office of Inspector General, "Audit," p. 10.

[31] This means that the individual is suspected of engaging in conduct constituting, preparing for, aiding in, or related to terrorism and/or terrorist activities.

[32] There are "limited exceptions to the reasonable suspicion requirement, which exist to support immigration and border screening by the Department of State and Department of Homeland Security." See Piehota, Testimony.

[33] Department of Justice, Office of Inspector General, "Audit," p. 3.

**Figure 2. Nominations and Rejections to Terrorist Screening Database,** FY2009–FY2013

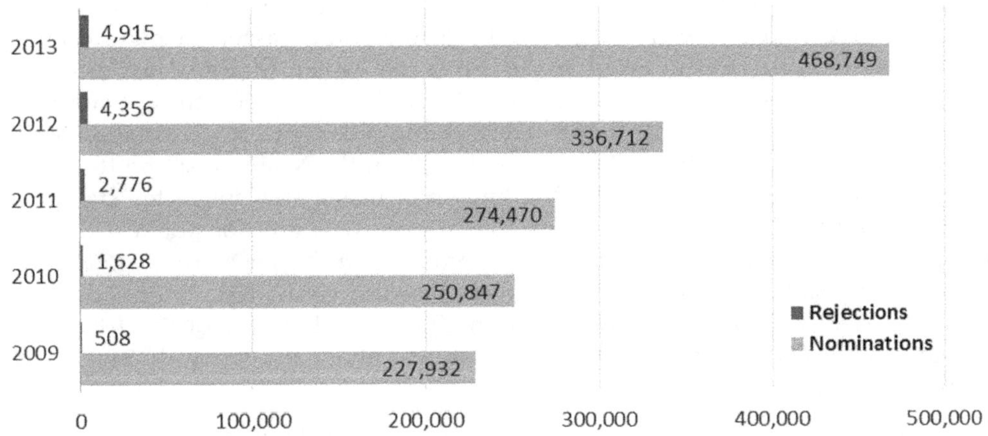


**Source:** CRS presentation of information from *Gulet Mohamed v. Eric Holder et al.*, "Defendant's Objections and Responses to Plaintiff's First Set of Interrogatories," U.S. District Court, Eastern District of Virginia, April 7, 2014.

**Notes:** In total, 1,558,710 nominations were made from FY2009 to FY2013; 14,183 were rejected (0.9%).

### Export

The TSC routinely exports watchlist information to federal agencies authorized to conduct terrorist screening. According to the TSC, this occurs as the information is processed: "seconds later, it shows up with our partners so they can do near-real-time screening."[34] According to the TSC, those partners consist of "five major U.S. Government agencies" that receive TSDB exports, which are subsets of the entire watchlist.[35] Each of the agencies gets a different portion of the TSDB that is "tailored to [its] mission, legal authorities, and information technology requirements."[36] Among the agencies whose screening systems make use of TSDB information are the following:

The **Department of State's** (DOS's) consular officers draw on TSDB information in the Consular Lookout and Support System (CLASS) used for passport and visa screening.

The **Transportation Security Administration** (TSA) uses information from the TSDB for aviation security screening. The No Fly List, the Selectee List, and the Expanded Selectee List are compared to passenger records using a program known as Secure Flight. The No Fly List includes identities of individuals who may present a threat

---

[34] U.S. Congress, House Committee on Homeland Security, Subcommittee on Transportation Security, *Safeguarding Privacy and Civil Liberties while Keeping Our Skies Safe,* hearing transcript, 113th Cong., 2nd sess., September 18, 2014, p. 24.

[35] Federal Bureau of Investigation, "Terrorist Screening Center: Frequently Asked Questions," September 25, 2015; Department of Justice, Office of Inspector General, "Audit," p. 9.

[36] Piehota, Testimony.

to civil aviation and national security. Listed individuals are not allowed to board a commercial aircraft "flying into, out of, over, or within United States airspace; this also includes point-to-point international flights operated by U.S. carriers."[37] (As discussed below, Customs and Border Protection [CBP] screens the passenger manifest before any international flight is allowed to depart to the United States.) The Selectee List includes individuals who must undergo additional security screening before being allowed to board a commercial aircraft. The minimum derogatory information requirements that form the basis for including an identity in the No Fly List and the Selectee List are "more stringent than the TSDB's known or reasonably suspected standard,"[38] although the specific criteria for inclusion on these lists are not publicly disclosed. The stricter criteria make these lists much smaller than the TSDB. In 2014, there were approximately 800,000 identities in the TSDB according to the FBI, roughly double the figure reported in 2008.[39] By comparison, in 2014 only about 8% of the TSDB identities—around 64,000—were on the No Fly List, and about 3%—roughly 24,000—were on the Selectee List.[40]

The Expanded Selectee List, an extra security measure developed in response to a failed attempt to trigger an explosive by a foreign terrorist onboard a U.S.-bound flight on December 25, 2009, screens against all TSDB records that include a person's first and last name and date of birth that are not already on the No Fly or Selectee lists.[41] This may be used at times of heightened terrorism threats, although TSA has not publicly explained when it relies on the Expanded Selectee List as opposed to the standard Selectee List to identify passengers for enhanced airport checkpoint screening.

**Customs and Border Protection** (CBP) owns and uses TECS (not an acronym), the main system that CBP officers employ at the border and elsewhere to screen arriving travelers and determine their admissibility.[42] TECS accepts "nearly all" records from the TSDB.[43] CBP also uses the Automated Targeting System (ATS), which is "a decision support tool that compares traveler, cargo, and conveyance information against law

[37] See Federal Bureau of Investigation, "Terrorist Screening Center: Frequently Asked Questions," September 25, 2015.

[38] Department of Homeland Security, Office of Inspector General, *Role of the No-Fly and Selectee Lists in Securing Commercial Aviation,* (redacted), July 2009, p. 9.

[39] U.S. Congress, House Committee on Homeland Security, Subcommittee on Transportation Security, *Safeguarding Privacy and Civil Liberties while Keeping Our Skies Safe,* hearing transcript, 113th Cong., 2nd sess., September 18, 2014, p. 25. According to media reporting, in 2013 there were about 700,000 people on the watchlist. See Scahill and Devereaux, "Watch Commander." See also Rick Kopel, (then) Principal Deputy Director, Terrorist Screening Center, Federal Bureau of Investigation, written statement before the House Homeland Security Committee, Subcommittee on Transportation Security and Infrastructure Protection, September 9, 2008.

[40] Piehota, Testimony.

[41] The Expanded Selectee List is not an official subset of the TSDB, however. See Department of Homeland Security Office of Inspector General, *Implementation and Coordination of TSA's Secure Flight Program,* (redacted), July 2012, p. 6; U. S. Government Accountability Office, *Secure Flight: TSA Should Take Additional Steps to Determine Program Effectiveness,* GAO-14-531, September 2014, p. 14 (Hereinafter: Government Accountability Office, *Secure Flight*).

[42] Department of Homeland Security, Office of Inspector General, *Role of the No-Fly and Selectee Lists in Securing Commercial Aviation,* (redacted), July 2009, p. 14.

[43] Department of Homeland Security, Office of Inspector General, *Implementation and Coordination of TSA's Secure Flight Program,* (redacted), July 2012, p. 6.

enforcement, intelligence, and other enforcement data using risk-based targeting scenarios and assessments."[44] As one of its functions, ATS "compares information about travelers and cargo arriving in, transiting through, or exiting the country, against law enforcement and intelligence databases" including information from the TSDB.[45] As its name suggests, Automated Targeting System-Passenger (ATS-P) is the portion of ATS focused on passengers, "for the identification of potential terrorists, transnational criminals, and, in some cases, other persons who pose a higher risk of violating U.S. law"[46] and is used by CBP personnel at the border, ports of entry, and elsewhere, including screening the passenger manifests of all U.S. bound international flights.[47]

**Rules-Based Screening—Looking for Potential Threats without Relying on Identities**

The federal government is not aware of all the identities of people with ties to terrorist groups who may threaten the United States. Thus, a watchlisting regimen founded on identities is inherently incomplete. In a push for a more complete sense of threat, CBP and TSA have established systems that assess the risk of particular travelers based on rules—"patterns identified as requiring additional scrutiny."[48] CBP's ATS includes such rules. CBP establishes "rules" for ATS "based on CBP officer experience, analysis of trends of suspicious activity, law enforcement cases and raw intelligence" and looks for travelers or cargo hewing to such patterns.[49] Additionally, TSA works with CBP data and also establishes its own rules based on intelligence analysis to create two watchlists within TSA's Secure Flight Program. These have not been publicly named.[50]

The **FBI** runs the National Crime Information Center's (NCIC's) database, which it has described as "an electronic clearinghouse of crime data that can be tapped into by virtually every criminal justice agency nationwide, 24 hours a day, 365 days a year."[51] The

[44] Department of Homeland Security, *Automated Targeting System—TSA/CBO Common Operating Picture, Phase II*, Privacy Impact Assessment Update, September 16, 2014, p. 1.

[45] Ibid.

[46] Department of Homeland Security, *Automated Targeting System*, Privacy Impact Assessment, June 1, 2012, p. 6.

[47] Department of Homeland Security, *Automated Targeting System—TSA/CBO Common Operating Picture, Phase II*, Privacy Impact Assessment Update, September 16, 2014, p. 1.

[48] Ibid., p. 2.

[49] Ibid.

[50] Government Accountability Office, *Secure Flight*, pp. 12–13.

[51] See https://www.fbi.gov/about-us/cjis/ncic. The FBI describes how NCIC is used by noting that "criminal justice agencies enter records into NCIC that are accessible to law enforcement agencies nationwide. For example, a law enforcement officer can search NCIC during a traffic stop to determine if the vehicle in question is stolen or if the driver is wanted by law enforcement. The system responds instantly. However, a positive response from NCIC is not probable cause for an officer to take action. NCIC policy requires the inquiring agency to make contact with the entering agency to verify the information is accurate and up-to-date. Once the record is confirmed, the inquiring agency may take action to arrest a fugitive, return a missing person, charge a subject with violation of a protection order, or recover stolen property."

NCIC includes 21 files. One of them, the "Known or Appropriately Suspected Terrorist File" includes TSDB records. The NCIC database is used for domestic law enforcement screening.[52]

The **Department of Defense** uses TSDB information to help screen people trying to enter military bases.[53]

### Screening

Employees from U.S. federal, state, and local law enforcement agencies who perform screening activities (screeners) check the identities of individuals they encounter in their daily work against specific subsets of the TSDB. Such queries happen either in-person or via submitted official (electronic or paper) forms. Examples include instances when

- foreign visitors and returning U.S. citizens enter the United States at a port of entry and are screened by CBP officers;
- state or local police pull over vehicles for moving violations and interact with drivers and passengers; and
- foreign applicants submit visa applications that are reviewed by Department of State officials.[54]

Every year, more than 1 billion queries are likely made against information in the TSDB.[55] Queries that yield possible matches between the identifying information provided by individuals and TSDB holdings are known as "encounters."[56] Screeners receive notification of possible matches via their specific screening databases.[57]

When a query produces an encounter, screeners are directed to contact the TSC. Employees in the TSC's 24-hour operations center perform additional research to track down any information that "may assist in making a conclusive identification."[58] (Screeners have access only to the identifying information available in the TSDB, while TSC analysts can search through additional datasets and intelligence to clarify a possible match.) If a positive match is made or if the TSC analysis is inconclusive, the FBI's Terrorist Screening Operations Unit coordinates how the government responds; "For example, [the unit] may deploy agents to interview and possibly apprehend the

[52] Ibid. Also see Federal Bureau of Investigation, "Terrorist Screening Center: Frequently Asked Questions," September 25, 2015.

[53] Federal Bureau of Investigation, "Terrorist Screening Center: Frequently Asked Questions," September 25, 2015. TSDB information is also shared with some foreign allies.

[54] Examples suggested in Department of Justice, Office of Inspector General, "Audit," p. 1.

[55] Ibid, p. 2.

[56] Ibid.

[57] Department of Justice, Office of Inspector General, "Audit," p. 4.

[58] Ibid., pp. 4–5.

subject."[59] Any new information collected from an encounter is forwarded to the TSC to enhance any related existing TSDB entry.[60]

## Visa and Air Traveler Screening

The use of TSDB information by federal agencies to thwart the international movement of terrorists is highlighted in efforts to screen foreigners who apply for U.S. visas and those who enter via the Visa Waiver Program (VWP), and in the general screening of air travelers.[61] In these instances, information from the TSDB helps to keep terrorists from using legitimate means of visitation and travel to find harbor in the United States.

### Overview of the Visa Screening Process

#### Immigration Law and Terrorism

Engaging in specified terrorist activity, as well as a broad range of activities in support of terrorism, generally bars the entry of a foreign national into the United States. The Immigration and Nationality Act (INA) expressly provides that aliens who have engaged or intend to engage in terrorist activity—either as an individual or as a member of a terrorist organization—are inadmissible. The INA allows the categorizations of individuals and groups as terrorists in a process that is distinct from diplomatic, foreign policy, or military policy considerations. The terror-related activities that would prevent someone from immigrating to the United States are applicable whether or not they are directed against the United States, and whether or not the foreign national's admission would pose a threat to U.S. security.

The statutory language permitting the exclusion of aliens on the basis of membership in organizations deemed subversive to national security dates back to the Immigration Act of March 3, 1903.[62] The Alien Registration Act of 1940 made past and current membership in proscribed organizations and subversive classes of aliens additional grounds for exclusion. When the various immigration and citizenship laws were unified and codified as the Immigration and Nationality Act of 1952 (INA),[63] the result was three separate grounds for exclusion that pertained to national security or political subversives.[64]

---

[59] Ibid., p. 5.

[60] Ibid. People seeking to have their names removed from the TSDB because of "difficulties experienced during travel screening at transportation hubs, such as airports, seaports, train stations, or U.S. border crossings" can use DHS's Traveler Redress Inquiry Program (DHS TRIP). See Federal Bureau of Investigation, "Terrorist Screening Center: Frequently Asked Questions," September 25, 2015. For more information on DHS TRIP, see https://www.dhs.gov/dhs-trip. See also the "Air Passenger Risk-Based Screening" section in this report.

[61] For information on the VWP, see CRS Report RL32221, *Visa Waiver Program*, by Alison Siskin.

[62] Even though the statutory definitions have been revised over time, for the purposes of this report the terms "excludeable" and "inadmissible" are used interchangeably, as are "exclusion" and "inadmissibility." In both instances, the meanings center on the basis for denying a visa or denying admission to the United States.

[63] Also known as the McCarran-Walter Act, P.L. 82-414.

[64] The Immigration and Nationality Act, which was passed as the McCarran-Walter Act of 1952, added 9 new grounds for exclusion along with 22 grounds that were in current law at that time. When President Harry Truman vetoed the McCarran-Walter Act, he specifically criticized the national security-related grounds.

The Immigration Amendments Act of 1990[65] streamlined and modernized the security, foreign policy, and political grounds for exclusion, and added a terrorism-related ground of exclusion to the INA. In part as a response to the 1993 World Trade Center bombing, Congress strengthened the anti-terrorism provisions in the INA through the Illegal Immigration Reform and Immigrant Responsibility Act[66] and the Antiterrorism and Effective Death Penalty Act.[67] The USA PATRIOT Act of 2001 and the REAL ID Act of 2005[68] continued the trend to expand the national security-related grounds for exclusion.[69]

There are two broad classes of foreign nationals that are issued visas:

- *Immigrants,* foreign nationals who wish to come to live permanently in the United States and are issued immigrant visas, and
- *Nonimmigrants,* foreign nationals who seek to come to the United States temporarily and are issued nonimmigrant visas.[70]

A visa applicant is required to submit his or her photograph and fingerprints, as well as full name (and any other name used or by which he or she has been known), age, gender, and the date and place of birth. Depending on the visa category, certain documents must be certified by the proper government authorities (e.g., birth certificates and marriage licenses). All prospective lawful permanent residents must submit to physical and mental examinations, and prospective nonimmigrants also may be required to have physical and mental examinations. These reviews are intended to ensure that aliens are not ineligible for visas or admission under the INA Section 212(a) grounds for inadmissibility.[71]

Many visitors, however, enter the United States without nonimmigrant visas through the VWP.[72] This provision of the INA allows the Attorney General to waive the visa documentary requirements for aliens coming as visitors from 38 countries. Aliens entering

Congress successfully overrode his veto, and he signed the Immigration and Nationality Act on June 17, 1952 (66 Stat. 163).

[65] P.L. 101-649.

[66] P.L. 104-208.

[67] P.L. 104-132.

[68] P.L. 107-56 and P.L. 109-13.

[69] CRS Report RL32564, *Immigration: Terrorist Grounds for Exclusion and Removal of Aliens,* by Michael John Garcia and Ruth Ellen Wasem.

[70] Humanitarian admissions, such as asylees, refugees, parolees, and other aliens granted relief from deportation, are handled separately under the Immigration and Nationality Act (INA). Persons granted asylum or refugee status are ultimately eligible to become lawful permanent residents. For more on refugees, see CRS Report RL31269, *Refugee Admissions and Resettlement Policy,* by Andorra Bruno. Illegal aliens or unauthorized aliens include those noncitizens who entered the United States without an official inspection at a port of entry, entered with fraudulent documents, or violated the terms of their visas after entering the United States. For more, see CRS Report R43892, Alien *Removals and Returns: Overview and Trends,* by Alison Siskin.

[71] The grounds of inadmissibility under INA §212(a) include health-related grounds, criminal history, security and terrorist concerns, public charge (e.g., indigence), seeking to work without proper labor certification, illegal entrants and immigration law violations, ineligibility for citizenship, and aliens who are illegally present or have previously been removed.

[72] CRS Report RL32221, *Visa Waiver Program,* by Alison Siskin.

through the VWP have been vetted through a system, known as the Electronic System for Travel Authorization (ESTA), that checks them against the TSDB.[73] (See "National Security and Public Safety Reviews" below.) As with all foreign nationals, CBP inspectors at the port of entry perform background checks and admissibility reviews that draw on information from the TSDB. (See "Export" and "Screening" above.)

### National Security and Public Safety Reviews

For some years, consular officers have been required to check the background *of all visa applicants* in the "lookout" databases and part of that process involves screening against information from the TSDB.[74]

The Department of State (DOS) specifically uses the Consular Lookout and Support System (CLASS) database, which surpassed 42.5 million records in 2012 and contains a subset of the TSDB. (See "Export" and "Screening" above.) Consular officers use name-searching algorithms to ensure matches between names of visa applicants and any derogatory information contained in CLASS. DOS reports that about 70% of the records in CLASS come from other agencies, including the Department of Homeland Security (DHS), the FBI, and the Drug Enforcement Administration. DOS also employs an automated CLASS search algorithm that runs the names of all visa applicants against the Consular Consolidated Database (CCD) to check for any prior visa applications, refusals, or issuances.[75] The CCD is a biometric and biographic database encompassing all visa applicants. Since February 2001, the CCD has stored photographs of all visa applicants in electronic form; since 2007, the CCD has stored 10-finger scans.[76] The digital photograph and the 10-finger electronic scan are the standard for biometric data collected by U.S. embassies and consulates.

DOS has relied on the Security Advisory Opinion (SAO) system, which requires a consular officer abroad to refer selected visa cases for greater review by intelligence and law enforcement agencies.[77] The current interagency procedures for alerting officials about foreign nationals who may be suspected terrorists, referred to in DOS nomenclature as Visa Viper, began after the 1993 World Trade Center bombing and were institutionalized by enactment of the Enhanced Border Security and Visa Entry Reform Act of 2002.

---

[73] P.L. 110-53 required DHS to implement an electronic travel authorization system and other enhancements to the VWP, and DHS established ESTA so that those traveling under the VWP would undergo a security screening before traveling to the United States. Travelers under the VWP may not travel to the United States without an approval from ESTA.

[74] Lookout databases store information on persons whose entry might pose a threat to the safety or security of the United States.

[75] Testimony of David T. Donahue, Deputy Assistant Secretary for Visa Services, in U.S. Congress, House Committee on Homeland Security, Subcommittee on Border and Maritime Security, *From the 9/11 Hijackers to Amine El-Khalifi: Terrorists and the Visa Overstay Problem*, 112th Cong., 2nd sess., March 6, 2012.

[76] Consular officers transmit the fingerprints taken during the visa process to CBP officers at ports of entry, enabling them to match the fingerprints of persons entering the United States.

[77] U.S. Congress, Senate Committee on Foreign Relations, Subcommittee on International Operations and Terrorism, *The Post 9/11 Visa Reforms and New Technology: Achieving the Necessary Security Improvements in a Global Environment*, hearing, October 23, 2003.

If consular officials receive information about a foreign national that causes concern, they send a Visa Viper cable (which is a dedicated and secure communication) to the National Counterterrorism Center (NCTC).

In a similar set of SAO procedures, consular officers send suspect names, identified by law enforcement and intelligence information, to the FBI for a name check program called Visa Condor.[78] There is also the "Terrorist Exclusion List," which lists organizations designated as terrorist-supporting and includes the names of individuals associated with these organizations.[79]

In June 2013, DOS launched an initiative known as "Kingfisher Expansion" (KFE) in partnership with the NCTC for conducting interagency counterterrorism screening of all visa applicants.[80] Under KFE protocols, the consular official submits the visa applicants' electronic visa applications as a "vetting package" to the NCTC. In turn, the NCTC uses an automated process to compare the vetting package with its holdings, most notably the Terrorist Identities Datamart Environment (TIDE) on known and suspected terrorists and terrorist groups. (For a brief discussion of TIDE, see "Verification of Identities for the TSDB and Export to Federal Data Systems" above.) A hit in KFE triggers a Washington-based interagency review of the visa application. KFE also conducts post-issuance reviews of valid visas to check for new information on emerging threats.[81]

Despite dipping somewhat in FY2013, the number of aliens denied nonimmigrant visas under terrorist grounds of inadmissibility has increased since the 1990s and mid-2000s. FY2012 was the peak year for immigrant denials based on national security grounds. As **Figure 3** shows, the general trends hold for immigrant and nonimmigrant exclusions.[82]

What about travelers from Visa Waiver Program (VWP) countries where their citizens do not need visas to travel to the United States?[83] In implementing the VWP, CBP uses the Electronic System for Travel Authorization (ESTA), a security vetting tool, to review prospective travelers from visa waiver countries "to determine if they pose a law enforcement or security risk before they board aircraft destined for the United States."[84] ESTA draws on records from the TSBD.

---

[78] Ibid.

[79] For further discussion of terrorist screening, see CRS Report RL32564, *Immigration: Terrorist Grounds for Exclusion and Removal of Aliens*, by Michael John Garcia and Ruth Ellen Wasem.

[80] KFE also coordinates with DHS (including CBP and U.S. Immigration and Customs Enforcement (ICE)), the FBI, and the FBI's Terrorist Screening Center.

[81] Testimony of Edward J. Ramotowski, Deputy Assistant Secretary for Visa Services, in U.S. Congress, House Committee on Oversight and Government Reform, Subcommittee on National Security, *Hearing on Securing the U.S. Border, B1/B2 Visas and Border Crossing Cards*, 113th Cong., 1st sess., November 14, 2013.

[82] Bureau of Consular Affairs, *Report of the Visa Office*, U.S. Department of State, Table XX (multiple years).

[83] See http://www.cbp.gov/travel/international-visitors/visa-waiver-program/visa-waiver-program-improvement-and-terrorist-travel-prevention-act-faq. For background on the Visa Waiver Program, see CRS Report RL32221, *Visa Waiver Program*, by Alison Siskin.

[84] For details see Customs and Border Protection, "Strengthening Security of the VWP through Enhancements to ESTA," press release.

In November 2014, DHS responded to concerns regarding terrorists entering the United States from VWP countries by expanding the information collected from VWP travelers through ESTA.[85] DHS has stated that ESTA has been a "highly effective security and vetting tool" enabling "DHS to deny travel under the VWP to thousands of prospective travelers who may pose a risk to the United States [presumably endangering national security or public safety], prior to those individuals boarding a U.S. bound aircraft."[86] However, since ESTA is a biographic and not a biometric security check and there is no interview by a consular officer, some contend that ESTA does not provide the same level of screening as a visa application.[87]

In addition to the enhancements of ESTA data elements discussed above, in 2015 DHS boosted the security criteria that countries "must meet to participate in the VWP."[88] Also, in December 2015 Congress passed legislation requiring changes to the VWP.[89] Among other changes, the legislation established new eligibility requirements for the VWP which, as implemented, modified what data were to be collected from travelers via ESTA.[90] Furthermore, as of April 2016 all foreign travelers participating in the VWP have to use e-Passports.[91]

---

85 P.L. 110-53. Department of Homeland Security, Customs and Border Protection, "ESTA - New questions to the ESTA application," CBP INFO Center, Washington, DC, November 3, 2014, https://help.cbp.gov/app/answers/detail/a_id/1756/~/esta—new-questions-to-the-esta-application.

86 Testimony of Francis Taylor, Under Secretary for Intelligence and Analysis, Department of Homeland Security, in U.S. Congress, House Committee on Homeland Security, *Terrorism Gone Viral: The Attack in Garland, Texas and Beyond*, 114th Cong., 1st Sess., June 3, 2015.

87 See CRS Report RL32221, *Visa Waiver Program*, by Alison Siskin.

88 Department of Homeland Security, "Statement by Secretary Jeh C. Johnson on House Homeland Security Committee Task Force Report on Combating Terrorist and Foreign Fighter Travel," press release, September 30, 2015 (Hereinafter: Johnson, "Statement on House Homeland Security").

89 See Consolidated Appropriations Act, 2016 (P.L. 114-113; H.R. 2029). For a discussion of the VWP provisions in the bill, see "Legislation in the 114th Congress," in CRS Report RL32221, *Visa Waiver Program*, by Alison Siskin.

90 Certain travelers are no longer eligible to travel or be admitted to the United States under the VWP. These include (1) nationals of VWP countries who have been present in Iraq, Syria, countries listed under specified designation lists, or countries deemed appropriate by the DHS Secretary (currently including Iran, Libya, Somalia, Sudan, and Yemen) at any time on or after March 1, 2011 (there are limited exceptions); and (2) nationals of VWP countries who are also nationals of Iraq, Syria, Iran, or Sudan. Travelers who fall under these restrictions are not barred from entering the United States, but they must obtain a visa from a U.S. Embassy or Consulate for such travel. See http://www.cbp.gov/travel/international-visitors/visa-waiver-program/visa-waiver-program-improvement-and-terrorist-travel-prevention-act-faq.

91 Such passports include "the security feature of an electronic chip, which holds all of a passenger's information including name, date of birth and other biographical information. This not only protects privacy and prevents identity theft, but also helps to safely identify a passenger, making travel safer and faster." See Department of Homeland Security, "Statement by Secretary Jeh C. Johnson on Strengthening Travel Security with E-Passports," press release, April 1, 2016.

**Figure 3. Foreign Nationals Denied Visas under Terrorist Grounds of Inadmissibility**
FY2000–FY2015

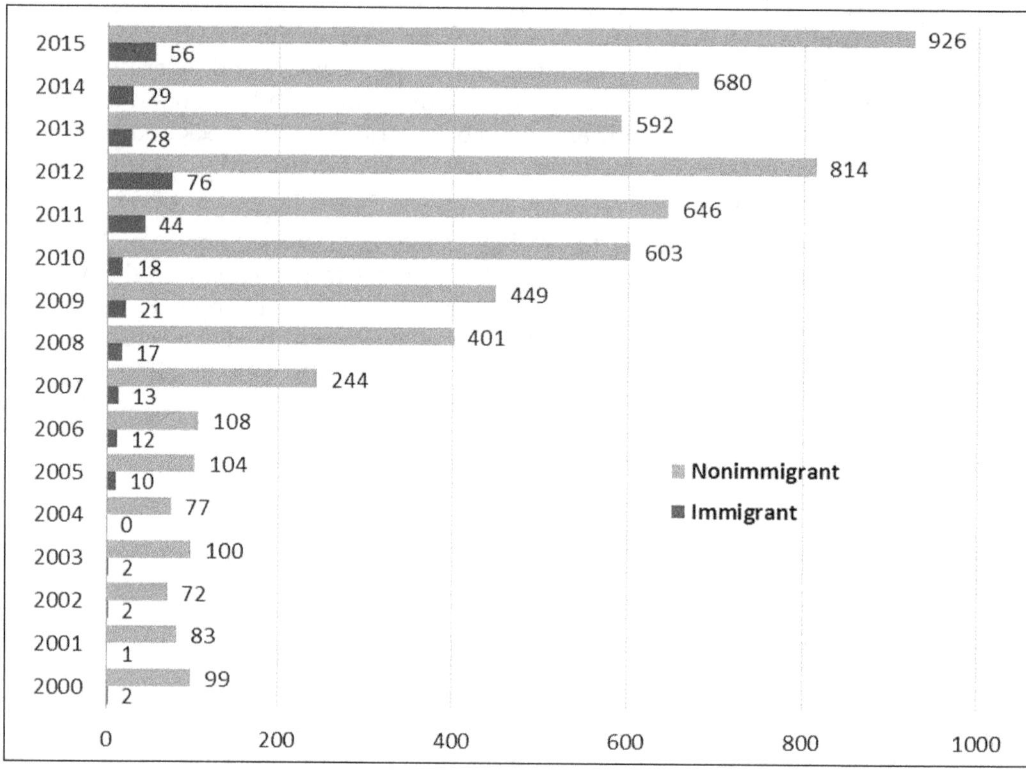


**Source:** CRS presentation of initial determination data from Table XX of the annual reports of the U.S. Department of State, Office of Visa Statistics (multiple years).

**Notes:** Data are initial determinations of inadmissibility. Some denials may be overcome with additional evidence. In 2000, the Department of State (DOS) issued 413,521 immigrant visas and 7.6 million nonimmigrant visas. In FY2015, DOS issued 531,463 immigrant visas, and 10.9 million nonimmigrant visas. Table I of the annual reports of the U.S. Department of State, Office of Visa Statistics (multiple years).

## Air Passenger Risk-Based Screening

TSA has initiated a number of risk-based passenger screening initiatives to focus its resources and apply directed measures based on intelligence-driven assessments of security risk. These efforts involve identifying known threats to aviation by comparing passenger names and birthdates to the No Fly and Selectee lists, and potentially the Expanded Selectee List, to deny boarding to No Fly matches and apply enhanced screening processes to Selectees. It also involves identifying low-risk travelers who can be routinely granted expedited physical screening so that TSA screening resources can be focused on passengers of unknown risk that TSA has no information about and on passengers that pose an elevated risk (i.e., Selectees).

### Identifying Low-Risk Travelers

In 2001, the Aviation and Transportation Security Act (P.L. 107-71) authorized TSA to "establish requirements to implement trusted passenger programs and use available technologies to expedite the security screening of passengers who participate in such programs, thereby allowing security screening personnel to focus on those passengers who should be subject to more extensive screening."

A cornerstone of TSA's risk-based initiatives created under this authority is the PreCheck program. PreCheck is TSA's latest version of a trusted traveler program.[92] Under PreCheck, participants vetted through a background check process (including screening against terrorist watchlist information) are processed through expedited screening lanes where they can keep shoes on and keep liquids and laptops inside carry-on bags. As of May 2016, PreCheck expedited screening lanes were available at more than 150 airports. The cost of background checks under the PreCheck program is recovered through application fees of $85 per passenger for a five-year membership. TSA's goal is to process 50% of passengers through PreCheck expedited screening lanes, thus reducing the need for standard security screening lanes.

A predecessor test program called the Registered Traveler program, which involved private vendors that issued and scanned participants' biometric credentials, was scrapped by TSA in 2009 because it failed to show a demonstrable security benefit. However, PreCheck has demonstrated improved screening efficiency, resulting in cost savings for TSA. TSA estimates annual savings in screener workforce costs totaling $110 million as a result of risk-based screening efficiencies.[93] Provisions in the FAA Extension, Safety, and Security Act of 2016 (P.L. 114-190) included language to expand the PreCheck program by involving private-sector entities in marketing and enrollment. Language in the bill would mandate that PreCheck screening lanes be open and available during peak and high-volume travel times.

One concern raised about PreCheck and the passenger screening process is the posting of instructions on publicly accessible Internet sites detailing how to decipher boarding passes to determine whether a passenger is a PreCheck participant, or a Selectee who must undergo thorough secondary screening. The lack of encryption and the limited capability TSA has to authenticate boarding passes and travel documents could be exploited to attempt to avoid detection of threat items by more extensive security measures. To address this concern, the DHS Office of Inspector General recommended in 2015 that TSA explore the feasibility of encrypting boarding passes and work to deploy functional credential authentication technologies at airport screening checkpoints.[94]

Other concerns raised over the PreCheck program include the lack of biometric identity authentication and the extensive use of a program called "managed inclusion" to route selected travelers not enrolled in the PreCheck program through designated PreCheck expedited screening lanes. In 2014, the Government Accountability Office (GAO) found

---

[92] See https://www.dhs.gov/trusted-traveler-comparison-chart.

[93] Department of Homeland Security, Transportation Security Administration, Fiscal Year 2016 Congressional Justification, Aviation Security.

[94] Department of Homeland Security, Office of Inspector General, *Use of Risk Assessment -within Secure Flight (Redacted)*, OIG-14-153, Washington, DC, July 2015, https://www.oig.dhs.gov/assets/Mgmt/2015/OIG_14-153_Jul15.pdf.

that TSA had not fully tested its managed inclusion practices, and recommended that TSA take steps to ensure and document that testing of the program adheres to established evaluation design practices.[95]

TSA phased out the managed inclusion program in the fall of 2015. Since September 2015, TSA behavior detection officers and explosives trace detection personnel no longer direct passengers not enrolled in PreCheck to expedited screening lanes. Selections based on evaluations by canine explosives detection teams continue, but TSA is moving toward offering expedited screening only to PreCheck program enrollees.[96]

In addition to passenger screening, TSA, in coordination with participating airlines and labor organizations representing airline pilots, has developed a known-crewmember program to expedite security screening of airline flight crews.[97] In July 2012, TSA expanded the program to include flight attendants.[98] The program is currently available at several airports in the United States, but is not available to foreign aircrews or at foreign airports.

### Behavioral Detection Approaches

TSA has developed a passenger behavior detection program to identify potential threats based on observed behavioral characteristics. TSA initiated early tests of its Screening Passengers by Observational Techniques program in 2003. By FY2012, the program deployed almost 3,000 Behavior Detection Officers at 176 airports, at an annual cost of about $200 million.

Despite its significant expansion, questions remain regarding the effectiveness of the behavioral detection program, and privacy advocates have cautioned that it could devolve into racial or ethnic profiling of passengers despite concerted efforts to focus solely on behaviors rather than individual passenger traits or characteristics. While some Members of Congress have sought to shutter the program, Congress has not approved legislation to do so. For example, H.Amdt. 127, an amendment to the FY2014 DHS appropriations measure that sought to eliminate funding for the program, failed to pass a floor vote in the 113th Congress. Congress also has not taken specific action to revamp the program, despite concerns raised by GAO and the DHS Office of Inspector General.[99] Congress has, however, repeatedly directed TSA to provide justification for the program and evidence of its utility and effectiveness, mostly through appropriations report language.

[95] U.S. Government Accountability Office, *Aviation Security: Rapid Growth in Expedited Passenger Screening Highlights Need to Plan Effective Security Assessments*, GAO-15-150, December 2014.

[96] "TSA Explains Confusion over PreCheck Policies," *TravelSkills*, September 23, 2015, http://travelskills.com/2015/09/23/tsa-explains-confusion-over-precheck-policies/.

[97] See http://www.knowncrewmember.org/Pages/Home.aspx.

[98] Transportation Security Administration, *Press Release: U.S. Airline Flight Attendants to Get Expedited Airport Screening in Second Stage of Known Crewmember Program*, July 27, 2012, http://www.tsa.gov/press/releases/2012/07/27/us-airline-flight-attendants-get-expedited-airport-screening-second-stage.

[99] U.S. Government Accountability Office, *Aviation Security: TSA Should Limit Future Funding for Behavior Detection Activities*, GAO-14-159, November 2013; Department of Homeland Security, Office of Inspector General, *Transportation Security Administration's Screening of Passengers by Observation Techniques (Redacted)*, OIG-13-91, Washington, DC, May 29, 2013; Department of Homeland Security, Statement of Charles K. Edwards, Deputy Inspector General, Before the United States House of Representatives, Committee on Homeland Security, Subcommittee on Transportation Security, November 13, 2013.

### Terrorist Watchlists in Aviation

After the failed bombing attempt of Northwest Airlines flight 253 on December 25, 2009, TSA modified security directives to require airlines to check passenger names against the No Fly List within two hours of being electronically notified of an urgent update, instead of allowing 24 hours to recheck the list. The event also accelerated the transfer of watchlist checks from the airlines to TSA under the Secure Flight program, the mechanism for vetting passenger name records against the No Fly and Selectee lists. In November 2010, DHS announced that 100% of passengers flying to or from U.S. airports were being vetted using Secure Flight.[100]

On international flights, Secure Flight operates in coordination with the use of watchlists maintained by CBP's National Targeting Center-Passenger, which relies on the Advance Passenger Information System, the ATS-P, and other tools to vet both inbound and outbound passenger manifests.

In addition to these systems, TSA conducts risk-based analysis of passenger data carried out by the airlines through use of the Computer-Assisted Passenger Prescreening System (CAPPS). In January 2015, TSA gave notification that it would start incorporating the results of CAPPS assessments, but not the underlying data used to make such assessments, into Secure Flight along with each passenger's full name, date of birth, and PreCheck traveler number (if applicable). These data were used within the Secure Flight program to perform risk-based analyses to determine whether passengers receive expedited, standard, or enhanced screening at airport checkpoints.[101] Use of Secure Flight to select passengers for expedited screening has been discontinued following concerns that the practice created security vulnerabilities and recommendations that it be discontinued by the DHS Office of Inspector General following an incident in which a convicted domestic terrorist was selected to receive expedited airport screening based on results of the TSA Secure Flight risk-based analysis.[102]

### Passenger Redress

The Intelligence Reform and Terrorism Prevention Act of 2004 (P.L. 108-458) required TSA and DHS to establish appeals procedures by which persons who are identified as security threats based on records in the TSDB may appeal such determinations and have such records modified, if warranted, to avoid recurrence. Also, provisions in the Implementing Recommendations of the 9/11 Commission Act of 2007 (P.L. 110-53) required DHS to establish an Office of Appeals and Redress to establish a timely and fair process for individuals who believe they have been delayed or prohibited from boarding a commercial aircraft because they were wrongly identified as a threat. DHS

[100] Department of Homeland Security, "DHS Now Vetting 100 Percent of Passengers On Flights Within Or Bound For U.S. Against Watchlists," press release, November 30, 2010.

[101] Department of Homeland Security, Transportation Security Administration, "Privacy Act of 1974; Department of Homeland Security Transportation Security Administration-DHS/TSA-019 Secure Flight Records System of Records," 80 *Federal Register* 233–239, January 5, 2015.

[102] Department of Homeland Security, Office of Inspector General, *Allegation of Granting Expedited Screening through TSA PreCheck Improperly (OSC File No. DI-14-3679) (Redacted)*, OIG-15-45, Washington, DC, March 15, 2015, https://www.oig.dhs.gov/assets/Mgmt/2015/OIG_15-45_Mar15.pdf

must maintain records of passengers and individuals who have been misidentified and have erroneous information corrected.[103]

To meet these statutory requirements, DHS established the DHS Traveler Redress Inquiry Program (DHS TRIP) as a mechanism for addressing situations in which individuals claim to have been inappropriately singled out.[104] The DHS TRIP program allows passengers seeking redress, or their representatives, to file complaints online or by mail.[105] After receiving the completed online questionnaire or the complaint form, DHS is to request supporting information within 30 days. Filers are given a control number that allows them to track the status of their inquiry using the Internet. If the investigation finds that the traveler was delayed due to a misidentification or name-matching issue, DHS is to describe the steps required to resolve the issue. For example, the traveler may be required to retain a copy of the DHS response letter and present it during the check-in process when traveling on airline flights. If a passenger disagrees with the resolution decision made by DHS, he or she may take further steps to appeal the decision.[106]

DHS has revised the manner in which redress cases are handled after a number of courts determined that the procedures for seeking redress violated individuals' rights to due process under the Constitution.[107] Under the revised redress process now in place, a U.S. person[108] who applies for redress from an allegedly erroneous inclusion on the No Fly List would receive an initial response letter indicating whether he or she is in fact on the No Fly List. If so, this letter would also notify the individual that he or she may elect to receive or submit additional information. These processes generally do not apply to foreign citizens as such individuals have no specific legal rights to redress under current law.

If the individual requests further information, DHS TRIP will forward the details of the case to the TSC Redress Office, which in turn would notify NCTC and the relevant nominating agencies that a redress submittal has included a request for additional information concerning an individual's placement on the No Fly List. The TSC Redress Office would then request an unclassified summary of information supporting an individual's placement on the No Fly List. Upon receipt of this information, the TSC would forward it to DHS TRIP, which would typically provide a second response to the redress seeker that would include details of the unclassified summary provided by the TSC. This second letter informs recipients that they may seek further review of their status and that they may submit any information supporting the position that their placement on the No Fly List is not warranted.

---

[103] See 49 U.S.C. §44926.

[104] See https://www.dhs.gov/dhs-trip.

[105] Complete instructions for filing complaints under the DHS TRIP program can be found at http://www.dhs.gov/one-stop-travelers-redress-process.

[106] Department of Homeland Security, "Privacy Act of 1974; Department of Homeland Security Transportation Security Administration- DHS/TSA-019 Secure Flight System of Records," 78 *Federal Register* 55270-55274, September 10, 2013.

[107] CRS Report R43730, *Terrorist Databases and the No Fly List: Procedural Due Process and Other Legal Issues*, by Jared P. Cole.

[108] U.S. person refers to a citizen or Lawful Permanent Resident.

The TSC Redress Office will review the relevant materials provided by federal agencies and the redress seeker and provide a recommendation to the TSA Administrator regarding whether or not the individual should remain on the No Fly List. The TSA Administrator would review that recommendation and issue a final decision to remove the individual from the No Fly List, maintain the individual on the list, or remand the case to TSC for further information. This final order would be sent to the individual petitioner and TSC. If the order removes the individual from the No Fly List, the TSC would update the relevant information in the TSDB.[109]

## List of Abbreviations

| | |
|---|---|
| ATS | Automated Targeting System |
| ATS-P | Automated Targeting System-Passenger |
| CAPPS | Computer-Assisted Passenger Prescreening System |
| CBP | Customs and Border Protection |
| CCD | Consular Consolidated Database |
| CLASS | Consular Lookout and Support System |
| DHS | Department of Homeland Security |
| DHS TRIP | Department of Homeland Security Traveler Redress Inquiry Program |
| DOS | Department of State |
| ESTA | Electronic System for Travel Authorization |
| FBI | Federal Bureau of Investigation |
| GAO | Government Accountability Office |
| INA | Immigration and Nationality Act |
| KFE | Kingfisher Expansion |
| KST | Known or Suspected Terrorist |
| NCIC | National Crime Information Center |
| NCTC | National Counterterrorism Center |
| SAO | Security Advisory Opinion |
| TIDE | Terrorist Identities Datamart Environment |
| TSA | Transportation Security Administration |
| TSC | Terrorist Screening Center |
| TSDB | Terrorist Screening Database |
| VWP | Visa Waiver Program |

[109] For further details on the revised redress procedures, see Declaration of G. Clayton Grigg, Deputy Director for Operations of the Terrorist Screening Center, Latif v. Holder (D. Or. 2015) (No. 3:10-cv-00750-BR 4), available at https://www.aclu.org/sites/default/files/field_document/253%20Declaration%20of%20G%20Clayton%20Grigg_0.pdf.

## Author Contact Information

Jerome P. Bjelopera
Specialist in Organized Crime and Terrorism
jbjelopera@crs.loc.gov, 7-0622

Alison Siskin
Specialist in Immigration Policy
asiskin@crs.loc.gov, 7-0260

Bart Elias
Specialist in Aviation Policy
belias@crs.loc.gov, 7-7771

## Acknowledgments

Ruth Ellen Wasem, former CRS Specialist in Immigration Policy, contributed to this report before she retired from CRS in June 2016.

# C. THE LONE WOLF AND THE INTERNET

# COMMENTARY

by
**Douglas C. Lovelace, Jr.**

Section C completes this volume by presenting an informative document addressing an important aspect of the online radicalization of terrorists. It is difficult to overstate the increasing importance of internet radicalization of lone wolf terrorists. The traditional venue for online radicalization has been terrorist organizations' websites. In 1998, twelve websites of terrorist organizations were known to exist. By 2003 that number had increased to 2,650, and by 2014, it had grown to over 9,800. The plethora of terrorist organizations with websites include Hamas, Hizbollah, al-Gama'a al Islamiyya, the Popular Front for the Liberation of Palestine, Palestinian Islamic Jihad, Boko Haram, Tupak-Amaru, Sendero Luminoso, Kahane Lives, Basque ETA, Real IRA, Aum Shinrikyo, ELN-Colombia, Liberation Tigers of Tamil Eelam, Armed Revolutionary Forces of Colombia, the Popular Democratic Liberation Front Party, the Kurdish Workers' Party, the Zapatista National Liberation Army, the Japanese Red Army, Islamic Movement of Uzbekistan Mujahedin, Chechens, Lashkar-e-Taiba, and al-Qaeda. As will be discussed later, many terrorist organizations have moved beyond passive websites into the proactive use of social media platforms to provide radical ideology as well as instruction in bomb making and the use of other weapons of terror.

The internet is a very accommodating tool for spreading radicalization and the means to act upon it. It is largely unregulated, reaches huge global audiences very inexpensively, provides a fair degree of anonymity, allows high volumes of information flows, and is multimedia and interactive. It is used to spread propaganda; create terrorist networks; radicalize, recruit and mobilize terrorists; raise funds to support terrorists; gather intelligence; and conduct cyberterrorism.

The trend in terrorist internet usage has been decidedly toward exploitation of the enormous utility of social media. This is especially true for motivating and training lone wolf terrorists. Social media affords virtual interactivity and is popular among demographic groups the members of which are vulnerable to radicalization. The use of YouTube for radicalization and terrorist instruction is increasing rapidly. Recognizing its attractiveness to younger cohorts and the easy dissemination of its contents, virtually all terrorist groups are now exploiting it.

As suggested above, the internet is being exploited increasingly to cultivate lone wolf terrorists: those who act alone in committing terroristic violence in support of a radical group, movement, or ideology, outside the command, control, or direct material support of a terrorist organization. In 2011, then President Obama stated that lone wolf terrorists constitute the most serious threat to U.S. domestic security. Since then, reflecting a focus on the lone wolf threat, law enforcement at various levels of government has arrested or otherwise eliminated many would-be or actual lone wolf terrorists. However, countering online radicalization is difficult in the United States, due in no small part to our commitment to the freedom of speech provided for in the First Amendment to the U.S. Constitution, as well as the individual protections afforded by the Fourth and Fifth Amendments.

To paraphrase Benjamin Franklin's well-known quote, those who would sacrifice freedom for security deserve neither. Nevertheless, many argue that the new reality requires a revised appreciation for the proper balance between security and freedom of speech and freedom from unreasonable search and seizure. Security is not provided by passively awaiting attacks and responding to them. Preventive and preemptive actions are required to thwart attacks. The final document offered in this volume, *The Advocacy of Terrorism on the Internet: Freedom of Speech Issues and the Material Support Statutes,* is a CRS report that addresses this very complex issue from a legal perspective. It seeks to answer the question raised by many, including some members of Congress, whether the federal government should attempt to restrict or prohibit internet speech that advocates terrorist acts.

The CRS report provides a very cogent discussion of how promotion of terrorism through internet speech might be restricted without unnecessary abridgement of the freedom granted by the First Amendment. The report correctly notes that not all speech is protected by the First Amendment. For example, fighting words, incitements to imminent violence, child pornography, and obscenity are restricted by the Federal Government without violating the U.S. Constitution. However, the report also correctly states that to lose its First Amendment protections, speech must be intended to incite imminent lawless action and must be likely to produce criminal acts. Any speech that falls short of meeting those criteria appears to be protected. However, the report provides some useful observations of possible limitations to the scope of that protection.

The report concludes with an examination of the possible application of material support to terrorist statutes and the Communications Decency Act as potential authorities for limiting internet advocacy of terrorism. Although brief, the discussions of these laws make fairly solid arguments for using them, albeit in limited circumstances, to reduce the exploitation and effectiveness of the internet as a terrorist radicalization and instructional tool. A reading of the CRS report assists the reader in understanding the many nuances of attempting to regulate internet speech that advocates and, arguably, materially supports terrorism.

# DOCUMENT NO. 10

# THE ADVOCACY OF TERRORISM ON THE INTERNET: FREEDOM OF SPEECH ISSUES AND THE MATERIAL SUPPORT STATUTES

**CRS Report R44626**

**Kathleen Ann Ruane**
Legislative Attorney

September 8, 2016

## Summary

The development of the Internet has revolutionized communications. It has never been easier to speak to wide audiences or to communicate with people that may be located more than half a world away from the speaker. However, like any neutral platform, the Internet can be used to many different ends, including illegal, offensive, or dangerous purposes. Terrorist groups, such as the Islamic State (IS, also referred to as ISIS or ISIL), Al Qaeda, Hamas, and Al Shabaab, use the Internet to disseminate their ideology, to recruit new members, and to take credit for attacks around the world. In addition, some people who are not members of these groups may view this content and could begin to sympathize with or to adhere to the violent philosophies these groups advocate. They might even act on these beliefs.

Several U.S. policymakers, including some Members of Congress, have expressed concern about the influence that terrorist advocacy may have upon those who view or read it. The ease with which such speech may be disseminated over the Internet, using popular social media services, has been highlighted by some observers as potentially increasing the ease by which persons who might otherwise have not been exposed to the ideology or recruitment efforts of terrorist entities may become radicalized. These concerns raise the question of whether it would be permissible for the federal government to restrict or prohibit the publication and distribution of speech that advocates the commission of terrorist acts when that speech appears on the Internet.

Significant First Amendment freedom of speech issues are raised by the prospect of government restrictions on the publication and distribution of speech, even speech that advocates terrorism. This report discusses relevant precedent concerning the extent to which advocacy of terrorism may be restricted in a manner consistent with the First Amendment's Freedom of Speech Clause. The report also discusses the potential application of the federal ban on the provision of material support to foreign terrorist organizations (FTOs) to the advocacy of terrorism, including as it relates to the dissemination of such advocacy via online services like Twitter or Facebook.

## Introduction

The development of the Internet has revolutionized communications.[1] It has never been easier to speak to wide audiences or to communicate with people who may be located more than half a world away from the speaker.[2] However, like any neutral platform, the Internet can be used for many different ends, including illegal, offensive, or dangerous purposes.[3] Terrorist groups, such as the Islamic State (IS, also referred to as ISIS or ISIL),[4] Al Qaeda,[5] Hamas,[6] and Al Shabaab,[7] use the Internet to disseminate their ideology, recruit new members, and take credit for attacks around the world. In addition, people who are not members of these groups may view such content and could begin to sympathize with or to adhere to the violent philosophies these groups advocate. They might even act on these beliefs.[8]

For example, it has been reported that the sermons of Anwar al Awlaki were instrumental in influencing the ideology of certain individuals accused of terrorist activities, including the perpetrators of the San Bernardino shooting and the Boston Marathon bombers.[9] Awlaki was a U.S. citizen who was targeted and killed by a drone strike on foreign soil.[10] Awlaki left behind numerous digital videos on websites like YouTube of himself preaching his interpretation of the Islamic faith.[11] Some of his videos expound upon less controversial topics such as respect for the holy month of Ramadan, the nature of marriage, or the relationship between Islam and Jesus Christ.[12] However,

[1] Protecting and Promoting the Open Internet, 80 Fed. Reg. 19738 (Apr. 13, 2015) ("The open Internet drives the American economy and serves, every day, as a critical tool for America's citizens to conduct commerce, communicate, educate, entertain, and engage in the world around them.").

[2] *Id.*

[3] *See* Fair Hous. Council v. Roommates.com, LLC, 521 F.3d 1157, 1169 (9th Cir. 2008) (noting that Internet content and service providers often provide neutral tools that may be used to carry out illegal acts or to communicate illegal content).

[4] Rick Gladstone and Vindu Goel, *ISIS Adept on Twitter, Study Finds,* N.Y. Times (Mar. 5, 2015), http://www.nytimes.com/2015/03/06/world/middleeast/isis-is-skilled-on-twitter-using-thousands-of-accounts-study-says.html?_r=0.

[5] Scott Shane, *The Lessons of Anwar al-Awlaki,* N.Y. Times (Aug. 27, 2015), http://www.nytimes.com/2015/08/30/magazine/the-lessons-of-anwar-al-awlaki.html.

[6] Gwen Ackerman, *Facebook Accused in $1 Billion Suit of Being Hamas Tool,* Bloomberg (Jul. 11, 2016), http://www.bloomberg.com/news/articles/2016-07-11/facebook-sued-for-1b-for-alleged-hamas-use-of-medium-for-terror.

[7] Harriet Alexander, *Tweeting Terrorism: How al-Shabaab Live Blogged the Nairobi Terrorist Attack,* The Telegraph (Sept. 22, 2013), http://www.telegraph.co.uk/news/worldnews/africaandindianocean/kenya/10326863/Tweeting-terrorism-How-al-Shabaab-live-blogged-the-Nairobi-attacks.html.

[8] *Id.*

[9] Shane, *supra* note 5.

[10] *Id.*

[11] *Id.*

[12] *Id.*

other videos depict Awlaki exhorting his followers never to trust a non-Muslim; that Muslims are at war with the United States; and, in a video entitled "Call to Jihad," that "it is every Muslim's religious duty to kill Americans."[13] It was messages like these, particularly the "Call to Jihad," that reportedly motivated the San Bernardino and Boston Marathon attackers.[14]

More broadly, the Islamic State organization has been known to use popular Internet services such as Twitter and YouTube to disseminate videos of its fighters executing prisoners, claim credit for organizing terrorist attacks such as the attack that occurred in Paris in November of 2015, and recruit new members to their cause.[15] IS personnel also disseminate high-quality electronic publications encouraging supporters to conduct violent attacks in their communities. Members of Hamas and Al Shabaab have reportedly used Facebook and Twitter to disseminate their ideology as well.[16] The media arm of Al Shabaab used Twitter to claim credit for the terrorist attack on the Westgate Shopping Mall in Nairobi, Kenya and distribute information and pictures of the attack while it remained ongoing.[17]

Speech advocating violence and terrorism is prohibited by the terms of service of Twitter, Facebook, and other social media outlets.[18] Sites like Twitter reportedly have increased their efforts to disable accounts that are associated with terrorist groups or the advocacy of terrorist ideologies. However, these efforts have not been wholly successful.[19] When one account is disabled, another might soon appear to replace it.

Many policymakers, including some Members of Congress, have expressed concern about the influence the speech of terrorist groups and the speech of others who advocate terrorism can have on those who view or read it.[20] Some policymakers have expressed particular concern regarding the ease by which persons who might otherwise not have

---

[13] *Id.*

[14] *Id. See also* Erik Eckholm, *ISIS Influence on Web Prompts Second Thoughts on First Amendment,* N.Y. Times (Dec. 27, 2015), *available at* http://www.nytimes.com/2015/12/28/us/isis-influence-on-web-prompts-second-thoughts-on-first-amendment.html. Awlaki also reportedly helped to create Inspire Magazine. Shane, *supra* footnote 5. Inspire Magazine, published by Al Qaeda in the Arabian Peninsula, is freely available on the Internet, and can be found via a simple Internet search on an engine like Google. Bob Drogin, *The 'Vanity Fair' of Al Qaeda,* L.A. Times (Nov. 26, 2010), http://articles.latimes.com/2010/nov/26/nation/la-na-terror-magazine-20101126. It is written in English and commonly defends perpetrators of terrorist attacks and encourages readers to commit terrorist acts. *Id.*

[15] Gladstone and Goel, *supra* note 4.

[16] Ackerman, *supra* note 6; Alexander, *supra* note 7.

[17] Alexander, *supra* note 7.

[18] *See, e.g., Twitter Rules,* https://support.twitter.com/articles/18311# (last visited, Aug. 26, 2016); *Facebook Terms of Service* https://www.facebook.com/terms (last visited Aug. 26, 2016); YouTube Community Guidelines https://www.youtube.com/yt/policyandsafety/communityguidelines.html (last visited Aug. 26, 2016).

[19] Mike Isaac, *Twitter Steps Up Efforts to Thwart Terrorists Tweets,* N.Y. Times (Feb. 5, 2016), http://www.nytimes.com/2016/02/06/technology/twitter-account-suspensions-terrorism.html.

[20] *See, e.g.,* Scott Shane, *Internet Firms Urged to Limit Work of Anwar al-Awlaki,* N.Y. Times (Dec. 18, 2015), http://www.nytimes.com/2015/12/19/us/politics/internet-firms-urged-to-limit-work-of-anwar-al-awlaki.html [hereinafter "Shane II"]; Eric Posner, *ISIS Gives Us No Choice But to Consider Limits on Speech,* Slate (Dec. 15, 2015) http://www.slate.com/articles/news_and_politics/view_from_chicago/2015/12/isis_s_online_radicalization_efforts_present_an_unprecedented_danger.html; Press Release, House Committee on Foreign Relations, Poe, Sherman, Royce, Engel: Shutdown Terrorists on Twitter (Mar. 12, 2015), https://democrats-foreignaffairs.house.gov/news/press-releases/poe-sherman-royce-engel-shut-down-terrorists-twitter. [hereinafter "Committee Member Press Release"]

been exposed to the ideology or recruitment efforts of terrorist entities may become radicalized.[21] These concerns raise the question of whether it would be permissible for the federal government to restrict or prohibit the publication and distribution of speech that advocates the commission of terrorist acts when that speech appears on the Internet.[22]

Significant First Amendment freedom of speech issues are raised by the prospect of government restrictions on the publication and distribution of speech, even speech that advocates terrorism. However, government restrictions on advocacy that is provided to foreign terrorist organizations as material support have been upheld as permissible. This report will discuss relevant precedent that may limit the extent to which advocacy of terrorism may be restricted. The report will also discuss the potential application of the federal ban on the provision of material support to foreign terrorist organizations (FTOs) to the advocacy of terrorism and the dissemination of such advocacy by online service providers like Twitter or Facebook.

## Constitutional Principles: Advocacy of Violence or Lawlessness Under the First Amendment

The First Amendment to the Constitution states that "Congress shall make no law ... abridging the freedom of speech...."[23] According to the Supreme Court, "the First Amendment [generally] means that government has no power to restrict expression because of its message, its ideas, its subject matter, or its content."[24] However, the freedom of speech is not absolute.[25] Some speech, including fighting words, incitements to imminent violence, child pornography, and obscenity can be restricted by the government without constitutional concern.[26]

Furthermore, courts do allow the government to place restrictions on protected speech under certain circumstances.[27] When a restriction applies to speech based upon its content[28] or upon the viewpoint expressed,[29] courts generally apply the highest level of scrutiny, known as strict scrutiny.[30] In order to satisfy strict scrutiny, a speech restriction

[21] *See* Committee Member Press Release, footnote 20.

[22] Posner, *supra* note 20; *but see,* David Post, *Protecting the First Amendment in the Internet Age,* Volokh Conspiracy, Wash. Post (Dec. 21, 2015), https://www.washingtonpost.com/news/volokh-conspiracy/wp/2015/12/21/protecting-the-first-amendment-in-the-internet-age/?utm_term=.cfe4340d93ad.

[23] U.S. Const. amend. I.

[24] Ashcroft v. Am. Civ. Liberties Union, 535 U.S. 564, 573 (2002) (internal quotation marks omitted).

[25] United States v. Stevens, 559 U.S. 460, 468 (2010).

[26] *Id.* (listing the traditionally recognized categories of speech that may be prohibited).

[27] For example, the government may place content-neutral time, place, and manner restrictions on speech as long as such restrictions serve a significant interest and are narrowly tailored to directly advance that interest. Ward v. Rock Against Racism, 491 U.S. 781 (1989).

[28] A law that restricted speech because of the subject matter discussed likely would be considered by a reviewing court to be a content-based restriction. Reed v. Town of Gilbert,__U.S.__, 135 S. Ct. 2218, 2227 (2015) ("Government regulation of speech is content based if a law applies to particular speech because of the topic discussed or the idea or message expressed.").

[29] Laws that single out speech expressing a particular viewpoint on a subject (e.g., negative views of a racial group) for special restriction are "viewpoint discriminatory" and a particularly egregious form of content discrimination. Rosenberger v. Rector and Visitors of Univ. of Va., 515 U.S. 819, 829 (1995) (finding that government discrimination among viewpoints is a "more blatant" and "egregious form of content discrimination").

[30] *Reed,* 135 S. Ct. at 227.

must directly advance a compelling government interest and it must be the least restrictive means for achieving that interest.[31] It is rare that a law will survive this level of scrutiny.[32] Generally, when a restriction is not directed at the content of speech or the viewpoint expressed, courts apply a less-exacting standard of scrutiny, known as intermediate scrutiny.[33] Content-neutral restrictions on protected speech will be upheld if the government can show that the restriction advances a substantial government interest and is narrowly tailored to achieve that interest.[34] In this way, the government is permitted to impose reasonable regulations on the time, place, and manner of speech.[35]

### Pure Advocacy of Violence and Law Breaking Under *Brandenburg v. Ohio*

In *Brandenburg v. Ohio*, the Supreme Court held that the First Amendment can protect the advocacy of lawbreaking and violence. *Brandenburg* overturned a conviction under Ohio's criminal syndicalism statute, invalidating that statute.[36] The statute, like other syndicalism laws, prohibited "advocat[ing] ... the duty, necessity, or propriety of crime, sabotage, violence, or unlawful methods of terrorism."[37] Members of the Ku Klux Klan had been convicted of violating that statute at a rally covered by a Cincinnati television station at the request of one of the Klan members.[38] At the rally, among other incendiary comments, one of the members said "We're not a revengent [sic] organization, but if our President, our Congress, our Supreme Court, continues to suppress the white, Caucasian race, it's possible that there might have to be some revengeance [sic] taken."[39] Other statements advocating violence were made, as well.

The Supreme Court overturned the convictions at issue because "the mere abstract teaching ... of the moral propriety or even moral necessity for a resort to force and violence is not the same as preparing a group for violent action" and cannot be punished

---

31 Sable Commc'n of Cali., Inc. v. FCC, 492 U.S. 115, 126 (1989).

32 Williams-Yulee v. Fla. Bar,__U.S.__, 135 S.Ct. 1656, 1666 (2015) (noting that it is the "rare case [] in which a speech restriction survives strict scrutiny").

33 See *Ward*, 491 U.S. at 797; United States v. O'Brien, 391 U.S. 367, 377 (1968) (sustaining regulations that burden speech where the government interest in enacting the regulation is unrelated to the suppression of speech).

34 *Ward*, 481 U.S. at 797 ("[E]ven in a public forum the government may impose reasonable restrictions on the time, place, or manner of protected speech, provided the restrictions are justified without reference to the content of the regulated speech, that they are narrowly tailored to serve a significant governmental interest, and that they leave open ample alternative channels for communication of the information.) (internal quotations omitted).

35 *Id.*

36 395 U.S. 444 (1969) (per curiam). *Brandenburg* overturned a previous decision, *Whitney v. California*, upholding California's criminal syndicalism statute, which was similar in substance to the Ohio statute struck down by *Brandenburg*. 274 U.S. 357 (1927). In upholding the constitutionality of California's statute, the *Whitney* Court gave great deference to the judgment of the state regarding the dangers presented by the speech at issue. *Id.* at 371. The state had declared that becoming a member of a group like the Communist Party "involves such danger to the public peace and the security of the state, that these acts should be penalized." *Id.* The Court said that it would not declare such judgment to be unconstitutional unless it was "an arbitrary or unreasonable attempt to exercise the authority vested in the State in the public interest." *Id. Whitney* was decided over forty years before *Brandenburg*, and the *Brandenburg* Court wrote that cases subsequent to *Whitney* had discredited the Court's ruling in that case. 395 U.S. at 447.

37 *Brandenburg*, 395 U.S. at 445.

38 *Id.*

39 *Id.* at 446.

by the government in a manner consistent with the First Amendment.[40] In order for speech inciting violence or lawlessness to fall outside of the ambit of the Free Speech Clause, the Court held that:

1. the speech must be directed at . . .
2. inciting "imminent lawless action" and
3. the speech must also be likely to produce such action.[41]

In other words, for punishment of speech advocating violence to be constitutional, the speaker must both intend to incite a violent or lawless action and that action must be likely to imminently occur as a result.[42] In so holding, the Court invalidated Ohio's criminal syndicalism statute,[43] reasoning that the statute failed to draw the distinction between "mere abstract teaching" and "preparing a group for violent action" and, therefore, swept too broadly.[44] Consequently, in order for a statute that restricts the advocacy of violence or lawlessness to be constitutional, the statute must apply only to speech meeting the standard announced by the Court.[45]

### Ambiguity in *Brandenburg*'s Scope

As indicated by the Court in *Brandenburg*, speech that is intended to incite violent action and is likely to imminently produce such action is not protected by the First Amendment and may freely be proscribed by the government. However, the Court did not elaborate upon what it might mean for speech to be "likely to imminently produce" unlawful action.[46] Therefore, it is unclear how imminent the violence advocated must be in order for speech to be able to be proscribed.[47]

In *Hess v. Indiana*, the Supreme Court provided some guidance regarding "imminence" pursuant to *Brandenburg*.[48] The defendant in *Hess* had been convicted of disorderly

[40] *Id.* at 448 (quoting Noto v. United States, 367 U.S. 290 (1961)).

[41] *Id.*

[42] *See, e.g.*, Bible Believers v. Wayne Cty., 805 F.3d 228, 244 (6th Cir. 2015) ("The right to freedom of speech provides that a state cannot proscribe advocacy of the use of force or of law violation except where such advocacy is directed to inciting or producing imminent lawless action and is likely to incite or produce such action.") (internal quotations omitted); Blum v. Holder, 744 F.3d 790, 802 (1st Cir, 2014) (finding that the Animal Enterprise Terrorism Act did not apply to expressive conduct protected by the First Amendment, including speech meeting *Brandenburg's*, standard); United States v. Bell, 414 F.3d 474 (3d Cir. 2005) (finding that, while speech meeting *Brandenburg's*, standard cannot be restricted, the speech at issue was false commercial speech that aided and abetted violations of the tax laws and, therefore, could be enjoined).

[43] *Brandenburg*, 395 U.S. at 450.

[44] *Id.* at 448.

[45] *Id.* at 448 n.2 (citing *Dennis v. United States*, 341 U.S. 494 (1951), which had upheld the constitutionality of the Smith Act, 18 U.S.C. § 2385, which prohibits advocating the overthrow of the United States government, and *Yates v. United States*, 354 U.S. 298 (1957), which overturned convictions under the Smith Act because the jury instructions had permitted punishment for pure advocacy "unrelated to its tendency to produce forcible action").

[46] *See* Michael Buchhandler-Raphael, *Overcriminalizing Speech*, 36 Cardozo L. Rev. 1667, 1678-80 (2015); Thomas Healy, Brandenbug *In a Time of Terror*, 84 Notre Dame L. Rev. 655, 681 (2009).

[47] Healy, *supra* note 46 at 681 ("For instance, what does imminence meant? Does it mean within a few hours . . . or does it indicate a longer time frame?").

[48] 414 U.S. 105 (1973) (per curiam).

conduct.[49] At an anti-war rally, he had been arrested for shouting "[we'll] take the [expletive] street later."[50] The Court overturned his conviction because his statement "amounted to nothing more than advocacy of illegal action at some indefinite future time" and his statements were not directed to any person or group of persons.[51] In the Court's words, "there was no evidence, or rational inference from the import of the language that his words were intended to produce and likely to produce *imminent* disorder."[52]

Some argue that the Court's decision in *Hess* indicated the Court viewed the "imminence" requirement to mean that violence must be likely to occur immediately as a result of the speech at issue.[53] The *Hess* Court apparently did not think that a threat to "take the street" at some later point to be imminent or likely enough to be punished under *Brandenburg*.[54]

However, state and federal courts have not always applied *Hess* or the imminence requirement of *Brandenburg* so strictly.[55] For example, in *People v. Rubin*, a California state court ruling, Rubin was charged with solicitation of murder.[56] During a press conference to protest a planned march by the Nazi Party through Skokie, Illinois, Rubin offered money to anyone who "kills, maims, or seriously injures a member of the American Nazi Party.... The fact of the matter is that we're deadly serious. This is not said in jest, we are deadly serious."[57] The trial court found that his speech was protected by the First Amendment, but the appeals court reversed.[58] After reciting *Brandenburg*'s standard, the state appeals court held the defendant's speech was directed to inciting lawless action, and that such action was likely to imminently occur, even though the march in Skokie was not scheduled to take place until five weeks after the defendant had spoken.[59] In justifying its holding, the court wrote that "time is a relative dimension and imminence a relative term, and the imminence of an event is related to its nature.... We think solicitation of murder in connection with a public event of this notoriety, even though five weeks away, can qualify as incitement to imminent lawless action."[60]

---

[49] *Id.*

[50] *Id.* at 106-07.

[51] *Id.* at 108-09.

[52] *Id.* at 109 (emphasis in original).

[53] *See* Buchhandler-Raphael, *supra* note 46 at 1677 ("In light of *Hess,* imminent means nothing but immediate action, which is an almost impossible burden to satisfy."); Marc Rohr, *Grand Illusion? The Brandenburg Test and Speech that Encourages or Facilitates Criminal Acts,* 38 Willamette L. Rev. 1, 18-19 (2002) (*"In Hess,* the Court did appear to require that the interval between speech and called-for response must be quite brief."); Kent Greenawalt, Speech, Crime, and the Uses of Language, 209 (1989) (finding that *Hess's* imminence interpretation was "very restrictive").

[54] This interpretation coincides with the plain meaning of the word "imminent," which generally means "close at hand in its incidence," seemingly requiring an immediate risk of the occurrence of violence. *Imminent,* Oxford English Dictionary (2016) http://www.oed.com/view/Entry/91904?redirectedFrom=imminent&.

[55] Healy, *supra* note 46, at 670-72 (noting cases that arguably misapplied *Brandenburg).*

[56] 96 Cal. App. 3d 968 (Cal. Ct. App. 1979). *See* Healy, *supra* note 46, at 671-72 (citing *People v. Rubin* as an example that lower courts have not strictly applied *Brandenburg's* imminence requirement).

[57] *Rubin,* 96 Cal. App. 3d at 972.

[58] *Id.*

[59] *Id.* at 977.

[60] *Id.* at 978.

The only other Supreme Court case to apply the standard announced in *Brandenburg* was *NAACP v. Claiborne Hardware*.[61] In that case, the Supreme Court overturned civil judgments against black defendants who had organized a boycott of white-owned businesses in a Mississippi town in order to protest discrimination and advocate for racial equality.[62] According to the lawsuit, one of the defendants, Charles Evers, had advocated the use of violence to enforce the boycott against unwilling participants.[63] Plaintiffs argued that Evers's advocacy of violence should make him liable to the plaintiffs for their losses resulting from the boycott.[64] The Court disagreed, stating "[this] Court has made clear ... that mere advocacy of the use of force or violence does not remove speech from the protection of the First Amendment."[65] The Court specifically noted that Evers's speech primarily consisted of a plea for black people to unify wherein strong language was used that might have been construed as advocacy of violence.[66] While the Court noted that "a substantial question would be presented whether Evers could be held liable for the consequences of that unlawful conduct" had immediate violence erupted from his speech, any violence that occurred happened weeks later.[67] The Court therefore concluded that Evers' speech was protected under the First Amendment.

However, the Court has also found that First Amendment protection for speech related to illegal activity has its limits. In *United States v. Williams*, the Court upheld the constitutionality of a statute that outlawed knowing offers to provide or requests to receive child pornography.[68] Citing *Brandenburg*, the Court noted that "there remains an important distinction between a proposal to engage in illegal activity and the abstract advocacy of illegality."[69] Distinguishing the statute from one that would raise issues under *Brandenburg*, the Court found that it did not ban the advocacy of the creation of child pornography, but instead prohibited what were essentially attempts to give or receive it.[70] Child pornography is not protected by the First Amendment.[71] In *Williams*, the Court held that offers to give or receive it are also categorically excluded from First Amendment protection.[72] For that reason, the Court found that the statute "[fell] well within constitutional bounds."[73] Because the Court found that the statute did not raise issues regarding permissible restrictions on the pure advocacy of violence or lawlessness, the precise boundaries of the *Brandenburg* standard remain unclear.

[61] 458 U.S. 886 (1982).

[62] *Id.* at 934.

[63] *Id.* at 926.

[64] *Id.* at 898.

[65] *Id.* at 927-28.

[66] *Id.* at 928.

[67] *Id.*

[68] 553 U.S. 285 (2008).

[69] *Id.* at 299.

[70] *Id.*

[71] New York v. Ferber, 458 U.S. 747, 764 (1982) (finding that child pornography is not protected speech).

[72] *Williams*, 553 U.S. at 299.

[73] *Id.*

### *Holder v. Humanitarian Law Project*

Beyond the issue of regulating advocacy of imminent lawlessness or violence, the more recent 2010 case of *Holder v. Humanitarian Law Project* ("*Humanitarian Law Project*") is also relevant to questions regarding the advocacy of terrorism, as the opinion analyzes the permissibility of burdening speech that may more generally benefit terrorist organizations. In *Humanitarian Law Project*, the Supreme Court upheld the constitutionality of the federal criminal prohibition on the provision of material support to entities that have been officially designated as foreign terrorist organizations (FTOs) by the United States.[74] The criminal prohibition applies to, among other forms of support, the provision of "personnel," "training," "service," and "expert advice and support" to designated entities."[75]

The plaintiffs in that case sought to provide certain services to FTOs, but feared that the provision of such services was barred by the law.[76] While the plaintiffs did not claim that the statute violated the First Amendment in all instances, they alleged that the law was constitutionally invalid if applied to the assistance they contemplated providing the FTOs, which was intended to assist those groups' legitimate, non-terrorism related activities.[77] In particular, the plaintiffs sought pre-enforcement review in order to ensure that they could teach these organizations how to apply for certain humanitarian aid, engage in political advocacy on behalf of minority groups represented by these organizations, and give legal advice regarding the negotiation of peace agreements.[78]

The Court agreed with the plaintiffs that the prohibition on the provision of material support extended not only to conduct, but also to speech in a manner that burdened the plaintiffs' First Amendment rights.[79] The majority acknowledged that the restriction was content-based, and accordingly applied "a more demanding standard" of scrutiny to the provision than would otherwise have been employed if it reached only conduct.[80] Nonetheless, the Court upheld the application of the statute to the speech in question.

The Court's assessment of the permissibility of the burden imposed on the plaintiffs' speech rights was informed by its reading of the underlying statute. The Court construed the material support statute as having been "carefully drawn to cover only a narrow category of speech to, under the direction of, or in coordination with foreign groups that the speaker knows to be terrorist organizations."[81] The fact that the statute covered speech coordinated with foreign terrorist groups, and not "independent advocacy" that

[74] 561 U.S. 1 (2010).

[75] *Id.* at 14; 18 U.S.C. § 2339B.

[76] *Humanitarian Law Project*, 561 U.S 1, 10-11 (2010).

[77] *Id.*

[78] *Id.*

[79] *Id.* at 28.

[80] *Id.* at 27-28.

[81] *Id.* at 26.

happened to support those groups, made it easier for the government to demonstrate that the restriction was narrowly tailored to advance the government's interest.[82]

Turning to the government's justification, the Court began its analysis by reiterating that Congress has a compelling interest in combating terrorism and protecting national security.[83] In banning the provision of all material support to foreign terrorist organizations, the Court observed that Congress had reasoned that any support provided to these organizations, even support not intended to aid in terrorist endeavors, can free resources to support terrorist activities.[84] The Court noted congressional findings that if American citizens provided material support to entities the U.S. government had identified as terrorist groups that activity may strain diplomatic relationships between the United States and countries in which the FTOs operate.[85] In the Court's view, official cooperation and interaction with non-governmental entities can lend legitimacy to terrorist groups, which might undermine the government's interest in combating those organizations.[86] When examining the support that the plaintiffs wished to provide to FTOs, the Court observed that "[a] foreign terrorist organization introduced to the structures of the international legal system might use the information to threaten, manipulate, and disrupt."[87] According to the Court, prohibiting the provision of material support to FTOs, therefore, directly advanced the government's compelling interest in combating terrorism, and because the prohibition applied only to material support coordinated with FTOs, the statute was narrowly tailored to achieve the government's compelling interest.

In reaching its conclusion upholding the statute, the Court emphasized that its holding applied only to the factual situation before the Court, and that the Court was not deciding the constitutionality of more difficult cases that might arise in other circumstances.[88] The Court also stated that it "in no way suggest[ed] ... that a regulation of *independent* speech"—i.e., speech that is not coordinated with a FTO– "would pass constitutional muster, even if the Government were to show that such speech benefits foreign terrorist organizations" or that a similar statute banning the provision of material support to a *domestic* organization would survive review.[89] The Court focused upon the significance of the fact that Congress had carefully crafted the statute to avoid burdening constitutional rights when enacting the law[90] and emphasized that Congress's views on matters of national security are entitled to "significant weight."[91]

---

[82] *Humanitarian Law Project,* 561 U.S. at 26.

[83] *Id.* at 28 ("Everyone agrees that the Government's interest in combating terrorism is an urgent objective of the highest order.") (internal quotations omitted).

[84] *Id.* at 29-30.

[85] *Id.* at 32.

[86] *Id.* at 30.

[87] *Id.* at 37.

[88] *Id.* at 39 ("All this is not to say that any future applications of the material-support statute to speech or advocacy will survive First Amendment scrutiny.").

[89] *Id.* (emphasis added).

[90] *Id.* at 35-36. Here the Court stressed again that "Congress has avoided any restriction on independent advocacy, or indeed any activities not directed to, coordinated with, or controlled by foreign terrorist group." *Id.* at 36.

[91] *Id.* at 36.

## Restricting the Advocacy of Terrorism on the Internet

Some have argued that it should be permissible to restrict advocacy of terrorism disseminated via the Internet under the First Amendment, including perhaps in situations where current case law suggests that significant constitutional questions might be raised.[92] Such advocates contend that eliminating or restricting such speech from the digital environment will reduce the risk of "self-radicalization"[93] and will restrict the ability of terrorist groups to use social media to spread their propaganda.[94]

### The Constitutionality of a Criminal Law that Would Wholly Prohibit Terrorist Advocacy

Under *Brandenburg*, it appears that laws that criminalize the dissemination of the pure advocacy of terrorism, without more, would likely be deemed unconstitutional.[95] Despite the ambiguities in its application, *Brandenburg* remains controlling precedent and has been cited by the Supreme Court as such.[96] Consequently, speech that does no more than independently advocate the moral propriety or the moral good of terrorist acts is likely protected by the First Amendment.[97] According to *Brandenburg*, statutes that fail to draw the distinction between abstract advocacy of violence and incitements directed at and likely to produce imminent lawless action sweep too broadly to be upheld.[98] Therefore, any law that would generally restrict the independent advocacy of terrorist action on the Internet, without narrowing its application to only that advocacy that meets *Brandenburg*'s definition of incitement, would likely be unconstitutional. The limiting language in the Supreme Court's majority opinion in *Humanitarian Law Project* appears to support this argument.[99] The Court stressed that the application of the

---

92 Eckholm, *supra* note 14; Posner, *supra* note 20.

93 Self-radicalization describes the process by which an individual, or group of individuals comes to adhere to and, eventually, act on extreme philosophies. *See Threats to the American Homeland After Killing Bin Laden: An Assessment: Hearing Before the H. Comm. on Homeland Security*, 112th Cong. 12 (2011) (statement of Evan Kohlmann, Flashpoint Global Partners) ("We are seeing individuals who are popping up who were not recruited by any individual cleric or any individual mosque. They are being motivated purely by what they see on the web.").

94 Eckholm, *supra* note 14 ("Recently, though, a few legal scholars, too, have engaged in what others call First Amendment heresy. What does clear and present danger mean when terrorists are provoking violence over the Internet? Should not the government have a way, they ask, to block messages that facilitate terrorist acts?"); Cass R. Sunstein, *Islamic State's Challenge to Free Speech*, BLOOMBERG VIEW (Nov. 28, 2015, 12:38 PM), https://www.bloomberg.com/view/articles/2015-11-23/islamic-state-s-challenge-to-free-speech (arguing that due to the dangers posed by the advocacy of terrorism, the constitutional test for restricting such advocacy may need to be reconsidered).

95 Brandenburg v. Ohio, 395 U.S. 444, 448 (1969) (per curiam) ("A statute which fails to draw [the distinction between abstract teaching of the moral propriety of violence and preparing a group for action] impermissibly intrudes upon the freedoms guaranteed by the First and Fourteenth Amendments.").

96 *See, e.g.*, United States v. Stevens, 559 U.S. 460, 468 (2010). (citing *Brandenburg* for the proposition that "incitement" is not protected by the First Amendment).

97 *Brandenburg*, 395 U.S. at 447.

98 *Id.* at 448.

99 *See* Eugene Volokh, *Speech That Aids Foreign Terrorist Organizations and Strict Scrutiny*, VOLOKH CONSPIRACY (June 21, 2010, 5:43 PM), http://volokh.com/2010/06/21/speech-that-aids-foreign-terrorist-organizations-and-strict-scrutiny/ ("We Americans must have the right to try to persuade our fellow citizens, and our government, that our government is on the wrong side in various foreign policy controversies, that groups that the government says are bad guys are actually good guys (or at least less bad than the really bad guys), or that we should change our policies about which kinds of support to the bad guys are barred and

prohibition on material support to FTOs was properly tailored to withstand scrutiny, in part, because the statute did not apply to independent advocacy of terrorism.[100] The Court stressed that it was not addressing whether Congress could burden independent advocacy, even if it could be shown that FTOs would benefit from that advocacy.[101]

Some have argued that speech that advocates terrorist acts is so inherently dangerous that it should be distinguished from other speech that advocates violence or law breaking.[102] These commentators posit that the government should be able to ban the dissemination of terrorist advocacy in the same way that the dissemination of child pornography is restricted.[103] The comparison to child pornography is likely inapt, however. While the technology that permits the identification and filtering of child pornography might be adapted to filter the advocacy of terrorism,[104] the constitutional justification for allowing the government to police the distribution of child pornography arguably does not justify treating the abstract advocacy of terrorism in a similar matter.

Child pornography, the depiction of a minor engaged in sexual conduct that is not necessarily obscene, is unprotected by the First Amendment.[105] The Supreme Court held that the possession and distribution of child pornography could be completely prohibited because the government has an overriding interest in destroying the market for speech that requires the injury and exploitation of children in order to create it.[106] However, the Court has held that this reasoning does not extend to pornography that merely *appears* to, but does not in actuality depict a child engaging in sexual conduct ("virtual child pornography").[107] In reaching this holding, the Court explained that restrictions that apply to pornography depicting actual children were upheld because the laws targeted the production of the work and the harm that it caused children, not

---

which are allowed. To do that, we need to be able to make arguments defending or even praising those groups, *even-when such arguments help designated foreign terrorist organizations . . .*") (emphasis in original).

100 Holder v. Humanitarian Law Project, 561 U.S. 1, 36 (2010) ("Finally, and most importantly, Congress has avoided any restriction on independent advocacy, or indeed any activities not directed to, coordinated with, or controlled by foreign terrorist groups.") (emphasis in original).

101 *Id.* at 39. *See also,* Volokh, *supra* note 99 ("To be sure, the majority doesn't hold that a ban on independent advocacy would be unconstitutional even though such a ban might be necessary to serve a compelling government interest; it expressly reserves that question. But I think that the majority's repeated stress that the law doesn't restrict independent advocacy suggests that the Court would indeed strike down such a ban that applied to independent advocacy.").

102 *See, e.g.,* Eckholm, *supra* note 14; Sunstein, *supranote* 94.

103 *See,* Posner, *supra* note 20 ("The idea would be to get out the word that looking at ISIS-related websites, like looking at websites that display child pornography, is strictly forbidden."); Shane II, *supra* note 20 (quoting Mark D. Wallace, a former diplomat, arguing that terrorist advocacy should be removed from the Internet similarly to child pornography).

104 *See, e.g.,* Ellen Nakashima, *There's a new tool to take down terrorism images online. But social-media companies are wary of it,* Wash. Post (June 21, 2016), https://www.washingtonpost.com/world/national-security/new-tool-to-take-down-terrorism-images-online-spurs-debate-on-what-constitutes-extremist-content/2016/06/20/0ca4f73a-3492-11e6-8758-d58e76e11b12_story.html.

105 *Ferber,* 458 U.S. at 764. The definition of "sexually explicit conduct" in the federal child pornography statute includes "lascivious exhibition of the genitals or pubic area of any person [under 18]" and "is not limited to nude exhibitions or exhibitions in which the outlines of those areas [are] discernible through clothing." 18 U.S.C. §§ 2256(2)(A)(v), 2252 note.

106 Osborne v. Ohio, 495 U.S. 103 (1990).

107 Ashcroft v. Free Speech Coal., 535 U.S. 234, 249 (2002). Virtual child pornography includes depictions that appear to be children, but are not. *Id.* at 241. They may be images of adults that are digitally altered to make the subject appear younger, or simply images of very young-looking adults. *Id.*

its content.[108] In the case of virtual depictions of child pornography, no children are harmed in the creation of the content.[109] The government had attempted to justify similar restrictions on virtual child pornography by arguing that such material, like actual child pornography, increased the risk that consumers of that content would victimize children in the future.[110] Addressing that concern, the Supreme Court reiterated that the government "may not prohibit speech because it increases the chance an unlawful act will be committed 'at some indefinite future time.' "[111]

Applying this reasoning to the advocacy of terrorist activity, it does not appear that the creation of speech that advocates terrorism always inherently harms someone in the course of its production in a way that would be similar to the creation of actual child pornography. To be sure, some terrorist propaganda depicts terrorist attacks or executions, but terrorist advocacy does not necessarily require someone to be harmed in order for the speech to occur.[112] Instead, the advocacy of terrorism, like virtual child pornography, arguably creates or increases a risk that a crime will be committed "at some indefinite future time."[113] And the Supreme Court has held that the government may not prohibit speech solely on the basis of that indefinite risk.[114]

### Can Terrorist Advocacy Be Restricted More Easily on the Internet?

Speech that advocates terrorism that is distributed via the Internet may pose a significant danger to the public due to the ease of propagation to people who might be willing to act on those messages.[115] For that reason, some lawmakers and scholars argue that courts should permit terrorist advocacy to be more easily restricted when the Internet is used to disseminate it.[116] The Supreme Court has recognized that "each medium of expression presents special First Amendment problems."[117] For example, the Court has permitted broadcast speech to be more easily regulated than speech via other mediums because, among other factors, broadcasted speech is uniquely accessible to children.[118]

The Supreme Court has yet to consider the specific question of whether the ease of dissemination of information over the Internet warrants treating advocacy of violence via that medium differently than the same speech communicated through other means.

---

[108] *Id.*

[109] *Id.*

[110] *Id.* at 253.

[111] *Id.*

[112] *See, e.g.*, Terrence McCoy, *ISIS, beheadings and the success of horrifying violence*, Wash. Post (June 13, 2014), https://www.washingtonpost.com/news/morning-mix/wp/2014/06/13/isis-beheadings-and-the-success-of-horrifying-violence/

[113] *Ashcroft*, 435 U.S. at 253.

[114] *Id.*

[115] Eckholm, *supra* note 14; Posner, *supra* note 20.

[116] *Id.*

[117] FCC v. Pacifica Found., 438 U.S. 726, 748 (1978).

[118] *Id.* at 749. In the Supreme Court's most recent opinion addressing the broadcast indecency rules, the Court did not reach the question of their constitutionality. FCC v. Fox Television,__U.S.__; 132 S.Ct. 2307 (2012). However, Justice Ginsburg filed a concurring opinion arguing that *Pacifica* was wrongly decided and invited its reconsideration. 132 S.Ct. at 2321 (Ginsburg, J. concurring).

However, the Court has had the opportunity to examine what standard of review should be applied to restrictions on Internet speech more generally.

In *Reno v. American Civil Liberties Union,* the Supreme Court struck down restrictions on the communication of indecent speech to minors.[119] In doing so, the Court held that content-based restrictions on Internet speech should be subject to strict scrutiny.[120] The Court examined whether the medium of the Internet, like the broadcast medium, justified greater latitude for the government to restrict speech on that platform and concluded that it did not.[121] Comparing the reasons for permitting greater restrictions on broadcasted speech to the medium of the Internet, the Court explained that broadcasted speech is uniquely accessible to children. Specifically, the Court noted that there is an appreciable risk that if indecent speech were broadcast at times when children would be likely to be in the audience, children might accidentally be exposed to that speech.[122] In contrast, the risk of accidentally encountering indecent speech on the Internet was, in the Court's assessment, far lower and did not justify departing from the general rules regarding content-based restrictions on speech.[123]

The Court therefore accorded the highest degree of protection to speech on the Internet because "the interest in encouraging freedom of expression in a democratic society outweighs any theoretical but unproven benefit of censorship."[124] Assuming that the Court would apply the same reasoning to a content-based restriction on the advocacy of terrorism, the fact that speech is distributed via the Internet would not seem to permit the government to more easily regulate its dissemination, under current case law.

## Application of Material Support Statutes to Advocacy of Terrorism

Under current law, the two federal statutes criminalizing material support for terrorism or foreign terrorist organizations, 18 U.S.C. §§ 2339A and 2339B, appear most relevant to online advocacy of terrorism. Neither statute squarely prohibits the advocacy of terrorism. But both statutes potentially cover non-tangible forms of support for terrorist activities or foreign terrorist groups, including through the recruitment of personnel or the provision of training, expert advice or assistance, funding, or financial services.[125] The material support statutes have been the most often prosecuted anti-terrorism offenses.[126] Section 2339A of Title 18 of the United States Code prohibits the provision of material support with the knowledge or intent that the support be used to carry out a terrorist attack.[127] Section 2339B prohibits the provision of material support

[119] *Reno,* 521 U.S. at 885. Indecent speech is speech that describes or depicts sexual or excretory organs or activities in a way that is patently offensive to the audience. *Pacifica,* 438 U.S. at 732.

[120] *Reno,* 521 U.S. at 885.

[121] *Id.* at 868-69.

[122] *Id.*

[123] *Id.* ("[T]he Internet is not as 'invasive' as radio or television. The District Court specifically found that 'communications over the Internet do not "invade" an individual's home or appear on one's computer screen unbidden. Users seldom encounter content 'by accident.' ") (internal citations omitted).

[124] *Id.* at 882.

[125] 18 U.S.C. § 2339A(b); 18 U.S.C. § 2339B(g).

[126] CRS Report R41333, *Terrorist Material Support: An Overview of 18 U.S.C. 2339A and 2339B,* by Charles Doyle.

[127] 18 U.S.C. §2339A.

to designated foreign terrorist organizations.[128] As previously discussed, the Supreme Court in *Humanitarian Law Project* held that material support provided in the form of certain kinds of speech under the direction or in coordination with foreign terrorist organizations in violation of section 2339B may be punished consistent with the First Amendment even if such support is for purposes other than advancing the group's terrorist activities.[129]

### Section 2339A: Material Support of Acts of Terrorism

Section 2339A of Title 18 of the U.S. Code prohibits:

1. (a) attempting to,
   (b) conspiring to, or
   (c) actually
2. (a) providing material support or resources, or
   (b) concealing or disguising
      i. the nature,
      ii. location,
      iii. source, or
      iv. ownership of material support or resources
3. knowing or intending that they be used
   (a) in preparation for,
   (b) in carrying out,
   (c) in preparation for concealment of an escape from, or
   (d) in carrying out the concealment of an escape from
4. an offense identified as a federal crime of terrorism, as enumerated by the statute.[130]

Material support or resources covers "any property, tangible or intangible, or service,"[131] but excludes medicine and religious material.[132] For the purposes of the discussion of whether the material support statutes can apply to the advocacy of terrorism, it is sufficient to note that the definition of material support explicitly includes "training" and "expert advice or assistance."[133] The statute defines training as the "instruction or teaching designed to impart a specific skill, as opposed to general knowledge,"[134] whereas expert advice and assistance is defined to mean "advice or assistance derived from

[128] 18 U.S.C. §2339B.

[129] Holder v. Humanitarian Law Project, 561 U.S. 1, 36 (2010).

[130] 18 U.S.C. §2339A.

[131] 18 U.S.C. § 2339A(b)(2)-(b)(3).

[132] *Id.*

[133] *Id.*

[134] *Id.*

scientific, technical, or other specialized knowledge."[135] Unlike the material support statute at issue in *Humanitarian Law Project*, which potentially applied to activities done in furtherance of a foreign entity's activities unrelated to terrorism, a requisite for application of Section 2339A is that the support was given with the knowledge or intention that it would be used to facilitate a terrorist crime.[136]

It seems that the provision of speech in the form of training or expert advice or assistance with the intent that it be used to support a specific act of terrorism can be constitutionally punished. Even when a violation of the law may take the form of speech, the Supreme Court has held that the Constitution is not necessarily a barrier to punishment.[137] For example, an agreement to violate the law may be punished as a criminal conspiracy, and an agreement to fix prices in a market might constitute a violation of the antitrust laws.[138] Constitutional challenges to the scope of Section 2339A, including those based on arguments that it is incompatible with the First Amendment, thus far have proven unsuccessful.[139]

### Section 2339B: Material Support of Designated Terrorist Organizations

Section 2339B of Title 18 of the United States Code predicates liability on material support provided to certain designated terrorist organizations, rather than to the commission of a specific crime of terrorism.[140] As acknowledged by the Supreme Court in *Humanitarian Law Project*, this difference may create closer constitutional questions when the statute is applied to speech.[141] Section 2339B outlaws:

1. (a) attempting to provide,

   (b) conspiring to provide, or

   (c) actually providing
2. material support or resources
3. to a foreign terrorist organization

---

[135] *Id.*

[136] *Id.* Convictions for a criminal violation of either Section 2339A or 2339B are punishable by imprisonment for not more than 15 years and/or a fine of not more than $250,000 (not more than $500,000 for an organizational defendant). *Id.;* 18 U.S.C. § 2339B. *See also* CRS Report R41334, *Terrorist Material Support: A Sketch of 18 U.S.C. 2339A and 2339B,* by Charles Doyle.

[137] Giboney v. Empire Storage & Ice Co., 336 U.S. 490, 498-502 (1949) ("[It] has never been deemed an abridgement of freedom of speech or press to make a course of conduct illegal merely because the conduct was in part initiated, evidenced, or carried out by means of language, either spoken, written, or printed.").

[138] *Id.* ("Such an expansive interpretation of the constitutional guaranties of speech and press would make it practically impossible ever to enforce laws against agreements in restraint of trade as well as many other agreements and conspiracies deemed injurious to society.").

[139] *See, e.g.,* United States v. Amawi, 545 F.Supp.2d 681 (N.D. Ohio 2008) (upholding Section 2339A against a challenge that the statute was constitutionally overbroad and could infringe lawful expression); United States v. Sattar, 314 F.Supp.3d 279, 305 (S.D.N. Y. 2004) ("There can be no doubt, in any event, that § 2339A is a legitimate exercise of Congress's power to enact criminal laws that reflect legitimate state interests in maintaining comprehensive controls over harmful, constitutionally unprotected conduct.") (internal quotations omitted). *See generally* CRS Report R41333, *Terrorist Material Support: An Overview of 18 U.S.C. 2339A and 2339B,* by Charles Doyle.

[140] 18 U.S.C. §2339B.

[141] 561 U.S. at 39.

4. knowing that the organization
    (a) has been designated a foreign terrorist organization, or
    (b) engages, or has engaged in "terrorism" or "terrorist activity."[142]

Section 2339B's definition for "material support" is the same definition that applies to Section 2339A and covers "any property, tangible or intangible, or service" and explicitly includes "training" and "expert advice or assistance."[143] The *Humanitarian Law Project* Court clarified that advocacy may only constitute material support when it is "concerted activity," i.e., activity in connection with or under the direction of an FTO.[144]

To violate Section 2339B, one need not intend to aid in a terrorist attack or to further an organization's terrorist activities.[145] One need only have "knowledge that the organization is a designated terrorist organization ... that the organization has engaged in terrorist activity ... or that the organization has engaged or engages in terrorism."[146]

### Advocacy Directed to, Coordinated with, Under the Direction of an FTO

Assuming that a particular type of terrorist advocacy is within the scope of the "material support" proscribed by Section 2339B (e.g., it involves training or the giving of expert advice), the primary question that remains is whether the speech at issue would constitute advocacy "directed to, coordinated with or controlled by" a FTO.[147] In examining the clarity of the statute in *Humanitarian Law Project* and holding that the statute was not impermissibly vague, the Court pointed out that, by its terms,

> [the] statute prohibits providing a service "to a foreign terrorist organization." The use of the word "to" indicates a connection between the service and the foreign group. We think a person of ordinary intelligence would understand that independently advocating for a cause is different from providing a service to a group that is advocating for that cause.[148]

However, the Court did acknowledge that it was leaving open "questions of exactly how much direction or coordination is necessary for an activity to constitute a 'service.' "[149] The majority decided that it would be more appropriate to address those questions when the particular factual situations arose.[150]

A 2013 case decided by the First Circuit Court of Appeals may indicate that some courts could be inclined to broadly interpret what it means to direct speech to, coordinate with,

---

142 18 U.S.C. § 2339B. In addition to criminal prosecutions, Section 2339B(c) permits the Attorney General or the Secretary of the Treasury to bring a civil suit to enjoin violations of this section.

143 18 U.S.C. § 2339B(g)(4).

144 *Humanitarian Law Project*, 561 U.S. at 24.

145 18 U.S.C. §2339B.

146 *Id.*; *Humanitarian Law Project*, 561 U.S. at 17-18.

147 *Humanitarian Law Project*, 561 U.S. at 6.

148 *Id.* at 24 (internal citations omitted).

149 *Id.*

150 *Id.*

or act under the direction of a FTO.[151] In that case, Tarek Mehanna was convicted of several terrorism-related charges, including for providing material support to Al Qaeda, an organization Mehanna knew to be a designated FTO.[152] Mehanna had traveled to Yemen in an attempt to join Al Qaeda, but had been unable to locate the training camp he sought.[153] Mehanna had also translated publicly available Arabic language documents, some of which were Al Qaeda-generated propaganda, into English and had posted his translations on a website that was sympathetic to Al Qaeda.[154] Mehanna argued that his translations were independent advocacy, protected by the First Amendment and that the jury had not been properly instructed regarding what it means to coordinate with an FTO under Section 2339B.[155]

The First Circuit upheld his convictions. In doing so, the court examined the trial judge's instructions to the jury regarding the First Amendment and the defendant's translations. The First Circuit noted that the trial judge had defined "coordination" by explaining that "[i]ndividuals who act entirely independently of the 'FTO' to advance its goals or objectives shall not be considered to be working under the FTO's direction."[156] The First Circuit could find no legal error with these jury instructions. In response to the contention that the jury should have been instructed that a direct connection between a FTO and a defendant must be proven in order for the defendant to have acted in coordination with the organization, the appeals court stated that neither the statute nor the Supreme Court's decision in *Humanitarian Law Project* required "a direct link" between a defendant and a FTO for a violation to occur.[157] Nonetheless, the appeals court did not explicitly hold that Mehanna's translational activities were sufficient to sustain his conviction.[158] At the same time, the court held that, even if the defendant's translational activities did not constitute an attempt to provide material support, the evidence surrounding his trip to Yemen in an attempt to join Al Qaeda supported his convictions.[159]

The *Mehanna* case does not provide definitive answers as to when speech activity that may benefit an FTO is sufficiently directed to, coordinated with, or under the direction of a FTO to be considered material support.[160] However, it does suggest that certain forms of speech-related activity might be considered to be material support, even if the

---

151 United States v. Mehanna, 735 F.3d 32 (1st Cir. 2013), *cert. denied*, 135 S. Ct. 49 (2014).

152 *Id.* at 41.

153 *Id.*

154 *Id.*

155 *Id.* at 47.

156 *Id.* at 48-49.

157 *Id.* at 50.

158 *Id.* at 51.

159 *Id.*

160 *See* Buchlander-Raphael, *supra* note 46 at 1683-84 ("Cognizant of the difficulties that the government's 'translation as service' theory posed for First Amendment jurisprudence, the court attempted to play down the significance of the translation-centric charge by characterizing it only as an 'alternative basis' for conviction."); Emily Goldberg Knox, *Note: The Slippery Slope of Material Support Prosecutions: Social Media Support to Terrorists,* 66 Hastings L.J. 295, 314-15 (In affirming Mehanna's conviction, the First Circuit held that the trial court adequately instructed the jury. However, the court skirted the need to decide anything about coordination by affirming Mehanna's conviction on the grounds that his trip to Yemen was sufficient to support a guilty verdict, even if his Internet activities were constitutionally protected.").

defendant never actually has direct contact with the FTO.[161] If speech can be material support when the defendant has never succeeded in making direct contact with the FTO, it seems unclear where the line might be drawn between independent advocacy of terrorism that the Supreme Court in *Humanitarian Law Project* suggested could not be restricted and advocacy of terrorism that constitutes a violation of Section 2339B.[162]

### The Application of Section 2339B to Social Media Services

Some observers have suggested the possibility that when members of FTOs obtain accounts for social media sites like Twitter and Facebook, those sites are providing a service to FTOs that constitutes material support in violation of Section 2339B.[163] Some FTOs have reportedly acquired social media accounts from social media companies.[164] One recent study estimated that over 30,000 accounts on Twitter were controlled by the Islamic State organization alone as of 2014.[165] Others have noted the apparent presence of other terrorist groups on Twitter and other social media outlets.[166] The outstanding questions appear to be whether providing a social media account could constitute material support and whether a social media company has knowledge sufficient to support a conviction.[167] However, it does not appear that the Department of Justice (DOJ) has ever brought a criminal or civil case against any social media outlet alleging such a violation.[168] As a result, there is no case law clarifying whether the statute can properly

161 *See* Buchhandler-Raphael, *supra* note 46 at 1683-84 (arguing that *Mehanna* "demonstrates how the prohibition against providing material support to FTOs criminalizes a lot of speech, despite the arguably weak causal link between the speech in question and the risk of future harm").

162 *See* Noah Feldman, *Courts Blur Line Between Violent Speech and Crime,* Bloomberg View (Jul. 12, 2016), https://www.bloomberg.com/view/articles/2016-07-12/courts-blur-line-between-violent-speech-and-crime ("Create a pro-Islamic State music video and post it on a known IS website and you could find yourself convicted of a crime, material support for terrorism.... The First Circuit should've analyzed whether Mehanna's translation activities counted as coordination. But it didn't ...").

163 *See* Fields v. Twitter, No. 16-cv-00213-WHO, 2016 U.S. Dist. LEXIS 105768 (N.D. Cal. Aug. 10, 2016); Compl. at 2-3, Force, et. al v. Facebook, No. 16 Civ. 05490 (S.D.N.Y. Jul. 10, 2016); *see also* Jacob Bogage, *Family of ISIS Paris Attack Victim Sues Google, Facebook, and Twitter,* Wash. Post (Jun 16, 2016), https://www.washingtonpost.com/news/the-switch/wp/2016/06/16/family-of-isis-paris-attack-victim-sues-google-facebook-and-twitter/; Knox, *supra* note 160, at 311 ("The plain language, legislative history, and legislative intent provide strong support for a broad understanding of the term 'service'" and it likely includes social media accounts); Zoe Bedell and Benjamin Wittes, *Tweeting Terrorists, Part II: Does it Violate the Law for Twitter to Let Terrorist Groups Have Accounts?,* Lawfare (Feb. 14, 2016, 6:35 PM), https://www.lawfareblog.com/tweeting-terrorists-part-ii-does-it-violate-law-twitter-let-terrorist-groups-have-accounts, [hereinafter "Bedell and Wittes Part II"]

164 *See* Knox, *supra* note 160, at 308-10; Zoe Bedell and Benjamin Wittes, *Tweeting Terrorists, Part I: Don't Look Now But a Lot of Terrorist Groups are Using Twitter,* Lawfare (Feb. 14, 2016, 5:05 PM), https://www.lawfareblog.com/tweeting-terrorists-part-i-dont-look-now-lot-terrorist-groups-are-using-twitter (taking note of the number of terrorist groups that appear to have affiliated and official Twitter accounts).

165 J.M. Berger, *The ISIS Twitter Census: Making Sense of ISIS's Use of Twitter,* Brookings Inst., (Mar. 6, 2015), https://www.brookings.edu/blog/order-from-chaos/2015/03/06/the-isis-twitter-census-making-sense-of-isiss-use-of-twitter/.

166 *See* Complaint at 2-3, Force, et al. v. Facebook, No. 16 Civ. 05490 (S.D.N.Y. filed Jul. 10, 2016); Jacob Bogage, *Family of ISIS Paris Attack Victim Sues Google, Facebook, and Twitter,* Wash. Post (Jun 16, 2016), https://www.washingtonpost.com/news/the-switch/wp/2016/06/16/family-of-isis-paris-attack-victim-sues-google-facebook-and-twitter/.

167 *See* Knox, *supra* note 160 at 310-21.

168 *See* Quintan Wiktorowicz, *Working to Counter Online Radicalization to Violence in the United States,* White House Blog (Feb. 5, 2013, 10:02 AM), https://www.whitehouse.gov/blog/2013/02/05/working-counter-online-radicalization-violence-united-states (noting that the Obama administration investigates and

be applied to social media companies whose generally available services are used by FTOs to communicate.

If a court were to evaluate whether Section 2339B can be applied to social media companies, one of the most difficult questions presented would be whether a social media site could be said to be acting in coordination with or under the direction of an FTO. As noted above, *Humanitarian Law Project* did not provide guidance as to the level of coordination necessary to constitute the provision of a service to a FTO under the statute.[169] *Mehanna* suggests that defendants need not have direct contact with the FTO in order for a violation to occur.[170] Websites generally do not engage in background checks or any other form of verification prior to permitting an account to be created.[171] Given the number of people who use their services, such verification may be impossible.[172] And given the difficult burden that would be imposed on social media companies in performing background checks on every user, a court may simply conclude that providing an account to a user who may happen to be affiliated with a FTOs may be insufficient in and of itself to rise to the level of "coordination" necessary to violate Section 2339B.[173] Nonetheless, a number of social media sites have policies to remove terrorist content or the accounts of terrorist groups.[174] Some have argued that because social media sites often fail to suspend accounts that are associated with FTOs, the government could argue that this failure is evidence of coordination with FTOs.[175] Without case law interpreting this question, it remains unclear whether the fact that terrorist groups and their representatives often are able to obtain and use social media accounts represents a sufficient connection between social media services and the terrorist groups to support a finding of the provision of material support.

---

prosecutes those "who use the Internet to recruit others to plan and carry out acts of violence." and works to inform citizens regarding the threats of terrorist activity online, but does not attempt to remove content from the Internet in its approach).

[169] *Humanitarian Law Project,* 561 U.S. at 24.

[170] *Mehanna,* 735 F. 3d at 50.

[171] *See, e.g.,* Chi. Lawyers' Comm. for Civ. Rights Under Law, Inc. v. Craigslist, 519 F.3d 666, 668-69 (7th Cir. 2008) (noting that "[every] month more than 30 million notices are posted" to Craigslist); Stats, Facebook (last visited Aug. 27, 2016), http://newsroom.fb.com/company-info/ ("1.13 billion daily active users on average for June 2016").

[172] *See Chi. Lawyers' Comm.,* 519 F. 3d at 668 ("An online service could hire a staff to vet the postings, but that would be expensive and may well be futile: if postings had to be reviewed before being put online, long delay could make the service much less useful . . .").

[173] *See also,* Gabe Rottman, *Hamas, Twitter and the First Amendment,* Am. Civ. Liberties Union (Nov. 21, 2012, 3:25PM), https://www.aclu.org/blog/hamas-twitter-and-first-amendment ("For de facto common carriers like Twitter, open to all, the provision of service is not 'coordinated' in the way the Court seems to argue is necessary, and it certainly does not suggest 'support' in the sense of concerted activity in furtherance of the goals of the designated terrorist organization.").

[174] *See* Katie Benner, *Twitter Suspends 235,000 More Accounts Over Extremism,* N.Y. Times (Aug. 18, 2016), http://www.nytimes.com/2016/08/19/technology/twitter-suspends-accounts-extremism.html?_r=0; Natalie Andrews and Deepa Seetharama, *Facebook Steps Up Efforts Against Terrorism,* Wall St. J. (Feb. 11, 2016), http://www.wsj.com/articles/facebook-steps-up-efforts-against-terrorism-1455237595.

[175] *See* Knox, *supra* note 160 at 316 ("The failure to suspend FTO accounts could be seen as a conscious decision that provides evidence of coordination, particularly as social media companies have the ability to monitor and proactively take down these accounts."); Bedell and Wittes Part II, *supra* footnote 163 (noting that the *Humanitarian Law Project* Court left unclear what coordination might mean, but arguing that "it's worth noting that even if the requisite relationship includes 'formal elements,' Twitter's relationship with its users—including Hezbollah, Hamas, and the PKK—is defined by precisely such elements, including a legal contract.").

In addition, in order to hold a social media company criminally or civilly liable for the provision of material support to an FTO under Section 2339B, the government must prove that the defendant knew that the organization to which the support was provided was a designated FTO or that the organization was engaged in terrorism.[176] Social media companies could be expected to argue that they do not have sufficient knowledge of a new user's affiliation with a FTO upon the activation of an account.[177] Over one billion people use Facebook,[178] and millions also use Twitter.[179] The companies do not, and might argue that they cannot, attempt to discover with any degree of certainty what users of its services will be terrorist affiliates prior to the activation of an account.[180]

Nonetheless, social media sites appear to be generally aware that their services are used by some percentage of their subscribers to disseminate terrorist advocacy and that they may be used by FTOs themselves. Twitter, Facebook, and other social media sites can and do disable accounts that violate their terms of service.[181] Certain violent speech, including speech that advocates or glorifies terrorism, violates the terms of service of these sites.[182] It has been reported that Twitter has recently increased the number of accounts that it has disabled for promoting terrorism.[183] Facebook has also reportedly removed posts that advocate terrorism and has disabled accounts for the same reason.[184] The fact that social media companies take steps to remove that content when it appears on their services may be evidence that they know that their services are being used by FTOs.[185] On the other hand, a social media website might not be sure if an account

---

[176] 18 U.S.C. § 2339B. *Humanitarian Law Project* did not address the question of what level of awareness would be sufficient to sustain a conviction under Section 2339B because the plaintiffs in that case did not dispute their knowledge that the groups at issue were FTOs. *Humanitarian Law Project*, 561 U.S. at 9-10.

[177] *See* Knox, *supra* note 160 at 319 ("Social media companies will reject any assertion that they knew they were providing a service to designated FTOs."); Zoe Bedell and Benjamin Wittes, *supra* note 163, https://www.lawfareblog.com/tweeting-terrorists-part-ii-does-it-violate-law-twitter-let-terrorist-groups-have-accounts ("One could imagine Twitter's arguing that the statute is vague as applied to it, because there is no way it reasonably can know which of the millions of users who sign up for its services are affiliated with designated foreign terrorist organizations.").

[178] Stats, Facebook (last visited Aug. 27, 2016), http://newsroom.fb.com/company-info/ ("1.13 billion daily active users on average for June 2016").

[179] @Twitter, Twitter (Dec. 18, 2012, 10:01AM), https://twitter.com/twitter/status/281051652235087872 (stating that Twitter now has over 200 Million users).

[180] *See* Knox, *supra* note 160 at 319 ("Social media companies will reject any assertion that they knew they were providing a service to designated FTOs."); Bedell and Wittes Part II, *supra* note 163; Gabe Rottman, Hamas, *Twitter and the First Amendment*, Am. Civ. Liberties Union (Nov. 21, 2012, 3:25PM), https://www.aclu.org/blog/hamas-twitter-and-first-amendment.

[181] *See, e.g.*, Benner, *supra* note 174; Ryan Lucas, *New Software Aims to Curb Extremism Online*, CQ.com (June 17, 2016, 3:04 PM) http://www.cq.com/doc/news-4912514?0.

[182] *See, e.g.*, Twitter Rules, https://support.twitter.com/articles/18311# (last visited, Aug. 26, 2016); Facebook Terms of Service https://www.facebook.com/terms (last visited Aug. 26, 2016); YouTube Community Guidelines https://www.youtube.com/yt/policyandsafety/communityguidelines.html (last visited Aug. 26, 2016).

[183] Benner, *supra* note 174.

[184] Andrews and Seetharama, *supra* footnote 174.

[185] *See* Knox, *supra* note 160 at 320 ("Furthermore, after the brutal execution of reporter James Foley, Twitter and YouTube began aggressively cracking down on accounts affiliated with ISIL. This swift and decisive action suggests that these companies have the ability to identify and shut down accounts affiliated with FTOs despite the large number of users.").

actually belongs to a FTO or is operated by another user identifying itself as the FTO.[186] It is unclear whether the general knowledge of social media sites that terrorist organizations are using their services, despite lacking actual knowledge that a particular account is used by a specific FTO, is sufficient to support a conviction for the provision of material support under Section 2339B.[187]

### Private Civil Lawsuits and Section 230 of the Communications Decency Act

Section 2333 of Title 18 of the United States Code permits U.S. citizens injured in their persons, property, or business by acts of international terrorism to recover treble damages.[188] Courts have interpreted violations of Section 2339A and 2339B to be acts of international terrorism for the purposes of Section 2333.[189] Recently, a number of lawsuits have been filed by private plaintiffs against social media websites alleging that they are providing material support to terrorist groups in violation of 18 U.S.C. § 2339B.[190] One such lawsuit was brought against Twitter and alleged that Twitter's dissemination of propaganda by the Islamic State organization led to a terrorist attack that caused the death of three government contractors at a training facility in Jordan.[191] In another lawsuit, the father of one of the Americans killed in the orchestrated terrorist attack in Paris in 2015 similarly accused Twitter, Google, and Facebook of providing material support to the Islamic State in violation of Section 2339B, arguing that without the services provided by these sites, "the explosive growth of ISIS over the last few years into the most-feared terrorist group in the world would not have been possible."[192]

Beyond the difficulty with determining whether social media companies can be held civilly liable for providing material support under the terms of Section 2339B, such private civil lawsuits may face an additional hurdle in attempting to hold social media services accountable for allowing FTOs to use them.[193] Section 230(c) of the Communications

---

[186] *See* Zoe Bedell and Benjamin Wittes, *Tweeting Terrorists, Part III: How Would Twitter Defend Itself Against a Material Support Prosecution?*, Lawfare (Feb. 14, 2016, 7:16 PM), https://www.lawfareblog.com/tweeting-terrorists-part-iii-how-would-twitter-defend-itself-against-material-support-prosecution ("Twitter might plausibly argue that it cannot know if the Hamas account really is run by Hamas or is, in fact, precisely the sort of independent advocacy the statute exempts.") [hereinafter "Bedell and Wittes Part III"]

[187] *Id.*

[188] 18 U.S.C. § 2333.

[189] *See* Boim v. Quranic Literacy Inst., 291 F.3d 1000, 1015 (7th Cir. 2002); Goldberg v. UBS, 609 F.Supp.2d 92, 114 (E.D. N.Y. 2010). *See also* CRS Report R41333, *Terrorist Material Support: An Overview of 18 U.S.C. 2339A and 2339B*, by Charles Doyle.

[190] Fields v. Twitter, No. 16-cv-00213-WHO, 2016 U.S. Dist. LEXIS 105768, at *3-*6 (N.D. Cal. Aug. 10, 2016); Complaint at 2-3, Force, et al. v. Facebook, No. 16 Civ. 05490 (S.D.N. Y. filed Jul. 10, 2016); Jacob Bogage, *Family of ISIS Paris Attack Victim Sues Google, Facebook, and Twitter*, Wash. Post (Jun 16, 2016), https://www.washingtonpost.com/news/the-switch/wp/2016/06/16/family-of-isis-paris-attack-victim-sues-google-facebook-and-twitter/.

[191] *Fields*, 2016 U.S. Dist. LEXIS 105768, at *3-*6.

[192] Jacob Bogage, *Family of ISIS Paris Attack Victim Sues Google, Facebook, and Twitter*, Wash. Post (Jun 16, 2016), https://www.washingtonpost.com/news/the-switch/wp/2016/06/16/family-of-isis-paris-attack-victim-sues-google-facebook-and-twitter/.

[193] *Fields*, 2016 U.S. Dist. LEXIS 105768, at *28. *See also* Cyrus Farivar, *It'll be very hard for terrorism victim's family to win lawsuit against Twitter*, arsTechnica (June 17, 2016, 5:00AM), http://arstechnica.com/tech-policy/2016/06/itll-be-very-hard-for-terrorism-victims-family-to-win-lawsuit-against-twitter/; Benjamin Wittes and Zoe Bedell, *Did Congress Immunize Twitter Against Lawsuits for Supporting ISIS?*, Lawfare (Jan. 22, 2016, 9:14AM), https://www.lawfareblog.com/did-congress-immunize-twitter-against-lawsuits-supporting-isis

Decency Act (CDA) prohibits holding interactive computer service providers liable for content provided by third parties.[194] While the liability shield does not apply to violations of the federal criminal law,[195] the U.S. Court of Appeals for the First Circuit recently held that, even when the civil lawsuit is based upon a violation of federal criminal law, Section 230's shield may bar recovery if the lawsuit seeks to treat a service provider as a publisher.[196] Consequently, even if social media service providers do violate Section 2339B when providing accounts to FTOs, it is possible that Section 230 of the CDA would shield them from civil liability for that violation.

### *Section 230 of the Communications Decency Act*

Section 230(c)(1) of the CDA states, in pertinent part, that "no provider or user of an interactive computer service shall be treated as the publisher or speaker of any information provided by another information content provider."[197] This language has been interpreted by courts to provide immunity from civil liability to providers and users of interactive computer services for content provided by third parties.[198] In creating this liability shield, Congress sought to preserve the robust and vibrant communication that occurs on the Internet and to "keep government interference to a minimum."[199] However, Section 230 is not an absolute bar to liability.[200]

A three-part test has been developed to determine whether a defendant is eligible for Section 230's protection. If the lawsuit is:

1. brought against and interactive computer service provider or user (e.g., a website like NYTimes.com, or a social media service, like Twitter or Facebook),[201]

---

("companies would, indeed, have powerful arguments for immunity under" Section 230). [hereinafter "Wittes and Bedell Section 230"]

194 47 U.S.C. § 230(c)(1).

195 47 U.S.C. § 230(e).

196 Doe v. Backpage.com, 817 F.3d 12, 22 (1st Cir. 2016) (holding that the plain meaning of Section 230(e)'s text compelled the conclusion that the exception from the liability shield for federal criminal cases did not apply to civil liability even when the civil suit was based upon a violation of federal criminal law).

197 47 U.S.C. § 230(c)(1). The liability shield is not available for violations of federal criminal law, intellectual property law, state civil and criminal laws that do not conflict with section 230, or the Electronic Communications Privacy Act of 1984 (ECPA), its amendments, or similar state laws to ECPA. 47 U.S.C. § 230(e).

198 Jones v. Dirty World Entertainment, 755 F.3d 398, 406 (6th Cir. 2014) ("Although §230(c)(1) does not explicitly mention immunity or a synonym thereof, this and other circuits have recognized the provision to protect internet service providers for the display of content created by someone else.") (citations omitted).

199 *Id.* at 407; *see also* 47 U.S.C. § 230(b)(2) ("It is the policy of the United States ... to preserve the vibrant and competitive free market that presently exists for the Internet and other interactive computer services, unfettered by Federal and State regulation.").

200 Fair Hous. Council v. Roommates.com, LLC, 521 F.3d 1157, 1164 (9th Cir. 2008) (stating that the statute did not "create a lawless no-man's-land on the Internet.").

201 An interactive computer service is defined by section 230 as "any information service, system, or access software provider that provides or enables computer access by multiple users to a computer server, including specifically a service or system that provides access to the Internet and such systems operated or services offered by libraries or educational institutions." 47 U.S.C. § 230(f)(2). This definition has been held by courts broadly to encompass websites, such as Backpage.com or Facebook, internet service providers, such as Verizon or Comcast, and all other types of computer services that provide a neutral platform for users of the service to communicate via the Internet. *See, e.g., Dirty World,* 755 F.3d at 407 ("These providers include broadband providers, hosting companies, and website operators like Dirty World and Richie."); Backpage.com v. Hoffman, No. 13-cv-03952, 2013 U.S. Dist. LEXIS 119811 (D.NJ 2013).

2. based upon information provided by another content provider, and

3. seeks to hold the defendant liable as a publisher or speaker of that content,

then Section 230's liability shield applies.[202] If it can be shown that the interactive computer service provider contributed to the development of the illegal content, Section 230's liability shield is not available.[203]

To date, only one court has ruled with regard to section 230's application to a lawsuit alleging material support of a FTO by a social media company. In *Fields v. Twitter*, the plaintiffs, family members of United States government contractors that were killed in a terrorist attack in Lebanon, alleged that the Islamic State organization used Twitter to spread propaganda, raise funds, and attract recruits, and that Twitter knowingly permitted such use of its services.[204] The plaintiffs further alleged that Twitter's provision of these services generally caused their injuries.[205] However, the plaintiffs did not specifically allege that the Islamic State used Twitter to recruit the person who committed the terrorist attack that injured the plaintiffs or that Twitter was used to plan the attack.[206] Instead, the plaintiffs alleged only that the attacker was generally inspired by propaganda that he had seen on Twitter.[207]

The United States District Court for the Northern District of California dismissed the plaintiffs' lawsuit, but gave the plaintiffs leave to amend their complaint.[208] In doing so, the court did not reach the question of whether Twitter actually had provided material support to a foreign terrorist organization. Instead, the district court dismissed the lawsuit because the court found that Section 230 of the CDA shielded Twitter from liability.[209]

The central argument in *Fields* with regard to Section 230 was whether the lawsuit was attempting to hold Twitter liable as a publisher.[210] To support their argument that the lawsuit was not targeting Twitter as a publisher, the plaintiffs offered two justifications. First, they argued that their lawsuit was not based upon the content of the speech disseminated by Twitter, but instead was based solely upon Twitter's provision of services in the form of Twitter accounts to the Islamic State organization.[211] Second, they alleged that because much of the organization's recruiting communication is accomplished via Twitter's Direct Messaging services, which are private communications between individual users, those direct messages are not "published" to the public and recovery

[202] *See* Klayman v. Zuckerberg, 753 F.3d 13554, 1357 (D.C. Cir. 2014).

[203] *Fair Hous. Council*, 521 F.3d at 1168 ("In other words, a website helps to develop unlawful content, and thus falls within the exception to section 230, if it contributes materially to the alleged illegality of the conduct.").

[204] Fields v. Twitter, No. 16-cv-00213-WHO, 2016 U.S. Dist. LEXIS 105768, at *3 (N.D. Cal. Aug. 10, 2016).

[205] *Id.* at *4-*6.

[206] *Id.*

[207] *Id.*

[208] *Id.* at *28.

[209] *Id.*

[210] *Id.* at *8. The plaintiffs in *Fields* did not dispute that Twitter was providing an interactive computer service. *Id.* Nor did the plaintiffs argue that the content that allegedly inspired the attack that injured them was provided by a third party. *Id.*

[211] *Id.* at *11.

based upon those communications cannot be barred by Section 230.[212] The district court rejected both arguments.

In rejecting the plaintiffs' provision of accounts theory of liability, the court noted previous cases analyzing the breadth of Section 230's liability shield have defined publishing broadly to include *any* decision related to what third-party content might be made available on a site or removed from it.[213] Generally, previous courts had applied that reasoning to specific offensive content and not to the decision of whether to provide access to a platform to specific persons.[214] However, the district court did not see a substantive distinction between the two concepts for the purposes of whether Twitter was being treated as a publisher. In the court's view, granting permission to a particular person to post whatever content that person liked was no less a publishing decision than allowing content to be posted in the first place, or removing content that the site decided violated its rules.[215] "Twitter's decisions to structure and operate itself as a platform … allowing for the freedom of expression [of] hundreds of millions of people around the world and to allow even ISIS to sign up for accounts on its social network," in the court's view, "reflect choices about what [third-party] content can appear on Twitter and in what form."[216] These were quintessential publishing decisions in the view of the court. Consequently, Section 230's liability shield applied.[217]

Turning to whether content that was not made publicly available was published for the purposes of Section 230, the court again was not convinced by the plaintiffs' arguments.[218] In making this determination, the court noted that Section 230 was first enacted to provide a liability shield for defamatory content posted by third parties.[219] Accordingly, the district court took into account that appeals courts have looked to

[212] *Id.* at *13.

[213] *Id.* at 17 (citing Klayman, 753 F.3d at 1359 ("the very essence of publishing is making the decision whether to print or retract a given piece of content"); *see generally* Fair Hous. Council v. Roommates.com, LLC, 521 F.3d 1157, 1170-71 (9th Cir. 2008) ('"determin[ing] whether or not to prevent [the] posting' of third-party material online is 'precisely the kind of activity' covered by the CDA").

[214] *Fields*, 2016 U.S. Dist. LEXIS 105768, at *17.

[215] *Id.* at *19. The court analogized this case to a recent First Circuit decision. *In Doe v.* Backpage.com, 817 F.3d 12 (1st Cir. 2016), plaintiffs had argued that Backpage.com was liable to them for violating the Trafficking Victims Protection Reauthorization Act because it had hosted advertisements whereby the plaintiffs were trafficked in violation of the statute. *Id.* at 15. The First Circuit held that Section 230(c)'s liability shield barred recovery because it "extends to the formulation of precisely the sort of website policies and practices" at issue in the case. *Id.* at 20. "Features such as these, which reflect choices about what content can appear on the website and in what form, are editorial choices that fall within the purview of traditional publisher functions." *Id.* at 21.

[216] *Fields*, 2016 U.S. Dist. LEXIS 105768, at *20 (internal citations and quotations omitted).

[217] The court also found two further deficiencies in the plaintiffs' argument that seeking to hold Twitter liable for providing accounts to FTOs was not an attempt to hold Twitter liable as a publisher. *Id.* at *13. First, the court found that much of the plaintiffs' complaint focused on content posted to Twitter by the Islamic State organization. *Id.* "In short, the theory of liability … is not that Twitter provides material support to ISIS by providing it with Twitter accounts, but that Twitter does so by 'knowingly permitt[ing] [ISIS] to use [those accounts] as a tool for spreading extremist propaganda … " which essentially sought to hold Twitter liable for content it published. *Id.* *16-*17. Furthermore, plaintiffs had not properly alleged causation. *Id.* at *22 ("[The] allegations in the [complaint] do not support a plausible inference of proximate causation between Twitter's provision of accounts to ISIS and the deaths of Fields and Creach.").

[218] *Id.* at *26.

[219] *Id.* ("As noted above, Congress enacted section 230(c)(1) in part to respond to a New York state court decision finding that an internet service provider could be held liable for defamation based on third-party content posted on its message boards.").

defamation law when determining the scope of the shield provided by Section 230.[220] Because, under defamation law, the term publication means to communicate to another person, other than the person defamed[221] the *Fields* court determined that in order for an interactive service provider to be treated as a publisher for the purposes of Section 230, the third-party content need not be made publicly available.[222] Section 230's liability shield therefore also applied to content communicated via Twitter's Direct Messaging service.

As noted above, similar private civil lawsuits alleging that social media sites provide material support to terrorist organizations are pending in court. It remains to be seen whether those cases will be decided similarly to *Fields v. Twitter*. However, *Fields* does suggest that reviewing courts may be inclined to continue the general trend of broadly applying the liability shield provided by Section 230 to civil suits brought against Internet platforms that display third-party content like Twitter, Facebook, and Google.[223] If so, they may provide a barrier to attempts to curb the advocacy of terrorism on the Internet through civil litigation.

## Author Contact Information

Kathleen Ann Ruane
Legislative Attorney
kruane@crs.loc.gov, 7-9135

[220] *Id.*

[221] *Fields*, 2016 U.S. Dist. LEXIS 105768, at *27 (citing Zeran v. America Online, 129 F.3d 327, 332 (4th Cir. 1997)).

[222] *Id.* The district court also noted a number of other cases where Section 230 was held to bar recovery for claims based upon the transmission of third-party content that was nonpublic and in which the courts did not question whether the content could be said to have been "published." *Id.* at *28 (citing Hung Tan Phan v. Lang Van Pham, 182 Cal. App. 4th 323, 324-28 (App. 2010); Delfino v. Agilent Techs., Inc., 145 Cal. App. 4th 790, 795-96, 804-08 (App. 2006); Beyond Sys., Inc. v. Keynetics, Inc., 422 F. Supp. 2d 523, 528, 536-37 (D. Md. 2006)).

[223] *See* Eric Goldman, *Section 230 Immunizes Twitter From Liability For ISIS's Terrorist Activities-Fields* v. Twitter, Tech. & Marketing L. Blog (Aug. 11, 2016), http://blog.ericgoldman.org/archives/2016/08/section-230-immunizes-twitter-from-liability-for-isiss-terrorist-activities-fields-v-twitter.htm ("There are other pending lawsuits against social media sites for materially supporting terrorists. *[Fields v. Twitter]* reinforces the likelihood that those cases will also fail for Section 230 and causation reasons."); *but see* Wittes and Bedell Section 230, *supra* note 193 (arguing that despite the fact that "companies would, indeed, have powerful arguments for immunity under" Section 230, the liability shield should not apply).

www.ingramcontent.com/pod-product-compliance
Lightning Source LLC
LaVergne TN
LVHW062111200926
848484LV00007B/1638